International Relations: Understanding Global Issues

International Relations: Understanding Global Issues

Peter A. Toma
University of Arizona

Robert F. Gorman
Southwest Texas State University

Brooks/Cole Publishing Company

Pacific Grove, California

Brooks/Cole Publishing Company
A Division of Wadsworth, Inc.

Printed in the United States of America
10 9 8 7 6 5 4 3 2

Library of Congress Cataloging-in-Publication Data
Toma, Peter A.
    International relations : understanding global issues / Peter A.
Toma, Robert F. Gorman.
       p.   cm.
    Includes bibliographical references and index.
    ISBN 0-534-14508-6
    1. International relations. I. Gorman, Robert F. II. Title.
JX1391.T66 1990
327—dc20   90-41262
                                        CIP

Sponsoring Editor: *Cynthia C. Stormer*
Project Development Editor: *Janet M. Hunter*
Editorial Assistant: *Cathleen Sue Collins*
Production Editor: *Penelope Sky*
Manuscript Editor: *Robin L. Witkin*
Permissions Editor: *Carline Haga*
Interior and Cover Design: *Katherine Minerva*
Art Coordinator: *Lisa Torri*
Interior Illustration: *Accurate Art*
Authors' Assistant: *Kelli Waldron*
Typesetting: *Execustaff*
Cover Printing: *Lehigh Press Lithographers*
Printing and Binding: *Arcata Graphics/Martinsburg*

For my students:
past, present, and future
P.A.T.

To the memory of
Thomas Hovet, Jr.,
colleague, friend, scholar, and global citizen
R.F.G.

About the Authors

Peter A. Toma is Professor Emeritus of political science and international relations at the University of Arizona, where he continues to teach. He is a former director of an EPDA institute in international affairs at the University of Arizona, and of an area program on Europe and the USSR at the National War College. Professor Toma has written and cowritten numerous books and articles, including *Socialist Authority: The Hungarian Experience* (1988).

Robert F. Gorman is Associate Professor of political science at Southwest Texas State University. He served on the U.S. State Department Council on Foreign Relations; conducted, under a Ford Foundation grant, research on international policy toward refugees and development in Africa; taught in Malaysia; and studied refugee and humanitarian issues throughout Southeast Asia. The author of many publications, Dr. Gorman is now preparing a book on American refugee policy.

Preface

In recent years, writers of international relations textbooks have tended to choose a particularly attractive theme or appealing paradigm as a means of taming a field that at times seems beyond domestication. Equally so, users of international relations texts—teachers and students alike—expect to find an overarching organizational principle that conveniently encompasses the wide interdisciplinary subject matter. Popular texts have been organized around power as the central driving force of international relations; around interdependence as a challenge to traditional power politics analysis; around perception and misperception as fundamental to the fashioning and interaction of foreign policies; around conflict and cooperation as constant, if alternative, explanations of state behavior; and around geopolitical and environmental determinism. Some authors trust to history as the primary basis for understanding the behavior of nations; others insist that a rigorous statistical approach to the study of interstate behavior is the only way to achieve a scientific explanation.

Too often, texts that represent a singular approach warp the subject matter to fit the organizing theory. We believe in an eclectic and issue-oriented approach to the study of international relations. No theory or theme holds a monopoly on truth, although many are powerfully attractive and worthy of study. We thus develop several themes as the book progresses, including the notions that the contemporary world is struggling through a transitional period where conflicting forces of continuity and change are at work; that conflict and cooperation coexist as tools of statecraft; that politics and economics interact to fashion the policies of nations; that old and new actors vie for influence on the international scene; that perception and misperception inform the direction of global politics; and that the study of international relations is rent by debates about whether realists, neo-realists, structuralists, pluralists, traditionalists, or behavioralists best understand the underlying dynamics of international relations.

Understanding international relations, then, requires some consideration of *competing* theories and themes. Our issue-oriented approach allows readers to explore and evaluate different theories about the functions and processes of international relations. In each chapter we provide essential history, basic concepts, and supporting empirical studies to illuminate the subject in general and in detail. Readings at the end of each chapter elaborate further on a particular theory or approach, to deepen the reader's understanding of relevant issues. A list of key terms and study questions in each chapter further helps students master the material. As an additional learning aid, the key terms are defined in the glossary at the end of the book.

Organization

This book consists of five basic parts. In Part I we establish a framework for understanding international relations, review its historical development, and discuss various ways of studying the subject. In Part II we examine the foreign policy-making process, first by reviewing the roles played by numerous international actors, and then by analyzing how decision-making processes work. In Part III we examine the instruments nations use in conducting their interrelations: diplomacy, psychological war, propaganda, terrorism, international organization, international law, and war. In Part IV we explore the basic issues that lead either to tension and conflict or to potential cooperation. In Part V we speculate upon the future of international relations.

In Part I we introduce a recurring theme: We live in an ever more interdependent world. In chapter 1 we use the example of the changing U.S. role in the international system, and explain three predominant schools of thought about how world society is structured and which aspects of it are most relevant to our discipline. In chapter 2 we develop a related theme: The growing interdependence of world communities challenges the traditional state system. We review the historic roots of the state system, discuss key concepts of tradition and change, and consider whether standard assumptions about the state, power, and the national interest can withstand the many forces of contemporary change. In chapter 3 we consider the ways in which international relations may be studied, taking a look at the role of theory building.

In Part II we explore the foreign policy making process. In chapter 4 we assess the relative capabilities of such actors as states, international organizations, nongovernmental agencies, corporations, churches, and individuals. In chapter 5 we further this examination by analyzing the decision-making processes nations use as they draw on their economic, military, political, and social capabilities to protect and advance their interests.

In Part III we examine the instruments that states use to influence other states. In chapter 6 we consider the role of nation-states in the world arena, and question why some states exert more influence than others, through diplomacy, negotiations, and bargaining. We weigh the relative advantages of secret and open diplomacy and of tacit and formal diplomacy, and discuss variations of bargaining and summitry; we relate each of these aspects to the larger issue of why some states are more inclined than others to use diplomacy instead of force in settling disputes. In chapter 7 we characterize the kinds of international actors that would be likely to use either psychological warfare, propaganda, or terrorism. We also assess the impact of variables on the exercise of influence. Here and in chapter 8 we note that technological advances have pushed the capacity for violence to new extremes. Our study of the causes of violence stresses human nature, the nature and organization of the state, and the nature of the international system. We find that in some instances violent outbreaks result from diminished prosperity, but there is no single cause-and-effect relationship that could be improved in order to achieve peace. The key issue is still whether existing treaties, conventions, and laws can prevent the increase of international terrorism. In chapter 9 we consider the fact that some nongovernmental and intergovernmental organizations have more power than some nation-states. In chapter 10, on international law and world order, the key question is whether the existing system can adequately handle the many transnational problems that individual nation-states either cannot or will not manage. In chapter 11 we examine monetary problems and their regional and bilateral solutions, looking at the disparity in trade relations, currency exchange, and capital investment between developed and less-developed countries.

As we see in Part IV, the issues of conflict in international relations are as numerous and complex as the cooperative efforts to resolve them. In chapter 12 we describe significant regional and bilateral issues, focusing on two that produce particular tension: the unequal development in rich and poor countries, and the global arms race. In chapter 13, we consider the fine line between cooperation and conflict, suggesting that when actors have mutual interests that can be furthered by cooperation, when the gains outweigh the losses, and when the number of players is small, then cooperation is not only possible but desirable.

In Part V, chapter 14, we reexamine economic, security, and ecological issues in terms of the perceptions that prevailed in the late 1980s, and anticipate the attitudes of the 1990s and beyond. Throughout the text we seek to understand the human phenomena that permeate all aspects of international relations. The issues we focus on are determined not by personal preference but by the latest scholarly literature.

We expect that our approach will lead to a broader understanding of world politics. We hope that it will stretch and broaden perspectives, rather than narrow them. In a world as diverse in its nations and cultures as our own, it is no surprise that there are so many different and competing perspectives on how they interact. Our issues orientation has allowed us to leave the richness and diversity of international relations, and the study of it, intact. Readers can only benefit.

Acknowledgments

We appreciate the following reviewers for giving their time and attention to helping us improve this book: Philip R. Baumann, Moorhead State University; F. Heath Cobb, Pierce College; William C. Cromwell, American University; Paul Dichl, University of Illinois, Urbana; Dick Ganzel, University of Nevada, Reno; Francis Hoole, Indiana University, Bloomington; Michael Huelshoff, University of Oregon, Eugene; John Iatrides, Southern Connecticut State University; Lawrence LeBlanc, Marquette University; David Mares, University of California, San Diego; George Quester, University of Maryland, Arlington; Gholam Razi, University of Houston; William Meyer, University of Delaware, Newark; Philip Rogers, George Washington University; and Raju G.C. Thomas, Marquette University.

Peter A. Toma
Robert F. Gorman

Contents

Part I
Understanding International Relations: Basic Concepts and Applications
1

■

Part II
Elements of Foreign Policy Making
89

Four
The Actors and Their Capabilities   90

Five
The Determinants and Processes of Foreign Policy Behavior   120

■

Part III
Instruments of Foreign Policy and State Behavior
157

Nine
International Organization 249

Ten
International Law 281

International Relations: Understanding Global Issues

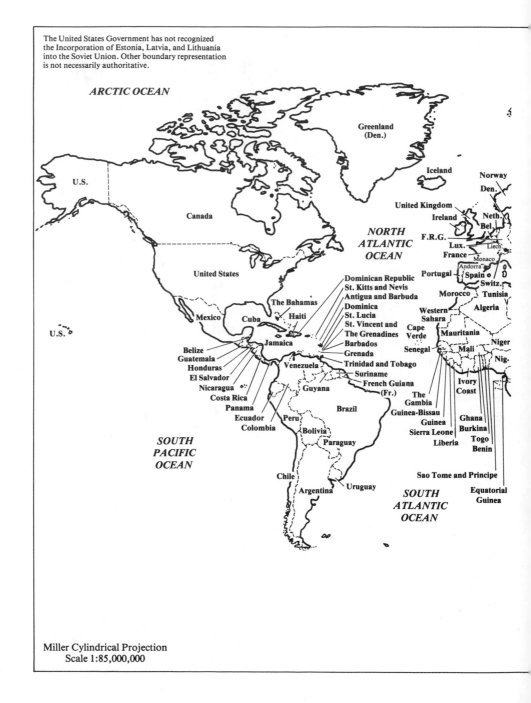

The United States Government has not recognized the Incorporation of Estonia, Latvia, and Lithuania into the Soviet Union. Other boundary representation is not necessarily authoritative.

ARCTIC OCEAN

Greenland
(Den.)

Iceland

Norway
Den.

United Kingdom
Ireland

Neth.
Bel.

NORTH ATLANTIC OCEAN

F.R.G.
Lux.
Liech.

France
Monaco

Andorra

Portugal

Spain

Switz.

Morocco

Tunisia

Western Sahara

Algeria

Mauritania

Niger

Cape Verde

Senegal

Mali

Nig.

U.S.

Canada

United States

Mexico

Cuba

The Bahamas

Haiti

Jamaica

Dominican Republic
St. Kitts and Nevis
Antigua and Barbuda
Dominica
St. Lucia
St. Vincent and
The Grenadines
Barbados
Grenada
Trinidad and Tobago

Belize
Guatemala
Honduras
El Salvador
Nicaragua
Costa Rica
Panama
Ecuador
Colombia

Venezuela

Suriname
French Guiana
(Fr.)

Guyana

Peru

Brazil

Bolivia

Paraguay

The Gambia
Guinea-Bissau
Guinea
Sierra Leone
Liberia

Ivory Coast

Ghana
Burkina
Togo
Benin

U.S.

SOUTH PACIFIC OCEAN

Chile

Argentina

Uruguay

Sao Tome and Principe

SOUTH ATLANTIC OCEAN

Equatorial Guinea

Miller Cylindrical Projection
Scale 1:85,000,000

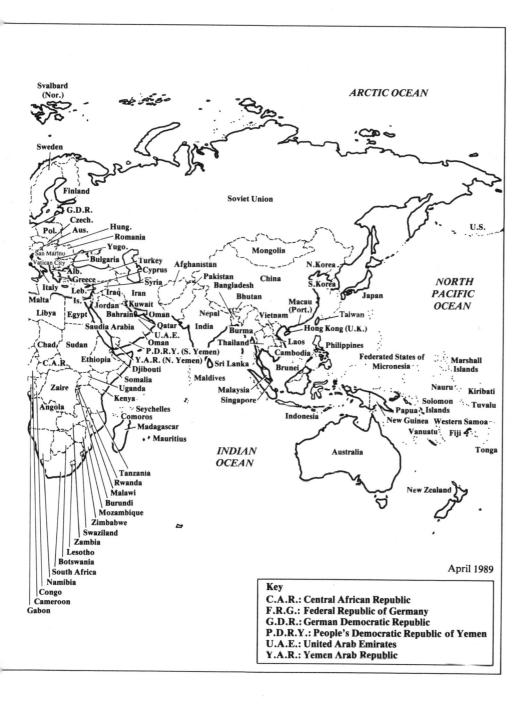

ARCTIC OCEAN

Svalbard
(Nor.)

Sweden

Finland

Soviet Union

U.S.

G.D.R.
Czech.
Pol. Aus. Hung.
Romania
Yugo.
San Marino
Vatican City Bulgaria Turkey
Alb. Cyprus
Greece Syria
Italy Leb. Iraq Iran
Malta Is. Jordan Kuwait
Libya Egypt Bahrain Oman
Saudia Arabia Qatar
U.A.E.
Oman
P.D.R.Y. (S. Yemen)
Y.A.R. (N. Yemen)
Djibouti
Somalia
Uganda
Kenya

Mongolia

N.Korea
S.Korea
Japan

NORTH
PACIFIC
OCEAN

Afghanistan
Pakistan
China
Bangladesh
Bhutan
Nepal
India
Burma
Thailand
Vietnam
Macau
(Port.)
Taiwan
Hong Kong (U.K.)
Laos
Cambodia
Philippines
Sri Lanka
Maldives
Brunei

Federated States of
Micronesia

Marshall
Islands

Chad Sudan
C.A.R.
Ethiopia
Zaire
Angola

Nauru
Kiribati
Solomon
Islands
Tuvalu
Papua
New Guinea
Western Samoa
Vanuatu
Fiji
Tonga

Malaysia
Singapore

Indonesia

Seychelles
Comoros
Madagascar
Mauritius

INDIAN
OCEAN

Australia

Tanzania
Rwanda
Malawi
Burundi
Mozambique
Zimbabwe
Swaziland
Zambia
Lesotho
Botswania
South Africa
Namibia
Congo
Cameroon
Gabon

New Zealand

April 1989

Key
C.A.R.: Central African Republic
F.R.G.: Federal Republic of Germany
G.D.R.: German Democratic Republic
P.D.R.Y.: People's Democratic Republic of Yemen
U.A.E.: United Arab Emirates
Y.A.R.: Yemen Arab Republic

Part I

Understanding International Relations: Basic Concepts and Applications

One
The Study of International Relations: A Thematic Introduction

Two
Sources of Continuity and Change in International Relations

Three
Theories and Approaches in the Study of International Relations

One

___
■

The Study of International Relations:
A Thematic Introduction

Before we begin the study of global issues, it is appropriate to ask what kind of world we have in mind, and what our role as Americans is in that world. The world we call the planet Earth is approximately 4 billion years old; earth's biosphere (a system of life and living organisms) is about 3 billion years old, while its sociosphere (a system of human beings in interaction) is only about 300,000 years old. In fact, we have only had records of human history for the past 5,000 years. From the beginning of human history, the world has been but a reflection of human behavior in interaction with the terrestrial habitat. Human behavior has also influenced the earth's ecosphere (the natural environment in which humans live). Thus, how individuals react to the world in which they live is not a function of that world but rather a reflection of themselves; that is, different people react differently to the same world. Patterns of political, economic, and social behavior have been discernible since ancient times; so it is possible and meaningful to trace continuity and change in human interaction, searching for patterns of similarities and differences. However, before any changes in the international political system can take place, certain identifiable global issues, which emerge as a result of demands by discontented segments (nations) of the global society and which challenge the international system's status quo must be resolved. We will focus on the contemporary issues that affect the changing international system and try to arrange them in a pattern that encompasses the prerequisites for the study of international relations (IR).

More than 5 billion people live in our world. They are organized into about 160 territorially based units, or states, that are spread across five continents. These people share a single ecosystem, they have similar needs and hopes, and they are subject to the rules of interdependent economic productivity and distribution. Whether we consider the world a "global village" as Marshal McLuhan has suggested or "Spaceship Earth" as Barbara Ward Jackson has proposed, it is clear that people all over the world have a lot in common. But these same people also differ greatly in terms of their political organizations, ideologies, standards of living, and cultures. These similarities and differences make for a rapidly changing and highly complex world society. Thus, a student of international relations must understand the global society as a whole.

Although the world's people are incurably diverse, they are also inescapably **inter-dependent.** For example, any major event that occurs anywhere in the world will have a significant impact on the lives of the American people, whether the event is a business (e.g., a drop in the value of the U.S. dollar on foreign exchange markets) or security matter (e.g., a hijacking or terrorist attack on U.S. citizens or commercial airlines), or a health-related (e.g., illicit drug trafficking to the United States) or cultural issue (e.g., the banning of U.S. printed and electronic media output in the People's Republic of China after the June 1989 suppression of student demonstrations for freedom and democracy). Similarly, major U.S. events will impact the global society as well. Today the farthest separated places on earth are less than a two-day flight apart by jet plane, and they are only about 40 minutes apart by guided missile. Instant worldwide communication via television using relayed earth communication satellites can cover almost any event anywhere in the world. Signs of growing interdependence are visible not only in communications, transportation, business, and military and political matters but also in science, technology, and medicine. While countries are becoming more interdependent in some areas, however, they are becoming less interdependent in others, such as language, education, religion, economics, and to some extent domestic politics.

In some areas of the world a growing nationalistic awareness hinders the process of interdependence and results in a more conflictual rather than consensual relationship with other members of the global society. This manifestation of anti-interdependence must not be confused with a nation's competitive force, which is an outgrowth of human nature. Striving for a position of power and strength in the world arena based on material well-being and affluent lifestyle is different from seeking leadership position based on ideological or religious beliefs. So far, a single ruler or organization has never controlled the global society. Although many rulers and organizations have tried, fortunately, not one has succeeded. Making our global society prosperous, free, and democratic does not necessitate rule by one person or organization. Or as Harlan Cleveland points out in the supplementary reading at the end of the chapter, "a nobody-in-charge world doesn't mean a leaderless world."[1] In the aftermath of World War II, a massive reorganization of the world began. But Cleveland believes that creative global institution building can be accomplished without a global war. The initiative should come from responsible, wise, and experienced "rethinkers" who could collectively sketch out a credible, workable system of peaceful change, not from governments or intergovernmental organizations. The ultimate goal would be to "rethink international governance," because no *one* country is capable of achieving this goal. Therefore, "the governments of leading nations have to exercise their leadership not by threatening or browbeating or invading or colonizing peoples that don't agree with them, but rather in ways that are more multilateral, more coherent, more consultative, and more consensual than ever."[2]

Is the United States Still Number One?

In the Fourth of July, 1989, edition of *USA WEEKEND,* popular writers Tom Peters and Bob Waterman offered their thoughts on America's position in the world. In spite of the many problems the country faces, Peters and Waterman believe that the United States is still number one. "Look at our economic and military strength, and our personal freedoms. Nobody in the world comes close, and U.S. culture is everywhere. You can travel to any country, including the USSR, and hear our music, and see our movies."[3] Interestingly enough, a poll conducted by *USA WEEKEND* about a month earlier showed that many Americans thought Japan was number one. Table 1.1, compiled by the same newspaper magazine, seems to confirm that result.

Table 1.1

Comparison of four industrial giants

	United States	Japan	USSR	West Germany
Population	247,498,000	123,231,000	287,015,000	60,162,000
Life expectancy (yrs)	75	78	69	75
Average work week (hrs)	41.0	46.8	39.0	40.5
Household income	$30,759	$38,200	$8,700	$20,875
Unemployment rate (%)	5.5	2.5	n/a	8.0
Space launches (in 1988)	12	3	90	7
Houses with phones (%)	92.5	100.0	28.5	81.0
Voting rate (%)	50.2	69.9	99.9	84.3
Divorces per 1,000 people	4.8	1.3	3.4	2
Murders per 100,000 people	8.300	1.500	0.444	4.400
Gross national product	$4.2 trillion	$1.9 trillion	$2 trillion	$698 billion
Defense (percentage of GNP)	6.6	1.0	14.0–16.0	5.0

SOURCES: Country Forecasts by Frost & Sullivan, *1989 Britannica Book of the Year, 1989 World Almanac, Statistical Abstract of the United States 1989* (Washington, D.C.: Census Bureau, 1990).

If the United States is doing so well, why are so many people talking about our decline? The answer seems relatively simple. At the end of World War II the United States became the world's preeminent power and continued as such into the late 1960s. That strength was built on three pillars: nuclear superiority, control of the world's energy industry, and the strength of the dollar in international trade and finance. For a considerable period after the war, the United States enjoyed a nuclear monopoly. Today the Soviet Union maintains a position of nuclear parity with the United States. In 1960, for example, the United States was responsible for almost one-half of the gross national product (GNP) of the world's market economies. Today it is responsible for only about one-third. In the 1950s the United States could intervene, with a minimal covert effort, to overthrow left-leaning governments (e.g., Guatemala) in many parts of Central America. Today in most Latin American countries, Washington has difficulty justifying the December 20, 1989 intervention in Panama that toppled the tinhorn dictator Manuel Noriega and then took him into custody on charges of conspiracy, racketeering, importing drugs, and travelling to further the conspiracy. In 1948, under the Marshall Plan, the United States provided (in today's dollars) almost $100 billion in grants to Western Europe. Now the United States is the world's largest debtor nation and could not consider undertaking a similar program in Eastern Europe. We must now tailor our economic policies to accommodate foreign creditors whose capital we cannot do without.[4]

Why did the decline in America's international standing take place? An oversimplified answer is because of America's complacency. It was inevitable that key industrial states, crushed in World War II, like West Germany, Great Britain, France, and Japan, would sooner or later regain a major place in the international system. It seems we had grown accustomed to being number one, and without any serious competition during the 1960s, also complacent. For the past two decades the media and critics at large have been complaining that the U.S. has lost its competitive edge in science and technology, economics, education, and communications. While the United States was becoming mired in the Vietnam conflict, Japan, Germany, Korea, Taiwan, and other countries were catching up in these fields and then forging ahead with greater competitiveness. Many U.S. high school and college students became more concerned with staying out of the military draft than with becoming rocket scientists. Our school systems began to place less emphasis on math and science, and as a result, U.S. schools still continue to produce students who end up at the bottom in international competition. It is no wonder, then, that American industry spends more than $20 billion annually to educate and retrain its workers.

In the meantime the world has become a web of interdependent nations that have no national boundaries when it comes to buying and selling, producing and consuming, and hiring and firing scientists, engineers, executives, and workers. Today's world is seeking a work force that understands the present generation of technology and can adapt to the next generation. The important question in the marketplace is no longer who you are, but what you know and what you can do. In the past American college or university graduates competed with one another for job opportunities; now they compete directly or indirectly with students from around the world, because companies are multinational and have branches worldwide and because many international students, competing on U.S. soil, are willing to take less pay and do more work. The connotation of an "interdependent" world raises many questions for Americans—young and old, rich and poor—about how to make the future more secure, more affluent, and freer.

Did the decline in America's global fortunes also initiate a shift in its foreign trade policy? Only in the mid-1970s, when the U.S. annual trade deficit began soaring into the tens of billions of dollars, did we begin to see just how many products were coming into this country from Germany, Korea, Taiwan, and Japan—and how much the foreign demand for American products was drying up. Since then, the U.S. share of the world market in automobiles has fallen from 76 to 24 percent; in machine tools, from 100 to 35 percent; in turntables, from 90 to 1 percent; and in color televisions, from 90 to 10 percent. Fewer new processes are invented in America, and therefore the United States is being pushed back into lower-productivity and lower-wage industries, while those countries that are technologically better capture larger market shares in the high-tech, high-productivity, and high-wage industries. As early as the 1950s and 1960s, cheap labor drew American investment and technology overseas. In effect, we exported jobs, and our technology went with them. In exchange, we got less expensive and eventually better products, stamped "made in Japan," "Germany," "Korea," "Hong Kong," or "Taiwan."

Gradually, the United States changed its foreign trade orientation from the developed to the **less developed or developing countries (LDCs)** of the world (see figure 1.1). Our exports and imports to LDCs were about 11 percent of GNP in 1970; that figure doubled in 1979 and peaked in 1981. Before World War II it was less than 5 percent. We have learned that an increase in international trade translates into enhanced economic prosperity through greater specialization and economies of scale. Interdependence also makes cooperation essential. Economic problems such as energy, food, security, population pressure, and financial stability are truly global in character and can only be effectively tackled through cooperation among nations. As a result of post-1973 income growth in the oil-producing countries, the less developed countries have become an increasingly important market for U.S. manufacturers. In 1982, for example, LDCs purchased $83 billion (about 40 percent) of U.S. merchandise exports, exceeding combined U.S. exports to Western Europe and Japan. Between 1975 and 1982 the value of U.S. exports to LDCs rose by about 11.5 percent per year, exceeding the increase in the value of U.S. exports to developed countries over the same period. Since 1982, however, U.S. exports to LDCs have remained about the same or dropped somewhat. In 1988, for example, LDCs purchased $95 billion worth of U.S. exports, or 40 percent of total U.S. merchandise exports.

Developing countries are an important market for U.S. agricultural goods. Of the $37 billion of agricultural products the United States exported in 1988, $19 billion (about

Developing countries often are divided into subcategories based on income level or stage of industrial development. In 1971 the United Nations established the category of the *least developed*—a group characterized by the exceptionally small size of the gross national product and manufacturing sector as well as a low literacy rate. These are mostly landlocked states or isolated islands, and many have limited physical resources and a declining population due to emigration. In 1980 the least developed countries together received an average of about twenty dollars of bilateral and multilateral official development assistance per inhabitant. The average for other developing countries was about ten dollars.

Developing Countries (Least developed countries are shown in boldface.)

Afghanistan	Burma	Dominica	Honduras
Algeria	**Burundi**	Dominican Republic	Hong Kong
Angola	Cambodia	Ecuador	India
Antigua and Barbuda	Cameroon	Egypt	Indonesia
Argentina	**Cape Verde**	**Equatorial Guinea**	Iran
The Bahamas	**Central African**	El Salvador	Iraq
Bahrain	**Republic**	**Ethiopia**	Ivory Coast
Bangladesh	**Chad**	Fiji	Jamaica
Barbados	Chile	Gabon	Jordan
Belize	China	**The Gambia**	Kenya
Benin	Colombia	Ghana	Kiribati
Bhutan	**Comoros**	Grenada	North Korea
Bolivia	Congo	Guatemala	South Korea
Botswana	Costa Rica	**Guinea**	Kuwait
Brazil	Cuba	**Guinea-Bissau**	Laos
Brunei	Cyprus	Guyana	Lebanon
Burkina	**Djibouti**	**Haiti**	**Lesotho**

Liberia	Nigeria	Saudi Arabia	Tunisia
Libya	Oman	Senegal	Tuvalu
Madagascar	Pakistan	Seychelles	**Uganda**
Malawi	Panama	**Sierra Leone**	United Arab
Malaysia	Papua New Guinea	Singapore	Emirates
Maldives	Paraguay	Solomon Islands	Uruguay
Mali	Peru	**Somalia**	Vanuatu
Malta	Philippines	Sri Lanka	Venezuela
Mauritania	Qatar	**Sudan**	Vietnam
Mauritius	**Rwanda**	Suriname	**Western Samoa**
Mexico	St. Cristopher	Swaziland	**Yemen (Aden)**
Morocco	and Nevis	Syria	**Yemen (Sanaa)**
Mozambique	St. Lucia	**Tanzania**	Zaire
Nepal	St. Vincent and	Thailand	Zambia
Nicaragua	the Grenadines	**Togo**	Zimbabwe
Niger	**Sao Tome and**	Tonga	
	Principe	Trinidad and Tobago	

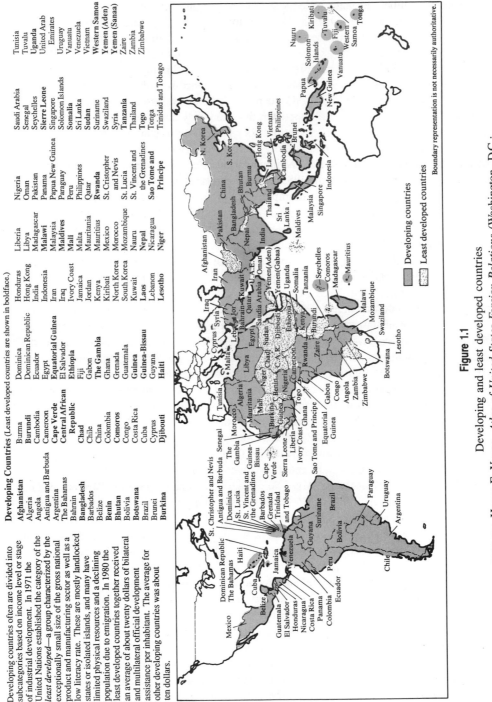

Figure 1.1

Developing and least developed countries

SOURCE: Harry F. Young, *Atlas of United States Foreign Relations* (Washington, D.C.: Department of State Publication 9350, December 1985). p. 69.

51 percent) went to LDCs; over half of U.S. wheat exports and more than 60 percent of rice exports went to LDCs. In 1988 about 20 percent of U.S. farm acreage was devoted to producing for LDC markets. During the same year U.S. private direct investment in the LDCs totaled $77 billion, about 24% of our total private direct investment abroad. As the less developed countries become more stable and more prosperous, they become more attractive candidates for investment.

However, when **OPEC (Organization of Petroleum Exporting Countries)** oil prices more than doubled in 1979–1980, which created great prosperity in the oil-producing countries, a crisis occurred in the oil-dependent countries, especially among the LDCs. The total **OECD (Organization for Economic Cooperation and Development)** current account balance swung from a 1978 surplus of $9 billion to a 1980 deficit of about $74 billion. The LDCs' current account deficit doubled to $62 billion in 1980, whereas OPEC's current account rose from a $5-billion to a $120-billion surplus. As debt accumulated in the LDCs, the rapid decline in oil prices and the 1983 worldwide recession impacted the U.S. economy. In the first eight months of 1982, for example, U.S. exports to Mexico dropped 26 percent, exports to Chile dropped 50 percent, and exports to Thailand dropped 25 percent. If we keep in mind that every $1-billion decrease in U.S. exports eliminates fifty to seventy thousand American jobs (after multiplier effects are taken into account), then we can see that the LDCs' economic hardships had a serious impact on the U.S. economy not only in terms of the accumulation of debt and the inability to repay it, but also in the areas of employment and trade.

On the other side of the trade ledger, the developing countries supply about 45 to 50 percent of the goods that the United States imports for its factories and consumers. In 1988 U.S. purchases amounted to $166 billion, rising from $41 billion in 1982 to $111 billion in 1987. The LDCs supply more than half of the bauxite, tin, and cobalt used by U.S. industry. The developing countries also supply more than half of U.S. imports of ten other strategic metals or minerals, (see figure 1.2), as well as all rubber, coffee, cocoa, and hard fibers. The intertwining of the European, Japanese, and U.S. economies with Third World economies is expected to increase in the 1990s.

As interdependence and global problems increase, the need for understanding U.S. opportunities and limitations in the global arena becomes indispensable. Beyond the demands of economics, the Third World is fundamental to U.S. aspirations for security and peace. The challenges of the past exemplified by the Soviet Union's political influence and military reach are being subjected to new challenges formulated in Mikhail Gorbachev's **new thinking** on Soviet foreign security policy. Gorbachev's commitment to interdependence indicates that areas of human activities have emerged in the contemporary world that no longer accommodate the traditional Marxist-Leninist principles. A new approach is required to secure further development of science and technology, to further integrate economic activities and to solve global problems. The Soviet "initiative" to deal with the "interdependence of survival" (which the Western world has practiced for the past twenty years) has political connotations that make the Soviet Union appear to be the champion of peace and disarmament and the protector of the LDCs that are being exploited by the capitalist West, especially by the United States. While the Soviet Union is extending a cooperative gesture to the United States in arms reduction, it is seeking to better trade relations, share scientific and technological knowledge, and exploit the differences among the Western allies. With the apparent decline of the Soviet military threat around the globe, our European allies, Japan, and Canada become more complacent and keener trade competitors. Thus free trade versus protectionism and trade wars become more poignant issues affecting U.S. policy makers, as we move into the twenty-first century. American producers and consumers can no longer

The United States produces most of the minerals used by American industry but depends on foreign suppliers to meet some or all of its needs for more than twenty of the eighty strategic and critical minerals included in the national defense stockpiles. Western Europe is more dependent on foreign mineral production than the United States;

Japan's dependence is almost total. The USSR is relatively self-sufficient in minerals.

The map shows the principal sources of ten nonfuel minerals for which the United States relies chiefly on imports and gives the supplier's share of total U.S. imports of the listed minerals in 1980–1983.

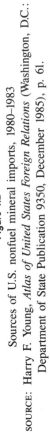

Mineral Imports, 1980-1983 (average percentage of apparent U.S. consumption)

75% asbestos

95% bauxite, alumina

86% chromium

94% cobalt

100% diamond (industrial, stone)

99% manganese

74% nickel

86% platinum group

75% tin

63% zinc

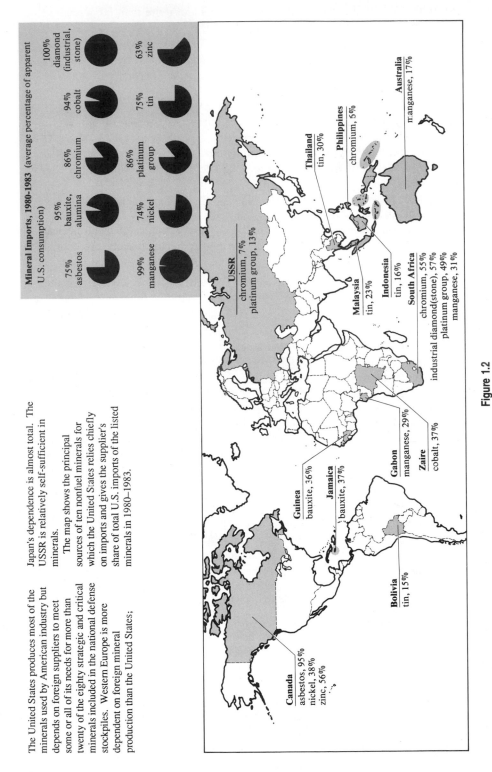

Canada
asbestos, 95%; nickel, 38%; zinc, 56%

Guinea
bauxite, 36%

Jamaica
bauxite, 37%

Bolivia
tin, 15%

Gabon
manganese, 29%

Zaire
cobalt, 37%

USSR
chromium, 7%; platinum group, 13%

Malaysia
tin, 23%

Indonesia
tin, 16%

South Africa
chromium, 55%; industrial diamond(stone), 57%; platinum group, 49%; manganese, 31%

Thailand
tin, 30%

Philippines
chromium, 5%

Australia
manganese, 17%

Figure 1.2

Sources of U.S. nonfuel mineral imports, 1980–1983

SOURCE: Harry F. Young, *Atlas of United States Foreign Relations* (Washington, D.C.: Department of State Publication 9350, December 1985), p. 61.

afford to look toward the future with old clichés, values, and practices. In fact, the U.S. government informs its citizens that it is their duty to develop a keen understanding of U.S. global responsibilities in order to preserve freedom, security, and individual well-being.

Why Study International Relations?

International relations is deeply relevant in our daily lives. Now this proposition may not be self-evident, and so, before we get about the business of trying to understand international relations, it is only fair that we try to justify why we should study it in the first place. The study of international relations is relevant and important for many reasons. Indeed, an individual's liberty, property, and job—even his or her life—may depend on events that occur in the relations between nations.

Deep in concrete-hardened missile silos in the desolate stretches of the American West and in remote areas of the Soviet Union, sitting atop powerful rockets, are enough nuclear warheads to convert the earth's lithosphere into a radioactive wasteland, destroying life as we know it on this incredibly fruitful planet. And the United States and the Soviet Union are not the only two members of the "nuclear club." China, Great Britain, France, India, Pakistan, Israel, and South Africa either have this frightening technology or they are perceived as having it. An individual may be complacent about the chances of these weapons actually being used, but the rapid spread of nuclear technology to the conflict-ridden areas of the world should not give anyone comfort. Still one might argue that the nuclear arms race has little relevance to life's everyday realities. And it is possible, especially for today's youth, to be totally unconcerned about the high incidence of conflict around the globe and whether they might be drafted and forced to fight a real war.

At the Vietnam Memorial in Washington, D. C., visitors quietly scan the list of fifty thousand names grimly etched in the somber black marble, searching perhaps for the name of a loved one. The vast majority of the dead commemorated there were young, college-age men. A war in a far-away, unfamiliar land claimed their lives. Today wars and regional conflicts continue to claim tens of thousands of lives (see figure 1.3).

The war between Iran and Iraq in the Persian Gulf claimed over 500,000 lives—by some estimates nearly ten times the number of Americans killed in Vietnam. A whole generation of Iranians and Iraqis have become cannon fodder, but for many Americans this was a forgotten war until 1987 when American naval forces were called on to protect neutral shipping from attack. Twelve Americans were killed when an Iraqi missile hit their ship. The Persian Gulf war suddenly took on new significance for the families of those dead servicemen. In Lebanon, 241 American marines, part of a peacekeeping force deployed to bring some stability to that war-torn land, were killed in a terrorist attack on their barracks. These examples suggest that war and regional conflicts continue to be an unfortunate but very real feature of modern international relations—a feature that promises to touch the lives of many young people, whether or not they recognize its relevance.

But suppose that the rumbles and rumors of war are but faint and distant sounds. In what other, more concrete and immediate way is international relations relevant to a college student? A few years ago, Texas college students complained when tuitions were doubled. An oil state, Texas had long relied on oil tax revenues to finance higher education. But in 1985–1986, Saudi Arabia decided to flood the market with its high-grade crude

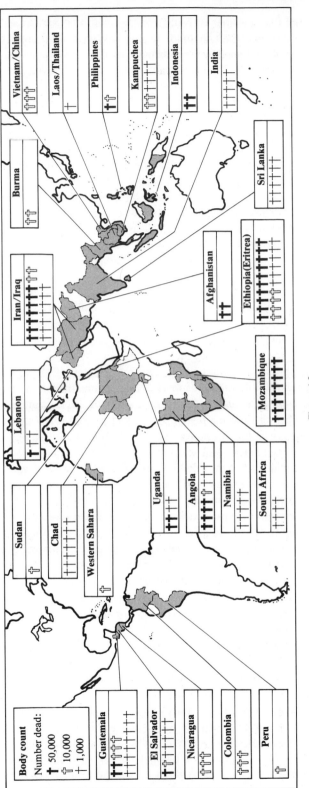

Figure 1.3
Casualties in the world's twenty-five wars (1963–1988)

SOURCE: "Turn South for the Killing Fields," *The Economist*, March 12, 1988, p. 182.
© 1988 The Economist Newspaper Ltd. All rights reserved.

and force global oil prices so low that non-OPEC producers, such as Great Britain and Mexico, could not afford to compete. As Saudi Arabia persisted in this policy, the price Texas received for a barrel of oil dipped by more than 50 percent, and state revenues declined precipitously. Suddenly, policies devised in Riyadh (Saudi Arabia's capital city) dictated policies made in the Texas legislature in Austin. Faced with a budget crisis, the Texas legislature was forced to raise tuitions to keep pace with the continuing costs of higher education. Consumers around the world benefited greatly from the lower prices they paid for gasoline, but the overall impact on Texas and other oil-rich states was negative.

The global economy increasingly dictates a range of domestic U.S. economic trends. The rate of foreign investment in the United States has grown dramatically in the last decade. By setting up shop in the United States, Japanese, British, and German companies avoid tariffs and duties that the U.S. government imposes on their goods. As a result, a much higher proportion of American college graduates will be working for foreign companies and in foreign-owned factories and businesses in years to come.

For individuals who like to travel, international relations presents a host of challenges. Travel documents, visas, and passports must be obtained in order to leave one country and enter another legally. Foreign currencies must be converted into the local currency. In addition, travelers are exposed to the dangers of hijacking and terrorist attack. Prudent travelers learn the location of the nearest embassy or consulate, just in case they run into difficulty in a foreign country.

There is precious little that we discuss—whether it is the weather, the quality of the air we breathe, the price of a cup of coffee, the sunburn we got over the weekend, or the stock market crash—that isn't affected in some way by international relations. Weather reports are commonly collected by weather satellites that are governed by international treaties; pollution spills that do not stop at a nation's borders cause international environmental and public health problems; a freeze in Brazil causes a hike in the price of coffee beans and in the cost of a cup of coffee in Akron; industrial pollutants deplete the global ozone layer, leading to a higher incidence of skin cancers; and fears about the shakiness of the American economy, its increasing debts, and growing trade deficits send the stock market into a 500-point tailspin.

International relations is relevant to our daily lives, and we deny this fact only at great peril. The world is a big and complicated place. No one government or country can claim to control or dominate it. In fact, perceptions about the world, about who is responsible for its problems, and about how these problems should be solved differ greatly from one country to another. As we noted earlier, most Americans like to see their country as number one. In reality, however, only one in twenty people is an American. Americans are a minority not only in terms of global population but also in terms of land mass, property, knowledge, and even power. In economic terms, depending on the base year chosen, the United States represents less than one-fourth of the world GNP and military expenditure, and the U.S. share of the world's energy and steel production is smaller still. The same can be said about the production of knowledge: Only about one-third of the Nobel Prize winners in the natural sciences, and a handful of the world's great inventors and discoverers, have been American. In spite of the great arsenal of modern weapons, much less than half of the world's potential for political and military power is under direct U.S. control.[5]

This American concern about the country's declining position in world politics is nothing new. Historian Arthur Schlesinger, Jr., reminds us that such anxieties have arisen periodically since the earliest days of the Republic. But this notion can be confusing, depending on the years and causes considered. For example, the United States has undergone a relative decline since the 1950s, but if the 1930s or the late 1960s are taken as the baseline, the decline in America's share of world product is *less*.[6] Similarly, misleading historical analogies and false anxieties can lead to retrenchment and self-fulfilling prophesies. For instance, images from the 1970s—such as gas-ration queues, Soviet troops in Afghanistan, and revolutionaries in Tehran taking hostages in the American embassy—raised fears that were exploited during the 1980 presidential election by Jimmy Carter's strategists under the slogan of getting rid of the malaise that had descended upon American society. But this characterization of the American people in the late 1970s is as misleading as the portrayal of American decline in the 1980s. The real causes of the nation's changing position in world politics are multipolarity and interdependence. As a result of multipolarity, power in the global economy has increasingly spread among other countries, particularly among U.S. allies. And as a consequence of the increased complexity of international interdependence, no *one* country has the potential to exercise decisive influence over the *whole* international system. Complexity, as we will learn in the chapters that follow, derives from more actors, more issues, greater interactions, and less hierarchy in international politics. To understand what has happened in the dynamic global arena, we must distinguish between influence over other countries and influence over outcomes in the international system as a whole. The United States still carries more leverage than other countries, but it carries less leverage than in the past because the increased complexity of interdependence makes the achievement of foreign policy goals more difficult.[7] Thus, while Japan has taken the lead in certain areas of high technology and has challenged the United States in markets long dominated by Americans, the United States remains at the forefront of new sources of economic power, even though it shares that position with Japan. Although Americans are justly concerned that the American education system does not yield enough scientists and engineers, few societies are so flexible that they could cope with a shortage of talent by importing and absorbing it.

What Is International Relations?

What is international relations, and how does it differ from other fields of study? **International relations** flow from contacts and interactions among countries, such as political interactions among governments, such as wars, alliances, diplomatic relations, negotiations, and threats of military force. Traditionally, students of international relations have studied these political interactions almost exclusively. However, economic, cultural, religious, racial and ethnic ties, and relations between people living in separately organized states may also fall within the proper sphere of international relations.[8]

As a field of study, international relations is relatively new and is difficult to define precisely. Although international relations first appeared as a field of study in American universities only about seventy years ago, the study of history, economics, and government (or politics) comes from the ancient Greeks. To be sure, even the ancients studied international relations but usually as an adjunct to history or politics. In most American universities, international relations is considered one of the major subfields of political science. But, in fact, many scholars who consider themselves students of international relations are not political scientists. International relations is interdisciplinary in character and, thus, defining its precise boundaries as a field is difficult.

Students of international relations include mathematicians (who build mathematical models of arms races), economists (who study the international trade and monetary system), psychologists (who study the role of perception in international decision making), lawyers (who study international law), theologians (who study the moral implications of international policy), historians (who study diplomatic history and the evolution of the state system), sociologists (who study group behavior among nations), and anthropologists (who study and compare the interactions of cultures). Even physicists and biologists study international relations. Physicists have been active in the nuclear weapons field and have voiced concerns about the impact of new weapons systems on international relations. Biologists, on the other hand, have studied theories of aggression in the animal kingdom and their applicability to international phenomena such as war. The unifying thread among students in these different fields is the study of interactions *between and among* separately constituted governments, societies, and peoples.

Charles McClelland defines international relations as follows:

> The outermost boundaries of international relations are suggested if we imagine *all* of the exchanges, transactions, contacts, flows of information, and actions of every kind going on at this moment of time between and among the separately constituted societies of the world. To this picture in the mind, we should add the effects created within societies from all such interflowing events in earlier times both of the immediate and the more remote past. Finally, the stream of these actions and responses should be conceived as moving on to the future of tomorrow and beyond, accompanied by the expectations, plans, and proposals of all observers of the phenomena.[9]

As McClelland suggests, important events occurring between and within states affect international relations. This concept raises another issue for the student of international relations to consider: the level-of-analysis problem. To add some clarity and order to the exploration of the various dimensions of international relations, it is useful to differentiate the five levels of analysis: the individual level, the subnational group level, the national level, the regional level, and the international (or systemic) level.[10] Clearly, individuals, especially key decision makers such as presidents and foreign ministers, have an impact on international relations. Their thoughts, perceptions, and attitudes can determine whether a nation goes to war or stays at peace. Certainly, the behaviors of subnational interest groups, bureaucracies, governmental departments, and agencies that influence or formulate a country's foreign policy should also be studied carefully. As we will see, **nation-states** are the dominant actors in international relations, and their behavior has attracted the greatest amount of interest among students and scholars. But nation-states also have regional relations; they form trade blocs, alliances, and international organizations to help achieve their mutual interests. These regional organizations, in turn, can affect the policies of nations. Finally, the nation-state lives in an international environment as well. The **international system** level encompasses all international interactions, regional systems, and the overall distribution of power between states. A state ignores the structure of the international system as a whole at its peril. The serious student of international relations should be interested in how the structure of the international system affects the behavior of states. In fact, not only should the serious student be interested in how entities at each level of analysis affect international relations, but also in how each level of analysis is affected by the other levels.

So, now we know that international relations is the study of states and other actors and their interaction at the five levels of analysis just described. But what about its history—how did the study of international relations develop in the United States? Unlike most other disciplines in the related social–behavioral sciences, international relations developed synthetically. That is, the discipline grew out of adjustments to changes in world politics and trends in the related social sciences, rather than out of experimentation and discovery. There was no series of logical steps that led to new, systematic advances. Nevertheless, by reviewing landmarks in the literature, we can identify at least three, or possibly five, stages of development that led to the present status of international relations.[11] In theoretical terms, consisting of both analysis and synthesis, international relations as a field of study went through three distinct periods of development: traditional, behavioral, and post-behavioral. However, in historical terms, international relations had as many as five phases of development.

During the first phase—also known as the historical phase (prior to World War I)—the emphasis was on reconstructing the past through documentary evidence and legalistic interpretations. There was a strong belief that the present had been formed from the past and that this trend could be projected into the future. Organization and a world order based on the peace settlement at Versailles were emphasized during the second phase (after World War I). The great powers interplay and the military strategy of geopolitics influenced the third phase of development (between the two world wars). The fourth phase developed after World War II within the context of a bipolar world overshadowed by ideology and the realist-versus-idealist controversy. In the late 1950s Hans Morgenthau's realist explanation that state actors, concerned with stability in a conflict-prone world system, maximize power in the name of national interest was challenged by the behavioralists as constituting a level-of-analysis problem. In this phase the main arguments focused on research methods. Until about 1970 the underlying realist assertion that nation-states were the *only* actors in the global arena was never challenged. Therefore, in the 1970s the post-behavioral, or fifth phase, developed into a triangular "inter-paradigm" debate (i.e., the realists versus the pluralists and structuralists), which focused on the assumption of a state-centric world. The realists were criticized for neglecting to deal with important actors such as intergovernmental organizations (IGOs) and nongovernmental organizations (NGOs), terrorists, ethnic groups, and religious movements. Realists were also accused of not paying attention to the state's transnational and interdependent role in a "cobweb" context of world societal relations.[12] During the 1970s the beleaguered realists regrouped their forces and, under the label to *neo-realists,* launched a counterattack with very different characteristics from traditional realism. They had adopted a structural mode of analysis that was antithetical to the traditional realism exported from Europe. During the 1980s, the behavioralists' criticisms of the realists led to the rediscovery of economics and its political impact on international relations. Hence, the new field of international relations called *international political economy,* which focuses attention on economic matters, nonstate actors, interdependence, and issue areas, became institutionalized. Neo-realists such as Robert Keohane and Stephen Krasner attempted to demonstrate their claim by studying the U.S. role in international finance as a function of world capitalist development. On the other hand, the Marxist version of international political economy, followed by scholars such as Immanuel Wallerstein, rejected both realism and neo-realism, focusing instead on dependency theory, imperialism, and the crises and contradictions in capitalism.

Another group of scholars called *global modelers* focused on the dynamics of global capitalism but were not influenced by neo-Marxist studies of imperialism and dependency. These scholars are mostly systems engineers and computer modelers who are concerned with world problems that transcend national boundaries, such as the population explosion and environmental degeneration. Their goal is to reconceptualize the planetary situation by including all aspects of an interdependent global environment. Although it is not part of the new field of international political economy, this orientation of ecologists is closely related to international political economy. National security studies, an altogether different focus of inquiry in international relations, has acquired a distinct status and empirical reference. This area has a following among scholars in international relations, scientists, engineers, politicians, and even theologians who are concerned with various aspects of nuclear weapons in a global situation.

These interdisciplinary interests represent a movement toward the human activity and social arrangements of a "global village."[13] Thus, the current scope of international relations has been broadened to include laypersons and professionals from other disciplines whose sometimes innocent concerns for a "safer and better world" lead them to study international relations. While a scientific orientation is now an institutionalized part of the discipline, the boundaries are blurred to such an extent that it is difficult to distinguish between the relevancy and irrelevancy of the voluminous studies surrounding international relations.

At the beginning of this chapter, we alluded to the complex nature of the world we live in and argued that in order to understand the various interactions taking place in the world society as a whole, we need certain professional tools to analyze or explain "the facts" responsible for the complex nature of the global system. Some problems arise at every stage of the process of explaining international phenomena. These problems can be both methodological (e.g., how should phenomena be observed, defined, measured, and compared?) and theoretical (e.g., what are the merits of analysis, what links phenomena, and what are the levels on which to conduct the analysis?). In both areas of endeavor—methodology and theory building—the IR discipline has come a long way. Today, the field contains three **paradigms** (or major explanations) of the international system and the world society as a whole: realism, pluralism, and structuralism. Throughout the 1980s the debate about the respective merits of these three schools of thought became a focal point in international relations.

According to the **realist school,** the world society is a system of "billiard ball" states in intermittent collision. Adherents of the **pluralist school** see the world society as a network of numerous crisscrossing relationships in a cobweblike arrangement. Members of the **structuralist school** view the world society as a many-headed octopus whose powerful tentacles constantly suck wealth from the weakened peripheries toward its powerful centers or heads—the major powers.[14] Each paradigm starts with a different image and arrives at a different conclusion, because the proponents have erected a theoretical structure that identifies actors, dynamics, and dependent variables in contradictory terms. These fundamental differences beg the question of whether the scope of international relations should be limited to state-centric international politics as the realists argue, or whether it should encompass additional actors such as the IGOs and NGOs as the pluralists maintain, or whether it should envelop the entire world system at all levels with an emphasis on the economic mode of production as the structuralists argue. The answer to this question will also determine whether concepts such as *deterrence* and *alliance* (in realist terms) are more important than *ethnicity* and *interdependence* (in pluralist terms), or *exploitation* and *dependence* (in structuralist terms).

There are, of course, several other perceptions and explanations of world society, which can be attributed to differences in methodology and conceptualization. There is no consensus in the IR discipline on how to observe, define, measure, compare, and classify phenomena. Therefore, in many instances the process becomes more or less a matter of individual choice. This is not to imply, however, that the field lacks structure, focus, or disciplinary rigor. Thus our task in this book is not to condemn or endorse these schools of thought but to identify them in their proper context and to compare them to other approaches, always with the prevailing question: What is new in the discipline of international relations?

As stated earlier, changes in international relations are not derived from laboratory experimentation (a series of logical steps leading to new and systematic advances in orderly progression) but from adjustments to changes in global politics. In other words, global transformations and emergent trends have produced new conditions and phenomena that must be analyzed and synthesized in order to be incorporated into the discipline as new knowledge. During this process, new issues and cleavages are addressed by testing old theories and approaches that are relevant to understanding the changes taking place in the global arena. Because change is endemic to international relations, emphasis must be placed not only on different approaches through which international phenomena are explained, but also on the factors that produce change and impact the political actors on the global stage. Therefore, unlike many other textbooks, ours does not follow one arbitrarily selected approach that we consider "the right approach," instead, we emphasize issues—new and old—that encompass all dimensions of contemporary international relations and the analytical perspectives that have been devised to understand them. Perhaps our strongest motivation for this issue-oriented approach has been the absence of a general theory and a lack of consensus among scholars about the exact scope and method of international relations. Thus, in the following thirteen chapters, we are not guided by who is right or wrong but by what students interested in the subject matter should know about new developments in international relations.

Harlan Cleveland

■

The Future of
International Governance
Managing a Nobody-in-Charge World

At the 1980 General Assembly of the World Future Society in Toronto, held jointly with the Canadian Association for Future Studies, the Canadian millionaire and public servant Maurice Strong sent us home with these parting words: "The bad news is that the world is coming to an end. The good news is, not yet—and not necessarily."

But we do stand at "the hinge of history." Economist Barbara Ward fashioned that phrase nearly twenty years ago. The biosphere of our inheritance and the technosphere of our creation are out of balance, she wrote. "The door of the future is opening onto a crisis more sudden, more global, more inescapable, more bewildering than any ever encountered by the human species. And one which will take decisive shape within the life span of children who are already born...."

Everything that has happened since those words were written reinforces their prescient wisdom.

The adjective *nuclear* already carried overtones of dread, casting malignant shadows on nice familiar nouns like *waste* and *safety* and *conflict*. But nobody had yet done the calculations that cause us now to argue whether the use of strategic weapons would produce a nuclear winter or merely a nuclear autumn.

Ward was writing before the latest evidence was in about the arrogance of our engineering—before Bhopal,

Harlan Cleveland is a professor at the University of Minnesota's Hubert H. Humphrey Institute of Public Affairs, Humphrey Center, 301 19th Avenue South, Minneapolis, Minnesota 55455. He has also served as U.S. Ambassador to NATO. This article is adapted from a presentation given at "Future Focus," the 1986 World Future Society conference in New York City. For more information on the "Rethinking International Governance" project, contact Professor Cleveland at the above address.
SOURCE: Adapted by permission of the publisher, *The Futurist*, Vol. 22, No. 3 (May–June) 1988, pp. 9–12.

before Chernobyl, before the *Challenger* exploded. She didn't know then that the buildup of carbon dioxide and other "greenhouse gases" in the global atmosphere will likely warm up the world enough to make a dust bowl out of Kansas and flood the world's seaports in an irreversible rising of the oceans.

It wasn't as clear then as it is now that (in Roger Revelle's memorable image) we humans are conducting a giant geophysical experiment of which we cannot even guess the outcome. At this hinge of history, what we do to the natural environment may, for the first time in world history, produce more global change than what Nature does to, and for, its human species.

Above all, we didn't realize back then how the explosive marriage of computers and telecommunications would require us to rethink the very fundaments of our philosophy, rethink an economics based on scarcity, rethink governance based on secrecy, rethink laws based on ownership, rethink management based on hierarchy.

Obstacles to Policy Making

The biggest changes that affect our capacity to cope are evident enough: the informatization of society and the internationalization of problems. Both seem to erect large obstacles to responsible policy making. Yet, these obstacles have mostly to do with the way each of us *thinks* about our informatized, internationalized world.

For example, it is hard to keep our *opportunities* in perspective. Information is rapidly becoming the dominant resource in "modern" and even "modernizing" societies. It is much more accessible than any previously dominant resource (land, minerals, energy) in the history of civilization. That should be good news for fairness. Yet, our ways of thinking, rooted in the hierarchical concepts of the age of administrative pyramids, inhibit the currently disadvantaged from taking advantage of the new information environment.

Our minds, which are trained in school to organize reality in distinct categories, are frustrated by *the blurring of distinctions* in the world outside our minds. This is especially true of the dividing line between "domestic" and "international." Because information flows so freely around so much of the globe, the content of international affairs is now predominantly the internal affairs of other nations; and the content of "domestic politics" is heavy with international impacts and implications. Yet, in the United States, for example, the issues of policy politics still tend to be publicly debated (and handled in Congress and the White

House) as though the line between "domestic" and "international" were not irretrievably blurred.

And it is hard, in thinking about the new information environment, to escape from *the entrenched metaphors of economics*. Information as such cannot be owned, much less monopolized, though delivery services can. Information therefore gives rise, not to exchange transactions in a traditional market, but to sharing transactions in a new kind of global commons for which we do not yet have a settled body of economic, legal, or political theory.

To manage these revolutions (of explosive power, of biotechnology, of informatics) while minimizing the dangers (from industrial and military accidents, from malign environmental change, from computerized crime, from the many genies escaping from scientists' bottles) will not only require our very best expert minds. To manage the macrotransition we are in will require policy makers to think more freshly, farther ahead, and more widely (which is to say globally) than every before.

In a democracy, citizens make public policy and governments carry it out, so it's the citizens who have to be the practical futurists. And since the policy-making citizens are just grown-up schoolchildren, today's schoolchildren had better also be growing up with a forward lean and a global perspective.

Our capacity to cope thus depends on our applied imagination, our specialized skills mixed with broad understandings, and especially on our sense of public responsibility, which means our *personal* responsibility for the *general* outcome.

Rethinking International Governance

What is needed today is an ambitious effort to "rethink international governance." We must examine, in its parts and their relations to each other, the international system as a whole.

In 1986, we began, at the University of Minnesota's Hubert H. Humphrey Institute of Public Affairs, a project to encourage this rethinking of international governance. The project is now well under way under the guidance of a corps of twenty-seven international generalists from twenty-two countries. I am indebted to three of my close American colleagues Lincoln Bloomfield, Geri Joseph, and Magda McHale—for parts of what follows.

Suppose that we were assigned to be the "postwar planning staff" in the middle of a great war. We wouldn't start, would we, by tinkering with the machinery of the United Nations, or by trying to reduce nuclear stockpiles by ratios that would leave us all as insecure as we were before the reductions, or by making marginal adjustments in a system of trade and money that is inherently unstable and unfair?

On the contrary, we would start by asking "After the UN, what?" and "After quantitative arms control, what?" and "After a defunct Bretton Woods system, what?" We would feel obligated, wouldn't we, to think comprehensively and globally about a system that spans security, development, economic management, human rights and responsibilities, the migration of peoples, and the mix of dangers and opportunities that stem from scientific discovery and technological innovation?

The trouble is: We cannot, this time, afford war as the prelude to thinking hard about peace. So we have to figure out how to do "postwar planning" without having the war first. We propose to make a start now on the premise that the world does not need, because it cannot survive, global war as a spur to creative global institution building.

We cannot expect governments, or intergovernmental organizations, to initiate this kind of root-and-branch rethinking. Except in times of deep crisis (such as a great depression or war), governments are, paradoxically, too "responsible" for peace to take the responsibility for change.

We thought that the best bet was to assemble for this purpose, from around the world, under nongovernmental auspices, an ad hoc "core group" of wise and experienced rethinkers, working together in a manner that does not engage whatever professional responsibilities they might otherwise be carrying, to sketch a credible, workable system of peaceful change.

Fragments of a Workable World

One starting point in imagining a workable world is to ask what already works.

As an offset to the daily diet of mayhem and disaster that passes as "news" in the mass media, we need to remind ourselves, and our future policy makers still in school, that some parts of the "international system" are working very well, and other parts tolerably well.

Not all of it is to everyone's taste; in a world mainly characterized by diversity, no outcome will be universally praiseworthy. But consider, as examples, these fragments of "a workable world":

- Weather forecasting, the eradication of some infectious diseases, international civil aviation, the allocation of the frequency spectrum, the uses of outer space (so far), Antarctica, the deep seabed (what's left of it), and the many other instances of, or efforts at, international technological cooperation.

- Multinational corporations, both "private" and "socialized," which operate across national boundaries so much more easily than governments seem able to do.
- European economic integration (as far as it goes).
- The string of agricultural research institutes around the world.
- The success (so far) of population limitation in most, though not all, developing countries.
- Cooperation and freedom for development in the Pacific Basin, where so many of the best examples of growth-with-fairness are to be found.
- The "globalization" of an efficient information flow (though not always a fair distribution of the benefits) in such fields as money exchange, commodity markets, airline reservations, and the coverage of news and sports.
- Subregional cooperation, such as the Mediterranean cleanup pushed by the UN Environmental Programme.
- Adjudication, by the International Court of Justice, of a few disputes. They are pitifully few, but one of them was the seemingly intractable Atlantic fisheries dispute between Canada and the United States.
- The more effective instances of UN peacekeeping and quiet diplomacy by international agents and outside-the-system mediators.

There is a good deal to start with here. Can we bottle the essence of what works and sprinkle it over what doesn't?

Managing the Global Commons

"Rethinking international governance" requires us to focus on the international "functions of the future," to analyze the new needs for cooperation on mutual security, on economic stability and fairness, on assuring justice and participation, on managing the global commons—the commons that now includes not only clouds and penguins and fish and deep-sea minerals, but also parking spaces at geosynchronous orbit, the gene pool of microorganisms, and the transborder flow of computerized data.

Cutting across the "functions of the future" are new technologies, the product of new scientific learnings in the life sciences and of the recent marriage of fast computers and global telecommunications. The new technologies deserve our special attention; they can make or break any effort to develop an up-to-date international system of peaceful change.

Many of the items on the contemporary agenda take the form of implicit or explicit threats to economic and political stability, to the global biosphere, or to the survival of the human race itself. Virtually all of these threats come not, as in the past, mainly from the workings of cruel but impersonal forces, acts of Fate or of God. They derive overwhelmingly from the hand and brain of man, whose scientific and technological prowess has spun off malign "externalities" ranging from overpopulation to the weapons of genocide.

It is still shocking, more than forty years later, to realize that the Manhattan Project, the huge secret organization that produced the atom bomb during World War II, did not employ on its staff a single person whose full-time assignment was to think hard about the implications if the project should succeed. No one was working on nuclear arms control—and we have been playing catch-up, not too successfully, ever since.

The perverse social impacts of the new technologies have spawned (even in the world's most powerful countries) feelings of inadequacy, even helplessness, of being swept along—sometimes for better but often for worse—on an unstoppable flood of innovations.

Technologies of Peace

Yet, it is beyond argument that technology, when asked the right questions, can work for peace as well as war, for social fairness as well as economic growth. We don't have to start with satellites for military reconnaissance and only belatedly say to ourselves, "Hey, wouldn't that product of military R&D be useful for verifying arms-control agreements?"

Why couldn't we start the other way around, by posing for the R&D community the requirements of a genuine peace system and then asking the scientists and engineers to address themselves to *that*? There are, surely, more than enough people with highly technical skills, especially young people, who would prefer to labor in the vineyards of peace than where the grapes of wrath are stored.

There are already some encouraging examples of what happens when you start with the benign technological options. Remote sensing from satellites has been used for mapping the Amazon, for crop forecasting, and for monitoring the destruction of rain forests and the outward creep of deserts. The resistant hybridized grains that help avert hunger are the product of another benign technology, and so is the chemical research that spurs the progress of population control in so many countries.

I was privileged to be in on the birth of the World Weather Watch, now perhaps the most successful example of global cooperation—which is why you never hear about it. It's the worldwide data system that delivers to your TV screen every night, through the cooperation of more than a hundred nations, a five-day forecast backed up with weather photos taken with orbiting cameras. During the 1960s, the system by which this is done was invented, proposed, deployed, and tested—the picture-taking satellites, the communications satellites, the faster computers. A quarter of a century ago, we were doing our social thinking *in parallel* with the technological R&D. It's not a lost art; we just seem to have forgotten where we put it.

We can hardly blame the scientists and engineers who chase after the grants and contracts in researching and developing the technologies of war, if we're not trying equally hard to create a demand for their skills and insights in fashioning the technologies of peace.

A World with Nobody in Charge

The political context for "rethinking international governance" is a world with nobody in charge. The puzzle we now face is strikingly similar to the problem so successfully confronted by Thomas Jefferson, James Madison, Alexander Hamilton, and company. Last year, the United States celebrated two hundred years of a constitution written to govern a large, diverse, developing nation through institutions designed to make sure that nobody would be in overall charge. In 1787 and beyond, that's what the separation of powers, the checks and balances, and the federal system were all about.

In 1988 and beyond, this century's third try at world order will also be an exercise in the management of pluralism, this time on a world scale. But if we're going to be living in a Madisonian world, the people of a nobody-in-charge society should find congenial work in helping to fashion institutions for a world with no nation or creed or race or ideology in charge, a world truly "safe for diversity," in the words of President John F. Kennedy.

A nobody-in-charge world doesn't mean a leaderless world. It just means that the governments of leading nations have to exercise their leadership not by threatening or browbeating or invading or colonizing peoples that don't agree with them, but rather in ways that are more multilateral, more coherent, more consultative, and more consensual than ever.

Study Questions

1. How would you describe the world according to characteristics such as the biosphere, ecosphere, and sociosphere?
2. What are some of the manifestations of growing interdependence and anti-interdependence?
3. How does Harlan Cleveland describe the "nobody-in-charge world"?
4. What is needed to build a future world with no one ruler or organization in charge? How can this be accomplished?
5. Why do Tom Peters and Bob Waterman believe that the United States is still number one?
6. What are the symptoms of U.S. decline of power in the international system?
7. How did interdependence contribute to the decline of U.S. power?
8. How did the decline in America's international standing affect its foreign trade policy?
9. Why are the less developed countries important to the U.S. economy?
10. How does the Soviet Union view interdependence?
11. Why should we study international relations?
12. How does the global economy dictate a range of domestic trends in the United States?
13. Why are anxieties about the decline of American power dangerous for policy making?
14. Why is it important to distinguish between influence over other countries and influence over outcomes in the global system?
15. What is international relations, and how does it differ from other fields of study?
16. What are the various levels of analysis in international relations?

17. What are the five stages of development that led to the present status of international relations?
18. What were IR's main achievements during the fifth or post-behavioral stage?
19. What is meant by the "rediscovery" of international political economy?
20. How do perceptions of the world society differ between realists, pluralists, and structuralists?
21. International relations developed synthetically, not organically. What does this statement mean?

Key Terms

interdependence

international relations

international system

less developed (or developing) countries (LDCs)

nation-state

new thinking

OECD (Organization for Economic Cooperation and Development)

OPEC (Organization of Petroleum Exporting Countries)

paradigm

pluralist school

realist school

structuralist school

Notes

1. Harlan Cleveland, "The Future of International Governance: Managing a Nobody-in-Charge World," *The Futurist,* May/June 1988, p. 12.
2. Ibid.
3. See interview with Tom Peters and Bob Waterman written by John Hillkirk, *USA WEEKEND,* 30 June–2 July 1989, 4–5.
4. See Charles William Maynes, "Coping with the '90s," *Foreign Policy,* no. 74 (Spring 1989): 42–62.
5. See Karl W. Deutsch, *The Analysis of International Relations,* 3rd ed. (Englewood Cliffs, N.J.: Prentice-Hall, 1988).
6. See Joseph S. Nye, Jr., "Understanding U.S. Strength," *Foreign Policy,* no. 72 (Fall 1988): 105–129.
7. Ibid., p. 108.
8. Charles McClelland, *Theory and the International System* (New York: Macmillan, 1966), p. 17.
9. Ibid., p. 20.
10. J. David Singer, "The Level-of-Analysis Problem in International Relations," in *The International System,* eds. Klaus Knorr and Sidney Verba (Princeton, N.J.: Princeton University Press, 1961), pp. 77–92.
11. For a complete and detailed explanation, see William C. Olson and Nicholas G. Onut, "The Growth of a Discipline: Reviewed," in *International Relations: British and American Perspectives,* ed. Steve Smith (Oxford: Basil Blackwell, 1985), pp. 1–18.

12. See, for example, Michael P. Sullivan, "Transnationalism, Power Politics, and the Realities of the Present System," in *Globalism versus Realism: International Relations Third Debate,* eds. Ray Maghroori and Bennet Ramberg (Boulder: Westview Press, 1982), pp. 195–221.
13. See, for example, J. David Singer, "The Responsibilities of Competence in the Global Village," *International Studies Quarterly* 29, no. 3 (1985): 245–262.
14. Michael Banks, "The Inter-Paradigm Debate" in *International Relations: A Handbook of Current Theory,* eds. Margot Light and A. J. R. Groom (London: Frances Pinter, 1985), p. 12.

Two

Sources of Continuity and Change
in International Relations

To a large extent, this book focuses on the contemporary institutions and processes—formal and otherwise—that facilitate international relations. But to understand contemporary international relations, we must study the past, because the modern international system and the rules by which it is governed are the result of centuries of evolution. Indeed, the interstate system is still anchored in traditional rules, concepts, and practices that are nearly three and a half centuries old.

As we embark on an exploration of politics in the global arena, we will study history and also reflect on one of the basic tensions that gives modern international relations much of its distinctive flavor, that is, the battle between the forces of continuity and the forces of change. The battle lines are rarely drawn with clarity; nor are the signs of battle readily apparent. But the forces of continuity and change are in constant struggle in much the same way as the ocean and the shore are in constant confrontation; the rocky promontories are not reduced to sand overnight, but the forces of change are ever at work, inexorably reshaping the environment. And so it is in relations among nations; the modern forces of change challenge the traditional forces of continuity.

What are these forces? The primary force of continuity in international relations is the nation-state, with its trappings of sovereignty and its marshaling of power in the pursuit of its national interests.[1] The forces of change include the emergence of a global economy, rapid technological advances, threats to the global environment, and the rising importance of nonstate actors as holders of power and influence. These forces of change have eroded the traditional foundations of the international order.

Indeed, some analysts predict that the state is dying, if not already dead. Some people insist that the nation-state is an anachronism, no longer relevant to the global problems confronting the international system today.[2] But is the state irrelevant? Is it an endangered species? As we will see later in this chapter, there is good reason to believe that, to paraphrase Mark Twain, reports about the death of the state have been greatly exaggerated. The purpose of this chapter, then, is twofold. First, we will review the historical development of international relations. Second, as we trace the evolution of the international system, we will identify and define basic concepts of continuity and change that the student of international relations should be familiar with in order to understand how the forces of change have challenged the traditional international order. To understand these questions, we first need to transport ourselves back in time to examine the origins of the state system and some of the key concepts on which it was built and still stands, however precariously.

Sources of Continuity

The Westphalian System

Most students of international relations argue that the modern state system can be traced back to the **Peace of Westphalia** in 1648, which brought an end to the Thirty Years War and to the dominance of the Church in the political life of Europe.[3] Although this event was an important turning point in the development of the state system, one should not conclude that states first came into existence then. Indeed, states and state systems can be identified throughout most of recorded human history in many parts of the world. Thanks to writers such as Thucydides, our knowledge of the Greek city-state system is perhaps the most extensive.[4] But interstate relations were also evident in ancient Egypt, in the dynastic politics of China, and in the subcontinent of India.[5] Nor was the state suddenly born in Europe in 1648. Rather, the Peace of Westphalia marked the completion of centuries of evolution, as relatively well-defined and generally larger geographic units coalesced from the fragmented feudal political order of the Middle Ages. The implications of the Peace of Westphalia were far-reaching; in effect, it established a number of basic principles on which the modern global international system is based. Several of these principles are described in the following paragraphs.

Sovereignty In the Middle Ages, debates about sovereignty and the appropriate authorities of religious and secular rulers were common. Some scholars held that true sovereignty resided in religious authorities, whereas others believed that political sovereignty could only truly exist in the secular realm. Perhaps the most dominant thinker of the time, Thomas Aquinas defined **sovereignty** as the ability to achieve one's will without hindrance or let. In other words, an entity could be sovereign only if its will was unrestrained by obstacles and if it did not need to ask for another's permission to do something. Logically, only God could meet the rigorous demands of such a definition. Derivatively, the pope, though frail and finite like all created things, could make the strongest claims to sovereignty as God's representative on earth. Kings held political authority and controlled business and economic activity, but they were accountable to the spiritual authorities, who were responsible for moral and religious matters.[6] The Church's influence did not stop there, though. Its teaching on usury (charging excessive interest on money), its disallowing of business on Sundays, its efforts to prevent war on Sundays and during holy seasons, even its teachings on divorce placed some constraints on the kings' abilities to control the political and economic aspects of their realms. But even if they resented the Church, kings also feared it. Kings who violated Church teachings could be excommunicated, that is, kicked out of the Church and denied its sacraments. Understandably, rulers were not keen about arousing the anger of the pope or his Church, and so most of them submitted to the Church's authority in these matters.

This situation did not appeal to everyone, however. As the Protestant Reformation gathered momentum in the 1500s, princes began to claim sovereignty for themselves. They were supported by a growing number of political thinkers who opposed the Church's interference in political affairs. In 1576 Jean Bodin, a French philosopher, argued that princes themselves were sovereign, and that only they should have the ultimate right and authority to control all people and events within the territory under their jurisdiction.[7] After the devastation of the religious wars, this principle of princely sovereignty seemed to be the only alternative to continued religious conflict. Indeed, by the end of the Thirty Years War in 1648, the European monarchs and princes had concluded that stability and peace depended on their ability to dictate even the religion of their state. Henceforth, neither the state's political or religious life could be dictated by an external power. Sovereignty came to mean the government's ability to control all of the country's internal and external affairs.

Inherent in the idea of sovereignty was that each state was equal and independent. No sovereign could claim to be more sovereign than another, and each was independent of the other, at least in theory. The monolithic sovereignty of a God working through his church on earth had given way to a theory of multiple sovereigns who did not need to seek permission to act. But this new system presented many hindrances and obstacles to the attainment of princely will. If no one could impose rules on a prince, then a prince could not ensure that his will would prevail in his relations with other sovereigns. Determining whose will prevailed became the primary task of international politics among sovereign states.

Today sovereignty refers to the right of a state to control its domestic and foreign affairs without external interference. Sovereign states alone have a legal right to take a person's life. Only they can legally wage war. They have the right to control the flow of people, money, and economic goods over their borders. They determine who their citizens will be and what laws will guide their behavior. State governments decide what treaties they will sign, and who they will make alliances with. Governments of fully sovereign states, in other words, make their own foreign policies.

Obligation   Sovereignty implied that rules could not be imposed on states without their consent. But the Peace of Westphalia also called for states to recognize the existence of respective rights and duties. If a prince expected other princes to respect his authority within his jurisdiction, then he must respect their rights in their jurisdictions. The right or privilege of sovereignty carried with it a reciprocal duty. For instance, once states had agreed to be bound by the terms of a treaty, they were expected to honor those terms. A system of international law, of norms that would guide state behavior, was essential to effectively maintain order among sovereigns. Moreover, recognition of the right of other sovereigns to exist was a necessary concession for the maintenance of the Westphalian system.

Recognition   The Westphalian system implied that the original signatories to its treaties were the only existing states. Also implicit in the system was that future sovereign states could enter the system formally only after being recognized by the existing states. In effect, the Westphalian system was Eurocentric: in legal terms, it effectively declared the rest of the world **terra nullis,** literally, territory legally belonging to no one. Of course, we know that extensive empires—such as the Chinese, the Aztecs, and the Zulus—existed in many other parts of the world at this time. But according to the European view, rulers of other nations throughout the world could not legitimately exercise authority without the recognition of European states. This powerful legal concept was backed by Europe's military, economic, and political power, and, in fact, Europe had begun to colonize the rest of the world even before Westphalia. By the end of the period of colonial expansion, the European states dominated the rest of the world. In the process, the Westphalian system became global in character and practice.

Although it has roots in the Westphalian system, recognition is still very much a part of international relations. Recognition by the great powers of Europe was really the key to obtaining sovereign status. Today any state may grant recognition to any other, and no one state's recognition is considered any more or less valid from a legal standpoint. Politically, however, recognition by the most powerful states is still more important than recognition by smaller powers. When Biafra declared its independence from Nigeria in 1967, it received recognition as a new state from a number of African countries, but it failed to receive recognition from major powers outside Africa. Three years later Biafra's war of independence was crushed by the Nigerian central government. Had Biafra received the recognition and support of the major European powers, or of at least one superpower, the outcome might have been different.

Recognition is a political act that implies certain legal consequences. When one state recognizes another, it acknowledges the right of the new state to sovereignty and the right of its government to participate in international relations, to send and receive diplomats, to have access to the domestic courts of the recognizing state, and so on. A distinction should be made between recognition of states and recognition of governments. When a new state is recognized, usually its government is recognized simultaneously as the state's legitimate government. Subsequent changes of government through constitutional means (for example, by elections) do not require further recognition. But what if a government is overthrown by revolution? Some governments believe that recognition should be extended automatically to any government that can demonstrate control over the country's population and territory. However, for political reasons, other governments might decide not to recognize a new government's claim to sovereignty—to pretend, in effect, that it does not have control over its territory. The United States, for instance, refused to recognize Mao Tse-tung's Communist government when it overthrew Chiang Kai-shek's Nationalist regime on mainland China in 1949. Instead, the U.S. government continued to recognize the Nationalist government of the Republic of China, which fled to the island of Formosa (Taiwan), despite the fact that nearly a billion Chinese lived on the mainland under the Communist government of the People's Republic. In 1979, the United States, bowing to political realities, finally recognized the People's Republic as the legitimate government of all China (including Taiwan). Formal diplomatic relations with the Nationalist government ceased, and diplomatic ties with the Communist government were established.

The U.S. treatment of China highlights the difference between de facto and de jure recognition. When an existing government formally recognizes another government, it extends **de jure recognition,** that is, recognition in law. But suppose that prior to this act, the government engages in direct negotiations with the government seeking recognition? This would constitute a form of **de facto recognition,** since direct negotiations with another government imply that it has legitimacy. This distinction is very important for some states. For instance, most of the Arab states deny the existence of both the State of Israel and its government. In the various negotiations that have taken place in order to achieve cease-fires after several Arab–Israeli wars, the representatives of the Arab states have refused to engage in direct bilateral negotiations with Israel, fearing that this might constitute recognition of the State of Israel. This explains why negotiations either have been mediated by third parties who shuttle back and forth between Israel and the Arab states (as exemplified by former Secretary of State Henry Kissinger's famous shuttle diplomacy of the early 1970s) or held under the direct auspices of the United Nations. According to a UN rule, membership in an international organization does not constitute recognition by all other members, nor do negotiations under the auspices of such a body constitute recognition. This explains why Israel and Iraq can sit next to each other in the UN General Assembly, even though Iraq denies the formal existence of Israel. Egypt is the only Arab state that formally recognizes Israel. This recognition took place when Anwar el-Sadat, the former president of Egypt, traveled to Israel, met directly with the government of Menachim Begin, and addressed the Israeli Knesset (legislative body). These were acts of recognition, in themselves, and were followed by the formal extension of diplomatic relations between Egypt and Israel.

Obviously, recognition is taken very seriously by many governments. Recognition is critical to full participation in international relations. It is a kind of legal rite of passage to statehood, and it is vigorously sought by those who do not have it. Those that have the power to give recognition—the existing states—often are selective in granting it. To understand its political importance, we need to define what is meant by the concept of *statehood,* and how it differs from the concept of *nationhood.*

The Nation, the State, and the Nation-State

To fully appreciate the development of the state system originating with the Peace of Westphalia, we must focus for a moment on the concepts of the *state,* the *nation,* and the *nation-state.* The terms are often used interchangeably, but there are technical differences between them. These differences are at the heart of many contemporary problems in the international system.

The nation   A **nation** consists of a group of people who share a common past, heritage, customs, and history as well as a common vision and aspiration for the future. Often they share a common religion, ethnic background, and language. Whichever of these factors is the basis for the sense of unity, a nation is a community of individuals that have developed a sense of common identity. This is the essence of **nationalism:** The sense of unity also implies a sense of separation from other nationalities.[8] The French people are a nation: They speak a common language, share a common culture, and take pride in their history. So do the English or Germans. Each people has its own identity that unifies them, but still distinguishes them from other peoples. Nationalism can be both a positive and a negative force. The drive to compete with other nations, to excel as a culture, to grow as an economic community can be generated by nationalist sentiment. But nationalism can be destructive, a source of international and domestic conflict, even a threat to the existence of governments. Nazi Germany is an example of destructive nationalism. However, failure to recognize popular nationalist sentiment can also cause problems. Not all people who share a sense of nation have their own states, nor do all states consist of people who have a single nationalistic outlook.

The state   A **state** possesses four key attributes: (1) a territory, (2) a population, (3) a government having jurisdiction over this territory and population, and most important, (4) recognition from other states. The population of a state may be homogeneous and share a common sense of nationalism, but this is not always the case. A state can exist without a common sense of community, of nationalism. Indeed, throughout much of Africa, states have emerged from the colonial era with boundaries that do not conform to demographic and ethnic realities. These states have a territory and a recognized government, but they lack a common historical heritage, language, ethnic background—in a word, they lack a sense of common national unity.[9] By comparison, many European states (Spain, France, and England, for instance) had begun to develop common senses of national unity before the formal advent of the state. In short, it is possible for a nation not to be a state, and for a state not to be a true nation.

The nation-state   Although the term "nation-state" is often used synonymously with the terms *state* and *nation,* technically it describes a nation that is recognized as a state. The true nation-state is one whose population is unified by a common sense of nationalism and whose government is recognized by other states. Most of the European nations are genuine nation-states. On the other hand, many newly independent African countries are still striving to establish a common sense of nationalism where none has existed. They are states, but not bona fide nations. In addition, there are still many peoples who have the attributes of nationhood but are not recognized as states. These groups might be called nonstate nations and include the Palestine Liberation Organization, the Kurds who straddle the borders of Turkey, Iran, and Iraq, and the Eritreans who have fought for independence from Ethiopia since 1962. Many other examples could be cited. The important thing to remember is that much of the conflict in the international system can be attributed to the lack of congruence between nationhood and statehood in the vast areas of the globe that have only recently been admitted into the Westphalian society of states.

Ordering the State System: Balancing Power

The competing sovereignties that emerged from the Peace of Westphalia could not exist in a total state of anarchy devoid of rules to guide their behavior. But each state existed in an arena in which it had to jealously guard its own interests. The only way a state could ensure that its interests would prevail over the interests of other states was to increase its power. With power, sovereigns could influence the course of international events, carve out colonial empires, and secure wealth, prosperity, and prestige for themselves and their people. But sovereigns who were intoxicated with the pursuit of power, and who wanted to wield it inflexibly on their fellow sovereigns, could be very disruptive. It was natural, then, that states would form alliances to prevent any one state from gaining **hegemony** over the rest of them, that is, to prevent any state from becoming so powerful that it could dictate policy to the other states or could even conquer them. It was natural, although not always perceived or done, that they would attempt to maintain a **balance of power** to prevent any one state from gaining control or hegemony. How do countries balance power? One way is to join alliances with other countries; another way is to increase the state's power to match or exceed that of another country. In either case, it is necessary to determine how much power one has relative to other countries. For that reason, it is important to explore, if only briefly, what the chief elements of power are.

The concept of power   **Power** is a resource that countries may use to achieve their goals, or to ensure that their interests prevail over those of other countries. Power refers to the ability to shape the environment and to control and influence the behavior of other people or governments. Every state has some degree of power; some have more, others less. Power, then, is relational. Even more important, it changes. It is the change in the degrees of power that different nations possess that marks their rise and decline.

Several sources or elements of power can be identified, if not always easily measured. For example, military power might be measured by the size of a country's armed forces and the amount of weapons at their disposal. But if the history of war reveals anything, it is that these are not always the most important indicators of power.[10] Other considerations such as the morale of soldiers, the quality of military leadership, the technological level of weapons, and the quality of strategy and logistics are often more decisive. Moreover, military considerations cannot be evaluated in isolation from other important measures of power.

A country's geographic location, its size, and its natural resources also play a key role.[11] A small country like Poland, which is situated on a plain in the traditional invasion routes through the continent of Europe, is bound to be in a less powerful position than a country like Great Britain whose insular position removed it from the heart of many conflicts in Europe. Large countries like the Soviet Union and the United States are less vulnerable to complete conquest and more likely to possess within their borders many of the resources that are indispensable to a strong economy.

On balance, industrialized countries are likely to be more powerful than agricultural ones, although the capacity to feed one's population is clearly an advantage. Likewise, heavily populated countries tend to be more powerful than their less heavily populated counterparts. But a large population can also be a burden if it is composed of many competing ethnic factions or is so very poor that the people are unproductive.

Some factors of power cannot be measured so easily. For instance, the morale of the population, the quality of the government and diplomacy, and the capacity to forge effective and stable alliances are not easily determined. Yet these factors can be crucial to the overall power position. Finally, a country's power is credible only if its leaders are willing to use it. Power can be converted into actual influence only if it is used or if the threat of its use is credible.

Balancing power   The art of balancing power depends to a large extent on measuring and comparing power. Because there is always uncertainty in this endeavor, countries tend to seek advantages in power rather than actual balances. Napoleon, for instance, upset the balance of power in Europe around the turn of the nineteenth century by trying to establish a French empire. Before and after his time, European countries sought to maintain delicate balances of power, to prevent hegemony, and to build a system of stability, order, and peace. But, as European countries found, sometimes hegemony can only be prevented by going to war. If peace was at times a by-product of the balance of power, a more overriding concern was to prevent hegemony by any single state or group of states.

At best a crude concept, the balance of power nevertheless provided a means by which European sovereigns could conduct statecraft, pursue diplomacy, and order their interrelations.[12] Although the nature of power and actual shifts in power have dramatically altered the traditional international order, many leaders are still guided by rough calculations of power and power balances in seeking the national interest. But a number of scholars no longer believe that the balance of power notion can adequately describe contemporary international relations. We will return to the basic issues in this debate momentarily, but first we need to examine the concept of the national interest and some of the factors that have affected the evolution of the international system.

The national interest   The concept of the **national interest** is not new, although it has varied somewhat over time.[13] At the time of the Peace of Westphalia, the national interest might have been best characterized as the interest of the sovereign, of the kings and princes of Europe themselves. However, as the modern state developed, sovereigns had to appeal more openly to the nationalism of their people. In some cases, the rise of democracy required that the national interest be formulated in somewhat more general terms that could find support in the public at large.

Essentially, the national interest represents the collective goals of a state, which include at a minimum maintaining political independence, economic stability, territorial preservation, and social stability.[14] In addition to these relatively defensive goals, states might also have more aggressive, offensive interests with respect to other states. Hans Morgenthau, a prominent scholar in the study of international relations, argued that the national interest, defined in terms of power, should not be viewed as a concrete, unchanging thing. Rather, it must be constantly redefined to reflect both domestic and foreign changes.[15] Careful leaders, he argued, should avoid equating the ideological aspirations of a state with practical calculations about the balance of power and the national interest. While much of this advice continues to be pertinent today, many scholars now emphasize that the national interest can no longer be defined as narrowly as it once was. Changes in the international system as a whole, they point out, now make it imperative for leaders to define the national interest in broader terms. At some point states must consider how their policies will preserve not only the nation but also the global economy and ecosystem in which the nation must survive. The national interest and the global interest, they argue, increasingly intersect in the contemporary world.[16]

Another criticism of the concept has less to do with the need to broaden the definition, than with its ambiguity. What precisely is the national interest, especially in pluralistic countries where many different groups and interests compete? How one goes about defending the national interest is the subject of a considerable debate. Domestic, economic, and political considerations often substantially affect how different businesses, political groups, and leaders define the national interest at any particular time. Thus, leaders often appeal to the national interest not as an objective guide to action but as an ex post facto justification of government policy, or even as a weapon to discredit domestic political opponents. As a student of international relations, you might question a leader's claim to be acting in the national interest, because this concept means many different things to different people.

Sources of Change

The Transition to the Modern International System

The concepts of state sovereignty, nationalism, power, the balance of power, and the national interest continue to have relevance for modern international politics, just as they were important concepts from the very beginning of the modern state system. But major changes over the past three centuries have modified their current roles. Even before the Peace of Westphalia, European nations had begun to colonize the world. In the 1500s, the Spanish and Portuguese were the first to embark on the establishment of colonial empires in South and Central America and Southeast Asia. The British and Dutch joined this game in the 1600s—Britain in the Americas and Holland in Asia. But the real scramble for colonies did not begin until after Westphalia. In the 1700s and 1800s many European countries expanded their political, economic, and military influence throughout the world. In this last phase of the colonial era, the effort to build colonial empires reached its most feverish level. By the time the European countries were beginning to bring most of Africa and much of Asia under colonial sway, the colonies in the Americas had gained their independence, often by waging revolutionary wars against the mother country. So it was that in 1776 the United States joined the community of nations, followed by Bolivia, Chile, and Argentina in the early 1800s. But even as these colonies struggled for independence, their aim was to join the society of nations that had originated in Europe. In other words, they sought recognition as sovereign states from existing European states. The Westphalian system had a powerful attraction.

As American states obtained independence, Europe turned its colonial designs with greater energy on Africa and Asia. The Dutch, Portuguese, and Spanish, who had long competed for the spice trade, were slowly eclipsed in Asia by the British and French, who extended their influence into Southeast Asia. Britain claimed control of India, Burma, and the Malay Peninsula. The French occupied Indochina. Even China and Japan, the two traditional Asian powers, were subjected to European economic predominance, if not outright colonial occupation. Africa, too, was carved up into spheres of colonial influence at the Berlin–West Africa Conference in 1884–1885. Belgium, Germany, and Italy joined France, Britain, and Portugal in the scramble for Africa. The Middle East, in turn, fell under the dominance of the Turkish-based Ottoman empire throughout most of the colonial era.

International politics in the three centuries following the Peace of Westphalia consisted first of the gradual extension of European influence throughout the globe, and then of the gradual decoupling of colonial territories from their European colonial masters. The Europeans' success in dominating the globe could be attributed to their superior military force, political organization, and economic sophistication. But perhaps more important was the general acceptance of the legal norms established by the Europeans. Colonies rejected European political domination, but they embraced the Westphalian state system, sought recognition from existing European states, and wanted all the trappings of sovereignty enjoyed by the nations of Europe.

In the twentieth century, dramatic events began to challenge the fundamental structure and customary practices of the traditional international system. The colonial edifices of the European states began to crack. With the end of World War I came the end of the German, Austro-Hungarian, and Ottoman empires. Austria-Hungary saw many of its territories given independence, while the Ottoman Empire's territories and Germany's African colonies were divided among the victorious European Allies. Under a mandate system created by the League of Nations after World War I, France and Britain assumed administrative control of most former possessions of Germany and Turkey. The pace of decolonization quickened after World War II, as France, Britain, Portugal, the Netherlands, and Belgium divested themselves of most of their colonial holdings. The emergence of two anticolonial superpowers, the United States and the Soviet Union, together with a UN system that encouraged the progressive attainment of independence for non-self-governing territories, and considerable pressure for independence from colonized peoples hastened the process of decolonization. Over a hundred new nations gained their independence, and European political influence, which had once been global, waned. Still the economic influence of the former colonial powers continued to be quite strong, because the newly independent countries depended to a large degree on the traditional trade patterns and economic ties that had been established during the colonial period. In addition, the remaining legal structures and international norms still bore the heavy imprint of the European-inspired Westphalian system. Thus, a strand of continuity existed in the midst of change.

The end of the colonial period was not the only significant development of the twentieth century. Other changes began to assault the traditional ways of doing things. Two global wars wracked the state system, and weapons of awesome destructive power introduced a new element of terror to the old balance of power. Economic, cultural, and societal interaction among states dramatically increased. Common threats to the global environment and unequal distribution of natural resources called for a reexamination of a limited definition of the national interest. Agriculturally oriented countries in the Southern Hemisphere resented global inequalities of wealth that favored the rich industrialized nations of the Northern Hemisphere, and called for the creation of a **New International Economic Order.**[17] The need to control potential conflicts and to facilitate the increased pace of international economic interactions led to the emergence of hundreds of new international organizations.[18] Global economic opportunities led businesses to look beyond their domestic markets to opportunities for foreign investment.[19] As a result, multinational corporations proliferated. The number and influence of nongovernmental agencies also rose to deal with contemporary humanitarian, social, and economic problems that increasingly transcended national boundaries.[20] The rise of terrorism is yet another example of new trends in international politics. In short, the sovereignty of nations seems assaulted by the forces of contemporary change on every front.

From Multipolarity to Bipolarity and Back Again

In the twentieth century the social and economic changes described in the preceding section were accompanied by significant shifts in the global distribution of power and by the emergence of ideology as a primary factor in the relations of nations. At the turn of the century, there were a number of major powers in the international system (including several European states, the United States, Russia, and Japan), each pursuing its national interests, sometimes through shifting sets of alliances. The international system exhibited **multipolarity;** that is, power was distributed among a number of countries. (See figure 2.1 for a pictorial representation of multipolarity.) This multipolar pattern of power distribution continued until World War II. That war had devastating consequences for most of the European powers and Japan. These countries dropped from the major power scene, at least temporarily, leaving a power vacuum that was quickly filled by two dominant countries— the United States and the Soviet Union. Indeed, the term **superpower** became a fashionable description of these two nations, which possessed overwhelming nuclear and conventional military power. The multipolar age was supplanted by a bipolar one, in which power was concentrated in two countries. When this happens, the international system is said to exhibit **bipolarity.**

If the superpowers had been content to play the traditional game of power rivalry, the emergence of a bipolar system might have been less of a shock to the international system. But the contest between the Soviet Union and the United States exceeded mere rivalry; it was viewed as an ideological struggle of global proportions. An **ideology** is a set of beliefs about how government should be organized and what kinds of policies it should pursue. From the Soviet Union's perspective, the system of capitalist exploitation perpetuated by the United States would eventually succumb to the forces of Marxist revolution and change. From the American perspective, freedom was threatened at every turn by "godless Communists." If freedom were to prevail, the communist threat had to be eliminated or at least contained. The superpowers' mutual fears and distrust led to a rigid bipolar alliance structure after World War II, as the smaller powers gathered under the banners of capitalism and communism. This bipolar period, which lasted into the 1950s and early 1960s, ushered in the **Cold War,** a time marked by periodically intense hostility, propaganda, and competition between the Eastern and Western blocs but never by direct military confrontation between the superpowers. In 1989 the remarkable changes that swept through the Soviet Union and Eastern Europe signaled an end to the Cold War. Whether these reforms will lead to a permanent end to the war or to a resumption of tensions still remains to be seen.

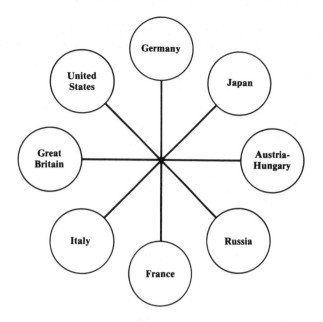

Figure 2.1

Pre–World War I multipolar distribution of power

The apparent end of the Cold War was preceded by the erosion of bipolarity and movement back toward a more multipolar world.

The structure of the post–World War II bipolar world is displayed in figure 2.2. Notice that the bipolar nature of this system was cemented by both bilateral agreements and multilateral regional security groups. The United States entered several security arrangements including the North Atlantic Treaty Organization (NATO); the Australia, New Zealand, and U.S. Pact (ANZUS); the Rio Pact, with Latin American countries; the Central Treaty Organization (CENTO), with Pakistan, Iran, Turkey, and the United Kingdom; and the Southeast Asian Treaty Organization (SEATO). The Soviet Union, in turn, sought support from the Warsaw Pact states, consisting primarily of its Eastern European allies, and from North Korea and the People's Republic of China through bilateral agreements.

The rigid character of the post–World War II bipolar system began to loosen as many of the former major powers, such as Japan, Germany, France, and Great Britain, revived. In addition, many newly independent nations were not prepared to participate in the East–West dispute, preferring to remain neutral or to play one side against the other. Strains in the superpowers' relations with their own allies became more apparent over time. China asserted its independence from Moscow, while Japan and the Western Europeans asserted their revived economic power in ways that challenged American commercial and financial supremacy. Some newly independent countries discovered that they could gain political and economic leverage by threatening to deny their oil to other countries. By the 1960s even the superpower monopoly on nuclear weapons—the most potent symbol of superpower status—had ended.

In recent years students of international relations have begun to see the world as composed of several different groups of countries, based on ideological orientation and level of economic development. One of the major differences in the post–World War II period, as we have just seen, was the **East–West dispute,** which was marked by the growing

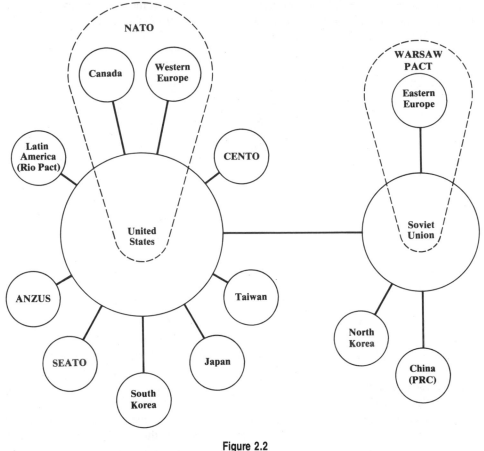

Figure 2.2
Post–World War II bipolar distribution of power

polarization between the Western capitalist countries led by the United States and the Eastern socialist ones led by the Soviet Union. Because of the very different ideologies and economic systems that have characterized, until recently, at least, the countries in these two blocs, they are often referred to as the First and Second Worlds. The **First World** consists of Western capitalist industrial democracies, including the United States, the countries of Western Europe, Japan, Australia, New Zealand, and Canada. The **Second World** includes the socialist powers of Eastern Europe and, of course, the Soviet Union. Although the First and Second Worlds continue to vary considerably in political and economic terms, they are similar in that they are fairly industrialized (if along different ideological lines) and relatively wealthy. Moreover, should liberalization and democratization of the Soviet Union and Eastern Europe continue, the chief differences between the Second and First Worlds will become less meaningful.

Over time, other divisions among nations have complicated the East–West dispute. The rapid decolonization in the 1950s and 1960s resulted in many new, independent countries that had little use for the East–West dispute. They believed that the most important problem in international relations was the disparity between their considerable poverty and the relative wealth of both the East and the West. As these countries pressed for more favorable treatment in the international economic system, they began to see their primary problem as a North–South issue based on levels of economic development, rather than on ideology. The term **North–South dispute** was coined because most of the wealthy countries were located in the Northern Hemisphere, whereas most of the poor countries were located in the Southern Hemisphere. Although some less developed countries took sides in the East–West dispute, a large number chose instead to pursue policies of **neutralism** or **nonalignment.** Others explicitly tried to exploit the East–West dispute by playing one side against the other in an effort to attract more resources from either side.

The poorer, less developed nations have been called the **Third World** to distinguish them from the more industrialized countries of the North. This label has never been satisfactory because of the considerable diversity among Third World countries. Included in this group, for instance, were China and India—two very populous and large countries with considerable economic potential. Less populous countries such as Chad and Mali, with few resources and much less promise of economic development, were also included. Despite the potentially bright prospects for their economies, Brazil, Chile, and Argentina were also considered Third World countries, as were Haiti and El Salvador, countries held tight in the grip of widespread and persistent poverty. In Asia, South Korea, Taiwan, and Singapore began to emerge as economic powerhouses. Corporations located manufacturing industries in these countries to take advantage of their significantly cheaper labor costs and high labor productivity. The emergence of the Organization of Petroleum Exporting Countries and the tremendous wealth that oil generated for oil-producing countries further accentuated the differences among Third World countries. Saudi Arabia and the Gulf States, fairly underpopulated countries, suddenly catapulted to the top of the global per capita income charts. Soon analysts of international politics began to differentiate between countries in the Third World that had a chance to industrialize and develop their economies and those poorest of the poor whose chances for development were far less favorable. This latter group has been called the **Fourth World**—the most underprivileged world of all.

These obvious differences in economic development among nations led the World Bank in recent years to classify countries into six categories instead of four.[21] The bank now distinguishes between industrial market economies and industrial nonmarket economies (of the socialist bloc), categories that correspond to the concepts of the First and Second Worlds, and separates the so-called Third World into four categories: high-income oil-exporting countries, upper-middle-income countries, middle-income countries, and low-income countries. The last category includes the most desperately poor countries. States falling into the latter two categories are known as less developed countries (LDCs).

Thus, today's world is no longer as bipolar as it once was. The United States and the Soviet Union cling to their superpower status, as domestic and foreign challenges to their power increase and as their own economic and military capacities decline. As this chapter's reading on Japan's effort to redefine its international role suggests, a growing number of new countries are pressing for attention, while many former powers and a number of new ones are asserting their power and influence. Multipolarity is being slowly reestablished. The trend away from rigid bipolarity is very pronounced and has been hastened by a recognition of the growing interdependence of states. The more complicated nature of power distributions in the contemporary world is depicted in figure 2.3.

Interdependence

One of the chief concepts used to describe the nature of the contemporary international system is *interdependence*. The concept suggests that states are not completely independent actors, instead they have become dependent on each other. No one state is wholly self-sufficient; each relies on the resources and products of the others. Policies pursued by one

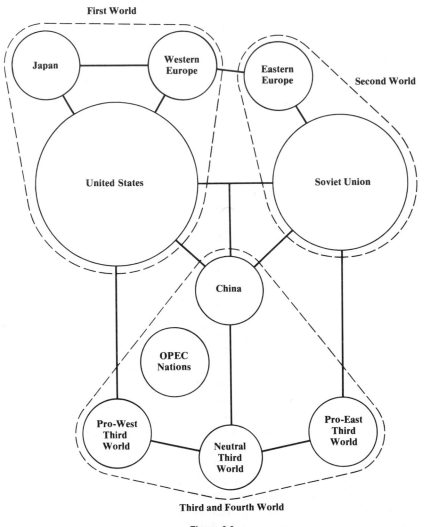

Figure 2.3
Contemporary distribution of global power

Part I   Understanding International Relations

state have immediate and often serious consequences for other states. Borders are more porous than ever to immigration, capital flows, trade, and terrorist activities. Even domestic policies have broader international implications. Poverty in Mexico leads to illegal immigration into the United States. The price of oil in Western Europe depends on political events in the Middle East. Higher oil prices devastate the economies of already poor countries in Africa, Asia, and Latin America. Ballooning U.S. budget deficits result in part from increased defense expenditures that have been seen as necessary to counter the external Soviet threat. The failure of savings and loan institutions in Ohio and Maryland creates tremors in financial markets throughout the globe. The world, in short, is growing increasingly interdependent, especially in nonmilitary spheres of activity.

Interdependence in the contemporary international system has three key characteristics: (1) the existence of many different channels of formal and informal contact between governments, peoples, and nongovernmental groups; (2) the absence of clear-cut priorities for an increasingly broad and more diverse number of global issues; and (3) the existence of constraints on the use of military force as the sole source of power.[22] In other words, in this century, international relations are increasingly affected by actors other than state governments.[23] Nations now face more numerous issues, and the distinction between domestic and foreign policies toward these issues is increasingly blurred. Finally, the ability to use military force effectively to resolve many of these complex issues has diminished. Modern interdependence calls for a reexamination of the traditional concept of the state, a reevaluation of the role and nature of power, and perhaps a redefinition of the once-parochial notion of the national interest.

Interdependence and the modern state   The claim of complexity is common to all ages. But complexity is, if anything, the hallmark of the present. George Washington and Peter the Great would no doubt be awed by the enormous responsibilities that their successors now shoulder. They would be impressed by the tremendous technological advances that have sped the pace of international interaction and made it more complicated. They would be startled by the tremendous array of new states, global businesses, international agencies, and nongovernmental groups whose interests must be considered in making foreign policy decisions. They would probably be annoyed at having to manage the vast bureaucracies that have evolved to cope with contemporary policy concerns. They would probably welcome a return to the days of leisurely contact between nations by legate and courier. In short they would probably agree that the modern requirements of statecraft are considerably more demanding than they were two centuries ago. In other words they would recognize that interdependence impinges on the traditional character of the state.

In theory states are sovereign, independent, and equal. Allowing for the fact that states have never been absolutely sovereign, independent, and equal in any other than a strictly legal sense, their physical inequality and mutual dependence are more apparent than ever. Tuvalu and Nauru, both members of the United Nations, are very tiny island nations with populations of only a few thousand each. They can hardly be seen as equal in any real sense with, say, China, with its population of a billion, or with the Soviet Union, with its vast territorial expanse. Nor can even the most powerful states be viewed as wholly independent actors. Almost all nations rely on goods or services imported from other countries to maintain their economic health. Even in arms development, states are not completely independent actors. Indeed, in a paradoxical way, states involved in arms races become dependent on their adversaries' moves and countermoves. Thus, states may theoretically be equal and independent, but in reality they are unequal and interdependent.

Does this mean that states are an endangered species? As we noted earlier in this chapter, some scholars think that the state is an anachronism and that other actors, such as corporations or international agencies, are better suited to manage international affairs. Is the state likely to disappear as the primary unit of organization in the international system? Two factors suggest that it will not. First, nationalism has been and continues to be one of the most potent forces of the twentieth century. Sovereignty may be a legal fiction, but millions of lives have been lost in the nationalistic wars of this century. Fictions having such real consequences are something more than fictions. As long as national fervor remains high, it is unlikely that the state will vanish, although particular multiethnic countries may succumb to internal demands for self-determination. Second, states still have the legal power to regulate the activities of all nongovernmental actors, whether they are corporations, nonprofit organizations, or international agencies. The corporate ability to resist regulation is not insignificant, but in recent years states have learned how to deal with corporations and have begun to develop codes of conduct for transnational organizations.[24]

The existence of interdependence does not necessarily augur for the demise of the interstate system. Instead, it may simply mean that states are no longer in as good a position as they once were to formulate foreign policies without considering the views of numerous, contending domestic political forces and weighing the impact that the policy will have on their allies and adversaries in the international arena.

Interdependence and power If the very existence of the state is not threatened by interdependence, there can be little doubt that the way states use power is constrained in an era of interdependence. As we noted earlier, power can be difficult to measure, and it becomes even more difficult in a context of interdependence. A monarch in the eighteenth century could calculate with some certainty his or her military strength and economic capacity to wage war relative to a potential adversary. However, as a result of industrialization and the emergence of a global economy, such calculations have become increasingly difficult to make.[25] Moreover, even if military power could be measured reliably, the ability to use it effectively in contemporary international relations is limited. Apart from a certain level of prestige gained by possessing it, the most devastating form of military power, nuclear weaponry, is viable for little more than as a deterrent to the use of similar weapons by others. Nuclear weaponry obviously cannot be used effectively to punish terrorists, to fight a guerrilla war, or to convince countries to lower tariffs on economic goods. The very destructive capacity of nuclear weapons limits their effectiveness even in the context of all-out warfare, especially if the other side also has them. Hence, the primary purpose for having such weapons is to prevent others from using them first. Similarly, military intervention by conventional forces cannot guarantee the flow of oil to Western markets from politically unstable Middle Eastern regimes. This is not to say that military force is completely irrelevant today. It can be used effectively under certain circumstances, as the U.S. invasions of Grenada and Panama demonstrated. But several other examples— such as Afghanistan, Vietnam, and Lebanon—suggest that superpower involvement in foreign civil wars can be indeterminate or even counterproductive. The political and economic consequences of the use of military force, then, must be carefully considered.

If military power is increasingly circumscribed today, economic power may be seen as becoming more important. But while economic power is an important component of a country's strength, it is as subject to the limits of interdependence as military power.

All countries have economic vulnerabilities; some have more than others. It is the distribution of these vulnerabilities that can give some states advantages over others in the use of economic power. For example, Japan's pro-Israeli policy changed almost overnight when the Arab oil-exporting countries threatened to cut off oil supplies during the 1973–1974 Middle East conflict. This about-face can be attributed to the fact that Japan imported about 90 percent of its oil from these countries. Only recently, in the wake of its growing economic might, has Japan begun to explore closer ties with Israel again. But as our reading in this chapter indicates, even a mighty economic power such as Japan continues to suffer from economic vulnerabilities.

Sellers of commodities can be economically vulnerable as well. They may desperately need the foreign exchange earned by the sale of their resources to maintain the health of their economies. In other words, vulnerabilities and dependencies are often mutual. Moreover, these vulnerabilities constantly change as economic forces, which are beyond the control of any single nation, change. Thus, the ability of a country to convert economic power into effective political influence shifts in conjunction with global economic realities.

Ultimately, the effective use of power in an age of interdependence hinges on the prudence and good judgment of leaders. It depends on their ability to adjust their foreign and domestic policies to the ever-changing and increasingly complicated network of economic and political relations between nations.

Interdependence and the national interest   The conditions of interdependence affect the traditional concept of the national interest in two ways: (1) by the growing influence of large numbers of domestic organizations with foreign interests, and (2) by the emergence of global economic and ecological concerns that transcend national boundaries. Let us consider each of these factors in greater detail.

First, in an age of global communication and rapid transportation, individuals now have access to many sources of information about international issues. Many individuals participate in nongovernmental organizations such as the League of the Red Cross and Red Crescent Societies, Rotary Club International, professional organizations, churches, and movements that create ties between people in different countries. People do not depend solely on information provided by their governments, and their views on key issues may be at odds with their government's interpretation. Multinational corporations have also grown in number, size, and influence. Governments must now consider the interests and views of this wide range of nongovernmental and corporate actors as they formulate a conception of the national interest. Many of these new actors have a considerable stake in the foreign policies pursued by their governments. Corporations may lobby hard for foreign policies that favor their investment position in other countries. In many cases the views of important and powerful domestic interest groups conflict with one another; thus, the definition of the national interest may depend on the outcome of a struggle between different domestic organizations with opposing foreign interests. On occasion the interests of a specific group may be at odds with what the government defines as the national interest. For instance, during the postindependence conflict in Angola, Gulf Oil Corporation did business with the ruling Marxist regime, and Cuban troops actually protected its Cabinda oil resources from attacks by the pro-Western rebel groups supported by the U.S. government.[26]

Second, economic and ecological security are now matters that clearly transcend national boundaries. The health of the global economy and ecosphere are essential to every nation's economic health and ecological survival. Industrial pollution in one country can adversely affect the ecology of another country. For instance, industrial pollutants from factories in Western Europe and the United States make their way into the upper atmosphere and drop as deadly acid rain on the dying forests and lakes of Scandinavia and Canada. Forest and fishery resources are a substantial component of these countries' economies. For them, acid rain is a major international issue.

Some students of international relations argue that the concept of the national interest must at some point acknowledge the interests common to all nations.[27] One scholar predicts that the twentieth century "marks the beginning of a fundamental shift in human history as the world's rapidly growing human population encounters environmental limits to growth on a global scale."[28] Global resource depletion also threatens the future health of the international economy. Population and economic growth, once seen as positive forces in international politics, now present dilemmas. They hasten depletion of finite resources, cause pollution of the environment, and overtax food production capacities. Some experts argue that growth potentially contains the seeds of its own destruction.[29] Not everyone looks at the future with such gloom, however. Some scholars believe that growth can be sustained without catastrophic dislocations until early in the next century.[30] But the existence of a debate about the possibility of global catastrophe should be instructive and cautionary. Common sense tells us that the world's natural resources are finite and that runaway population growth will have negative consequences.

The key question is whether nations will choose to respond to future scarcities as completely isolated political units seeking only to maximize the interests of their own populations or whether a greater degree of international cooperation will emerge to manage economic and ecological problems that are common to all. Many analysts who first alerted the world to the potential consequences of unlimited growth have concluded that an effective response to these problems can lie only in the creation of new international institutions to cope with the global agenda.[31] Others believe that growth is still a positive good and that those who forecast doom are exaggerating. According to this viewpoint, not only will new systems of global management do no good, they will also add more layers of inefficiency to an already bloated international bureaucracy.[32]

Basic Issues of Continuity and Change

In this chapter we have reviewed several traditional concepts that have undergirded the international system. Chief among them were sovereignty, the state, the nation, and the balance of power. A brief review of the historical development of the state system has shown that many changes have led to a greater degree of economic and ecological interdependence among states. But states persist, as does their pursuit of power. Their persistence in the face of change raises a number of issues that we encourage the reader to consider: How will the clash between the forces of tradition and the forces of change be resolved? Will the state sink into oblivion as the forces of change overwhelm it or will it adapt? How relevant are power and the balance of power as principles on which to base foreign policies in an age of interdependence? Is interdependence an inevitable or irreversible process? If the state cannot cope with the demands of contemporary change, what other form of organization might be more effective? regional or global governments? corporations?

We cannot easily predict the future of the international system, but we can draw some conclusions about the past and about current trends. First, the state has been resilient and malleable. At first, states were indistinguishable from the monarchs who ruled them.

Louis XIV's claim "L'état, c'est moi," "I am the state," was not a mere boast; it was a reality. Although monarchies fell during the transition to democracy, the state managed to survive. If anything, the state was strengthened by the growth of modern nationalism. Even the break-up of the colonial systems did not challenge the state system, rather it led to an explosion of new independent states. Nor did two global wars in this century destroy the state. To be sure, European leaders realized that global wars of that sort could no longer be tolerated, and they began creating new European institutions to integrate their economies so that war between them would be unthinkable. They set about making themselves so economically interdependent that a war could not be planned, let alone carried out. Indeed, no wars have been fought in Europe for the past forty years. Instead a Common Market has bound Western European nations ever more closely together. But European states persist, they have adapted, cooperated, and integrated their economies. They have ceded bits and pieces of their sovereignty to the European Communities. But the states remain, as does the sense of nation.[33] The English, French, Germans, and Italians still retain a strong sense of nationalism. Even in this example of the most intense historical effort ever at economic integration, complete political integration has not been attained. This suggests that the state is quite adaptable to change; it bends and stretches but resists breaking. In Eastern Europe, resurgent nationalism and greater assertion of national autonomy suggest that, even after years of Soviet hegemony, the people retain a strong national identity. The state and the nation persist in the midst of remarkable change. Indeed, rising nationalist sentiments within various Soviet socialist republics, such as Azerbaijan, Latvia, Lithuania, and Estonia, challenge Russian mastery over the widespread territory of the Soviet Union.

Second, the nature of power and the states' ability to use it has changed. Power is still relevant—even crucial—to modern international relations. Indeed, even the staunchest advocates of interdependence admit that the pursuit of power is still a state's fundamental goal. They do not differ from realists such as Hans Morgenthau on this question. Realists believe that power and the pursuit of power is the state's primary motivation as it pursues its national interests in cooperation and conflict with other states. Advocates of interdependence differ from realists in their interpretation of what kinds of power can be effectively employed under conditions of interdependence.[34] Even the realists began to reconsider the role of military force in the power equation after the emergence of oil as a tool of foreign policy.[35] However, power is clearly more difficult to measure than ever before, and the outcome of power contests is even harder to predict. Thus, calculating and maintaining balances of power is also less certain. The art of statecraft is more complicated than ever as the number of states and nonstate actors proliferates. State leaders still think and act in terms of rough calculations of power, but these processes are now conditioned by concerns about interdependencies and mutual vulnerabilities.

What of the future? Is interdependence a permanent condition? It is hard to read a newspaper, listen to a speech on foreign policy, or watch television news commentaries without seeing or hearing a reference to our "increasingly interdependent world." It is commonplace to hear that the world is interdependent and becoming more so. Whether this attitude reflects a hope or an empirical prediction is not as clear. In any case, there is no guarantee that interdependence will lead to cooperation instead of greater conflict.[36] Nor is there any guarantee that the world will continue to grow more interdependent. Indeed, one aspect of interdependence is a high level of commercial activity among states. But pressure for higher tariffs to protect domestic industries from foreign competition is increasing in many countries. As protectionism gains strength, economic interdependence will be reduced. In other words, as long as the state remains a basic unit of economic activity, with its own currency, fiscal and monetary policy, and domestic political forces, the degree to which it is subject to interdependence is at least partially under its own control. Many states are still able to choose a policy of isolation or insulation, rather than interdependence, at least in the economic arena. But economic and ecological interdependence are likely to remain important constraints for most states.

The case of Japan, which is addressed in this chapter's reading by Soroos, vividly illustrates the problems of interdependence for a modern nation-state. Traditionally an isolationist state, Japan now faces the problem of adapting to a global economy. By most measures it has adapted very well, surging into second place behind the United States in terms of its gross national product. But Japan's economy is vulnerable. It rests on a very shaky resource base, depends on imported commodities to sustain its manufacturing sector, and remains vulnerable to the hostile trade policies of other governments. Japan's success in trade has unleashed resentment in the United States and Europe, where many people believe that Japanese commercial gains have been achieved unfairly and at others' expense.

Soroos also demonstrates how domestic efforts to internationalize or broaden Japanese outlooks on the world run counter to its traditionally insular culture. Indeed, Japan's key to success thus far may be the tight-knit, exclusive nature of its culture, which reinforces loyalty to Japanese products and discourages openness to foreign goods. But future success calls for more openness to the world, lest Japan's access to Western markets be denied by disgruntled trade partners. Like most other nations, Japan faces the tension of the competing forces of continuity and change. Japanese nationalism, tradition, and culture are strong sources of continuity. But Japan is locked into an interdependent global economy that it cannot control and that calls for change. Once a source of strength, Japan's cultural tendencies now threaten continued economic success.

Japan is not alone in its efforts to cope with the demands of an interdependent world. Every country faces a similar challenge. Some nations will manage their situations better than others, but none can really avoid the constantly changing and interrelated political and economic forces that influence contemporary international relations.

Summary

The forces of continuity and the forces of change are at the heart of the debate between those who see the need for a more cosmopolitan world order and those who continue to advocate a narrower, self-interested, parochial definition of the national interest. Two basic realities now face the international system. On the one hand, the state still exists; sovereignty continues to be a formidable obstacle to the realization of a globally oriented political order, and policy makers continue to act in the name of the sovereign state. On the other hand, there is a growing awareness of the interconnectedness of the world and of the common interests that citizens of all nations share.[37] New avenues of communication and contact between peoples and nations have emerged.

We live in a time of paradox: The contemporary international system is fundamentally different from and similar to the system that emerged in the century or so after the Peace of Westphalia. A basic tension exists between the old and the new realities. We live in a time of transition, in an age of struggle between the traditional forces of continuity and the contemporary requirements of change.

Marvin S. Soroos

■

Global Interdependence and the Responsibilities of States: Learning from the Japanese Experience

Global Responsibilities in an Interdependent World

The multiple and complex ways in which states are dependent upon one another are arguably the most compelling feature of the contemporary world order. Some forms of interdependence came about by conscious design. . . . Other forms of interdependence occur because the natural resources of the planet, such as petroleum, minerals, fertile land, and plant species, are concentrated in a few countries rather than being dispersed evenly throughout the world. Still other types of interdependence arise out of problems that spill across national boundaries, examples being epidemics of contagious diseases and static-causing radio signals. Interdependence is also present where there are conflicting uses of international commons, such as the oceans, seabed, outer space, and airwaves. Finally, new forms of interdependence can arise from the introduction of technologies, as has been the case in nuclear weapons, communication satellites, computers, and genetics.

Interdependence is not intrinsically either a desirable or undesirable condition. Some types of international interdependence, such as economic exchanges, are pregnant with opportunities for nations to work together to achieve what they could not acting on their own. Other types of interdependence are fraught with costs and dangers, as in the phenomenon of transnational acid precipitation in North America and Europe and the uneasy nuclear "balance of terror" prevailing between the United States and the Soviet

SOURCE: This article first appeared in *Journal of Peace Research* 25, 1 (1988). Reprinted by permission in abridged form. © *Journal of Peace Research*, 1988, pp. 17–29.

Union. The extent to which interdependence furthers the interests of the countries that are caught up in it depends on how effectively the situation is managed. The rewards of most positive forms of interdependence will be realized only if steps are taken to ensure that the conflicts, disputes, and tensions that arise over the terms of cooperation do not cause the relationship to sour. On the other hand, the potentially negative, and sometimes even catastrophic, consequences of other forms of interdependence can be averted by responsible behavior of several actors. . . .

Japan as a Case Study in Global Responsibility

Japan is an interesting, if hardly typical, case for discussing the global responsibilities of states in an interdependent world. Through the ages, what limited contacts Japan has had with the outside world have usually been cautious and rather awkward, with periodic and often abrupt shifts between openness, withdrawal, and on occasion, aggressiveness. . . .

In recent years Japanese leaders and people. . . have pondered several anomalies in Japan's relationship to the outside world. First, despite rising to second place in the economical ranking of the nations of the free world, and being categorized as an "economic superpower," Japan has been a rather passive and uninfluential participant in the major arenas of world politics. Second, even though Japan's post–World War II economic growth and prosperity are heavily dependent on international commerce, the Japanese are criticized for contributing relatively little to the maintenance of the international system that has made it possible. And third, for having cast their destiny with the outside world economically, the Japanese have a continuing reputation for being an insular people who are not at ease interacting with peoples of foreign cultures. Thus, the Japanese find themselves faced with the challenge of redefining the responsibilities their country has to the outside world, while as a people opening themselves up socially and culturally through a process that is referred to as *kokusaika* in Japanese, which translates into the English term "internationalization." . . .

Although public opinion polls reveal that there is considerable support for assuming greater international responsibilities. . ., internationalist tendencies are offset by nationalistic sentiments that are deeply held by a sizable segment of the population. Concern has been expressed that Japanese culture will be irreparably damaged as a result of the internationalizing process. Misgivings have also been aired about the unidirectional nature of the endeavor in which Japan is being asked to adapt to the Western cultures, with little expectation of reciprocation.

Japan's Vulnerabilities

. . . [Japan imports] 50 percent of the caloric intake of its people and virtually all of its petroleum, iron ore, copper, bauxite, and nickel. [It] would have great difficulty compensating for substantial cutbacks from its major sources of supply. To pay for its vital imports, Japan depends on markets for its exports that have been opened by substantial reductions in trade restrictions since World War II.

Japan is in an enviable position in view of the prosperity of its people, the competitiveness of its products in international markets, a mounting trade surplus . . .and status as the world's leading lender nation. Nevertheless, concern is widespread that Japan's good fortune could unravel unless steps are taken to deal with its vulnerabilities, which are basically of two types. First, events or developments that do not involve Japan directly may nevertheless destabilize the international economic and political order in ways that could have serious consequences for Japan. Such was the case when war broke out between Iran and Iraq, two countries on whom Japan has depended for sizable shares of its oil imports. . . .

A second type of vulnerability exists in Japan's relationships with the countries that it relies on for economic welfare and military security. Japan's large trade surpluses have strained relations with the United States and Western Europe and sparked proposals for protectionist trade legislation that could cut deeply into the market for Japanese exports. In the realm of security, even though development of its armed forces is constrained by its constitution, Japan has come under criticism, especially in the United States, for being a free rider on defense matters. The policy of the Japanese government over the past two decades of limiting expenditures on its security forces to 1 percent of the GNP is cited as one of the reasons for Japan's economic success in contrast to the relatively stagnant economy of the United States where defense expenditures approach 7 percent of the GNP. . . .

Envy over Japan's rapid rise to the status of economic superpower is another cause of resentment both in the developed world which is being overtaken and in the Third World countries where Japan is criticized for having some of the same imperialistic tendencies as the United States. . . . Resentments in Southeast Asia arise from the influx of Japanese businessmen, bankers, and engineers, triggering demonstrations on the occasion of visits by Japanese leaders. Japanese business activity in China has been the target of student riots.

. . .In order to minimize these vulnerabilities, Japanese leaders are committed to having Japan play a greater role in maintaining the international system which has been so beneficial for the country, while at the same trying to improve the international image of Japan and internationalize the Japanese people.

Japan's Expanding International Role

The role played by Japan in world politics has lagged far behind its evolution as an economic superpower. During the period of reconstruction after World War II when memories of Japanese aggression were still vivid, it was to be expected that Japan would concentrate on its internal problems. Foreign policy was conducted cautiously so as not to offend other states, in particular those that were most important to Japan. Thus, Japan seemed reluctant to take a stand on issues before world opinion had congealed. But by the 1970s, the asymmetry between Japan's economic and political roles in the world had become less defensible. . . .

If states such as Japan, which lack the means to exert themselves in a forceful way militarily, are to play a significant role in shaping the course of world politics, it will be largely through skillful and creative diplomacy. Recent Japanese. . .leaders have tried to project their country more vigorously, both through the frequency of their diplomatic missions and a greater willingness to take an independent stance on international issues. . . .

Japan has been in the forefront of international efforts to resolve several of the more tense regional conflicts, [especially] the Iran–Iraq war. . . .

Japan has placed considerable stock in the United Nations both as a preserver of peace that is critical to its international economic activity and as an arena in which Japan can expand its role in world politics. . . . Japan's financial contributions to the organization are now second only to the United States, and its share of the assessments have risen from 2.19 percent in 1956 to 10.84 percent in 1986. . . .

Foreign economic assistance has played prominently in Japan's strategy for improving its image as a responsible member of the international community. Japan's level of foreign assistance was quite low up through the mid-1970s. . . . What aid was given was closely tied to the promotion of Japanese exports. . . . But. . .Japan. . .not only doubled its official development assistance by 1980, [it] also untied many of the strings attached to it and. . .distributed it more widely around the world. . . . The proportions of aid being given on concessional terms. . .increased, as [did] the share disbursed through multilateral organizations. . . .

Internationalizing Japanese Society

Diplomatic initiatives to enhance Japan's role as an active participant in the world's political arenas can bear significant results in the short term. However, internationalizing Japanese society is inevitably a protracted process because it entails fundamental changes in deeply rooted social and cultural tendencies. Over the long run, a failure to make progress on internationalization may undermine efforts of Japanese leaders to project their country more confidently and constructively in international political arenas. . . .

On several readily observable measures of internationalization, contemporary Japan compares favorably with other developed societies. Newspapers and television have at least as extensive coverage of international news as their foreign counterparts. Numerous Japanese scholars are well informed on intellectual developments in Western societies. In being liberally introduced to the history and culture of both West and East, Japanese schoolchildren learn more about a broader range of civilizations than students in most other countries. Six years of English language training is part of the required curriculum of Japanese students. . . . The Japanese government has begun a program to increase [the number of foreign students studying in Japan]. . . .

What then is lacking in Japan's internationalization that explains the persistence of the issue both inside and outside Japan? One answer lies in the way the Japanese have traditionally viewed themselves as being a separate and distinctive group of people, much more so than do other national societies that have not been isolated from the outside world for as much of their history. It is noteworthy that until 1945 the Japanese had not been subjected to a foreign invasion or occupation of their land. In addition, Japanese derive more of their personal identity from their group affiliations than is the case in the more individualistic Western societies. The most encompassing group identity of Japanese is with their national society as a whole, which one becomes a member of only through birth and being socialized into it. This exclusivity is widely resented by outsiders who interpret it, perhaps incorrectly, as a form of arrogance, condescension, and even racism or tribalism. While contact with foreigners either in Japan or abroad would seem to break down this sense of separation, it may sometimes have the opposite effect of reinforcing the Japanese belief in their distinctiveness. . . .

These traits of the Japanese people not only limit the extent to which they understand and interact with foreign peoples but also reduce the degree to which Japan and the Japanese are known to the outside world. Cultural tendencies such as these, which have evolved over centuries, are susceptible only to the most gradual changes.

Toward Definitions of Global Responsibility. . .

What insights from the Japanese case study can be applied to the larger problems of defining the international responsibilities of states in an interdependent world and what it means for a population to be internationalized?. . .

In general terms, the fulfillment of global responsibilities implies that states are obliged to do what is in their means to help address international problems of regional or global scope, while minimizing if not eliminating ways they add to the severity or complexity of such problems. . . . For example, initiatives to mediate conflicts arising between other states, as the Japanese have done for Iran and Iraq, can be exercises in global responsibility as can restraint in the uses of coercion and force in the conduct of foreign policy. . . . In the economic realm, responsibility dictates not giving in to pressures for. . .trade policies that would transfer the costs of dealing with domestic problems to other countries through the use of import restrictions, export subsidies, or currency devaluations. Foreign assistance, especially of an economic or technical nature, can also be a major contribution to managing interdependence. . . .

Can a globally responsible foreign policy be pursued by the leaders of a country without a sympathetic and supportive population? In Japan the presumption has been that it cannot be done effectively over the long run, thus the call of the government for the Japanese people to "internationalize." What it means to internationalize the country has been a subject of continuing debate in Japan for more than a century. . . . While the Japanese are rather up-front in recognizing the problems they have in relating to foreign people, their limitations are by no means unique. . . .

The extent to which a population is internationalized is a combination of many characteristics. Perhaps foremost is the question of how cosmopolitan are the *values* of a society. . . . *Information* is a second element of internationalization. How well informed is a population on the cultures of foreign countries, major developments taking place abroad, or the principal issues before the United Nations? Person-to-person *contact* with foreign people, either in their country or in one's own, is a third aspect of internationalization. Internationalization also implies having the requisite *skills* for interacting and getting along with other people of diverse cultures. . . .

Conclusion

The recent efforts of the Japanese to define a constructive and responsible role for their nation in an increasingly interdependent global community illustrate several . . . conceptions of peace. Having experienced the devastation of modern warfare, including the horrors of atomic blasts over two of their cities, Japanese leaders and people have been a persuasive collective voice for a world free from war. The reluctance of contemporary Japanese to prepare for war, . . . is consistent with the [concept] of negative peace, although skeptics would argue that Japan is simply taking advantage of the United States's commitment to come to its defense.

The economic successes of Japan may serve as an example for other countries to reassess the wisdom and competitive feasibility of much higher levels of military expenditures.

The outline of the responsibilities of states to address cooperatively the agenda of problems that confront the world community, which was drawn from the Japanese case study, includes a number of positive and associative ways that governments can work together to improve the quality of life not only for their own populations but also for the peoples of other countries. And in doing so, they also diminish markedly the risk of war. The emphasis being placed on internationalizing the Japanese people in ways that will enable them to more successfully react and relate to people of foreign cultures is also an affirmative endeavor that has implications for what peace is rather than what it is not, and for bringing people peacefully together rather than keeping them at a distance. . . .

Study Questions

1. What are the chief forces of tradition and change in international relations?
2. What was the Peace of Westphalia, and why was it important?
3. What is sovereignty? Is it still a relevant concept?
4. Discuss the concept of *recognition*. What is the difference between de jure and de facto recognition? Provide examples.
5. What is the difference between a state, a nation, and a nation-state? Name examples of each.
6. How would you define *power*? What are some key elements of power?
7. What is the balance of power? What is its purpose?
8. What is the national interest? What problems do you see with this concept?
9. What are some of the key changes that took place in the twentieth century that altered the traditional international order?
10. Define and discuss the importance of bipolarity and multipolarity.
11. What is meant by the First, Second, Third, and Fourth Worlds? Provide examples of each.
12. What does *interdependence* mean?
13. How does interdependence challenge the power of states? Does it call for a new definition of the national interest? How? Why?
14. Do you think today's national leaders have an easier or more difficult job than the monarchs of old in coping with international relations? Why?
15. In your opinion, is the nation-state a major hindrance to a better world, or is it the only real source of order in the international system? Would we be better off with a world government, or one based on the dominance of corporations?
16. Drawing on the Soroos article, how would you characterize Japan's response to global interdependence? In what ways might Japan's situation be similar to or different from that of the United States?

Key Terms

balance of power

bipolarity

Cold War

de facto recognition

de jure recognition

East–West dispute

First World

Fourth World

hegemony

ideology

multipolarity

nation

national interest

nationalism

neutralism

New International Economic Order

nonalignment

North–South dispute

Peace of Westphalia

power

Second World

sovereignty

state

superpower

terra nullis

Third World

Notes

1. Hans Morgenthau, *Politics Among Nations: The Struggle for Power and Peace,* 4th ed. (New York: Knopf, 1967).
2. For a discussion of the views of several corporate advocates who make this argument, see Richard Barnet and Ronald Muller, *Global Reach: The Power of the Multinational Corporation* (New York: Simon & Schuster, 1974), pp. 15–20.
3. James Stegenga and W. Andrew Axline, *The Global Community: A Brief Introduction to International Relations,* 2nd ed. (New York: Harper & Row, 1982).
4. Thucydides, *A History of the Peloponnesian Wars* (New York: Modern Library, 1951).
5. See, for instance, Kautilya, *Arthasastra,* 3rd ed., trans. R. Shamasastry (Mysore, India: Wesleyan Mission Press, 1929), in which the struggles of India's principalities are carefully analyzed.
6. St. Thomas Aquinas, *De Regno, Ad Regem Cypri* (On Kingship, to the King of Cyprus), trans. G. B. Phelan and T. Eschman (Toronto: Pontifical Institute of Medieval Studies, 1949). See also Dino Bigongiari, *The Political Ideas of St. Thomas Aquinas* (New York: Hafner Press, 1953). For an excellent discussion of the concept of sovereignty, see Harold Laski, *Studies in the Problem of Sovereignty* (New Haven: Yale University Press, 1917).
7. Jean Bodin, *Six Books of the Commonwealth* (1576), abr. and trans. M. J. Tooley (New York: Barnes and Noble, 1967).
8. Hans Kohn, *The Idea of Nationalism* (New York: Macmillan, 1961).
9. Saadia Touval, *The Boundary Politics of Independent Africa* (Cambridge: Harvard University Press, 1972).
10. See Edward Gibbon, *The Decline and Fall of the Roman Empire,* 3 vols. (New York: Random House, n.d.) for a monumental history of the Western World from 180–1453 A.D. and for some keen insights into the rather common occurrence of smaller forces decisively beating substantially larger ones.
11. For a classical treatment of the role of geographical variables of national power, see Nicholas Spykman, *The Geography of Peace* (New York: Harcourt, Brace, and Company, 1944).

12. Morton A. Kaplan, *System and Process in International Politics* (New York: Wiley, 1957).

13. Charles Beard, *The Idea of the National Interest* (New York: Macmillan, 1934). For a more recent analysis, see Friedrich Kratochwil, "On the Notion of Interest in International Relations," *International Organization* 36 (Winter 1982): 1–30.

14. James N. Rosenau, *The Scientific Study of Foreign Policy* (New York: Free Press, 1971).

15. Morgenthau, *Politics Among Nations,* pp. 5–8.

16. Lester Brown, *World Without Borders* (New York: Random House, 1972); idem, *The Twenty-Ninth Day* (New York: Norton, 1978).

17. See Ervin Laszlo, Robert Baker, Jr., Elliott Eisenberg, and Venkata Raman, *The Objectives of the New International Economic Order* (New York: Pergamon Press for UNITAR, 1978).

18. Harold Jacobsen, *Networks of Interdependence: International Organizations and the Global Political System* (New York: Knopf, 1984), p. 9.

19. For an explanation of the various motives for foreign investment, particularly with regard to the theory of the product life cycle, see Barnet and Mueller, *Global Reach,* especially pp. 129–133.

20. For an in-depth discussion of the role of nongovernmental actors, see Richard Mansbach, Yale Ferguson, and Donald Lampert, *The Web of World Politics: Nonstate Actors in the Global System* (Englewood Cliffs, N.J.: Prentice-Hall, 1976).

21. World Bank, *World Development Report* (Washington, D.C.: World Bank, 1986), pp. 175–179.

22. Robert Keohane and Joseph Nye, *Power and Interdependence: World Politics and Transition* (Boston: Little, Brown, 1977), pp. 24–29.

23. Mansbach, Ferguson, and Lampert, *The Web of World Politics.*

24. See Robert Blake and Richard Walters, *The Politics of Global Economic Relations* (Englewood Cliffs, N.J.: Prentice-Hall, 1983), pp. 125–132, for a discussion of steps that host countries and the UN have taken to monitor and influence the activities of multinationals. See also Stephen Krasner, *Defending the National Interest* (Princeton: Princeton University Press, 1978), for an excellent treatment of the relations between governments and corporations from a statecentric perspective.

25. Keohane and Nye, *Power and Interdependence,* p. 225.

26. Robert Barnet, *Real Security: Restoring American Power in a Dangerous Decade* (New York: Simon & Schuster, 1981), p. 69.

27. Richard Sterling, *Macropolitics: International Relations in a Global Society* (New York: Knopf, 1974), p. 3. For a classic treatment on human–milieu relations, see Harold Sprout and Margaret Sprout, *The Ecological Perspective on Human Affairs* (Princeton: Princeton University Press, 1965).

28. Dennis Pirages, *The New Context for International Relations: Global Ecopolitics* (North Scituate, Mass.: Duxbury Press, 1978), p. 4.

29. Donella Meadows, Donald Meadows, Jorgen Randers, and William W. Behrens III, *The Limits to Growth* (New York: Universe Books, 1972).

30. Herman Kahn, William Brown, and Leon Martel, *The Next Two Hundred Years* (New York: Morrow, 1976).

31. Jan Tinbergen, Antony Dolman, and Jan van Ettinger, *Reshaping the International Order* (New York: Dutton, 1976); Gerald O. Barney, *The Global 2000 Report to the President,* vol. 1 (Washington, D.C.: Government Printing Office, 1980).

32. See, for instance, Wilfred Beckerman, *In Defense of Economic Growth* (London: Cape, 1974); Herman Kahn, *The Coming Boom* (New York: Simon & Schuster, 1982); and Alvin Toffler, *The Third Wave* (New York: Morrow, 1980).

33. For a discussion of the process of economic integration in Europe and its effects on political integration, see Leon Lindberg and Stuart Scheingold, *Europe's Would-Be Polity: Patterns of Change in the European Community* (Englewood Cliffs, N.J.: Prentice-Hall, 1970); and Niels Sonntag and Kevin Featherstone, "Problems of Political Integration," *Journal of Common Market Studies* 22, no. 3 (March 1984): 269–282.

34. Keohane and Nye, *Power and Interdependence,* pp. 11–19.

35. Hans Morgenthau, "The New Diplomacy of Movement," *Encounter* 3, no. 2 (August 1974): 56.

36. See, for instance, Bruce Russett, "Conflicts and Integration," Chap. 12 in *International Regions and the International System* (Chicago: Rand McNally, 1967), especially at pp. 198–201.

37. James K. Oliver, "The Balance of Power Heritage of 'Interdependence' and 'Traditionalism,'" *International Studies Quarterly* 26, no. 3 (September 1982): 373–396. Oliver argues that differences between the traditionalists (e.g., realists) and the advocates of interdependence are really less substantial than is sometimes suggested. In a sense, both world views are tenable in the modern age, each describing a certain reality. This fact only underscores the argument of this chapter that the forces of tradition and change coexist and that the outcome of the clash between them, for now, is not easily predicted.

Three

■

Theories and Approaches in the Study of International Relations

In this chapter we will explore the use of theory as a way of understanding international relations. We will see that theory helps us make sense of the behavior of various international actors. We will also see that theories are based on different perceptions, images, and opinions about the world. In other words, they are based on different interpretations of facts and events. Because not everyone shares the same opinions, perceptions, and beliefs, competing theories of international relations are bound to arise. Similarly, a number of different and contending approaches to describing and explaining international behavior have emerged. The result is that international relations does not have a single, all-explanatory, overarching theory. Instead, a number of "islands" of theory deal with different subjects such as war, arms races, negotiations, decision making, and economic integration.

There are even different methods of collecting, analyzing, and interpreting information. Some students of international relations prefer traditional and qualitative methods of study, whereas others use more scientific and quantitative approaches. To understand the role of theory building in international relations then, we must pay attention both to *what* we want to know and to *how* we should approach knowing it.

What Is Theory?

Theory is the key mechanism used to organize and order facts into data, because it helps identify important data. Theories are used to define, label, and classify the phenomena of international relations. Like other academic disciplines, international relations depends on sets of conceptual units, called taxonomies or classifications to facilitate study, analysis, and understanding. This process enables scholars to collaborate with one another and to engage in cumulative learning and theory building.

According to *Webster's Third New International Dictionary, theory* has its origin in the Greek *theōrein,* or "to look at." Indeed, theories are a way of looking at and understanding the world we live in. Theory, then, is a body of empirical, logically interconnected generalizations aimed at describing, explaining, and predicting events in our world. Generally speaking, theory in international relations does a better job of describing and explaining, than of predicting, events.

When we develop theories about our world, a complex mental process unfolds as we observe, relate, and analyze different events. Although presumably based on fact, theories are affected by our perceptions, values, beliefs, and cognitions.

The Building Blocks of Theory

Facts

Perceptual theorists believe that what is real or unreal in the international arena depends on the *interpretation* that is given to the facts by authoritative decision makers, rather than on the facts alone. The **facts** do not speak for themselves; they are given meaning by each interpreter from his or her analytical point of view. Consequently, rather than springing from reality, facts are actually pieces of information that an international actor selects as having importance while rejecting other pieces of information as lacking importance. *Facts* are thus subjectively defined and are a phenomenon of perceptions.[1] In other words, actors in the international arena impose facts on reality. Hence, reality will always depend on the actor's perceptions and the questions he or she chooses to ask.

Values, Beliefs, and Cognitions

We can distinguish between three types of knowledge in international relations: evaluative (values), affective (beliefs), and cognitive (cognitions). A **value** is a preference for one state of reality over another. Values do not specify what is but rather what ought to be; they are judgments about the goals that ought to be pursued in political life and about the moral quality of political objects and events. For example, despite the cooperation among the World War II allies, the United States did not trust the Soviet Union enough to share atomic secrets, in part because the USSR's Marxist-Leninist values were antithetical to values held by American policy makers.

A **belief** is a conviction that a description of reality is true, proven, or known. A belief is not the same as a value. Affections and feelings are often expressed under a belief as symbols of attachment, involvement, alienation, rejection, identification, amity, and enmity about political objects. A belief is a configuration of ideas and attitudes bound together by some form of constraint or functional interdependence.[2]

A **cognition** is information derived from the environment that can be substantiated through physical evidence or perceptual observation. Cognitions are empirical beliefs about the nature of people, politics, and international actors and their interactions. Cognitions are key elements in establishing perceptual systems and in changing those systems. For example, when two actors in the international arena disagree on an issue, each tries to sway the other by introducing cognitions that will revise his or her beliefs and values. The assumption is that when actors behave rationally, cognitive evidence can change stubborn beliefs and values that might otherwise lead them to misperceptions. Yet research findings in a variety of studies show that deeply held values and beliefs are highly resistant to change through new cognitions.[3] To illustrate the very different way in which facts can be interpreted through different perceptual systems, values, and cognitions, let's consider the 1986 U.S.–Libyan dispute.

The U.S.-Libyan Dispute: Facts and Perceptions

On Sunday, March 23, 1986, at 4:30 A.M. Eastern Standard Time, U.S. aircraft and ships began Operation Prairie Fire, a series of naval maneuvers in the Mediterranean Sea near the Gulf of Sidra (see figure 3.1). Libya claims that its territorial sea extends to the so-called line of death across the wide mouth of the Gulf of Sidra, thus extending far beyond the customary twelve-mile territorial sea limit recognized by most nations, including the United States. On Monday, March 24, at 1:00 P.M., three U.S. ships crossed this "line of death" in the Gulf of Sidra, but continued to respect a twelve-mile territorial limit. At 2:52 P.M. Libya launched two antiaircraft (SA-5) missiles from the Surt missile site at U.S. planes in the Gulf of Sidra. At 6:00 P.M. two Libyan MiG-25s ventured into the gulf, but turned back. At 7:45 P.M. another SA-5 was launched from the Surt base. At 8:14 P.M. the Libyans launched one or two more SA-25s, but no U.S. planes were hit. At 9:26 P.M. two U.S. A-6 Intruders from the aircraft carrier *America* retaliated with Harpoon missiles and Rockeye bombs and destroyed a Libyan attack boat in the gulf inside the "line of death." At 10:06 P.M. two A-7 planes from the carrier *Saratoga* launched high-speed antiradiation missiles, called HARMs, at the Surt missile site. At 11:15 P.M. A-6 bombers attacked a second Libyan patrol boat, forcing it to turn back to Benghazi.

On Tuesday, March 25, at 1:15 A.M. Aegis radar cruiser *Yorktown* fired two Harpoon missiles at a third Libyan patrol boat north of the "line of death." At 1:54 A.M. two U.S. A-7s from the Saratoga launched two more HARMs at Surt, and on the same morning between 8:07 and 11:00 A.M. U.S. aircraft struck at two Libyan vessels, destroying one near Benghazi. On Thursday, March 27, at 4:30 P.M. (11:30 P.M. Libyan time), the United States ended the Gulf of Sidra maneuvers.

Did Operation Prairie Fire resolve the issue of whether the twelve-mile territorial sea limit or the much broader Libyan claim was valid? The issue has never been tested in any international court or forum. So, for the United States, the exercises were meant to emphasize that free navigation on the "open sea" would be enforced by military power, if necessary. According to a radio broadcast from Tripoli, however, the incident meant that "We [Libyans] will impose our sovereignty on the Gulf of Sidra with our blood!"

These incidents in the Gulf of Sidra caused two diametrically opposed perceptual systems to vie for support in the international arena. In Washington the exercise was hailed as protecting the right of free passage in international waters and as punishing Libya for its sponsorship of international terrorism. In Tripoli Col. Muammar Gaddafi proclaimed victory, and Libyan radio exhorted, "Oh, heroes of our Arab nation, let your missiles and suicide cells pursue American terrorist embassies and interests wherever they may be!"[4]

The battle of Sidra left a few smoking Libyan boats and a large question mark: Did America's slap at Gaddafi deter or encourage further terrorism? Washington, as well as the majority of the American people, believed that the display of American muscle would induce Gaddafi to be reluctant to support, if not completely opposed to, further terrorism. By April 7, 1986, three days after the West Berlin disco bombing that left an American serviceman and a Turkish woman dead, the Reagan administration was convinced that Libyan support of international terrorism had not ceased and decided that the time for action had arrived (see table 3.1). During April 11–14, UN Ambassador Vernon Walters was dispatched to Western Europe to win the backing of U.S. allies for a raid on Libya. On April 14 at 7:00 P.M. E.S.T., the United States carried out a surgical air attack on designated targets in the Tripoli and Benghazi areas of Libya.

In his televised address following the attack on Libya, President Ronald Reagan asserted that the air strike "will not only diminish Colonel Gaddafi's capacity to export

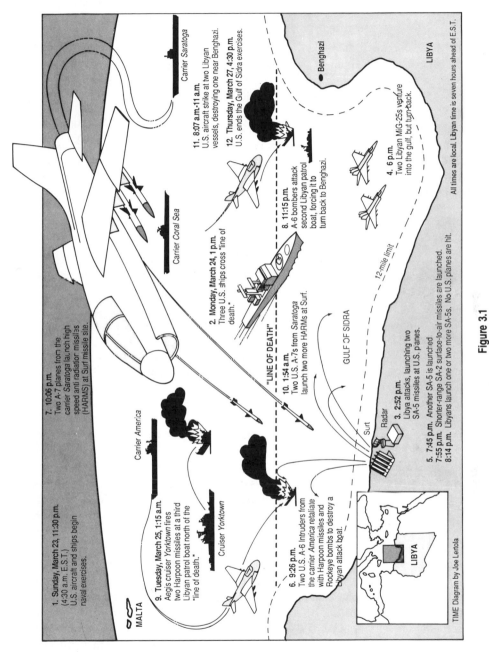

Figure 3.1

The Gulf of Sidra maneuvers

SOURCE: *TIME*, April 28, 1986, pp. 16–17. Copyright 1986 Time, Inc. Reprinted by permission.

The following labels and annotations appear in the figure:

1. **Sunday, March 23, 11:30 p.m.** (4:30 a.m. E.S.T.) U.S. aircraft and ships begin naval exercises.

2. **Monday, March 24, 1 p.m.** Three U.S. ships cross "line of death."

3. **2:52 p.m.** Another SA-5 is launched.

4. **6 p.m.** Two Libyan MiG-25s venture into the gulf, but turn back.

5. **7:45 p.m.** Shorter-range SA-2 surface-to-air missiles are launched.
   7:55 p.m. Shorter-range SA-2 surface-to-air missiles are launched.
   8:14 p.m. Libyans launch one or two more SA-5s. No U.S. planes are hit.

6. **9:26 p.m.** Two U.S. A-6 Intruders from the carrier *America* retaliate with Harpoon missiles and Rockeye bombs to destroy a Libyan attack boat.

7. **10:06 p.m.** Two A-7 planes from the carrier *Saratoga* launch high speed and radiator missiles (HARMs) at Surf missile site.

8. **11:15 p.m.** A-6 bombers attack second Libyan patrol boat, forcing it to turn back to Benghazi.

9. **Tuesday, March 25, 1:15 a.m.** Aegis cruiser *Yorktown* fires two Harpoon missiles at a third Libyan patrol boat north of the "line of death."

10. **1:54 a.m.** Two U.S. A-7s from *Saratoga* launch two more HARMs at Surf.

11. **8:07 a.m.–11 a.m.** U.S. aircraft strike at two Libyan vessels, destroying one near Benghazi.

12. **Thursday, March 27, 4:30 p.m.** U.S. ends the Gulf of Sidra exercises.

3. 2:52 p.m. Libya attacks, launching two SA-5 missiles at U.S. planes.

"LINE OF DEATH"

GULF OF SIDRA

12-mile limit

All times are local. Libyan time is seven hours ahead of E.S.T.

Carrier *Saratoga*

Carrier *Coral Sea*

Carrier *America*

Cruiser *Yorktown*

MALTA

Surf

Radar

• Benghazi

LIBYA

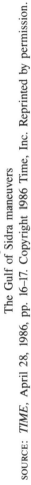

LIBYA

TIME Diagram by Joe Lertola

Table 3.1

Operation El Dorado Canyon

Date and Time	Event
April 5	The La Belle discotheque bombing in West Berlin implicates Libyan agents in the terrorist act.[a]
April 7	In response President Reagan approves plan by the Joint Chiefs of Staff for surgical bombing strikes against Libya—contingent however on sought changes by the Libyan Government or American allies in their policies on terrorism.[b]
April 7–14	The Pentagon planners make preparation for carrying out a raid on Libya subject to Presidential "reconfirmation."[c]
April 11–14	President Reagan sends UN Ambassador Vernon A. Walters to European capitals to seek support for possible U.S. action against Libya and to discuss Libyan involvement in terrorism.[d] With reluctance Britain backs Reagan's plan, permitting the use of British-based planes for the attack, however, France and Spain reject the request to use their airspace while West Germany and Italy are opposed to the raids in general.[e]
April 12	Malta proposes to an emergency meeting of the UN Security Council that the Secretary General intervene to stave off new United States–Libyan clashes. After a four hour closed session, the council recessed for the weekend.[f]
April 13	President Reagan gives final authorization for the strike.[g]
April 14 12:00–1:00 P.M. E.S.T.	U.S. F-111 bombers, KC-135 Stratotankers, and EF-111 Ravens take off from Lakenheath, Mildenhall, Fairford and Upper Heyford airbases in Britain and head for Libya, skirting France and Spain.[h]
7:00 P.M. E.S.T.	A-7s and F-18s from the Coral Sea and the American carriers disable Libyan radar sites with HARM and Shrike missiles. F-111s from Great Britain are accounted for except for one. Using surprise and electronic jamming, A-6s from carriers strike at targets in and near Benghazi.[i]
7:30 P.M. E.S.T.	President Reagan in a broadcast address refers to Operation El Dorado Canyon a success.[j]

SOURCES: [a]*The New York Times*, 4/11/86, pp. 1 and 10; [b]*ibid.*, 4/15/86, p. 11; [c]*ibid.*, 4/10/86, pp. 1 and 23; [d]*ibid.*, 4/13/86, pp. 1 and 13; [e]*Newsweek*, 4/28/86, p. 38; [f]*The New York Times*, 4/13/86, p. 18; [g]*ibid.*, 4/15/86, p. 11; [h]*Newsweek*, 4/28/86, pp. 26–28 and 31; [i]*The New York Times*, 4/15/86, pp. 1 and 11; [j]*The New York Times*, 4/15/86, p. 10.

terror, it will provide him with incentives and reason to alter his criminal behavior." For whatever reason, that argument won the support of only three U.S. allies: Great Britain, Canada, and Israel. All the others counseled against a raid and France and Spain even refused to let American F-111s fly over their territory on the mission. In the United States, by contrast, an overwhelming 71 percent of 1,007 adults polled approved of the strike, as opposed to only 20 percent who disapproved and 9 percent who were not sure.[5] In Great Britain, Market and Opinion Research International surveyed 1,051 people for the London *Times*: 66 percent were against the air strike, and only 29 percent approved while 5 percent remained unsure.[6] In France, 49 percent of those surveyed were opposed to the air strike and only 39 percent were in favor. There were demonstrations against the U.S. attack on Libya in many major cities of the Western alliance and in most nonaligned countries of the world. The most notable dissenter in the United States was former President Jimmy Carter, who predicted in an off-the-cuff remark that the raid would make Gaddafi "a hero in the Arab world and a worse menace than ever."

Even though most Arab leaders mistrust Gaddafi, they see themselves as part of the Arab family when he is under attack from the West. In the Middle East families pull together to confront a common enemy even if the family members hate one another. Indeed, the struggle with the Arab world is more complex than some of the leaders in Washington would have us believe. The March 14 National Security Council decision, dubbed Operation Prairie Fire and the April 7 decision were couched in the perceptual framework that Washington would be safe from either Soviet or Arab reprisal. The U.S. decision makers perceived the Soviet Union as more interested in the new round of arms control talks with the United States than in supporting Libya. Washington had quietly informed Moscow in advance of its intentions in the Gulf of Sidra and when the attacks were launched, the Soviets made themselves almost invisible—they kept one communications ship anchored at Surt, and it was lighted up like a Christmas tree so that the U.S. Sixth Fleet would avoid it. Besides, the Soviet Union had no military commitments to defend Libya. After the attack, however, the General Secretary of the Communist Party of the Soviet Union, Mikhail Gorbachev, denounced the U.S. "imperial, bandit act" and then offered to withdraw Soviet naval forces if the United States did as well. This ploy was scarcely plausible.

As for potential Arab reprisals, American officials did not believe that Arab oil producers whose economies were reeling under precipitous declines in oil prices could afford to retaliate. In addition U.S. officials believed that Egypt's Hosni Mubarak, the only other Arab leader who could have complicated matters, was under siege in his own country and therefore was not likely to undertake risky foreign adventures. As it turned out, their perceptions were correct in both cases. Verbal criticisms—some stronger than others—came from the Arab leaders, but none seemed anxious to support Gaddafi beyond words.

Gaddafi perceives himself as a desert visionary who is destined to restore Arabs to their past glory. He feels that he has inherited the "Pan-Arab" legacy of former Egyptian leader Gamal Abdel Nasser and that his ultimate mission is to confront former Western colonial powers in the name of all Arab peoples and of Islam. This belief underlies his support of the Palestinian cause and of Palestinian terrorists. While some Arab leaders dismiss him as overly ambitious and incautious, others see him as a hero.

Contrary to Washington's expectations, Gaddafi survived the air attack on his residence and an attempted military coup, which the U.S. attack was calculated to touch off. Two weeks after the attack Gaddafi was in full command in Libya and was hailed as a martyr throughout the non-Western world. In public speeches and radio addresses, Gaddafi raged at President Reagan and Prime Minister Margaret Thatcher, calling them "child murderers," and announced to the Western world that "we will not kill your children, we are not like you." In the meantime, Libyan-sponsored terrorist activities continued in Lebanon, Sudan, England, and elsewhere.

These incidents in Libya during March and April 1986 raised several questions. Was the United States intruding into Libyan territory when the three U.S. ships crossed the "line of death"? In launching military operations in the Gulf of Sidra, was the United States spoiling for a fight? Why wasn't the international status of the waters of the Gulf of Sidra tested in an international court or forum? Did the damages inflicted on Libya by the Sixth Fleet deter international terrorism? Did the United States follow the advice of its Western allies against a raid on Libya? Did world public opinion favor or oppose the U.S. raid? Is the concept of terrorism the same for the United States as it is for other nations? Decision makers' responses to these questions varied according to their perceptual systems. Most people consider their own **perceptions** to be real (true) and opponents' perceptions to be at least partly false. Everybody responds to events as they perceive them, based on their prior experience and on what they hope will happen.[7] What humans, including international decision makers, perceive may or may not correspond to reality. Thus, what matters is not how real actions are in international relations, but how real they appear to be to the actors in the international arena and how those actors respond to them.[8] Whether it is Ronald Reagan or Muammar Gaddafi, each leader's perceptual system supports itself with an array of data and historical analyses that need no further substantiation. Each leader regards the other's perceptual system as inaccurate and dishonest.

In summary, we have seen that perception is a dynamic process. It is determined not only by the outside world, but also by the perceiver's culture, attitudes, expectations, needs, experiences, and other attributes. In short, perception is subjective. The processes of perception are connected with a range of other mental processes that influence future perceptions, thus forming a closed circle. Most of the time, our habits-of-mind help defend our ego and our opinions, find consonance rather than dissonance, and give meaning and predictability to the world. Because in international relations we are often concerned with the behavior of people in groups or organizations, the two levels of analysis—the individual as such, and the person as a role-player in an organization—will frequently be linked through the perceptual process. If the groups belong to different countries or cultures, then they are further divided by language, values, **images,** history, and other factors that influence their perceptions of each other and of the situation. Ultimately, such differences will also affect the key players in the international arena: the decision makers.[9]

Approaches to Building Theory

Hypotheses

Almost all theories start with some effort to observe the world, to find causes, meaning, and order in the operations of social and natural phenomena. In dealing with political and social events, developing theories is more difficult because they are not easily subjected to controlled experiment. And yet, despite varying perceptions, images, and beliefs, regularities in political behavior and in international relations do seem to exist. As people see the regularities, they begin to formulate **hypotheses,** that is, guesses about causal relationships between events. For instance, if we see many cases of *extended deterrence,* in which the policy makers of one state (the defender) threaten the use of force against another state (the potential attacker) in an attempt to prevent that state from using military force against the defender's ally (the protégé), we might hypothesize that under certain conditions extended deterrence is likely to succeed.

As Paul K. Huth points out in the supplementary reading, extended deterrence is greatly strengthened if the defender has the military capability to deny the attacker a quick victory and turn the conflict into a protracted struggle. In other words, a potential attacker's calculus of military costs seems to focus on whether military force can be used to achieve decisive results at relatively low cost.

Although some people will be content to accept a hypothesis on the basis of a few historical examples, others will demand further investigation. They may want to have more proof, for instance, that *military balance* is a powerful explanatory variable in the analysis of deterrence. As they test their hypotheses—that is, check their predictions about conditions under which potential attackers will refrain from aggression against actual observations— they are engaged in the process of theory building.

Traditionalism, Behavioralism, and the Scientific Method

All students of international relations engage in hypothesizing and theory building. Those who rely on their own knowledge of history, politics, law, and foreign affairs are known as **traditionalists.** In contrast to the traditionalists, scholars who approach the study of international relations in a more scientific and quantitative manner are known as **behavioralists.** To test which theories and hypotheses best accord with actual behavior in the international system, behavioralists rely on the scientific method, a model of inquiry that proceeds according to the following steps:

1. A *hypothesis* (or assumption) is formed about the relation of one variable to another. (A variable is something that varies, and the variation is thought to influence a particular state of being [i.e., variation] in something else.) For example: International cooperation increases with economic aid. It has a subject (the variable, *international cooperation*), a connective verb (a relationship, *increases*), and an object (the variable, *economic aid*).
2. An *evaluation* is performed to compare the measured relationship with the original hypothesis.
3. *Suggestions* are made about the significance of the findings, factors involved in the test that may have distorted the results, and other hypotheses that the inquiry brings to mind.[10]

To accomplish the first step in the process of scientific methodology (that is, to test hypotheses), the behavioralist must first collect reliable data.[11] For all practical purposes, there are two types of data: descriptive versus measurable, or soft versus hard. Whereas descriptive or **soft data** are subjective or normative, measurable or **hard data** are more objective or empirical. For example, the data about U.S. intentions in the Gulf of Sidra were subjective, giving the impression that the air attack on Libyan targets was a just retaliation for terrorism. The events describing U.S. attempts to gain the support of her allies prior to the April 14 air attack on Libya were also subjective or soft data. However, the information based on the public opinion polls taken in the United States, Great Britain, and France represents measurable or hard data on American misperceptions of her Western European allies. The characterizations of Muammar Gaddafi and the Arabs are value judgments, without any supporting evidence based on in-depth studies.

At this juncture, we should point out that in international relations both types of data are of great significance. Therefore, the exclusion of subjective data, such as ideas, motives, feelings, attitudes, intentions, desires, and purposes, from the study of international relations would seriously limit our ability to perceive the complexities of interaction in the international system. However, behavioralists prefer to tackle the second category of data, that is, *empirical* or observable, quantifiable hard data. One of the many reasons for this preference is that these data are measurable and thus presumably less vulnerable to misperception or misinterpretation.

It is not always easy, however, to collect hard data. Sometimes the data are simply not available, or they can only be estimated. Studies dealing with future trends suffer from this problem; researchers can only guess at future trends based on the best available current evidence.[12] In all international relations research the maxim is to collect and classify data that resemble the "real world" and that are relevant to the researcher's initial hypothesis.

Once the researcher has collected the data, they must be standardized and analyzed. Data analysis involves piecing the data into useful categories—a process known as comparison (e.g., comparing a set of data for one country to a set of data for another). The type of analysis, statistical techniques, or computer applications a researcher performs will depend on the research inquiry, as well as on the method he or she used to collect the data, and on the complexity of the hypothesis.[13]

While the ultimate goal of a behavioralist researcher in international relations is to rely on data that can be tested, verified, and reproduced to acquire accurate and dependable knowledge, many traditionalists question whether this objective can be realistically attained, since as they see it, international relationships and interactions are not *directly* observable or easily subjected to controlled scientific experiments. Traditionalists argue that certain situations or developments in international relations simply do not lend themselves to quantification. The philosophical implications of issues such as the arms race, world poverty, hunger, the deterioration of the earth's ecological system, the struggle for independence, and the existence of terrorism suggest that human actions (interaction by actors in the international arena) and social aspirations are impelled by belief, even though the believer may be only vaguely aware of his or her intellectual premises.

The researcher no less than the decision maker is affected by these subconscious values. According to the traditionalists, the subject matter of international relations often concerns religious, moral, and highly political issues of order, justice, freedom, and equality. From a traditionalist perspective, the goals of American foreign policy should be "a world free of fear and war; a world open to ideas, open to the exchange of goods and people; a world in which no people, great or small, live in angry isolation; a world free of hatred and discrimination; a world of independent nations. . .a world that provides sure and equitable means for the peaceful settlement of disputes and moves steadily to a rule of law; a world of equal rights and equal opportunities for all, in which the personal freedoms essential to the dignity of man are secure."[14]

The behavioralist researcher, on the other hand, will try to quantify, if possible, concepts such as *freedom, well-being,* and *independence.* For example, if the economic well-being of a nation might be measured by income, gross national product, cost of living, purchasing power, square footage of housing, ownership of cars, household goods, and so on, nations can then be ranked according to scores of highest achievement. However, such quantified measurement and ranking may not explain whether members of the highest ranking nation in terms of economic well-being are also the happiest, most satisfied, most moral, or judicious. In this gray area the traditionalist researcher's judgments will be dominant, although the evidence for his or her assertions and conclusions may be lacking.

While both behavioral (quantitative) and traditional (qualitative) methods of study are valuable, quantitative techniques to study international phenomena have become more popular and influential. Those scholars who emphasize quantitative techniques in their research are usually concerned with three problems: (1) systematic classification of nations, (2) identification of typical patterns among types of nations, and (3) identification of factors responsible for the changing relationships among nations. Quantitative research methods have been used to chart the flow of transactions within and between regions and to explain the transformation of alliances, the causes of war, the dimensions of conflict, and the conditions under which different degrees of international integration emerge.[15]

How, then, should one build theory in international relations? To begin with, the traditionalist and behavioralist approaches both seem to have value. Normative (qualitative) and empirical (quantitative) approaches can help devise and assess theories of international behavior. However, neither approach has achieved a breakthrough in devising a general theory of international relations.[16] Instead a number of pretheories or paradigms have emerged that often rely on both traditional and behavioral methods of study. A **paradigm** is an intellectual framework that structures one's thinking about a set of phenomena; that is, a cognitive map that helps organize reality and make sense of the multitude of events that occur in the world each day. Three paradigms—realism, structuralism, and pluralism—dominate the study of international relations.

Contending Paradigms or Pretheories in Contemporary International Relations

Realism

Although theorizing about the nature of interstate relations can be traced to ancient times, the modern study of international politics was ushered in by World War I, when the first philosophical differences erupted between **idealists** or (utopians) and **realists** in what we refer to as the traditional stage of the study of international relations.[17] Both schools of thought were concerned with preventing another international war. The American idealists emphasized international legal rights and obligations, preservation of international peace, cooperation based on moral principles, trust in human nature, and the rational behavior of people. Idealists opposed balance-of-power politics, national armaments, the use of force, secret alliances, and geopolitical spheres of influence. The realists, on the other hand, stressed power and interest based on national security and diplomacy backed by military force. Their arguments centered around the relative merits of the national interest, legal institutions, and moral precepts as criteria for guiding and evaluating international behavior.[18] After World War II, realism became the dominant approach to the study of international relations.

The realists, together with the idealists and even many behavioralists, treated the world system as a structure comprised of nation-states whose governments interacted through their foreign policies. Realists assumed that all actors in the system understood that their roles were within the static structures of the state system. States and governments were central international actors responsible for the flow of influence (power) along the formally established tributaries of the international system. This conceptual rigidity did not allow for the dynamics and change that occur in the relationships among governments and other actors.

Realism did not begin to falter, however, until the early 1970s when **post-behavioralism** challenged the assumptions of a **state-centric** world. At the end of the decade realism was competing with structuralism and pluralism as general explanations of international politics. By the early 1980s the realists had not only sustained various attacks by advocates of other paradigms, but they had regrouped and counterattacked under the banner of *neo-realism*. Neo-realism differs from traditional realism in that it is more open to the use of behavioral research techniques. Still whether in its traditional or newer garb, realism no longer dominates thinking and theorizing about international politics; it is joined by the structuralist and pluralist paradigms.

Structuralism

Structuralists start out with the assumption that human behavior cannot be understood merely by examining an individual's motivation and intention, because when these factors are combined, human behavior creates structures that individuals may not be aware of. For example, when people walk across a field, they may create a path unintentionally and others who follow the path then reproduce it. This process of reproduction is neither conscious nor intentional. Structuralists characterize language in similar terms. No individual consciously establishes the rules of language and no individual can change those rules. Yet, when language is used, people reproduce its structure.[19] Thus structuralism is based on holist methodology, which argues that social interaction creates systems that are defined by enduring characteristics.

In the 1970s Immanuel Wallerstein used the idea of center–periphery relations as an organizing device for looking at world history. His thesis was that understanding world history requires a structured model that embraces political and economic elements. According to his findings, centralized empires have been the dominating mode of economic and political organization. When empires collapse, they are replaced by decentralized world systems, which in turn disintegrate when a political unit seizes control and creates a new empire. Since the sixteenth century, however, a set of strong core states in Europe has dominated a large number of weak peripheral states in the rest of the world. This dominance has persisted for several centuries because of the balance of power favoring the strong states. Divisions such as class, nationality, race, and ethnic group are a product of the structure of the world political and economic system—a system that reinforces the weak peripheral states' dependency on the strong.[20]

Pluralism

The pluralist approach in international politics developed in the 1970s as a response to the realists' belief that international politics involved relations among states of strikingly similar character and behavior. At first pluralism characterized the international systems in terms of transnational relations conducted among a kaleidoscope of nonstate actors.[21] The pluralist approach, however, lacked a structural focus, and therefore the main advocates of **transnationalism** resurrected the state and made interdependence their centerpiece for characterizing contemporary relations among states. They made it clear, however, that relations among states are not determined by the distribution of power as the realists have claimed. In contrast to the structuralists' assertions, the pluralists view the world as a multicentric rather than state-centric or global-centric system of relationships. Pluralists emphasize the role of multinational companies and interdependence in trade, the structure of conflict, ethnicity, group identity, and the self-determination of nonstate actors. For example, ethnic-based community groups in Lebanon, Cyprus, or Sri Lanka appear to be more powerful than the state because the loyalty and identity of the people hearken to the ethnic group rather than to the state. These kinds of conflicts are domestic rather than interstate in character, although they have considerable international implications. Pluralists believe that the separation of domestic and international relationships is not only misleading but harmful to the accurate understanding of much international conflict today.

Comparing the Paradigms

These three major analytic frameworks—realism, structuralism, and pluralism—are incompatible or contradictory in their outlook on world society. Each paradigm has an independently coherent explanation about the images of how international relations functions. The paradigms disagree on the concept and role of actors, the dynamics of interaction in the system, and on the task and scope of international relations. For example, realists consider states to be the only actors; pluralists recognize states as actors and a host of nonstate actors as well, ranging from international governmental organizations to nongovernmental organizations; and structuralists see economic classes as the major actors in the global arena. As far as the dynamics of international relations is concerned, realists see force as the main factor, pluralists see complex social movements as the main factor, and structuralists see economics as the main factor. Realists believe that the task of international relations is to explain what states do, pluralists believe that it is to explain major world events, and structuralists believe that the main task is to explain the gap between rich and poor nations. The scope of the study of international relations, according to realists, is the politics of the sovereign nations defined in a state-centric fashion. Pluralists consider a wide range of subjects, including the behavior of states, multinational corporations, markets, ethnic groups, and the people. Structuralists have the widest boundaries of all; they emphasize the unity of the entire global system at all levels, focus on the economic modes of production, and look at international politics only as a secondary phenomenon. All three paradigms have their own peculiar conceptual focuses. For example, realism relies heavily on deterrence and alliances; pluralism relies on ethnicity and interdependence; and structuralism relies on exploitation and dependency. All three paradigms employ concepts such as *power, sovereignty,* and *law* with similar meanings, but *imperialism,* the *state,* and *hegemony* are used very differently.[22] Together these similarities and differences in conceptualization represent an attempt by theorists to analyze and synthesize the behavior of the human race, that is, to divide the world society into identifiable units of analysis whose patterns of interaction can be examined and explained in a systematic way. Each paradigm has contributed to the process of theory building, and each has advanced our knowledge of state or nonstate actors' behavior in international relations.

Normative Approaches to the Study of International Relations

Advocates of the realist, structuralist, and pluralist paradigms use a variety of normative approaches to understand international relations. The major objective of these approaches is to address questions of justice, rights, duties, and obligations. While they differ in philosophical orientation, attitude, and argument, these approaches are similar in the use and analysis of data, logic, and the role of judgment. They are nonscientific and nonquantitative, and they reject the methodologies employed by behavioralists. The normative approaches were common between the two world wars; their influence declined after World War II, regaining momentum during the 1970s and 1980s. The historical, legal, and cosmopolitan approaches are among the better-known normative methods.

The Historical Approach

Followers of the historical approach use one of the oldest methods of evaluating evidence from international relations. The purpose of the **historical approach** is to reconstruct the past on the basis of documentary evidence in order to provide explanations of how events and conditions grow and develop over time and how these events and conditions are related.

Many behavioral scientists have questioned the ability of the historical approach to make predictions in international relations. They argue that the relevance of past experience to gauging future trends also depends on the rate and scale of change through time. If the kind of behavior at issue exhibits relatively stable patterns through a given time span, then precedents are more trustworthy guides than in periods of rapid and radical change. Since we seem to live in an age of revolutionary change, certain critics assert that nearly all historical experience has lost some predictive value, thus making the application of the historical approach to the study of international relations of only limited relevance. In other words, our world changes so rapidly that the meaning of international events and conditions can scarcely be analyzed and understood in time to apply the lessons to related developments.[23]

The Legal Approach

Adherents of the legal approach assume that all disputes, even in international politics, are legal contests. Therefore, the international courts and international law, which are viewed as morally superior to international politics, are responsible for these conflicts. Phrases such as "peace through law" and "peace through institutions" are central to the legal approach, because they represent the desire to build a global system based on international organizations and the law.

Whereas before and after World War II the legal approach focused on the problems of war, that focus shifted to human rights in the 1970s and 1980s. Advocates argued for the need to develop international conventions, such as the Universal Declaration of Human Rights and the Helsinki Accords, that went beyond mere statements of aspiration to impose legal duties on states even in the treatment of their own citizens.[24] The legal approach today shows a continuing interest in developing humanitarian law, promoting justice, protecting the global environment, and maintaining world public order.

The Cosmopolitan Approach

Advocates of the **cosmopolitan approach** seek to extend the framework of morality globally to all actors in the international arena, not just to the state or within the state. The aim is to revive the moral fabric in international interaction that was removed by the realists' moral skepticism. According to this approach, relations among nations ought to be constrained by a principle of distributive justice. National interests should not be slavishly adhered to if they result in substantial injustice or harm to other nations or peoples.

Like the legal approach, the cosmopolitan approach seeks to promote economic, civil, and political rights. The logic and structure of the argument is that no other rights can be enjoyed unless basic rights, such as access to food and health care, political participation, and freedom of movement, are secured. The responsibility for guaranteeing the basic rights of all members of the international society is matched by a duty to protect others from deprivation and to aid those who are deprived. Consequently, the developed world has a responsibility toward the less developed world, which may in fact call for redistribution of wealth and even reorganization of the international economic system.[25]

Nonnormative Approaches to the Study of International Relations

Of the nonnormative approaches to the study of international relations, the power approach, the closely related balance of power approach, and the geopolitical approach are most often associated with the realist paradigm. The systems approach has characterized most of the work done by structuralists, but pluralists and realists have also adopted this approach at different times. Pluralists have tended to favor the functionalist, communications, and decision-making approaches. But these distinctions are not hard and fast. Indeed, advocates of each paradigm have used nearly all of these approaches at one time or another.

The Power Approach

The best-known exponent of the power approach was the late Hans J. Morgenthau. In Morgenthau's estimation, the distinguishing element of international politics is the aspiration for **power.**[26] The desire to dominate is part of human nature and part of all human associations, from the family through fraternal and professional associations and from local associations to the state itself. **National interests,** in particular, must be defined in terms of power. The national interest, according to Morgenthau, must always stand above, and therefore absorb, the limited and parochial claims of subnational groups, even if these groups seek to interpret the national interest in their own terms.[27] Since every nation by virtue of its geographic position, historic objectives, and relationship to other power centers possesses a conglomerate of strategic interests, a realistic foreign policy must attempt to safeguard these claims, which, in Morgenthau's language, means a foreign policy congruent with the national interest. Very often, however, leaders—either by personal choice or because of influence exerted by certain pressure groups—choose "abstract moral principles" as their guide in making foreign policy. Morgenthau condemns this practice as "unreal," because these abstract principles do not reflect a state's power interests. The real nature of such abstract policies is concealed by ideology. In Morgenthau's estimation, political ideologies arc only disguises for the realities inherent in the struggle for power.[28]

In harmony with Morgenthau's views, most realists (or more recently, neo-realists) treat international relations as the study of nearly anarchic relations among sovereign political entities—the nation-states.[29] These states recognize no supreme international judge or arbiter, and they may resort to the use of power or to threats of force to protect and promote what they consider to be their vital interests. Thus, realists posit that the nature of the state is to acquire as much power as it can because of the dangerous and anarchic world in which it exists. If a state is to succeed, it has little choice but to make the acquisition of power its chief aim. Power is thus a means to an end but it is also an end in itself, because only with power will a state be well placed to pursue other goals such as peace and prosperity. Needless to say, this makes international relations conflictual rather than consensual. Cooperation among the states in the world arena is possible but only when it serves the national interest defined in terms of power. For example, realists believe that no state would go to war if the leaders knew they would lose more than they would gain. Realists believe that all wars could be avoided if their outcome could be discovered in advance.

As we noted in chapter 2, realists, or more accurately neo-realists, who follow the power approach to the study of international relations are substantial in numbers and impressive in the influence they exert on the profession—an influence that has been equaled only by the pluralists.[30] But the problem with realism lies in the conception of power itself. Some critics argue that the concept of power is essentially an unquantifiable phenomenon and that it cannot be empirically tested or verified. For example, in terms of verifying a state's power, only those resources that seem likely to prove useful in future specific situations, like the size of the military, can be counted. However, there is no guarantee that the quality, capability, and determination of the fighting forces will meet the highest standards, and thus they remain at best only rough indicators of power. Consequently, states cannot maximize their power; they can only try to acquire resources that they think will prove to be an asset.

Similarly, there is no validity to the assumption that leaders can discern where a state's interest, defined in terms of power, really lies. Leaders can only use their judgment based on the information available. Whether a state action is directed toward maximizing power cannot be empirically tested. Terms such as *struggle for power* do not tell us very much about the means, capabilities, relationships, process, and quantity of power. Instead of viewing power as a principal factor responsible for all actions in international relations, some scholars see the use of power mainly as a way of influencing other actors. However, even this dynamic interpretation is limited because it overlooks the factors that condition one actor to seek to influence another actor's behavior. In addition, it does not answer some questions relating to the determination of national goals or governmental decision-making processes, or questions dealing with trade relations, export credits, and investment incentives, to cite only a few examples.

The Balance of Power Approach

This approach is an offshoot of the classical concept of power. Most studies on the subject consider the aim of the **balance of power** approach to "hold all states in check," that is to not allow any state to become too strong or capable of taking over the territory of another state. Other studies, however, go as far as stating that a true balance of power leads to international peace.[31]

According to the classical concept of the balance of power, the safety of all nations was assured only if no one nation or group of nations was permitted to achieve a preponderance of power; if, in other words, a rough balance was achieved. Whenever this balance threatened to break down, a "balancer" (usually a major power) would try to restore the shaky equilibrium by entering into an alliance with other weaker states so that a new balance of power could be achieved. Before the Second World War, Great Britain played the balancer with variable success for nearly three-hundred years. *Pax Britannica* meant that Britain was able to tip the scales by allying herself with weaker nations against whatever state or combination of states threatened to become predominant.[32]

This classical concept of the balance of power as practiced by Great Britain was a process of checking power with power. The method used to accomplish this aim was the formation of alliances and counteralliances. The equal distribution of power among states belonging to different alliances was sufficient to deter the would-be attacker from pursuing its expansionist goals. Peace was thus achieved as a result of the balancing act among the states belonging to these alliances. Under this concept, the balancer was assumed to be motivated not by national interests but by international altruism, that is, a desire to maintain peace and world order. Of course, Morgenthau disagreed with this supposition. He argued that it was not the balance of power itself but the "international consensus" upon which it was built that preserved international peace.[33] Morgenthau considered the balance of power approach "uncertain" because no completely reliable means of measuring, evaluating, and comparing power existed, "unreal" because leaders tried to compensate for its uncertainty by aiming for superiority rather than equality in power, and "inadequate" because it did not take into account the restraining influence of the basic intellectual unity and moral consensus prevailing among European states from 1648 to 1914.[34] Similarly, according to A. F. K. Organski, wars have been most likely to occur when there was an approaching balance between the dominant nation and a major challenger. Peace, on the other hand, has been most likely when one bloc has enjoyed a decided preponderance over the others.[35]

The classical balance of power approach further assumes that the partners in the alliance are static (rather than changing) components of the international equilibrium. This supposition is partially responsible for the gradual decline of the effectiveness of the balance of power approach to the study of international relations. As we have already pointed out, nation-states are almost never static; some are expanding, while others are contracting. Because of the variability of natural resources, population, science, technology, economic capacity, and armaments, the classical balance of power approach that served Great Britain for three centuries now fails to provide a satisfactory understanding of international relations or a reliable yardstick for measuring international behavior.[36]

The Geopolitical Approach

The **geopolitical approach** is closely related to the state-centric theory of realism and its central concept of power. However, in this approach, the main source of power is the environment. The approach is based on the assumption that space, topography, location, and climate interact with population, communications, industry, and technology to produce power. Advocates of the geopolitical approach include determinists, such as Ratzel, Mahan, and Mackinder, who believe that the environment determines political developments, and nondeterminists, such as Harold and Margaret Sprout, who see the environment as only one factor, albeit an important one, in conditioning politics.

State power, according to Friedrich Ratzel, a German geographer, was largely derived from its spatial situation. The state, as an organism in space and contingent on adaptation to environmental conditions, was a product of organic evolution. From this conception the wide geographical space or **Lebensraum** was a necessary condition of state viability in the modern world. Whereas Ratzel viewed land as the ultimate source of strength, the American naval strategist Alfred Mahan viewed sea power as the key to control of space. Mahan's objective was to call the United States to follow Britain's imperial example as a sea power, so that it might fulfill its Manifest Destiny beyond the shores of North America. British geographer Alfred Mackinder synthesized and further developed the ideas of Ratzel, Kjellen, and Mahan to arrive at his own geopolitical conclusions. According to Mackinder's analysis, the uneasy and unstable balance between the pivotal area of East Central Europe and the Asian and European fringes was the key to international unrest. He recommended that the maritime powers prevent an alliance between continental Europe and the Russian empire. With this in mind, Mackinder coined the concepts *heartland* for Eastern Europe and *world-island* for Europe, Asia, and Africa. His basic thesis was that whoever rules Eastern Europe rules the heartland, whoever rules the heartland commands the world-island, and whoever rules the world-island commands the world.[37] Whereas Mahan saw naval power as the main source of national power, Mackinder saw the technology of land transport, air power, and outer-space exploration as crucial factors in national power.

Following Mackinder's thesis, other students of geopolitics suggested that the rimland of Eurasia might prove strategically more important than the heartland, if new centers of industrial power and communications were created along the circumference of the Eurasian land mass. The *rimland* concept contributed to the theoretical foundations of George F. Kennan's influential postwar proposal that the United States adopt a policy of containment to thwart Soviet imperialism.[38]

As this discussion suggests, the determinist aspect of the geopolitical approach starts out with the assumption that humans are products of their environment and that their ideas, motives, and interests are merely reflections of the environment. Opposing this genuinely deterministic school of geopolitics are the behavioralists, who hold that the environment does not compel people to do anything. The environment, or *milieu* as they usually call it, is simply there, "clay at the disposal of man, the builder."[39] According to the founders of the *ecological triad,* we need to look at the ongoing policy–choice processes of the individual entity, its environment, and entity–environment interrelationships to explain international behavior. As Harold and Margaret Sprout explained, there are three types of relationships between the entity and the environment: environmental possibilism, environmental probabilism, and cognitive behavioralism.[40]

Possibilism is a method whereby the analyst interprets the properties of the physical environment in the light of human knowledge, equipment, and social organization. Possibilists calculate what is actually possible, or will become possible, at a given place and time in terms of (1) the distribution and variation of the social factors of the environment, (2) the state of technology and the prospects of technological change, and (3) the social structures permitting technological change and advancement. In this respect the potential of a country such as Japan for influencing the world arena of politics appears to be much greater than that of India, whose population and territory are several times larger than Japan's. Large territories and large populations are not always an asset. A state with a large population that is predominantly uneducated and unskilled and a large landmass that is rich in natural resources but undeveloped cannot play the same role in world affairs as a state with high technological and scientific achievement and great potential for industrial growth. As Harold Sprout has pointed out, "the more efficient a people's equipment, and the greater their skills, the greater becomes their potential capacity to master the limitations of the nonhuman environment—and do so at a price compatible with their conception of a tolerable standard of living."[41] Thus, the contemporary possibilist in international relations is less concerned with location, distance, space, terrain, climate, and natural resources and more interested in who needs what and how to go about getting it within the international system.

Environmental probabilism is based on certain assumptions about motivation and knowledge of the environment.[42] According to the Sprouts, as decision makers view their environment, its characteristics provide hints as to the probability of certain outcomes. The environment presents the decision maker not only with what is possible but also with what course of action is more or less likely under certain circumstances. Most, if not all, human activity in this perspective is affected by the uneven distribution of human and nonhuman resources.

Entity–environment relationships are based, according to the Sprouts, on possibilism and probabilism. The environment provides a number of behavioral–choice possibilities that do not determine the entity's choice but limit it. The Sprouts also emphasize the importance of the decision makers' psychological milieu.[43] How decision makers see the environment will affect the content of their image of the world and therefore the entire decision-making process. Although political decisions are based on leaders' perceptions of their milieu, results of these decisions are limited by the objective nature of the operational environment as well.

The Systems Approach

Although the systems approach was used by students of international relations before the application of the scientific method, the approach is now closely associated with behavioralism and scientific politics. There is no coherent and unambiguous statement about the characteristics of the systems approach in international relations. There is a large body of concepts, but there is no body of rules spelling out how a systems approach should be implemented. Nevertheless, the systems perspective enables us to understand the elements or parts of international relations and how they are interconnected.[44]

There are many definitions of a *system,* but they all emphasize interrelationships among units that are part of a whole. The early followers of the systems approach, such as Morgenthau, adhered to the state-centric model. Not until Morton Kaplan, who produced one of the first major works using the systems approach, was the state-centric model subjected to behavioralist type of investigation. Kaplan identified the existence of a system in terms of the occurrence of behavioral regularities between defined sets of variables.[45]

Research on the structure of the international system gradually convinced some scholars that the state-centric perspective was inadequate and deceiving.[46] Hence scholars began to extend their concentration to a number of nonstate actors. Their justification was simply that the state-centric model did not reflect realities in the existing world. James Rosenau addressed this problem by focusing on the concept of *linkage,* which he defined as a "recurrent sequence of behavior that originates in one system and is reacted to in another."[47] Through the linkage concept, Rosenau demonstrated that certain issues cut across the boundaries between domestic and foreign policies. The linkage concept was similar to the concept of *permeability* developed by John H. Herz, who argued in the late 1950s that the nation-state was no longer a defensible unit because of the development of nuclear weapons.[48] Similar concerns were expressed by scholars following the systems approach, who argued that global problems such as war, population growth, depletion of natural resources, and the deterioration of the environment could not be successfully treated as separate and separable problems.[49] This perspective argues that the survival of the human race is in jeopardy because of its refusal to consider the finite nature of the earth.[50]

In the early 1970s a new "transnationalist" view developed among the international relations scholars. According to transnationalists, nation-states are not the only actors in the international arena. Other actors included intergovernmental and nongovernmental organizations, cartels, terrorists, and hijackers. Moreover, the impact of war, population pressures, pollution, depletion of natural resources, and the use of the sea and outer space on the international system has changed the structure and the relationships among the actors in the system. Increases in the frequency of travel, migration, trade, investment, and the transfer of technology also produce greater interdependence. Finally, transnationalists posit that war, especially thermonuclear war, is no longer a viable option for foreign policy decision makers. A drastic change in the weapons systems resulted in both a change in the nature of warfare and a shift toward the dominant role of economic power in the international system.

This brings us to the third and most recent perspective of the systems approach, which is known alternatively as the world systems or *globology* approach. The world system perspective focuses attention on individuals as units of a highly complex network of cross-cutting relationships within a world society. Although these relationships have always been present, they have increased in modern times under the pressure of technological change. World system advocates compare international relations to a network of cobwebs, each cobweb representing a system with complex relationships. World society consists of millions of these cobwebs, which transcend geographical boundaries.[51] The emergence of the world system perspective rests to a large extent on the contemporary importance of political economy issues and a decreasing predominance of military–security issues.[52]

The development of the systems approach has opened up new vistas for inquiry into the political process, encouraged writers to think theoretically, precipitated attempts to test systems propositions at an empirical level, and generated new thinking in international relations.

The Functionalist Approach

Functionalism is predicated on the argument that violence, population explosion, pollution, depletion of natural resources, poverty, ignorance, chaos, anarchy, and other pathological characteristics will not be eliminated or reduced in international politics until greater social, economic, and political cooperation is achieved in the international system. No country or region can insulate itself against their effects. The task, then, is to find new ways of political organization other than those based on power or territorial sovereignty. Functionalists advocate the creation of international organizations based on increased cooperation through communication, trade, cultural exchange, tourism, and education. They allege that such cooperative intercourse will slowly build confidence in international institutions and erode the rigidity of national boundaries. The resulting increases in economic performance and alleviation of tensions should pave the way for greater prosperity and a sturdier peace. The sovereignty of nations will thus slowly erode, and people will eventually shift their loyalty to international institutions.

The assumption here, of course, is that greater interaction among nations necessarily leads to understanding and cooperation and that sharing in modern scientific and technological achievements creates more tranquility throughout the world. However, there is some ground for fearing that reliance on modern communication and other technological devices is steadily increasing rather than decreasing world problems.[53] For further discussion of the functionalist approach as it relates to international organizations and regional integration, see chapters 9 and 13.

The Communications Approach

According to Karl Deutsch, one of the chief proponents of the **communications approach,** power is no longer the key variable in the explanation of political phenomena. Instead of power, the essence of politics becomes "the dependable coordination of human efforts and expectations for the attainment of the goals of the society."[54] International politics, therefore, is not necessarily limited to security concerns as the dominant objectives and motivations of states. The chief advantage of this approach is that it is not restricted to any one level of analysis but is equally relevant for groups, peoples, and organizations of any size, including the nation-state.

The greatest contributions of the communications approach have been in the study of economic and political **integration.** Integration refers to the process whereby many different political or economic units (such as states) try to unify themselves. The progress made by countries in integrating their economies can be judged by examining the flow of international transactions such as trade, tourists, mail, and migration. Deutsch and his associates argue that integration can result in amalgamated or pluralist security communities. The United States is a good example of an amalgamated security community, because it has a single federal government exercising central political control over a continent-size region. Pluralist security communities, on the other hand, have no central political authority, rather they are loosely affiliated national units that cooperate toward common security ends. For example, Western European countries are friendly to one another and thus do not fortify their borders but move toward integration. Indeed, as we will see in chapter 13, Western Europe is the best contemporary example of efforts by separate sovereign states to integrate their economies. The communications approach has relied to a very large extent on the European case as an example of how increased transactions across borders can break down the traditional and arbitrary boundaries of the state system.

The Decision-Making Approach

This approach focuses attention on the behavior of the decision makers involved in the formulation and execution of foreign policy. From the **decision-making** approach perspective, the "real and objective world" matters less than the perceptions of decision makers.[55] Richard C. Snyder, the father of the decision-making approach, asserts that "the key to the explanation of why the state behaves the way it does lies in the way its decision makers define their situation."[56] In other words, there is no need even to attempt to describe "objective realities," if the subjective perceptions of decision makers are the appropriate focus for any explanation of state behavior. Thus, the so-called national interest is little more, according to the decision-making school of thought, than the subjective perceptions of the decision makers.[57]

The decision-making process is an important variable. Snyder's emphasis on the close relationship between the making of decisions and their content has been of great importance in the development of foreign policy analysis. To explain a foreign policy decision, the analyst must understand the process by which the decision is made. The analyst must investigate the relationship between the process and the decisions that emerge from it. This means that he or she must know the perceptions, attitudes, and beliefs of individual decision makers, how information is collected and analyzed in governmental and bureaucratic settings, and the domestic and international political circumstances that affect individuals, governments, and bureaucracies.

How exactly do governments make policy? As we point out in chapter 5, policy making is a complex process. Graham Allison, for example, has argued that at different times decisions are made in different ways. He identifies three basic processes or models that explain how decisions are made: the rational actor model, the organizational process model, and the governmental or bureaucratic politics model.[58] According to the **rational actor model,** policy makers carefully define foreign policy problems, seek wide information about foreign policy situations, identify the nation's critical interests in the situation, consider all available alternative courses of action, select the policy options that seem to best serve the country's interests, implement the policy, evaluate its success, and if the policy fails, select a better one. Critics, however, assert that the assumptions implicit in such a model are unrealistic because decision makers rarely have sufficient information or time to follow through on this sort of process.[59] They contend that most political decisions are not arrived at rationally and comprehensively and are not designed to promote society's common good. In most cases, these decisions are marginal steps to bring about gradual change, to close political gaps, and to avert or control crises.[60]

In the **organizational process model** Allison assumes that "the government consists of a conglomerate of semifeudal, loosely allied organizations, each with a substantial life of its own."[61] Thus, foreign policy is understood to be the product or "the outputs of large organizations, functioning according to standard patterns of behavior," rather than the deliberate choices of a unified governmental actor.[62]

The third model, the governmental or **bureaucratic politics model**

sees no unitary actor but many actors as players—players who act in terms of no consistent set of strategic objectives but rather according to various conceptions of national, organizational, and personal goals; players who make government decisions not by a single rational choice but by the pulling and hauling that is politics.[63]

Accordingly, foreign policy is considered neither as governmental choice nor as organizational output but as a consequence of various bargaining games among key players within the government bureaucracy.

On the whole, the decision-making approach has been absorbed into the practice of foreign policy analysis. The bad habits it challenged have largely been abandoned and the new ones it proposed have been incorporated into the working assumptions of diplomats and other decision makers.[64] Have the concepts and categories offered by the decision-making approach facilitated a better understanding of foreign policy? The answer is a resounding yes.[65] Nevertheless, some issues and criticisms have been raised in connection with the clarity of this approach. Some critics question the assumption that foreign policy consists of conscious, isolatable decisions. Indeed, to some, foreign policy decisions appear to be a seamless web of actions and reactions.[66] If this is so, what criteria can be used to identify key decisions? Answers to these questions must be quite subjective. In the final analysis the decision-making approach appears to have been a valuable exercise for scholars and for those who are actively engaged in the formulation and implementation of foreign policy.

Summary

The foregoing discussion shows that the discipline of international relations has produced a considerable range of methodologies, paradigms, theories, and study approaches. As global issues expanded and the number of actors proliferated, so too have the number of approaches, each with its own concepts and assumptions about the nature of international political interaction. This review of study approaches is not exhaustive. Some scholars use perception as an organizational theme to explain international behavior.[67] Others combine game theory with the balance of power and the decision-making approaches.[68] Still others use the bargaining approach.[69] The choice and application of approaches varies from scholar to scholar, depending on the methodological orientation they have and the specific aims of their studies.

As students of international relations, we are dealing with a rich, wide subject matter. The approaches we have reviewed in this chapter are equally rich and diverse. Each approach sheds a different light on the behavior of actors in international relations. Each contributes some knowledge of and insight into the conduct of international relations. Each helps describe and explain some aspect of our complex world and, on rare occasions, perhaps even helps predict the outcome of international events.

Paul K. Huth

Extended Deterrence and the Outbreak of War

To threaten or resort to the use of military force is a critical foreign policy decision for the leadership of a country. Policy makers have often believed that national interests extended beyond the defense of their own country to include the security of other states. As a result, when such countries were the targets of an attack, policy makers have threatened military retaliation against the potential aggressor in an attempt to deter the attack. The effective use of extended deterrent threats, however, is not easily achieved.

A potential aggressor's uncertainty as to the willingness of the deterrer to risk war over the defense of another state can weaken the credibility of deterrence....

The security dilemma can lead policy makers to overestimate the hostile intentions and threats posed by the military capabilities and actions of other states. In a situation of extended deterrence the intended defensive military actions of the deterrer can be perceived by the potential aggressor as an offensive threat and thereby provoke a spiral of military escalation....

A deterrer must strike a balance between actions that demonstrate resolve and enhance the credibility of threats and the provocation of the potential aggressor. In this study I will test hypotheses on historical cases of extended deterrence from 1885 to 1984 in an attempt to identify the conditions under which extended deterrence is likely to succeed or fail.

Concept of Extended Deterrence

In this study cases of extended-immediate deterrence will be analyzed. The concept of *deterrence* will be defined as follows:

SOURCE: *American Political Science Review* 82, no. 2 (June 1988): 423–439. Reprinted by permission of the journal and the author.

1. *Deterrence:* A policy of deterrence seeks to convince an adversary by the threat of military retaliation that the costs of resorting to the use of military force to achieve foreign policy objectives will outweigh the benefits... The deterrer's threat of retaliation may be based on either the military capability to repulse an attack and thereby deny the attacker its battlefield objectives and prevent the loss of territory or the capability to inflict heavy military losses on the attacker in a protracted armed conflict of attrition...

2. *Extended deterrence:* A confrontation in which the policy makers of one state (defender) threaten the use of force against another state (potential attacker) in an attempt to prevent that state from using military force against an ally—or territory controlled by an ally (protégé)—of the defender. The objective of extended deterrence is to protect other countries and territories from attack, as opposed to preventing a direct attack on one's own national territory.

3. *Extended-immediate deterrence:* A confrontation that is characterized by the following:
   a. A potential attacker is actively considering the use of force against a protégé of the defender.
   b. Policy makers of the defender state are aware of the threat directed at the protégé.
   c. Policy makers of the defender state, either explicitly or by the movement of military forces, threaten the use of retaliatory force in an attempt to prevent the use of force by the potential attacker...

An extended-immediate deterrence confrontation entails an overt threat and counterthreat by potential attacker and defender. In contrast, *extended-general deterrence* refers to an adversarial relationship between states in which the threat of an armed conflict over the security of another country exists but the potential attacker is neither engaged in a dispute that threatens war nor has issued coercive threats or initiated military preparations for the use of force. Extended-general deterrence is maintained by arms races, the formation of alliances, and in the declaratory statements of foreign policy leaders as to their country's security interests. For example, U.S. troops are deployed in South Korea as a deterrent to a potential North Korean attack and statements by U.S. leaders of the intent to defend the Persian Gulf are designed to counter a potential Soviet threat to countries in the region.

Fifty-eight cases of extended-immediate deterrence were identified for the period 1885–1984. In a majority of cases both the potential attacker and defender were great powers, while in a small number of cases both states were regional powers. Twenty-four cases were coded as failures of deterrence while the remaining thirty-four cases were coded as successful deterrence...

Assumptions

The decision-making calculus of the potential attacker is based on certain assumptions.

Offense and Defense

The objectives of the potential attacker in threatening the use of force against the protégé represent a combination of both offensive and defensive goals. Analytically, it may be possible to draw a relatively clear distinction between these two opposing motives; but in the actual calculations of the potential attacker the two are often closely interconnected. Defensive motives determine the minimal goals to be pursued by the potential attacker, while offensive motives define the more ambitious maximum goals to be pursued. The important implication is that in most international disputes and crises there is an opportunity for diplomacy and negotiations to contribute to conflict resolution because the potential attacker is not motivated solely by far-reaching and aggressive aims.

Force and Negotiation

In deciding whether to challenge the deterrent threats of the defender, it is assumed that the potential attacker will consider two alternative courses of action:

1. reliance on military threats and the use of force to resolve the conflict with the defender and protégé
2. reliance on negotiations and diplomacy to resolve the conflict with the defender and protégé

...These two courses of action define the basic structure of the conflict for the potential attacker, in which the choice is between the coercive strategy of standing firm behind its demands, or the accommodative strategy of cooperating and making concessions to the defender's bargaining position... A number of variants can be identified for each of these two courses of action and the potential attacker may combine the two policies in the initial stages of the confrontation; but once the intentions of the defender are determined, a fundamental decision will be made by the potential attacker as to what policy to adopt. As a result, these two courses of action become policy alternatives at this crucial point in the confrontation with the defender.

Bargaining Reputation

The potential attacker will be sensitive to how the outcome of the confrontation with the defender will affect its own bargaining reputation. Bargaining reputation can be defined as the willingness of a state's foreign policy leadership to risk armed conflict in pursuit of political goals and to refuse to concede to the demands of adversaries under coercive pressure. Bargaining reputation is important because policy makers very often believe that their actions and behavior in a particular confrontation will be interpreted by other states as a general indicator of their resolve... The political leadership's bargaining reputation has both domestic as well as international consequences. Domestically, the leadership's political stature and influence within the elite and broader population will depend in part on its record of managing difficult foreign policy issues and international crises. A successful record will enhance the leadership's political stature and authority, whereas a record of weakness and setbacks in foreign policy will diminish the leadership's political position. Internationally, a strong bargaining reputation will increase a state's position of leadership, influence with allies, and the credibility of coercive threats directed at adversaries; while a weak bargaining reputation will have the reverse impact. The important implication for a potential attacker is that the desire to protect its bargaining reputation will be an important factor in a decision whether to challenge the defender's deterrent threat.

Costs and Gains

The final decision of the potential attacker will be based on a comparison of the likely costs and benefits of the two alternative policy choices. The course of action with greater expected gains (or fewer losses) will be adopted by the potential attacker.

Hypotheses on Extended Deterrence

To be deterred the potential attacker must conclude that the defender's deterrent actions are both credible and stable. A *credible* deterrent depends on whether the defender possesses the military capabilities sufficient to inflict high military costs on the attacker in an armed conflict (battlefield casualties, destruction and depletion of arms and equipment, damage to and potential loss of territory) and the intention to use those capabilities if necessary. A *stable* deterrent does not increase the potential attacker's fear of a preemptive military strike and thus provoke rapid military escalation and avoids engaging the bargaining reputation of the potential attacker to such an extent that it makes it more difficult for the potential attacker to back down from its coercive bargaining position.

Four sets of variables can be identified that are likely to play a critical role in determining the credibility and stability of the defender's deterrent actions. These four sets of variables are hypothesized to play a crucial role in the potential attacker's calculus of deterrence:

1. the balance of military forces between potential attacker and defender
2. the interests at stake for the defender in protecting the protégé
3. the past behavior of the defender in confrontations with states
4. the bargaining behavior of the defender during the immediate deterrence confrontation with the potential attacker

The Military Balance

Immediate deterrence is likely to succeed when the potential attacker estimates that the probability of success is relatively low and the costs high in resorting to the use of sustained military force to achieve foreign policy objectives. The potential attacker is likely to consider three alternative options for using military force:

1. limited aims strategy
2. rapid offensive attack strategy
3. attrition strategy. . .

The objectives of a limited aims strategy is to seize control of disputed territory held by an opponent. The key to success for the potential attacker is to achieve tactical, if not strategic, surprise in the use of force. The potential attacker is then in a position either to overwhelm the under-prepared forces of the opponent or to occupy the disputed territory before the opponent has the opportunity to send in reinforcements and build up local defenses. The goal of the attacker is to limit, if not avoid, direct engagement with the military strength of the opponent and instead use force where local superiority prevails.

The second military option for the potential attacker is the strategy of rapid offensive attack in which the objective is to defeat the opponent's armed forces decisively. The goal is not to minimize armed conflict with the adversary and to take control of disputed territory but to engage the armed forces of the adversary in a series of large-scale battles so that its armed forces can be defeated. The assumption of the potential attacker is that if the armed forces of the adversary can be defeated in a rapid and decisive manner, the

adversary will be forced to surrender before it can mobilize the economy and civilian population for war or before allies can effectively intervene in support of the target of the attack.

The third military option available to a potential attacker is the strategy of attrition. The objective is similar to that of the rapid offensive attack: the decisive defeat of the armed forces of the adversary. The prinicipal difference between the two strategies, however, is the time required to achieve military victory. With a strategy of attrition, the attacker does not anticipate a series of rapid victories but a protracted conflict in which the goal is to wear down and outlast the adversary by being able to withstand heavy military losses better. . . .

If the potential attacker's policy makers believe that military force can be successfully employed in a quick and decisive attack, then the probability of deterrence success will decrease. Conversely, if the policy makers estimate that military force cannot be successfully employed in a quick and relatively low-cost attack, then deterrence is more likely to prevail. Calculations regarding the outcome of a protracted war are not likely to have a critical impact on deterrence outcomes since policy makers do not generally initiate an armed conflict with the intention of engaging in a war of attrition. The immediate balance of forces (defense against the limited aims strategy or the rapid offensive attack designed to defeat the protégé before the defender can intervene) and the short-term balance of forces (defense against the strategy of rapid offensive attack in which the attacker seeks to defeat both the defnder and protégé) should be positively related to the success of extended-immediate deterrence.

Hypothesis 1 The probability of extended deterrence success increases as the balance of military forces improves for the defender. The immediate and short-term balance of forces will have a greater impact on deterrence outcomes than will the long-term balance of forces.

The deterrent value of nuclear weapons is a controversial and important question. The credibility of a nuclear threat will depend on the political–military situation in which it might be employed. For purposes of self-defense and to deter the use of nuclear weapons by another state against one's own territory, the threat of nuclear retaliation is likely to function as a credible deterrent, given a secure secondstrike capability. . . However, in this study, of the fifteen cases in which the defender possessed nuclear weapons, the potential attacker in fourteen cases was a nonnuclear power. (The only exception is the 1979 case of the People's Republic of China as the potential attacker and the Soviet

Union as the defender of Vietnam.) The critical question, then, is what extended deterrent value do nuclear weapons exert when the potential target is a nonnuclear power? In such situations it is argued that the deterrent impact will be minimal for a number of reasons. First, the use of nuclear weapons would risk provoking strong criticism and denunciation both internationally and domestically (in twelve of fifteen cases the nuclear power defender was the United States, the United Kingdom, or France). Second, nuclear use would be likely to increase the incentives for horizontal nuclear proliferation, which the nuclear powers have consistently opposed. Third, the likelihood of collateral damage to civilians would act as a strong constraint. In summary, the combination of salient political, military, and ethical questions about the immediate and long-term consequences of nuclear use by the defender against a nonnuclear power raise serious doubts as to the credibility of such a decision.

Hypothesis 2 The possession of nuclear weapons and the latent threat of nuclear use by the defender will not have a significant impact on extended deterrence outcomes when the potential attacker is a nonnuclear power.

Interests at Stake for the Defender

The potential attacker's uncertainty as to the intentions of the defender are inherent in a situation of extended deterrence. If the policy makers of the potential attacker are to believe that the defender is willing to incur the costs of armed conflict in defense of the protégé, they must be convinced that the issues at stake are vital enough to the defender to justify those costs. If the potential attacker does not believe that the defender has important interests at risk in defending the protégé, then the credibility of extended deterrence will be questioned...

The value of the protégé to the defender can be determined in part by the political, military, and economic ties that link the defender to the protégé. The stronger those ties, the more important they are to the defender to maintain and protect. The presence of a military alliance between defender and protégé indicates that the defender has reputational interests at stake. The credibility of the alliance commitment for the defender can be linked to the defender's concern to maintain a reputation for honoring agreements with states and a reputation for a willingness to use force in support of allies when threatened. The failure to honor an alliance if the protégé is the target of an unprovoked attack risks signaling to other states that the defender is reluctant to use force if its own security is not directly threatened. As a result, not only may the defender's security commitments to other states be questioned, but the defender may also

subsequently find it more difficult to secure allies in support of its own defense. In the period from 1816–1965, 76 percent of allied nations that were attacked received armed support, whereas only 17 percent of nonallied states received such support...

Hypothesis 3 The probability of extended deterrence success will increase if the defender has an alliance with the protégé.

Military arms transfers from defender to protégé also indicate that reputational interests are at stake for the defender. The greater the degree to which the protégé relies exclusively on the defender for arms imports, the more likely it is that the defender will be viewed by other states as developing a sphere of influence and closer political ties with that country....

Hypothesis 4 The probability of extended deterrence success will increase as the protégé's reliance on arms transfers from the defender increases.

The protégé may also be economically important to the defender. High levels of foreign trade between defender and protégé indicate some of the potential economic costs to be incurred if the protégé is forced by the attacker to cut its ties with the defender. Exports from the defender to the protégé contribute to higher levels of domestic employment and output, while imports from the protégé may represent important sources of raw materials or products that cannot be produced as efficiently domestically.

Hypothesis 5 The probability of extended deterrence success will increase as the protégé's share of the defender's foreign trade increases.

Bargaining Behavior of the Defender

The potential attacker's uncertainty as to the defender's intentions and sensitivity to threats and challenges indicate that the defender's bargaining behavior can play a critical role in the success or failure of deterrence. An effective bargaining strategy by the defender can reduce the potential attacker's uncertainty and thereby enhance credibility, whereas ineffective strategies can reduce credibility or provoke the potential attacker. The optimal bargaining strategy will enhance the credibility of the defender's deterrent actions while avoiding the provocation of the potential attacker. There are two principal dimensions to the bargaining process in the confrontation between the potential attacker and defender: (1) diplomacy and negotiations and (2) military preparations and movement of forces.

For both dimensions of the bargaining process three general strategies are available to the defender ranging from conciliation and minimal military actions to an unyielding position in negotiations and maximum military preparations. The three strategies of military escalation by the defender are

1. *Policy of strength:* The defender responds to the military actions of the potential attacker with greater-than-equal levels of military preparedness.
2. *Policy of tit for tat:* The defender responds to the military actions of the potential attacker with equal levels of military preparedness.
3. *Policy of caution:* The defender responds to the military actions of the potential attacker with less-than-equal levels of military preparedness. . .

The three strategies of diplomacy and negotiations for the defender are

1. *Bullying policy:* The defender adopts an unyielding position in support of its demands and does not reciprocate accommodative initiatives by the potential attacker.
2. *Firm-but-flexible policy:* The defender adopts a mixed policy of refusing to concede to the repeated demands and threats of the potential attacker while also proposing to compromise based on reciprocal concessions.
3. *Conciliatory policy:* The defender adopts a policy of proposed concessions despite the lack of reciprocation by the potential attacker. . .

Caution in military actions by the defender will minimize the risks of provocation due to the security dilemma and thereby enhance deterrence stability. Similarly, conciliation in negotiations by the defender will avoid engaging the potential attacker's bargaining reputation, which will also enhance deterrence stability. The critical problem, however, with these two strategies is that they assume, or are designed to deal with, a potential attacker motivated by defensive goals only. As a result such policies fail to recognize that the potential attacker is also likely to be considering more ambitious offensive objectives; thus deterrence stability is increased but at the expense of deterrence credibility. The reverse problem exists when the defender adopts a bullying negotiating strategy or a policy of strength in military preparedness. An unyielding diplomatic stance clearly signals the defender's intention to support the protégé and possibly risk armed conflict; but the defender's refusal to propose or consider some form of limited concessions is likely to increase the potential attacker's concern that a retreat will be viewed by other states

as capitulation under pressure. A policy of military strength will put the defender in a favorable military position to intervene if deterrence should fail; but it may also increase the chances of deterrence failure by provoking either further escalation by the potential attacker and fears of a preemptive strike or the potential attacker's determination to avoid signs of retreat under maximum coercive pressure. Diplomatically and militarily, these two strategies are optimal for enhancing credibility if the potential attacker is motivated solely by offensive aims; but if the security dilemma and defensive objectives are also an important component of the potential attacker's calculus, then such policies risk provocation.

The optimal strategy for balancing credibility and stability is to pursue a policy of reciprocity. Diplomatically, reciprocity signals to the potential attacker the determination of the defender to support the protégé while at the same time signaling the defender's intention to not coerce or force the potential attacker to accept a settlement that is clearly one-sided. Proposals for negotiations and limited compromise may therefore offer a way for the potential attacker to back down in the confrontation with minimum damage to its bargaining reputation. Tit-for-tat military escalation signals both the defender's intention to use force if the protégé is attacked and the increased capability to act promptly if necessary but does not place the potential attacker in a highly vulnerable military position.

Hypothesis 6 A policy by the defender of tit for tat in military escalation will increase the probability of extended deterrence success in comparison to alternative policies.

Hypothesis 7 A firm-but-flexible policy of diplomacy and negotiations by the defender will increase the probability of extended deterrence success in comparison to alternative policies.

Past Behavior of the Defender

The bargaining behavior of the defender provides a direct means by which to signal to the potential attacker the defender's intentions to support the protégé. The potential attacker, however, may also draw on the past behavior of the defender in international confrontations to help determine the defender's willingness to risk armed conflict or to concede under coercive pressure. If security commitments are interdependent . . ., a defender's past actions in a confrontation should have an impact on the potential attacker's assessment of the defender's likely behavior in the extended-immediate deterrence conflict. If the defender has backed down in a previous conflict and conceded to the demands of the opponent in order to avoid an armed conflict, the credibility of the defender's extended deterrent actions is more likely to be questioned. If the defender, however, did not concede under coercive pressure then the credibility of the defender's extended deterrent actions should be enhanced. . . .

Hypothesis 8 The past behavior of the defender in those confrontations in which the current potential attacker was directly involved will have a greater impact on deterrence outcomes than in those cases in which the current potential attacker was not directly involved.

Consistent with the logic underlying the hypotheses on bargaining behavior, a past record of firm-but-flexible bargaining by the defender should increase the probability of deterrence success in comparison to a past record of conciliation or bullying. A past record of making concessions under coercive pressure and an unwillingness to risk armed conflict should contribute to the weakening of the defender's future credibility; while a past record of intransigence and bullying will have already imposed domestic political as well as international costs on the potential attacker. As a result, the potential attacker should be even more determined to protect its bargaining reputation and avoid another retreat before the defender. . .

Hypothesis 9 In past confrontations between defender and potential attacker firm-but-flexible bargaining by the defender will enhance the deterrence actions of the defender in the next confrontation between the two states. If the defender, however, adopted a bullying or conciliatory strategy, then the probability of deterrence failure in the next confrontation will increase.

Measurement of Variables

The dependent variable was coded as either deterrence success (one) or failure (zero). . .

. . . In this study, due to the limits of data availability, military capabilities will be measured as simply the ratio of defender–protégé forces to potential attacker forces. Three different operational measures were constructed. First, the immediate balance of forces includes those ground forces (number of troops) of the defender–protégé and potential attacker that can be deployed in the battlefield at the very outset of an armed conflict. The *immediate balance* is defined as those land forces of the potential attacker in a position to initiate an attack directly and those land forces of defender–protégé in a position to repulse such an attack

directly. To be in a position to engage in combat directly, the opposing troops must be either concentrated and mobilized for combat at the point of likely attack or be capable of mobilization for immediate combat from forward positions to the point of attack. . . . Second, the *short-term balance* is defined as the capacity of the potential attacker and defender–protégé to reinforce and augment the immediate balance of forces through the mobilization of each country's standing ground and air forces and first class of trained reserves. The third measure is the *long-term balance* of forces, which is defined as the capacity of each side to build up its existing armed forces and to maintain that increased level of fighting strength by the mobilization of the economy and population for a protracted war. The composite national capabilities index. . . was adopted by multiplying each state's existing military capabilities (share of world total military personnel and expenditures) by the sum of that state's industrial and demographic size (share of world total steel production, industrial fuel consumption, urban and total population). The deterrent value of nuclear weapons for the defender was recorded as one for those cases in which the defender possessed nuclear weapons and zero for the remaining cases.

The military and economic ties between defender and protégé were measured as follows: First, the existence of an *alliance* between the two states was coded with a value of one, the absence of an alliance was coded with a value of zero. Second, *military arms transfer ties* was defined as the share of arms imported by the protégé from the defender as a percentage of total arms imported over a three-year period prior to the case of extended deterrence. The percentage share was calculated on a 10-point scale ranging from 1 (0–10%) to 10 (91–100%). Third, *economic ties* were measured as the protégé's share of the defender's total merchandise exports and imports over a three-year period. . .

The following categories were utilized to code the outcomes of previous cases of attempted extended deterrence for the defender:

1. *Success:* Defender stands firm in support of protégé and potential attacker refrains from attack.
2. *Failure but armed support:* Deterrence fails, and protégé is attacked; but defender does intervene with military force to protect protégé.
3. *Capitulation:* Deterrence fails, but defender does not intervene with military force to protect protégé.

Categories 1 and 2 represent indicators of a past record of firmness for the defender, while category 3 indicates a record of weakness. In the statistical analysis a value of one was recorded for each case with one of the three possible outcomes listed above, while a value of zero was recorded for each case in which there was no past attempt at extended deterrence for the defender.

The following categories will be utilized to describe the outcomes of the most recent past confrontation between the defender and potential attacker:

1. *Diplomatic put-down:* The defender adopts a bullying bargaining strategy or forces the potential attacker to make critical concessions in order to avoid an armed conflict, or both.
2. *Stalemate:* The defender and potential attacker avoid a direct military confrontation, but firm-but-flexible bargaining by the defender fails to achieve any agreement with the potential attacker resolving the underlying issues in disupte.
3. *Diplomatic defeat:* The defender retreats under the pressure of the potential attacker and concedes on the critical issues in dispute in order to avoid becoming involved in a direct military confrontation...

To determine which outcome applied to the past behavior of the defender, a detailed summary of diplomatic negotiations was recorded for each past case and then examined to determine to what extent the defender had conceded to the demands of the potential attacker. The distinction between a put-down by the defender and a stalemate is based on whether the potential attacker was forced to make critical concessions or the defender rebuffed proposals for compromise. In the case of a stalemate both sides tacitly agree not to press their demands further and the immediate confrontation is allowed to deescalate as neither side is forced to back down and accept the demands or position of its opponent. The defender adopts a firm-but-flexible bargaining strategy; but the potential attacker is not interested in a compromise settlement, and therefore the issues in contention remain unresolved. To test the hypothesis that a record of past conciliation or bullying with the potential attacker reduces the likelihood of deterrence success, those cases in which the defender has either backed down and accepted a diplomatic defeat or the potential attacker has done so will be examined. To test the hypothesis that a record of firm-but-flexible bargaining enhances the likelihood of deterrence success, those cases in which the past behavior of the defender is coded as a stalemate will be analyzed....

To operationalize the diplomatic and military strategies adopted by the defender, a detailed chronological summary of the negotiating process and military actions of each state was compiled for each case. To determine which diplomatic strategy was pursued by the defender, the record

of the negotiating process was broken down into a series of sequential exchanges between defender and potential attacker from the beginning to the end of the dispute.... A value of one was recorded for each case in which the defender adopted a firm-but-flexible negotiating strategy and a value of zero for those cases in which alternative strategies were adopted. For example, in the Anglo–Russian dispute over the northern Afghan border in 1885 the British pursued a firm-but-flexible strategy by proposing to the Russians that the Panjdeh territory would be conceded only if Afghanistan was to retain control over disputed territory that was strategically vital. In contrast, in the confrontation between Russia and Japan over Korea and Manchuria in 1903–1904, the Russian government refused to negotiate over Russian rights in Manchuria; while at the same time it sought to place severe constraints on Japanese rights in Korea...

To determine which strategy of military escalation was pursued by the defender, the summary of military actions was broken down chronologically into a series of moves and countermoves by each side. The military moves of defender and potential attacker were then categorized according to the following scale of escalation:

1. symbolic show of force, display of military presence
2. demonstration of military capabilities
3. build-up of military forces
4. positioning of forces for immediate use
5. preparation of forces for immediate use
6. mobilization of forces for war

For each round of move and countermove, the response of the defender was coded as either *greater than, equal to,* or *less than,* the military actions of the defender.... For those cases in which the defender adopted a policy of tit for tat a value of one was recorded, while a value of zero was assigned to those cases in which a policy of strength or caution was adopted. For example, Libyan armed intervention in the Chadian Civil War in 1983 and preparation to advance on the capital was reciprocated by the airlifting of French troops to the Chadian capital and their deployment along the so-called red line north of the capital. In contrast, in the Czech crisis of 1938 German mobilization of ground and air forces for an attack against Czechoslovakia was countered only by precautionary naval measures on the part of the British and, as a result, Britain was not in a position to defend Czechoslovakia if it was attacked. A tit-for-tat policy would have required that the British expeditionary force be sent to France and then be deployed and mobilized to carry out with French forces a counteroffensive along the Franco–German border...

Data Analysis

The model specified for empirical testing included four variables: the military balance, the value of the protégé to the defender, the bargaining behavior of the defender, and the past behavior of the defender. These four sets of variables represent two fundamental components in the potential attacker's calculus of deterrence: (1) the military capabilities of the defender to protect the protégé and (2) the likely intention of the defender to use force to protect the protégé. Probit analysis was utilized to determine which of the alternative indicators for each set of variables provided the greatest degree of relative explanatory power. The hypotheses as formulated in the preceding section represent the expected results of the empirical testing. . . .

The final equation is presented in table 1. Overall, the results of the probit analysis indicate generally strong support for the hypotheses as formulated. The principal findings can be summarized as follows:

1. The balance of forces had an important impact on deterrence outcomes. As hypothesis 1 predicted, the immediate and short-term balance of forces had a positive impact on the probability of deterrence success, whereas the long-term balance of forces had no significant impact. The most effective military deterrent seems to be the capacity of the defender to repulse an attack and deny the adversary its military objectives from the very outset to early stages of an armed confrontation. Conventional deterrence based on a denial capability is much more effective than the threat

of punishment in a protracted armed conflict. In addition, the possession of nuclear weapons by the defender (hypothesis 2) did not have a significant impact on deterrence outcomes when the target was a nonnuclear power.

2. Strategies of crisis bargaining play an important role in the success or failure of deterrence. As argued in hypotheses 6 and 7, the adoption of a policy of tit for tat in military escalation and a firm-but-flexible diplomatic strategy are the most effective bargaining strategies in contributing to deterrence success. These results indicate that bargaining behavior based on a policy of reciprocity can signal to the potential attacker the defender's determination to protect the protégé, without provoking the potential attacker. These results support a growing body of experimental and comparative historical research that concludes that reciprocity is a robust strategy for inducing cooperation among adversaries. . .

3. Consistent with hypothesis 8, the past behavior of the defender in the most recent confrontation with the potential attacker had a significant effect on deterrence outcomes; whereas the past behavior of the defender in deterrence cases with other states did not. Hypothesis 9 was partially supported by the empirical evidence: a record of past conciliation and of backing down under pressure or of bullying by the defender reduced the likelihood of deterrence success. A past outcome of firm-but-flexible bargaining and stalemate between defender and potential attacker, however, did not increase the probability of deterrence success, contrary to the expectations of hypothesis 9.

Table 1
Probit analysis of deterrence outcomes

Explanatory Variable	Estimated Coefficient	Standard Error
Constant	−1.67	—
Military balance		
Immediate balance of forces	0.55	.28[a]
Short-term balance of forces	0.83	.36[b]
Bargaining behavior		
Firm-but-flexible diplomacy	0.97	.45[b]
Tit-for-tat military escalation	0.98	.46[b]
Reputation from past behavior[c]		
Defender backs down	−1.15	.64[a]
Defender intransigence	−0.86	.49[a]

Note: Percentage of predictions correct = 84; number of cases = 58.

[a] Significant at the 95.0% confidence level, one-tailed test.

[b] Significant at the 97.5% confidence level, one-tailed test.

[c] Those cases in which the defender and potential attacker were adversaries in a previous confrontation.

4. The only set of hypotheses not supported by empirical testing were those linking high levels of political–military and economic ties between defender and protégé to deterrence success (3–5). The reason would seem to be the strong impact of bargaining behavior on influencing the potential attacker's estimate of defender intentions and interests at stake. High levels of arms transfers and foreign trade between defender and protégé represent an indirect basis for estimating the defender's interests at stake. The bargaining behavior of the defender, however, provides a more immediate and direct indicator of the defender's intent to support the protégé, which the potential attacker is likely to infer reflects the importance of the interests at stake for the defender. Alliance ties have little independent deterrent impact, it would seem, since the importance of the alliance for the potential attacker rests largely on the immediate and short-term military contribution of the defender to the protégé, which is reflected in the balance of forces. The long-term political and military costs to the defender of not honoring an alliance commitment do not seem to be that salient to the potential attacker.

In order to help interpret the results in table 1 additional tables are presented that report the marginal impact of changes in each variable while holding all other variables in the equation at their mean value. In table 2 the impact of changes in the immediate and short-term balance of forces is reported. For example, a change in the immediate balance of forces from a one-to-four disadvantage to an equal balance of forces for the defender increases the probability of deterrence success by 16 percent; while the change from an equal balance to a three-to-one advantage for the defender increases the likelihood of deterrence success by 27 percent. Similar results are obtained when the short-term balance of forces is examined.

The results presented in table 3 indicate that crisis bargaining plays a critical role in determining the success or failure of deterrence. These results lend strong support to the argument that despite the potential problems of misperception and cognitive biases. . . in a crisis or confrontation, policy makers can still effectively signal and clarify intentions by means of diplomatic and military actions. For example, the adoption of a firm-but-flexible diplomatic strategy increased the probability of deterrence success by 32 percent. A strategy of tit for tat in responding to the military escalation of the potential attacker increased the chances of success by 33 percent.

The defender's past behavior also plays a critical role in deterrence outcomes. If the defender was forced by the potential attacker to concede to its demands under military pressure in a previous confrontation, then the deterrent threats and actions of the defender lacked credibility in the next dispute between the two states. As the results in the bottom third of table 3 indicate, if the defender has backed

Table 2
The impact of the balance of military forces on deterrence

Balance of Military Forces	Change in Ratio of Defender–Protégé Forces to Potential Attacker Forces	Percentage Change in Probability of Successful Deterrence
Immediate	0.25–0.50	5
	0.50–0.75	5
	0.75 1.00	6
	1.00–1.50	9
	1.50–2.00	8
	2.00–3.00	10
	3.00–5.00	6
Short-term	0.25–0.50	6
	0.50–0.75	5
	0.75–1.00	4
	1.00–1.50	7
	1.50–2.00	6
	2.00–3.00	8
	3.00–5.00	9

Note. The marginal impact of each variable is calculated by changing its value while holding all other variables in the model (table 1) at ther mean value. The change in the location on the cumulative standard normal distribution is then converted into the percentage change in the probability of successful deterrence.

Table 3
The impact of bargaining strategies and past behavior on deterrence

Strategies and Behavior	Percentage Change in Probability of Successful Deterrence
Bargaining strategy	
Firm-but-flexible diplomacy [a]	+32
Defender military escalation	
Tit for tat [b]	+33
Past confrontation outcome	
Defender backs down [c]	−42
Defender intransigence or put-down [c]	−32

Note: The marginal impact of each variable is calculated by changing its value while holding all other variables in the model (table 1) at their mean value. The change in the location on the cumulative standard normal distribution is then converted into the percentage change in the probability of successful deterrence.
[a] As opposed to a bullying or conciliatory strategy.
[b] As opposed to exceeding or failing to match escalation of the potential attacker.
[c] As opposed to stalemate or no past confrontation.

down, the probability of deterrence success decreases by 42 percent. A reputation for unyielding firmness and bullying, however, is not to the advantage of the defender (just as it is not an effective bargaining strategy for immediate deterrence). If the defender adopted a bullying strategy (diplomatic put-down) in the last encounter with the potential attacker, the probability of deterrence success also decreased —by 32 percent. The reason seems to be that having been bullied previously, the potential attacker was less likely to retreat in the future and suffer further damage to its bargaining reputation. For example, the decision by Russia to go to war in defense of Serbia in 1914 was strongly influenced by the diplomatic setbacks that Russia suffered at the hands of Germany in previous confrontations in 1909 and 1912–1913...

Conclusion

The defense of allies from external threats is an enduring feature of the competition between states for spheres of influence in the international system. Extended deterrence, however, can be a very difficult and demanding task for foreign policy leaders. In this study we have found that a potential attacker's calculus of military costs seems to focus on whether military force can be used to achieve decisive results at relatively low cost. Extended deterrence is greatly strengthened, therefore, if the defender has the military capability to deny the attacker a quick victory and turn the conflict into a protracted struggle. While a number of recent case studies have questioned whether the military balance is a powerful explanatory variable in the analysis of deterrence

outcomes..., the results of this study strongly suggest that the balance of forces is an important variable in a potential attacker's calculus of deterrence.

Uncertainty in estimating the intentions of the defender in a situation of extended deterrence is a critical problem confronting a potential attacker. One way in which the defender can signal its intentions and reduce uncertainty is through the bargaining process. A tit-for-tat policy of military escalation not only signals the defender's willingness to use force if necessary, it also has an important impact on the immediate balance of forces. The movement and positioning of military forces by the defender in many cases of extended deterrence erased a local imbalance of forces in favor of the potential attacker and established a formidable tripwire deterrent capability in which the use of force by the potential attacker would necessarily result in the direct engagement of the defender's armed forces. As a result, the ability of the potential attacker to achieve quick and decisive results with the use of force was greatly reduced and the military costs increased...

Deterrence success, however, is not only a question of the defender possessing and demonstrating the intent to use powerful military forces. The critical role that a firm-but-flexible diplomatic strategy played in deterrence success strongly suggests that the political costs of inaction are also an important factor in the potential attacker's calculus of gains and losses... The emphasis in deterrence theory has been on the requirements of the defender to possess strong military forces and to demonstrate the intent to use force. It is important to recognize, however, that estimates of only the military costs of using force provide a partial and incomplete explanation of deterrence outcomes in a number of cases. The political costs for the potential attacker of not pressing ahead with the use of force, defined in terms of bargaining reputation, need to be recognized as central to successful crisis management. By combining firmness with conditional proposals of limited compromise, the immediate confrontation can be deescalated and the potential attacker can retreat from its threat to use force without reinforcing the appearance of capitulation due to coercive pressure. The credible threat of military force is required to convince the potential attacker that the military costs of changing the status quo are high, but skillful diplomacy is also required to assure the potential attacker that the political costs of continued peace are acceptable. . . .

Study Questions

1. Why is theory important in international relations?
2. What is the difference between a value, a belief, and a cognition?
3. How do we distinguish between perception and reality?
4. What are facts and how do they acquire meaning in international relations?
5. Distinguish between the modes of analysis described in this chapter and description, explanation, and projection.
6. What does it mean to hypothesize?
7. What type of knowledge do we seek in international relations?
8. Distinguish between behavioral and traditional research methods in terms of data collection and mode of analysis.
9. Explain the similarities and differences between the three paradigms: realism, pluralism, and structuralism.
10. What do we mean by *approach* to the study of international relations?
11. Explain the salient features and characteristics of international relations during the traditional, behavioral, and post-behavioral periods.
12. Who are the realists, neo-realists, idealists, traditionalists, behavioralists, and structuralists?
13. What are the salient features of the historial approach?
14. What are the main features of the legal approach?
15. What is the cosmopolitan approach?
16. What are the salient features of the power approach?
17. What do we mean by the *national interest* and how can it be demonstrated?
18. Why are the followers of the power approach called realists and what is the realistic view of international relations?
19. What are the salient features of the classical balance of power approach?
20. Why was the classical balance of power approach considered obsolete?
21. What is the contemporary model of the balance of power approach followed by the realists?
22. Why is the geopolitical approach determinist in orientation?
23. Who are the environmental possibilists, and what is their approach to the study of international relations?
24. What is the *ecological triad*?
25. Describe the difference between the state-centric model of the systems approach and the *linkage* type.
26. Under the systems approach, why is it important to shift focus from a state system to a conception of world society and its basic constituent, the individual?

27. What are transnationalism, interdependence, and globalism?
28. What are the main features of the functional approach?
29. What are the aims of the communications approach?
30. What three major developments in the communications approach made it significant for the study of international relations?
31. What are the aims of the decision-making approach?
32. What are the analytical component parts of the decision-making process?
33. Explain the rational actor or choice model of the decision-making process.
34. Explain the organizational process model.
35. Explain the governmental or bureaucratic politics model of the decision-making process.

Key Terms

balance of power	Lebensraum
behavioralist	national interests
belief	organizational process model
bureaucratic politics model	paradigm
cognition	perceptions
communications approach	possibilism
cosmopolitan approach	post-behavioralism
decision-making approach	power
facts	rational actor model
functionalism	realists
geopolitical approach	soft data
hard data	state-centrism
historical approach	theory
hypothesis	traditionalists
idealists	transnationalism
image	value
integration	

Notes

1. See David Easton, *The Political System* (New York: Knopf, 1953), p. 53.
2. See Philip E. Converse, "The Nature of Belief Systems in Mass Public" in *Ideology and Discontent,* ed. David E. Apter (New York: Free Press, 1964), p. 207.
3. See Leon Festinger, *The Theory of Cognitive Dissonance* (Stanford: Stanford University Press, 1962).
4. Richard Stengel, "Sailing in Harm's Way," *TIME,* 7 April 1986, p. 20.
5. Yankelovich/Clancy, Shulman, "Hitting the Source," *TIME* 28 April 1986, p. 26.
6. Ibid.
7. See Harold Sprout and Margaret Sprout, *The Ecological Perspective on Human Affairs* (Princeton: Princeton University Press, 1965), p. 29.

8. For a better understanding of the perceptual process and some psychological dimensions of perception, see Albert E. Eldridge, *Images of Conflict* (New York: St. Martin's Press, 1979), pp. 1–40; and Robert Jervis, *Perception and Misperception in International Relations* (Princeton: Princeton University Press, 1976).

9. For a general study in social psychology that stresses various aspects of social cognition, see B. H. Rowen and J. Z. Rubin, *Social Psychology* (New York: Wiley, 1983). For a "cognitive maps" approach, especially in the study of political leaders and their outlook, see R. Axelrod, ed., *The Structure of Decision: The Cognitive Maps of Political Elites* (Princeton: Princeton University Press, 1976); and D. Stuart and Harvey Starr, "The Inherent 'Bad Faith Model' Reconsidered: Dulles, Kennedy and Kissinger," *Political Psychology* 3, no. 3/4, (1981, 1982): 1–33.

10. For further elaboration of the scientific method, see Kenneth R. Hoover, *The Elements of Social Scientific Thinking* (New York: St. Martin's Press, 1976), pp. 33–35.

11. See Bernard Berelson and Gary A. Steimer, *Human Behavior* (New York: Harcourt, Brace and World, 1967).

12. See Julian L. Simon and Paul Burstein, *Basic Research Methods in Social Science,* 3rd ed. (New York: Random House, 1985), p. 225.

13. New data in international relations are becoming available on a rapidly increasing scale. It is appropriate, therefore, to ask where students of international relations can find relevant data that could be used for their own research to meet the requirements of a term paper, if not something more ambitious. Perhaps the most useful category of data is *aggregate data,* such as social, economic, or demographic statistics, census data, and the like, that are gathered by governments or private organizations for their own operational purposes; from sources such as those in the following list, students can learn about the social structure and process of a country and its rate of change during a certain period and under certain conditions.

   A. Frequently used and annually updated aggregate data have been gathered in the UN's *Statistical Yearbook, Demographic Yearbook,* and *Yearbook of International Trade Statistics;* the *Political Handbook of the World* edited by Arthur S. Banks; the International Monetary Fund's *Balance of Payments Yearbook* and *Direction of Trade;* various reports by the World Bank such as the *World Debt Tables;* the International Labor Organization's *Yearbook of Labor Statistics; Compendium of Data for World System Analysis* by Bornschier and Heintz; and *International Political Economy Yearbook* by W. Ladd Hollist and F. Lamond Tullis.

   B. Some older classics include the *Cross-Polity Survey* by Arthur S. Banks and Robert Textor; the *World Handbook of Political and Social Indicators* by Bruce M. Russett and his associates or the same title by Lewis Taylor and Michael Hudson; and finally, *Dimensions of Conflict Behavior Within and Between Nations* by Rudolph Rummel and Raymond Tanter.

   C. For events data sets to model processes of international interaction and to forecast the course of future international developments, see the *World Events Interaction Survey* (WEIS) developed initially by Charles McClelland, and the *Conflict and Peace Data Bank* (COPDAB) compiled under the direction of Edward Azar. The application of various events data sets is brilliantly demonstrated in *Describing Foreign Policy Behavior* edited by Patrick Gallahan, Linda P. Brady, and Margaret G. Hermann.

   D. For further explanations of the use and manipulation of aggregate data, see *Social Science Research: A Handbook for Students* by Gerald S. Fermun and Jack Levin;

Basic Research Methods in Social Science by Julian L. Simon and Paul Burstein; *Comparing Nations: The Use of Quantitative Data in Cross-National Research* edited by Richard L. Merritt and Stein Rokkan; and *Quantitative International Politics* edited by J. David Singer.

   E. In addition, statistics provide valuable research data; see *Nations on Record: United Nations General Assembly Roll-Call Votes, 1946–1973,* serial collections of the Inter-University Consortium for Political and Social Research at the University of Michigan; or the UN roll-call votes published during each UN session in the *Index to Proceedings of the General Assembly.* Public opinion polls from many countries on a variety of issues are also available in the journal *World Public Opinion Update.*

   F. New secondary data such as ratios, rank-order profiles, statistical distributions, and correlations are available in studies such as *State of the World* by Lester R. Brown and his collaborators; *the Global 2000 Report to the President of U.S.* by G. O. Barney; *Mankind at the Turning Point* by M. Mesarovic and E. Protel; and *Atlas of United States Foreign Relations* by Harry F. Young of the Department of State's Bureau of Public Affairs.

   G. Finally, for information about world events, see *Deadline Data on World Affairs* and *Keesing's* or the *Handbook of Economic Statistics 1986* put together by the Central Intelligence Agency; the series *International Development Resource Books* published by Greenwood Press; the *MERIP Reports* on the Middle East; or the publications on the arms race and arms control by the Stockholm International Peace Research Institute.

14. U.S. Department of State, Bureau of Public Affairs, *How Foreign Policy Is Made,* Department of State publication 7707 (Washington, D.C.: Government Printing Office, 1969), p. 23.

15. See, for example, John E. Mueller, ed., *Approaches to Measurement in International Relations: A Non-Evangelical Survey* (New York: Meredith Corp., 1969).

16. See Charles A. McClelland, *A Design for International Research: Scope, Theory, and Methods and Relevance,* monograph 10 (Philadelphia: American Academy of Political and Social Science, 1970), p. 72; and James N. Rosenau, "Pre-Theories and Theories of Foreign Policy," in *Approaches to Comparative and International Politics,* ed. R. Barry Farrell (Evanston, Ill.: Northwestern University Press, 1966), pp. 27–92.

17. For a general survey of approaches to the study of international relations, see James E. Dougherty and Robert L. Pfaltzgraff, Jr., *Contending Theories of International Relations* (Philadelphia: Lippincott, 1971).

18. See, for example, Hans J. Morgenthau, "Another 'Great Debate': The National Interest of the United States," *American Political Science Review* XLVI, no. 4 (December 1952): 961–988; Thomas I. Cook and Malcolm Moos, *Power Through Purpose: The Realism of Idealism as a Basis for Foreign Policy* (Baltimore: Johns Hopkins Press, 1954); and Kenneth W. Thompson, *Political Realism and the Crisis of World Politics: An American Approach to Foreign Policy* (Princeton: Princeton University Press, 1960).

19. See Richard Little, "Structuralism and Neo-Realism," in *International Relations: A Handbook of Current Theory,* eds. Margot Light and A. J. R. Groom (London: Frances Pinter, 1985), p. 76.

20. Immanuel Wallerstein, *The Modern World System: Capitalist Agriculture and the Origins of the European World Economy in the 16th Century* (New York: Academic Press, 1974); idem, *The Modern World System II: Mercantilism and the Consolidation of the European World Economy 1600–1750* (New York: Academic Press, 1980).

21. See, for example, Robert O. Keohane and Joseph S. Nye, *Power and Interdependence: World Politics in Transition* (Boston: Little, Brown, 1977); and Richard W. Mansbach, Yale H. Ferguson, and Donald E. Lampert, *The Web of World Politics: Non-State Actors in the Global System* (Englewood Cliffs, N.J.: Prentice-Hall, 1976).

22. For further explanation, see Michael Banks, "The Inter-Paradigm Debate," in *International Relations: A Handbook of Current Theory,* eds. Margot Light and A. J. R. Groom (London: Frances Pinter, 1985), pp. 7–26.

23. See Charles A. McClelland, "Systems and History in International Relations: Some Perspectives for Empirical Research and Theory," *General Systems* III (1958): 229.

24. Thomas Buergenthall and J. H. Hall, eds., *Human Rights, International Law and the Helsinki Accords* (Montclair, N.J.: Allanheld, Osmon & Co., 1977).

25. See Charles R. Beitz, *Political Theory and International Relations* (Princeton: Princeton University Press, 1979); John W. Burton, *Dear Survivors* (Boulder: Westview, 1983); Johann Galtung, *The True Worlds: A Transnational Perspective* (New York: Free Press, 1980).

26. Hans J. Morgenthau, "International Politics as a Struggle for Power," Part II of *Politics Among Nations* (New York: Knopf, 1951).

27. For an analysis of the national interest, see Morgenthau, "Another 'Great Debate,'" pp. 961–988.

28. For an analysis of political ideologies, see Hans J. Morgenthau, *Politics Among Nations,* 3rd ed. (New York: Knopf, 1960), pp. 86–96.

29. For a pro and con argument on power politics, see Trevor Taylor, ed., *Approaches and Theory in International Relations* (London: Longman, 1978), pp. 122–140.

30. For example, Raymond Aron, *Peace and War: A Theory of International Relations* (New York: Doubleday, 1966); Zbigniew Brzezinski, *Game Plan* (New York: Atlantic Monthly Press, 1986); Inis L. Claude, Jr., *Power and International Relations* (New York: Random House, 1962); John N. Herz, *International Politics in the Atomic Age* (New York: Columbia University Press, 1962); Stanley Hoffman, *The State of War* (New York: Praeger, 1965); George F. Kennan, *Realities of American Foreign Policy* (New York: Norton, 1966); Richard N. Rosecrance, *International Relations: Peace or War* (New York: McGraw-Hill, 1973); John W. Spanier, *Games Nations Play,* 5th ed. (New York: Holt, Rinehart & Winston, 1984); John G. Stoessinger, *The Might of Nations,* 8th ed. (New York: Random House, 1986); Kenneth W. Thompson, *Political Realism and the Crisis of World Politics* (Princeton: Princeton University Press, 1960); and Kenneth N. Waltz, *Man, the State and War* (New York: Columbia University Press, 1954).

31. At least two empirical studies examining the stability of the balance of power during the Bismarckian period of history confirmed that "unbalanced relationships are more likely to be unstable" than balanced ones. See Brian Healy and Arthur Stein, "The Balance of Power in International History," *Journal of Conflict Resolution* 17, no. 1 (March 1973): 33–61; and Richard J. Stoll, "Bloc Concentration and the Balance of Power," *Journal of Conflict Resolution* 28, no. 1 (March 1984): 25–50.

32. See Stoessinger, *The Might of Nations,* p. 24.

33. Hans J. Morgenthau, *Politics Among Nations,* 4th ed. (New York: Knopf, 1967), p. 214.

34. Ibid., chap. 14; see also Dougherty and Pfaltzgraff, *Contending Theories of International Relations,* p. 34.

35. A. F. K. Organski, *World Politics* (New York: Knopf, 1958), pp. 292–338.

36. See John H. Herz, "Balance System and Balance Policies in a Nuclear and Bipolar Age," *Journal of International Affairs* XIX, no. 1 (1960): 39–41.

37. Alfred Mackinder, *Democratic Ideals and Reality* (New York: Norton, 1962), p. 150.

38. See Stephen B. Jones, "Global Strategic Views," *Geographical Review* XLV (October 1955): 492–508.

39. Harold Sprout and Margaret Sprout, *Man–Milieu Relationship Hypotheses in the Context of International Politics* (Princeton: Center of International Studies, Princeton University, 1956), p. 39.

40. Harold Sprout and Margaret Sprout, *An Ecological Paradigm for the Study of International Politics* (Princeton: Center of International Studies, Princeton University, 1968), pp. 11–21.

41. Harold Sprout and Margaret Sprout, "Geography and International Politics in an Era of Revolutionary Change," *Journal of Conflict Resolution* IV, no. 1 (March 1960): 156–157.

42. Sprout and Sprout, *Man–Milieu Relationship Hypotheses,* p. 50.

43. Sprout and Sprout, *The Ecological Perspective on Human Affairs,* p. 140.

44. See N. Jordan, "Some Thinking About 'Systems,'" in *Systems Analysis,* ed. S. L. Optner (Hammondsworth, England: Penguin Books, 1973), p. 61.

45. Morton A. Kaplan, *System and Process in International Politics* (New York: Wiley, 1964), pp. 4–24.

46. J. David Singer, S. Bremer, and J. Stuckey, "Capability Distribution Uncertainty and Major Power War, 1820–1965," in *Peace War and Numbers,* ed. Bruce Russett (Newbury Park, Calif.: Sage, 1972); Maurice A. East, "Status Discrepancy and Violence in the International System: An Empirical Analysis," in *The Analysis of International Politics,* eds. James N. Rosenau, Vincent Davis, and Maurice A. East (New York: Free Press, 1972); and M. Wallace, *War and Rank Among Nations* (Lexington, Mass.: Heath, 1973).

47. James N. Rosenau, ed., *Linkage Politics* (New York: Free Press, 1969), p. 45. See also Arthur A. Stein, "The Politics of Linkage," *World Politics* XXXIII, no. 1 (1980): 62–81.

48. John H. Herz, *International Politics in the Atomic Age* (New York: Columbia University Press, 1959).

49. Richard A. Falk, *This Endangered Planet: Prospects and Proposals for Human Survival* (New York: Vintage Books, 1972), pp. 94–98.

50. Donella H. Meadows, Dennis Meadows, Jørgen Randers, and William H. Behrens, *The Limits to Growth* (New York: Universe Books, 1972).

51. John W. Burton, *World Society* (Cambridge: Cambridge University Press, 1972), pp. 351ff.

52. W. Ladd Hollist and James N. Rosenau, "World System Debates," *International Studies Quarterly* XXV, no. 1 (1981): 6.

53. For evidence suggesting that interactions between the actors on the international stage have not necessarily increased global solidarity and promoted international peace, see W. Andrew Axline and James A. Stegenga, *The Global Community* (New York: Dodd, Mead, 1972), pp. 117–120.

54. Karl W. Deutsch, *The Nerves of Government: Models of Political Communication and Control* (Glencoe, Ill.: Free Press, 1963), p. 124.

55. See Richard C. Snyder, H. W. Bruck, and Burton M. Sapin, "Decision Making as an Approach to the Study of International Politics," *Foreign Policy Analysis,* series no. 3 (Princeton: Princeton University Press, 1954). The study was later reprinted in Richard C. Snyder, H. W. Bruck, and Burton M. Sapin, *Foreign Policy Decision-Making: An Approach to the Study of International Politics* (New York: Free Press, 1962).

56. Snyder, Bruck, and Sapin, *Foreign Policy Decision-Making,* p. 65.

57. C. F. Friedrich Kratochwil, "On the Notion of 'Interest' in International Relations," *International Organizations* 36, no. 1 (1982): 1–30.

58. Graham T. Allison, *Essence of Decision: Explaining the Cuban Missile Crisis* (Boston: Little, Brown, 1971), pp. 3–4.

59. See Sidney Verba, "Assumptions of Rationality and Non-Rationality in Models of the International System," in *The International System, Theoretical Essays,* eds. Klaus Knorr and Sidney Verba (Princeton: Princeton University Press, 1961).

60. See Herbert Simon, *Administrative Behavior: A Study of Decision-Making Processes in Administrative Organization,* 2nd ed. (New York: Macmillan, 1958).

61. Ibid., p. 67.

62. Ibid.

63. Ibid., p. 144.

64. James N. Rosenau, "The Premises and Promises of Decision-Making Analysis," in *Contemporary Political Analysis,* ed. James C. Charlesworth (New York: Free Press, 1967), p. 211.

65. See R. Pettman, *Human Behavior and World Politics* (London: Macmillan, 1975), p. 32.

66. See R. E. Jones, *Analyzing Foreign Policy* (London: Routledge & Kegan Paul, 1970), pp. 36–38.

67. Walter S. Jones, *The Logic of International Relations,* 5th ed. (Boston: Little, Brown, 1985).

68. John Spanier, *Games Nations Play,* 5th ed. (New York: Holt, Rinehart & Winston, 1984).

69. Michael P. Sullivan, *International Relations: Theories and Evidence* (Englewood Cliffs, N.J.: Prentice-Hall, 1976), pp. 252–300.

Part II

Elements of Foreign Policy Making

Four
The Actors and Their Capabilities

Five
The Determinants and Processes of Foreign Policy Behavior

Four

The Actors and Their Capabilities

Consider the following events: Argentina invades the Falkland Islands precipitating a seventy-four-day war with the United Kingdom. Terrorists bomb an American military compound in Beirut, Lebanon, killing 241 marines. Motorola Corporation withdraws its investments from South Africa. Ronald Reagan and Mikhail Gorbachev sign the Intermediate Nuclear Force Treaty. NATO ministers meet to discuss how this treaty will affect West European security. The World Health Organization announces the eradication of smallpox. Pope John Paul II travels to India for meetings with religious and government figures. Dr. Robert Gale leads an international team of doctors and technicians from fifteen countries to help the Soviet Union's medical establishment cope with the health effects of the Chernobyl nuclear reactor accident. Musicians hold a global rock concert to raise money for famine victims in Africa. CARE and Catholic Relief Services deliver food assistance to starving Ethiopians. Television news networks and the print media report on the American raid on Tripoli, Libya. A delegation of Australian aborigines travels to Libya seeking financial support for taking their land claims case against the Australian government to the International Court of Justice.

What do these seemingly unrelated incidents have in common? Little, except that each is an example of an actor in international relations. States (governments), terrorists, corporations, heads of government, regional security organizations, international organizations, religious figures, individuals, and celebrities, nongovernmental agencies, and indigenous groups are, or could be, actors in international relations. On any given day there are hundreds of globally significant events such as these in which different individuals and organizations interact. These events and interactions are the real stuff of international relations. In this chapter we will identify the basic actors in international relations and explore the actual capabilities, powers, and influences that each actor possesses as they interact with one another.

Background and Basic Concepts

The Actors: Some Initial Considerations

An actor in international relations may be defined as any entity whose actions have an impact beyond the borders of a single country. The significance of the impact, of course, may vary considerably. Almost without exception, states—or more precisely, governments—are actors in international relations. Even states that seek isolation from the international arena engage in actions that have impacts beyond their borders. But this definition is not limited to governments. Many other actors also must be recognized. Following our definition, private agencies that raise money for the poor or homeless in their own country are not engaging in international relations. However, those agencies that raise money and operate programs for people in other countries are engaging in international relations, and thus are actors in the world arena. Businesses that engage in foreign exports or that have overseas subsidiaries are international actors, but those companies that only have domestic operations and that are not involved in international trade are not international actors. A national liberation group may or may not be an international actor, depending on its activities. If the group seeks assistance from foreign governments or engages in terrorist activities against foreign citizens either in its own country or overseas, it could be considered an international actor. Obviously, almost any group could become an international actor, but at any given time only some of them actually are.

Before the emergence of the modern state system at the Peace of Westphalia, many different kinds of entities played a role in global politics. Empires, popes, other key individuals, mercenaries, clans, tribes, trading and business groups, pirates, and guilds were involved in international relations. Westphalia ushered in an age of state dominance in international politics. States were seen as the only legitimate legal actors, and many of the other entities lost significance. By the nineteenth century, however, new actors emerged on the global stage. The first intergovernmental organizations (IGOs) began to appear in the 1800s. Nongovernmental organizations (NGOs) also began to appear in greater numbers in the second half of the nineteenth century.[1] International politics, which had been perceived as the almost exclusive domain of kings and other sovereigns, was progressively being populated by new and different actors. Nor were strictly interstate relations the same. As decolonization occurred, large numbers of new, small, weak countries burst onto the international scene. The upshot was that interstate relations grew increasingly more complex and could no longer be divorced, practically speaking, from the influence of IGOs, multinational business enterprises, and NGOs. Nevertheless, in international relations, the state still dominates patterns of interaction among these various actors. The state creates IGOs to serve purposes that it deems necessary. Corporations do not owe their existence to states, but they do have a parent country and must enter into agreements with other countries before they can set up business operations in them. Nongovernmental organizations do not owe their existence to states either, but they are governed by the laws of their parent country and of the countries in which they run programs or have affiliate organizations.

It is important, then, to distinguish between primary and secondary actors in international relations. There can be little doubt that states (or rather governments acting in the name of states) are the **primary actors.** The first example cited in the opening paragraph of this chapter—the Falkland Islands—involved two nation-states employing violent actions against each other over a long-standing dispute that had not been settled by peaceful means. Argentina and the United Kingdom, together with more than 160 other countries, are the primary actors in international relations. Only they can go to war, tax people, and legally take life. Only they are legally sovereign, and they ultimately determine the laws that regulate the behavior of other actors. While states are the primary actors, they are not equally influential (as Miller points out in the supplemental reading at the end of this chapter), nor are they always more influential than other kinds of actors such as certain corporations or international organizations. Indeed, as we saw in chapter 1, states may exist juridically (as legal entities), but they may have very little common sense of unity or even a de facto ability to exercise control over the territory they legally govern. This problem is especially apparent among the recently independent states of the Third World, which leads some scholars to draw a basic distinction between juridical and de facto states.[2] In addition, on rare occasions a state may try to withdraw from international relations altogether, insulating itself as much as possible from outside interference and cutting off all trade and diplomatic ties. Albania, for instance, has largely withdrawn from international relations. China tried during its cultural revolution in the 1960s. But most states find it difficult, unrealistic, and impractical to withdraw from international relations. Most states do participate, and as a group they constitute the highest and in some ways the most basic unit of international relations. Other actors must be aware of this basic fact in order to achieve their own ends in the global arena.

The **secondary actors** in international relations have grown in number and influence in the last century, so much so that some people believe that these actors may have undermined the capacity of states to dictate the pace of world affairs.[3] Whether this is true is still a matter of debate. What cannot be doubted is that many more and different kinds of players now exist on the international scene, including liberation, insurgent, and terrorist organizations, IGOs, NGOs, religious figures, celebrities, and other individuals. Somewhat begrudgingly, states have extended a certain degree of legal personality to some of these entities, especially to IGOs. States have even slowly accorded limited rights and duties to individuals, who were once considered mere objects rather than subjects of international law.

Because states or governments are still the predominant actors in world affairs, most students of international relations spend more time analyzing nations' capabilities than those of the other actors.[4] But an overemphasis on the power of states misrepresents a more complex reality in which other actors exercise influence, sometimes very considerable influence, on world affairs. In trying to assess the importance, role, and capabilities of states and nonstate actors in the international arena, it is useful to differentiate between high politics and low politics. **High politics** refers to key political, military, and national security aspects of international relations, such as decisions about war, peace treaties, military alliances, arms control, dispute resolution, and so on.[5] High politics has been dominated by U.S.–Soviet ideological, political, and military competition. By contrast, **low politics** concerns routine economic relations, cultural exchanges, international travel, tourism, and communications between countries. Nonstate actors typically are more involved in low politics. But IGOs and terrorist and insurgent groups can be key players in high politics as well. Indeed, as the Cold War tensions recede and economics becomes a greater preoccupation internationally, the preeminence of high politics may diminish and the role of secondary actors may grow in stature. In this chapter we will explore the capabilities of states and those of the other actors as well, but let us begin with the kingpins of the high political agenda: the states.

Assessing the Capabilities of States

Virtually all of the planet's landmass and even a significant amount of its oceans, lies under the legal jurisdiction of states. Over 160 in number, states come in a huge variety of sizes and have markedly different capabilities. Some states, such as the United States, the Soviet Union, and Japan, are very wealthy. Others, such as Chad, Ethiopia, and Haiti, are very poor. Some countries are very large in terms of geographical area. The United States, Canada, and the Soviet Union, for instance, stretch across continents, while Australia is a continent unto itself. On the other hand, some countries, such as the Maldive Islands, Kiribati, and Grenada, are small island nations. Similarly, some countries are populous and others are not. China has over a billion people and India's population approaches 800 million. On the other hand, Nauru and Tuvalu each have only a few thousand people. Obviously, a large, heavily populated, rich country will be better able to influence international relations than a small, sparsely populated, poor one. It is very important to study the elements of power (or as we refer to it in this chapter, the capabilities of states) in order to understand international relations better.

Power   As we pointed out in chapter 2, power is a resource that governments seek in order to have greater success in achieving their goals. While power can be thought of as a resource to be accumulated, it can also be seen as a *capacity* to shape the world in one's image, that is, to have control over other actors and, ultimately, over the outcome of international events.[6] As the term *capacity* implies, power can also be seen as being potential or actual in character; in other words, not every country uses all of its power all of the time.[7] Whether seen as a resource or as a capacity, the presumed end of power from the standpoint of any one country is to convince other countries and actors to conform to its will and to control the pace of international events. More specifically, states use power to attain certain goals, such as economic prosperity, social stability, territorial preservation, and on occasion, territorial expansion.

Elements of power   We have also seen that there are several elements of power; that is, several capacities or attributes that characterize powerful countries. A large population, substantial geographical area, significant economic wealth, and a strong military are capabilities that clearly affect a nation's power.[8] Table 4.1 illustrates the importance of these elements. Indeed, one would be hard pressed to find a truly powerful country that does not possess at least one or two of the indicators of power represented in the table. The table also illustrates degrees of power. Not surprisingly, for instance, only two countries—the United States and the Soviet Union—are ranked in the top five countries on all five lists. Superpower status, it seems, is correlated with high rankings on these measures of power. Major power status is also reflected in the table. The People's Republic of China (PRC) and India appear on all five lists, although not always in the top five rankings. The Federal Republic of Germany (FRG) or West Germany, the United Kingdom (UK), Italy, Iran, and France are ranked in the top twenty on four lists, whereas five countries (Brazil, Japan, Mexico, Canada, and Poland) appear on three lists. While exact gradations of power are difficult to define based on these measures and rankings alone, they do help illustrate in a general and crude way the degrees of power that nations have. Similarly, countries with very small populations, a limited land area, a low gross national product (GNP), low levels of military spending, and small armed forces are not likely to wield significant global influence.

Let us examine the key measures of power more closely. A big population enables a country to maintain a large army. Referring to table 4.1, we can see that eleven of the most populous countries also rank in the top twenty countries in terms of the size of their armed forces. Similarly, a large geographical area may help insulate a country from foreign invasions and increase the resource base for its economy. A strong economy, in turn, enables a country to compete effectively in international trade during peacetime and to manufacture weapons during wartime. There is, for instance, a strong correlation between countries with large GNPs and those with high military spending. Of the top twenty-ranked countries in GNP, seventeen are also in the top twenty in military spending.

However, countries that have only one of these attributes may be at a disadvantage. For example, a country with a huge population but a small landmass and a poor economy may find its population a burden. Conversely, a country with a huge geographical area that is sparsely populated may find it difficult to effectively exploit its resources and protect its land.

Each component of power, in turn, consists of several other factors. Geographical size alone does not make a nation powerful. For instance, nine of the twenty largest countries listed in table 4.1, fail to appear in the top twenty countries on the other indicators of power. Small countries may be well endowed with mineral resources and fertile agricultural land, whereas large ones may contain vast areas of unusable deserts (i.e., Chad and Sudan) or jungles (i.e., Zaire). In addition, the location of a country and its geographical features and climate may lend it certain advantages. Switzerland, for instance, is not very large in terms of population or geographical area, but its mountainous location, together with its policy of neutrality, has insulated it from foreign attackers. On the other hand, landlocked countries, such as Czechoslovakia, Bolivia, and Zimbabwe, which have no direct access to the sea, may find themselves in a more vulnerable position in terms of international trade than coastal nations. In our age of nuclear weapons, high technology, and rapid transportation, the importance of geography has diminished somewhat from a military standpoint. Mountain ranges and oceans are no protection against intercontinental ballistic

Table 4.1

Top twenty ranking countries on selected indicators of power

Population			Area			Gross National Product		
Rank	Country	Population (thousands)	Rank	Country	Area (1,000 sq. km.)	Rank	Country	GNP (in millions of U.S. dollars)
1	PRC (China)	1,054,000	1	Soviet Union	22,402	1	United States	3,765,000
2	India	781,400	2	Canada	9,976	2	Soviet Union	2,060,000
3	Soviet Union	281,100	3	PRC (China)	9,561	3	Japan	1,292,000
4	United States	241,600	4	United States	9,363	4	West Germany	697,200
5	Indonesia	166,400	5	Brazil	8,152	5	France	539,500
6	Brazil	138,400	6	Australia	7,687	6	United Kingdom	482,500
7	Japan	121,500	7	India	3,288	7	Italy	373,100
8	Bangladesh	103,200	8	Argentina	2,767	8	Canada	340,800
9	Nigeria	103,100	9	Sudan	2,506	9	PRC (China)	321,100
10	Pakistan	99,200	10	Algeria	2,382	10	Poland	235,200
11	Mexico	80,200	11	Zaire	2,345	11	Brazil	212,300
12	Vietnam	63,300	12	Saudi Arabia	2,150	12	India	200,500
13	West Germany	60,900	13	Mexico	1,973	13	East Germany	168,600
14	Philippines	57,300	14	Indonesia	1,919	14	Spain	164,400
15	Italy	57,200	15	Libya	1,760	15	Australia	159,800
16	United Kingdom	56,700	16	Iran	1,648	16	Iran	158,800
17	France	55,400	17	Mongolia	1,565	17	Mexico	144,200
18	Thailand	52,600	18	Peru	1,285	18	Netherlands	139,300
19	Turkey	51,500	19	Chad	1,284	19	Czechoslovakia	132,700
20	Egypt	49,700	20	Niger	1,267	20	Romania	120,600

(continues)

Part II Elements of Foreign Policy Making

	Military Spending	Military Spending (in millions of U.S. dollars)		Armed Forces	Armed Forces (thousands)
Rank	Country		Rank	Country	
1	Soviet Union	330,000[a]	1	Soviet Union	5,227.0
2	United States	288,400	2	PRC (China)	3,200.0
3	France	34,500	3	United States	2,158.0
4	West Germany	34,200	4	India	1,262.0
5	United Kingdom	31,800	5	Iraq	1,000.0
6	Japan	25,400	6	Vietnam	900.0
7	Italy	16,800	7	North Korea	838.0
8	Saudi Arabia	16,200	8	Turkey	654.5
9	Iraq	14,000	9	Iran	654.4
10	East Germany	11,600	10	South Korea	629.0
11	India	9,650	11	France	547.0
12	Iran	9,000	12	West Germany	495.0
13	Canada	8,800	13	Pakistan	481.0
14	Spain	7,500	14	Taiwan	424.0
15	Netherlands	6,503	15	Syria	407.0
16	Poland	5,900	16	Poland	394.0
17	South Korea	5,700	17	Italy	388.0
18	PRC (China)	5,600	18	Spain	325.0
19	Czechoslovakia	5,400	19	Ethiopia	320.0
20	Australia	5,300	20	United Kingdom	319.0

[a] The figure for Soviet military spending is calculated at 16 percent of the Soviet GNP

SOURCES: Population and area are from *World Development Report* (Washington, D.C.: World Bank, 1988), pp. 222–223. Military data are drawn from *The Military Balance, 1988–9* (London: Institute for Strategic Studies).

missiles. However, geographical factors continue to be important in the acquisition or maintenance of economic power.

Other things being equal, a large population is an important contributor to national power. But other demographic factors must also be taken into account. If too much of the population is under the age of fifteen or over sixty, its productive capacity will be limited. In many Third World countries, for instance, half or more of the population are under the age of fifteen. Children and the aged make many demands on a country's economy for education and health care. Similarly, an ethnically homogeneous population is likely to be more stable than one consisting of many ethnic divisions. Grossly inequitable distributions of income and wealth may also make a society more unstable, prone to internal turmoil, and vulnerable to revolution. Nigeria, for instance, ranks ninth among states in population size but suffers from ethnic divisions, political instability, civil war, and a significant disparity in the distribution of economic wealth. An uneducated, poorly trained, or illiterate population clearly contributes less to national power than an educated, skilled, and technologically sophisticated population. Thus, a country with a smaller, more productive population is likely to be more powerful than one with a larger, less productive population. Israel, a very small country in terms of area and population, has managed to prevail in several Middle East wars against much larger countries such as Egypt and Syria.

As we have seen, a country's economy can be affected by geographical and demographic considerations. Several material factors such as the availability of human and natural resources are also critical to a robust economy. Among the necessary resources, food and energy are perhaps the most important. A nation that cannot produce enough to feed its population is vulnerable. Similarly, adequate domestic supplies of oil, coal, or other sources of energy are critical to a nation's power base. Without these resources, nations become vulnerable to outside political pressure. Japan, for instance, relies heavily on imports of Middle East oil; so when the Arab petroleum-exporting countries embargoed oil shipments to countries with a pro-Israeli policy, Japan shifted almost overnight to a more pro-Arab posture. Resource availability is clearly essential, but even more important is the ability to exploit resources—to convert them into useful products. An industrial economy depends on adequate economic infrastructures including roads, communications systems, ports, energy production facilities, and a skilled work force capable of managing these systems.

While population, land, and wealth are key elements of national power, they are by no means the only elements. Military strength is obviously a key component of national power.[9] Without a military capability, states would be vulnerable to foreign domination. Military strength is based on or affected by a country's geographical position, population, and economic capacities. For instance, a country's capacity to produce weapons is closely tied to its industrial capabilities, just as the size of its armed forces depends to some extent on the size of its population.

However, a state's military capability is based on much more than the size of its army or its capacity to produce weapons. Very strong countries with large armies have been overcome by smaller, weaker nations.[10] The United States lost the war in Vietnam. The Soviet Union failed to conquer liberation forces in Afghanistan. In both wars the morale of the opposing forces and the military and political tactics of each side played a large role in the weaker nation's ability to resist the military might of a superpower.[11] National morale, the soldiers' morale, strategy, and tactics can play decisive roles in military conflicts, as can the quality of military leadership. Thus, a nation's military capability is really a complex mix of qualitative and quantitative factors.

All but a few nations have sought to develop military capabilities in order to promote their security and preserve their interests.[12] This is one of the more significant facts of international relations, and it sets states apart from other international actors that are not in a position to field an armed force. Of course, insurgent and belligerent groups are an exception, but their goal is to gain control of the state or to receive recognition that would give greater legitimacy to their military operations.

States with a weak military capability may choose to compensate through diplomatic strategies, such as securing militarily powerful allies. The quality of a country's diplomacy may pay dividends in both the political and economic spheres. If a nation is deficient in natural resources, for example, it may seek access to them through commodity agreements with other nations. In addition to diplomatic skill, the capability of the entire governmental apparatus is also an important variable in a nation's power. An efficient bureaucracy and a carefully designed decision-making process are critical to the successful application of a nation's power. The government's ability to extract and mobilize resources is also a key variable.[13] A country should seek policies with respect to other states and international actors that are commensurate with its economic, political, and military capabilities. For example, if a state's military capability is ineffective, it courts disaster if it initiates wars with stronger neighbors.

Policy making, then, becomes a very important capacity. This subject is explored further in chapter 5, but it is important to stress here that a nation's power is mediated through its government. The experience, efficiency, and dedication of a government's decision makers determines to a significant degree how successfully a country marshals its power, achieves its interests, and preserves and protects its society. But above all, the government must have **legitimacy** in the eyes of its citizens. If the government's authority is questioned, if it is not perceived as legitimate, it will not be able to survive for long. A significant component of a nation's power is that its government is capable of maintaining the loyalty of its citizens. A country whose government and the people are at war with one another is unlikely to wield significant influence in world affairs.

To summarize, a country's power (capabilities) varies with a number of factors including population size, geographic size, location and topography, resource availabilities, economic vitality, agricultural self-sufficiency, industrial capacity, size of the armed forces, sophistication and quantity of weaponry, quality of military leadership, quality of diplomacy, capacity to enter into effective alliances, quality of the government, and morale and loyalty of its population and armed forces. Some of these elements—such as population size, geography, and natural resource availability—are material in character. We might call them **natural capabilities.** Other factors—such as military sophistication, industrial capacity, and economic vitality—deal with a country's ability to exploit its natural capabilities. We might call these factors **synthetic capabilities.** Still other elements—such as national morale or the quality of government and leadership—are more psychological in character. They might be called **psychological capabilities.**[14] Countries vary substantially in terms of these three kinds of capabilities. As nations seek to expand their political influence, increase their economic wealth, and preserve their political independence, territorial integrity, and societal cohesiveness, they rely on all of these capabilities.

But we have yet to answer a very practical question: Which kinds of capabilities are most reliable in achieving such goals or in helping a state prevail in disputes with other countries? For answers to this question, we need to turn to the results of behavioral research. One study, which explored the history of militarized disputes and wars during the period of 1816 to 1976, arrived at some interesting findings.[15] It focused on three major capabilities: population, industrial capacity, and military capability. With regard to success in militarized disputes and wars, this study found that a country's industrial base was more critical than military allocations. In fact, countries that had overallocated resources to the military sector as compared to the industrial sector on the eve of wars were defeated more often than they were victorious. On the other hand, the study found that the number of military personnel as a fraction of the population was important to success in wars but not in militarized disputes. Apparently, a heavy industrial base during peacetime was the strongest predictor of success in both disputes and wars. Countries that overallocate resources to the military sector may be depriving the economic sector and relying too heavily on the notion that big armies mean big influence in peacetime. However, this study did confirm that large armies were a key factor in actually winning wars.[16]

Other studies seem to confirm that the synthetic capabilities are critical to the outcomes of conflicts. A country's political development, its ability to extract resources from its population, is often the key to the success of apparently less powerful countries engaged in conflicts with apparently more powerful ones.[17] Israel, which on paper should be overwhelmed by the superior population, military strength, and resource capability of the Arab world, has prevailed in large part because of the superior extractive (synthetic) capacities of its government.

Historical studies seem to confirm the conclusion that a nation's synthetic capabilities play a major role in the rise and fall of nations. The strongest military powers in any given age tend to be those countries with strong, growing economic bases. Even more important are the relative rates of economic, industrial, and military power among governments. A country may be more powerful than in earlier times, but if the other nations' capabilities are growing at a faster rate, it will actually lose ground in relation to them. Coupled with technological developments and innovations, these shifting rates of economic development lead to changes in the global power balance. Countries that take on too many global commitments, wars, and foreign adventures usually overreach their economic capacity. Heavy military investment deprives them of resources that could be devoted to productive pursuits. By contrast, if their adversaries are investing more heavily in the industrial and economic spheres rather than in the military arena, then they are likely to rise to prominence as the older, spent military powers decline.[18]

The tendency to equate a nation's power with brute force or military strength alone should be avoided. As we have just seen, military strength is an important consideration in wartime. It may also be important during peacetime as a deterrent to aggressive countries that might otherwise be tempted to exert military force on weaker neighbors over certain disputes. But military force, or coercive threats, constitute only a small subset of the thousands of interactions states engage in.[19] Truly powerful countries use their economic power and diplomatic influence to persuade other countries to adopt policies more consistent with their own.[20] Persuasion is often a more effective method. The concept of power, then, is one that has many faces. One face is the battleship, the tank—of military force. Another, less obvious one is the oil tanker, the merchant vessel, or the bustling port—of economic strength. Still another is the diplomat, who, while representing his or her country's military and economic power, artfully persuades diplomats of other countries with the written and spoken word.

No country is all-powerful, no matter which face one examines. All nations must interact with one another as they make their way. Some are better endowed and better organized and so have greater success in achieving their own interests, in controlling events, and in affecting how the world is organized.[21]

But even this is an oversimplistic and idealized representation of power in international relations, because states not only compete with one another, but they also must increasingly take into account the capabilities of other nonstate actors such as corporations, IGOs, NGOs, and individuals. We must turn our attention for the moment then to the types of capabilities these other actors possess.

Assessing the Capabilities of Nonstate Actors

Like states, nonstate actors possess certain capabilities that enable them to have influence in international relations. As we have seen, population, military capacity, geographical factors, and economic wealth are key factors in the power of states. With the exception of military capacity, the capabilities of nonstate actors can also be defined in these terms. Most nonstate actors have a population base (defined as a membership or work force), financial resources, and some kind of a geographical base, often involving more than one country. The Catholic church, for instance, has hundreds of millions of adherents in virtually every country around the globe and a rather staggering degree of financial wealth. Similarly, multinational corporations employ millions of people throughout the world and control billions of dollars of assets.[22] Some corporations have subsidiaries in dozens of foreign countries. Thus, a decision made at the headquarters of a multinational corporation may affect the lives of people in many other countries. A corporation such as General Motors, which employs more than eight hundred thousand people, has gross annual sales that exceed the gross national product of all but a dozen countries, serves literally millions of customers around the world, and has a vast global management network, is bound to exercise considerable influence on the countries in which it operates, especially in terms of its investment and management decisions. Other nonstate actors, such as terrorist organizations, IGOs, and NGOs, have financial resources, a geographical base and reach, and memberships. Let us take a closer look at each of these nonstate actors, starting with multinational corporations.

Multinational corporations   **Multinational corporations** are increasingly important actors on the international scene. Whether Motorola pulls its investments out of South Africa or Honda opens new plants in the United States, corporate decisions about where to invest or disinvest can have a significant economic impact on the countries concerned. Multinational corporations (MNCs) are distinguished by three characteristics: (1) they are big, (2) they have business operations in at least one but usually many more countries, and (3) their **subsidiaries** in other countries are subordinate to the home office in the parent country.[23] For all of these reasons, corporations can play an influential role in international relations.

Let's take a look at the size factor first. If the wealth of nations (based on gross national product) is compared to that of corporations (based on gross annual sales), the result is a surprising one as table 4.2 illustrates. Dozens of MNCs are wealthier than over half of the countries in the world, Exxon, Royal Dutch Petrol, and General Motors have gross annual sales that match the GNP of Austria, Romania, Yugoslavia, or Iran. Indeed, as table 4.2 shows, forty of the wealthiest one-hundred economic entities in the world are MNCs. Clearly, these are not only wealthy but also very powerful organizations. Indeed, their number, size, and scope has grown in the last several decades.[24]

The fact that MNCs are big is further enhanced by the fact that they have business operations in many countries (hence the term *multinational*). No one country can control the MNCs' business and economic activities. The subsidiary branches ultimately owe their allegiance to the home office in the parent country. The idea of national businesses with specific national loyalties has been swiftly overtaken by businesses that presumably have a more cosmopolitan flavor but that still retain the same overriding concern as their nationalistic precursors—making a profit. Indeed businesses become multinational to make money by reducing costs and diversifying their risks. Although they have a country of origin—a parent country—their investment decisions are not always consistent with the parent country's interests. Despite some misgivings, many host countries have welcomed corporate investments as a way to stimulate economic growth. But there are many drawbacks in inviting corporate investment, especially for poorer countries that are less able to monitor corporate activities. For these countries, opening their economies to external penetration by corporations can be a double-edged sword. Corporations can be formidable competitors to the parent country and the host countries as well.

However, several factors limit the MNCs' capacity to exercise all of their potential influence on international relations. First, MNCs compete primarily with other corporations rather than with states. The focus of corporate activity is to win markets and to outperform business competitors. If MNCs could ever unify or pool their rather impressive resources, they would be formidable indeed. But they tend to be a rather diverse, competitive group. For instance, although American multinational corporations are still numerically in the majority, non-American corporations are gradually increasing in relative number. Particularly interesting has been the emergence of a growing number of Third World multinationals.[25] Second, although MNCs have substantial economic power, it is difficult to see how it might be translated into political influence. Indeed, one expert has observed that, apart from a few isolated examples such as oil corporations, MNCs have not had a significant impact

Table 4.2

Comparative wealth of countries and multinational corporations

Rank	Country/ Multinational Corporation	Gross National Product/Sales (million $U.S.)	Rank	Country/ Multinational Corporation	Gross National Product/Sales (million $U.S.)
1	United States	3,056,900	51	Algeria	45,345
2	Soviet Union	1,563,000	52	*Ford Motor*	44,455
3	Japan	1,190,000	53	Philippines	41,676
4	West Germany	757,085	54	*Texaco*	41,147
5	France	627,306	55	Greece	40,888
6	United Kingdom	530,725	56	*IBM*	40,810
7	PRC (China)	302,500	57	Thailand	38,526
8	Canada	279,089	58	Colombia	38,186
9	Brazil	274,740	59	*Sears Roebuck*	35,883
10	Spain	204,240	60	*Dupont*	35,769
11	Mexico	196,350	61	Egypt	34,427
12	India	184,128	62	*Nissho Iwai*	33,067
13	Australia	169,037	63	Pakistan	33,024
14	Saudi Arabia	156,382	64	Kuwait	30,437
15	Netherlands	154,257	65	*Cargill*	30,000
16	Poland	145,610	66	*Phibro-Salomon*	29,757
17	East Germany	117,270	67	*Standard Oil Ind.*	29,494
18	Sweden	115,409	68	*Standard Oil Ca.*	29,182
19	Switzerland	108,556	69	*BP Oil*	29,173
20	Belgium	107,877	70	United Arab Emirates	29,168
21	*Exxon*	97,288	71	*Gulf Oil*	28,887
22	Argentina	89,490	72	*Atlantic Richfield*	27,455
23	Indonesia	89,450	73	Libya	27,120
24	Czechoslovakia	85,140	74	Iraq	27,100
25	South Africa	82,339	75	Malaysia	26,811
26	Nigeria	77,217	76	*General Electric*	26,797
27	*Royal Dutch Petrol*	77,123	77	New Zealand	25,391
28	South Korea	75,090	78	Chile	25,158
29	*General Motors*	74,582	79	*ENI* (Italy)	25,022
30	Austria	74,468	80	Portugal	24,719
31	Romania	71,090	81	*ERI* (Italy)	24,518
32	Yugoslavia	70,530	82	*Toyota*	22,927
33	Iran	69,700	83	Peru	22,040
34	*AT&T*	69,403	84	*Chevron*	22,000
35	Venezuela	69,068	85	Israel	21,210
36	*Mitsui*	64,439	86	*Unilever*	20,599
37	Turkey	63,746	87	*Arco*	20,000
38	Denmark	63,138	88	*Shell Oil*	19,883
39	*Mitsubishi*	62,984	89	*INI* (Spain)	18,271
40	*Mobil*	58,988	90	*Elf Aquitaine*	18,188
41	Norway	58,844	91	*Veda Aktiengeselisch*	18,058
42	Hungary	55,420	92	*Conoco*	18,000
43	*Iton C*	53,618	93	Morocco	17,575
44	Finland	52,349	94	Ireland	17,569
45	*Mobil Oil Corporation*	50,607	95	*U.S. Steel*	17,523
46	Taiwan	49,364	96	North Korea	17,500
47	*Marubewi*	47,869	97	*Toyomenka Kaisha*	17,465
48	*British Petrol*	47,102	98	Cuba	17,400
49	*Sumitomo*	46,968	99	*Hitachi Ltd.*	17,392
50	Bulgaria	46,030	100	Syria	15,892

SOURCES: Country GNP from Ruth L. Sivard, *World Military and Social Expenditures, 1985* (Washington, D.C.: World Priorities, 1986). Company sales from Ward's Business Directory, vol. 3, *Major International Companies, 1985* (Detroit: Gale Research, Inc., 1985).

on international politics.[26] Rather, when MNCs have exerted influence over political situations, they have done so not as independent actors, but as instruments of their home governments.[27] Other studies show that MNCs usually have rather narrow, specific economic objectives, while governments often expect much broader, positive results from investments.[28] Tensions between governments and MNCs, then, may be a product of these different economic expectations rather than a result of MNC efforts to manipulate host country politics. Third, corporations are subject to the states' legal authority. The MNCs may find ways to outmaneuver this legal authority, but the states have the ultimate regulatory authority. Finally, MNCs have no direct capacity (or in most cases even an interest) to protect themselves by developing a military capacity. They rely instead on governments to maintain law and order, which is indispensable to the maintenance of a healthy investment climate. If these factors limit the MNCs' capacity to exercise influence in international relations, they do not change the fact that corporations have considerable economic power, and that MNCs can individually and collectively influence the decisions of governments in ways that will protect their interests.

Students of international relations have tried to determine which actor—states or corporations—is dominant in their mutual relations. In the early 1970s many experts were convinced that corporations had eclipsed the states' capacity to exercise sovereignty.[29] By the late 1970s, however, a "new orthodoxy" emerged as scholars began to stress the resurgence of the state and to conclude that corporations had been put back on a leash.[30] Governments were regulating corporations, forming national business enterprises and cartels to compete with them, nationalizing foreign holdings, and developing transnational codes of conduct for MNCs.

Other experts dissent from the new orthodoxy, believing that the resurgence of the state may be more apparent than real. One study finds that MNCs have been able to ignore and circumvent numerous regulations through various legal and illegal means (e.g., negotiated exemptions, management manipulations, bribery). In so doing, MNCs have demonstrated an ability to maintain control over their operations, despite governmental efforts to ensure greater **indigenization** (local control) of corporate interests.[31] States have responded with considerable vigor to the challenge posed by corporations, however, MNCs have demonstrated considerable agility in resisting governments that have tried to regulate and control their holdings. This is an ongoing struggle that is likely to continue for some time without a decisive victor, because states and MNCs have rather formidable capabilities that can be employed to resist one another.

Churches Like multinational corporations, churches are transnational in character in that they have congregations in many different countries. A central hierarchy or congress of national church organizations may exist to set church policy and make doctrinal decisions that apply to members around the world. The Catholic church, which was very influential in international relations during the Middle Ages, is a classic example of a transnational organization. Other churches are much more decentralized. Buddhism and Islam, for instance, have no central church hierarchy but are nonetheless very influential religions. Table 4.3 provides a size breakdown of the world's major religions. The "population" of a church is only a crude measure of its global influence. A church cannot call on its population in quite the same way a country can: It cannot draft them, send them to war, or tax them in any direct way. Participation in a church is voluntary, whereas citizenship carries certain civic and legal obligations. Still, it would be a mistake to discount the role of the world's major religions and church organizations in international relations.

Table 4.3

The population base of major world religions

Christianity	
Roman Catholicism	628,000,000
Protestantism	373,000,000
Eastern Orthodox	63,000,000
Total	1,064,000,000
Islam	554,000,000
Hinduism	461,000,000
Buddhism	250,000,000
Confucianism	158,000,000
Shinto	32,000,000
Taoism	20,000,000
Judaism	17,000,000

SOURCE: *The World Almanac and Book of Facts* (New York: Newspaper Enterprise Association, 1986), p. 336. The membership criteria used by each group varies. Catholics use baptism, while Protestants count only those who have formally joined a church. Most other religions do not keep formal records, so these figures are only rough estimates.

Let us consider for a moment the largest single church organization in the world: the Catholic church. Although it may be less influential in international politics today than it was in the past, it is an important global actor. The church's diplomatic arm is still very active. The Vatican maintains formal diplomatic relations with many states and has interceded as a mediator in disputes between countries with large Catholic populations. For instance, the Vatican mediated a dispute between Argentina and Chile over territorial rights in the Beagle Channel. In addition, as table 4.3 shows, the Catholic church claims over 600 million adherents around the world. Of course, as Joseph Stalin once observed, the church has no "divisions," no army or military structure, but an active pope such as John Paul II can exert political influence. For instance, a word from John Paul II could get Poland's Solidarity labor movement (which, ironically, now governs Poland) to exercise restraint and even cooperate with Poland's communist former government. Although the communist government welcomed conciliatory efforts by Pope John Paul II, who is a Pole, they were less pleased with his criticism of the government's human rights record and social policies.

The power of the Catholic church extends beyond a Polish pope's influence in his homeland. The church has taken a strong position in the nuclear arms debate, and its teachings on moral and social questions clearly have a political impact. Even when the church acts on matters that are solely within its jurisdiction, such as in canonization of saints, it can create a political stir. In June 1988, Rome canonized 117 Vietnamese and foreign Roman Catholic martyrs persecuted by Vietnamese rulers during the seventeenth and eighteenth centuries. The current government in Hanoi viewed this action as a glorification of the colonial period and protested it as interference in Vietnam's national sovereignty and belittlement of its prestige. The government summoned Vietnam's Catholic bishops to Hanoi and lodged a formal protest against them.

The Catholic church is only one example of the impact of churches and religion on international politics. Many other religious organizations have significant influence on international politics. The Lutheran church, for instance, is very active in Scandinavian countries—such as Denmark, Finland, Iceland, Norway, and Sweden—where Lutherans constitute as much as 90 percent of the population. Cooperation among Nordic countries is enhanced by this religious commonality. Similarly, Islam remains a powerful influence in policies pursued by many governments in Africa, the Middle East, and Asia. In many countries Islam is the official religion, and a global pan-Islamic conference is now held annually so that governments in the Islamic world can discuss their differences and coordinate their policies. Where religion is a common bond, churches can promote greater cooperation among nations.

But history teaches us that religions have also been the occasion of bitter conflict as well. Nor is such conflict a thing of the past, as several contemporary examples suggest. The Dalai Lama, the exiled political and religious leader of Tibet, is a religious figure who continues to command significant support among Tibetan activists who call for Tibetan independence and oppose Chinese occupation. During 1987–1988, trouble flared in Tibet as Buddhist monks, followers of the Dalai Lama, led often violent protests against Chinese occupation. In India Sikh religious groups have engaged Indian troops in violent gun battles. In the Middle East conflicts between Jews and Arabs within Israel and among Israel and her neighbors occasion considerable violence. As long as religion remains a part of the human experience, churches will play a role in the incidence of conflict and in efforts to promote peace within and among nations.

Nongovernmental organizations   In recent years, private, nonprofit, nongovernmental groups have joined corporations as increasingly vocal and influential actors on the international scene.[32] More numerous even than MNCs, NGOs deal with every conceivable aspect of international relations. Their influence on big issues such as war and peace may only be marginal today, but in countless other areas such as humanitarian aid, education, science, social affairs, cultural and economic development, religion, medicine, and law their contributions have been significant. In other words, NGOs tend to be more active in low politics than in high politics. Nongovernmental organizations derive their influence from their knowledge of and expertise in particular subjects that are of international significance and concern. In this way they can serve as international interest groups, as focal points for the mobilization and articulation of interests shared by people living in different countries. Nongovernmental organizations often have affiliated organizations, which have the same or at least similar goals, in more than one country. Nongovernmental organizations have access to private and public resources to fund their activities. They lobby governments and international agencies to effect policies that are consistent with the organization's objectives. They are not in a position to exercise physical coercion—to force governments to do anything—but they do increasingly function as the moral and ethical conscience of international relations, prodding governments to take steps more consistent with humanitarian values and reminding them when they fail to do so. The work of organizations such as the Red Cross, Amnesty International, and The Lawyers Committee for Human Rights are especially noteworthy, but similar efforts by literally hundreds of NGOs are also significant. Governments may not always pay much attention to world opinion when it varies with national interests, but NGOs are closing the gap between domestic and world opinion. When pressures come not only from world opinion but from domestically based organizations that are tied to global NGO networks, states may find it increasingly difficult to remain deaf to NGO appeals.

In the areas of human rights, humanitarian aid, development assistance, and scientific cooperation, to mention a few, nongovernmental organizations are especially significant. Indeed, many governments now rely on them to implement humanitarian assistance projects. When the United States sent food to famine-stricken Ethiopia in 1985, CARE, Catholic Relief Services, and other private voluntary organizations distributed it. Thus, NGOs do not always, or even most of the time, find themselves in an adversarial role with governments. Rather, they are often engaged in joint efforts to meet mutual humanitarian objectives.

Intergovernmental organizations   Unlike MNCs or NGOs, intergovernmental organizations are created by states and thus are directly answerable to them. Nevertheless, IGOs have increased dramatically in number in this century and have been important actors in dealing with routine interactions among states and at times with more critical political disputes. Hundreds of IGOs deal with almost every conceivable aspect of international relations. They spend hundreds of millions of dollars every year on peacekeeping, social and humanitarian welfare, economic development programs, cultural and scientific exchanges, and many other activities. An IGO's capabilities depend on the mandate given it by its member-states. Its capabilities depend on the size of its budget, the scope of its activities, the number of its members, and the ongoing support (political as well as financial) that its members are willing to provide. It is important to distinguish here between success and influence. An IGO with a limited mandate may be very successful in achieving the objectives for which it was created. But if its charge deals with rather routine matters, its influence cannot be viewed as too significant. On the other hand, an IGO may have a rather extensive mandate (such as the United Nations, the Organization of African Unity, or the European Communities) and be only marginally successful in pursuing all of its objectives. However, an intergovernmental organization may exercise considerable influence on certain issues and prove to be a very useful tool for resolving states' differences on these issues. Such an organization might be considerably more influential than its apparently more successful counterpart with a limited mandate.

The historical and contemporary role of IGOs in international relations is explored in much greater depth in chapter 9. For now we merely want to underscore that IGOs often mediate disputes between nations, initiate literally hundreds of international conferences annually, and coordinate cooperative efforts in the humanitarian and development fields. Despite recent cutbacks, their budgets are at substantially higher levels today than four decades ago, and the number of functions that states have delegated to them has also expanded greatly. In short, IGOs are more broadly active today than ever before in coordinating and facilitating international relations, even if their capacity to act autonomously is constrained by their constitutional link to the states that created them.[33]

Terrorist and insurgent groups   Terrorists are increasingly visible actors in international relations.[34] They sometimes act as individuals but more commonly as agents of organized political groups that are seeking to overthrow existing governments, seize power from them, and gain recognition from the international community. The Palestine Liberation Organization and its various splinters and factions command the loyalty of significant numbers of people, some of whom are terrorists. Liberation groups can influence world events and affect the foreign policies of nations. These groups may or may not be recognized as legitimate by other nations, but there can be little doubt, especially in recent years, that liberation groups have a significant impact on world affairs.[35]

The success of such groups often depends on the degree of foreign support they can attract. For instance, the *contras,* an insurgent group in Nicaragua, depended almost solely on the United States for aid to fight a guerrilla war against their country's Sandinista government. The contras' power, and their ability to challenge the Sandinista government—which lost power in a recent democratic election—was closely related to U.S. congressional grants of military assistance and CIA support. Insurgent groups can ultimately be successful only if they can capture the support of the local populations. Thus, in addition to outside aid, popular support is a critical dimension of an insurgent group's capabilities. Groups that lack both outside and internal support are unlikely to fare well. Those having both support systems are likely to be more successful. Assuming that some degree of popular domestic support exists for such groups, the outcome of contests between insurgent groups and existing governments to a large extent depends on which contestant other countries choose to support. Thus, although insurgent groups such as the African National Congress in South Africa and the *contras* of Nicaragua have much greater visibility in recent years, they could not have made headway without the support of outside governments. In short, groups that can insinuate themselves into the larger international political agenda are more likely to survive, and in these circumstances the policies of states will be most decisive in the outcome of their quests for power.

Terrorism, in particular, like insurgent activities more generally, has waxed and waned over the years. States have been increasingly preoccupied by terrorism in the 1980s. Whether we refer to the hijackings of the 1960s or the bombings, kidnappings, and assassinations of the 1980s, threats of violence and violence itself are the terrorists' primary tools. They have captured the attention of the global news media, excited military retaliation between governments victimized by terrorism and those thought to be responsible for sponsoring terrorism, caused the dismissal of diplomats, reduced tourism and travel to certain parts of the world, and elicited counterterrorist programs in many countries.[36] Terrorist networks exist within and between countries. International financing networks help and arm terrorists. Certain governments, such as Iran, Libya, and Syria, actually promote this activity, making it even more difficult to control. Terrorism has become an integral part of international politics. Unlike other nonstate actors, however, terrorists are actively engaged in the high political game of war, coercion, violence, and force.[37] They initiate violence against citizens of certain countries and have become, in turn, the direct target of retaliation by the governments of those countries. We undertake a more extensive discussion of terrorism in chapter 7.

Individuals Assessing the capabilities of individuals as international actors is perhaps more difficult than the assessments we have conducted thus far.[38] Individuals are the most basic building block of international society. In the final analysis, all other actors are composed of individuals. There are about 5 billion individuals on our planet today, and they are all affected by international relations. Only a small proportion of the world's people, however, are actually engaged in international relations in some capacity, and of them only a small number are in very high positions of authority. Usually individuals do not become involved in international relations in their own capacity but rather as members of groups that have specific interests, views, and objectives. The president of a nation signs an international treaty not as an individual in his or her own right, but as the head of state—as the representative of the nation. A corporate executive agrees to an investment program in another country as a representative of the corporation. The secretary-general of the United Nations functions as an intermediary between states based on the official capacity of the position. Nevertheless, there can be little doubt that personality is a strong factor in how well individuals function in these positions.

It is important to study not only the individual, but also the role that he or she fills within the various kinds of groups (i.e., governments, NGOs, IGOs) that interact at the international level.[39] Nevertheless, it is the personal initiative, foresight, and charisma of individuals interacting with one another within and between groups that ultimately drives all politics, including international politics. Thus, we must consider how people think, perceive, and react in different roles to fully understand the interaction of states and nonstate actors. And we must not ignore individuals outside the collective setting. People-to-people contacts are also important. Every tourist is an ambassador for his or her country. Whether people spread good will or ill is not an insignificant issue, because the attitudes we have as individuals toward people of other nations multiplied many times over become the attitudes of one group or nation toward another.

Several examples help to illustrate the different ways in which individuals can make a mark on international relations. As we noted at the beginning of this chapter, perhaps the most effective international emissary in the Chernobyl nuclear accident was the American physician Robert Gale, whose efforts to save nuclear accident victims near the city of Kiev eventually overshadowed the more negative diplomatic interchanges between the Soviet and Western governments. Acting on his own initiative and with the aid of another individual, prominent American industrialist Armand Hammer, who has long-standing ties with leaders of the Soviet Union, Gale demonstrated that concerned people could have a positive impact on world affairs. (Gale is also the head of a private organization that monitors international needs for bone marrow transplants.)

Other individuals have also made significant positive contributions in international relations. Bob Geldof, the Irish rock star, was the driving force behind the organization of the Live Aid concert that raised about $100 million for African famine relief. Live Aid was courted by UN agencies and private voluntary organizations that coordinate and implement famine relief efforts, while African governments vied for a piece of Live Aid's resources. Unlike states, Live Aid cannot make war or sign a treaty, but it would be erroneous to suggest that it is not an important, if new, actor on the international scene.

Similarly, an old holy man living in exile in Paris became the most powerful political force in the undoing of the Shah of Iran in the late 1970s. His name was Ayatollah Khomeini, and his influence has since been felt not only in Iran but throughout the Middle East and the world. Even before Khomeini returned triumphantly to his homeland, the words he uttered from exile in Paris held more sway with the Iranian people than the edicts of the Shah, who, as far as the international community was concerned, was still the legal sovereign. In this case an individual—to be sure a very influential religious figure—successfully challenged the legitimacy of what had been one of the most imposing and powerful governments in the Middle East.

Basic Issues

In the following supplementary readings several basic issues are addressed: (1) Does the modern state effectively perform its traditional functions? (2) Are nonstate actors eroding the capacity of states to control international relations? and (3) What role should the state play in the future? In the Miller and Brown essays we find agreement and disagreement on these issues.

The continuing debate about the role of the state and other actors in the international system has excited the interest of many students of international relations. This debate is part of a larger debate between globalists who stress the growing interdependence in international relations and realists who stress the continuing predominance of states.[40] Globalists, such as Seyom Brown, believe that the role of states is slowly being eroded by nonstate actors. Others underscore this opinion, arguing that states are becoming less relevant in our contemporary global system, which is increasingly marked by "cascading interdependence."[41] Miller, and the realists, on the other hand, believe that interdependence is largely a myth, and that the state remains the centerpiece of international relations.[42]

Another aspect of the debate concerns the issue of self-determination, which has been a continuing concern in recent literature.[43] The concept of **self-determination** calls on states to grant independence to peoples who wish to control their own destiny. This powerful concept formed the under-pinning of the decolonization of the world after World War II. Unfortunately, many ethnic groups around the world still aspire to self-determination. Many of these claims are against the newly independent countries of the Third World themselves. Most claims to self-determination are opposed by states that assert sovereign jurisdiction over their lands and that jealously guard their right of territorial integrity. Many of the conflicts that have wracked the international system in recent years originated in disputes between governments and secessionist groups that seek either to overthrow or to gain independence from an existing government. Often, secessionist groups will resort to guerrilla war or terrorism to promote their cause. One might dispute the right of the Palestine Liberation Organization, South Molluccans, the Sikhs of India, or Tamils of Sri Lanka to kill innocent civilians in order to achieve their goals of self-determination, but no one would deny that insurgent groups such as these have become increasingly visible actors in international relations. As Miller points out, however, groups do not challenge the state system itself, but rather the existence of individual countries.

Summary

Today there are no neat and clean divisions of interaction in the international system. Rather, as we have previously noted, the world has come to resemble a cobweb of interactions between many different kinds of actors.[44] It is still possible, of course, to identify patterns of behavior, such as the sending and receiving of diplomats, which are exclusively interstate activities. But interstate relations are being increasingly influenced by other nonstate actors. Military decisions and issues of war and peace, for instance, though still predominantly an interstate affair, often involve other actors. Many of today's international conflicts involve nonstate, insurgent, liberation, or terrorist groups. Similarly, in an area like arms control, churches and interest groups have become increasingly involved. Consider, for example, the U.S. Catholic Bishops' Pastoral letter on nuclear war or the various nuclear freeze and disarmament movements that have sprouted up in the United States and Europe in recent years.[45] Certainly in the less political, more economic sphere corporations, IGOs, and NGOs have been even more centrally involved. Each has an interest, a stake, and a role to play. How successful each actor is depends, as we have seen, on its capabilities.

As we leave our discussion of the actors in international relations, consider whether states are losing their capacity to control international relations. Are the nonstate actors slowly eroding state sovereignty? The evidence seems mixed. What is clear is that this century has been marked by the rapid proliferation of both state and nonstate actors. Nationalism continues to be a strong force in international relations, but international cooperation has also emerged to deal with problems that no single nation can solve on its own. Nonstate actors are clearly a permanent feature of the international landscape, and no doubt will continue to be essential ingredients to the effective operation of technical, economic, and humanitarian aspects of international affairs. Intergovernmental organizations, insurgent organizations, and terrorist groups, on the other hand, will no doubt continue to be important players in the arena of high politics. But the capabilities of states are yet to be overshadowed. States have accommodated their behavior to account for nonstate actors.

This accommodation has sometimes fostered cooperative relations, and sometimes conflict, between state and nonstate actors. But nonstate actors have accommodated their behavior as well. For better or worse, states still ultimately govern international system. This is a central reality of contemporary international relations. However, two other realities are equally clear. First, today's world is more complex, and no actor, even the most powerful state, can achieve its interests without taking into account the capabilities of the expanding and diverse range of state and nonstate actors that now populate the global arena. Second, as the role of economics in international politics grows, nonstate actors will play an increasingly important role in international relations in the next decade and well into the next century.

J. D. B. Miller

The Sovereign State and Its Future

...This article looks at some of the major developments involving the sovereign state in the past twenty-five years, considers the extent to which we can regard it as a significant category in the light of major differences between states in size, resources, and so forth, examines the advantages which it has in contemporary international relations, together with its characteristic domestic role, and asks what influences threaten its persistence and stability.

...[With the appearance of so many new states in recent years,] the question of...[their viability has been raised]. What is viability? It is obviously not the capacity to live without trading with others, or without seeking investment and aid from them; and it does not depend on getting help only on the strictest commercial terms. It is not being able to muster a modern defense force with the latest weapons. It is not balancing the budget or being able to repay all the loans which have been contracted. If viability is any or all of these thing, most modern states do not possess it. Yet they are regarded as independent and sovereign, or sufficiently so to be accepted.

It is now clear that there is no minimum size for a sovereign state. What matters is not so much the combination of resources which the prospective state can command as the approach likely to be taken toward it by its former colonial power, by its neighbors, by the major powers of the day, and by international organizations. If these approaches are favorable,...then the new state can be accepted into the community of existing states, can be provided with bilateral and multilateral aid of various kinds, and can form

SOURCE: From *International Journal* 39 (Summer 1984), pp. 284–301. Reprinted by permission in abridged form.

associations with other states of roughly like mind about international issues.

...A further development...which has given extra status to the newer sovereign states is the emergence of new groupings among them, designed to provide more weight and significance than the members could exert on their own. The Organization of African Unity (OAU), the Association of South-East Asian Nations (ASEAN), and the South Pacific Forum are examples. The most significant has been the so-called Group of 77, now containing many more members than that original number.... The effect of these bodies has been to enlarge, not restrict, the significance of the individual sovereign state, even when it is small and unimportant. The Group of 77 provides strength which [small] states could not secure on their own, while the regional bodies give them opportunities for expression which they would not get in more numerous company....

Just as international organizations in the United Nations complex have proved susceptible to management by sovereign states, rather than the other way round, so attempts at supranationalism and integration have proved to be susceptible—fatally so, in most cases—to the pressures and interests of the states composing them. Most of these projects have disappeared....

Summing up the effects of these developments in the past twenty-five years, one can say that we have a great many more sovereign states; that most of them are former colonies of the European powers; that some of them are very small; that this does not seem to have affected their capacity to survive; that there is a marked tendency for smaller states to be able to outface major states on political issues of vital importance; that there has been a considerable increase in associations of the newer states; that international organizations have become largely subservient to the demands of the Group of 77; and that in these organizations, as in attempts at supranational structures, the member states have been the dominant elements.

It is important, in using the term *sovereign states,* to recognize that they come in all shapes and sizes, and that, in practice, one is quite dissimilar from another.... If the dissimilarity between states is so marked, how can we call the sovereign state a significant category in human affairs? Are we justified in saying that there is such a thing as the sovereign state...?

The answer is to be found in both the international and domestic contexts. In the international, the first reason for regarding the sovereign state as a significant category is that the formal equality between states which is the foundation of diplomacy brings opportunities to the weak and restrictions to the strong. It stands in the way of the kind of universalized brutality which might otherwise characterize the international scene. It is a fiction, but a necessary and desirable fiction. It can provide time for an answer, caution about a provocation, the occasion for discussion, the necessity for formality, and the recognition of difficulties which draconian action might cause. It is no guarantee that violence will not be used or that reason will prevail. But it encourages the use of civilized procedures whereby disputes can be talked about and negotiations can continue. Such opportunities occur only while conditions are normal, that is, while warfare is not actually in progress; sometimes they are forsworn through the conviction of one state that it cannot be seen in company with another, as in the attitude of the Arab states toward Israel or that of the United States toward Cuba. They are nevertheless a valuable element in international relations. Without the assumption that there are sovereign states and that they are all equal for purposes of discourse, relationships would be much more tortured than they are.

Again, it can be argued from international experience that the sovereign state is significant because it is the way in which peoples have, voluntarily and involuntarily, organized their main connections with one another. Large masses of people are organized into states, roughly representing common interests. To a great extent, international relations are organized officially, not only in terms of these states' relationships with each other, but also in terms of the associations between groups of states, arranged regionally and in other ways representing presumed common interests. Small states, as we have seen, can augment their status in this way; large states court the groups of small states in order to achieve their ends in bilateral and multilateral negotiations. . . .

The domestic circumstances of sovereign states also show how effective is this form of social organization, and why it persists. If again we take the smaller excolonial states, those which would have once been regarded as unviable and incapable of sustaining their independence, we can see that the great majority can handle their own affairs, even if they do not conform to the highest standards which Western countries set themselves. There is now an interdependence of governmental methods, a confluence of lifestyles among the leaders of states, which helps to provide a certain minimum standard of government. This minimum is frequently provided by armies, which are the local custodians of order in unsettled and ethnically divided societies. One may not like military rule, but it is at least a recognizable form which need not consist solely of tyranny and which may provide the foundation on which a more pluralistic domestic system of government can be built. In addition, it is characteristic of the domestic structures of small states today that these are sustained in greater or less degree by international aid, which enables certain standards of administration and provision to be kept up. . . .

The satisfaction of peoples is the ultimate justification for the existence of sovereign states. . . . The family, the village, [and] the province have not shown themselves capable of providing citizens with the services which, at the present stage of technology and scientific development, they have a right to expect. . . . It is simply not the case that villages and their surrounding areas can produce much beyond foodstuffs; the products of higher technology, the social services which modern peoples demand, the protective arrangements which their industries require, can be provided only by the sovereign state. It is the state which acquires armaments, which regulates the currency, which encourages investment and contracts foreign loans, which makes alliances and conducts diplomatic démarches, which prohibits the entry of foreigners into the labor market, and which pays the forces who march past on national days. These are indispensable services. A perfect society might not need them; but the societies which we have are convinced that they are important.

. . .The sovereign state is clearly an institution which we keep having more of and which we can probably not do without. . . . For the time being and for as far ahead as we can see, we are landed with this entity which, while it can take all shapes and sizes, has a basic identity in terms of formal position in the eyes of other states and of the services which it provides for its citizens; these cannot be effectively furnished by other bodies in the same degree and to the same level. Experience suggests that [states] must exist. But what influences threaten the persistence and stability of the sovereign state?

In looking for them, we can quickly dismiss some which have been advanced as implacable enemies. These include international organizations and multinational corporations, which some imaginative projections have cast as bodies so powerful that they can subdue and in some respects replace the state. . . . International organizations and multinational corporations do make demands on Third World states; but these demands need not be met, and they can be resisted with quite significant weapons. If they are not met, there is little that the corporations and international organizations can do, except to withdraw their services from the state in question. . . .

We can disregard the notion, once popular among specialists in international relations, that there is an ineluctable force called integration, which destroys weak states in a particular area by causing them to seek incorporation with one another, or with neighboring strong states, in order to achieve a unit capable of standing on its own. It has proved to be inadequate in various Latin American situations. Only in respect of the European Communities does it appear to possess any force. . . . The point to keep in mind is that the status of [the] sovereign state provides opportunities for seeking survival that may transcend seemingly inevitable tendencies toward integration.

. . .We are left with genuine threats to the future of particular sovereign states, though not, I should think, to the institution of the sovereign state as such. Foremost among these is the problem of internal disunity, arising from resistance by ethnic minorities to the domination of groups which they regard as discriminatory and tyrannical. Some of these problems, in long-established states, can be disregarded; there would be a Spain if the Basques obtained their independence, and a France if Corsica were lost. However, what sort of Canada would there be without Quebec? And how much would Britain be changed without Scotland? Even in these instances of well-attested threats from minority movements, there would still be the likelihood that the main part of the state would survive, just as the Federal Republic of Germany survive[d] as a fair imitation of the Weimar Republic in spite of the amputation of East Germany. The real danger exists in new states in which ethnic conflict of a communal character was barely kept in check by the colonial masters, and in which the basis of the state rests on uneasy foundations. . . .

Yet it is fair to say that the dangers of disunity, while obvious from the direction taken by domestic politics in so many new states, have so far only rarely caused the destruction of states or even their dismemberment. Among the new states, India is the one case in which a major province, Pakistan, has been shorn off to satisfy an ethnic minority. . . . Indonesia and Nigeria have experienced insurrections, and India and Malaysia racial riots of disturbing proportions; but all four remain as sovereign states. Sri Lanka. . .has had disastrous ethnic clashes between Tamils and Sinhalese, but continues to exist as a single state. While ethnic conflict may in extreme cases destroy a state, it normally embitters relations between the communities, but does not prevent the government. . .from continuing in control.

There are at least two other grave dangers which sovereign states may experience. One is quarrels with neighbors. The Third World is replete with these. . .The quarrels may be about boundaries, ethnic differences, access to resources, and a variety of other issues. . . . It can be asserted, however, that although these quarrels threaten particular states, they do not threaten the sovereign state as an institution, any more than minority demands for separate states by Basques in Spain or Tamils in Sri Lanka may do. If anything, such dangers to existing states can lead only to the creation of more states, or of stronger ones, not to a blotting out of states as such.

A further threat to some states is incapacity to find the resources which will enable them to survive. This is a genuine problem of viability. It involves the degree of trade, investment, and foreign aid which a country can attract, rather than any quantification of its natural resources. . . .

Such problems and threats are genuine. . . . They [cause states] to cooperate in bodies like ASEAN and the OAU, but this cooperation involves a strong sense of the need to preserve national identity and independence. It would be foolish to expect anything else in the next quarter of a century.

Seyom Brown

The World Polity and the Nation-State

. . .The world polity, which can no longer be defined simply as a nation-state system, is turning into a polyarchy. The institutions and individuals who can "deliver the goods" across national borders and who therefore are both primary objects and actors in the diplomatic arena may or may not be official agencies of the nation-state in whose jurisdiction they reside or are permitted to operate. Increasingly, the nation-state system operates as a *sub*system, in competition with other subsystems, of a polyarchical world polity.

The dominant role of nation-states in the preservation of order and the allocation of values in the world polity is being challenged by other entities and movements—subnational, transnational, and supranational—which, relatively speaking, will continue to gain in appeal, authority, and power.

This is not to say that human communities are anywhere near ready to discard the organized nation-state as the performer of essential security and welfare functions or that relations between national governments are becoming peripheral to world politics.

The Nation-State System: An Appreciation

The nation-state system has two dimensions: (1) a "domestic" dimension, or the relations of the people within a country with one another and with the institutions of government; and (2) an "international" dimension, or the relations of one country with other countries.

SOURCE: From *International Journal* 39 (Summer 1984), pp. 509–528. Reprinted by permission in abridged form.

Each of the territorially demarcated countries into which all the people of the world now are divided. . .is supposed to retain sovereignty, in the sense of full legal authority, over what happens in that country. Each claims to be a self-governing community—a state—and generally is recognized by other such communities as having this independent political status. In each of these nation-states, ultimate authority and power are assumed to be lodged in a central government which is responsible for ensuring that the basic requirements of community life are maintained for the human beings within its jurisdiction—namely, law and order, . . .conditions that encourage industry and commerce, processes for maintaining community norms of justice, controls on the use of natural resources and the natural environment, and a common cultural base, especially language.

Despite the existence of alternative foci of social identification—religions, transnational ethnic and cultural groups, ideological movements—the government of the country within which individuals reside usually has an overriding claim on their loyalty. Only the government of one's own country has generally recognized authority and power to require an individual to put his own life at stake to defend the common interests of the population. It is primarily that same government which, in the name of law and order and justice, issues and implements the basic rules of social interaction which are to prevail throughout the country's territory. . . .

In the ideally functioning nation-state system, international relations are supposed to be restrained by the system's norm of state sovereignty: No country, no world or regional organization, no foreign citizen or organization has the right to act within the territory of another country without its consent. Intervention is not supposed to take place without permission. And any privileges obtained by foreigners to act within the territorial jurisdiction are supposed to be negotiated. In fact, of course, such sovereignty is often violated. Smaller, weaker countries are coerced by the more powerful into granting them privileges of access and entry; and to guard against this intervention from a hostile state, potential victims form alliances with powerful friendly countries, sometimes establishing a degree of dependence on their protectors which, paradoxically, requires them to accept an oppressive foreign presence, albeit voluntarily.

Nation-States and Public Order

Each nation-state has the responsibility for maintaining sufficiently peaceful conditions within its own jurisdiction to allow the inhabitants to engage in their normal domestic pursuits—agriculture, industry, trade, and cultural and family life—secure from violent attacks on themselves or their possessions.

To perform this public order function adequately, the central government of the nation-state normally is accorded a monopoly of violent weapons available in the country; or, short of such monopolization of violence, the central government is always expected to be able to overwhelm any private or local violence. The central government of the nation-state is also the locus of the main capabilities for protecting the territorial unit from outsiders who might penetrate its borders and violate persons or property—the function usually referred to as defending the "territorial integrity" of the country. . . .

Because of the unequal military power of countries, some of them are unable to satisfy their external security requirements without accepting material or direct help from friendly countries in order to balance the military power of an enemy. Thus, inherent in the right and expectation of national self-defense of the territorial unit is the right to form alliances. . . .

In reality, the function of maintaining public order in the world polity is still performed, however inadequately, through the operation of the nation-state system. There is no other institution, and no process other than voluntary negotiations among states to organize a balance of power, with the capacity to organize countervailing military power against a determined and powerful aggressor nation.

Nation-States and Commerce

The separate nation-states also create the basic conditions for economic relations within and between communities. The territorial confines of a nation-state, . . .usually mark the boundaries of highly organized trading communities or "markets." Foreigners usually must receive the permission of the national government to sell in its market and usually must convert their own currencies into the special national currency of the market in order to pay for purchases.

As communities of coordinated economic activity, the nation-states are specially responsible for providing for the construction and availability of transportation and communications networks to facilitate commerce within their jurisdictions and between them. . . .

International coordination to establish "rules of the road" and to avoid congestion has. . .been found to be highly desirable in the transportation and communications fields. Some of the most important "functional" international institutions operate in these fields. . . . Some of these agencies have been given international licensing authority; but the power to impose sanctions on violators of international rules is retained by national governments or their subunits. . . .

Nation-States and the Use of Natural Resources and the Environment

One of the main reasons for having systems of governance—states—is to control access to and exploitation of the natural resources used by a community, so that members can be assured of appropriate shares, vulnerable resources are kept in usable condition, and exhaustible resources are not too rapidly depleted. Because the location of natural resources is not always congruent with the borders of nation-states, coordination and cooperation among groups of them is often in their mutual self-interest. The nation-state system accordingly has developed associations of resource users in various fields. But, as is characteristic of all the functions where coordination has proved necessary, adherence to common standards and rules is voluntary. . . .

Nation-States and the Maintenance of Diverse Cultures

One of the most important functions the nation-state performs for human society is the provision of a home for particular ways of life. Under the protection of a particular legal-political system whose sovereignty is respected by other countries, special rules of morality, religious practice, language, music, and artistic and architectural creation can be encouraged and reserved in the face of those who may not sufficiently value the national culture. If such autonomous enclaves of culture were not provided with adequate protection, many of the cultural groups that now maintain their uniqueness might be homogenized into larger and more aggressive world cultures. The loss of cultural integrity is feared especially by societies that require disciplined adherence to religious rituals and specific family and sexual mores. The national governments representing these societies often attempt to prevent foreign telecommunications broadcasts and the free dissemination of literature from other cultures and frequently maintain tight restrictions on the activities of tourists and foreign commercial enterprises within their societies. . . .

The Nation-State System as an Inadequate Subsystem of the World Polity

The nation-state system has indeed proved to be a remarkably durable human invention—dating, in the eyes of many historians, back to the Treaty of Westphalia (1648) which ended the wars of religion—and there is no prospect of its total collapse so long as the great powers avoid stumbling into World War III. However, day by day the evidence grows that neither the separate nation-states nor the system of relations between them can adequately perform the standard tasks of governance. A manifestation of this inadequacy is the proliferation of transnational and subnational organizations and movements—representing diverse religious, ethnic, geographic, economic, and professional groups and interests—which are allocating resources and values and managing conflict (often unsuccessfully) within and among themselves, and as often as not bypassing the institutions of the central national government. Increasingly, the span of political authority and legal control of the nation-states are revealed to be incongruent with the intense clusters of interaction between peoples. "Nations," as it were, do not match states; economies have become disjoined from polities; those who profoundly affect one another's lives are often not politically or legally accountable to one another.

Deficiencies as a World Order System

The ability of the nation-state system to maintain world public order and to preserve the sovereign independence of its members, large and small, has depended on credible alliance commitments designed to redress imbalances of military power which might tempt aggressor nations. The viability of this equilibrating mechanism of the system has been cast into severe doubt by the development of weapons that have made all states—even the superpowers— unconditionally vulnerable to virtually total destruction. . . .

Deficiencies as a Regulator of the Transnational Economy

The ability of the nation-state system to ensure that public safety, orderly commerce, social justice, and cultural integrity are sustained within the territorial confines of particular countries is undermined when national policies for regulating the national market can be ignored or overwhelmed by buyers and sellers unaccountable to the political and legal institutions of the nation. . . .

The incapacity of national governments and the governments of local subdivisions of nation-states to regulate the transnational economy does not bode well for the effectiveness of social policies designed to transfer resources and other benefits from the more successful competitive members of society to those handicapped in some way for competition in the market. If corporations are able to relocate production facilities to avoid paying high wages and benefits to their labor forces and to avoid high taxes, or if they can avoid local taxes by transnational relocations of financial assets within the corporation, then, in many countries, the fruits of decades of domestic political struggle

to legislate "progressive" redistributions of income will be left to wither.

Developing countries anxious to attract foreign investment and manufacturing subsidiaries—despite standard Third World rhetoric against the multinational corporation— are competing with each other to assure international corporate managers that there will be few onerous restrictions on their activities and that they will not have to hand over a large part of the subsidiary's earnings to the host-country government.

A more subtle effect of the overbearing influence of the transnational economy on society is its erosion of diverse cultural forms. The global market tends to be a great homogenizer. . . . Cultural uniqueness is often economically inefficient, and its preservation therefore requires intervention in the name of the community's noneconomic values. The preservation of cultural diversity has been one of the main contributions of the nation-state system to world society. . . . [But] the increasingly inadequate reach of national governments into the functioning of the transnational economy, involving as it often does a loss of control over what comes into the domestic market, is depriving world society of perhaps its only existing effective means of husbanding the pluralism that has hitherto stimulated mankind's proudest accomplishments in the realms of philosophy, literature, fine arts, science, and even technological-economic development.

Insufficient Ability to Protect the Natural Environment

. . . Humans have learned to produce large-scale and severe alterations of the environment affecting the health of ecosystems that traverse national lines and are sometimes global in scope. Yet in most regions of the globe there are no legal mechanisms which the nationals of an affected country can invoke to compel actors engaging in disturbing actions in another country's jurisdiction, or even in such "commons" as the high seas or outer space, to consult with them or to be held in any way internationally accountable for the damage inflicted on commonly used resources.

Prognosis: Anarchy or Polyarchy?

A situation of anarchy prevails where individuals or groups are accountable to no one but themselves for what they do to others. In the world polity, under the nation-state system, while there might at times and places have seemed to be virtual anarchy between the states, the states themselves. . . have been able to maintain relatively effective systems of governance within their borders. Nevertheless, the conditions necessary to avoid anarchy even within the nation-states are being undermined by new material and social forces which neither the separate national governments nor the nation-state *system* seem able to contain.

First, given today's military technologies, war, if it does break out between certain nation-states, can rapidly... become total war—leaving a heap of smoldering radioactive rubble where civilization once held sway.

Second, because of the growing interdependence of states and the swiftness with which resources and other assets can be transferred in and out of national jurisdictions by transnational corporate enterprises and financial networks, national polities have been losing a good part of their capacity for self-government. The most powerful economic actors and agencies...can affect the lives of large numbers of the world's population, while remaining substantially impervious to controls legislated by popular parliaments and not legally accountable to any agencies representing the interests of the communities they affect.

Third, technological developments have given nation-states an increasing ability to disrupt the conditions of life within each other's jurisdictions through environmental actions, which are transmitted through nature's vast web of interlinked ecosystems. The conventional instruments of statecraft...appear inadequate to the task of subordinating environment-damaging technologies to the civil needs of the world polity or even to the purposes of domestic polities.

A drift toward anarchy is certainly plausible.... [However], where national governments have been losing their grip, provincial or local governments have been moving in to take up the slack, often negotiating trade and investment arrangements with similar subunits of government in other countries. Where public organizations have faltered in providing essential social amenities to inhabitants of national or local commonwealths, nongovernmental associations of self-help (often catering to members of particular religious or ethnic groups) have stepped into the void. Moreover, unregulated markets are hardly anarchic; the regime of supply and demand, where it holds sway, creates its own incentives for public order, stability of contract and monetary relationships, and even a certain amount of justice.

Not anarchy but *polyarchy* is the more appropriate concept for describing and understanding the emergent patterns in the world polity. In a polyarchic system there is no dominant structure for managing cooperation and conflict. Nation-states, subnational groups, transnational special interests, and communities, all compete for the support and loyalty of individuals....

The model for such a world system is the modern, ethnically diverse greater metropolitan area, such as New York or Los Angeles. These megalopolises comprise numerous municipal and special-purpose jurisdictions, many of which overlap, but they lack a strong central government for the whole metropolitan area. The polyarchic "global city" could exhibit an analogous structure. Public services—physical safety, education, cultural activities, public utilities—could be largely provided within locally demarcated political units (some of them still the smaller nation-states of the traditional international system); but where a high degree of coordination is required across national boundaries—air travel and telecommunications, and the use of the oceans, great river systems, the atmosphere, and outer space—multinational or transnational institutions, with memberships and spans of control congruent with the interdependent relationships, could be accorded the responsibility for coordination, rule making, and even rule enforcement.

The nation-states surely have a crucial role to play in the polyarchic world as far ahead as we can see. But it is time that we start to view them as only one element of the world polity rather than its essence.

Study Questions

1. What criterion determines whether an entity can be called an international actor?
2. What are primary and secondary actors? Give examples and explain.
3. What kinds of capabilities are likely to increase a country's power?
4. How does geography affect a country's power?
5. Does a large population necessarily make a country powerful? Explain.
6. Discuss the role of economic and military factors in determining a country's power.
7. What are some intangible or psychological elements of a country's power?
8. Discuss the differences between natural, synthetic, and psychological elements of power. Give examples of each.

9. Which of these three major types of power seems to be the most important factor in success in disputes and wars?
10. What is meant by the terms *high politics* and *low politics*? Why is this distinction important in studying the role of nonstate actors?
11. Name the key characteristics of multinational corporations.
12. Why are MNCs increasingly influential actors in international relations?
13. What factors limit the capacity of MNCs to develop state power?
14. In international relations today, which is the more powerful actor—states or MNCs?
15. Why are intergovernmental organizations considered secondary actors?
16. In what ways do IGOs affect international relations?
17. In what ways can individuals become actors in international relations?
18. What activities are nongovernmental organizations most likely to pursue? What kinds of influence do they have? Why?
19. Under what circumstances are insurgent groups likely to succeed? least likely to succeed?
20. How do terrorists influence international relations?
21. Is conflict limited to relations between states? In what ways might other actors cause conflict? In what ways might they help to resolve it?
22. Does the modern state effectively perform its functions? Contrast Miller's and Brown's views in your answer.
23. Are nonstate actors in a position to supplant the power of the state? Cite arguments made by Miller and Brown.
24. According to Brown and Miller, what key functions do states perform? Do they perform these functions well?
25. Do you believe, as Brown does, that the state system is inadequate? Why or why not?
26. What does Brown mean by the term *polyarchy*?
27. What are the differences between globalists and realists in terms of the future of the state as the dominant international actor?
28. Do claims to self-determination threaten the state system? Why or why not?
29. Why doesn't Miller think that corporations are a threat to states, or that regional integration will make states obsolete?

Key Terms

high politics	primary actors
indigenization	psychological capabilities
legitimacy	secondary actors
low politics	self-determination
multinational corporations	subsidiaries
natural capabilities	synthetic capabilities

Notes

1. It should be noted that the origins of at least one nongovernmental organization, the Rosicrucian Order, can be traced back to the 1600s. For a discussion of the growth

of NGOs, see Kjell Skjelsbaek, "The Growth of International Nongovernmental Organizations in the Twentieth Century," *International Organization* 25 (Summer 1971): 420–442.

2. Robert H. Jackson and Carl S. Rosberg, "Why Africa's Weak States Persist: The Empirical and the Juridical in Statehood," *World Politics* 35, no. 1 (October 1982): 1–24. In this article, the authors explore various definitions of the state and draw heavily on the distinction between actual and legal capacities to govern.

3. The most exhaustive theoretical discussion of nonstate actors and the challenges they present to states can be found in Richard W. Mansbach, Yale H. Ferguson, and Donald E. Lampert, *The Web of World Politics: Non-State Actors in the Global System* (Englewood Cliffs, N.J.: Prentice-Hall, 1976).

4. The literature, for instance, on nonstate actors as *nonstate actors* is rather sparse. Two notable works touching on a range of nonstate actors include Mansbach, Ferguson, and Lampert, *The Web of World Politics;* and Phillip Taylor, *Non-State Actors in International Politics: From Transregional to Sub-State Organizations* (Boulder: Westview, 1984). Other works on particular actors are available, including works on terrorism, multinational corporations, intergovernmental organizations, and nongovernmental organizations. Many of these sources are cited in this reference list.

5. See Taylor, *Non-State Actors in International Politics,* pp. 203–209.

6. Jeffrey Hart, "Three Approaches to the Measurement of Power in International Relations," *International Organization* 30 (1976): 289–305, especially p. 303.

7. D. Baldwin, "Power Analysis and World Politics," *World Politics* 31 (1979): 161–194.

8. For efforts to measure power, see Ray Cline, *World Power Assessment: A Calculus of Strategic Drift* (Boulder: Westview, 1977); and, Wayne Ferris, *The Power Capabilities of Nation-States* (Lexington, Mass.: Heath, 1973).

9. For a careful discussion of those circumstances in which military power, expenditures, and allocations are important, see Frank W. Wayman, J. David Singer, and Gary Goertz, "Capabilities, Allocations, and Success in Militarized Disputes and Wars, 1916–1976," *International Studies Quarterly* 27, no. 4 (December 1983): 497–515.

10. Stephen Rosen, "War, Power, and the Willingness to Suffer," in *Peace, War, and Numbers,* ed. Bruce Russett (Newbury Park, Calif.: Sage, 1972), pp. 167–183; A. F. K. Organski and J. Kugler, "Davids and Goliaths: Predicting Outcomes of International Wars," *Comparative Political Studies* 11, no. 2 (1978): 141–180; and A. Mack, "Why Big Nations Lose Small Wars: The Politics of Asymmetrical Conflict," *World Politics* 27 (1975): 175–200.

11. See A. Mack, "Why Big Nations Lose Small Wars," especially pp. 177–179 and passim for a discussion of the Vietnam case in particular.

12. Examples of states that have not sought such a capability include Costa Rica, Iceland, and Gambia. Ironically, the latter recently became federated with its larger neighbor, Senegal. Before the federation the president of Gambia was forced to turn to Senegal for assistance to put down a coup attempt, because Gambia had no domestic forces.

13. For greater elaboration on the role of the extractive capability, see Organski and Kugler, "Davids and Goliaths"; and Alan C. Lamborn, "Power and the Politics of Extraction," *International Studies Quarterly* 27, no. 2 (1983): 125–146.

14. This typology of the elements of national power is employed in Walter Jones, *The Logic of International Relations* (Boston: Little, Brown, 1985), pp. 248–258.

15. Wayman, Singer, and Goertz, "Capabilities, Allocations, and Success," pp. 497–513.

16. Ibid., pp. 504–508.

17. Organski and Kugler, "Davids and Goliaths," pp. 143–145, 175.

18. Paul Kennedy, *The Rise and Fall of the Great Powers: Economic Change and Military Conflict from 1500–2000* (London: Fontana Press, 1988).

19. See, for instance, the rather diverse number and types of interaction catalogued in the World Events Interaction Survey (a research project and data bank). This survey is described in McClelland, C. A., and G. Hoggard, "Conflict Patterns in Interaction among Nations," in J. N. Rosenau, ed., *International Politics and Foreign Policy* (New York: Free Press, 1969), pp. 711–724.

20. For an insightful discussion of the use of persuasion, see Baldwin, "Power Analysis and World Politics," pp. 163–175. Baldwin also stresses the need to view power not as some absolute capacity, but rather situationally and contextually as actors, issues, and circumstances change (at pp. 192–193).

21. See Donald Puchala and Stuart Fagan, "International Politics in the 1970s: The Search for a Perspective," *International Organization* 28, no. 2 (Spring 1974). They argue that high politics, or security politics as they refer to it, no longer adequately explains international relations, which now includes many transnational and integrative processes not dominated by security considerations.

22. See Taylor, *Non-State Actors in International Politics,* pp. 203–209.

23. David H. Blake and Robert S. Walters, *The Politics of Global Economic Relations* (Englewood Cliffs, N.J.: Prentice-Hall, 1983), pp. 87–88. Depending on the restrictiveness of the definition employed, the number of corporations around the world ranges from about five hundred to over ten thousand.

24. For an authoritative treatment of MNCs, see Robert Gilpin, *U.S. Power and the Multinational Corporation: The Political Economy of Foreign Direct Investment* (New York: Basic Books, 1975).

25. See Krishna Kumar, "Third World Multinationals: A Growing Force in International Relations," *International Studies Quarterly* 26, no. 3 (1982): 397–424.

26. See Robert Gilpin, "The Politics of Transnational Economic Relations," in *Globalism Versus Realism: International Relations' Third Debate,* Ray Maghroori and Bennet Ramberg, eds. (Boulder: Westview, 1982), p. 191.

27. Ibid.

28. Anant Negandhi, "Multinational Corporations and Host Government Relationships: Comparative Study of Conflict and Conflicting Issues," *Human Relations* 33, no. 8 (1980): 517–541.

29. Raymond Vernon, *Sovereignty at Bay* (New York: Basic Books, 1971).

30. Theodore Moran, *Multinational Corporations and the Politics of Dependence: Copper in Chile* (Princeton: Princeton University Press, 1974): C. Fred Bergsten, "Coming Investment Wars?" *Foreign Affairs* 53, no. 1 (1974): 136–138. For an excellent discussion of the "new orthodoxy," see Thomas Biersteker, "The Illusion of State Power: Transnational Corporations and the Neutralization of Host-Country Legislation," *Journal of Peace Research* 17, no. 3 (1980): 207–221. Biersteker dissents from the new orthodoxy, arguing that MNCs have considerable capabilities to resist the reassertion of state regulation over their activities.

31. Biersteker, "The Illusion of State Power," pp. 213–219.

32. Recently, the literature on NGOs has grown. Key works include Landrum Bolling with Craig Smith, *Private Foreign Aid: U.S. Private Philanthropy* (Boulder: Westview, 1983); John Sommer, *Beyond Charity: U.S. Voluntary Aid for a Changing World* (Washington,

D.C.: Overseas Development Council, 1977); and Robert Gorman, *Private Voluntary Organizations as Agents of Development* (Boulder: Westview, 1985).

33. For an extensive discussion on the role of IGOs, see Taylor, *Non-State Actors in International Politics.*

34. For an informative treatment on the terrorism phenomenon, see Yonah Alexander, *International Terrorism: National, Regional and Global Perspectives* (New York: Praeger, 1981).

35. See Michael Sullivan, "Transnationalism, Power Politics, and the Realities of the Present System," in *Globalism vs. Realism: International Relations' Third Debate,* eds. Ray Maghroori and Bennett Ramberg (Boulder: Westview, 1982), p. 201.

36. Arve Ofri, "Intelligence and Counterterrorism," *Orbis* 28, no. 1 (Spring 1984): 41–52.

37. Jerome Corsi, "Terrorism as a Desperate Game: Fear, Bargaining, and Communications in the Terrorist Event," *Journal of Conflict Resolution* (March 1981): 25, no. 1, pp. 47–86.

38. For an eloquent exposition on the role of the individual in international relations, see Isaak Hummel, *Individuals and World Politics* (Pacific Grove, Calif.: Brooks/Cole, 1975), pp. 3–19. See also J. W. Burton, "The Individual as the Unit of Explanation in International Relations," *International Studies Newsletter* 10, no. 1 (1983): 1–17. Another very insightful treatment of the individual as a unit of analysis can be found in Patrick Morgan, *Theories and Approaches to International Politics: What Are We to Think?* 3rd ed. (New Brunswick, N.J.: Transaction Books, 1981), pp. 41–106. Morgan playfully points out how difficult it is to construct broad explanatory theories using the individual as the unit of analysis.

39. James Rosenau, "A Pre-Theory Revisited: World Politics in an Era of Cascading Interdependence," *International Studies Quarterly* 28, no. 3 (September 1984): 267–271, 290–300.

40. A useful collection of articles on this subject can be found in Ray Maghroori and Bennet Ramberg, eds., *Globalism Versus Realism: International Relations' Third Debate* (Boulder: Westview, 1982).

41. Rosenau, "A Pre-Theory Revisited," pp. 263–267.

42. Kenneth Waltz, "The Myth of National Interdependence," in *The International Corporation,* ed. Charles P. Kindleberger (Cambridge: MIT Press, 1970), pp. 205–223. Another highly readable analysis supporting the proposition of the continued predominance of the state is Hedley Bull, "The State's Positive Role in World Affairs," *Daedalus* 108, no. 4 (1979): 111–123. Corroborating Bull's view is the argument of Richard Haass, "The Primacy of the State. . .Or Revising the Revisionists," *Daedalus* 108, no. 4 (1979): 125–138.

43. See, for instance, H. E. Chebabi, "Self-Determination, Territorial Integrity, and the Falkland Islands," *Political Science Quarterly* 100, no. 2 (Summer 1985): 211–225; and M. Islam, "Secessionist Self-Determination," *Journal of Peace Research* 22, no. 3 (1985): 211–220.

44. The cobweb model of international relations was introduced in John W. Burton, A. J. R. Groom, C. R. Mitchell, and A. V. S. DeReuck, *The Study of World Society: A London Perspective,* occasional paper no. 1 (Pittsburgh: International Studies Association, 1974).

45. Susan Okin, "Taking the Bishops Seriously," *World Politics* 36, no. 4 (July 1984): 527–554.

Five

The Determinants and Processes of Foreign Policy Behavior

Statesmen and scholars agree that foreign policy activities vary from one state to another and from one type of government to another. They also agree that the aim of foreign policy is to affect the behavior of another actor in the international arena. However, they do *not* agree on exactly what foreign policy should include. There are almost as many definitions of foreign policy as there are writers on the subject. We will view **foreign policy** as a set of authoritative decisions taken in the name of the state that are inteded to achieve certain goals in the international arena. In other words, *foreign* in foreign policy applies to anything beyond the legal boundaries of a particular state; and *policy* we define as a guide to action intended to realize the goals a state (i.e., authoritative decision makers) has set for itself. Policy is made through a process called decision making. In international relations, decision making is a neverending process of reaction and adjustment that links every state—large or small, rich or poor—to every other state through a network of communications.

Perhaps the best way to understand foreign policy is to determine how different states make foreign policy decisions and then to compare these methods. Over the past twenty years or so, research findings from comparative foreign policy analysis have helped us develop a better understanding of the factors and variables that shape nation-state behavior.[1] These findings attempt to answer the key question in foreign policy: Why do nation-states do what they do? Available concepts and analytical tools can describe, at least in general terms, the patterns of the foreign policy behavior of individual countries. Whereas a state's foreign policy will vary from issue to issue, from situation to situation, and from time to time, the same analytical tools and concepts can be used to explain all foreign policies. In other words, foreign policy behavior can be analyzed in terms of regularities and patterns that are derived from common structures and processes of foreign policy making.[2] As we explore why nation-states act as they do in the international arena, it will become more and more evident that there are a host of influences responsible for the differences in foreign policy behavior of nation-states.

Our aim in this chapter is twofold: (1) to develop a framework for classifying the various determinants of foreign policy behavior, and (2) to take a closer look at the foreign policy–making process. While it is true that the institutions and procedures involved in foreign policy making differ from country to country, our concern here is not the legal–formal aspect of the foreign policy process, but rather the dynamic one underlying the decision process in all political systems.

Determinants of Nation-State Behavior

James Rosenau, perhaps the best-known advocate of the comparative study of foreign policy, claims that all possible influences on foreign policy (independent variables) can be classified into five categories: (1) idiosyncratic (having to do with the characteristics of individual decision makers), (2) role (of decision makers), (3) governmental, (4) societal, and (5) systemic influences.[3] These categories raise two questions: (1) Are the categories all-encompassing (as far as the influences on foreign policy behavior are concerned)? and (2) Which category will carry more weight in the decision-making process of a particular state in formulating and implementing foreign policy goals and objectives? While some scholars of comparative foreign policy, like David Singer or Frederic Pearson, for example, use a simpler scheme for explaining foreign policy behavior in terms of two or three sets of variables, others, like Robert North or Charles Hermann, rely on a more elaborate one—employing six sets of variables. Following Rosenau's conceptual design, we have lumped these sets of variables into three levels of analysis: (1) the systemic level (which examines the external factors influencing the nation-state within the international system), (2) the national attribute level (which examines internal factors of the state), and (3) the idiosyncratic level (which examines factors associated with personality characteristics unique to the decision makers of the state). Let us summarize some of the factors under these three levels of analysis.

Systemic Factors

Systemic factors are those influences on a state's policies that arise from the state's international environment, such as geographical "realities," international actions occurring abroad, and structural characteristics of the global system. Geographical factors include size, location, number of borders to be defended, topography, and the degree of access to various points on the globe. As we have already seen in previous chapters, *geography* can affect a nation-state's foreign policy behavior either positively or negatively. Countries with access to the sea and control of strategic waterways (e.g., Egypt's Suez Canal) have an advantage compared to landlocked countries (e.g., Chad) that are remote from the main arteries of communication lines. However, technological advances can transform today's advantages into tomorrow's disadvantages. For example, super tankers and giant aircraft carriers have diminished the importance of the Suez Canal, while Chad may still enjoy benefits from the discovery of precious mineral resources in its territory. In the contemporary world, technology can neutralize geographical factors to a great extent. For instance, military strategy is no longer calculated by such terms as the *hinterland* and the *heartland,* but by *nuclear retaliation* and *lead time.* Referring to Cuba, Nikita S. Khrushchev, former party leader and head of the Soviet government, boasted more than twenty years ago that the Soviet Union had the capability of defending its interests six thousand miles away—far beyond its own borders. He clearly implied that the Soviet Union did not need common borders with Cuba to defend the island.[4]

In some instances geography influences the formulation of certain new policies, but in other instances already established policies define the importance of geography. In early June 1987, at the Venice Economic Summit, the seven members of the industrialized world (the U.S., the U.K., Japan, France, FRG, Italy, and Canada) worried about the Persian Gulf because of the importance they attached to industrial development through the free flow of oil from that region. Should the industrialized world become less dependent on oil, however, the Middle East would lose some of its intrinsic value. Research findings are divided on whether geographic proximity promotes conflict or cooperation. Some analysts have concluded that geographic proximity increases conflict,[5] whereas other analysts maintain that it has increased interstate cooperation, ranging from trade to tourism and diplomatic contacts.[6] Perhaps the best example of the two opposing roles of geographic proximity can be found on the borders between the United States and Canada and between the Soviet Union and the People's Republic of China. Canadian–U.S. relations are cooperative, whereas Soviet–Sino relations are fraught with tension, hostility, and conflict.

Cooperation or conflict among nation-states can be studied in not only a geographic sense but also in a political, economic, or cultural sense. The degree of similarity and difference between nation-states (i.e., the "distance" between them) can be a significant index for measuring the volume and types of transactions among the multitude of actors in the international system. Numerous scholars have hypothesized that the more similar countries are in terms of their political, economic, and cultural characteristics, the greater the levels of trade, communications, and other *interactions* are likely to be between them.[7] This does not mean, however, that countries with dissimilar characteristics have no intense interactions. The example of the United States and the Soviet Union clearly shows a continuous interaction in political, economic, and cultural activities. Thus we may conclude that even conflict systems contain elements of cooperation.

As we pointed out earlier, systemic thinking emphasizes wholeness; that is, when we look at the international system we are looking at the patterns of interactions among the actors. Interdependence emphasizes the links or interconnections among the units of a system. Such links can also influence foreign policy. This second systemic factor, international **interdependence** or interaction has two different effects on foreign policy. First, it causes nations to be more sensitive to developments in other nations. For example, in 1986 a chemical company in Switzerland polluted the Rhine River. This situation damaged the fishing and tourist industries farther downstream (all the way to the delta in the Netherlands) and frustrated and angered the citizens and governments of the neighboring countries. Of course, the degree of sensitivity depends on how quickly changes in one country (i.e., reparations offered by the Swiss chemical company) bring about changes in another (e.g., cooperation in the cleanup procedures in West Germany), and how positive the results are. Second, interdependence may cause countries to be vulnerable to the effects of the resulting changes in other countries.[8] For example, the chemical company and the Swiss government were vulnerable even after the cleanup, the damages to the Rhine River may be long-lasting, and the spillover effects are deeply rooted.

Interdependence can cause conflict. In the late 1970s and the 1980s Japan ignored warnings about dumping goods on the U.S. and Western European markets. In the United States Japan's actions provoked congressional reaction, threatening trade wars with Japan, even if those trade wars could lead to higher unemployment and a recession in both the United States and Japan.

A third systemic factor affecting the behavior of the actors in foreign policy making is the structure of the global system, especially with regard to conflict and war. Although there is no consensus on how unipolarity, bipolarity, and multipolarity influence conflict and war, there is general agreement that the overall system structure limits the options of both large and small powers.[9]

The role of the **international system structure** can be examined at the regional and global levels. For example, in the Middle East a struggle for regional dominance dates from the eighth- to eleventh-century movement of the capital of the Islamic caliphate, or empire, from Arabia to Damascus to Baghdad and finally to Cairo. Outside powers such as Persia and the Ottoman Empire tried to intervene in this Arab system but without success.

Rivalries persisted in this region until fairly recently; in 1988 three new alliances were created, with Saudi Arabia playing a dominant role. The prolonged competition had produced intrigues, summit meetings, and aspirations for Islamic and Arab unity, as well as wars and assassinations.[10]

Regional disputes can restrain national leaders' choices if those disputes are within the *sphere of influence* but outside the interests of the major powers. For example, Gorbachev's visit to several client states, including Cuba, in 1989 resulted in the announcement of the unilateral reduction of Soviet armed forces in Eastern Europe and a reminder to Fidel Castro that the USSR's program of *perestroika* and *glasnost* does not look favorably on the spreading of violent revolutions in the hemisphere. As long as a major power has client states in its sphere of influence, it can assert its will without great resistance. Another example is the 1973 conflict between Israel and Egypt. In contrast to the Iran-Iraq war, which had lasted almost a decade—because both countries were outside any sphere of influence—the 1973 conflict between Egypt and Israel was of short duration because both countries were client states in a sphere of influence of two rival superpowers and were subject to their orders. In the East-West regional arrangements before the 1900s, it was safe to argue that the Soviet Union exercised a much stricter influence over Western European states than did the United States. In the Western Hemisphere, however, U.S. influence is much more assertive. Leaders' choices in Africa or the Middle East are much less constrained because they are outside the sphere of influence of the major actors. Although some former colonial powers continue to exercise regional influence—France, for example, continues to play a significant role in the security of West and Central African states, such as Chad—their source of power is more bilateral than systemic.

External environment can influence a country's involvement in various commercial activities as well. For example, all states are subject to international trade regulations, international monetary policies, international communications, and privileges and sanctions by international organizations. To understand the structure of the system, we need to know the number of state actors, the relative size of those actors, and the existence of nonstate actors and alliances built by various bonds or linkages between two or more states.[11]

Let us first consider the effects of alliances on the foreign policy behavior of nation-states. Alliances can reveal the distribution of friendship and hostility, as well as the military capabilities of member nations. Alliances combine elements of cooperation and conflict. Formalized in written treaties, alliances are formed to ensure cooperation in security or military affairs. They are distinguished from other forms of international cooperation because their members perceive a third party to be a mutual enemy or security problem. United States forces in Europe, for instance, have been referred to as "trip-wire forces" because an attack on Western Europe would involve American troops and military support. Consequently, American troops represent a deterrence against the threat of a potential Soviet attack on members of the North Atlantic Treaty Organization (NATO) in Western Europe. A similar arrangement holds true for the Warsaw Pact (or WTO, Warsaw Treaty Organization), established in 1955 as a response to West Germany's entry into NATO. The WTO serves the security interests of the Soviet Union and her Eastern European allies. While alliances are often used to balance power among nations, they are no guarantee of peaceful relations between their member states.[12] It is not unusual for coalition partners to go to war against each other. For example, the Soviet Union has invaded the territory of two WTO members,

Hungary in 1956 and Czechoslovakia in 1968; and the conflict between Greece and Turkey over Cyprus and skirmishes between Iceland and Great Britain over fishing rights are examples of rivalry among NATO members. As long as the WTO countries are perceived as a major threat to the Western industrialized countries, however, the unity among NATO members is very high compared to a period of detente or *perestroika,* when alliance unity tends to decline and interbloc "fraternization," trade, cultural exchanges increase.

Whereas leading members of an alliance may provide a protective shield or a "nuclear umbrella" to the smaller members, there is always a danger that the stronger nations can be dragged into conflicts through reckless actions by their weaker partners. According to former Secretary of State Henry Kissinger, both the United States and the Soviet Union could have been dragged into a conflict during the 1973 Yom Kippur war, when the Soviet Union threatened to intervene on behalf of its informal coalition partner Egypt, if the United States failed to prevent its client Israel from defeating Egypt.

For different reasons, states may also try to go it alone; that is, states may avoid alliances by following a neutral policy or by attempting to withdraw from the international system of states as much as possible. Many newly emerging nation-states have chosen a nonaligned foreign policy. With the mushrooming number of states in the international arena, newly emerging countries could choose to ally themselves either with the Western or Eastern (Soviet) bloc or to remain nonaligned. Most chose the latter course, and the nonaligned movement, which began at the Bandung (Indonesia) conference in 1955, gave these states a bargaining position in international organizations, such as the United Nations, where they asserted themselves and sought concessions from both the Eastern and Western blocs. A good example of the nonaligned movement's current role in the international system can be seen in the workings of the **Geneva Group of Seventy-Seven** (G 77), which functions as a caucus for approximately 120 less developed countries. They are a potent voting bloc to be reckoned with in the UN and other international organizations. Because of their sheer numbers, no UN measure can be passed without their support.

In summary, the effects of systemic factors on foreign policy behavior range from involvement in war to international trade, communications, diplomatic relations, the formation of alliances, nonalignment, and other interactions between nation-states. The structure of the international system may give the impression that there is no room for manipulation by policy makers outside the major actors' sphere of influence. Although the superpowers exercise enormous influence, especially in the military sphere of their capabilities (the nuclear umbrella, for instance), other kinds of decisions by smaller actors, especially among the Third World states, illustrate the ebb and flow of systemic forces.

National Attribute Factors

The characteristics, or national attributes, of a state influence its foreign policy behavior. National attributes include demographic, economic, military, and governmental influences. Whereas the systemic factors affect the external environment of a state's foreign policy behavior, the **national attribute factors** arise from its domestic environment.

Under demographic attributes, for example, are the size, motivation, skills, levels of education, and homogeneity of a country's population, and the way they affect the human resources available to its government. As we pointed out in chapter 3, the considerable difference between Japan's and India's capabilities is not due to topography, which makes India richer in natural resources, but to human resources commensurate with a technologically advanced society, which gives Japan the status of an advanced major power. With only about one-sixth of the population of India, Japan produces about six times more in goods and services than India. While size does effect a state's capacity to act, its physical area or population alone is not a very accurate indicator of its capability in foreign policy. The combination of size, economic development, and political accountability is much more reliable for measuring differences in foreign policy behavior. For example, in early July 1941, Japan decided to seek expansion in Southeast Asia even at the risk of war with the United States. This decision was reached incrementally by the Imperial Conference and for the Japanese military it meant survival. After the freeze on Japanese assets in the United States of July 1941, and the cancellation of shipments of oil, scrap-iron and other industrial goods from the United States, Japan's economy was in shambles and her ability to wage war was in jeopardy. Japan was also lacking rice, tin, bauxite, nickel, rubber and other raw materials normally imported from the Dutch East Indies (now Indonesia) and Malays. The United States, Great Britain and the Netherlands made it known that the embargo and freezing of assets would be lifted ony if Japan withdrew from both China and Indochina (now Vietnam, Laos and Kampuchea). Japanese military high command demanded that either strategic supplies be restored by a peaceful settlement with the Western powers, or access to them would be secured by force. But the choice of a negotiated settlement was not feasible to the political leaders in the West or in Tokyo. As a result, the Imperial government on December 7, 1941, staged a surprise attack on U.S. naval facilities at Pearl Harbor.[13] What this example illustrates is referred to by Robert C. North and Nazli Choucri as *lateral pressure*. According to this concept, rising population, advancing technology, and inadequate access to resources are responsible not only for food shortages and the depletion of some basic resources, but also for the uneven access to basic resources of different societies and states, and also perhaps for international conflict and violence. In this respect, national attributes provide valuable data for studying the processes that lead to war.[14]

What Japan was willing and able to do in 1941 because of U.S. pressure, it would not and could not repeat in 1973, when the OPEC countries used pressure on Japan and other Western industrial nations to cut off petroleum supplies. To ease the pressure, according to Pearson and Rochester, Tokyo abandoned its previous pro-Israeli line on the Palestinian issue. The changes in conditions and situations in 1973 made Japan highly accommodative. Thus, changes in foreign policy are not traceable only to demographic attributes of a country but to economic, military, and governmental ones, especially such attributes as the availability of technology and financial resources to exploit or create substitutes for natural resources, military capability, ethnic and social diversity, as well as public opinion and internal political stability.[15]

Whether a country is homogeneous or heterogeneous will make a great difference in the conduct of an effective foreign policy. A case in point is Lebanon's foreign policy. For centuries, Lebanon had maintained a careful balancing act between Moslems and Christians which earned it the title of "Middle Eastern Switzerland." After the Palestinian exodus to Lebanon in 1967, the fragile balance was shattered, making it virtually impossible for any Lebanese government to conduct a sound foreign policy. The tragic events leading to the disintegration of the Christian-controlled Lebanese state in the late 1970s and early 1980s, are a prime example of how ethnic and religious rivalries can affect a state's foreign policy behavior. In 1976 the Arab League sent Syrian peacekeeping troops to Lebanon to protect Christian enclaves against homeless Palestinians living in refugee camps. These Palestinians, along with their Lebanese Muslim allies, threatened to take control of Lebanon. However, because Israel sought to control part of Lebanon along the Israeli border and had the support of the Christian groups, by 1981 Syria was openly siding with the Muslim Lebanese and had moved missiles into the Bekaa Valley to counter Israeli air support of the Christians. Allowing the Christians to gain control of key access points on the road to Damascus could have been interpreted as giving Israel a strategic advantage, so Syria opted to shift its protective role to the Muslims

Chapter Five   The Determinants and Processes of Foreign Policy Behavior

and thus continue to play a tricky balancing game for fear of war with Israel. For over a decade the tangled web of ethnic and religious conflict turned Lebanon into a haven for terrorism and chaos and provoked interventions by both its neighbors Israel and Syria.

Many economic characteristics can affect a state's foreign policy; some are more important than others. When we look at differences in nations' foreign policy behavior, the more important variables include the size of the economy, its wealth or economic development, and its mode of economic organization (e.g., capitalist, socialist, or communist). Economic size is usually measured in terms of a nation's GNP (or the estimated total value of goods and services produced in a year). Therefore, differences will be quite noticeable between technologically advanced industrial nations and agricultural countries that have little or no industrial base.

The size of a nation's economy is often determined by its technological development or economic wealth. A lack of these factors limits a state's resources and capacity to act. As we saw in chapter 4, there seems to be a direct correlation between a state's economic size, its overall wealth (i.e., the total amount of income available per person, measured as per capita GNP), and its resources and capacity to act. Several studies have found that smaller, economically underdeveloped states are at a disadvantage when compared with larger, richer states. Larger and wealthier states are much more involved in diplomacy and transnational politics through governmental as well as nongovernmental organizations than smaller and/or poorer ones.[16] Poorer states are handicapped in many other ways; for example, they are restricted by a lack of information and by their processing capability, which prevents them from responding accurately and quickly to their external environment.[17] It is not surprising, therefore, that the United Nations is their major source for contacts with the outside world.

Finally, how does the organization of a state's economic system affect its foreign policy behavior? Some theorists argue that **capitalism** (i.e., the economic system emphasizing private ownership of capital and the mode of production) is based on heavy military expenditures, which serve to maintain prosperity at home while fighting communism abroad. Monopolistic capitalism, according to the critics, generates a surplus that can be absorbed only by government spending and taxation.[18] They also argue that foreign trade and investment are essential to the survival of modern capitalism, and that capitalist countries use **neocolonialism** to create spheres of influence for the purpose of securing foreign markets or commodities in the LDCs. Most of these arguments, however, have been refuted by other scholars.[19] Similarly, the predictions by Lenin and other communist prophets that capitalist states would become hostile enemies pitted against each other in competition for resources and markets of less developed societies is nothing more than an ideological diatribe. During World War II the Soviet Union and the United States were allies, but since the end of the war, just the opposite has been the case. So much so that several socialist countries, including the Soviet Union, have envied the prosperous, viable, and harmonious relationship that continues to exist among the leading industrial (capitalist) countries of the West.

Communism (an economic system of state ownership of capital and the mode of production) adheres to a foreign policy that seeks to establish a class dictatorship (by the workers' party elite who believe in proletarian internationalism). Thus the foreign policy of communist states is, at least in theory, based more on class antagonism and less on foreign trade and investment activities. Foreign trade and investment are used more for political gains, especially since Mikhail Gorbachev introduced his "New Political Thinking" in Soviet foreign policy. The principles of **new thinking** were erected on two main pillars: *perestroika* (or restructuring) and *glasnost* (or openness). Both are part and parcel of Soviet socialism, which Gorbachev believes can be turned back into a viable system that can perform on a level with other advanced (capitalist) nations. While *glasnost* is supposed to provide political freedom and liberalization, *perestroika* is supposed to create the incentives for economic restructuring to make the Soviet economy both modern and efficient. Any resemblance to capitalist practices is simply shrugged aside as "deideologization," because not even ideology must interfere with Soviet foreign policy. Certain aspects of Soviet *new thinking* about international relations suggest a scaling-down of Soviet external ambitions, including the past endorsement of class warfare (revolutions), proletarian internationalism, and limited sovereignty (the Brezhnev doctrine). As a result, several hard-line socialist states, such as Cuba, North Korea, and the People's Republic of China, are reluctant to follow the Soviet example and find it difficult to reconcile economic reforms with orthodox Marxist–Leninist principles.

Social democratic states follow another type of economic system, which advocates some measure of state ownership of capital and a mode of production (e.g., major banking and transportation) but without a class dictatorship. They maintain a foreign policy based on democratic principles and international cooperation. Such countries as Sweden, Denmark, Portugal, Australia, Iceland, and New Zealand have close ties with the Third World, supporting their position on various issues of economic development and racism. Working through the world organization of social democratic parties, social democratic states have influenced many intergovernmental organizations and national actors with their progressive programs.

Although economic issues are becoming of increasing importance in foreign policy, security concerns outweigh economic concerns because they can involve a nation's identity and entire existence. The most costly outlay of national revenues is undoubtedly for security. In 1985, for example, the aggregate annual outlays of revenues for weapons exceeded $1 trillion, which is triple the $300 billion spent in 1972.[20] In 1982 the world spent $1.3 million a minute for military purposes.[21] Lebanon, Laos, Vietnam, Kampuchea, South Yemen, and North Korea, with a per capita GNP of $500 or less in 1982, spent over 10 percent of their GNP on military expenditures.[22] The point here is not so much that those countries that can least afford to will spend money on armaments, but that every nation-state, rich or poor, relies on military security. Military security concerns play an important role in shaping a state's foreign policy. How so?

Whether it is called the **military-industrial complex** (a phrase coined by President Dwight D. Eisenhower, in his last public address in 1960) or "Soviet military power," military interests are articulated in both the American and Soviet societies by industrial managers (state or private). These interests attempt to ensure the growth, power, prosperity, and technological preeminence of the arms manufacturing industries they control. In the Soviet Union arms producers share interests with their clients in the Soviet armed forces and the decision makers within the hierarchy of the Communist party.[23] In the United States pressure groups interested in military spending concentrate their activities on issues that will create a favorable climate for the support of high military expenditures. The chief aims in both the United States and the Soviet Union are the same: to build a strong military might for security purposes. However, the process for achieving those goals will vary considerably between the two political systems.[24]

Many variables enter into the calculation of rating or measuring military power. Ranking nations according to the size of their armed forces, the number of various types of weapons, the skill levels of their armed personnel, and their research and development efforts can be useful. However, such an exercise cannot dependably predict power relations among states. For example, in terms of military expenditures, the Soviet Union spends twice as much on armaments and has almost twice as many men and women in uniform as does the United States. It would appear then that the Soviet Union is the world's number one military power. However, it frequently has been argued that in terms of the relative quality of personnel and weaponry, as well as the capabilities of allies, the United States is either on a par with or somewhat ahead of the Soviet Union. Military power ratings are similarly deceptive among the countries in the Middle East. Israel spends 25 percent of its GNP on defense. Syria and Egypt spend less than half of this, but their combined armies are five times larger than Israel's. Yet Israel has enjoyed superior technology and skill levels, the potential of total mobilization, and high motivation, which makes Israeli military power superior to that of Syria and Egypt. As American experience in Vietnam showed, the country with the largest number of armed forces and the most sophisticated military technology does not necessarily win the conflict. Other variables may be more decisive than military factors taken alone.

One variable that may make or break a state's foreign policy (especially in democracies or open political systems) is societal support. Human resources and economic and military wealth capabilities do not count for much if the government cannot mobilize them. Before commenting on the influence the public has on foreign policy behavior, let us consider whether the type of governmental system matters in shaping foreign policy behavior. One view of global politics is that it does not matter much whether states are dictatorships or democracies, because the pressures of the international system or other national attributes largely determine foreign policy. This perspective argues that an elite determines national interests and that domestic politics and mass public opinion play only secondary roles. Other scholars argue that domestic politics and the type of political system play a significant role in determining a nation's foreign policy. Somewhere between these two extremes is the point of view that the type of governmental system matters to a certain degree in shaping foreign policy behavior "because all political leaders, whether presiding in open or closed political systems, are concerned to some extent about their domestic political environment."[25] Closer scrutiny will reveal, however, that there is considerable difference between closed and open political systems with respect to who governs and how and when public opinion affects policy.[26] Because of the many interests exerting pressures on one another in a democracy, all governmental leaders seek societal support to remain in office, gain control of government, and then implement their policies. Democratic governments must hear and respond to the demands and needs of society. In other words, governmental leaders are restricted in their choices of policy not only by systemic factors and other national attribute factors but by societal pressures exerted by interest groups and public opinion.[27] Although leaders in dictatorships are concerned to some extent about their domestic political involvement, the domestic pressures are greater in democracies. These leaders must contend with a wider circle of relevant actors, some controlling the purse strings (the Congress),[28] others poking around for news stories (the media),[29] others seeking to take their jobs away (political rivals), and still others complaining about their loss of jobs or illegal immigration.

There is an ongoing debate in the international relations literature about the importance of governmental variables in shaping foreign policy. It has been hypothesized that the type of governmental system (closed or open) is related to the propensity to fight wars, the flexibility of policy, and efficiency and discretion.[30] For example, dictatorships are viewed as decisive, swift, and flexible, whereas democracies are often seen as slow to act, susceptible to emotionalism, and relatively inflexible.[31] Dictatorships are also seen as more efficient and decisive than democracies because they do not have to depend on the democratic checks and balances. Critics of democratic foreign policy processes often blame the Congress and the media for jeopardizing the discretion and secrecy that are often required to conduct effective foreign policy.

Whether in democratic or dictatorial systems, the role, organization, and function of bureaucracy is important. Bureaucratic rivalries within governments are not uncommon, and they affect a country's ability to implement its foreign policy. For example, rivalries between branches in the U.S. armed services or between the Red Army and the Soviet Strategic Rocket Forces are well documented.[32]

Whether a country enjoys internal political stability can also have a significant bearing on its foreign policy behavior. A national government in turmoil due to domestic upheaval becomes suspect to friends and foes alike. Those parties that want to protect their investments and credits will try to strengthen a government under pressure and restore stability through bilateral or multilateral actions; on the other hand, those interested in a change of government will support government's internal enemies through various clandestine actions.

Idiosyncratic Factors

Whatever a country's situation in the international environment or its particular national attributes, whether its government is open or closed, its economy weak or strong, its foreign policy is assumed to be made ultimately by individuals responsible for authoritative decisions. According to this reasoning, individual decision makers are capable of shaping world events, and so we must try to understand their role in the foreign policy process. The question still remains, however, whether governmental decisions, and their consequences, would have occurred *regardless* of the identity of the authoritative decision makers. Environmental determinists would probably argue that "objective environmental constraints" and "historical forces" are larger than any single individual. But, non-determinists would argue that personal characteristics of foreign policy decision makers are the most important single factor in shaping foreign policy. As Margaret Hermann observed, the difference between these two schools of thought can be found in the centuries old "great man" (or woman) versus "zeitgeist" debate. However, research on leadership indicates that neither position is tenable by itself because leadership qualities are determined by *both* the characteristics of the individual and the characteristics of the situation.

As we pointed out in chapter 3 (under environmental possibilitism), not all decision makers see their environment in the same way. Depending on their perceptual system, what is real to one decision maker may not be real to another decision maker. Decision makers, under normal conditions, do not respond to the objective facts of the situation, but to their image of the situation.

Other types of individual-level variables that can affect foreign policy behavior include "personality traits or dispositions" such as cognitive complexity, dogmatism, displacement of private motives onto public objects, and ego-defensive behavior. Whether the individual is active or passive, positive or negative, tolerant or domineering, rational or impulsive, can have important implications for foreign policy decisions. For example, Woodrow Wilson's unwillingness to compromise with political opponents in crucial situations (e.g., the ratification of the Treaty of Versailles in 1919) was, according to one study, a result of his competition with and aggression toward his father.[33] Studies of other key national leaders suggest that there is a psychological environment within which individual and idiosyncratic factors in affect foreign policy behavior.[34] However, to understand foreign policy behavior, both types of factors—objective (systemic and national attribute) and subjective (idiosyncratic)—must be considered. In many cases, the institutional role of the policy makers can be as important in affecting their individual characteristics as the inherited and acquired personality traits.

A leader's personal charisma and magnetism are not always considered typical idiosyncratic factors because they can also be derived by skillfully manipulating political factors in the environment. Therefore, as long as the environment is amenable to manipulation, the leader's invincibility is practically guaranteed. For example, Mikhail Gorbachev's *new thinking* in Soviet foreign policy is predicated not so much on the greatness of the man himself as on the system of one-party monopoly on power, the Communist party of the Soviet Union, that he and his followers control. As long as this monopoly on power remains intact and Gorbachev's program is able to satisfy the party leaders, his charismatic popularity and the success of his program are assured. However, should his new thinking fail to achieve this goal, Gorbachev may become a victim of his own program and thus turn the Soviet Union back to prereform days, as happened in the People's Republic of China after the government crushed the student-inspired freedom movement in June 1989. Should this become the scenario in the near future, one could then argue that a country's foreign policy can change in certain circumstances, but the "continuities" remain.

In-depth psychological and personality-oriented studies of foreign policy making point out that private motives are displaced onto public objects. That is to say, decision makers impose their private (idiosyncratic) personality drives onto the world around them. Depending on their personalities, political leaders may be more or less willing to take risks, cooperate, or go to war. According to one study, a country's foreign policy tends to be more aggressive in those cases in which decision makers have a stronger need to exhibit power and have very ideological or black-or-white views about their friends and adversaries. When decision makers have a more complex view of the world, however, their government's policies will tend to be more cooperative.[35]

Idiosyncratic factors can also affect foreign policy when the right person turns out to be in the right place at the right time. **Rapprochement** (a reconciliation of interests of rival states after a period of estrangement) between the United States and the People's Republic of China toward the end of the U.S. involvement in Vietnam was more feasible under the Nixon administration than in preceding ones because of Nixon's strong anticommunist record. Similarly, the return of occupied Sinai territory to Egypt in 1979 was more easily accomplished by Israeli Prime Minister Menachem Begin, a staunch hawk and former terrorist leader in the struggle for independence, than it would have been for the less conservative leaders of the labor party. When conservatives make concessions, it is less likely to be viewed as appeasement of aggressive states.

Another important idiosyncratic attribute is the individual's physical and mental ability. This is particularly true when we deal with older political leaders who are susceptible to the strains of office. For example, Charles de Gaulle (who died at age seventy-nine), Josip Broz Tito (age eighty-eight), Mao Tse-tung (age eighty-four), Jomo Kenyatta (age eighty-five), and Leonid Brezhnev (age seventy-five) remained in office to a very advanced age. The question is whether their perceptions, determinations, and decisions, reflected an impaired physical and mental health problem. Critics of Franklin Roosevelt claim that he was too ill during the 1945 Yalta Conference to negotiate effectively with Joseph Stalin. Woodrow Wilson's stroke, shortly after his return from the Paris Peace Conference in 1919, weakened his control over governmental decisions. Similarly, during the Suez crisis of 1956, British Prime Minister Anthony Eden was suffering from hypertension and other nervous disorders that impaired his decision making abilities.

Regardless of whether the causes of idiosyncratic factors are biological (innate genetic characteristics) or environmental (i.e., cultural), they still affect foreign policy behavior. They can be the cause for aggression or cooperation. Some ethologists (scientists who study animal behavior) argue that there is a strong biological basis for human behavior and that we can find the causes for that behavior in studying the evolution of human beings. Others argue that the genetic or biological impact is either very small or nonexistent. For our purposes, however, international relations, not ethology, can explain why nations go to war or why they act cooperatively in the world arena.

So far, we have seen that there is a considerable interaction among individuals, states, and systemic factors when we attempt to explain a nation's foreign policy behavior. Systemic factors are particularly important in affecting alignment behavior. National attribute factors are dominant in affecting the scope of foreign policy. Idiosyncratic factors are significant in explaining the aspects of foreign policy affected by the subjective–psychological characteristics of the policy makers. Seldom is one set of factors responsible for the particular formulation of foreign policy. Many cause–effect relationships affect all three sets of factors in foreign policy making. For example, when the United States invaded Grenada on October 25, 1983, the action could be attributed to (1) a growing threat to American subjects on the island where only three days before a violent coup had taken place; (2) assumptions that a new and undisputedly pro-Marxist government with close ties to Havana and the Soviet bloc countries would come into existence (in other words, a change in the international system); (3) pressures brought by a request from five Caribbean nations for a joint invasion of Grenada; (4) numerous interest groups in the United States that were critical of the administration's soft stance toward international communist expansion (i.e., national attributes) and that supported the request for intervention; and perhaps (5) President Reagan's own hawkish position, cultivated over a long period, to be strong and determined against communist aggression (i.e., idiosyncratic factors).

The continuous flow of information from a multitude of sources which might impact on the individual foreign policy decision maker—surrounded by systemic, national attribute, and idiosyncratic factors—makes it extremely difficult to determine which one of these factors plays a primary and which ones a secondary role in the shaping of foreign policy of a country. As it will become evident in the second part of this chapter, "information processing" i.e., how information is handled by individuals, and groups of individuals, in decision making is a complex matter that leads to some set of judgments about the world and some set of actions by the decision makers.

The Foreign Policy–Making Process

We have examined several determinants (or ends and means) of foreign policy behavior. We have noted that both systemic and national attribute factors affect (constrain) a state's actions; however, we have also pointed out that foreign policy behavior is subject to idiosyncratic factors. In other words, authoritative decision makers must make choices among foreign policy ends and means that will be determined by objective (systemic and national attributes) subjective (or idiosyncratic) conditions of the environment. As table 5.1 points out, all three sets of factors intermingle (or overlap) as a country's foreign policy makers consider how their state should relate to other states. Information (a vast, ongoing wave

Table 5.1

Determinants of nation-state behavior

Factors	Characteristics	
Objective Systemic	International interactions: diplomatic relations, distance transactions, trade, travel, cultural exchange, environmental cooperation	International system structure: major powers, alliances, coalitions, international organizations, nongovernmental and governmental organizations, regional arrangements, legal precedence (international law, or IL)
National Attribute	Economic: size, wealth, level of development and productivity, mode or organization	Military: defense posture (expenditures), size of armed forces, size and types of weapons, skill levels, research and development
	Demographic: size, motivation, skills, level of education, homogeneity of population	Governmental: closed/open political system, bureaucratic organizations, political accountability, party politics, social structure, societal pressures (interest groups, public opinion, media)
Subjective Idiosyncratic	Leadership personality: psychological environment, physical and mental ability, personality traits, experiences, cultural–value norms, attitudes and belief systems	

of signals, facts, and noise) coming in from the *objective* international environment is interpreted (through subjective or idiosyncratic factors) by leaders as it is passed along through government agencies and subjected to a variety of domestic political pressures (national attributes). The result of this process is, as figure 5.1 points out, some set of judgments about the world and some set of actions. Our immediate aim is to shed some light on what is done with this information, which has an important bearing on the quality of those judgments and the effectiveness of those actions. In other words, our focus will be on the decision-making process of foreign policy making.

Given that institutions and procedures involved in foreign policy making differ from country to country, we are less interested in the legal-formal aspects of the foreign policy process and more interested in the dynamic aspects that are based on the intellectual and psychological factors underlying the decision process in all political systems. This should enable us to look *inside* the foreign policy process, and see how leaders responsible for foreign policy make decisions under different circumstances.

At the beginning of this chapter, in an attempt to define foreign policy, we noted that the *process* involves people's (authoritative and decision makers) decisions about and actions on choices to achieve certain goals through certain means. How they will exercise those choices depends to a great extent on how they perceive and define a situation. We also alluded to the fact that as long as states interact in the international system, the foreign policy process is constantly in motion. There is a prevailing popular notion, mostly propagated by politicians and the media, that each country has a single, conscious foreign policy or master plan containing a set of goals and strategies responsible for the conduct of its external affairs. In the United States, for example, such master blueprints of foreign policy appeared under the headings of the Great Design (under Roosevelt in 1945), the Truman doctrine (in 1947), detente (under Nixon in the mid-1970s), human rights (under Carter in the late 1970s), or peace through strength (under Reagan in the 1980s). It is customary for every U.S. president, either in the inaugural address or the first state of the union address, to outline the nation's foreign policy for the four-year period. Studies show that no matter how much a leadership tries to establish a single, overall foreign policy, sooner or later the decisions taken will deviate from the blueprint because of the fluidity and complexity of interactions in the international system. In other words, the grand plan idea in foreign policy may be appealing for public consumption, but for all practical purposes it often turns into a myth.[36] Consequently, the foreign policy of any country must be viewed realistically as a series of many decisions, that may coalesce in a coherent way, but that most likely will not. According to the school of **comparative foreign policy analysis,** these multitudes of foreign policy decisions confronting a national government are conceptualized under three approaches: macro-decisions, micro-decisions and crisis decisions.[37]

Types of Foreign Policy Decisions

Macro-decisions provide a general outline to be used as directives by the governmental organizations responsible for daily, routine decisions leading to the implementation of foreign policy. Any decision can be broken down into a predecisional stage, a formulation stage, and an implementation stage. The macro-decisions represent the first stage, encompassing the perceptions and attitudes of the leadership groups responsible for the country's foreign policy. These decisions involve position statements by the leaders on major, ongoing policy issues. For example, the United States has global interests that require constant attention. To assist the various players in the government bureaucracy

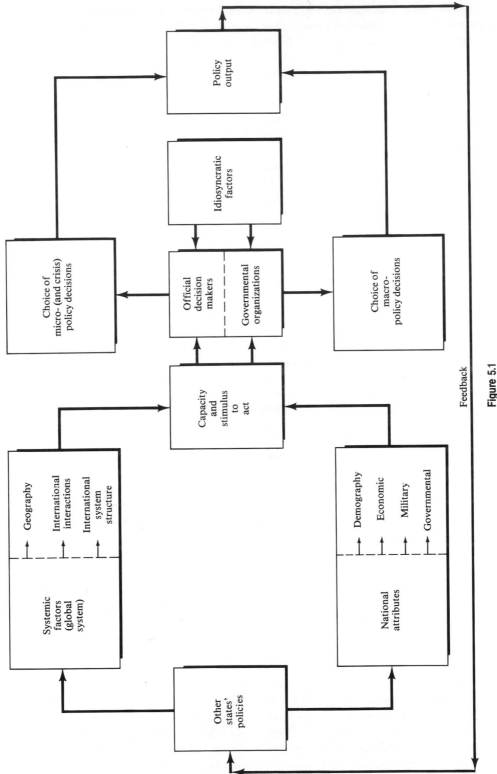

Figure 5.1
The foreign policy–making process

carry out foreign policy smoothly, macro-decisions provide the guidelines for routine operations. Macro-decisions usually take place in situations that have been known and monitored for quite some time and, therefore, come as no surprise to anyone involved in the complex process of decision making.

Micro-decisions, which are also known as administrative decisions, are usually handled at the lower levels of the organization network by individuals other than the political leadership. As pointed out by Pearson and Rochester, such decisions are narrow in scope, low threat in seriousness, and therefore do not require the attention of the authoritative decision makers at the top level. Micro-decisions usually follow the guidelines set by macro-decisions.

A myriad of foreign policy decisions are carried out every day on a routine basis by employees with different ranks in the bureaucratic hierarchy of foreign policy making. Many of them follow a standard set of guidelines or simple rules of procedure. For example, the U.S. Department of State receives and sends out over one thousand cables a day from and to American diplomatic and consular officials abroad; however, the secretary of state may see less than a dozen, and the president sees only one or two. The rest of the cables are handled routinely by the members of the bureaucratic hierarchy.[38]

Crisis decisions, like macro-decisions, involve a small but very high level of decision making. They are made in situations of threat and potential gravity. Often crisis decisions must address problems having an element of surprise and a short time frame in which to reach a decision.[39] For example, the U.S. response to the threat of American lives during the attempted communist takeover of Grenada in October 1983 and President Kennedy's response to the Cuban missile crisis in October 1962, both required a concerted effort by the American political leadership and some consultations with the allies to deal with the crisis situations. The decisions had to be swiftly made even though they had potentially far-reaching consequences. On the other hand, the Iranian hostage crisis faced by the Carter administration in 1979–1980, lasted 444 days. The peculiarity of this case rests with the unprecedented breach of one of the most sacred rules of international conduct, that is, the diplomatic immunity from host government seizure and punishment.

The determination of a *crisis situation* varies according to the characteristics of the decision situation. Charles Hermann, for example, has identified eight possible decision situations (crisis, innovative, inertia, circumstantial, reflexive, deliberative, routinized, and administrative). Some scholars argue that most of what happens in foreign policy is *crisis management,* such as responding to situations that may have grave consequences, have occurred somewhere in the global system, and have an indirect impact on the security or well-being of a nation-state. In other words, as long as that situation has no major impact on a country, decision makers (or units) do not have to involve top-level foreign policy makers. The assumption here is that foreign policy is a continuous flow of interactions at all decision-unit levels where various types of decisions blend together into a coherent policy.

Types of Decision-Making Processes

Most followers of the comparative foreign policy school of thought identify three different types of decision-making processes: the rational actor model, the organizational process model, and the governmental or bureaucratic politics model.[40]

According to Graham Allison, when faced with a decision-making situation (or a problem that requires resolution), rational actors follow a series of intellectual steps that help them choose among the alternatives that have been calculated to maximize achievement of the desired goals; only then do they take the action necessary to implement the decision. In other words, the rational actors apparently follow a process in which they (1) define a situation that calls for a decision after an objective consideration of facts; (2) specify the goals by ranking them according to priorities; (3) consider all available means for reaching the objectives, (4) select the one objective that will maximize the goal achievement, and (5) take the well-calculated action to implement the decision. The assumption here is that governments consist of united, purposive strategists who, in possession of full information, calculate and implement actions on the basis of how best to maximize power and security. This assumption ignores possible dissent among the policy makers or disagreements in interpretations of costs and benefits based on ideological and cultural differences, as well as other constraints associated with the broad determinants of human behavior such as perception, socialization, personality development, intelligence, attitudes, and values. The **rational actor model** is considered to be an ideal type of decision-making process that seldom conforms to everyday reality. Nevertheless, decision makers who only approximate this model can be said to act more, or less, rationally.

In the **bureaucratic politics model,** governments are viewed as being composed of many parts, including both individuals and organizations. Consequently, decisions are not seen as the products of a rational, intellectual process but rather of the interaction, adjustment, and politics of people and organizations. In other words, foreign policy is a result of a political process consisting of bargaining, compromise, adjustment, arm twisting, favoritism, and sometimes even unethical methods used for political or personal gain. The central argument is that administrative *units* in the organizational structure of foreign policy making develop their own perceptions and vested interests. They tend to socialize with their employees and thereby present condensed or even distorted views of an issue. Intrabureaucratic conflicts may therefore become as problematical as interstate conflicts. This model helps to explain, for instance, the clashes between national security advisers and secretaries of state in the U.S. government. As Bert Rockman points out:

> The United States possesses two foreign ministers within the same government: the one who heads the Department of State, and the one who is the assistant to the president for national security affairs. The former heads a classically contoured bureaucracy...[the latter] has come to be seen as the president's personal spokesman as well as an influential molder, and sometime executor, of his policy choices...The NSC [National Security Council] is a fast track. In contrast, the State Department can be a ponderously slow escalator. One setting is oriented to solving problems, the other to raising them. One is more oriented to attaining a bottom line, the other to journeying down a bottomless pit.[41]

What emerges is, therefore, a process in which each participant or player sees different aspects of the same issue under consideration, has different stakes (or interests) in the game, and takes a different position.[42] As we noted in chapter 3, although individual players in the process try to act in a rational way, in the final analysis rationality will depend to a large extent on the perceptions and interpretations of facts and realities describing a situation. A state's foreign policy behavior is, therefore, not that of a monolithic actor whose participants in the process see everything alike, but a result of a set of "decision games" to formulate foreign policy followed by "action games" to implement that policy. The implementation of the policy may or may not reflect the original decision because of the complexity of human beings as participants in the process.

Reflecting on the determinants of foreign policy, especially the national attribute factors, it is fair to argue that most, if not all, foreign policy is developed with an eye to domestic problems. Depending on the type of political system, the players (or participants) in the decision-making process of foreign policy are playing different roles and exerting different influences on different types of decisions under consideration. The most important players, of course, are always at the top of the pyramid or in the center of a circle, depending on the form and shape of the illustration depicting the flow chart of the decision-making process. The less important players will be lower in that pyramid or farther from the center of the circle. Regardless of the type of situation requiring action, some scholars argue that foreign policy decisions emerge from the structured bargaining and bureaucratic games played by these participants.[43] In the third model, or the organizational process model, decisions are made through a quasimechanical reference to past decisions, precedence, routines, or governmental roles, based on the standard operating procedures of governmental organizations. These organizations rely on past experiences, rule books, guidelines, and directives to teach employees how things should be done in their organization. The **organizational process model** assumes that every government is made up of a conglomerate of loosely allied organizations that function according to standard patterns of behavior and that are fairly predictable because of their bureaucratic nature. While it all looks clear-cut and simple, a closer scrutiny of the individual decision maker will reveal that he or she is affected by idiosyncratic factors as well as by organizational and role influences.

In every governmental organization engaged in foreign policy making, the individual acting in any **role** (i.e., his or her policy making responsibilities toward a functionally defined decision-making unit) processes information. This information will inevitably result in communications that incorporate some of the individual's idiosyncratic attributes, no matter how objective he or she is. By the time information from the field is processed through the organization's bureaucratic network and presented in a condensed fashion to the authoritative decision makers, it very likely will include preferences, biases, distortions, and omissions.

In the international system with more than 160 nation-states and hundreds of non-governmental organizations all producing information through interacting with one another, it is relatively easy to see how decision makers can be overwhelmed with information. Thus, the individual in the organizational process of foreign policy making must identify the important information. In many instances an individual's behavior will be less affected by legal statutes, constitutions, job descriptions, and position within an organization and more affected by the expectations of co-workers, both superiors and subordinates. (Consider, for example, Lt. Col. Oliver North's perception of his role in the U.S. National Security Council during 1981–1986.) Some individuals in the organizational process who want to retain their positions or advance their careers may behave as they think others expect them to behave. Still other individuals are expected to follow the needs and requirements of their organizational setting rather than their personal convictions. A recent example of subordinating personal convictions to those of the organization is Henry Kissinger; as national security adviser and then as secretary of state in the Nixon administration, he was the chief architect and advocate of detente with the Soviet Union. However, after he left the office of secretary of state in 1976, Kissinger became an ardent critic of Soviet abuses of detente and unwittingly a critic of his own well-intentioned policy. Kissinger's role as national security adviser and as secretary of state illustrates that members of different organizations see different sides of a situation, depending on how that situation affects their organization. As Allison observed, where you stand depends on where you sit.

According to Allison's organizational process model, each organization within a government has a narrow range of interests and priorities, and each sees its interests as similar to and necessary ingredients of some "national interests." Because they are deeply concerned with organizational health, members are expected to demonstrate how successful their organization is; that is, how well they follow standard operating procedures (to cut down on uncertainty and risk) and how well they serve the decision makers in providing them with useful information. However, this latter activity can be used as a double-edged sword. It can involve withholding information that could embarrass the organization or implementing top-level decisions in the best interest of the organization rather than in the spirit of the decision handed down from the top.[44]

Although it is true that only the individual is capable of acting on behalf of the state, it is also a given that many individuals involved in foreign policy making act within the limitations of their particular role and are affected by the immediate environment of the decision unit. Foreign policy decisions are seldom the product of a single individual. As we have already tried to demonstrate, foreign policy decisions are usually a result of a complex process involving many individuals who act on behalf of different decision units and carry out their activities or responsibilities in an interaction with other individuals and organizations. As members of a small group, all individuals experience certain pressures to conform to the group's view and, therefore, not to challenge it. In this process of *partisan mutual adjustment* the perceptions of the individual may be changed to fit the collective views within the group. The individual's conformity to small-group views is a phenomenon called **groupthink**.[45] Typically, a decision-making organization will experience overloads; that is, more information comes in, more decisions must be made more rapidly, and more directives have to go out. Despite precautionary measures, communications channels may break down, resulting in delays and increasingly isolating the decision makers from events in the field, which in turn, may cause them to go into crisis and to engage in crisis behavior. In other words, their perceptions become polarized; they cannot think more than one or two moves ahead; they may become dominated by fear-motivated projections; they may tend to overreact and thus enter an escalation spiral. This phenomenon is what Irving Janis meant by *groupthink* behavior.[46] One of the symptoms of this behavior is the creation of an illusion of security, because group conformity leads individual members to suppress any personal doubts they may have about a situation involving risk taking.[47] For example, in the case of the surprise attack on Pearl Harbor, the "clubby" atmosphere that prevailed among the American admirals in Hawaii prevented any individual objection or opposition to a collective feeling of invincibility, despite several prior intelligence clues indicating a possible Japanese raid on the harbor.[48] A more recent failure in the foreign policy advisory process, as a consequence of Janis's groupthink syndrome, involves the diversion of profits to the Nicaraguan "freedom fighters" derived from the sale of arms to Iran. In the hearings before the Select Committee of the U.S. Senate and House of Representatives, Rear Admiral Poindexter (former national security advisor) testified (July 17, 1987) that the reason he thought of the National Security Council (NSC) as an ivory tower was that several other governmental organizations involved in foreign policy making refused to cooperate in proposing high-risk decisions to the president. According to Poindexter, the members of those organizations are interested in protecting their "own turf" and are unwilling to change their tranquil (routine) conditions for a policy involving high risks. In other words, they prefer to do business as usual and not respond to (or ignore) certain challenges in the global system. On the other hand, Poindexter saw the role of the NSC, (which serves only the president), as responding to all challenges affecting U.S. interests, even if they constitute high-risk decisions. For this reason, Poindexter apparently took it upon himself and a close-knit group of lower-level decision makers to carry out a clandestine operation without informing the president or the Congress. The attempt ended not only in failure but also in investigations by the Congress and a special prosecutor.

Another symptom of groupthink involves the group members' righteous feelings and self-esteem, leading them to conclude that the group's decisions could only be sound and flawless. In other words, the groupthink process not only causes individuals to act less rationally than they might if they were on their own, but it can also lead to a shared illusion of unanimity, rationalization, and self-censorship of doubts and counterarguments. Of course, whether any small group in the foreign policy decision-making process follows the characteristics of the groupthink phenomenon will depend on the group leader, who may or may not promote the creation of groupthink. As the reading selection by Paul A. Anderson reveals, John F. Kennedy was a good example of how to develop a consensus of top advisers in support of an improved covert invasion in March 1961—generally known as the Bay of Pigs decision. The groupthink system of "self-appointed mindguards" is clearly evident from Bobby Kennedy's admonition to Schlesinger: "You may be right or you may be wrong, but the president has made his mind up. Don't push it any further. Now is the time for everyone to help him all they can."[49] In the **Cuban missile crisis** decision, however, because the task environment was very different (i.e., to determine how to respond to an *external* event rather than to create an event), Kennedy consciously removed himself from several sessions of the Executive Committee, so that his presence would not inhibit the review of a large number of options and arguments presented at the meetings.

Finally, it may be asked, what role, if any, does morality play in foreign policy? It is not unusual for any state in the world to make foreign policy statements laced with moral principles. Such policy statements frequently invoke a positive response from the internal environment of the state and sometimes even from the external one. However, ethical norms and moral judgments are also used with great seriousness on the formulation level of decision making. In the Cuban missile crisis decision, for example, both Assistant Undersecretary of State George W. Ball and U.S. Attorney General Robert F. Kennedy argued strongly against engaging in a surprise attack on Cuba on moral and humanitarian grounds.[50] Similarly, when testifying on behalf of U.S. involvement in Vietnam, Secretary of State Dean Rusk argued convincingly that because of treaty obligations, the United States had a moral commitment to support South Vietnam against the North Vietnamese regulars infiltrating the South. Even if there is a fine line between morality and self-interest, there is ample evidence that foreign policy makers, especially at the top level of the organizational hierarchy, use moral considerations in their deliberations. Of course, whether actions taken on moral grounds will be appreciated by other actors in the international system depends greatly on the political system and its ideological orientation. President Carter's human rights policy was perhaps admired by the American people, but it was resented and criticized by some governments and people in Latin America and elsewhere. Some countries interpreted the policy as an imposition of American values on their cultures. When the Carter administration refused to provide military or economic assistance to certain authoritarian regimes in Latin America because of human rights violations, those regimes were able to obtain such assistance from other technologically advanced countries for whom the business opportunities were more important than moral considerations. The lesson that emerges from this and similar experiences is that there are no universally accepted moral codes that would be acceptable to all nation-states.

With this in mind, let us consider the so-called Machiavellian principles of political expediency. Ever since 1513, when Niccolo Machiavelli formulated the "theory of state craft" for his prince, many statesmen and diplomats followed the maxim that "the ends of the state justify its means." Under this rule of conduct, some actors can justify practically anything that is carried out in the name of a noble cause. Terrorism in the name of seeking independence or indiscriminate bombings and violations of sovereignty in the name of national survival represent acts that are heroic to one group and immoral to another, depending on who commits the act. In some political systems, such as a democracy, frequent application of the ends-justify-the-means doctrine can be both counterproductive in foreign policy and damaging to the very foundations of the democratic system. But here we encounter a dilemma: Can a democracy relinquish certain operations that sometimes require immoral acts (e.g., covert operations), even if it means sacrificing success for morality in foreign policy? All democracies struggle with this difficult question.

Summary

In this chapter we have examined a series of environments (external as well as internal), contexts, sources, and determinants of influence, and limits on the foreign policy–making process. We started out with the global system and ended with an examination of the individual as an actor and his or her psychological environment. We argued that the systemic factors—geography, international interactions, and the international system structure— and the national attribute factors—demographic, economic, military, and governmental characteristics—are objective conditions that impose limits on a state's capacity to act no matter who is at the helm or what type of governmental system a country has. However, we also maintained that subjective conditions (i.e., idiosyncratic factors, such as differences in leadership personality, temperament, and other characteristics) can also have an important impact on foreign policy. Although in a crisis situation one particular set of factors (e.g., idiosyncratic ones) could be considered the main influence on foreign policy, all three sets of factors operate simultaneously in most instances.

We pointed out that foreign policy is not a single overall plan, but rather a series of decisions that tend to fall into three categories: macro-decisions, micro-decisions, and crisis decisions. Whereas macro-decisions involve determinants of a broad, general nature and normally occur in a setting in which the need for a decision has been anticipated, micro-decisions involve consensuses that are narrow in scope and low in risk taking and that are handled at the lower layers of the governmental organization dealing with foreign policy. Crisis decisions, on the other hand, are characterized by a sense of high threat, an element of surprise, and a short time frame and involve officials at the highest levels. References to states (acting through their national government) as policy makers are in most cases symbolic expressions, usually by journalists who are less concerned with the process and more with the substance of foreign policy. States are organizations, not organisms capable of making decisions; they do not possess values, attitudes, and motivations that underlie international actions taken in their name. Only human beings are capable of the behavior conventionally attributed to the nation-state or the government as a sovereign entity. Therefore in examining foreign policy decisions, our focus must be on people acting either as individuals or as part of a group.

Following Graham Allison's typology of the decision-making process, we distinguished between the rational actor, the bureaucratic politics, and the organizational process models.

Whereas the rational actor model is based on a number of ideal assumptions (i.e., government officials carefully define the situation, specify goals, consider all possible alternative means of achieving these goals, select the final alternative, implement the decisions, and evaluate the consequence for the nation), the other two models are more realistic, treating the foreign policy establishment as a collection of individuals, groups, and organizations that may or may not act rationally and that respond to external as well as domestic stimuli. In the bureaucratic politics model, the government response to situations is largely a result of bargaining among the players in a hierarchical organization of foreign policy. The bargaining and the results of the decision-making process (i.e., the decision games and the action games) are affected by limits such as the organizational process (individual roles) and the individual political skill of the players (their idiosyncracies). The latter is responsible for the complexities that make the predecisional, formulational, and implementation stages of any decision differ from country to country. The nonrational factors can and usually do operate at all stages of the decision process. The problems associated with the idiosyncratic factors of the individual decision maker are often compounded in group or organizational decision making. Groupthink can result not only in less rational acts but also in biased images of the world, rationalization, and false self-esteem. Another source of irrational behavior in foreign policy making is reliance on morality. It is questionable whether the values and ethical considerations of one country can be imposed on another. Similarly, it is difficult to justify questionable means if they are in the pursuit of noble ends. Yet it is imperative to recognize that in a world with many cultural and ideological differences, some states will rely more heavily on moral principles in foreign policy than others.

Paul A. Anderson

███

Normal Failures in the Foreign Policy Advisory Process

Making a decision is a risky act. With the future uncertain, the "best" often ambiguous, our reasoning capabilities limited, and our knowledge always incomplete (and often wrong), mistakes, errors, and failures are inevitable. Organizations are networks of fallible decision makers, and they can magnify the risks by making the decisions of an individual depend on the fallible and error-prone decisions of others. An organization need not, however, be the simple sum of its unreliable parts. John Von Neuman[1] showed that a properly organized collection of unreliable parts can be more reliable than any of its components. Whether any organization is an optimal arrangement of its parts is doubtful. What is clear is that some ways of organizing individuals are better than others, and a great deal of attention has been focused on how organizations in the private and public sector ought to be organized.

Among the most critical decisions any government makes are foreign policy decisions where issues of peace and war are at stake. How the U.S. government ought to make those decisions has been a consistent topic of debate among policy makers, scholars, and political observers. Since the Second World War, for example, six official studies have made recommendations for improving the conduct of U.S. foreign policy,[2] and with the advent of each new administration (and often within a president's term of office), the administrative machinery of foreign and national security policy making is reorganized. A good deal of the attention to the issue has focused on the problem of presidential choice and the administrative machinery for advising presidents.[3]

Paul A. Anderson teaches in the Department of Social Studies at Carnegie-Mellon University, Pittsburgh.
SOURCE: *World Affairs* 146, no. 2 (Fall 1983): 148–174. Reprinted by permission.

A president is forced to make foreign policy decisions with the benefit of very little direct, personal, firsthand knowledge. Presidents must rely on others for advice and counsel, and the information and alternatives a president receives are largely organizational products. The quality of that advice is critical to the quality of the decision.[4] . . .

Advisory Systems and Presidents

Every president develops a system to cope with the decision-making and information-processing demands in foreign affairs. Since 1946, that system has been built around the National Security Council. The NSC is a statutory shell and presidents are given broad flexibility in how they choose to make use of it. George, Nelson, and Destler describe systematically how recent presidents have chosen to structure the system which provides them advice and counsel on foreign affairs issues.[5] There are also more limited descriptions of individual presidents or individual decisions.[6] A central issue which has not received systematic attention is why presidents adopt the advisory system they do. An understanding of this is central in understanding the relationship between advisory systems and decision-making failures.

The existing literature tends to assume that the structure of counsel and advice is a simple function of presidential style and personality: Eisenhower was a general, Kennedy enjoyed freewheeling discussions, and Nixon disliked face-to-face confrontations.[7] To be sure, individual differences are important in explaining differences between presidential advisory systems, but more than personality must be involved. For example, during the first three years of the Nixon administration there were at least ten structural changes to the system of NSC committees and review groups. Unless there were a series of "new" Nixons, personality and style do not provide much leverage in understanding so much change. Moreover, "official" descriptions of advisory systems are just as much a fiction as are formal organization charts. Presidents use a variety of strategies in deciding how to decide.[8] Although the NSC system under Nixon is generally viewed as a single Kissinger-dominated system, Kohl identified six different patterns of policy making during the Nixon administration.[9]

A different perspective on the issue is provided by theories of information processing in organizations.[10] Governing imposes severe information-processing demands on a president, and no individual has the cognitive capacity to process all the information required to govern effectively. Organizing is a solution to that problem: large tasks are decomposed into smaller tasks, a division of labor allows individual expertise and specialties to be exploited, and standard operating procedures help to ensure coordination among the various organizational subunits. The NSC system and the Executive Office of the President are the organizational forms which manage the information-processing tasks of governing. They are organizations designed with presidential interests in mind to solve an administrative problem.

An advisory system, then, is a solution to the problem of managing complex information-processing and decision-making tasks. If the organization of the White House for foreign policy is viewed as a solution to a problem, then understanding why presidents come to adopt the advisory structures they do reduces to understanding the problem that an advisory system is intended to solve. While many factors contribute to a solution to the management problem, including the personal style of the president, tradition, and domestic politics, two factors are critical in the present context: presidential interests and the environment of policy making. If the purpose of policy making is to achieve foreign policy goals in the larger international environment, then the administrative problem solving which defines advisory structures can be seen as the president's attempt to achieve management goals in the environment of policy making. Just as we cannot understand why presidents adopt the policy stances they do without knowing their policy goals and the world political environment, we cannot understand the choice of advisory strategies without understanding presidential needs and interests with respect to decision making and the bureaucratic environment of policy making.

The View from the White House

The task environment a president faces is remarkably stable from administration to administration. The institutional presidency remains relatively constant regardless of who might be sitting in the Oval Office. The major institutions, with their parochial interests, remain in place, and the organizational structures which link the White House with the permanent bureaucracy, primarily the Office of Management and Budget and the Executive Office of the President, are heavily populated with career civil servants.

There are four elements of the task environment of policy making which shape presidential solutions to the problem of managing the decision-making process: policy interests, resources, opportunities, and demands.

All presidents come into office with a set of policy goals and interests which comprise the agenda for the administration.[11] The agenda represents the list of things to which the administration must attend. Some of the items on the agenda are specific policy proposals, but other items are more general: critical issues, doctrines, priorities, and high-

level goals. A president faces the problem of translating these frequently amorphous policy interests into concrete actions, getting the larger organization of the U.S. government to pay attention to the issues, and ensuring that acceptable results are achieved.

The institution of the presidency provides the occupant of the office with a variety of resources, both symbolic and real, to enable him to achieve policy goals.[12] They include the prestige and authority which comes with the office; a "bully pulpit" from which to define issues, direct attention, and practice the art of persuasion; the administrative authority to make decisions and give orders; the power to define the premises and presumptions on which others are to make their decisions; and his personal time and attention.

The flow of issues and information in an organization provides choice opportunities or situations which call for an organizational choice.[13] These choice opportunities provide presidents with the opportunity to achieve their policy goals and interests. A president, however, does not have the power to define every choice opportunity, and policy issues frequently come embedded in substantive problems or in bureaucratic conflicts. As a result, a president faces messy problems which only partially overlap with the policy interests on his agenda. These opportunities for presidential choice come in three varieties: some come from the foreign affairs bureaucracy and tend to reflect organizational interests, some opportunities arise because of the action of other governments, and some arise because of the personal actions of the president.

The final element of the task environment consists of demands. Presidential interest and attention are not just resources the president may use to influence others; they represent valuable resources which other officials can use in the bureaucratic bargaining game. The result is a competition among members of the bureaucracy for the limited time and attention of the White House. Presidential attention is also useful for lower level actors as a way to decrease uncertainty, and to receive direction and permission to take action. A further source of demands on the office of the president are other actors with their own agendas, resources, and opportunities. Government action does not always require presidential decision, and maintaining control over the action of powerful "others" places heavy demands on the presidency and the White House.

This rough specification of the task environment of policy making is the first part of the definition of the problem facing a president. The second part of the problem definition is the decision-making needs and interests of a president. The advisory structures a president adopts will reflect an attempt to further presidential decision-making interests in the complex and frequently unfriendly environment of policy making.

Existing work on presidential interests with respect to decision making, particularly the work of George and of Janis, presumes a particular presidential interest: Presidents are presumed to be disinterested deciders with a single overriding interest in discovering the "best" course of action.[14] Presidents, however, have a variety of legitimate interests which include minimizing decision-making costs, holding political coalitions together, persuading organizational subunits to accept presidential directives, and achieving substantive policy goals. While George recognizes the importance of these other considerations, his view is that a president's central interest in "high-quality decisions" can be separated from other interests.[15] Presidents are forced to exchange decision quality for management of time and the forging of a consensus of their advisers. It seems unlikely, however, that such a clean analytic separation can be drawn in the complex setting of policy making. As Greenstein suggests, the politics of decision making permeate the information-processing tasks to the extent that timely decisions and political support become part of the definition of a high-quality decision.[16]

A president in his role as chief executive has important interests which go beyond making choices. Leadership means, among other things, making the organization do things it would not otherwise have done. It means bargaining, persuading, pulling, and hauling. It means educating other participants as well as being educated by them. The attributes of presidential leadership, a vision of a better future, a sense of the possibilities, and the ability to move the nation toward that future, do not encourage individuals with a passive orientation. Presidents are elected to govern and manage change, and all presidents have a central interest in controlling the executive branch and in getting their programs and policies implemented. While presidents have a real interest in receiving a wide-ranging assessment of issues, interests, alternatives, and consequences, no president has an interest in seeing those assessments interfere with managing and leading.

This is a rough outline of the view from the White House. Presidents have a set of policy goals they would like to accomplish. They face an environment which is a mixture of opportunities and obstacles. Their problem is to choose advisory and decision-making procedures which will allow them to achieve their policy-making interests given the larger environment of the policy process. . . .

Postmortems and Normal Failures

A failure of the decision-making process is invariably signaled by a disastrous outcome. The disasters produced by a normal failure are no different than the disasters produced by systemic failures. Normal failures do not announce themselves. Distinguishing systemic from normal failures requires an examination of the process which led to the failure. Systemic failures will be characterized by a breakdown of the decision-making process, normal failures by an inappropriate, though adequately executed, procedure. Because any disaster could have been prevented had the decision makers behaved differently, disastrous outcomes are invariably classified as arising from a systemic failure. It is conceivable, however, that what appear to be malfunctions of the advisory process are more appropriately viewed as decision-making strategies inappropriate for the particular task environment, that is, as normal failures. One such candidate for a normal failure is the 1961 Bay of Pigs debacle. The most well-developed systemic-failure explanation of the policy-making failure is provided by Janis' groupthink syndrome.[17] Groupthink-induced failures fall within the class of systemic failures because they involve defective information processing brought on by pressures for conformity in policy-making groups.[18]

The CIA–sponsored invasion of Cuba in 1961 was a classic fiasco, without a doubt. The president of the United States approved a plan to use U.S.–trained Cuban exile groups to invade Cuba, spark a general uprising, and overthrow the Castro government with the understanding that the central role played by the U.S. government would be secret. It was to be a replay of the 1954 overthrow of the Guatemalan government, but it turned out to be anything but a replay of that successful covert CIA operation. The poorly trained and equipped exiles were overwhelmed by the Cuban militia, the flimsy U.S. cover story was quickly torn to shreds, and the new administration was held up to public scorn and criticism.

The debacle was not only that the attempt was so unsuccessful, but that it was even tried. A careful analysis of the decision demonstrates that the process which led to the attempt involved a series of blunders and outright mistakes. Janis identifies six major miscalculations which could have been corrected had the decision-making group been more critical and probing:[19] (1) that no one would know the U.S. was involved; (2) that the Cuban air force was ineffectual; (3) that the invasion force was willing and able to carry out the invasion without direct U.S. support; (4) that the Cuban army was so weak that the invasion force could establish a beachhead; (5) that the invasion would touch off a popular uprising against Castro; and (6) even if the initial assault failed, that the brigade could retreat to the mountains and carry on a guerrilla war against Castro. In diagnosing the failure, Janis points to the lack of vigilant information processing among Kennedy and his advisers. From his perspective the Bay of Pigs decision was a systemic failure brought about by psychological pressures for consensus and conformity within the decision-making group; it was an extraordinary failure of the advisory process and required an explanation in terms of extraordinary factors.

But was the Bay of Pigs decision the result of a systemic failure of the advisory process? Wyden's recent analysis of the Bay of Pigs incident casts some doubt on Janis's interpretation of an advisory process undone by psychological pressures.[20] First, critical discussion was not absent from the series of decision-making meetings. Kennedy rejected the initial CIA plan as too spectacular, and in doing so, identified a key tradeoff between the risk of disclosure and the risk of failure: A large-scale invasion with U.S. air support would have the greatest chance of success, but the U.S. role could not then be hidden; a quiet invasion would attract less attention to the United States but would have a greater chance of failure. According to Wyden, Kennedy rejected the large-scale invasion and asked that the military and political risks be brought into a more acceptable balance.[21] Moreover, the evidence indicates that Kennedy made the key decisions alone, somewhat reluctantly, and with a great deal of thought. Certainly these bits of evidence do not support the conclusion that the Bay of Pigs decision was exemplary. They do, however, suggest that the decision-making process which led to the Bay of Pigs did not suffer a complete breakdown.

If the Bay of Pigs decision is to be viewed as a normal failure, the first task is to identify the decision-making strategy. Wyden's analysis suggests a two-stage decision-making procedure.[22] The first part of the process involved a closed decision-making process and a president who was acting as a disinterested decider. The CIA members of the policy-making group acted as advocates attempting to convince the president and his advisers that their plan represented an efficient means for achieving the common goal of doing something about Castro. Once Kennedy had accepted the concept of a CIA–sponsored invasion of Cuba, he shifted from his disinterested decider role to one which emphasized getting his advisers to agree on a plan with a minimal risk of failure. Throughout both phases the policy process

remained closed. The first phase lasted from the time Kennedy was first informed of the plan, within weeks of his election, until March 11, 1961. On that date a meeting was held during which Kennedy rejected the initial plans, which called for a large-scale invasion, and requested a plan which better achieved the goal of keeping the U.S. hand hidden. After that meeting, a National Security Action memorandum summarized the decision:

> The president expects to authorize U.S. support for an appropriate number of patriotic Cubans to return to their homeland. He believes that the best possible plan, from the point of view of combined military, political, and psychological considerations has not yet been presented, and new proposals are to be concerted promptly. Action: Central Intelligence Agency with appropriate consultation.[23]

Once Kennedy had made the decision to go ahead with an acceptable version of the CIA plan, the incentives and motives of the players shifted. For the CIA, the goal was to design a plan which would be minimally acceptable to the president. Kennedy had the dual objectives of persuading the CIA to make appropriate modifications to their original proposal and to develop a consensus of his top advisers in support of an improved covert invasion. In time, Kennedy achieved both. The CIA produced a plan which appeared to have an acceptable political risk, and he forged a consensus in support of his proposal. Nevertheless, when it was time to make the final decision, he did not rush to judgment, but made his decision with what appeared to be a great deal of reluctance.

In retrospect, it is clear that the decision strategy adopted in this circumstance was inappropriate for the task environment. Kennedy overestimated the coherence of the CIA's planning, as well as their operational abilities. The key decision, that an acceptable plan could be developed and successfully executed, changed the policy problem into one of finding a particular solution to the problem of getting rid of Castro. It thus became almost an issue of implementing a presidential decision rather than a continued exercise in evaluating alternative courses of action. From this perspective, there was no extraordinary breakdown of the policy advisory process. The real mistake was in believing that the CIA could develop a coherent workable plan.

For the Bay of Pigs decision to be an instance of a normal failure, the following proposition must be supported: The decision-making strategy adopted in the Bay of Pigs decision fell within the range of reasonable solutions to the problems of managing the decision-making process. The most compelling case that the decision making was grossly defective is provided by the groupthink syndrome. In developing his groupthink explanation of the Bay of Pigs decision, Janis lists six symptoms of groupthink which were displayed during that time: (1) the illusion of invulnerability, (2) the illusion of unanimity, (3) the suppression of personal doubts, (4) self-appointed mindguards, (5) docility fostered by suave leadership, and (6) the taboo against antagonizing valuable new members. The normal failure perspective suggests that four (and perhaps five) of the symptoms of groupthink are merely reflections of the normal and ordinary operation of the foreign policy decision-making process and are probably to be found in most situations involving a decision-making strategy with a closed-policy process.

Conflict and consensus are key factors in making any governmental decision. The foreign policy issues which confront a government are sufficiently important and complex that there are always grounds on which reasonable people can disagree. While conflict can be useful in ensuring that a full range of views is explored, uncontrolled conflict will paralyze an organization into inaction.[24] Although optimal decision-making procedures may require policy goals to be operational with fully specified tradeoffs, the costs involved make agreement on a comprehensive representation of goals and interests exceedingly unlikely for two reasons. First, the information-processing requirements of such a task would overwhelm the individual cognitive capacities of the participants. Second, because reasonable people will disagree, even if individuals had the cognitive capacity to perform the task, it is unlikely they would reach agreement. As a result, organizations develop strategies for controlling policy conflict. Among the conflict-controlling strategies identified by Cyert and March are sequential attention to goals, the use of acceptable-level decision rules, and feedback-react decision procedures.[25] Each of these strategies has the effect of limiting the information-processing demands on decision makers, as well as minimizing goal conflict.

Strategies for controlling decision-making conflict in organizations have the effect of making consensus an important attribute of any decision. The point is not that all conflict is swept aside, or that everyone must agree with every decision: Conflict still persists. From a leadership perspective, consensus is a desirable attribute for several reasons. First, a consensus gives some assurance that the decision is not ill founded. While consensus does not represent a guarantee, for even a group can be wrong, the willingness of individuals to go along does signal something. Second,

a consensus gives a leader some assurance that the decisions will be faithfully implemented. Few presidential decisions are self-implementing, and a president has a greater assurance that the actions of others will reflect the spirit of his decision when they have concurred in it. Finally, consensus represents the costs of bargaining in an essentially political environment. Presidents would probably prefer not to have to bargain, to compromise, and to forge a consensus of advisers, but in a policy environment where presidential favor is not the only source of power, consensus is the cost of governing. The issue "is not so much that a consensus is a necessary condition before a policy can be adopted as that the advocates of a particular policy attempt to build a consensus as a means of getting their policy adopted."[26]

Incentives to limit decision-making conflict and forge a consensus can be seen as underlying five of the six symptoms of groupthink in the Bay of Pigs decision-making process. The illusion of unanimity occurs when "the group leader and the members support each other, playing up the areas of convergence in their thinking, at the expense of fully exploring divergences that might disrupt the unity of the group."[27] Fully exploring divergences in a decision-making group will have the effect of bringing conflict and disagreement into the open. While some conflict and disagreement is a good thing, exploring divergences fully will tend to create conflict which cannot be reasonably resolved. It is difficult and costly to make a group of independent individuals with different goals and different value tradeoffs reach unanimous agreement. No decision maker has an interest in raising issues which cannot be resolved.

A second symptom of groupthink is the suppression of personal doubts. This, too, can be seen as a natural consequence of the value complexity of policy making. Few policy issues lend themselves to certainty, and any decision maker is bound to have some doubts about any course of action. If every individual expressed all his doubts about every decision, common agreement would rarely be achieved. While complete self-censorship is clearly undesirable, every choice will involve some lingering doubt among some advisers.[28]

Janis's third symptom of groupthink is the presence of "self-appointed mindguards." Janis cites Bobby Kennedy's admonition to Schlesinger's expression of doubt: "You may be right or you may be wrong, but the president has made his mind up. Don't push it any further. Now is the time for everyone to help him all they can."[29] Janis presents this as a grave violation of appropriate behavior. Perhaps in this situation it was. It could also have been Bobby Kennedy's way of reminding Schlesinger that he had lost in the policy game, that his views had not prevailed, and that it was inappropriate for him to continue to fight the issue when the president had made his decision. The norms of appropriate behavior also include the injunction that, once decided, an issue should stay decided, and losers should not attempt to continue the policy debate in an attempt to change the decision. Given the high costs of reaching agreement, leaders have a strong incentive to demand that their subordinates accept presidential decisions. In this instance, JFK had already signaled his intention to approve an "acceptable" invasion plan in the National Security Decision Memorandum quoted above, and in that context, it is not suprising that Bobby Kennedy attempted to silence Schlesinger's concerns.

"Docility fostered by suave leadership" is the fifth symptom of groupthink which can also be seen as a natural consequence of the decision-making strategy. Janis argues that JFK's leadership style, particularly at the April 4, 1961 meeting, in which an open straw vote was taken, tended to coerce unwilling advisers to accept the plan. There seems little doubt that Kennedy manipulated the discussion, that his intention was not to hold a full and thorough airing of different views. It seems likely he had made an "in principle" decision to go ahead, and he wanted a consensus of his advisers in support of his decision. In evaluating JFK's performance, it is critical to remember that this was not the first meeting on this issue. The participants had made their views known in a series of previous meetings. It was very unlikely that another round would have uncovered any new information which would have changed any minds. The evidence from a whole series of presidents and presidential decisions suggests that this sort of manipulation is not uncommon. The importance of a consensus from a management perspective makes holding a meeting "for the record" a useful device for gaining the official commitment of subordinates to a presidential decision.

Two symptoms of groupthink remain unexplained from a normal failure perspective: the illusion of invulnerability, and the taboo against antagonizing valuable new members. The taboo against antagonizing new members could be seen as a manifestation of the need to control and limit conflict in decision-making groups, but that interpretation is even more speculative than the preceding claims and is probably best left alone. There is no reason to expect the normal incentives of policy making would tend to produce an illusion of invulnerability among the members of a decision-making group. But that by itself does not strike at the core of the present argument. The point is not that the Bay of Pigs decision was a good decision, or that psychological pressures for conformity are irrelevant in understanding the behavior of the decision makers. Instead, the point is that the symptoms of extraordinary failure of the process of policy making may not be so extraordinary after all, but simply reflections of the normal and ordinary operation of a particular decision-making strategy.

The still fragmentary evidence suggests that JFK adopted a two-phase decision-making strategy within the context of a closed policy-making group. During the first phase he acted as a disinterested decider, critically examining the proposals of his advisers. After a series of meetings during which the invasion plan was modified at his request, JFK made up his mind. At that point, the decision strategy shifted. He was no longer interested in exploring divergent viewpoints. Instead, he was interested in getting a consensus behind a course of action. Once he had forged an agreement among his advisors, he was left with the final choice. This sort of decision-making style would be sufficient to generate most of the symptoms of groupthink. But was it within the realm of reasonable solutions to the administrative problem of deciding how to decide?

There are grounds for thinking that the decision-making strategy was within the bounds of normality. In fact, a good case can be made that Kennedy used almost the same decision-making strategy in the Cuban missile crisis. Much has been made of the lessons JFK learned from the Bay of Pigs debacle and how those lessons shaped his behavior during the missile crisis.[30] Recently revealed aspects of Kennedy's behavior during the missile crisis suggest that the lessons had less to do with encouraging high-quality information processing and more to do with whom he could trust. During the first few days of the crisis, Kennedy appeared to act as a disinterested decider, just as he had during the Bay of Pigs. Moreover, the policy process was kept relatively closed: Except for RFK and Sorenson, the membership of the ExCom (Executive Committee) was not so different from the Bay of Pigs group, although it is true that a broader spectrum of lower-level officials was allowed to participate. By the evening of the third day JFK indicated his provisional decision in favor of a blockade, just as he had made the "in principle" decision in favor of the invasion.[31] Just as he had in the Bay of Pigs decision, JFK wanted a consensus in support of his preferred course of action, so he sent the group back with the clear signal that a blockade was his preferred course of action. The next two days were spent forging a consensus in support of a blockade. While unanimity was not achieved, RFK, McGeorge Bundy, and Robert McNamara were able to get the air strike advocates to agree that a blockade was an acceptable, though second-best, course of action. The meeting at which the official decision was reached resembled a Greek drama: The participants read their scripted parts and the plot moved inexorably toward the predetermined outcome.[32]

Later in the crisis, when it became necessary to face the prospect of trading U.S. missiles in Turkey for Soviet missiles in Cuba, JFK offered Khrushchev an informal, under-the-table deal. He would promise to remove the missiles from Turkey in trade for the Soviet missiles in Cuba. This, on Allison's analysis, was the crucial concession which resolved the crisis.[33] The only condition Kennedy placed on the swap was that it could not be made part of the public record. The trade would have to be implicit. What is striking about the "deal" is that not only was it withheld from the public, it was also withheld from the full membership of the ExCom. Only JFK's most trusted advisers were aware that Bobby Kennedy had made the offer to Dobrynin.[34] When making that critical choice, it seems JFK had no interest in a full and critical discussion of the issues with the ExCom.

Thus, the pattern of decision making in the Cuban missile crisis shares a number of strong similarities with the decision-making style of the Bay of Pigs decision. Moreover, the missile crisis displayed a number of the same symptoms of groupthink. Clearly Kennedy was the same "suave" leader with the ability to manipulate a group of high-level advisers. There were clearly pressures to silence diverging points of view in the case of Adlai Stevenson. Had the outcome been seen as a failure, there would have been many who could have pointed to suppressed personal doubts. Self-appointed mindguards operated to limit dissent and objection once the president had made his decision. Clearly, the Cuban missile crisis was not just a replay of the Bay of Pigs. There were significant differences in the quality of the information processing which lay behind the decision. But that is not the issue. The decision-making strategy was almost identical, but the task environment was different. In the Bay of Pigs decision, the CIA came to the president with a fully developed plan of action. From the CIA's perspective, their task was to get Kennedy to let them do what they wanted to do. By choosing a closed policy-making process, Kennedy undermined the ability of others to successfully challenge the CIA. In the Cuban missile crisis, the task environment was very different. The problem was not to evaluate the claims of a group which attempted to convince a president to let them act, but to determine how to respond to an external event. This being the case, the specialization and division of labor which hindered outside evaluations of the CIA's invasion plans actually contributed to the quality of the alternatives presented to Kennedy. Each part of the organization was able to proffer a solution which reflected that subunit's particular capabilities, and the conflict between different advocates helped clarify the issues for Kennedy. Thus from a normal failure perspective the

big difference between the Bay of Pigs and the missile crisis was not the decision-making strategy or the quality of the information processing, but the task environment. The strategy was appropriate in the environment of the missile crisis; it was inappropriate in the environment of the Bay of Pigs.

Conclusions

Making a decision is a risky act and failures are bound to occur. Determining the cause of failures and designing improved decision-making procedures requires more than simply examining the disasters and deciding what decision makers should have done differently. Failures come in several varieties, and determining causes and designing improvements requires an appreciation of the varieties of ways the system can fail to work. The implications of the argument for research seem clear:

1. It is not enough to examine failures. Descriptions of failures provide no information about what distinguishes them from successes.

2. The way in which a president sets about getting information and advice is a reflection of diverse presidential interests and the task environment of the policy process. Understanding the solution to the administrative problem requires understanding the diversity of presidential interests, the complexities and dynamics of the task environment of policy making, and the range of available solutions to the problem of deciding how to decide. Our existing knowledge of these aspects is surprisingly limited, and largely based on secondhand sources. We need to develop better, more systematic ways to exploit the rich archival records now becoming available.

3. Lists of presidential interests, task environments, and policy-making strategies are not enough. Some failures occur because the decision-making process does not always work as it should. Other failures occur because the decision-making strategy is inappropriate for the task environment. We need a better developed understanding of the differences. We need to understand how task environments interact with decision-making strategies, and we need to know how decision processes fail.

4. Prescriptions presume theories able to support counterfactuals about policy-making strategies and task environments. If we are to be taken seriously as institutional designers, then we must be able to make sensible claims about the effects of our designs. Too much of the prescriptive work on organizations (and here I am thinking primarily of the various "snake oils" which get peddled to organizations in the private sector) lacks a strong empirical

and theoretical basis. The issues of how presidents make foreign policy decisions are too important to be left to the carnival barkers.

Notes

This paper was prepared for delivery at the 1983 Annual Meeting of the American Political Science Association, Chicago, Illinois, September 1–4, 1983.

1. J. Von Neuman, "Probabilistic Logics and the Synthesis of Reliable Organisms from Unreliable Components," in C. E. Shannon and J. McCarthy (eds.), *Automota Studies,* (Princeton: Princeton University Press, 1956).

2. G. T. Allison and P. Szanton, *Remaking Foreign Policy* (New York: Basic Books, 1976).

3. W. I. Bacchus, "Obstacles to Reform in Foreign Affairs: The Case of NSAM 341," *Orbis* 18, 1974, pp. 266–276; K. C. Clark and L. F. Legere (eds.), *The President and the Management of National Security* (New York: Praeger, 1969); I. M. Destler, *Presidents, Bureaucrats and Foreign Policy* (Princeton: Princeton University Press, 1972), and "National Security II: The Rise of the Assistant (1961–1981)", in H. Heclo and L. M. Salamon (eds.) *The Illusion of Presidential Government* (Boulder, CO: Westview Press, 1981); A. L. George, *Presidential Decisionmaking in Foreign Policy: The Effective Use of Information and Advice* (Boulder, CO: Westview Press, 1980); P. Y. Hammond, "The National Security Council as a Device for Interdepartmental Coordination: An Interpretation and Appraisal," *American Political Science Review* 54 (1960): 899–910; S. Hess, *Organizing the Presidency* (Washington, D.C.: Brookings Institution, 1976); H. M. Jackson (ed.) *The National Security Council: Jackson Subcommittee Papers on Policy Making at the Presidential Level* (New York: Praeger, 1965); R. T. Johnson, *Managing the White House: An Intimate Study of the Presidency* (New York: Harper & Row, 1974); A. K. Nelson, "National Security I: Inventing a Process (1945–1960)," in H. Heclo and L. M. Salamon (eds.) *The Illusion of Presidential Government* (Boulder, CO: Westview Press, 1981).

4. The most personal factors a president can bring to a decision setting are personal interest (which focuses the attention of others on the issue) and high-level goals and objectives (which identify certain outcomes as desirable).

5. A. L. George, *Presidential Decisionmaking,* 1980; Nelson, "National Security I," 1981; Destler, "National Security II," 1981.

6. W. L. Kohl, "The Nixon–Kissinger Foreign Policy System and U.S.-European Relations: Patterns of Policy Making," *World Politics* 28 (1975); F. I. Greenstein, *The Hidden Hand Presidency* (New York: Basic Books, 1982); R. H. Immerman, "The Anatomy of the Decision Not to Fight: Multiple Advocacy or Presidential Choice?" presented at the 1982 Annual Meeting of the American Political Science Association; L. Berman, *Planning a Tragedy: The Americanization of the War in Vietnam* (New York: Norton, 1982).

7. Destler, *Presidents, Bureaucrats and Foreign Policy,* 1972; Johnson, *Managing the White House,* 1974; Hess, *Organizing the Presidency,* 1976; George, *Presidential Decisionmaking,* 1980.

8. Greenstein, *The Hidden-Hand Presidency,* 1982.

9. Kohl, "The Nixon-Kissinger Foreign Policy System," 1975.

10. J. G. March and H. A. Simon, *Organizations* (New York: Wiley, 1958); H. A. Simon, *Administrative Behavior* (New York: Free Press, 1976).

11. P. C. Light, *The President's Agenda: Domestic Policy Choice from Kennedy to Carter (with notes on Ronald Reagan)* (Baltimore: Johns Hopkins University Press, 1982).

12. R. E. Neustadt, *Presidential Power: The Politics of Leadership from FDR to Carter* (New York: Wiley, 1980; J. Helmer, "The Presidential Office: Velvet Fist in an Iron Glove," in H. Heclo and L. M. Salamon (eds.) *The Illusion of Presidential Government,* 1981; Hess, *Organizing the Presidency,* 1976.

13. M. D. Cohen, J. G. March, and J. P. Olsen, "A Garbage Can Model of Organizational Choice," *Administrative Science Quarterly* 17 (1972): 1–26.

14. George, *Presidential Decisionmaking,* 1980; I. L. Janis, *Groupthink,* 2nd ed. (Boston: Houghton Mifflin, 1982).

15. George, *Presidential Decisionmaking.*

16. Greenstein, *The Hidden-Hand Presidency.*

17. Janis, *Groupthink.*

18. L. Gelb, with R. K. Betts, *The Irony of Vietnam: The System Worked* (Washington, D.C.: Brookings Institution, 1979). His analysis suggests that that may have been a normal failure.

19. Janis, *Groupthink.*

20. P. Wyden, *Bay of Pigs: The Untold Story* (New York: Simon and Schuster, 1979).

21. Ibid., p. 101.

22. Ibid.

23. Ibid., p. 101.

24. George, *Presidential Decisionmaking;* M. D. Cohen, "The Power of Parallel Thinking," *Journal of Economic Behavior and Organization* 2 (1981): 285–306.

25. R. Cyert and J. G. March, *A Behavioral Theory of the Firm* (Englewood Cliffs: Prentice-Hall, 1963).

26. R. Hilsman, "The Foreign Policy Consensus: An Interim Research Report," *Journal of Conflict Resolution* 3 (1959): 371.

27. Janis, *Groupthink,* p. 37.

28. Evidence of the suppression of personal doubt would seem to be a highly unreliable indicator of a failure of the policy process. If certainty is a scarce condition in policy making, then every decision involves some doubt. When the outcome of the decision is seen as a disaster, individuals would have a natural tendency to remember their doubts and uncertainties. When the outcome of the decision is seen as a success, the reverse tendency would tend to magnify the certainty with which the decision makers anticipated the outcome. Thus the incidence of the suppression of personal doubt will tend to be overrepresented in policy failures and ignored in policy successes.

29. Janis, *Groupthink,* p. 40.

30. T. C. Sorensen, *Kennedy* (New York: Harper & Row, 1965); R. E. Neustadt and G. T. Allison, "Afterword," in R. F. Kennedy, *Thirteen Days* (New York: Norton, 1971); George, *Presidential Decisionmaking.*

31. D. Detzer, *The Brink: Cuban Missile Crisis, 1962* (New York: Thomas Y. Crowell, 1979); G. T. Allison, *Essence of Decision: Explaining the Cuban Missile Crisis* (Boston: Little, Brown, 1971).

32. Allison, *Essence of Decision,* p. 208.

33. Ibid., pp. 229–230.

34. A. M. Schlesinger, Jr., *Robert Kennedy and His Times* (New York: Ballantine, 1978). He was first to suggest that knowledge of the informal swap was closely held. His account was confirmed by the principles in a *Time Magazine* essay detailing the lessons of the crisis in 1982 (Rusk, McNamara, Ball, Gilpatric, Sorensen, and Bundy, 1982).

Study Questions

1. What do we mean by *foreign policy*?
2. What are the main postulates of the comparative foreign policy school of thought?
3. What are the key categories influencing foreign policy behavior?
4. Explain the phenomena under the systemic factors.
5. What does *distance* signify in conflict or cooperation among nation-states?
6. Explain the variations of the international system structure.
7. Why have most less developed nations followed a policy of nonalignment?
8. What are the characteristics of a major actor in the international system?
9. What are the differences between unipolar, bipolar, and multipolar system structure?
10. What is the meaning of *sphere of influence*?
11. Give some examples of national attributes.
12. Why is demography important as a national attribute?
13. How can economic characteristics affect a state's foreign policy?
14. Why is the economic system important in the determination of foreign policy behavior?
15. Why are military characteristics difficult to measure?
16. Why does the governmental system matter in shaping foreign policy behavior?
17. What is the impact of public opinion and mass media on foreign policy behavior in closed and open political systems?
18. How does internal political stability affect foreign policy?
19. Explain the phenomena under idiosyncratic factors.
20. Why is the psychological environment important in understanding foreign policy behavior?
21. How does displacement of private motives onto public objects manifest itself?

22. Why is the physical and mental ability of the policy maker important?
23. Why do we refer to idiosyncratic characteristics as part of the subjective conditions of the environment?
24. What do we mean by the foreign policy process?
25. Explain the meaning of *macro-decisions* and *micro-decisions* in foreign policy behavior.
26. How do *crisis decisions* differ from macro- and micro-decisions?
27. Distinguish between the rational actor model and the bureaucratic politics and the organizational process models of decision making.
28. Why is *role* important in the nonrational models of the decision-making process?
29. What do we mean by the phenomenon *groupthink*?
30. Explain the characteristics of groupthink.
31. What role does morality play in foreign policy?
32. What are the main issues concerning comparative foreign policy analysis?
33. What are the reasons for normal failures in the foreign policy advisory process?
34. Compare the Bay of Pigs decision with that of the Cuban missile crisis decision in the Kennedy administration. Why was one a failure and the other a success?

Key Terms

bureaucratic politics model
capitalism
communism
comparative foreign policy analysis
crisis decision
Cuban missile crisis
foreign policy
Geneva Group of Seventy-Seven (G 77)
groupthink
idiosyncratic factors
interdependence
international system structure

macro-decision
micro-decision
military-industrial complex
national attribute factors
neocolonialism
new thinking
organizational process model
rapprochement
rational actor model
role
systemic factors

Notes

1. For efforts to arrive at a more comprehensive theory of comparative foreign policy, see chap. 3, pp. 38ff. See also Charles W. Kegley, Jr., *The Comparative Study of Foreign Policy: Paradise Lost?* (Columbia: University of South Carolina, 1980); James N. Rosenau, P. Burgess, and C. F. Hermann, "The Adaptation of Foreign Policy Research," *International Relations Quarterly* 17 (1973): 119–144; J. Wilkenfield, G. W. Hopple, P. J. Rossa, and S. J. Andriole, *Foreign Policy Behavior* (Newbury Park, Calif.: Sage, 1980); M. A. East, S. A. Salmore, and C. F. Hermann, *Why Nations Act: Theoretical Perspectives for Comparative Foreign Policy Studies* (Newbury Park, Calif.: Sage, 1978); P. McGowan and H. Shapiro, *The Comparative Study of Foreign Policy* (Newbury Park, Calif.: Sage, 1973); P. Callahan, L. P. Brady, and M. G. Hermann, eds., *Describing*

Foreign Policy Behavior (Newbury Park, Calif.: Sage, 1982); *Sage International Yearbook of Foreign Policy* (Newbury Park, Calif.: Sage, 1973–1985); and *International Studies Notes,* XIII, no. 2 (Spring 1987): 31–55.

2. See, for example, Frederic S. Pearson and J. Martin Rochester, *International Relations: The Global Condition in the Late Twentieth Century* (Reading, Mass.: Addison-Wesley, 1984), pp. 146ff.

3. James N. Rosenau, "Pre-Theories and Theories of Foreign Policy" in *The Scientific Study of Foreign Policy,* rev. ed., ed. James N. Rosenau (London: Frances Pinter, 1980), pp. 115–169.

4. For the impact of technology on geography in international politics, see Raymond F. Hopkins and Richard W. Mansbach, *Structure and Process in International Politics* (New York: Harper & Row, 1975), pp. 148ff.

5. See, for example, Kenneth Boulding, *Conflict and Defense: A General Theory* (New York: Harper & Row, 1962); Quincy Wright, *A Study of War* (Chicago: University of Chicago Press, 1965); and Frederic S. Pearson, "Geographic Proximity and Foreign Military Intervention," *Journal of Conflict Resolution* 18 (September 1974): 432–460.

6. See, for example, Steven J. Brams, "Transaction Flows in the International System," *American Political Science Review* 60 (December 1966): 880–898; Richard L. Merritt, "Distance and Interaction Among Political Communities," *General Systems Yearbook* 9 (1964): 255–263; and Bruce M. Russett, *International Regions and the International System: A Study in Political Ecology* (Chicago: Rand McNally, 1967), pp. 200–201.

7. See Rudolph J. Rummel, *The Dimensions of Nations* (Newbury Park, Calif.: Sage, 1972), pp. 407–410.

8. Robert Keohane and Joseph Nye, *Power and Interdependence: World Politics in Transition* (Boston: Little, Brown, 1977), chap. 1.

9. See, for example, Michael P. Sullivan, *International Relations: Theories and Evidence* (Englewood Cliffs, N.J.: Prentice-Hall, 1976), pp. 169–200; A. F. K. Organski and Jacek Kugler, *The War Ledger* (Chicago: University of Chicago Press, 1980); and Randolph M. Siverson and Michael R. Tennefess, "Power, Alliance, and the Escalation of International Conflict, 1851–1965," *American Political Science Review* LXXVIII, no. 4 (December 1984): 1057–1069.

10. Pearson and Rochester, *International Relations,* pp. 158–159.

11. Bruce Russett and Harvey Starr, *World Politics: The Menu for Choice* (New York: W. H. Freeman, 1985), pp. 94–95.

12. Bruce Bueno de Mesquita, *The War Trap* (New Haven: Yale University Press, 1981).

13. See Bruce M. Russett, "Pearl Harbor: Deterrence Theory and Decision Theory," *Journal of Peace Research,* no. 2 (1967): 89–106.

14. See Nazli Choucri and Robert C. North, *Nations in Conflict* (San Francisco: W. H. Freeman, 1975).

15. See Pearson and Rochester, *International Relations,* p. 162.

16. See Maurice A. East, "Size and Foreign Policy Behavior: A Test of Two Models," *World Politics* 25 (1973): 556–576; and Harold K. Jacobson, *Networks of Interdependence* (New York: Knopf, 1979), p. 54.

17. See, for example, Yaacov Vertzberger, "Bureaucratic-Organizational Politics and Information Processing in a Developing State, *International Studies Quarterly* 28 (1984): 69–95.

18. Paul A. Baran and Paul M. Sweezy, *Monopoly Capital: An Essay on the American Economy and Social Order* (Harmondsworth, England: Pelican Publishing House,

1968). It is interesting to note, however, that in 1978, for example, the Soviet Union was in fourth place, after Iraq, Israel, and Saudi Arabia, whereas the United States was in eighth place in defense expenditure spending, or less than half of the Soviet Union's as a percentage of GNP. See Pearson and Rochester, *International Relations,* table 5.1, p. 165.

19. See, for example, Benjamin J. Cohen, *The Question of Imperialism* (New York: Basic Books, 1973), chap. 4; Frederic S. Pearson, "American Military Intervention Abroad: A Test of Economic and Non-economic Explanations," in *The Politics of Aid, Trade and Investment,* eds. Satish Raichur and Craig Liske (New York: Wiley, 1976), chap. 2; and Bruce M. Russett and Elizabeth C. Hanson, *Interest and Ideology: The Foreign Policy Beliefs of American Businessmen* (San Francisco: W. H. Freeman, 1975), chap. 5.

20. U.S. Arms Control and Disarmament Agency, *World Military Expenditures and Arms Transfers 1975–1985* (Washington, D.C.: Government Printing Office, 1987).

21. Ruth Leger Sivard, *World Military and Social Expenditures 1983* (Washington, D.C.: World Priorities, 1983).

22. U.S. Arms Control and Disarmament Agency, *World Military Expenditures and Arms Transfers 1972–1982* (Washington, D.C.: Government Printing Office, 1984), p. 4.

23. See Vernon V. Aspaturian, "The Soviet Military–Industrial Complex: Does It Exist?" in *Testing the Theory of the Military–Industrial Complex,* ed. Steven J. Rosen (Lexington, Mass.: Heath, 1973).

24. For the role of special interest groups engaged in the support of military spending, see Stanley Lieberson, "An Empirical Study of Military–Industrial Linkages," in *Testing the Theory of the Military–Industrial Complex,* ed. Steven J. Rosen (Lexington, Mass.: Heath, 1973).

25. See Pearson and Rochester, *International Relations,* p. 169.

26. See, for example, Robert A. Dahl, *Who Governs? Democracy and Power in an American City* (New Haven: Yale University Press, 1961); and Benjamin Page and Robert Shapiro, "Effects of Public Opinion on Policy," *American Political Science Review* 77, no. 1 (March 1983): 175–190.

27. See Charles W. Kegley, Jr., and Eugene R. Wittkopf, "Beyond Consensus: The Domestic Context of American Foreign Policy," *International Journal* (Canada), XXXVIII, no. 4 (1983–1984): 77–106; James N. Rosenau and Ole R. Holsti, "U.S. Leadership in a Shrinking World: The Breakdown of Consensuses and the Emergence of Conflicting Belief Systems," *World Politics* XXXV, no. 3 (April 1983): 368–392; and Steven L. Spiegel, "Religious Components of U.S. Middle East Policy," *Journal of International Affairs* 36, no. 2 (1982): 235–246.

28. See Hrach Gregorian, "Assessing Congressional Involvement in Foreign Policy: Lessons of the Post-Vietnam Period," *Review of Politics* XLVI, no. 1 (1984): 91–112.

29. See Lloyd N. Cutler, "Foreign Policy on Deadline," *Foreign Policy* no. 56 (Fall 1984): 113–128.

30. Pearson and Rochester, *International Relations,* p. 167.

31. See, for example, George F. Kennan, *American Diplomacy, 1900–1950* (Chicago: University of Chicago Press, 1951), pp. 59ff; and Townsend Hoopes, *The Limits of Intervention* (New York: McKay, 1973), chap. 4. This contention is, however, refuted by Avner Yaniv, "Domestic Structure and External Flexibility: A Systemic Restatement of a Neglected Theme," *Millennium* 8, no. 1 (1979): 25–37.

32. See Arnold Kanter, *Defense Politics: A Budgetary Perspective* (Chicago: University of Chicago Press, 1979); and Aspaturian, "The Soviet Military–Industrial Complex."

33. Alexander L. George and Juliette George, *Woodrow Wilson and Colonel House: A Personality Study* (New York: Dover, 1964), pp. 320ff.

34. For example, David McLellan, "The 'Operational Code' Approach to the Study of Political Leaders: Dean Acheson's Philosophical and Instrumental Beliefs," *Canadian Journal of Political Science* 4 (1971): 52–75; Ole R. Holsti, "The 'Operational Code' Approach to the Study of Political Leaders: John Foster Dulles' Philosophical and Instrumental Beliefs," *Canadian Journal of Political Science* 3 (1970): 123–157; Stephen G. Walker, "The Interface Between Beliefs and Behavior: Henry Kissinger's Operational Code and the Vietnam War," *Journal of Conflict Resolution* 21 (1977): 129–168; and Margaret G. Hermann, "Effects of Personal Characteristics of Political Leaders on Foreign Policy," in *Why Nations Act: Theoretical Perspectives for Comparative Foreign Policy Studies,* eds. Maurice A. East, Stephen A. Salmore, and Charles F. Hermann, (Newbury Park, Calif.: Sage, 1978), pp. 49–68.

35. Margaret G. Hermann, *A Psychological Examination of Political Leaders* (New York: Free Press, 1976).

36. See, for example, Roger Hilsman, *To Move a Nation: The Politics of Foreign Policy in the Administration of John F. Kennedy* (Garden City, N.Y.: Doubleday, 1967), p. 5.

37. Pearson and Rochester, *International Relations,* p. 186.

38. See Lincoln P. Bloomfield, *The Foreign Policy Process: A Modern Primer* (Englewood Cliffs, N.J.: Prentice-Hall, 1982), pp. 143ff.

39. The three-dimensional definition of "crisis"—short time, high threat, and surprise—is derived from Charles F. Hermann's conceptualization in *International Crisis: Insights from Behavioral Research* (New York: Free Press, 1972).

40. See Graham T. Allison, *Essence of Decision* (Boston: Little, Brown, 1971).

41. Bert A. Rockman, "America's *Departments* of State: Irregular and Regular Syndromes of Policy Making," *American Political Science Review* LXXV, no. 4 (1981): 911–912. It should be noted, however, that whatever system of advice and decision making exists, the president ultimately determines foreign policy.

42. See Christopher Hill and Margot Light, "Foreign Policy Analysis" in *International Relations: A Handbook of Current Theory,* eds. Margot Light and A. J. R. Groom (London: Frances Pinter, 1985), p. 160.

43. See Hilsman, *To Move a Nation.* For the application of the bureaucratic politics model to understanding information processing in the decision-making context of a developing country, India, see Vertzberger, "Bureaucratic-Organizational Politics and Information Processing."

44. For a criticism of bureaucratic politics engaged in pursuing self-interests, see Morton H. Halperin, *Bureaucratic Politics and Foreign Policy* (Washington, D.C.: Brookings Institution, 1947).

45. See Irving L. Janis, *Groupthink,* 2nd ed. (Boston: Houghton Mifflin, 1982).

46. Irving L. Janis, *Victims of Groupthink* (Boston: Houghton Mifflin, 1982); and A. N. Oppenheim, "Psychological Aspects," in *International Relations: A Handbook of Current Theory,* eds. Margot Light and A. J. R. Groom (London: Frances Pinter, 1985), p. 208.

47. See Janis, *Victims of Groupthink,* p. 157; and Ronald Steel, "The Kennedys and the Missile Crisis," in *Readings in American Foreign Policy: A Bureaucratic Perspective,* eds. Morton H. Halperin and Arnold Kanter (Boston: Little, Brown, 1973), p. 205.

48. See Roberta Wohlstetter, *Pearl Harbor: Warning and Decision* (Stanford: Stanford University Press, 1962); see also Jack S. Levy, "Misperception and the Causes of War," *World Politics* 36 (October 1983): 76–99.
49. Paul A. Anderson, "Normal Failures in the Foreign Policy Advisory Process," *World Affairs* 146, no. 2 (Fall 1983): 168, Janis, *Groupthink,* p. 40.
50. See Janis, *Victims of Groupthink,* p. 157; and Steel, "The Kennedys and the Missile Crisis," p. 205.

Part III

■

Instruments of Foreign Policy and State Behavior

Six

Diplomacy, Negotiation, and Bargaining

Diplomacy has almost as many meanings in international relations as there are writers on the subject. Some writers view it as "an art of conducting negotiations in the process of implementing foreign policy."[1] Others use it interchangeably with foreign policy involving the entire foreign relations process.[2] Or still others see it as "the *process* or *method* by which governments pursue foreign policy."[3] Russett and Starr, for example, argue that "the central feature of diplomacy is its communicative function."[4] Richard Rosecrance, however, cautions that "diplomacy refers specifically to the use of accredited officials for intergovernmental communication, not simply to communications links between states."[5] Whichever definition is used, logically there is no diplomacy without diplomats. We suggest the following definition of **diplomacy:** The conduct of relations between nation-states through their accredited officials for the purpose of advancing the interests of the appointing state. Although in popular usage *diplomacy* is used interchangeably with *negotiation,* as we will see, the two terms have different, more precise applications.

The history of diplomacy predates modern international relations by centuries. It can be traced back to ancient times in China, India, and Egypt when it primarily involved the delivery of messages and warnings, the pleading of causes, and the transfer of gifts from one tribal chief to another. These crude diplomatic practices were refined and institutionalized in ancient Greece and Rome. Envoys became not only messengers but negotiators. However, the first permanent legations were not established until the fourteenth century under a system of independent city-states in what is now Italy. This ambassadorial system rapidly spread to the rest of Europe. During the seventeenth and eighteenth centuries, two types of diplomatic representatives existed: ambassadors, who vied for precedence and protocol; and semiofficial agents, whose functions and access to authoritative sources of information were more limited. It was not until the Congress of Vienna in 1815 and three years later at Aix-la-Chapelle that serious efforts were made to simplify the classification of diplomatic agents and formalize their functions. Four categories of representatives were established: (1) ambassador extraordinary and plenipotentiary, and papal legate and nuncio; (2) envoy extraordinary, minister plenipotentiary, and papal internuncio; (3) minister resident; and (4) chargé d'affaires and chargé d'affaires ad interim. Precedence was based on the rank of the appointment conferred by the home government and on seniority of service in the particular capital. The most senior diplomat became the dean (or doyen) of the diplomatic corps.[6] Finally, a century and a half later, at the Vienna conferences on Diplomatic Privileges and Immunities

(1961) and on Consular Relations (1963), comprehensive agreements covering nearly all aspects of diplomatic activity were signed. These conferences divided the heads of diplomatic missions into three general categories. The first two categories comprise ambassadors and ministers, respectively, who are accredited (officially presented) to the head of the host state. The third category is made up of chargé d'affaires, who are accredited to the foreign ministers (or secretary of state) of the host country. Once diplomatic relations are established between two governments by mutual consent, ambassadors and ministers are exchanged. They represent the head of state of the sending state and are received by the head of state of the host country.

All diplomats enjoy certain privileges and immunities. Although they are expected to comply voluntarily with the host state's laws and regulations, they are exempt from its criminal and civil jurisdiction, as well as from its taxation. Embassies are immune from searches, and ambassadors' premises are viewed as small islands of sovereignty of the sending state. In recent years, however, these principles have been ignored by some countries as the hostage taking of American embassy personnel in Tehran, Iran, in 1979–1981 illustrated.

The Role of the Embassy and the Ambassador

No country maintains **embassies** (i.e., permanent seats of mission) in every nation-state. The superpowers maintain the largest number of overseas missions followed by several other major powers. Figure 6.1 shows U.S diplomatic and consular representation throughout the world. Most nations maintain legations with the largest states, with immediate neighbors, or with the United Nations. However, most countries are too poor to maintain extensive diplomatic establishments. For instance, no African country maintains embassies in all other African countries. Rather, they contact fellow African governments on an ad hoc basis or through their representatives in the Organization of African Unity and the UN.

American embassies overseas range in size from several hundred personnel in major world capitals to just a few individuals in smaller, less important nation-states. Embassies are headed by the ambassador, who is responsible for all personnel. Embassies are staffed with foreign service officers, military personnel, and civil servants from departments such as agriculture and commerce or consular offices. The United States Information Agency provides officers responsible for the dissemination of information, while the CIA and the National Security Agency supply officers responsible for intelligence gathering. (See figure 6.2 for a breakdown of personnel within the U.S. Embassy in Venezuela.) The bulk of work at an embassy, however, is carried out by locally hired employees whose functions include registering the births, deaths, and marriages of citizens of the sending state residing in the host country; issuing, validating, and replacing passports; demanding the extradition of criminals claimed to be under the jurisdiction of the sending state; and generally providing protection to the person, property, and other interests of citizens of the sending state. Other routine activities involve attending social and ceremonial affairs, such as luncheons, benefits, cocktail parties, ground-breaking ceremonies, and the like.

The role of diplomats can be broken down into several major categories. First, diplomats play an important symbolic role. They represent the interests of the sending state. They are expected to attend formal state functions, such as inaugurations, funerals of important leaders, and so on. Second, and closely related to the symbolic role, is the legal representation function. Diplomats represent the legal interests of their fellow citizens who

A U.S. mission in a foreign country is classified as an embassy if the permanent chief of mission has the rank of ambassador. U.S. embassies usually consist of political, economic, consular, and administrative sections staffed by members of the Foreign Service and the Department of State and, depending on need, of specialized sections employing personnel from other departments and agencies. The Foreign Commercial Service of the Department of Commerce is responsible for commercial program activity in sixty-six countries, and the Foreign Agricultural Service of the Department of Agriculture has officers posted at embassies in nearly forty countries.

The ambassador is the personal representative of the President. He or she must represent U.S. policy to the host government and coordinate and integrate the activities of all U.S. personnel in the host country (with the exception of military personnel under area command). The ambassador is assisted in these duties by the country team comprising the heads of the various embassy elements. The ambassador reports to the President and receives instructions through the Secretary of State.

In June 1985 there were 108 Americans employed in the Embassy and other offices in Caracas, Venezuela, and the consulate in Maracaibo. By comparison, the U.S. staff at the Embassy in London numbered 266, and in Brazzaville, People's Republic of the Congo, twenty-one. Most of the Americans assigned to the mission in Venezuela were members of the Foreign Service. There were about thirty civilian and military employees of the Department of Defense.

Chief of Mission
Ambassador
Personal Representative of the President

Deputy Chief of Mission
Minister—Counselor

Country Team

Mission Unit	Agricultural trade office	Agricultural counselor	Public affairs counselor	Commercial counselor	Political counselor	Economic counselor	Administrative counselor	Consul general	Defense attache	Head of military group (advisory)	Other agencies present: Drug Enforcement Agency Inter-American Geodetic Survey Internal Revenue Service	U.S. consulate in Maracaibo, U.S. staff: 3 State 1 USIA
Home Agency	Agriculture	Agriculture	USIA	Commerce	Department of State				Defense	Defense		

Figure 6.1
Diplomatic and consular representation

SOURCE: Harry F. Young, *Atlas of United States Foreign Relations* (Washington, D.C.: Department of State Publication 9350, December 1985), p. 8.

The United States normally accredits an ambassador (or a chief of mission of lesser rank) to each country with which the United States has diplomatic relations. In May 1985 the number of countries to which the United States had an accredited diplomatic mission was 153. Contacts with Bhutan, Maldives, and Vanuatu are maintained through embassies in neighboring countries or at the United Nations.

The United States has no diplomatic relations with Albania, Angola, Cambodia, Cuba, Iran, Mongolia, North Korea, Vietnam. and Yemen (Aden). In Cuba the United States maintains a U.S. Interests Section in the Swiss Embassy. All U.S. Embassy activities in Libya were suspended and U.S. personnel were withdrawn on May 2, 1980, but relations were not severed.

Consular posts provide various services for Americans in foreign countries and issue visas to foreigners for travel to the United States. Each embassy has a consular section, and there are separate consular facilities (see map).

Other Permanent U.S. Foreign Service Posts

U.S. Mission to the United Nations (New York)

U.S. Mission to the European Office of the United Nations and other international organizations (Geneva)

Permanent U.S. Mission to the Organization of American States (Washington, D.C.)

U.S. Mission to Berlin

U.S. Mission to the North Atlantic Treaty Organization (Brussels)

U.S. Mission to the UN Agencies for Food and Agriculture (Rome)

U.S. Mission to the Organization for Economic Cooperation and Development (Paris)

U.S. Mission to the European Communities (Brussels)

U.S. Mission to International Organizations in Vienna

U.S. Mission to the International Civil Aviation Organization (Montreal)

U.S. Observer Mission to the UN Educational, Scientific and Cultural Organization (Paris)

The United States has not recognized the incorporation of Estonia, Latvia, and Lithuania into the U.S.S.R. Boundary representation is not necessarily authoritative.

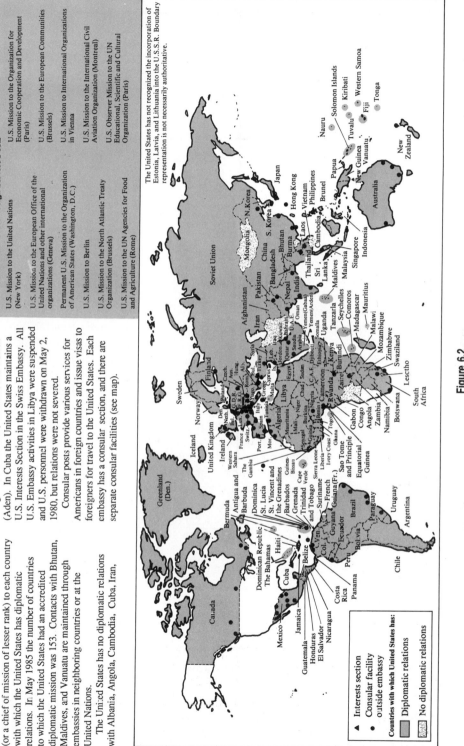

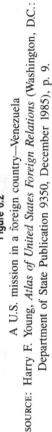

Figure 6.2

A U.S. mission in a foreign country—Venezuela

SOURCE: Harry F. Young, *Atlas of United States Foreign Relations* (Washington, D.C.: Department of State Publication 9350, December 1985), p. 9.

are traveling or living in the country. They may also be empowered to enter into negotiations or to sign agreements. Third, diplomats, especially consular officers, perform important economic functions. They attempt to identify opportunities for business ventures, trade, and investment for their nationals in the host country. Fourth, diplomats perform important political and information-gathering functions. They monitor political developments, analyze media reports, stay in touch with important governmental and opposition figures, and collect data on public opinion, economic, and security trends, which are analyzed and reported back to their home state. This important reporting function is described in greater detail in the following section. Finally, to attain these goals, diplomats and embassies must have a smooth administrative apparatus. Embassies are miniature bureaucracies, and as such, diplomats must have not only legal, political, and economic skills, but also a capacity for administration.

Reporting

The embassy's substantive functions are reporting and negotiating. Since the process of negotiations is central to diplomacy, we will return to it in greater detail later in this chapter. What is being reported home could be called intelligence, thus justifying the cliché that most embassy members are legalized spies. Economic attachés, for example, report general information on the host state's economic conditions. Political officers report about political activities and movements pertaining to the country's political stability. Military reporting depends greatly on the strategic location of the host state and on the friendly, neutral, or potentially hostile position of the government toward the sending state. Military attachés, for example, report information about the host state's military force, its morale, the quantity and quality of its weapons systems, and its military organization. Social and cultural reporting about class structures, ethnic, religious, and other minority movements as well as demographic problems are closely tailored to supplement the political, economic, and military reports. Even informal activities of embassy personnel such as luncheons, or casual conversations with host VIPs at cocktail parties and other social functions, are recorded in a "memorandum of conversation" and reported to the home office.

Information gathering at any embassy results in large quantities of "raw intelligence," which is sorted, verified, analyzed, evaluated, and synthesized into an estimate or evaluation of the host country's political situation. Information gathering is conducted overtly and covertly. The former is called diplomatic reporting; the latter is often referred to as spying.

The Ambassador

As the highest ranking official of the embassy, the **ambassador** is the personal representative of the government of the sending state. He or she is viewed by the host state as the official spokesperson for the sending state. In the nineteenth and early twentieth centuries ambassadors were professional people of intelligence, wealth, high morals, integrity, and skill in languages and diplomatic protocol, which placed them in an international fraternity of diplomats whose prestige was recognized throughout the world. Perhaps for this reason Sir Henry Wotton, an ambassador of King James I of England in the seventeenth century, allegedly referred to "an ambassador as an honest man who is sent to lie abroad for the good of his country."[7] The implication being that the ambassador was an honest man, but publicly he was dedicated to commit an "official lie." Perhaps the greatest authority on diplomacy, Sir Harold Nicolson, wrote: "The worst kind of diplomatists are missionaries, fanatics, and lawyers; the best kind are the reasonable and humane skeptics."[8] Honesty in diplomacy, in those days, did not mean telling everything the diplomat knew.

Judging by Nicolson's standards, contemporary diplomats are but amateurs in statecraft. According to Nicolson, a diplomat should be "a man of experience, integrity and intelligence, a man, above all who is not swayed by emotion or prejudice, who is profoundly modest in all his dealings, who is guided only by a sense of public duty, and who understands the perils of cleverness and the virtues of reason, moderation, discretion and tact."[9] Referring to the contemporary diplomatic scene, Nicolson added, "Mere clerks are not expected to exhibit all these difficult tasks at once."[10] The need for more highly qualified diplomats is echoed by many contemporary diplomats, including Charles Maechling, Jr. (see the first supplemental selection in this chapter), who is critical of the prevailing conditions that make diplomacy lose its luster and usefulenss. Maechling warns modern diplomats to learn to "operate in a goldfish bowl."

The rapid scientific and technological changes in the latter part of this century are also reflected in the transformation of the role of the embassy and the diplomatic service. The increase in the number of nation-states and their network of communications had also resulted in a commensurate growth in the size and complexity of embassies around the world. Although embassy duties are handled by a large number of specialists, the work they perform has changed diplomacy from an art to a management process.[11] Today, the role of an ambassador has changed appreciably. Since it is feasible for any top-ranking official to reach any part of the globe in the same day and transact sensitive business with his or her counter-part, governments are no longer dependent on their ambassadors to perform such tasks. Instant communication between the home office and the embassy and the use of supersonic jets and hot lines have changed the function of an ambassador from a negotiator to a reporter. As soon as information and the ambassador's interpretation of it are received, decisions are made in national capitals. Even on minor matters the local ambassador possesses little power, because states and societies are more interdependent and the issues are increasingly complex. Before World War II, the outcome of negotiations had practically no direct impact on the people at home unless it led to war. Today, however, most problems being negotiated can only be solved with the assistance of many other nations because they directly affect the people in a region or the entire world. For example, strategic arms reduction, tariff and monetary problems, air travel and communication regulations, pollution prevention, and security against terrorism are common problems that require common solutions. Because these problems impinge directly on a state's domestic politics, political leaders feel more comfortable when political appointees rather than diplomats conduct the negotiations for finding solutions to these problems. Some have gone so far as to ask: "Is the international society reaching the point where it can dispense with diplomacy?"[12] In the second supplemental reading in this chapter, Elmer Plischke, a distinguished ex-diplomat and scholar, observed that despite changes in the role of ambassadors, which reflect material changes in the conduct of foreign policy, it would be a mistake to write off the importance of the evolving diplomacy and the mitigating role of the ambassador. Much depends on the ambassador's ability and adaptability to the new conditions prevailing in the world today. Some ambassadors, for example, are known as *centralizers* because they act as the clearinghouse for information processing and try to orchestrate differences of opinion in the reports they receive, discourage staff initiatives and disagreements, and seek unanimity and conformity in action. On the opposite side are the *decentralizers,* that is, ambassadors who delegate responsibilities and who encourage diversity in reports they receive.

Another visible issue in the operation of an embassy is whether the ambassador is a career diplomat rising through the ranks of the Foreign Service or a political appointee.

In comparison to other major open political systems, the United States has a relatively large proportion (about one-third) of ambassadors who are politically appointed. In many cases such ambassadors lack firsthand experience regarding the operations of an embassy abroad; they are often only superficially familiar with the culture and language of the host state, and they are perceived by the foreign service personnel as outsiders who deprive qualified senior foreign service officers of job opportunities. The upshot is that large numbers of political appointees lead to low morale in the professional diplomatic corps. Although their political and business connections may enable political appointees to have access to members of Congress and the chief executive himself, the disadvantages they bring often outweigh the advantages.

Characteristics of New Diplomacy

The origin of *new* diplomacy can be found in the pronouncements and practices of President Woodrow Wilson immediately after World War I. **New diplomacy** as practiced by Wilson was a reaction to the old diplomacy of the great European powers. Old (also known as secret or French) diplomacy was based on the notion that the great powers carried more weight in deciding world problems than the smaller powers, which were subordinated to them. It further assumed that negotiations, a central feature of diplomacy, would be carried out by a corps of professionally trained diplomats who spoke the same language and adhered to the same rules of operation, including secrecy. Wilson's major objections to the old-style diplomacy were that secret diplomacy was a devious and dishonest business resulting in secret treaties and opposing alliances, which he thought were responsible for the outbreak of the war. Thus Wilson called for "open treaties, openly arrived at." In practice, new diplomacy was supposed to expose negotiations to the public at open conferences such as the League of Nations (the predecessor to the United Nations), with the mass media observing every step of the process. However, this process of open negotiations soon undermined the utility of diplomacy, because nations resorted to using public forums as a means of propaganda rather than problem solving or conflict resolution. After World War II, many nation-states developed a hybrid form of diplomacy, sometimes referred to as new diplomacy, which was quite different from both the old diplomacy and the idealist Wilson type of diplomacy. What are the characteristics of this diplomacy?

Summit and Shuttle Diplomacy

Because of the convenience of modern technology and the diminishing pivotal status of the ambassador abroad, the larger powers have tended to bypass Foreign Service personnel and ambassadors and conduct more of their business through special envoys, intermediaries, and high-level officials such as foreign ministers or secretaries of state.[13] Such was the case in 1974 with former Secretary of State Henry Kissinger and later in 1978 with Secretary Cyrus Vance in the Middle East. This practice has been dubbed **shuttle diplomacy.** The diplomats are briefed on the issues by State Department specialists but usually do not take part in the negotiations. In the Middle East examples, the secretaries of state were acting as diplomats.

Occasionally, diplomacy will take the form of **summit diplomacy,** which refers to an actual visit by a head of state to another country to negotiate personally with that country's leaders. Examples of direct personal negotiations between national leaders include Khrushchev and Kennedy at Vienna in 1961; Nixon and Chou En-lai at Peking in 1972; Nixon and Brezhnev at Moscow in 1972; Carter, Begin, and Sadat at Camp David in 1978; Reagan and Gorbachev at Reykjavík in 1986, at Washington, D.C. in 1987, and at Moscow in 1988; and Bush and Gorbachev at Malta in 1989 and at Washington, D.C. in 1990. This form of diplomatic activity, which was also used during the classical period by the monarchs of Europe, has been applauded and criticized. (For an extended discussion of summit diplomacy, see the supplemental reading by Elmer Plischke at the end of this chapter.) Whereas direct, personal contact between heads of state can lead to greater understanding and can speed up the negotiation process (as was the case between President Ford and Secretary-General of the Communist Party of the Soviet Union Brezhnev at Vladivostok in 1974), it can also lead to misunderstanding, denunciation, and myopia (as was the case at Reykjavík in 1986). Chief executives are seldom experts in international affairs. They lack the know-how of diplomatic procedures, the feel for cultural traits, and the finesse that skilled diplomats are able to bring to the negotiating table. Hurriedly and ill-prepared summitries (such as the one at Reykjavík) can lead to dire consequences. Elaborate presummit briefings and agreements in principle between the negotiating parties are a must for achieving success instead of the theatrics of summitry.[14]

Secret Versus Open Diplomacy

We referred to new diplomacy as a hybrid form, combining secret (or more precisely private) negotiations with public declarations of what had been achieved in those negotiations. Summitry is a good example of this form of diplomacy with the exception that negotiations are conducted between politicians instead of between professional diplomats. It involves the "media event" characteristics that on balance cater more to public consumption than to secret diplomacy, because shortly after the summitry, press conferences are held and various versions of the negotiations are made public. If, on the other hand, the Kissinger example is typical of the hybrid form of diplomacy, then it is reasonable to assume that it can be effective, even if it means skipping over the embassy personnel and ambassadors to conduct negotiations through shuttle diplomacy on a cabinet level. As Russett and Starr put it:

> Kissinger was a master of the private conversation and the public spectacle. He personified a return to the traditional diplomacy of the past, in the sense of hard bargaining in private and secret trips and agreements (which were revealed to the public after their completion) and a style that combined the use of force with the use of words to bring about an agreement with which every side could live but one that required every side to make concessions and compromises.[15]

This type of diplomacy presumably would disarm those who argue that secrecy in the negotiating process is imperative, and those, like Charles Maechling, who maintain that contemporary diplomats must learn how to "operate in a goldfish bowl" in front of television and other public fora. For those who follow one extreme or another, there is a difference between foreign policy making that aims to exercise influence in order to achieve desired results on a daily, routine basis (which is practiced by all actors who play the game in the global arena) and foreign policy making that aims to resolve serious and pressing problems through peaceful compromises (which should be carried out privately and discretely by able diplomats).

Bilateral Versus Multilateral Diplomacy

Before the late nineteenth century, states emphasized bilateral (two-country) diplomacy. Until then multilateral diplomacy (the simultaneous meeting of representatives of several countries) was mostly limited to peace conferences following major wars. However, after World War I, bilateral exchanges gave way to multilateral relations.[16] With the increase in sovereign nation-states after World War II from 50 to over 160, the increase in regional and world problems, and the proliferation of intergovernmental organizations, multilateral diplomacy has become a daily occurrence in such forums as the UN and the European Community. As in the case of secret versus open diplomacy, multilateral diplomacy has supporters and critics. The supporters argue that open participation of the diplomats is constructive in furthering democratic principles in international organizations, whereas critics maintain that large open forums are not effective in solving serious problems and may actually make matters worse.

Negotiation and Bargaining

Even though we have used *negotiation* interchangeably with *diplomacy,* we did so only to demonstrate that negotiation is diplomacy's chief instrument or raison d'être. Without the former the latter would be meaningless.

Negotiation—a formal form of interaction through which individuals explicitly try to reach some sort of agreement—is the first stage in a process seeking to find resolution to a problem. The second stage of the same process is called *bargaining.* Because bargaining and negotiation are major mechanisms of conflict resolution in our society, many social psychologists treat the two terms as synonymous.[17] In our case, however, the emphasis will be on the process, and therefore we will differentiate between negotiation and bargaining as two stages in the same process.

Before negotiation can commence, the parties must have an identical common interest in bringing about a new arrangement or object on an issue of conflict, or a complementary interest in an exchange of different objects that the parties cannot obtain by themselves but can only grant to each other.[18] At times, governments will enter into negotiations even when they are aware that there is no shared basis of interest. For example, not entering into negotiations because of domestic political demands or image making abroad could be damaging to government. Other reasons could include gaining propaganda advantages at the opponent's expense, sizing up the opponent, gaining information, misleading or deceiving the opponent, "maintaining contact," or using the talk as a substitute for the possibility of violent action.[19] As these observations suggest, the goals of negotiation are not always limited to seeking an agreement. To achieve an agreement of some kind between two parties, the negotiations are described as "serious." However, the two parties may not share the same view regarding the prospects of a negotiated agreement. When one party is more anxious to commence negotiations, the other party may attempt to gain concessions as a payment for entering into negotiations. Therefore, a precondition for successful negotiation is that parties negotiate "in good faith"; that is, they explicitly spell out terms for agreement.

Gordon Craig and Alexander George distinguish among four kinds of agreements in which states act to regulate their relations:

1. **Extension agreements** (e.g., tariff agreements), which provide a formal ratification and continuation of existing arrangements.

2. **Normalization agreements** (e.g., the reestablishment of diplomatic relations after a breach of relations), which terminate an abnormal situation in relations between two parties.
3. **Redistribution agreements** (e.g., preferential trade agreements), which benefit one party at the expense of another.
4. **Innovation agreements** (e.g., the European Economic Community, or EEC, in 1958, or the General Agreement on Tariffs and Trade, or GATT, in 1947), which call for new arrangements that benefit both parties but not always equally.[20]

Each of these different types of agreements requires a different negotiating process that entails a number of tasks and purposes. Before the parties commit themselves to enter into negotiations, the actors must agree on a time, place, agendum, conference arrangements, and the diplomatic level at which the discussions will be held. Disagreements on some of these procedural matters can be interpreted as a sign of how far apart the two parties are on the substantive issues. In the Korean truce negotiations of 1951, the Vietnam peace talks in the early 1970s, and the Geneva conference following the Arab–Israeli War of October 1973, procedural issues over the shape of the conference table and placement of the participants were of symbolic importance and of considerable disagreement among the parties.

In the opening stages of a negotiation, or during the exploratory discussions, the opposing parties attempt to define issues and the common interests that have brought them to the negotiating table. At this juncture the two sides attempt to verify or correct their earlier assumptions and beliefs regarding the prospects of an agreement. Each negotiator seeks a clear, authoritative, specific statement of the other side's demands. It is generally understood at this stage of the negotiating process that each side will state its maximum terms for an agreement (more than actually expected), so that there will be room for adjustment and modification—compromise—during the course of persuasion and bargaining. Also during this stage one party may ask for a general assurance that under certain conditions the other party will be willing to temper some of its demands. In other words, the earlier stage of negotiations is used for probing, jockeying, mutual confidence building, and what Ikle has called establishing the "rules of accommodation."

After the parameters for maximum demands have been set, each negotiator seeks to find out from the other side the minimum objectives that it is willing to accept—also known as the **resistance point**. To ascertain an opponent's resistance point is perhaps the most difficult aspect of the negotiation process. The reasons are obvious; to reveal the negotiator's minimal demands prematurely could jeopardize a successful negotiation. That is why negotiation requires skill, patience, and careful calculation. If the negotiators feel that the gap between the resistance points is too great, a stalemate develops that can lead either to the discontinuance of the negotiations or further probing to change each side's resistance points. If further negotiations continue in a stalemate, one or both sides may resort to propaganda maneuvers or they may agree to report back to their governments and ask for new instructions. As a last resort, they may break off the negotiations temporarily or permanently.

We should make a distinction between *formal* and *informal* or tacit negotiation. When states are unwilling to be explicit in their interests, or pursue formal negotiation and prefer instead to use hints and guesswork, then they are using **tacit** (informal) **negotiation** techniques. States use tacit negotiation for posturing purposes to spread propaganda, gather intelligence, and to influence third parties. Tacit negotiation is often employed to influence another government's future behavior. For example, in 1980, while the popular Polish labor union *Solidarnosc* was negotiating for recognition and political rights with the Jaruzelski government, the frequent Soviet naval and military maneuvers on the Polish border were intended as a signal to Solidarity leaders that the Soviet Union was willing and able to intervene in Poland's internal affairs to save the Soviet style of socialism.[21]

Formal negotiations take place when both parties in the negotiation process agree on at least some initial terms. Frequently, however, the negotiating parties—through face-to-face meetings, cables, or third-party intermediaries—have conflicting terms and preferences. If the differences are too great, the parties may choose to call off further negotiations. However, if the costs of no agreement are too high, they may move on to the second stage: bargaining over the actual terms of the agreement. Should they opt for bargaining, then certain preliminary issues of advantage or disadvantage to one side or the other must be settled. For example, issues such as the location of the negotiations, the parties to be represented at the negotiations, or even the shape of the bargaining table have to be resolved before bargaining can begin in earnest. Above all, before they engage in the bargaining process, the parties must believe that there is a potential agreement somewhere within the settlement range.

Bargaining can be viewed as a means of resolving differences over proposed terms of agreements between negotiating parties through some sort of compromise. For bargaining to take place, the terms proposed by both parties must be diametrically opposed to each other; otherwise they would have no issue for bargaining. The aim is for one side to influence its opponent into agreeing to its terms and to minimize costs and concessions if they have to be made.

The Bargaining Process

This process involves games and debates, as well as persuasion, promises, commitments, threats, and rewards. An able bargainer must have a clear idea of the client's priorities. He or she must also have minimum and maximum limits within which to operate before reaching an agreement. The objective is for each bargaining party to reach an agreement that would maximize the client's goals and minimize the opponent's demands. In other words, in a bargaining situation the aim is to push toward your opponent's minimum and your maximum set of proposed terms. With both bargainers trying to maximize their priorities, the outcome will depend on factors such as the ability to gauge the opponent's position, the ability to accurately assess the tools of influence available to the opponent, as well as the skill with which the opponent bargains. Whether or not a bargaining strategy will be effective, depends on the bargaining position of the bargainer. If you are negotiating from a position of weakness, if you are not wanted or needed in an agreement, or if your moves are poorly timed, bargaining effectiveness is likely to be reduced.[22]

Commitments (or promises) and threats are the two basic moves in bargaining. If you make a **commitment**, you are trying to change the opponent's expectations about your future conduct by changing your incentives. If, on the other hand, you issue a threat, you are trying to change the opponent's expectations about the payoffs that would result from your making certain choices. In other words, a commitment is a move to convince an opponent that you will maintain your current position, or implement your prediction, by making it less difficult for the opponent and more difficult for yourself. A **threat** is a prediction addressed to your opponent that he or she will suffer certain consequences if he or she does not comply with your wishes.[23] For example, in 1980 President Carter threatened the Soviet government with cutting off the sale of wheat if Soviet troops were not withdrawn from Afghanistan. The Soveit Union refused, and Carter carried out his threat by imposing the grain embargo. In 1981, however, President Reagan lifted the grain embargo as a reward for Soviet concessions in Poland. Furthermore, he recognized the fact that other countries such as Argentina, Australia, Canada, and New Zealand were willing and able to sell more grain to the Soviet Union than the United States could deliver and that the bargaining influence under the Carter administration was a failure.

As Roger Fisher and William Ury point out, it is more difficult to compel than to deter certain behavior on the part of another state.[24] **Compellance** means to persuade the other side to do something it does not want to do, either to continue a desired behavior or to stop some undesired behavior (e.g., the United States attempting to influence Israel to negotiate with the Palestinians). **Deterrence**, on the other hand, means to discourage the other side from doing something it might want to do (e.g., the United States attempting to discourage Israel from building new settlements in the occupied West Bank territory). Whereas a successful compellance requires the influenced party to make something happen, successful deterrence consists of nothing happening.[25]

To be successful, commitments or threats must be credible and potent. Unless the opponent believes that the bargainer making the commitments or threats has the capability and willingness to carry them out, they are meaningless. Otherwise the bargainer for the targeted state may perceive the threat or commitment as bluffing. If the opponent calls the bargainer's bluff, then the bluff maker must be prepared to deliver, if it values its future credibility. Thus a commitment or threat must be both believable and sufficiently potent in the eyes of the opponent's bargainer. Former Secretary of State Kissinger's attempt, in the early 1970s when he negotiated the Basic Agreements, to influence the Soviet Union to perceive and practice the concept of detente in a similar manner as the United States is a case in point. Kissinger's linkage theory to gain military and political concessions from the Soviet Union (e.g., SALT I) for American economic and technological support had credibility but lacked potency. The United States demonstrated its sincerity by rewarding the Soviet Union before any changes in Soviet behavior had occurred. Actually the bargaining strategy backfired because the American incentives Kissinger offered were insufficient to induce a change in Soviet behavior.[26] In other words, commitments and threats that might be credible but lack potency are just as likely to fail as those that have potency but lack credibility.

How can governments enhance the credibility of their threats and their commitments? Thomas Schelling, for example, suggested a number of ways to achieve this result. He considered the "act of commitment" central to a successful bargaining process. Therefore, he proposed to reinforce the declarations of intent with the kinds of tacit bargaining actions that we alluded to earlier, such as using troop mobilizations or budgetary allocations, demonstrating sealift capabilities, or sending a high-ranking diplomat abroad to lend credence and authority to the commitments. Schelling is particularly fond of the "burn all your bridges behind you" approach. Doing this makes clear to the other side that if they take a particular action you will have no choice but to carry out the threat.[27] The presence of American troops in West Germany is an example of the U.S. *trip-wire commitment* to convince the Soviets that any military aggression on their part against NATO allies would automatically trigger a U.S. response. The idea is to make a commitment by keeping your options open, while convincing the other side that all avenues of retreat from your threat have been closed off.[28]

There are at least three concepts in recent studies that explain the bargaining process as one that helps the negotiator to do better—not necessarily to win. First is the *game theory* notion of *nonzero-sum* encounters where the outcome to each of the two players totals other than zero.[29] The object is to transform zero-sum solutions into positive-sum solutions or a *variable-sum* game. In **zero-sum** games one person's gain equals the other's loss—in other words, the net change is always zero.

An example is the contest for sovereignty between Great Britain and Argentina over the Falkland Islands (Islas Malvinas). Because two states are claiming the island but only one can exercise sovereignty, as a result of the 1982 conflict, Britain so far is the winner and Argentina the loser. If, on the other hand, the two nations involved in a dispute over the Falkland Islands could come to realize that each is interested in the resources, then they might be able to bargain for an agreement whereby one could own the islands but the other would share in the benefits of the resources. The result would be a positive-sum situation (or **variable-sum game**), in which each party comes out with some benefits; no one comes out ahead, but both parties come away better off than before. The same result could be achieved, if, for instance, the island could be partitioned between Great Britain and Argentina—in which case, both countries could be declared winners.

The second concept, known as *Homans's theorem,* describes the method of the bargaining process as changing from a zero-sum to a nonzero-sum situation: "The more the items at stake can be divided into goods valued more by one party than they cost to the other and goods valued more by the other party than they cost to the first, the greater the chances of successful outcomes."[30] The assumption is that items are evaluated differently by different parties and that these evaluations can be changed by instruments such as persuasion, inducement, alternatives, and reorganization of ideas. During the first phase of diplomacy or negotiation, the actor must discover and convey these different evaluations, and then in the second stage, or bargaining, he or she must alter and group them so that they fit together into a potential agreement. Homans's argument is that in the bargaining process negotiating parties do not seek to prevail over each other's arguments by persuading them to change their basic views, but instead they rely on persuasion to arrange the elements of these views into a common decision.[31]

The third concept applicable to the bargaining process is "toughness" and "softness," or as Craig and George refer to them: *Optimizing* and *accommodative* approaches to the bargaining process. The actor in the bargaining process using the tough bargaining tactics is less likely to disclose the real resistance point of his or her government, than the actor following the soft approach to the bargaining process, and feels no obligation to reciprocate concessions.

Whichever approach or models of bargaining are applied, certain lessons can be helpful to any bargainer. One method used by Kissinger and others before him is known as *fractionation* or *compartmentalization.* This occurs when problems are broken down into smaller parts, separating smaller problems from bigger ones. This enables the bargainers to resolve some of the smaller problems peaceably and amiably, while building an atmosphere of confidence, and thus move on to bigger and tougher problems in an atmosphere of good will and cooperation. The prerequisite to such conflict bargaining is that the parties remove the game element from the process and learn to cooperate with each other in a step-by-step fashion of making concessions based on compromises.[32]

Another valuable lesson in bargaining comes from Gen. Edward L. Rowny, former special adviser to the president and the secretary of state for arms control matters. In his many years of negotiating experience with the Soviets, General Rowny recommends the following guidelines: Remember the objective; keep secrets; bear in mind the differences between the two political systems; beware of "Greeks bearing gifts"; remember that for the Soviets form means substance; do not be deceived by the Soviet "fear of being invaded;" beware of eleventh-hour negotiating; do not be deceived by words; and do not misinterpret the human element.

How does a person become a successful bargainer? According to Roger Fisher, persuasion, commitment, empathy, and reliance on the legitimacy of claims seem to work much better than threats or the use of force. The bargainer should always be concerned with precedent and reciprocity to appear consistent with principles when appealing to values held by the opponent. One way to do this is to use international law and international organizations. Recent studies show, however, that the effectiveness of both is declining. While the UN does better in managing conflicts than the International Court of Justice in The Hague, the record of success is poor in both cases.[33] Considering that more than two-thirds of the UN's membership is made up of developing countries who are also members of the nonaligned movement raises the question: How well has nonalignment served the newly developed countries of Asia and Africa as a diplomatic strategy? As Prof. Satish Kumar of India pointed out, "nonalignment as a diplomatic strategy has failed to meet the individual security needs of the members of the movement."[34] In 1979 at the Havana Non-Aligned Summit, for example, more than one-third of the ninety-two members had some sort of link with one great power or another.

Instruments of International Bargaining

The two most influential instruments of international bargaining are the use of military capabilities and economic resources. While the former is generally a coercive or punishment-oriented means of influence, the latter is an indirect means of influence whose objective is to exploit the vulnerability of other states.

In addition to coercive influence, military capabilities can also be used for rewards. For example, military assistance is an important component of American, European, and Soviet aid programs to the developing nations. Although the United States lags behind the Soviet Union in the total volume of arms transfer, for many years prior to 1978 the United States was in first place. France, Britain, Israel, Italy, South Africa, and other arms-producing states are important arms suppliers to the LDCs. There is no shortage of arms on the world market today, therefore, the ability of powerful states to influence Third World governments is limited to those countries that lack cash or barter and are solely dependent on aid.[35] Another way to reward states with military capabilities is to ask them to join in a military alliance. Weaker states, for example, with less sophisticated military capabilities may accept the deterrent umbrella of a stronger state by signing a formal treaty of alliance as a security measure against a potential common enemy.[36]

Military capabilities are usually employed in bargaining to achieve a deterrent effect. The concept of *deterrence* generally implies a preventive action against possible military aggression by making the potential aggressor aware that the cost of an aggression may outweigh the benefits. If deterrence fails, the game changes from the use of diplomacy to the use of force. An aggressor will usually rely on force because he or she expects to benefit from the new distribution of security, political control, territory, status, and wealth after force has been used. States are influenced by the threat of force because they fear what they will lose if others use force. The military technique of influence, therefore, is to achieve political ends, unless an aggressor's objective is to destory an opponent, in which case influence plays no role. However, when a state threatens to hurt an opponent, then the aim is to break the opponent's will to resist, that is, to influence the opponent's behavior into submission. Thus, military deterrence has become a very useful instrument of bargaining, practiced by all nations perceiving threats from potential enemies. Therefore, to prevent future aggression, many nations rationalize military spending as a necessary evil to maintain the peace by preparing for war. Studies show, however, that in the past superior states have often failed to deter attacks from weaker states.[37]

As a matter of logic, it is easier for a nation to convince its opponents that it will carry out a threat to protect its homeland than it is to convince them that it will carry out a threat to protect another state. Although strong, visible military ties combined with economic interdependence are the best guarantees for deterrence,[38] there are situations when authoritative decision makers who are inclined to use aggressive foreign policies miscalculate the costs and benefits and thus are willing to commit aggression.[39] In the final analysis, the decision makers' perception or misperception of the situation will determine the outcome of deterrence.

It is interesting to note that the use of threat or actual conventional military force retains a greater deterrent value than the threat of use or actual use of nuclear weapons. States having sufficient nuclear capabilities cannot credibly threaten to use or actually use them without inviting destruction by a retaliatory attack, or expect devastation so great that there is no territory, population, or wealth to be gained after their use. To put it another way, nuclear weapons have little utility if they must actually be used. Nuclear deterrence has a separate logic and language from that of the conventional use of military capabilities. In the 1950s when the United States maintained nuclear superiority, nuclear deterrence meant **massive retaliation** against the Soviet Union for even the smallest conventional aggression in Western Europe. In the 1960s, when the Soviet Union was gaining nuclear parity with the United States, deterrence was based on the concept of **mutually assured destruction (MAD)**, which meant that both sides were supposedly convinced that a first nuclear strike by one side on the homeland of the other would be suicidal, causing the state that suffered the first blow to retaliate with a second strike that would produce unacceptable damage to the aggressor. In other words, the process of nuclear deterrence was the same as the process of conventional military deterrence, namely, to convince an opponent not to attack. In the late 1970s and early 1980s, however, some American strategists considered the Soviet military doctrine (seeking military victory through the use of a nuclear weapons system), the building of shelters and antiballistic missile defenses, as well as the increase in the number and megatonnage of offensive ballistic missiles as an attempt to develop not just a deterrent but a war capability, which signaled a clear departure from the MAD concept.[40] Thus in the 1980s the United States opted for the research and development of a *strategic defense initiative* (SDI or as the media calls it, "Star Wars").

The second most important instrument of international bargaining is the economic means of influence. No state is self-sufficient today; each one has economic needs. Most states require petroleum, rubber, tin, cocoa, coffee, tea, copper, uranium, and other precious metals that are only produced in a few countries. A similar situation applies to food, technology, and the products of technology. States that lack resources and commodities depend on others, and therefore are vulnerable to economic influence. Nevertheless, the desire of every state is to be economically as independent as possible.

Just as military influence in the bargaining process, economic influence can be used either to reward or punish. States employ various techniques or tactics to control the flow of goods, services, and resources. For example, if a state wants to cut down on imports or make them more expensive, it can impose **tariffs**, or taxes levied on imported goods usually for the protection of the country's domestic industries. High tariffs will discourage trade from abroad; low tariffs will encourage it. A similar technique to punish a trading partner is to impose **quotas** on goods. It is important to distinguish between self-imposed and officially imposed quotas. For example, in the mid-1980s, Japanese automobile manufacturers imposed their own quotas on cars manufactured in Japan for export to the United States. On the other hand, the United States has imposed quotas at various times on sugar from Cuba, certain textiles from the People's Republic of China, lumber from Canada, and steel from Poland.

Other methods for controlling trade include **boycotts**, which refer to the refusal of a country to purchase goods to import products from another state (for example, when the U.S. refused to import *Stolichnaya* vodka from the Soviet Union after the invasion of Afghanistan in 1980). An **embargo**, which is the opposite of a boycott, may also be used. Embargoes occur when a state refuses to export needed goods to another state (for example, grain from the United States to the Soviet Union in 1980 or the Arab petroleum embargo of Western nations in 1974, following the Yom Kippur war).

Manipulation of loans and credits to stimulate buying by lowering prices is a somewhat milder form of punishment (for example, the competition between American- and Japanese-manufactured cars in the mid-1980s). Another example is a monetary policy to make the goods of one state more or less expensive depending on the devaluation or reevaluation of the state's currency (for example, in 1986–1987 the U.S. dollar was devalued by 25 percent which made the Japanese-manufactured cars increase in price 10 to 20 percent). Other methods of punishment are more extreme, such as expropriation or freezing of a foreign state's assets. For example, after the overthrow of the shah of Iran in early 1979, the United States froze all Iranian assets as a response to claims by owners and creditors against the Iranian government. Another extreme method is nationalization of corporate properties owned by nationals of foreign governments. For example, the action taken by the Manley government in Jamaica during the 1970s, which led to a denial of American loans and other economic pressures against Jamaica resulting in a decline in the Jamaican economy and eventual defeat of the Manley government in a 1980 election.

An example of economic influence used as a reward is the **most-favored-nation principle** (MFN), which is based on nondiscrimination in trade and extends tariff concessions agreed to by the signatories to all nations participating in the reciprocal system. The insertion of an MFN clause in a trade agreement means that the parties are not attempting to establish a bilateral preferential arrangement that would discriminate against other trading partners. In the United States, the president may withhold the application of the clause from trade with nations that discriminate against American exports. In 1974, for example, Congress used (by means of the Jackson–Vanik amendment) this power to withhold MFN treatment from the Soviet Union in an attempt to influence Soviet policy on the emigration of its Jewish citizens. However, the attempt failed because the Soviets refused to accept the trade agreement that granted them MFN status on the condition that they allow more Jews to leave the country. In fact, after 1975 the Soviets toughened their stance on emigration. The most popular technique of economic reward is foreign aid, in which transfer of economic goods or services are transferred from the donor to the recipient. The goods and services include commodity, money, or technical assistance. Foreign aid can be administered as **bilateral aid** (i.e., one state to another) **or multilateral aid** (i.e., aid given through international organizations such as the UN, the World Bank, the Inter-American Development Bank). Bilateral aid makes it easier for the donor to exert influence on the recipient. Hence, Third World recipients have preferred multilateral aid. Bilateral aid can be used for military assistance, economic development, or relief (in the event of a disaster such as earthquake). There are four types of bilateral aid: nonrepayable outright grants; long-term, low-interest loans; sales on credit or reduced prices; and technical assistance (by providing cost-free technical advisers and skilled personnel). Because of the influence donor countries exert on recipients, all types of aid programs have some "strings" attached. The type of aid, and the kinds of strings, depends on the bargaining position of both the donor and the recipient.

Summary

In chapter 5 we examined the dynamics of the foreign policy–making process. In this chapter we were concerned with how the major actors (nation-states) deal with one another and exert influence over one another through the techniques or instruments called diplomacy, negotiation, and bargaining. Although different types of actors interact in the international system (including terrorists, IGOs, and NGOs), our focus has been on nation-states because they alone can have accredited diplomatic representatives (long term or ad hoc). Because of advanced communications and travel technology, the role of the ambassador as a country's representative has been taken over by high-ranking public officials engaging in summit and shuttle diplomacy. Coupled with these is a trend toward greater public and multilateral diplomacy rather than secret and bilateral diplomacy.

Negotiation and bargaining are two processes by which diplomats attempt to influence other states. Negotiation can be brought to a successful conclusion when both parties find that agreement is preferable to conflict. However, if the parties disagree on the specific terms they try to negotiate, then bargaining begins as each side tries to strike a final agreement as far from their own minimum demands (resistance point) and as close to their maximum demands as possible. Contesting negotiators–bargainers may or may not be able or willing to define the issues in the same manner, or enter into a process consisting of a gradual convergence toward a compromise solution, or make reasonable cost–benefit calculations on issues and of bargaining time, or agree on relative bargaining power. The bargaining tactics involve threats and punishments or promises and rewards.

As far as the instruments of international bargaining are concerned, states usually rely on military and economic resources. Both enable a state to bargain through rewards and punishments. The recent trend has been more toward the use of economic tactics in bargaining than military ones. Although international negotiations and bargaining are part of diplomacy, the latter is a process that only national governments engage in—whereas the former can be carried out by a variety of actors that often lack territorial integrity and sovereignty.

Charles Maechling, Jr.

■

The Future of Diplomacy and Diplomats

Diplomacy stands at a crossroads in the turbulent 1980s and with it the future of the career service. No one questions the need for a corps of trained foreign service professionals to represent the nation overseas, or the role of the State Department as the formal vehicle for conducting foreign relations, but in practice the department's leadership role in foreign affairs within the government is increasingly subject to challenge. Not only has there been a shift in bureaucratic power from the State Department to the National Security Council, but in many eyes the department is viewed as merely a bureaucratic mechanism to formalize policies and implement decisions arrived at through other channels.

Fifty years ago, in the aftermath of the world war that shattered the old order in Europe, Sir Harold Nicolson sought to identify the reasons for the inability of diplomacy to solve the pressing problems of the postwar era. He set down his answer in a small book titled *Diplomacy,* subsequently updated in his Chichele Lectures at Oxford in 1953, which called for a return to the traditional methods of the old diplomacy, which he defined as the "conduct of relations between civilized states." With impeccable literary grace— and remarkable selectivity of historical example—he traced the evolution of the diplomatic method from its origins in the Greek city-states, through Byzantium, Venice and eighteenth-century France, to its apotheosis in Edwardian Europe. He concluded his analysis by scathingly enumerating the anarchical and barbaric forces that were threatening to destroy it.

Charles Maechling, Jr., an international lawyer, was on the 7th floor of the Department of State 1961–1967.
SOURCE: *Foreign Service Journal* 38, no. 1 (1981): pp. 17–22. Reprinted by permission of the author.

In Nicolson's idealized picture the old diplomacy, grounded in the European system of nation-states, was the outgrowth of a natural hierarchy of power, in which larger states assumed responsibility for the conduct of smaller states, and diplomatic intercourse was entrusted to a corps of professionals who ensured that relations were conducted according to principles of "courtesy, confidence, and discretion." Nicolson seems to equate the diplomatic method almost exclusively with negotiation, though not in the operational sense we think of today; he saw it as a continuous, confidential, and discreet process of adjusting relationships and differences between sovereigns. He says nothing about other aspects of diplomatic representation—military, commercial, public information. The reporting function is taken for granted.

Nicolson saw the primary threat to traditional diplomacy as originating not so much from the breakup of colonial empires or dramatic advances in transportation and communication, disruptive as these were to the civilized tenor and measured pace of diplomatic intercourse, as from the rise of popular democracy and the application to the conduct of external affairs of the "ideas and practices which in the conduct of internal affairs, had for generations been regarded as the essentials of liberal democracy." In brief, like his later American counterpart George Kennan, Nicolson bewailed the intrusion of domestic factors into the conduct of foreign relations.

Today, Nicolson's historical perspective seems almost ludicrously culture-bound and his standards of international behavior unbelievably artificial. (Can the term *responsibility* be seriously applied to the three partitions of Poland? to the rape of the Danish duchies by Prussia? to the repeated invasions of Italy by France? to the suppression of the Hungarian rising by Russia?) Profoundly disturbed by the impact of messianic Wilsonian idealism on the peace negotiations of 1919, and the rejection of the Versailles treaty by the Senate, Nicolson viewed the diplomatic method as one of the last entrenchments of civilization—an extension of the upper-class norms of Edwardian Europe, whose stratified class distinctions and traditions of civility he unconsciously extrapolated to the international arena. In order to nail down the indispensability of his class and educational tradition to diplomacy, he rather artfully narrowed the definition of the diplomatic function to exclude such difficult and inconvenient areas as the economics and technology that had already transformed European society and were rapidly revolutionizing warfare.

Dismayed by the League of Nations—and even more by the United Nations—Nicolson regarded their proceedings not as part of the "negotiating" (i.e., diplomatic) process but as "exercises in forensic propaganda." Appalled by the "diplomacy by insult or diplomacy by loudspeaker" which first made an appearance in the era of the fascist dictators, he equally rejected the intrusions of popularly elected politicians, especially American ones.

Nicolson's analysis (if it can be flattered by such an appellation) is useful today for its advocacy of certain timeless virtues in the conduct of relations between states—reliability, truthfulness, discretion, firmness, and consistency. Where his analysis failed fifty years ago—and where similar attempts fail today—is in its incomplete comprehension of the underlying idiom of history and human development, of which relations between governments and modalities of international intercourse can only be a reflection. Today the forces destructive of the old diplomacy that were operative in the 1920s and 1930s have been intensified and multiplied many times over. A return to the past is impossible.

The crisis confronting diplomacy in the 1980s can only be understood as part of the much larger crisis confronting the nation-state. Despite all the frenzied manifestations of nationalism and the proliferation of new nations, the basic reality to the latter part of the twentieth century is that "One World" is rapidly becoming a fact. The steady and inexorable shrinkage of the planet to the dimensions of a global village, combined with quantum leaps in the advance of technology and the social and economic development of hitherto backward regions is daily making the nation-state more obsolete at every level of international intercourse. As this process accelerates, the traditional modalities and instrumentalities have become too narrow and stereotyped to accommodate the traffic.

At the risk of belaboring the obvious, here are some of the factors that are rapidly changing the shape of diplomacy:

1. The revolution in communications and transportation

This is not merely a question of the extension overseas of the long arm of the executive branch, thereby reducing the importance of ambassadors and diplomatic missions. Of far greater impact are the multilevel channels of communications and transportation that now bind societies together, and saturate them with information on every facet of political, economic, and social life. The proliferation of news and information media—ranging from scholarly and technical journals at one end of the spectrum to radio and television at the other—has created so many information outlets that no significant development can be kept in isolation and analyzed for long.

In addition, the breadth of media coverage now dwarfs official coverage to the point of making the latter hopelessly narrow, no matter how much deeper its penetration. Mass communication also unleashes governmental propaganda, directed at a nation's own citizens, neighboring countries, and the rest of the world, on an unparalleled scale. Air transportation has compressed the time frame of international intercourse and made isolation of criminal activities inside national boundaries impossible.

2. Extension of the role of government

In every nation today, whether socialist or nominally free, the role of government in regulating the social and economic welfare of its citizens has projected the state into every level of commercial and financial life. In the United States, a governmental interest is present in a whole range of transactions untouched by government thirty years ago. This has generated corresponding pressures on government from the business, labor, and societal sectors affected. Government has everywhere extended its control over society and the person to the point where even in free societies the citizen has little redress except at election time. The effect on foreign relations is to expand government's constitutional mandate to intervene in transactions and activities extending overseas.

3. Advanced technology

The transformation of warfare by science and technology has not only created a "balance of terror" in nuclear armaments, but made the technology factor a crucial element in military readiness and comparative military strength. It is also transforming industry all over the world, on the one hand increasing productivity, on the other increasing energy consumption and vulnerability to economic and military disruption. The march of technology introduces an element of perpetual change into society, strongly accentuating the interdependence factor, discussed later.

4. Global interdependence

The voracity of advanced industrial societies for fuel and raw materials has made national self-sufficiency a thing of the past. The economies of advanced industrial societies like the United States, Japan, and Western Europe have become vulnerable. But dependence on foreign energy sources is only one aspect of the *interdependence* of advanced industrial societies on each other and the Third World. For nearly all countries, exports provide the foreign exchange to pay for food, fuel, and other imports on which the standard of living, and in a few cases like Britain and Japan, the physical survival of the population, depends. Economic self-sufficiency is almost everywhere an idle dream, except at the price of return to a subsistence economy and a medieval way of life. Environmental effects are also global in character, inextricably linked in such matters as toxic discharges and oil spills to the economic life of industrial societies. Moreover, multilevel relationships between nations now continue through periods of extreme political hostility and even war.

5. Egalitarianism—mass education

A rising level of general education and social equality has become both a precondition and inevitable consequence of technological progress and economic development. As mass education takes hold there is no way of containing popular participation in the governing process, however crude or indirect. There is no longer any way of containing ideas—and ideologies. Even the most repressive governments pay involuntary tribute to popular sentiment by feeling the need to justify their policies. Egalitarianism is replacing stratification by class whether or not accompanied by political freedoms.

6. Acceleration of change

Every nation, whether advanced or less developed, now stands on a moving walkway from which it falls off at its peril. Economic development is the name of the game in the Third World, and technological progress in the advanced industrial countries. Together with mass education, they stimulate societal change and fuel rising expectations. Constant political and economic adjustment becomes necessary to make society work, introducing a component of instability into foreign relations as well.

The convergence of these factors produces effects that make obsolete the conduct of foreign relations as a distinct and separate field of political activity. Internal and external affairs are now inextricably mixed up. Overseas developments frequently dictate popular responses at variance with foreign policy goals or commitments; these translate into internal political imperatives that cannot help but interfere with the steady pursuit of foreign policy goals.

The points of impact where overseas developments strike the domestic economy and social structure have now multiplied to the point where it has become virtually impossible for an administration to consistently pursue foreign policy goals without being subject to pressure from special interest groups, usually applied through Congress.

There is, of course, nothing new in the role that special interest pressures play in the formation of foreign policy—witness the effects of tariff policy and racial discrimination on U.S. relations with Japan during the 1920s; of the China lobby on U.S. relations in East Asia during the 1950s. What is different today is the degree to which the breakdown of a native American ethos has lowered resistance to ethnic, racial, and special interest particularity. This trend has been so encouraged by governmental demagoguery that decision making, both in the domestic and foreign fields, is in danger of being paralyzed by pressures at best irrelevant and at worst actually inimical to the national interest. In the last four years alone, the influence of the Greek lobby on arms sales to Turkey, of the Jewish lobby on West Bank settlement, of the farm lobby on the grain embargo against the Soviet Union, of the black lobby on relations with South Africa, and of the steel and automobile industries on competing Japanese imports has each been allowed total latitude of influence, without regard to countervailing strategic or political considerations. This intrusion of special interest pleading into the policy-making process is of course given full exposure by the press and mass media, thereby reinforcing pressure on members of Congress who might otherwise feel free to exercise independent judgment.

A second consequence has been the proliferation of nongovernmental links between countries. Every region, and especially the advanced industrial areas, is now interconnected with a complex network of economic, communications, and societal ties no longer susceptible of containment within established channels of government. The transactions of the international banking community in any given week now totally swamp the capacity of the leading industrial nations to trace them, let alone control them. Technology flow proceeds at so many levels, and by so many different routes, that the export control system can only hope to cover major categories of military equipment and then imperfectly.

To the extent that states extend their regulatory coverage to a given field of activity, that coverage now automatically spills over into foreign territory, creating conflicts of jurisdiction and ripple effects on foreign relations. The U.S. government now asserts the right to regulate *any* overseas economic activity, including stock and commodity trading that has a substantial effect within the United States. The statutory mandate of U.S. regulatory agencies to enforce the antitrust laws and curtail unfair trade practices has led them to police transactions in the stream of U.S. foreign commerce that not only fall within the jurisdictions of foreign governments but are regarded as perfectly legal by those governments.

Some agencies of government, hitherto regarded as exclusively domestic in character, now conduct their own specialized forms of foreign relations, using State Department channels for communications purposes only. The Departments of Justice and Treasury regularly conduct business with counterpart ministries overseas without going through diplomatic channels, and frequently make assertions of U.S. jurisdiction that are regarded by foreign governments as trespasses on sovereignty. Base rights and status-of-forces agreements are negotiated by the Defense Department, and scientific agreements by the National Science Foundation and White House science office, under only the loosest of supervision by the State Department, which has neither the personnel nor the expertise to assert effective control.

One little-noticed example of agency independence took place in 1975 when Secretary Kissinger was engaged in a delicate bit of carrot-and-stick trading with the Soviets. Without informing State, the chairman of the U.S. Maritime Commission negotiated an agreement with the Soviet government establishing reciprocal access to a limited number of ports in each country for U.S. and Soviet-flag vessels. Kissinger was infuriated but had to back down—the Maritime Commission is covered by a statutory mandate unlimited in scope, its chairman is not part of the executive branch.

A side effect of the multiplication of financial and economic relationships and the corresponding spread of governmental regulation has been the introduction of law and legal approaches into areas of foreign relations hitherto the province of traditional diplomacy. Contributing has been the breakdown of European hegemony and the challenge to the consensual methods of the old diplomacy posed in international forums by the socialist *bloc* and the more radical regimes of the Third World. As a result, the American style of international agreement, based on a contractual model that aims at covering every conceivable contingency, is gradually replacing the traditional European-style treaty or agreement, which tends to be tersely worded and aimed primarily at defining the intent of the parties. Moreover, the multilevel nature of international relationships has entangled virtually every act of state in a thicket of legal complexity—witness the recent inability of the U.S. government to take prompt action in freeing Iranian government assets and pursuing the ill-gotten wealth of the shah....

...Within the United States the complexity of the subject matter of diplomacy has opened the way to formation of a new foreign policy elite of full-time specialists in defense and foreign affairs matters, centered in foundations, universities and think tanks. Special interest pressures exerted through Congress and other public channels by business, labor or farm groups at least reflect legitimate economic and societal interests that in any event would have to find expression through the political process. Their objectives are tangible and their methods plainly visible. Much more elusive are the goals and methods of the new elite, which has replaced the traditional establishment of bankers, politicians

and lawyers. Its members employ words and ideas as weapons, gauge success and failure by the influence they exert over the political leadership, and camouflage a remorseless quest for power and riches under a protective mantle of selfless scholarship.

The creation of an outside community of academic specialists capable of infiltrating the bureaucracy and imposing its ideas on experienced military and civilian leaders is unique to the United States. Originally confined to areas of science, technology and advanced engineering, where expert advice could only be obtained from outside the government, the thirst for ostensibly objective scientific opinion has now spread to areas of foreign relations formerly reserved to the diplomatic practitioners. No other country would permit the career ranks of its government to be infiltrated by theoreticians with free license to impose their ideas on foreign policy and no accountability for the success or failure of their advice except to the politician who for a brief period gives them employment.

Unlike the old establishment, with deep roots in society and no personal advantage to be gained from public service other than enhanced standing in the community, the new elite is dominated by ambitious intellectuals whose entire life is wrapped up in their professional achievements, and whose ambitions—social and financial, as well as academic—depend on the influence they can exert on the decisionmaking process. Secure in tenured positions, with no obligation to actually educate, its more influential members are given facilities, research assistance, and travel opportunities on a scale impossible for business and professional men in other fields to match. Battening on government or industry grants, they have the mobility to shuttle from outside consultancies to inside policy jobs in a way denied to professionals locked into corporations and law firms by business commitments, retirement plans and shareholdings. Their continued access to colleagues in power is assured by the community's operation as both personnel recruiting ground and source of future employment.

The ascent to power of this new elite has a conspiratorial side inimical to good government. The financing of some of its leaders has been concealed from public view and is on a scale that leaves them in some degree captive to the policy biases of their patrons. The links between Kissinger, the Rockefeller interests and the late shah certainly distorted U.S. policy toward Iran. The Trilateral Commission, while certainly not a conspiracy in the crude sense portrayed by the right-wing fringe, was nevertheless converted into an *instrumentality* advancing the political fortunes of Governor Jimmy Carter at an early stage of his presidential candidacy—with the predictable result that after

Carter was elected to office key national security jobs were given to the commission's directorate, headed by Zbigniew Brzezinski, who in effect dictated his options in accordance with their own predilections and those of their sponsors.

The creative talents of the more gifted members of the new elite should not blind the public to the fact that they have imported values into government that are alien to the American tradition in both the figurative and literal sense. Their addiction to grand designs and resounding formulations, coupled with Old World affinities and hatreds brought over in their baggage, has severely damaged the American reputation for pragmatism, candor and moral principle. Their public pronouncements sometimes betray a shocking ignorance of the Constitution and separation of powers. Their personal traits, ranging from paranoia and deviousness to loose-lipped braggadocio, have repeatedly poisoned the climate of confidence so essential to a healthy relationship between colleagues and allies. As a result, honest reporting and the frank interchange of conflicting viewpoints have been made extremely hazardous for senior officials with careers at stake.

These strands come together in the phenomenal growth of the NSC, headed by the president's national security adviser, at the expense of the secretary and Department of State. The interrelationship between foreign and domestic affairs, often invoked by apologists to justify this trend, is not the determinative factor—that connection is divisible by the very nature of government and, until recently, was never permitted to diminish the supremacy of the secretary in his own sphere. The intractable new development is the encroachment of powerful departments and agencies with legitimate interests and independent statutory missions in the foreign affairs field that give them a degree of operational autonomy impossible for the department to control. The need for a coordinating mechanism to weigh the diverse interests and present balanced policy options to the president is obvious. Repeated efforts to endow the secretary of state with enough authority to exercise a coordinating role have run into a wall of departmental and congressional resistance. The rise of the NSC has been the inevitable result.

What do these lessons portend for the future? Can diplomacy survive the welter of conflicting forces that threaten to swamp it? Will the career services disintegrate into an aggregation of specialists bound together at the top by the small minority of managerial generalists who have managed to rise above the specialties that gave them a head start in the first place?. . .

Operating in a Goldfish Bowl

Sooner or later the department is going to have to tighten its rules on public disclosure or risk having its hand forced at every turn of the diplomatic wheel. Foreign governments have now become quite expert at manipulating the media; and the media are now locked into a competitive cycle that makes them willing collaborators. Absent official authorization, the standard reply of the working level to all requests for information from the press should be "no comment," and referral of the questioner to the department's spokesman. The "anonymous official source" label should be especially avoided: it has been thoroughly abused by the press in the form of unverifiable inventions.

Even the most inflexible traditionalist now understands that policies and negotiating positions must be formulated with unexpected exposure in mind. Sooner or later, the proliferation of leakage points and the compulsion of even the most authoritarian government to show achievement, or at least purposeful activity, makes disclosure inevitable. Less understood is that the currency of private undertakings and corridor assurances on which diplomats set such store is now of such transient and uncertain value as to be almost worthless. Statements on the public record, no matter how opaque or misleading, provide the only firm basis from which to derive the intentions of other governments and frame the policies of one's own. For a brief period at least, these represent a commitment by the leadership to its own people and the rest of the world.

If any conclusion is possible, a prediction can be made that the diplomat of the future is doomed to perform his functions in precisely the atmosphere that Harold Nicolson so justly abhorred. The profession has become both impossibly demanding and physically dangerous; the amenities and privileges to diplomatic life greatly attenuated. The consolation is that no other profession provides such a ringside seat to history in the making—and a chance to make history oneself.

Elmer Plischke

American Ambassadors—An Obsolete Species? Some Alternatives to Traditional Diplomatic Representation

Evolving diplomacy—and the mutating role of the ambassador—reflects material changes in the conduct of foreign affairs. Among the more important are improvements in the technology of international communication an transportation; expanding relationships of governments to people abroad as well as at home; mistreatment of emissaries, threats of terrorism, and decline in compliance with the precepts of the Vienna conventions on diplomatic and consular status and immunities; and both quantitative and qualitative proliferation—of the society of nations (with the emergence of more than one-hundred new states since World War II, including many microstates), of national interests, and of the functioning of the global diplomatic community.[1] . . .

Ambassador J. Robert Schaetzel argues that if the ambassador is regarded as "an endangered species," the implication is that his status is worth preserving, and suggests that, even though the ambassador may not be obsolete, he is obsolescent—that he "is in the way of becoming one of the world's anachronisms." He deplores "the timeless charade of formal social activity which has become synonymous with diplomacy," and the peculiar American process of appointing its ambassadors (naming noncareerists as ranking diplomats and widespread use of presidential special envoys), and he maintains:

> In a word, the ambassador is out of the serious play. He is rarely viewed as the best channel

Elmer Plischke is the foremost authority in the United States on the practice of modern diplomacy. Ex-diplomat, and writer of numerous books and articles on the conduct of diplomacy, he is professor emeritus, University of Maryland; adjunct professor, Gettysburg College; and adjunct scholar, American Enterprise Institute.
SOURCE: *World Affairs* 147, no. 1 (Summer 1984): 2–23. Reprinted by permission.

of communication with the head of government, he is not charged with the critical negotiating tasks, he is subordinated to visiting Washington officials and negotiating experts (visitors would be amazed if he had the temerity to offer substantive views), and—to make the message unmistakably clear—his expected duties are those of the hosteler.

He contends, therefore, that "the ambassador of the future will play a more limited role than the pompous illusion of the president's alter ego abroad, or the inflated image of the policy maker working in tight partnership with the secretary of state."[2]

While it may be questioned whether this is a valid interpretation of the functioning of accredited envoys, there is little doubt that profound change in the conduct of foreign relations in recent decades impinges on their contemporary status. Two of these developments, as they relate to the traditional bilateral representation of the resident ambassador and his mission, warrant special consideration—increasing diplomacy at both higher political and more particularized technical levels, and growing resort to multipartite negotiations. The fundamental issues that need to be addressed are whether summit, subsummit, technical, and multipartite conference diplomacy are replacing or supplementing classical diplomacy, and whether they are desirable, necessary, and productive foreign relations processes.

Some, especially professional diplomats, deplore what they deem to be the diminishing pivotal status of the resident ambassador abroad. However, of the four functional strata of diplomacy—the summit, ministerial, traditional or professional, and technical—there is little question that the traditional remains the basic, most widely employed for the primal functions of representation, communicating, reporting, and servicing of nationals and their interests abroad, but also for policy recommendation and often for bilateral negotiation. Nevertheless, in this century, especially in recent decades, the other levels and multipartite conferencing have gained in usage and public attention.

Summit Diplomacy

In earlier times reigning monarchs personally managed both their external and internal affairs. Chronicles of the past recount the foreign relations exploits of emperors, kings, princes, and churchmen, as well as presidents, premiers, chancellors, and dictators. For centuries they determined foreign policy and communicated and negotiated with other foreign leaders. As the modern state system developed, especially with the growth of democratic governance, chiefs of state came to play a less determinate role in foreign relations, and relied more on others—their heads of government, cabinet ministers, and eventually corps of professional diplomats. It is erroneous to maintain that personal diplomacy at the summit and ministerial levels is a new phenomenon. Its remarkable resurgence since the 1970s, affecting the functioning of the traditional ambassador evidences, rather, characterization by new titles, increased usage, unique forms, and popularization if not glamorization in the news media and public consciousness.

Although the expression *summit diplomacy* first came to be popularly employed in the 1950s,[3] as a form of state practice it is as old as history itself. Often conceived as pertaining primarily to top-level conferencing, it encompasses six distinguishable functions: making and enunciating policy, communicating personally with foreign leaders, commissioning personal representatives or special envoys, receiving visiting summit leaders, and undertaking such visits and tours abroad, in addition to participating in informal meetings and formal conferences. . . .

Summit conferencing has been subjected to especially severe criticism—because it supersedes the traditional diplomatic process, because the president is regarded as inadequately qualified or prepared for the particular venture, or because it fails to satisfy popular expectations or to produce sufficiently gratifying results. All too often the consequences are memorialized in pretentious communiqués, official reports, personal memoirs, or an amorphous "spirit of" Camp David, Geneva, Glassboro, or Manila. At the conclusion of one of the East–West meetings, Joseph Alsop cautioned that "we must wait and see whether a lot, or a little, or less than nothing at all was accomplished there."[4] President Eisenhower reportedly informed his cabinet in 1953: "This idea of the president of the United States going personally abroad to negotiate—it's just damn stupid. Every time the president has gone abroad to get into the details of these things, he's lost his shirt."[5] Nevertheless, during the next seven years, he went abroad at least a dozen times to engage in such conferencing. Others are more optimistic about meetings. During World War II, precluding that Big-Three Tehran Conference, Prime Minister Churchill wrote Stalin that wartime plans "can only be settled between the heads of governments and states with their high expert authorities at their side."[6] Presidents vary in their ability to withstand the lure of the summit. They all succumb to it, but they differ in their enthusiasm.

One of the staunchest cases for summit conferencing has been made by British diplomatist Lord Hankey—who personally attended five hundred sessions of international conferences and meetings in an official capacity. He declared that solutions to international problems frequently require resources "beyond those of the most competent and qualified diplomatist," and therefore:

> can only be settled in conference by persons who have their hand on the pulse of the political conditions and currents of thought in their respective countries; who have at immediate disposal all the technical knowledge which governments possess; who know how far they can persuade their fellow-countrymen to go in the direction of compromise; and who, insomuch as they have to defend their policy before their respective parliaments, are alone in a position to make real concessions.

He also claims that at Paris in 1919 "in a single day's conference more was accomplished to bring about unity of policy than could have been effected in weeks of inter-communication by ordinary diplomatic methods."[7] The crux of the matter is whether the president has the potentiality of accomplishing something not equally achievable by regular diplomats, and whether this is worth the time and risk.

Ministerial Diplomacy

Foreign ministers also engage personally in a great deal of international representation, conferencing, and other diplomatic activities. They not only exercise the customary function of meeting in their national capitals with foreign ambassadors, but also engage in fact-finding consultation tours abroad, spearhead troubleshooting missions, occasionally shuttle between foreign capitals, and attend many international conferences and sessions of international agencies. The secretary of state, for example, has headed American delegations to United Nations–sponsored global conclaves, the most important inter-American conferences, the post–World War II Council of Foreign Ministers sessions, and other diplomatic gatherings.

Because much international organization machinery since the 1930s functions regularly at the ministerial level—constituting institutionalized subsummit conferencing mechanisms—the secretary of state normally has attended sessions of such agencies as the United Nations General Assembly and the councils created to implement the North Atlantic and Manila Pacts, the CENTO and ANZUS treaties, and the inter-American defense system. Similarly, foreign ministers systematically represent their governments in sessions of the Council of Europe, the European Community, the League of Arab States, the Organization of African Unity, and other agencies. Ministerial-level representation also is common in the International Bank, the International Monetary Fund, and regional financial institutions. . . .

More recently, Dean Rusk achieved the record of fifty-two trips abroad in the 1960s, for approximately 125 consultations, meetings, and conferences, traveling nearly six hundred thousand miles, and spending more than 375 days en route and at the discussion table. During the 1970s, William P. Rogers, Henry Kissinger, Cyrus Vance, and Edmund Muskie undertook approximately sixty-five foreign missions, in addition to attending many regularized sessions of ministerial international agencies. This amounts to nearly one foreign trip every two months. In less than three and a half years, Secretary Kissinger averaged roughly ten per year. Many of these foreign ventures require the secretary to engage in multiple negotiations or individual consultation with the leaders of half a dozen or more countries within the span of a few days.

The role of the secretary is unique in that under the authority of his office he may consult and negotiate with foreign governments on his own initiative. Yet, as international spokesman for the United States, he is the agent of the president, and in this sense technically all of his diplomatic ventures abroad are in the nature of special diplomatic missions. They bear the approval or tacit consent of the president; sometimes they are specially commissioned by him, and therefore the secretary often represents, not himself, but the president. Consequently, although he occupies a ranking position at the subsummit, on these occasions he actually functions at the summit, and usually the diplomatic tasks he undertakes transcend those of traditional ambassadors, in terms of level of representation and reception and breadth of competence. Despite the hazards of ministerial diplomacy—such as overuse, long absence from the home government, and displacement of experienced diplomats— Norman L. Hill stresses its more obvious advantages:[8]

> The secretary's authority is necessarily broader than that of any subordinate so that he can negotiate without the need for extensive instructions. Furthermore, he may feel that he can negotiate with a picture of the world scene in his mind, . . .whereas an ambassador is more limited in his range of views. The modern secretary, too, may feel. . .that "talking face to face is the best way yet invented for enabling men to understand each other."

Technical Diplomacy

Another innovation of the twentieth century is the increasing involvement of technicians and specialists in diplomatic practice, either as members of diplomatic teams or as primary negotiators. In the first capacity, they are appointed as constituents of resident missions abroad and include experts on a variety of matters—agricultural, budgetary, consular, cultural, financial, foreign aid and assistance, health, intelligence, labor, legal, military, petroleum, refugee, scientific, trade, and other foreign affairs. This is exemplified by the appointment of commercial, military, treasury, and other functional attachés. Or they are attached to the staffs of conference representatives, and serve as counselors to delegates or as principals in the subsidiary machinery of these forums, such as conference committees, subcommittees, or technical drafting services. In this guise they are essentially advisory and auxiliary to the chief of mission or conference delegate and do not disadvantage the traditional diplomat.

In the second capacity, on the other hand, sometimes these specialists serve as primary representatives in negotiations on technical—as distinguished from political or diplomatic—matters. Because the scope of international concerns has broadened so enormously in recent decades and encompasses so many highly specialized subjects—as noted later—a great deal of contemporary foreign relations focusing on them must be handled by experts, and the diplomatic need is met either by recruiting them into the professional foreign service, by encouraging diplomats to specialize, or by appointing outside experts to particular diplomatic assignments. The more governments deal internationally with such technical matters, the more they are likely to bypass the resident diplomat and turn to specialists to cope with them.

Conference Diplomacy

. . .The shrinkage of world horizons, the Industrial Revolution and the resulting flow of trade, the achievements of scientific discovery and the technological revolution, and the growing interaction of states on an array of cultural, economic, financial, humanitarian, social, and technical as well as political, security, and legal affairs have broadened the scope of diplomacy enormously. In earlier times diplomatic relations were generally restricted to peace making, territorial disposition and boundaries, commerce and navigation, immigration, citizenship, extradition, and a limited number of other matters, which generally could be handled by the diplomats. States now negotiate with one another on a comprehensive spectrum of issues. These range, for example, from alliances to atomic waste disposal, from outer space and seabed resources to cell biology, from disarmament to preserving endangered species, from trade promotion to copyright problems, and including such more esoteric subjects as air hydrology, crashworthiness, crystallography, desert locusts, folklore, legal metrology, radio wavelengths, spent fuel storage, and unifying technical nomenclature. In recent years international conferences on law creation, peaceful settlement of disputes, and crisis management have also increased, but now interrelations entail virtually every subject in which the modern government harbors any official concern. This broadening of the substance of international affairs has augmented not only the functional quality, but also the degree of diplomatic contact and the number of bilateral and multilateral meetings, and has engendered the need for technical experts in the negotiation process.

Conference diplomacy, evolved to cope with these requisites, generally circumvents the bilateral functions of resident ambassadors. It assumes the form of ad hoc gatherings, occasional or regularized meetings, or periodic sessions of deliberative agencies of international organizations. For descriptive taxonomical purposes, international meetings and conferences may be grouped into complex categories distinguished on the basis of their composition, subject matter, timing, objectives, and other differentiating factors.[9]

One of its mutations—called "parliamentary diplomacy," which is characterized as institutionalized conferencing—is conducted within permanent mechanisms founded on agreed constitutive acts, like the United Nations and the nearly seventy-five other multipartite public international institutions in which the United States participates. In a single year, the government has been scheduled to send delegations to nearly 650 sessions of such organizations. Aside from the United Nations system, among the most numerous were those of the Organization for Economic Cooperation and Development (approximately 145 sessions), the North Atlantic Treaty Organization (more than 60), and the Organizations of American States (some 30 to 35). American representatives also attended at least forty meetings of commodity, fishery, and wildlife preservation agencies. In recent years the United States has been represented annually in the sessions of more than three hundred international institutions and their subsidiaries, many of a very specialized nature. In addition, in the past decade the United States has attended a series of UN–sponsored ad hoc

assemblages, dealing with such worldwide problems as aging, assistance to less developed countries, energy resources, mankind's habitat, human rights, population, refugees, science and technological development, and the status of women.

Delegates to such conferences and international agencies vary—including chiefs of state and government, cabinet ministers, special high-level representatives, ambassadors, other professional diplomats, and technical experts. Whereas many delegates are career diplomats, sometimes on assignments additional to their regular resident missions, the preponderant majority are on special assignment to the delegation at a particular conference or agency session. The cumulative consequence is that a major share of contemporary diplomacy is handled by this multipartite alternative to the traditional resident diplomatic mission, and American participants are largely special appointees rather than resident ambassadors, although many are professional diplomats assigned to permanent or special missions accredited to particular agencies (including the United Nations, several of its specialized agencies, the Organization of American States, the European Communities, and the North Atlantic Treaty Organization) or to deal with important functional issues (such as arms control, the law of the sea, and trade relations). While the typical resident emissary may not be centrally involved in this multipartite conferencing, many professional diplomats serve on negotiating delegations and their staffs. Thus, although the traditional ambassador may be bypassed, the diplomats are not.

Occasionally American representation in international conferencing escalates to the highest levels. The president and secretary of state may attend those meetings and conferences that they regard as warranting their personal participation, reflecting not only on their own persuasions, but also the pressures brought by other world leaders, the exigencies of the times, and in the case of the secretary of state, the specification of ministerial representation mandated for particular international agencies.

Quantitatively, summit conferencing is relatively rare. Beginning with Wilson's venture to Paris in 1919, the president has met with other world leaders in approximately 120 international conferences and meetings—one-third convened in the United States and the rest abroad. More than half are bipartite meetings. The multipartite range from the early trips of Presidents Coolidge to Havana in 1928, and Roosevelt to Buenos Aires in 1936—to address inter-American assemblages—to Roosevelt's wartime conclaves with Churchill, Stalin, and Chiang Kai-shek; the East–West summit conferences at Geneva in 1955 and Paris in 1960;

Western Big Three and Four Power meetings in 1953, 1959, and 1979; and occasional NATO sessions. Others include convocations of the presidents of the American republics, a series of economic talks by the leaders of the Western industrial powers, and a number of ad hoc conclaves like the seven-power Manila Conference to deal with the war in Vietnam in 1966, and the North–South Cancun Conference on international development in 1981.

Some summit meetings, like Kennedy's encounter with Khrushchev in Vienna in 1961 and Johnson's meeting with Kosygin in Glassboro in 1967, are informal. Occasionally they are devoted to signing ceremonies, such as those concerned with strategic weapons agreements—Nixon in Moscow, 1972; Ford in Valdivostok, 1974; and Carter in Vienna, 1979. Others are more formal conclaves, including those convened at Tehran, Yalta, and Potsdam during World War II and the Four Power East–West conferences at Geneva and Paris. Although the president is the primary representative of the nation in such conferences and meetings, he is usually accompanied by the secretary of state and a team of other top-level advisers and professional diplomats, unless the talks are very informal.

It is unrealistic to presume that the community of nations could handle, by traditional bilateral representation, the needs that are currently served each year by these hundreds of individual conferences and sessions of international agencies. Many involve the interests and actions of dozens of states (sometimes numbering more than 150), and some take months and even years of arduous negotiation.[10] In other words, much contemporary diplomatic business now dealt with by international conferencing could not be adequately handled by traditional missions and processes on a bipartite basis. This is far from saying that the customary function of resident ambassadors is no longer either necessary or important. Nor does it imply that many matters are not managed more effectively or successfully by classical processes.

* * *

Despite criticism of summit, ministerial, technical, and conference diplomacy, and the effects their development may have on the prestige and morale of the traditional ambassador and careeer diplomatic staffs, these alternative processes are bound to flourish. They parallel and reinforce classical diplomacy—each serving a useful purpose and all essential to the conduct of foreign relations in this complex age. They impact less on the quantitative than on certain qualitative aspects of regular resident emissaries—which creates a challenge, but not necessarily a threat, to the species. There are generic as well as practical limits to the capacities of traditional ambassadors in contemporary diplomacy. This does not suggest that they are either unnecessary or redundant. But their role may be modified in direct relation to the desirability of negotiating in a multipartite forum, the need to discuss technical issues, and the degree to which the president elects to become his own secretary of state, or the latter presumes to become his own ambassador. Even in such cases career diplomats—as distinguished from resident ambassadors—serve an essential purpose. As a matter of principle, the issue is less a question of whether the ambassador can handle, but whether he is best for, the diplomatic assignment.

Though widespread, time-tested, often useful, sometimes necessary, and above all, newsworthy, summit and subsummit diplomacy is by no means a magic elixir for international problem solving or malady.[11] It is not, warned President Reagan, "the cure for everything that's wrong in the world."[12] So far as summit diplomacy is concerned, Dean Rusk, noting the fundamental distinction between presidential visits abroad and involvement of the president in summit negotiations, argues that:

> The president, as Chief of State of the United States, can and ought to undertake a limited and carefully planned program of state visits, short in duration, and aimed at the exchange of courtesy and respect as a tangible expression of the good will of the American people. But negotiation at the chief-of-government level is quite another matter. It is not easily accommodated among the peculiarities of our constitutional system; it diverts time and energy from exactly the point at which we can spare it least; it does not give us effective negotiation; such experience as we have had with summit diplomacy does not encourage the view that it contributes to the advancement of American interests.

And he warns against permitting summit diplomacy to become "a debilitating or dangerous habit."[13] Despite its inherent media attraction, it should not be regarded as the consummate narcotic of the assuagement of international ailments. Much of the diplomatic diagnosis, prescription, and pharmaceutics must be, and is, left to others—to the professionals, including the resident ambassador.

While it may be contended that diplomacy at the summit, ministerial, and technical levels, and around the international conference table, supplements rather than supplants that of regular resident ambassadors, it is equally arguable that often it supersedes traditional participants, and therefore militates against their interests and functions—but without rendering them obsolete or useless. Their capacity is not diminished, either absolutely or relatively, but rather it has sustained some impediment to potential accretion and proliferation. If the function of these alternative levels of diplomacy and multilateral conferencing were solely the domain of traditional resident ambassadors, the results would not necessarily be better and, in the case of conferencing, the cost, in time and funds, would be prohibitive.

In short, the functioning of the traditional ambassador remains traditional, whereas the untraditional needs of diplomacy evoke new techniques to cope with them. Like most human institutions diplomacy is dynamic, designed to facilitate interstate relations as they change. Whatever emerges as "the new diplomacy"—in any era—is itself mutable and therefore likely never to approximate perfectability. To paraphrase Tennyson, "the old order changeth, yielding place to the new"—which, perhaps, is the most immutable of the traditions in diplomacy.

Notes

1. For commentary on "the new diplomacy," see the essays of Hermann F. Eilts, Harold Nicolson, Robert J. Pranger, and others presented in Elmer Plischke, ed., *Modern Diplomacy: The Art and the Artisans* (Washington, D.C.: American Enterprise Institute, 1979), Chapters 1 and 2. The impact of international terrorism on contemporary diplomacy is illustrated in Martin F. Herz, ed., *Diplomats and Terrorists: What Works, What Doesn't—A Symposium* (Washington, D.C.: Institute for the Study of Diplomacy, Georgetown University, 1982); in the growing literature on terrorism and skyjacking, such as the works of Yonah Alexander, Robert A. Friedlander, Brian M. Jenkins, Walter Laqueur, and others; and in the issues of *Terrorism: An International Journal* (quarterly, 1977).

2. J. Robert Schaetzel, "Is the Ambassador an Endangered Species, or Merely Obsolete?" in *Commission of the Government for the Conduct of Foreign Policy,* Appendices, vol. 6, pp. 328, 333.

3. The press first began to use the expression *summit conference* in relation to the Geneva East–West Conference of 1955, but the term *summit* was employed two years earlier by Winston Churchill in a foreign policy address to the House of Commons; see Hansard, *Parliamentary Debates,* 5th Series, vol. 515 (1953), p. 897. The word *summit* actually was used as early as 1943, when in a joint statement of President Roosevelt and Prime Minister Churchill, at the conclusion of the first Quebec Conference, they declared that it was indispensable for the unity of aim and method to be maintained "at the summit of the war direction." See United States Senate, *A Decade of American Foreign Policy: Basic Documents, 1941–49,* Senate Document No. 123, 81st Congress, 1st Session (1950), p. 7.

4. *Washington Post,* June 28, 1967.

5. See Emmet J. Hughes, *The Ordeal of Power* (New York: Atheneum, 1963), p. 151.

6. USSR Ministry of Foreign Affairs, *Correspondence Between the Chairman of the Council of Ministers of the USSR and the Presidents of the U.S.A. and the Prime Ministers of Great Britain During the Great Patriotic War of 1941–1945* (Moscow: Foreign Languages Publishing House, 1957), vol. 1, p. 81.

7. Lord Maurice Hankey, *Diplomacy by Conference* (London: Smith, 1920), p. 38.

8. Norman L. Hill, *Mr. Secretary of State* (New York: Random House, 1963), p. 111.

9. A chart of conferencing types, consisting of five general groupings composed of primary conference categories and subsidiary subcategories—totaling seventy-five distinct types is presented in Plischke, "International Conferencing and the Summit: Macro-Analysis of Presidential Participation," *ORBIS,* vol. 14 (Fall 1970), pp. 682–683.

10. The United Nations Conference on the Law of the Sea, for example, consisted of a series of three conclaves. The first and second were held in 1958 and 1963. Then, following five years of preparatory work in the General Assembly and an organizational session in New York in December 1973, the Third Law of the Sea Conference, attended by some 160 states, has met in one or more protracted sessions each year since 1974, constituting one of the lengthiest and largest international conferences on record.

11. Summary commentary of the advantages and disadvantages of diplomacy at the summit are provided in Keith Eubank, *The Summit Conferences, 1919–1960* (Norman: University of Oklahoma Press, 1966), chapter 15; and Elmer Plischke, *Summit Diplomacy: Personal Diplomacy of the President of the United States* (College Park, Md.: Bureau of Governmental Research, University of Maryland, 1958), chapter 7—republished Westport, Conn.: Greenwood, 1974.

12. *New York Times,* July 29, 1982, p. A 18.

13. Dean Rusk, "The President," *Foreign Affairs,* vol 38 (April 1960), pp. 360–361.

Study Questions

1. What do we mean by *diplomacy*?
2. How did diplomacy evolve?
3. What are the ranks and privileges of diplomats?
4. How is an American embassy organized?
5. What does reporting at an embassy entail?
6. Compare the role and function of the contemporary ambassador with that in the nineteenth century.
7. What does Charles Maechling, Jr., mean by "goldfish bowl" operation of a diplomat?
8. How did scientific and technological changes transform the role of the embassy and the diplomatic service?
9. Can international society dispense with diplomacy?
10. How does Elmer Plischke answer that question?
11. What is the difference between a centralizer and decentralizer?
12. What is the difference between a career diplomat and a political appointee?
13. Explain the difference between *old* and *new* diplomacy.
14. What are the characteristics of summit and shuttle diplomacy?
15. What are the characteristics of secret and open diplomacy?
16. What are the characteristics of bilateral and multilateral diplomacy?
17. What is the difference between negotiation and bargaining?
18. What are the requirements before negotiation can commence?
19. What are the four kinds of agreements in which states act to regulate their relations?
20. What is meant by the *resistance point*?
21. What do we mean by *tacit negotiation*?
22. What are commitments and rewards in the bargaining process?
23. What are threats and punishments in the bargaining process?
24. What is the difference between zero-sum and positive-sum or variable-sum games?
25. Explain Homans's theorem.
26. What is the difference between a "tough" and a "soft" stance in the bargaining process?
27. Explain the difference between the use of conventional military capabilities in bargaining and nuclear deterrence.
28. Explain the concept of MAD.
29. Why is the economic means of influence an indirect method and military capability a direct method?
30. What are the objectives of economic resources in the bargaining process?
31. How can tariffs influence bargaining?
32. How can quotas influence the bargaining process?
33. What is the difference between a boycott and an embargo as a method of controlling trade?
34. How can economic aid be used in the bargaining process?

Key Terms

ambassador

bargaining

bilateral aid

boycott

commitment
compellance
diplomacy
deterrence
embargo
embassy
extension agreement
innovation agreement
massive retaliation
most-favored-nation principle (MFN)
multilateral aid
mutually assured destruction (MAD)
negotiation

new diplomacy
normalization agreement
quota
redistribution agreement
resistance point
shuttle diplomacy
summit diplomacy
tacit negotiation
tariff
threat
variable-sum game
zero-sum game

Notes

1. Robert D. Cantor, *Introduction to International Politics* (Itasca, Ill.: F. E. Peacock, 1976), p. 105.
2. Jack C. Plano and Roy Olton, *The International Relations Dictionary,* 3rd ed. (Santa Barbara, Calif.: ABC-CLIO, 1982), p. 234.
3. William C. Olson, ed., *The Theory and Practice of International Relations,* 7th ed. (Englewood Cliffs, N.J.: Prentice-Hall, 1987), p. 149.
4. Bruce Russett and Harvey Starr, *World Politics: The Menu for Choice,* 2nd ed. (New York: W. H. Freeman, 1985), p. 163.
5. See Richard N. Rosecrance, "Diplomacy," in *International Encyclopedia of the Social Sciences,* vol. 4, ed. David L. Sills (New York: Macmillan, 1968), p. 187.
6. See Sir Harold Nicolson, *Diplomacy,* 3rd ed. (New York: Oxford University Press, 1964), pp. 28, 31–33. For a concise but thorough treatment of the concept of diplomacy from the seventeenth century to the present, see Gordon A. Craig and Alexander L. George, *Force and Statecraft: Diplomatic Problems of Our Time* (New York: Oxford University Press, 1983), Part I.
7. Quoted by Kenneth W. Thompson, "The Ethical Dimensions of Diplomacy," *The Review of Politics* 43, no. 6 (1984): 373. Also cited in Arthur Lall, *Modern International Negotiation* (New York: Columbia University Press, 1966), p. 151.
8. Nicolson, *Diplomacy,* p. 50.
9. Ibid., p. 55.
10. Ibid., p. 76.
11. See Gilbert R. Winham, "Negotiation as a Management Process," *World Politics* 30, no. 1 (October 1977): 87–114.
12. Alan M. James, "Diplomacy and International Society," *International Relations* VI, no. 6 (November 1980): 932.
13. See Henry Kissinger's memoirs, *White House Years* (Boston: Little, Brown, 1979); and idem, *Years of Upheaval* (Boston: Little, Brown, 1982).
14. See George Ball's criticism in his *Diplomacy for a Crowded World* (Boston: Little, Brown, 1976), especially pp. 35–36.
15. Russett and Starr, *World Politics,* p. 165.

16. Michael K. O'Leary, "Linkages Between Domestic and International Politics in Underdeveloped Nations," in *Linkage Politics*, ed. James N. Rosenau (New York: Free Press, 1969), pp. 324–346; and Elmer Plischke, *Microstates in World Affairs* (Washington, D.C.: American Enterprise Institute, 1977), chap. 4.

17. See, for example, Jeffrey Z. Rubin and Bert R. Brown, *The Social Psychology of Bargaining and Negotiation* (New York: Academic Press, 1975).

18. See Fred Charles Ikle, "Negotiation," in *International Encyclopedia of the Social Sciences*, vol. 11, ed. David L. Sills (New York: Macmillan, 1968), pp. 117–120.

19. See Craig and George, *Force and Statecraft*, pp. 157–158.

20. *Ibid.*, pp. 158–159.

21. For a discussion of *interventionary diplomacy*, see Richard Falk, "The Menace of the New Cycle of Interventionary Diplomacy," *Journal of Peace Research* XVII, no. 3 (1980): 201–205.

22. Frederic S. Pearson and J. Martin Rochester, *International Relations* (Reading, Mass.: Addison-Wesley, 1985), p. 229. For an explanation of how to negotiate arms reduction with the Soviet Union, see "Negotiation from Strength: An Interview with Eugene Rostow," *Fletcher Forum*, Summer 1983, pp. 228–238, and Edward L. Rowny, "Negotiating with the Soviet Union: Then and Now" (Washington, D.C.: Department of State Bureau of Public Affairs, Current Policy No. 1088, June 30, 1988).

23. Ikle, "Negotiation," p. 118. For a case study demonstrating the role of commitment as bargaining leverage, see William Mark Habeeb and I. William Zartman, *The Panama Canal Negotiations* (Washington, D.C.: Johns Hopkins Foreign Policy Institute, 1986).

24. Roger Fisher and William Ury, *Getting to Yes* (New York: Penguin, 1983).

25. See Thomas C. Schelling, *Arms and Influence* (New Haven: Yale University Press, 1966), pp. 69–78.

26. For an analysis of Kissinger's commitments and rewards, see Alexander L. George, "Domestic Constraints on Regime Change in U.S. Foreign Policy: The Need for Policy Legitimacy" in *Change in the International System*, ed. Ole R. Holsti, Randolph M. Siverson, and Alexander L. George (Boulder: Westview, 1980), pp. 251–258.

27. Thomas C. Schelling, *The Strategy of Conflict* (Cambridge: Harvard University Press, 1960).

28. Pearson and Rochester, *International Relations*, p. 232.

29. See I. William Zartman and Maureen R. Berman, *The Practical Negotiator* (New Haven: Yale University Press, 1982), pp. 12–15.

30. George Homans, *Social Behavior* (New York: Harcourt Brace Jovanovich, 1961), p. 62.

31. For additional literature on game theory, see, for example, Anatol Rapoport, *Fights, Games, and Debates* (Ann Arbor: University of Michigan Press, 1960); John von Neumann and Oscar Morgenstern, *Theory of Games and Economic Behavior* (Princeton: Princeton University Press, 1964); and M. Shubik, G. Crewer, and E. Savage, *The Literature of Gaming Simulation and Model-Building: Index on Critical Abstracts* (Santa Monica, Calif: Rand Corporation, 1972).

32. See Roger Fisher's handbook on international conflict situation, *International Conflict for Beginners* (New York: Harper & Row, 1969). It is interesting to note that not every player (e.g., the Soviet Union) considers compromise a viable form of negotiations. See, for example, Bennett Ramberg, "Tactical Advantages of Opening Positioning Strategies: Lessons from the Seabed Arms Control Talks 1967–1970," in *The Negotiation Process: Theories and Applications*, ed. I. William Zartman (Newbury Park, Calif.: Sage, 1988), pp. 136–148.

33. For a treatment of the International Court of Justice, see A. LeRoy Bennett, *International Organizations,* 2nd ed. (Englewood Cliffs, N.J.: Prentice-Hall, 1980), chap. 8; and Ernst B. Haas, "Regime Decay: Conflict Management and International Organizations, 1945–81, *International Organization* 37, no. 2 (1983): 189–256.

34. See Satish Kumar, "Non-Alignment as a Diplomatic Strategy," *International Studies* XX, no. 1–2 (January–June 1981): 117.

35. See Bruno S. Frey, "Weapons Exports and Aid to Developing Countries," *Journal of Peace Science* I, no. 2 (1975): 117–126.

36. See Jack S. Levy, "Alliance Formation and War Behavior," *Journal of Conflict Resolution* 25 no. 4 (December 1981): 581–613.

37. See, for example, Raoul Naroll, *Military Deterrence in History* (Albany: State University of New York, 1974), p. 328; and Wayne Ferris, *The Power Capabilities of Nation-States* (Lexington, Mass.: Heath, 1973).

38. Bruce M. Russett, "The Calculus of Deterrence," *Journal of Conflict Resolution* VII, no. 2 (June 1963): 97–109.

39. Arthur A. Stein, "When Misperception Matters," *World Politics* 34, no. 4 (July 1982): 505–526; Jack S. Levy, "Misperception and the Causes of War: Theoretical Linkages and Analytical Problems," *World Politics* 36, no. 1 (1983): 76–99; and Robert Jervis, "Deterrence and Perception," *International Security* 7, no. 3 (Winter 1982/1983): 3–30.

40. For an example of this apprehension, see Richard Pipes, "Why the Soviet Union Thinks It Could Fight and Win a Nuclear War," *Commentary* 64, no. 1 (July 1977): 21–34.

Seven

■

Psychological Warfare, Propaganda, and Terrorism

International relations has often been described as a series of games in which players (political actors) compete for various stakes. How successful a given player is depends ultimately on the amount of influence that can be exerted on the other players in terms of shaping their behavior in a desired fashion.[1] Some means of influence are direct and open; others are indirect and very subtle. In this chapter we will examine two instruments of foreign policy that are designed to influence the opinions and behavior of foreign peoples and state actors in desired directions through means other than the employment of a nation's political, economic, and military resources. These two instruments are psychological warfare and propaganda. A third technique we will examine is terrorism. *Nonstate* actors employ terrorism usually as a revolutionary technique carried out by disgruntled individuals acting against existing governments. The purpose of terrorism is to create fear, panic, and paralysis in international relations. Although the first two techniques appear to be nonviolent as compared to the third technique, they actually complement one another and overlap in many aspects.

Psychological Warfare

In 1920 the British military analyst and historian J. F. C. Fuller wrote that traditional means of warfare may in time be "replaced by a purely psychological warfare, wherein weapons are not even used or battlefields sought . . . but rather the corruption of the human reason, the dimming of the human intellect, and the disintegration of the moral and spiritual life of one nation by the influence of the will of another is accomplished."[2] Twenty years later the concept was made operational among the major foes involved in World War II. During that time **psychological warfare** was limited to military dissemination of propaganda to specific target audiences to undermine popular morale in the enemy state or to attain a given military mission. As a result, many propagandists served with or were under the auspices of the armed forces.

In the United States after World War II all military psychological warfare units were disbanded. Not until 1948 was a civilian-sponsored program authorized by the Congress under the jurisdiction of the Department of State; this program continued until 1953, when the U.S. Information Agency (USIA) was established as a quasiautonomous organization. The concept of psychological warfare acquired a new meaning and a new purpose. During the **Cold War,** psychological warfare became an important "perceptual" battleground in which Western capitalist and Eastern socialist countries presented their ways of life to each other's citizens and to other countries around the world as superior. If the Soviet Union could convince Americans and West Europeans that communism was the way of the future, or if Americans could convince Soviet and East European citizens that freedom in a capitalist society was more wholesome, battles could be won without resorting to military force. To promote a positive image in foreign countries, nation-states (especially major powers) engage in various kinds of cultural and information programs. The United States, for example, sponsors the Voice of America and many cultural activities through the USIA. The Soviet Union, on the other hand, has Radio Moscow, nation "friendship" societies, and a special section of the Communist party called the International Department that finances a large number of international conferences, protest demonstrations, and rallies favoring Soviet interests in foreign policy around the world.[3] The "weapons" employed in this psychological battleground include radio, television, films, public rallies, demonstrations, slogans, posters, books, newspapers and magazines, news conferences, and other means for influencing the thinking and emotions of opinion makers or the masses. Psychological warfare directed at the masses seeks to evoke emotional responses such as fear, hatred, horror, or fellowship; that is, it seems to build stereotyped images in the minds of the recipients.

However, psychological warfare may also include symbolic acts of violence and terror designed to intimidate or persuade adversaries to adjust their behavior. Under this definition psychological warfare would include various undercover activities such as espionage or subversion, assassination and other forms of state-sponsored terrorism, and censorship, when they are designed to mold the opinion or behavior of specific groups.

Intelligence requirements for effective psychological warfare operations vary depending on whether the political system operates in an open or closed society. The more authoritarian a political system, the greater its reliance on controls, censorship, and clandestine operations. In either case three major types of intelligence are required: (1) background data concerning the predispositions and weaknesses of the target; (2) propaganda output derived from various writings, speeches of leading adversaries, and press releases; and (3) evaluation of the effects of psychological warfare in more or less open societies where public opinion polling and market surveys are useful means for measuring results. Evaluation of the impact of psychological warfare techniques in closed societies can only be done by clandestine means. In this respect, authoritarian and dictatorial regimes have enjoyed a marked advantage over democracies in the implementation of programs of psychological warfare.

Although psychological warfare is often carried out by covert (secret) means, not all **covert operations** fall in the category of psychological warfare. Often they are an extension of diplomacy and are intended to achieve specific political or military goals, not just a psychological advantage. Covert activities are usually carried out by operatives of intelligence organizations in an attempt to influence the political process of a nation in a desirable way. Since undercover activities constitute interference in the domestic affairs of other nations, they are illegal and, if discovered, counterproductive. Therefore, nations that engage in covert activities (i.e., practically every nation in the world) must carefully weigh the cost–benefit ratio involved in such operations. In the United States, clandestine operations are directed by the National Security Council (NSC). Under the Nixon and Ford administrations five individuals (the NSC adviser, the CIA director, the undersecretary of state for political affairs, deputy secretary of defense, and the chairman of the Joint Chiefs of Staff), known as the 40 Committee, headed clandestine operations; they had access to the funds and resources necessary to conduct covert political and paramilitary operations throughout the world. Similar groups had headed covert operations before and after the establishment of the 40 Committee to produce favorable results in the implementation of U.S. foreign policy. It is difficult to prove or disprove the effectiveness of American clandestine operations abroad because of their limited number and the secrecy surrounding them. One well-known success story was the 1953 backing of a coup to oust Premier Mohammad Mossadegh in Iran in support of Mohammad Reza Pahlavi, thus giving American oil interests a greater share in Iranian oil resources.[4] A more recent success was the support given Corazon Aquino in her bid for power against former President Ferdinand Marcos in 1986. During the 1986 presidential campaign, which precipitated Marcos's ouster, the Reagan administration openly maintained cordial relations with the former dictator, however, behind the scenes it did everything legally possible to undermine his position. The payoff was a rare victory for democracy through a peaceful transition of power. While most of the credit for the virtually bloodless uprising belongs to the Filipino people, it could not have been accomplished without the strong bipartisan support in the U.S. Congress in response to a foreign policy crisis concerning the Philippines.[5] Of course, U.S. covert operations have failed, including the Bay of Pigs in 1961 and the attempt to rescue the American hostages in Tehran in 1980. In the summer of 1987 a more recent fiasco was brought to light before a select congressional committee during the Iran–*contra* hearings. This debacle confirmed the assertion that covert operations are often a direct contradiction of the political values they ostensibly seek to preserve. In a democracy secret operations run the high risk of failure and as such are subject to criticism and condemnation not only by the political opposition, but also by the public for not having been consulted on the matter. Perhaps for this and similar reasons, the Reagan administration abstained from a 1988 covert operation leading to a possible assassination of Col. Manuel Noriega and instead opted for using psychological warfare to dispose of the Panamanian dictator who had been indicted on illicit drug trafficking. These tactics proved inadequate to oust Noriega, and therefore, on December 20, 1989, the Bush administration intervened in Panama militarily to depose the self-appointed dictator and eventually brought him to the United States for trial on twelve counts of conspiracy.

In closed societies, where manipulative game playing goes hand in hand with the political system dictating to the people, covert operations are viewed as a natural extension of foreign policy, provided that the benefits outweigh the costs. In this respect the Soviet Union is a good example. Since its inception, the Committee for State Security (KGB) has maintained a **disinformation** department that forges documents, plants newspaper reports, spreads rumors and word-of-mouth horror stories, and conducts similar nefarious activities.[6] The KGB encompasses both domestic- and foreign-intelligence operations, which are both offensive and defensive in nature and designed to influence internal and external policies of other governments. The KGB agents not only seek out enemy agents, but also target unfriendly political leaders for all types of compromises and, in some instances, for assassination. Soviet covert activities include the overthrow of provocative governments and the support of friendly regimes. The difference is, however, that in the Soviet Union there are no charges, indictments, hearings, or public trials of the exposed players involved in covert games, as occurs, for example, in the United States. Again, the information about the success or failure of Soviet undercover activities is skimpy at best. The removal of Edward Gierek from the party and the government after he failed to effectively quash the demonstrations in major industrial Polish cities in the late 1970s and the appointment of

General Wojciech Jaruzelski as the Polish head of government is an example of successful Soviet involvement in Polish internal and external affairs. However, Soviet attempts to replace one leader with another in Afghanistan in the late 1970s, in order to protect socialism in that country and perhaps to stem the tide of Islamic fundamentalism threatening Soviet control have been a definite failure. An all-out Soviet invasion of Afghanistan occurred in December 1979.[7] Finally, on April 14, 1988, in Geneva, representatives of the governments of Pakistan and Afghanistan signed three bilateral agreements intended to end the war in Afghanistan. The United States and the Soviet Union, as states-guarantors, signed an additional "Declaration on International Guarantees." These documents, collectively known as the Geneva Accords, came into force on May 15, 1988, the date the Soviet Union began withdrawing its troops. Even so, the final chapter on Soviet involvement in Afghanistan has yet to be written. According to the accords, during the withdrawal phase the USSR can oversupply its own forces with enough weapons and material to last a decade and then leave it all behind when they depart. Moscow could then invoke the agreement signed by the two superpowers, claiming to have voluntarily ceased supplying the Afghan army and calling on the United States to halt its aid to the *mujahedeen*.[8] Of course, the classical example of Soviet covert operations took place in 1967–1968 in Czechoslovakia. First, it took Soviet intervention and "dirty tricks" to arrange a coup to replace the orthodox party leader Antonín Novotný in 1967 with the liberal Alexander Dubček. In August 1968, however, it was the failure of Soviet influence on the Dubček regime that brought about the imprisonment of Dubček and his associates and the military invasion of Czechoslovakia by the Warsaw Pact countries.

In all these instances the Soviet Union also unleashed an intensive media campaign with two objectives in mind: (1) to evoke a friendly response toward the USSR as the champion of peace and defender of socialism, and (2) to shift the blame onto domestic reactionaries supported by outside imperialist interests. In most cases, however, the indigenous population was clever enough to identify the real culprit, which compelled the Soviet Union to maintain a forceful rule of power.

Whether psychological warfare is considered a peaceful or violent means of influencing the opinions and behavior of targeted audiences, it can be effective only when its techniques are credible, clearly understood, and elicit a response within the capability of the target audience. What is credible is determined by the audience, not by the content of a message or action used for propaganda purposes.

Propaganda

In many ways **propaganda** is part of psychological warfare because it involves using symbols to deliberately manipulate other people's values and behavior.[9] Its main objectives are the strengthening of friendly support, the shaping or altering of attitudes and perceptions of ideas or events, the weakening or undermining of unfriendly foreign governments or their policies, and the counteracting of the unfriendly propaganda of other countries. When the latter is in operation, we refer to it as *counterpropaganda*.

On occasions, propaganda is equated with education; this is a gross oversimplification. Propaganda uses a set of prefabricated arguments and symbols designed to control the thinking, emotions, and actions of individuals; whereas education aims to present "all" sides of an issue and lets the individual decide who is right or wrong, what is good or bad.

Until recently, for example, in Soviet schools the Marxist–Leninist interpretation of international events was based on materialistic determinism that permitted only one "scientific" answer; that is, the answer endorsed by the party elite and disseminated through the channels of institutional control to all levels of the Soviet society. Thus, opinions were streamlined into repeating what others (meaning the party elite) had already endorsed for the masses. In this respect what we call *propaganda* may have legitimately been *education* in the Soviet Union because from their perspective that was the way the system worked.

The history of propaganda dates back to ancient times when primates learned to articulate and communicate with one another. In Western civilization propaganda and counterpropaganda appear to have existed in the Greek city-states about 500 B.C., where they were used by lawyers, demagogues, and politicians. Propaganda continued to be used until modern times to support and legitimize policies of all nations. The only difference is that some rely on it more heavily than others. Propaganda is especially favored during wars or crisis situations. In World War II, for example, each of the major contending governments made massive outlays for both domestic and foreign propaganda, and they all competed in the applications of various propaganda techniques. Since then every major power has had its ministry of propaganda—now called ministry of culture, enlightenment, or information—or some functional equivalent. Since the creation of the Soviet state, more money was spent on propaganda than weapons until the emergence of the costly, sophisticated thermonuclear weapons systems. The Soviet Union and other authoritarian and dictatorial political systems also had their official mechanisms for censorship, information control, and news management. Through such instruments as the USIA and Voice of America (VOA), the United States has sought to explain its policies to citizens of foreign nations; the aim is to create favorable responses from the general publics so that their governments will be encouraged to seek or maintain friendly relations with the United States. For example, VOA broadcasts penetrated deep into the Soviet Union even before the systematic jamming was discontinued in the spring of 1987. Of course, propaganda through the electronic media is used by numerous other countries that can afford to beam their messages to different audiences throughout the world.

To be effective, propaganda must be relevant, credible to the recipients, frequently repeated, simple, consistent, interesting, identifiable with a local or national situation, and disguised so the audience does not recognize it as propaganda. Propaganda may take the form of an appeal to the idealism of the recipients; it may be factual but distorted through careful selection, or it may be based on outright falsehoods.[10]

Propaganda is considered an integral part of international relations. Most parts of the globe are now easily accessible, economically and militarily interdependent, and provided with sophisticated tools of news gathering, telecommunications, and travel, which enable instant transmission of symbols or events to any point on the earth. In this fast-moving world it is possible to accentuate the peculiarities of different cultural, economic, and political patterns that are often in conflict and therefore subject to propaganda and exploitation. Symbols and perceptions are an important part of modern diplomacy. Nation-states are affected not only by verbal symbols but also by the economic and military inducements that the propagandist can apply in conjunction with the symbols. Symbols, according to several studies, are likely to be persuasive if they appeal simultaneously to people's identities, belief structures, and consciences.[11] For example, in order to seize the emotional initiative and maintain effective power, the Ayatollah Khomeini aroused both the animosities and the consciences of his followers and of neutrals by "satanizing" the aims of his opponents (especially the United States) while idealizing his own objectives.

The media propagandists use to reach the public are similar to those employed in psychological warfare. They include newspapers, magazines, radio, television, film, posters, billboards, handbills, speeches, rumors, flags, monuments, street names, postage stamps, awards and prizes, front organizations, international coalitions, international movements, and so on. This abridged version of a long list of media or channels of propaganda suggests that all nations, even the smallest and poorest ones, have access to the use of propaganda.

As noted in chapter 6, the availability and scope of the electronic and print media, as well as the involvement of legislatures in foreign policy, especially in the Western nations, has weakened the role of diplomacy and strengthened the role of propaganda. It is customary now to grant television time to national leaders visiting democratic countries to speak directly to the population. Interviews conducted by the print and electronic media, particularly in the United States, with VIPs from other countries, including potential enemies, provide an excellent opportunity for these individuals to articulate views that may differ from the policies of the host government and thus allow them to influence the thinking, emotions, and behavior of the citizens of the host country. For example, ABC's "Nightline" has hosted Georgi Arbatov, the head of the U.S.–Canada Institute of the Community party of the Soviet Union, or Vladimir Posner, a former American citizen now in charge of propaganda programming and broadcasting from Moscow, who in their frequent appearances speak freely to American audiences and skillfully attempt to influence their attitudes toward the Soviet Union. Similarly, CBS made special arrangements on its "Face the Nation" program for satellite hookup to have Comandante Ortega of Nicaragua promote his policies and to criticize U.S. policies toward Central America. On another occasion Soviet Minister of Foreign Affairs Eduard Shevardnadze appeared on the evening news to place the blame on the United States for being unwilling to remove seventy-two Pershing IIs from West Germany and thus jeopardizing an agreement on short-range strategic weapons. These examples differ significantly from diplomacy in its traditional form. The media are now used to influence public opinion even by leaders of a nation's adversaries. In a Western democracy this can play a significant role in the shaping of foreign policy. Ironically, in the Soviet Union and other closed political systems where public opinion plays a lesser role in foreign policy making, the channels of propaganda, including the print and electronic media, are either restricted or prohibited from affording the same privileges to prominent persons from unfriendly nations. Only on two occasions—during the 1971 and the 1988 summit meetings in Moscow—when the Kremlin leaders were pleading for U.S. support and cooperation, were former Presidents Nixon and Reagan allowed to address the Soviet people on television. However, a relatively recent development in the Soviet Union, popularly known as *glasnost* (or openness) and *perestroika* (or restructuring), has had a direct effect on Soviet propaganda techniques. As global communications and television diplomacy begin to play an increasingly important role in foreign and domestic policy, the Soviet Union is girding itself for the time when the possibility of Soviet citizens' watching foreign television programs of their own choosing may become a reality. In 1988, for example, the Soviet Union suspended the jamming of broadcasts by Radio Liberty. Preparations for the eventuality of a freer choice of information are being undertaken in both the ideological and technological fields. According to the new official strategy, based on General Secretary Mikhail Gorbachev's *new thinking,* Communists in the past were dogmatic, made mistakes, failed to act when they should have or acted too late, ignored major challenges, and suppressed human rights. Now they must avoid perpetuating old errors, see the world as it really is, analyze the challenges they have failed to meet, and draw a lesson from it all for the future.[12] In other words, old ineffective methods of propaganda, based on outmoded ideological principles, must be replaced by new techniques that consider the role of public opinion abroad and at home. As a result of *glasnost,* Soviet citizens were encouraged to express their opinions not only on domestic issues, but to a limited extent on foreign policy issues as well. In 1987, for example, Soviet citizens who relied on foreign radio broadcasts or word of mouth for information on Afghanistan differed significantly from those whose information came from the official Soviet media and the party's agitation and propaganda division. Evidence of negative public opinion on Afghanistan surfaced more frequently in letters to the editors of official publications. By 1988, when the decision was made to withdraw Soviet troops from Afghanistan, Gorbachev described the war as a "bleeding wound" and a contradiction to the spirit of *perestroika.* It is important to note, however, that in 1988, the war was no longer solely a matter of foreign policy (because the conflict had had a far-reaching domestic impact in the Soviet Union) and that all media maintained the policy position prescribed by the officialdom.

Perhaps the most successful propaganda coup engineered by Mikhail Gorbachev was in June 1989 during his visit to Bonn, West Germany. The world press referred to it as "historic" and the rapprochement contained in a joint declaration signed by Gorbachev and Chancellor Kohl as the beginning of "the creation of a Europe of peace and cooperation— of a European peace order or of a Common European House—in which there is also room for the United States and Canada."[13] The first section of the declaration stresses the need for a *new thinking,* which also explains the metaphor of the "Common European House," representing the fateful ties between the occupants who are obliged to live together under a common roof. According to this new thinking, the (national) rooms are in need of renovation—the doors must be enlarged, and architects and craftspeople with similar ideas must be found to complete the renovation. In practical terms, the West German government would further improve its relations with the Soviet Union to a culmination of relations between "two great powers," meaning the Soviet Union and the Federal Republic of Germany, not the United States.

Aware of his commitment to the Warsaw Pact allies, Gorbachev referred to the "people of the Federal Republic of Germany" and not to the Germans, thus illuminating the interpretive scope of the right of self-determination. Conversely, Kohl's *Deutschlandpolitik,* which concentrates on human rights more than on the "territorial questions," assured Gorbachev that Bonn did not intend to make East Germany feel uncertain and therefore complicate matters for Gorbachev. In his speech, Gorbachev made it clear that both German states can "decide for themselves" and "the future is more elastic than the past," which is consistent with the existing Soviet proposal on the dissolution of the blocs. Thus the idea of European security—Soviet style—first initiated in 1949 by Stalin's foreign minister, Vyacheslav Molotov, is being successfully pursued by Mikhail Gorbachev. It is consistent with Gorbachev's new political thinking in foreign policy. In summary, Gorbachev's foreign policy calls for an end to the arms race, a 50-percent reduction in U.S. and Soviet strategic offensive weapons; easing of tension in the Third World; increased economic and technical assistance to the developing nations (LDCs) through international organizations such as the International Monetary Fund, the World Bank, and others; elimination of outstanding world debts owed by the developing nations; restructuring of the world economic system along the lines advocated by the Group of Seventy-Seven (a voting caucus of approximately 120 Third World LDCs that meets before official sessions of the UN General Assembly to decide on a common course of action); ecological cooperation on a global basis with the industrialized nations providing the use of new technologies; and the respect for the security of every state, as well as the realization of human rights of all peoples in those states.

The aim of Gorbachev's *new thinking* is to promote the image of the Soviet Union as the champion of peace and disarmament and the protector of the LDCs against capitalist exploitation, while extending a cooperative gesture to the capitalist West in economic and trade relations, arms reduction, and cultural exchanges. It is the latter aim that Gorbachev so successfully exploited during his visit to West Germany. Realizing that the Soviet Union is in dire need of modernizing and strengthening its economy, some "Kremlin watchers" are expressing doubts about the sincerity of Gorbachev's new thinking because they believe his primary goal is *perestroika* or the restructuring of the Soviet system.[14] When Gorbachev took over the general secretariat of the party in 1985, two considerations dominated his thinking: (1) a radical change was required if the Soviet system was not to slide further into stagnation and backwardness, and (2) the Soviet regime had to be turned into a viable system again, able to perform on a level with other industrially advanced nations. Thus, it appears that the strategy since 1985 has been to strengthen socialism in the Soviet Union by transforming the system into a viable, technologically advanced superpower able to compete with any nation on earth. According to Gorbachev, the use of any peaceful means, even if they resemble capitalism, must be exploited and utilized to achieve this goal. Hence, propaganda becomes a significant tool of Soviet foreign policy.

One of the more subtle and effective methods of propaganda can be seen in sports. The Soviet Union, the German Democratic Republic, and Cuba are famous for exploiting their sport achievements during the Olympic Games. The XXII Olympiad in 1980 held in Moscow was a prime example of how to make the socialist system look superior to the capitalist system. The United States and a few other Western countries boycotted the games because of the Soviet invasion of Afghanistan. The Soviets interpreted this boycott as meaning that the American athletes were inferior to Soviet athletes. On the other hand, when the Soviet Union refused to send its delegations to the XXIII Olympics held in Los Angeles in 1984, the Soviet propaganda ploy was lack of security and threats to the athletes from Jewish and dissident organizations in the United States. In other words, the Soviet Union embarked on a propaganda line at home and abroad that life in the United States was unsafe and that the U.S. government could not cope with anarchy.

Terrorism

On September 8, 1972, UN Secretary-General Kurt Waldheim asked for inclusion in the General Assembly agenda an item titled "Measures to prevent terrorism and other forms of violence which endanger or take innocent human lives or jeopardize fundamental freedoms." He urged an end to senseless and destructive violence and asked that the world community continue "to exert its utmost influence in seeking peaceful ways" to find solutions to the problems underlying acts of **terrorism.** Waldheim's request evoked angry opposition and protests against considering terrorism without considering its cause. Two weeks later the secretary-general tried again but without success, and to pacify the opposition, he assured the protesters that he did not intend to circumvent principles already enunciated by the General Assembly regarding colonial and dependent peoples seeking independence and liberation.[15]

In December 1985 the General Assembly adopted a resolution "to prevent international terrorism which endangers or takes innocent human lives or jeopardizes fundamental freedoms and to study the underlying causes of those forms of terrorism and acts of violence which lie in misery, frustration, grievance, and despair and which cause some people to sacrifice human lives, including their own in an attempt to effect radical changes."[16] Although the resolution deals with terrorism, it avoids defining it for political reasons. While condemning terrorism, the resolution attributes acts of terrorism to injustice and frustration. In April 1974, after a quarter of a century or so of debating the issue, the UN finally agreed on a definition of **aggression** that includes a clause (Article 6) that states that peoples struggling for "self-determination" have the right to resort to all available means, including armed struggle.[17] Did the UN purposefully avoid defining *terrorism* so that it could get support for the condemnation, as well as sympathy for its acts (because the overwhelming majority of UN members are new states that used all types of nonpeaceful means in their struggle for self-determination)? Or were the members sensitive to the idea that it may take twenty-five years or more to define terrorism, just as it did aggression?

Whatever the reasons, there is no general agreement among political leaders, scholars, or laypersons on a definition of terrorism. For example, one U.S. official defined it as "the use of violence for purposes of political extortion, coercion, and publicity for a political cause."[18] Several scholars offer similar definitions.[19] The problem with this type of definition, however, is that it does not adequately delineate between the authorized use of violence by state and nonstate units. While there is documentation that several countries aid and abate terrorists, there is no clear evidence that they engage directly in terrorism. For example, assertions were made that Libya maintained, within it borders, camps capable of training five thousand terrorists at a time.[20] Similarly, allegations have been made that "an ever-increasing flow of arms and ammunition, manufactured in the Soviet Union, Czechoslovakia, and East Germany, have been shipped to the PLO via East Germany and Hungary."[21] It is also known that the United States has supported perpetrators of violence, which it calls "freedom fighters," in Afghanistan and Nicaragua, and Israel funneled millions of dollars of support to the Christian militia in Lebanon. Are all these countries engaged in terrorism? The answer is no, if the perpetrators are irregular soldiers who wage war against regular military forces and targets. They are then called *guerrillas,* not terrorists.[22]

Who Are the Terrorists?

There is a fine line between terrorism and **guerrilla warfare,** but both rely on violence by nongovernmental actors. In Northern Ireland, for example, the followers of the Provisional Irish Republican Army engage in terrorism and guerrilla warfare, depending on the acts they commit. They use both techniques to achieve national emancipation with the objective of forcibly eradicating British control in Northern Ireland and establishing Irish unity. Guerrilla warfare against British troops, with weapons obtained from communist countries as well as from the United States, is coupled with terrorism against innocent and defenseless civilians. Whether the revolutionaries in Ireland, the *mujahedeen* in Afghanistan, the *contras* in Nicaragua, the African National Congress in South Africa, or the Palestine Liberation Organization (PLO) in Lebanon act as freedom fighters or terrorists depends on what they do. Generally speaking, if they engage in warfare against military targets on their home territory to achieve national self-determination, they are *guerrillas.* However, if they engage in intentional use of force against innocent victims to instill fear and paralysis in the society, then they are *terrorists,* regardless of whether their cause is just.

There are more than fifty terrorist groups or organizations operating in different parts of the world today. For example, in the Middle East, there are at least a dozen or so; in

Western Europe about fifteen; in Latin America as many as seventeen; in Asia seven; and in Africa at least one. Among the better-known terrorist organizations in the Middle East are the Abu Nidal Organization—one of many PLO splinter groups, which is not only the most dangerous terrorist organization in existence, but one that would like to dispose of all nonmilitant Palestinians who are willing to reach any compromise with Israel, including Yasir Arafat, head of the largest faction of the PLO, called Fatah; the Lebanese Armed Revolutionary Faction; the Arab Organization of 15 May; the Democratic Front for the Liberation of Palestine; Hizballah or Islamic Jihad; the Palestine Liberation Front; and the Popular Front for the Liberation of Palestine. In Western Europe there is the Provisional Irish Republican Army, the Basque Fatherland and Liberty, Direct Action in France, the Armenian Secret Army for the Liberation of Armenia, Revolutionary Cells and the Red Army Faction in the Federal Republic of Germany, the Red Brigade in Italy, and the Revolutionary Organization 17 November in Greece. Latin America has its share of such groups, too: Shining Path in Peru, the Manuel Rodriguez Patriotic Front in Chile, the 19th of April Movement, the Ricardo Franco Front and the Ché Guevara Faction of the National Liberation Army in Colombia, and the Farabundo Marti National Liberation Front in El Salvador. In Asia the best-known terrorist groups are Chukaku-Ha and the Japanese Red Army (JRA) in Japan, the Liberation Tigers of Tamil Eelam in Sri Lanka, the New People's Army in the Philippines, and the Dal Khalsa and the Dashmesh Regiment in India. In Africa, it is the African National Congress (ANC). These are some of the terrorist organizations that engage in either internal or international terrorism.

The U.S. government defines international terrorism as "the premeditated use of violence against nocombatant targets for political purposes, involving citizens or territory of more than one country."[23] Both internal and international terrorism are often combined with guerrilla warfare, since all three are carried out by nongovernmental actors in the international system. International terrorism, of course, has a greater impact on the conduct of foreign policy among nations than internal terrorism. International terrorism can affect an entire region (e.g., the Middle East or Latin America) or the entire international system (e.g., consider the impact of terrorism in the Persian Gulf on the supply of energy resources worldwide). Furthermore, the psychology of terrorism is such that internal terrorism can trigger an encouragement and motivation for similar acts by other terrorist organizations around the world. It is difficult to identify and document an organized international center, headed by a directorate, which is masterminding all terrorist activities around the world. Yet, in addition to the many allegations, the existence of state-sponsored international terrorism can be documented. At a trial in London in October 1986, for example, evidence revealed direct links between the man arrested for planting a bomb in April 1986 at London's Heathrow Airport on an El Al plane carrying over 350 passengers (230 of whom were Americans) and senior Syrian government officials. In June 1986, at Madrid's airport, another individual was arrested for placing a bomb on an El Al plane. He admitted to being a member of the Abu Musa Organization, a PLO splinter group created with Syrian backing and headquartered in Damascus. In November 1986 a Berlin court produced evidence tying terrorists held in connection with the March 1986 bombing of the German–Arab Friendship Society in West Berlin to the Syrian embassy in East Berlin, to Syrian intelligence officials in Damascus, and to the terrorists who tried to blow up the El Al plane in London.[24]

Theoretically, it is possible to distinguish further among three types of terrorism, although they frequently overlap. One such variant is organizational terrorism, which applies mostly to small, tightly knit, politically homogeneous groups. Such groups are incapable of developing popular support for their radical positions and therefore resort to terrorism to gain influence. Examples include the Red Army Faction and the Revolutionary Cells in West Germany, the Red Brigades in Italy, Direct Action in France, and 17 November in Greece. Other groups of this type have become transnational in their terrorist reach. The most notorious example of an organizational-type of transnational terrorist group is the Abu Nidal Organization. Others include the Japanese Red Army and the Armenian Secret Army for the Liberation of Armenia.

Another type of terrorism is conducted within the context of insurgencies, which can be ethnic separatist or countrywide. Typically, they are wide-scale revolts against the established government conducted by paramilitary or guerrilla forces operating within the boundaries of the state under seige. These insurgent forces, however, frequently have a terrorist component that is seeking to undermine the government's credibility, legitimacy, and public support by directing terror at civilians. A good example is the New People's Army, the military wing of the Communist party of the Philippines. In addition to insurgent activity the New People's Army conducts terror to demonstrate that the Philippine government cannot protect its people.

A third type is state-sponsored terrorism, which involves direct sponsorship and abatement of terrorist groups and their actions by sovereign states. State sponsorship makes this terrorism deadlier, lengthens the reach of the terrorist activities, and is a matter of growing international concern. The most notorious state sponsors of terrorism are Iran, Afghanistan, and Libya. Syria was previously in this rank; however, following revelations in European courts of its involvement in terrorist acts in 1985–1986, international pressure forced Syria to adhere more closely to the international conduct prescribed by international law and agreements. State sponsorship of terrorism can take place at various levels: (1) by conducting actual terrorist operations (e.g., Afghanistan sending its agents into Pakistan to conduct an extensive bombing campaign); (2) by providing encouragement, direction, and material assistance to terrorist groups conducting their own attacks, which are also in the sponsoring state's interest (e.g., Iran and Libya have frequently used terrorist surrogates to carry out their vendettas throughout the world); (3) by providing weapons, explosives, training, safe passage, safe haven, and ideological justification (e.g., North Korea, South Yemen, and several Soviet bloc countries [before 1990] provided such support to various types of terrorist groups).

These states sponsor terrorism for varying reasons. Some states do so to achieve foreign policy objectives that could not otherwise be achieved through conventional political or military means. Some states sponsor terrorism to create or expand their power and influence among ideological or religious movements, or as a means of establishing credentials with revolutionary movements worldwide. Still other state-sponsored terrorist incidents are designed to stifle domestic opposition through selective assassination of dissidents abroad. For the most part, state sponsors of terrorism attempt to hide their involvement through proxies and other means. Their actions frequently are difficult to trace, so they can maintain respectability and legitimacy in the world community while covertly sponsoring subversion and terror to achieve their goals.[25]

Terrorism is neither a legal nor a legitimate instrument of state policy. Hence, once evidence linking states to the sponsorship of terrorism is made public, other states may choose to publicly condemn and punish them. As a result of the public evidence of Syrian support for terrorism, the European Community foreign ministers (with the exception of Greece) agreed on November 10, 1986, to take initial, limited action against Syria, including an end to arms sales. The United Kingdom broke off relations, and West Germany downgraded its diplomatic ties and cut off certain aid and trade connections. Similarly, the United States, a few days later, recalled its ambassador to Syria, cut off all forms of economic assistance, and reduced its trade. While Syria and Libya, so far, are the only countries implicated in providing support for terrorism in Europe, there are indictments against several other countries for rendering support to international terrorism. They include Cuba, Nicaragua, North Korea, Iran, and South Yemen. Allegations levelled against these states include giving terrorists weapons, training, and money; providing terrorists sanctuary, even in their embassies; and attempting to block international sanctions against terrorists, thus legitimizing their cause.[26]

Why would certain nation-states resort to international terrorism as an instrument of foreign policy? One explanation is the changing pattern of international conflict combined with the cost of warfare. Former Israeli Ambassador to the United States Benjamin Netanyahu, for example, argues that the waging of war has become increasingly expensive and risky because it can lead to a direct nuclear confrontation between the two superpowers or escalation in conventional war among smaller states (see note 26). Therefore, he claims that terrorism is a war waged by proxy. "It permits regimes to engage in aggression while evading responsibility or retaliation." While states may wish to sponsor terrorism, they do so at their peril. Political groups employ terrorism for their own ends. Syria or the Soviet Union may seek to destabilize Western economies and find that terrorists help do this. Therefore, they may support such activities to these ends. But terrorism is not easily controlled; it can lash out at almost any country or government. It is, in other words, difficult to control terrorists as an instrument of foreign policy. Moreover, the definite identification of a state such as Iran, Syria, or Libya as a supporter of terrorism will invite retaliation by other states.

The Impact of International Terrorism on the United States

According to numerous trend analyses, international terrorism has been on the rise throughout the 1970s and 1980s, although there have been peaks and lulls. Some earlier studies show that a total of 3,336 terrorist incidents occurred between 1968 and 1979—or an average of 303 incidents per year.[27] The same intelligence analysts showed a yearly increase from 500 incidents during the period 1979 to 1983 to 780 incidents in 1985.[28] An earlier study revealed that terrorist operations had a high success rate in achieving their immediate goals relative to the costs they incurred. Sixty-three major kidnappings and barricade operations between 1968 and 1974 resulted in an 87 percent success rate in seizing hostages, a 79 percent probability of all members of the terrorist team escaping punishment or death, a 40 percent chance of at least some demands being met, a 29 percent chance of full compliance with their demands, and an almost 100 percent probability of obtaining major publicity. During the same period terrorists suffered casualties in only 14 percent of all incidents.[29]

As figure 7.1 shows, international terrorist incidents continued to increase in the 1980s in spite of the added countermeasures taken by the international community to deal more resolutely with the problem. Since 1980, nearly 6,000 terrorist incidents have occurred

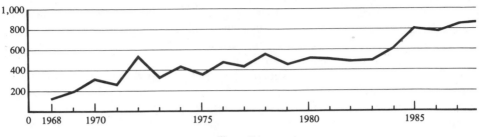

Figure 7.1
Trend of international terrorist incidents
SOURCE: Office of the Secretary of State, Ambassador at Large for Counterterrorism,
Patterns of Global Terrorism: 1988 (Washington, D.C.: Department of State
Publication 9705, March 1989), p. 2.

worldwide, leaving more than 4,000 people dead and 11,000 wounded. (Figure 7.2 shows the trend in casualties caused by terrorist incidents.) The bombing of PAN AM Flight 103 in December 1988, killing 270 persons (among them 189 Americans), made the year 1988 the highest in the number of incidents (855) and the number of fatalities (658). The Middle East had the highest number of incidents of international terrorism, 313 attacks, or 36 percent of the total worldwide. Asia, primarily due to terrorist attacks by the Soviet-backed regime in Afghanistan against targets in Pakistan, held second place with 194 incidents, or 22 percent; Western Europe remained in third place with 150 incidents. Terrorism in Latin America increased 35 percent in 1988 to a total of 146 attacks, 88 of them in Colombia. Africa remained in fifth place with 52 attacks, or 6 percent. Attacks against American citizens or property, which accounted for 20 to 25 percent of the worldwide total, rose from 149 in 1987 to 185 in 1988; most took place in Latin America.[30] Figure 7.3 shows terrorist incidents by region from 1980 to 1988.

Although there were more American casualties caused by terrorist attacks in the Middle East and Western Europe, the greatest number of incidents involving American citizens or property was in Latin America. Of the 146 international terrorist attacks in Latin America during 1988, 73 percent or 110 of 146 incidents involved U.S. personnel or facilities. However, in Latin America political violence is usually caused by guerrilla warfare and internal strife, rather than by international terrorism as such. As the supplemental reading "Terrorism, Inflation, and Debt Threaten Democracy in Peru" points out, in the Andean region much of the political violence is drug-related because the terrorists and guerrillas provide protection to the narcotics traffickers in return for money and arms used against authorities.

The most confusing picture of international terrorism emerges in the Middle East where terrorist acts are carried out by individuals and small groups for their own political or religious objectives, as well as by identifiable terrorist organizations and in some cases even by states using terrorism as a deliberate instrument of foreign policy. These terrorist acts had a spillover effect in many parts of the world (see figure 7.4). Iran has used terrorism as a deliberate instrument to subvert the policies of various Arab governments. Terrorism has also been used between Arab governments (e.g., Libya against Egypt) and between Palestinian groups (e.g., the various ultramilitant PLO splinter groups against the Fatah). Modern

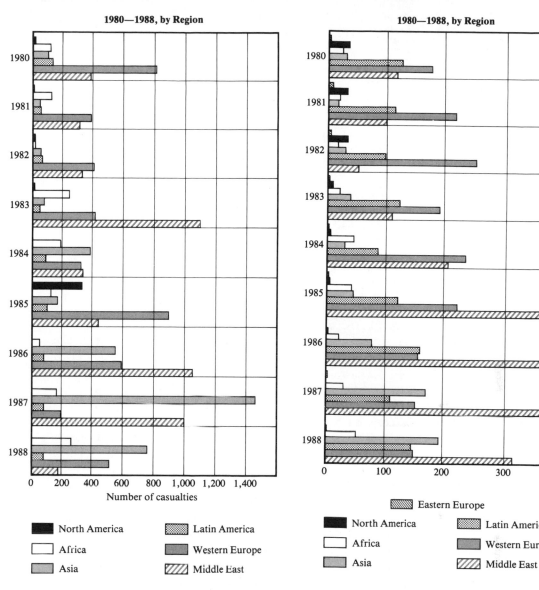

Figure 7.2

Trend of casualties caused by international terrorist incidents
SOURCE: Office of the Secretary of State, Ambassador
at Large for Counterterrorism, *Patterns of Global
Terrorism: 1988* (Washington, D.C.: Department
of State Publication 9705, March 1989), p. 9.

Figure 7.3

International terrorist incidents by region
SOURCE: Office of the Secretary of State, Ambassador
at Large for Counterterrorism, *Patterns of Global
Terrorism: 1988* (Washington, D.C.: Department
of State Publication 9705, March 1989), p. 2.

terrorism started in the Middle East in the late 1940s as part of the Arab–Israeli dispute over Palestine. Today, however, the Palestinian struggle with Israel is no longer the primary cause of terrorism in the Middle East. On several occasions, after the bloodiest and most publicized incidents, spokesmen for the PLO, including Yasir Arafat, denounced the attacks or distanced the PLO from them. On December 14, 1988, Yasir Arafat, speaking in Geneva

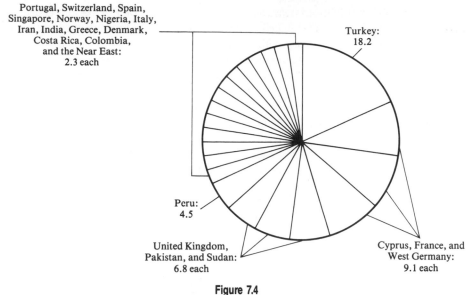

Figure 7.4
International terrorism, 1988
Middle East spillover by location
SOURCE: Office of the Secretary of State, Ambassador at Large for Counterterrorism,
Patterns of Global Terrorism: 1988 (Washington, D.C.: Department of State
Publication 9705, March 1989), p. 11.

as chairman of the PLO, accepted UN Security Council Resolutions 242 and 338, recognized Israel's right to exist, and renounced terrorism. This represents a fundamental change in PLO position, fulfilling longstanding U.S. conditions for the start of a substantive dialogue with the PLO.

After the Israeli invasion of Lebanon in 1983, when the Palestinians were driven from that country, terrorism and guerrilla warfare in Lebanon acquired new dimensions and new players. Now, it is a struggle between pro-Syrian Lebanese Shi'ites and the remnants of Palestinians in Beirut, between the Israeli-backed South Lebanese Army (Christians) and the pro-Iranian Lebanese Shi'ites and PLO splinter groups, and between Syrian forces and pro-Iranian Lebanese Shi'ites in the Bekaa Valley of Lebanon. Recently very few incidents had a direct relationship to the traditional Arab–Israeli dispute and of those that took place, responsibility for some was claimed by other than the Fatah. Many of the incidents, especially kidnappings, are deliberate instruments of state action through terrorist organizations aided by those states. For example, pro-Iranian Shia groups in Lebanon have engaged in killing and kidnapping French citizens, Americans, Germans, Soviet officials, English citizens and others, simply because Iran's official policy statements accused those countries of helping Iran's archenemy, Iraq, in waging war against Iran.

A relatively new development, called the *Palestinian uprising,* or **intifada,** in the Israeli-occupied West Bank and Gaza Strip began in December 1987 and continued into 1989. Acts of intifada violence are of an entirely different dimension and seriousness. In most cases, militant Palestinian youth attacked a variety of military and civilian symbols of the occupation primarily using stones and on occasions even Molotov cocktails and knives. In some cases Israeli settlers retaliated against Palestinians by forming vigilante groups and hunting the Palestinians down with firearms. During 1988, for example, 11 Israelis and more than 360 Palestinians were killed and hundreds more injured in sporadic clashes between Palestinian protestors and Israeli troops and settlers.[31] In the vast majority of events, it is difficult to assign specific responsibility for specific acts of violence and thus to apply the recognized norms of terrorism. Therefore, the intifada as a whole should be viewed primarily as civil insurrection that contains elements of terrorism in specific cases.

In South Asia, like in Latin America, international terrorism plays a less important role than internal terrorism and violence caused by separatist movements. The latter is of great concern to India where the Sikh separatists have committed numerous terrorist acts (in 1986 about six hundred people were killed and since then the numbers have escalated) with the objective of achieving recognition and an independent homeland in the Punjab. Conversely, the pro-Indian Tamil minority in Sri Lanka, which is supported by India and which acts against the government of Sri Lanka, has committed terrorist acts against the majority of the population. In July 1987 Indian Prime Minister Rajiv Gandhi visited Sri Lanka and made a commitment to refrain from future support of Tamil-sponsored terrorism. Pakistan, on the other hand, has suffered from international terrorism. For example, the September 1986 attack on the PAN AM airplane at the Karachi airport was allegedly carried out by the Abu Nidal Organization with Libyan support.[32]

Although its overseas installations have been vulnerable to terrorist attacks, U.S. territory, in general, has been more immune from terrorist incidents than that of most other countries. The success can be attributed to effective intelligence and law enforcement work and the desire by various U.S. minority groups to seek redress of their grievances through democratic means rather than terrorism. In general, it is safe to argue that although the number of attacks against U.S. citizens and installations was on the increase, the number of Americans killed or wounded in terrorist attacks was on a decline in the mid-1980s. However, if we consider the objectives of terrorism in international relations, we must conclude that to kill a great number of people is not what the terrorists are after. In the last two decades, for example, only 15 to 20 percent of the many thousands of terrorist incidents involved fatalities, and of those, 67 percent involved only one casualty.[33] While it would appear that terrorists have been successful in achieving their immediate goals as planned, they have been unsuccessful so far in reaching their long-term objectives. As one expert on terrorism notes: "There is no known case in modern history of a small terrorist group seizing political power."[34]

Terrorism today is directed primarily against industrialized democracies. This has been substantiated by intelligence reports and hard data. Before 1981, for example, 33 percent of all international terrorist attacks occurred in Western Europe and 10 percent in North America; 44 percent of all incidents involved the United States.[35] Terrorists often view the United States as either the main culprit or a power broker that can sway decisions in other countries to satisfy terrorist demands. Furthermore, the United States is perceived not only as a superpower but as the leader of the industrialized democracies. The fact that Western democracies in general, and the United States in particular, not only tolerate but promote diverse political views and a free media that thrives on controversy also stimulates an environment conducive to terrorist exploitation. Above all else, terrorists prize the audience that the Western media gives them when they cover terrorist incidents.

To Negotiate or Not to Negotiate?

In spite of the strong belief in democratic principles, or perhaps because of it, as the supplemental reading by L. Paul Bremer III reveals, the official U.S. policy is *not* to negotiate with terrorists. Other Western democracies, however, do not have the same policy. For example, Italy, West Germany, the United Kingdom, Spain, and France have negotiated with terrorists or with countries rendering support to terrorist groups. The United States has as well, but it was not made public until the revelations by the U.S. Attorney General Edwin Meese in November 1986, when his office uncovered certain documents leading to the Iran–*contra* debacle. The various investigations and congressional hearings that followed in 1987 provided clear evidence that the United States had secretly engaged in arms-for-hostages sales with Iran via Israel and other intermediaries. Perhaps the best illustration of the dual-track American approach to international terrorism is the U.S. air strike in April 1986 on Libyan installations in Tripoli and Benghazi, which it undertook ostensibly to deter further terrorist attacks. Although 60 percent of the respondents in the United Kingdom were against the U.S. bombing raid, the British government approved the use of British airfields to launch the raid. In the rest of Western Europe, however, the initial government and popular reaction was largely negative, objecting to the rash, Rambo-like use of force rather than diplomacy. Since then, at the Tokyo Summit (on May 5, 1986) the members of the European Community pledged to cooperate in the struggle against international terrorism and consequently placed all sorts of restrictions curtailing their diplomatic, cultural, and trade relations with Libya. Apparently members of the European Community, with the exception of Greece and certain reservations from France, took this action only after the evidence proving the Libyan connection between their people's bureau (embassy) in East Berlin and the terrorists in the April 5, 1986, bombing of a discotheque in West Berlin was exposed.

A recent study has argued that a no-negotiation strategy is *not best in all situations.* The efficiency of this strategy depends on the risk attitudes of the terrorists and appears to be best for groups that prefer risks. Groups that are adverse to risks may be approached for successful negotiations. To decrease the chance of concession, increase the commando force's effectiveness, and decrease the number of incidents, governments must make the contemplated actions unattractive to terrorists at the planning stage.[36]

In the United States numerous organizations and agencies deal with international terrorism. In June 1985 during the TWA hijacking a Task Force on Combating Terrorism was created. The following year, the Department of State coordinated an Anti-Terrorist Assistance program with about fifty foreign governments, and the CIA and other agencies increased their intelligence effort to obtain more accurate information on various terrorist activities around the world. Simultaneously, the U.S. Special Operations Forces beefed up their counterterrorist units in cooperation with other friendly governments. The Congress passed the Omnibus Diplomatic Security and Anti-Terrorism Act of 1986, which provided funds for security to diplomatic missions abroad and laws covering terrorist crimes committed against American citizens abroad. In addition, the Federal Bureau of Investigation, the Alcohol, Tobacco, and Fire Arms Bureau of Treasury, the Immigration and Naturalization Service, Customs, the Federal Aviation Administration, and others are involved in the prevention of terrorist acts in the United States and abroad. Other states have antiterrorism units as well.

As the supplemental reading on "Terrorism: Its Evolving Nature" points out, U.S. counterterrorism policy has three main elements. First, the United States makes no concessions to terrorists holding official or private American citizens hostage. Second, the

United States works with other countries to put pressure on the countries that support terrorism to persuade them that such support is not cost-free. Third, the United States cooperates with friendly countries to develop practical measures to counter terrorism.[37]

Since U.S. official policy is not to negotiate with terrorists, what measures are being taken against terrorists? According to L. Paul Bremer, III, former ambassador at large for counterterrorism, the U.S. strategy stresses certain practical measures complemented with actions against the states that sponsor the terrorists. The practical measures include the identification, location, and tracking of terrorists, followed by apprehension and legal procedures (i.e., punishment). These practical measures are reinforced through diplomatic, economic, and military actions against the states that support terrorism. The reasoning behind this strategy is that the community of nations must increase the political, economic, and military costs of helping terrorists until the sponsoring states cannot afford to pay them any longer.[38] The effectiveness of these practical measures is difficult to assess at this juncture. We know, however, that on November 1, 1989, the Iranian Majlis, or parliament, unanimously approved a law allowing the Tehran government to arrest Americans deemed to have acted against Iranian interests anywhere in the world and bring them to the Islamic Republic for trial by no-jury courts.

To what extent can international law deal with terrorism? Some scholars argue that international law is as ineffective as political and diplomatic avenues in dealing with terrorists.[39] For example, radical groups—some of which have been responsible for terrorist acts—have tried to gain recognition as combatants under the laws of war, which would exempt them from charges of criminal acts and accord them the rights of a prisoner of war. As a result of the Geneva Diplomatic Conference on the Reaffirmation of International Humanitarian Law Applicable in Armed Conflict (1977), the PLO and other freedom fighters may now claim the benefits of the laws of war. The document was adopted by ninety-nine nations, with eleven (including the United States) abstaining, and only Israel dissenting. According to the Geneva convention, soldiers must distinguish themselves from civilians by wearing uniforms and carrying their weapons openly. This requirement places a serious restriction on the PLO renegades who are committed to terrorist acts outside the laws and customs of war. On the other hand, the UN Convention against the taking of hostages, adopted by the General Assembly in 1979 and reaffirmed by the Security Council in 1985, gives members of national liberation movements the status of combatants (not terrorists), and therefore, they may take hostages; they are protected by the laws of war; and they are excluded from the convention.

Perhaps the strongest law is encompassed in the 1973 Convention on the Prevention and Punishment of Crimes Against Internationally Protected Persons, Including Diplomatic Agents. The convention, signed by more than sixty states, requires governments to make criminal certain violent acts directed against such persons or their property and to extradite or prosecute suspected offenders found in their territory.

Summary

In one respect all three instruments of foreign policy—psychological warfare, propaganda, and terrorism—deal with the perceptions of the actors in the global system and the people at large. All three instruments are designed to influence people's thinking, emotions, and actions, and all three use symbolic acts to elicit desired responses from their target groups.

Propaganda and psychological warfare seek to shape or alter attitudes and perceptions of ideas or events through deliberate manipulation by means of written or verbal symbols. Terrorism, on the other hand, seeks to evoke emotional responses such as fear, hatred, horror, and intimidation through assassination, bombing, armed attack, kidnapping, skyjacking, and arson.

Psychological warfare is a form of persuasion carried out by most nation-states using various kinds of cultural and information programs. In closed societies psychological warfare is used to screen information for domestic consumption and, as a popular instrument of foreign policy combined with propaganda, to influence the thinking and emotions of targeted audiences to support the country's foreign policy.

Success or failure of psychological warfare is contingent on both a nation's intelligence capabilities and the conditions in the target country. Covert or undercover operations are an integral part of psychological warfare, especially in closed societies. These operations are designed to influence the external policies of other governments and, in some countries, for domestic intelligence operations. In this respect, then, psychological warfare as an instrument of foreign policy can be used for peaceful as well as nonpeaceful purposes. Propaganda, on the other hand, is a strictly peaceful means of influencing other people's values and behavior through deliberate manipulation of symbols. Print and electronic media are the preferred channels of communication aimed at implanting data, ideas, or images in human minds to influence the thinking, emotions, or actions of targeted groups.

Of the three instruments of foreign policy, terrorism is the most enigmatic and problematical. Industrial democracies in Europe, with a long history of domestic terrorism, see it as a criminal problem. Israel, on the other hand, at war with its Arab neighbors, sees it as a form of warfare demanding a military response—a view increasingly prevalent in the United States.[40] More nations in the world community are neutral on the issue of terrorism than are for or against it. Consequently, the application of treaties, conventions, and domestic and international law to acts of terrorism has limited effectiveness because of the lack of enforcement. For this and other reasons, therefore, authorities on terrorism reject the notion that it can be controlled or wiped out entirely. In the near future, they see it as a problem of management rather than of resolution. As one expert put it: "We foresee in the last decade of this century an era in which three modes of armed conflict could coexist: first, limited conventional war of the kind we saw in the Falklands or Grenada; second, the classic rural guerrilla warfare we see in Central America; and third, increasingly, international terrorism . . . Warfare will not be confined by national borders; rather, local belligerents will mobilize external help with terrorists in their employ carrying out warfare around the world."[41]

Should this prognosis hold true, industrialized democracies, according to the findings of another study, will find it more difficult than authoritarian and dictatorial systems to cope with terrorism. According to a recent study, "the forces which produce a reversal of terrorism are stronger in repressive environments than they are in environments more conducive to moderate reform."[42] Apparently, many psychologists feel that terrorists are not punishable. They can be jailed or martyred but, from their point of view, never punished. (The editor of the Peruvian newsmagazine *Caretas* supports this view. His interview is presented as a supplemental reading to this chapter.) Terrorism, with some exceptions, is like crime. In open societies it goes on with its ups and downs but is never completely eliminated. During the summer months in Europe four U.S. citizens may fall victim to terrorism, while in New York City alone the number of people dying from gunshot wounds inflicted during a crime may be one-hundred times that many. There is a difference however;

rapists and murderers do not become martyrs and they do not have a long list of new criminals anxiously waiting to fill their shoes. Terrorism, like crime, could be "solved" if people in industrialized democracies were to choose to change their lifestyles and political systems for an oppressive type where every act could be monitored and controlled, but that is not in the nature or interest of the Western world. Freedom of movement, access to funds, guns, sanctuary, and the media—all integral aspects of Western democracy—are essential requirements for the success of terrorism. The dilemma for democracy may be contained in the following riddle: How can terrorism be destroyed without destroying democracy? Thus as has been suggested elsewhere, industrialized democracies must unite in purpose and action to control or stamp out terrorism.

L. Paul Bremer III

Terrorism: Its Evolving Nature

Following is a statement by L. Paul Bremer III, Ambassador at Large for Counterterrorism, before the House Foreign Affairs Committee, Washington, D.C., February 9, 1989.

The callous destruction of Pan Am Flight 103 on December 21, 1988, was a terrible international tragedy. The victims were not only the passengers and crew on the plane and the villagers in Lockerbie [Scotland] but also their relatives, friends, and all those who were touched by this horrible act. We deeply regret the loss families and friends of those on Pan Am 103 have suffered, and we share their anguish. And we share the pain of the people of Lockerbie who also lost friends and relatives.

We are determined to do everything in our power to see that this cowardly, senseless act will not go unpunished. We are committed to bringing the perpetrators to justice. Working with the British and other governments, we will follow every lead until we have answers. It may take time— there are not always quick answers in these cases—but I am confident that by using all of our resources, we will succeed in locating the murderers. Then we will exert all efforts to bring them to justice.

Right now investigators from the FBI [Federal Bureau of Investigation] are in Lockerbie, in London, in Frankfurt, and elsewhere working closely with their counterparts. We have established a task force within the intelligence community to mobilize our assets worldwide to gather information on potential suspects. We have approached dozens of other governments through intelligence and diplomatic channels for their assistance.

SOURCE: U.S. Department of State Bureau of Public Affairs, Current Policy No. 1151, March 1989.

Because the case is under investigation, and hopefully will eventually lead to trial, I am sure you will understand that I am not able to discuss the details of the investigation itself. However, I am optimistic that in the end, we will succeed.

In your February 3 letter of invitation to appear before the committee, you asked me to address a variety of topics. Some of these, including the adequacy of the Foreign Airport Security Act, an overall evaluation of the required foreign airport security assessments, and several others can be addressed more authoritatively by my colleagues from the FAA [Federal Aviation Administration]. Consequently, I defer to them on these matters.

However, three of the topics raised in your letter are directly relevant to my area of responsibility, and I would like to respond to them. They include

- an assessment of the current international terrorism threat to U.S. interests and civilians
- an overview and status of the U.S. government's counterterrorism policy
- the extent of international cooperation with the U.S. government on practical antiterrorism measures

The Terrorist Threat

Let us begin with the threat which terrorism poses to U.S. interests today.

Our preliminary analysis of the data for 1988 indicates that there were almost nine hundred international terrorist incidents last year, a new record. Terrorism clearly remains a major international problem.

The international nature of the terrorist threat is poignantly highlighted by the passenger list from Pan Am 103. Citizens of almost twenty nations died as a result of this single tragic event. Overall, international terrorism claimed the lives of almost four hundred people last year.

In dealing with international terrorism, we must— and do—constantly evaluate the nature of the threat, which changes markedly over time. As we take steps to reduce our vulnerability to terrorist attack, terrorists continue to try to find new "weak links" in the security chain which they can exploit. There are no quick fixes in this business.

For example, as the committee is aware, the international aviation community has made considerable progress in making it more difficult for hijackers to introduce weapons into the cabin of an aircraft. The tightened security and inspection procedures envisioned by the Foreign Airport Security Act of 1985, which your committee helped initiate, played a useful role in this security effort. As a result, there has been a significant drop in the number of hijackings. In 1986 and 1987 there was a total of three hijackings worldwide.

But while hijackings are down, aircraft sabotage is up. In 1986 and 1987 there were six explosions aboard aircraft resulting in 135 deaths. For the first time, we have had more incidents of sabotage than hijacking. And now we must add Pan Am 103 to this tragic toll.

New technology makes an impact on the counterterrorism front. In some instances, technical advances like plastic explosives help terrorists. On the other hand, our counterterrorism efforts are strengthened by the availability of new technology, such as the thermal neutron analyzer machines, to detect such explosives. The evolution of technology will go forward. So we must continue to anticipate how terrorists might try to turn technology to their advantage.

Our basic goal is constant. We seek to deter and prevent terrorist attacks. In the event of a terrorist incident, we seek the apprehension, prosecution, and punishment of those responsible. Our government has developed a counterterrorist policy to deal with the broad worldwide terrorist threat and its evolving nature.

Overview of U.S. Counterterrorism Policy

American counterterrorist policy stands on three solid pillars.

First, we will not accede to terrorist demands. We will not pay ransom, pardon convicted terrorists, or pressure other countries to give in to terrorist demands. In other words, we will make no deals. But we will talk to anyone authoritative—anywhere, anytime—about the welfare and unconditional release of our hostages.

Second, we have taken the lead in pressuring states which support terrorist groups and use terrorism as part of their foreign policy. We have shown these states that they will be penalized for supporting terrorism. The United States will not tolerate their aiding and abetting terrorist groups by supplying them with weapons, money, passports, training bases, and safehouses.

Third, we are imposing the rule of law on terrorists for their criminal actions. Good police work is catching terrorists, and they are being brought to trial. Since 1986, the United States has had a law which enables our law enforcement agencies to better combat terrorism overseas. Popularly called a "long arm" statute, the law makes it a federal crime to kill, injure, threaten, detain, or seize an American citizen anywhere in the world in order to compel a third person or government to accede to a terrorist's demands.

U.S. Policy: How Is It Working?

So we have a clear and comprehensive counterterrorist policy. How is it working?

Let us look first at the "no concessions" element of our policy. Obviously, this element of our policy was damaged by the Iran–*contra* affair. However, since then, we have made crystal clear our government's steadfast commitment to the "no deals" principle. No country, no group should believe there is gain in trying to blackmail the United States.

Based on my own meetings with counterterrorism officials and experts from other countries and in this country, I believe we have largely recovered the credibility lost by the Iran–*contra* affair. The international counterterrorism community understands our position, and there is strong bipartisan support here for our policy of firmness in dealing with terrorists. I hope and believe that the new administration will continue to benefit from this high level of support by the American people.

We have enjoyed an important measure of success on the second ingredient of our policy—pressuring states which support terrorism. As a result, some of the more notorious state supporters of terrorism have attempted—publicly at least—to distance themselves from terrorism.

Our 1986 airstrike on Libya's terrorist camp was the watershed event in the world's fight against terrorist-supporting states. European nations followed our lead against Libya by imposing political, economic, and security measures against the Gaddafi regime. European Community members expelled more than one hundred Libyan "diplomats" and restricted the movements of other Libyan "diplomatic" and "consular" personnel. These moves severely damaged Libya's European network dedicated to supporting international terrorism.

Gaddafi learned that his support for international terrorism would not be cost-free, and he changed his behavior which, after all, was the objective of our attack. Libya's involvement in terrorism declined from nineteen incidents in 1986 to six in 1987 and another six in 1988.

However, we must remain particularly vigilant regarding Gaddafi. There is reason to believe that Libya continues support for terrorism, albeit in a more subtle, less flagrant fashion. Moreover, Libya's continued work on a chemical weapons production facility emphasizes the need for extremely careful monitoring of Gaddafi's actions.

Syria, another long-time supporter of terrorism, also felt the pressure of our counterterrorism strategy. In late 1986, British and West German courts established Syrian complicity in terrorist attacks in London and West Berlin. Together with Great Britain, the United States joined an international campaign employing diplomatic, political, and economic sanctions to convince Syria to reduce its link to terrorist groups.

These efforts worked. In 1985 Syria was implicated in thirty-four terrorist incidents but in 1986 only six. In 1987 a year after our pressures, we detected Syria's hand in only one incident and in none in 1988. Moreover, Syria expelled the violent Abu Nidal Organization from Damascus in June 1987—a major victory for our counterterrorist policies.

These efforts may not force these nations to cease entirely their support for terrorist groups. Indeed, both Libya and Syria continue to provide such support. But a concerted, vigorous Western strategy does make them move more cautiously and become more circumspect.

The third and final element of our counterterrorism policy—using the rule of law against terrorists and encouraging others to do the same—is maturing into a potent weapon for two basic reasons. First, there has been a sea change in international attitudes toward terrorists. Second, governments have decided to provide law enforcement agencies the resources necessary to deter terrorism.

Not long ago, many usually responsible countries granted terrorists dispensation for their crimes. Ironically, terrorists were perceived as victims of those vague forces called "oppression" and "imperialism"—victims, or worse, romantic adventurers whose behavior should be indulged.

No longer is this true. Terrorists began to lose this international indulgence as they widened their circle of targets in the late 1970s. In some instances, they even attacked their sympathizers and supporters. The shock of such actions turned indulgence to revulsion.

And as popular disgust mounted, politicians finally insisted on action to counter the terrorists. Law enforcement agencies were given the resources to do their jobs. National police departments now have the surveillance gear, the communications equipment, and the money for overtime to gather intelligence and to track and arrest terrorists. As a result, more and more terrorists are being brought to trial and convicted. For example:

- On November 3, 1988, a Maltese court sentenced the sole surviving terrorist in the November 1985 hijacking of an Egyptian airliner to twenty-five years imprisonment—the maximum sentence under Maltese law. The surviving hijacker belonged to the Abu Nidal Organization.
- On October 27, 1988, a Sudanese court passed the death sentence on five Palestinian terrorists for their attack this year on Khartoum's Acropole Hotel and the Sudan Club. These five were also members of the Abu Nidal Organization.

- In July 1988 a Pakistan court convicted five terrorists for an Abu Nidal Organization attack against a Pan Am airliner in Karachi in September 1986.
- A French court convicted, *in absentia,* on October 20, 1988, the notorious Fatah terrorist Colonel Hawari to ten years—the maximum allowed under French law—for complicity to transport arms, ammunition, and explosives and for criminal associations.
- A West German court is currently trying Muhammad Hamadei, a Lebanese terrorist implicated in the 1985 TWA hijacking which resulted in the murder of an innocent American seaman, Robert Stethem.
- Here in Washington, D.C., Fawaz Younis, a Lebanese terrorist will soon go on trial for holding American citizens hostage when he led the 1985 hijacking of a Royal Jordanian Airlines flight.
- In Greece authorities will soon decide on Muhammad Rashid's extradition to this country where he is wanted for planting a bomb in 1982 on a Pan Am airliner. His extradition to the United States would be an important indication of Greece's adherence to its stated policy of combating terrorism.

In short, the United States has a counterterrorism policy in place and it works. However, it is obvious that we cannot succeed alone. Many of the essential ingredients in combating terrorism—gathering intelligence information, monitoring the movements of suspected terrorists, intercepting and apprehending terrorists—require effective international cooperation.

International Cooperation in Counterterrorism

As terrorists expand their activities, and as international repugnance to terrorist acts intensifies, nations increasingly regard terrorism as a collective threat and a common problem. The desire to promote international cooperation, already strong, was particularly evident in the aftermath of the attack on Pan Am 103.

International condemnation of the sabotage of Pan Am 103 was swift and emphatic. Many individual nations condemned the attack. The secretary general of the United Nations issued a statement in late December 1988 expressing "outrage" at the attack. This statement was echoed by the president of the Security Council, speaking on behalf of the council, who condemned the attack and called on all states to assist in the apprehension and prosecution of those responsible. Similarly, the twelve members of the European

Community released a joint statement deploring the sabotage of Pan Am 103.

The sabotage of Pan Am 103 has emphasized the need for prompt action to strengthen further aviation security measures. The FAA immediately issued orders for increased security measures on American carriers to deal with the new situations. But we cannot solve the problem alone. It is clear that we need to encourage the adoption of more stringent security measures throughout the aviation community.

Improving Aviation Security

To pursue this work, the international community is turning to the International Civil Aviation Organization (ICAO), an agency of the UN system based in Montreal. ICAO is the acknowledged body responsible for setting standards in the field of civil aviation and is, therefore, the appropriate forum for international followup to Pan Am 103.

On January 24 the United Kingdom and the United States jointly announced that, in response to the destruction of Pan Am 103, they were requesting a special session of the ICAO council to pursue ways "to improve international aviation security procedures." On January 30 the ICAO council decided to hold such a special session on February 15–16, 1989, to discuss ways to counter the growing trend of sabotage against civil aviation. A number of ICAO members—including the United States, the United Kingdom, the Federal Republic of Germany, Australia, and Switzerland —will be represented by their ministers of transportation at this meeting.

We expect representatives at this special ministerial-level council meeting to begin by reviewing briefly the existing aviation security measures. Aviation standards, as defined and adopted by ICAO members, are contained in annex 17 to the Chicago convention (which established ICAO in 1944).

Over the years, a great deal of important work has been done to improve the measures in annex 17, which should not be overlooked. For example, following the June 1985 hijacking of TWA 847, annex 17 was exhaustively reviewed. In December 1985 annex 17 was amended to include a number of provisions intended to prevent the use of weapons or dangerous devices aimed at causing bodily harm and damage to property aboard aircraft.

In 1986 ICAO's Unlawful Interference Committee reviewed ICAO's security standards to ensure that they were updated promptly as necessary. This committee, with support from the ICAO Secretariat, identified four areas that warranted priority attention as particularly vulnerable to placement of explosive devices. These included ramp security, weapons detection, cargo/mail/small parcel handling, and courier service.

Work on aviation security standards has continued in ICAO's Aviation Security Panel, which reports to the Unlawful Interference Committee. This panel has identified several priorities for work in ICAO. These include security controls to detect devices which might be carried by unsuspecting parties unwittingly acting as couriers for terrorists and passenger management methods to ensure that passengers leave nothing behind on an aircraft.

Much of this work will continue and intensify as ICAO defines new approaches to security. To facilitate this work, we hope that the February 15–16 ministerial council session will endorse a plan of work that establishes priorities for technical work in ICAO. These priorities include:

- detection of sabotage devices, especially explosives
- comprehensive screening of checked baggage
- comprehensive screening of passengers and hand baggage
- controlling access to aircraft by ground personnel
- establishing a new ICAO service available to members at their request to assess security at individual airports and to recommend improvements as necessary

We also expect the ministerial will review the status of security-related training provided by ICAO.

Finally, we expect the ICAO ministerial will discuss the need for increased attention to "tagging" plastic explosives for detection. Relatively little technical work has been pursued to date in this area. However, the tragedy of Pan Am 103 emphasizes both the urgency and importance of such work.

The ICAO council meeting next week will bring together some of the world's foremost authorities in aviation security. Their meeting underscores the commitment of the international community to continue the worldwide fight against terrorism. The combination of this political will and technical expertise lends considerable momentum to the important work in ICAO on aviation security, which has and will continue to make significant progress.

Handling Terrorist Threats

I know a number of members are interested in our government's policy on handling terrorist threats.

Each week, we receive literally dozens of threats— most of them directed at American officials abroad. We urgently and carefully analyze them. If a threat is deemed credible, we take immediate steps to counter the threat by getting the information into the hands of people who can take steps to counter the threat. For example, in the case of a threat to an airline, we get that information into the hands of airport security officials responsible for aviation security. This is the purpose of the FAA security alert bulletins sent to airline corporate security officials and to airport security officials.

We do not routinely make terrorist threats public. To do so would encourage "copycat" terrorist threats which could initially cause panic and disrupt air services and, in the end, cause indifference to the alerts themselves. As it is, we already receive on the average three threats to American airports or airlines each day.

Nor is it our policy to selectively alert people to terrorist threats. If we have a credible and specific terrorist threat to an airline which cannot be countered effectively on the spot, then our policy is to recommend that the airline cancel the flight. Otherwise, we would issue a public travel advisory to the American traveling public. It is not our policy to alert government officials and not the general public to such a threat. There is, and can be, no double standard.

While priority attention will continue on aviation security, we cannot overlook work in other vital areas. As the *Achille Lauro* tragedy demonstrates all too clearly, passenger ships are also vulnerable to terrorism, including sabotage. The International Maritime Organization (IMO) already has taken a number of steps to enhance maritime security. IMO security measures were analyzed in detail at the October 1988 meeting of the IMO Maritime Safety Committee, which agreed to review these measures annually. During 1989 the IMO will sponsor at least two regional security seminars—one in the Caribbean and one in the Mediterranean. These seminars will offer training and assistance in states' application of IMO security measures. We fully support this work in IMO and will participate actively in these seminars.

Mr. Chairman, my remarks thus far have been addressed to the topics you identified in your letter of invitation as of particular interest to the committee. Permit me, however, to include a reference to an indispensable component of our counterterrorism effort, namely our antiterrorist assistance (ATA) program, a program this committee was instrumental in establishing.

Antiterrorist Assistance Program

Since its inception in 1984, ATA has trained over 650 students from twenty-eight nations in advanced civil aviation security or airport police management. Both courses are offered at the Transportation Safety Institute—an FAA facility in Oklahoma City—and include a mixture of classroom instruction supplemented by on-the-scene instruction at major U.S. airports.

Countering the existing threats to international civil aviation requires an effective aviation security program which includes well-trained staff supplemented by a variety of technical aids. Any such system has built-in redundancy and recognizes that the most critical element in aviation security is the well-motivated employee who takes his or her duties seriously. We are confident that our basic ATA teaching program is sound and contributes to the building of such a system. It teaches the interdependence and supplemental effects of people, dogs, and existing electronic technology such as x-rays. We will incorporate into our training, as they emerge, the "lessons learned" from the Pan Am 103 bombing.

Bomb-detector dogs already hold a critical role in aviation security as part of a comprehensive effort to detect plastic explosives. There are limits, however, to what can be done with sniffer dogs. Dogs are capable of detecting plastic explosives, but they present logistical problems. At large airports such as those in the United States and Europe, dogs provide only part of the solution. Since the ATA program generally works with less developed nations, which often have small international airports, some of the problems presented by using detector dogs at major international airports may pose fewer difficulties at the smaller airports.

We are working to broaden the scope of our aviation security training, such as that offered through the ATA program. During FY [fiscal year] 1988, the United States worked with the French to improve aviation security in West Africa, with the Canadians to do the same at Manila International, and with the British in broad-based counterterrorism training for Pakistan. In cooperation with South Korea, we organized a conference of Pacific rim nations to establish enhanced aviation security standards before and during last year's Summer Olympic period.

The ATA program, with the range of training that it can offer, is a vital element in the U.S. response to the threat posed by international terrorism. For FY 1990, the president is seeking $10.017 million to support ATA training. These funds will finance training for some 1,500 recipients from twenty-five nations and provide a modest amount of training-related equipment.

The ATA program also works with the FAA's assessment of airports as provided under the Foreign Airport Security Act. The Department of State and the FAA cooperate closely in this FAA airport assessment program. Embassy officials are routinely involved in scheduling these assessments and facilitating the work of the FAA security officials during their visit. When deficiencies are identified in an airport's security program by the FAA officials, as they were in Caracas in the summer of 1988, State and FAA work together to develop an effective assistance program. State, through its antiterrorism assistance program, generally offers training in advanced civil aviation security or airport police management to help correct any such deficiencies. FAA, under its own authorities, provides related assistance. In the case of Caracas, the problems identified were corrected to FAA's satisfaction before the ninety-day-notice period expired.

Research and Development

In addition to training under the ATA program, we are continuing our work in research and development (R&D). One priority is to identify and develop new technology to apply to the process of examining baggage so that materials such as plastic explosives can be more consistently detected. While the first models are only now in production, the thermal neutron analyzer developed for the FAA offers real promise as a means of ensuring that plastic explosives cannot evade detection.

On behalf of the U.S. government, the State Department coordinates and funds a national counterterrorism research and development program. In FY 1990, we will be seeking $6 million to support this interagency program.

Included in the R&D program are projects to develop new forms of less expensive and more widely applicable detectors to identify plastic explosives or chemical/biological agents in closed containers. I hope that members of this committee will continue to support this program.

Another example of our R&D efforts at State is the Bureau of Diplomatic Security's funding for the development of a high-technology "sniffer" to detect nitrogen vapors, such as those emitted by explosives in automobiles, packages, luggage, or persons. The first operating models of this equipment, developed under contracts with Thermedics, Inc. totaling nearly $7 million, will be delivered to the State Department this summer. This equipment will be applied as part of our program to protect high-threat posts and to ensure the security of the secretary as he travels. This equipment offers promise as the possible basis for other prototypes which would be applicable for use in checking airline passengers, their luggage, and carry-on items.

Terrorism remains a major international problem. While we continue to make progress in countering terrorism in some areas, new dimensions to this problem emerge with dismaying frequency. There is no single magic solution to this international scourge. Yet our political will is strong, our available resources are carefully used, and our technical expertise is among the best in the world. We remain deeply committed to our concerted effort to combat terrorism, as are the members of the committee. We greatly appreciate your support which is essential if we are to prevail.

Terrorism, Inflation, and Debt Threaten Democracy in Peru

This World Press Dialogue with Enrique Zileri, editor of the newsmagazine *Caretas* of Lima and new chairman of the London-based International Press Institute, was conducted by editorial consultant Alfred Balk:

Have Peru's problems become the most explosive in Latin America?   Except for Central America, yes. Peru embodies many of the most acute problems of the Third World. We have suffered eight years of terrorism from the Shining Path guerrilla group and others. We are faced with a huge foreign debt and all of the accompanying complications, including a decline of new investment. Inflation has accelerated. Population growth continues. Our long tradition of military intervention adds a further worry.

Is narcotics traffic behind many of your problems?   The drug business is a major concern. We are a large producer of coca leaf, but we are not major refiners of cocaine. Drug traffickers' planes come into the country daily—by the dozens—from Colombia. Yet that has not caused us nearly the havoc suffered by that country. Peruvian drug dealers have not indulged in political assassinations, except for shooting officials in little towns in coca-producing areas. They kill rivals but not government ministers.

The U.S. State Department wants us to spray the coca plantations with herbicides, but we have resisted, pending more testing. Aid to fight the drug business has almost doubled, to $27 million, but this is a pittance compared with the $1 billion a year that the business earns.

It is a complicated problem. Impoverished peasants move into coca-growing areas to earn a living. Out of

sympathy or fear, some join forces with the Shining Path, which collects protection money from the drug dealers for allowing their planes to land. From the guerrillas' moralistic standpoint, they do good by diverting the drugs away from domestic consumption and forcing coca growers to produce some food.

Is protection money a major source of the guerrillas' revenue?   It is very difficult to tell. The Shining Path is, in many ways, a beggars' army. It does not receive weapons from abroad for ideological reasons. It tells its members to take their victims' guns, or to attack small police stations for their weapons.

These people are very fierce, very cruel, messianic, almost fundamentalist in their fervor. They apply the Maoist technique of establishing a revolutionary base in an area, killing the authorities there, terrorizing the population, and proselytizing from it. It's terrible. Of the ten to fifteen thousand people they have killed in Peru, the vast majority were peasants caught in the crossfire.

To the guerrillas, every other revolutionary movement is tainted: Cuba, the Soviet "imperialists," China. They consider China the worst. They are orphans of the Gang of Four, unredeemed Maoists, the only "pure" revolutionaries.

How much of the country do the terrorists control?   There is no area the armed forces or police cannot go into if they want. When they do, the guerrillas simply retreat. They are strongest in the very poor, remote, backward areas that are difficult to aid. They blow up whatever you try to build. Besides dynamiting electrification projects, which they do all of the time, they have destroyed experimental farms of international repute.

Sometimes they carry out hit-and-run assassinations in Lima. In one case the head of our electoral college, a revered elderly man thought not to have an enemy in world, was gunned down but by some miracle managed to survive. In 1983, in a horrible case of mistaken identity, eight journalists visiting a remote community were hacked to death.

How bad is the economy?   Over the past year, inflation has totaled 1,000 percent. People now carry money in shopping bags like they used to in Argentina or prewar Italy or Germany. Gross national product has dropped 4 percent, and real incomes 40 percent. Incomes average only $750 a year, with fantastic disparities. Our magazine has doubled in price and lost circulation.

What went wrong?   The country was swayed by a very charismatic leader: President Alan García. He was young and articulate and, at the time of his election in 1985,

SOURCE: *World Press Review* 36, no. 1 (January 1989): 33–35.
Reprinted by permission.

promised a new era of economic growth. The government used its reserves to stimulate phenomenal growth—9 percent in 1986, more than 6.5 percent in 1987, an unmatched performance in Latin America. Factories imported more and more materials to meet demand. We paid for those imports with exports: García announced in 1985 that no more than 10 percent of export revenues would be allocated to servicing the nation's foreign debt.

Then came a trade slowdown, particularly with the U.S. We fell into both fiscal and foreign-trade deficits. We couldn't service our foreign debt. Nobody would lend us money. We couldn't even import food, and Peru depends on imported food—some $300 million worth a year.

By early 1987, advisers were telling the president to start cooling the economy: "You have to husband your reserves. You're going to lose popularity. Start talking with the international financial community. You've made your point."

But García said no to the International Monetary Fund (IMF), claiming, "We don't negotiate." Peru stopped paying the banks. We kept on spending. García remained fantastically popular. He said that internal investment would carry us through, but of course it couldn't.

How has he tried to adjust?
By mid-1987 he knew he had to apply the brakes and it wouldn't look good, so he tried to nationalize the banks. This triggered an incredible upheaval. About half of the country was middle-of-the-road and said no. The press said we would now have to deal with the state banks for everything—they could put the squeeze on us anytime they want. Then writer Mario Vargas Llosa stepped into the political arena and denounced this as an authoritarian move to buckle the press and all of the opposition; the rationale was that if you have the banks, you have everything.

García has, by default, recreated the right-of-center. Previous surveys showed that it made up no more than 15 percent of the electorate. Suddenly it surged to 50 percent, clearly against nationalizing the banks. García's approval rating, an extraordinary 90 percent in 1985–1986, now is less than 15 percent—a dangerous level in a country wracked by terrorist violence.

What is Peru's foreign-debt policy now?
We resumed payments to the World Bank on multilateral, long-term development loans—up to 20 percent of export revenues. This still left a negative flow with the World Bank. Our finance minister talked with the bank's president Barber Conable, who was very tough. The IMF also has sent a mission to Peru. It is trying to help us put a program together, and in as face-saving a way as possible to try to hook us up somehow to the international community. The problem is that we are close to reaching $1 billion in back payments to the IMF. If debt restructuring leaves us with that size arrears, we can't manage.

García's timing was wrong. The world is not ready for García's approach. But debt relief—interest relief—is in the air, and in two years a change may occur.

Where does the military stand now?
There was a coup scare in October—probably a false one. García asked a general who is a good friend, had been a chief of staff, and headed one of five military regions, to check into rumors. The general apparently went around phoning other high officials of the army and asking, in effect, what's this about a coup? They did not appreciate this and called for his resignation, although they were aware that he was close to the president.

So relations between the armed forces and the government are cool. I may be terribly mistaken, but I don't see the conditions for a coup now. Usually coups occur when things are looking up. The armed forces have their hands full with the Shining Path insurgency. They were in power for twelve years, until 1980, and know how lonely it can get.

If the 1990 election, in which García cannot run, results in a victory by the moderate leftist Alfonso Barrantes, then the script could change. Barrantes is very popular, but his mixed United Left coalition includes the same type of radicals who backed Chilean President Salvador Allende before his overthrow. They don't clearly renounce violence, as Barrantes does.

What impact has Vargas Llosa had at this early stage of the campaign?
Surveys show him doing well. Barrantes has been leading in the polls, followed by Vargas Llosa, and then by the government party man Luis Alva Castro. But no one has been formally nominated by a party yet, and there is a large undecided vote. Former President Fernando Belaúnde Terry also is rising in surveys. Latin America is full of senior, seventy-year-old cabinet men like him who have run again. He says he is not running. But he is celebrating all kinds of anniversaries that keep him in the public eye.

Can García still aspire to Latin American leadership?
After taking office, he was very popular in many countries. I was with him on several trips where he was a smash hit. In Mexico he played the guitar with mariachis. He was upstaging other presidents. Now there is a friendly relationship, and the ideas are there, but people are saying, Look what's happened to him in his own country.

Has population control progressed?
Only in attempts, not results. Visitors have been astonished to see family-planning

commercials on television. One legislative chamber approved a bill allowing voluntary sterilization of women, but it got stalled in the other chamber. These things really are quite remarkable. In spite of the fact that the Pope has visited the continent twice, and in spite of the official position of the Roman Catholic church, there is movement. The church is becoming increasingly divided. The tragedy is that women still have four or five children, their health is endangered, and they can't get help.

What is Peru's relationship with the Soviet bloc? Peru has granted fishing rights to a large Soviet fleet, and the pre-1980 military government bought tanks and jets from the Soviet bloc. This commercial relationship continues. The financial concessions with such arrangements usually are very generous, while shifting away from a weapon usually is expensive. The García government also has bought Kalashnikov rifles from North Korea, at a fantastically low price—for the police, not the armed forces. The government remains very conscious of Peru's nonaligned status and rights.

What about relations with the U.S.? In 1985, our president got into a finger-pointing session with Secretary of State George Shultz after delivering a speech to the United Nations violently criticizing Reagan administration policies and perceptions of the Third World. But García also praised Jefferson, Lincoln, Roosevelt, and Kennedy. He was saying, "I'm not anti-Yankee; I'm anti-Reagan." Now the hope is that the more cosmopolitan George Bush will not emulate Reagan, and that officials considered hawks will be out of the picture. García's position is that there is a chance for a new beginning.

What future do you see for democracy in Latin America? If the situation continues as it is, the outlook is bleak—really bleak—although for a time it looked promising. García is seen as a troublemaker, a rebel, and our economy is seen as a mess. But look at Mexico and Argentina, not to mention Brazil. Everybody is in a mess.

If there is no real social and economic relief, democracy in these countries will disintegrate. There must first of all be debt relief, then something quite dramatic—perhaps a new Marshall Plan—to create a better base for investment. Latin American debt has been a key to the decline of international trade. Since 1980, trade has slipped tremendously as Latin America became a net exporter of capital. That can't go on. This is a huge issue, with interest bills piling up and all of our economies, including yours in the U.S., suffering.

What opportunities does Peru offer? We have fabulous economic frontiers. We know the location of immense mineral treasures but don't exploit them. We have potential riches in fishing, where state-owned operations now work at half-capacity. We have a huge, state-owned dry region awaiting irrigation. As Chile and New Zealand have discovered, Southern Hemisphere countries have natural advantages as winter produce exporters. We already sell $10 million worth of asparagus, which has become a delicacy. Our kiwi fruit can get to market two months before New Zealand's and surpasses California's in quality. If we all worked together, we could make a lot of investors, and ourselves, rich.

Study Questions

1. What do we mean by *psychological warfare*?
2. What is the difference between psychological warfare used during wartime and during peacetime?
3. What are the "weapons" employed in the two variations of psychological warfare?
4. What type of intelligence is required for psychological warfare?
5. Why is psychological warfare more suitable to authoritarian systems of government and less suitable to democratic systems?
6. Does the United States engage in covert activities? Give examples.
7. How does the Soviet Union wage covert operations?
8. What are some of the Soviet examples of undercover activities?
9. What do we mean by *propaganda*?
10. What are the main objectives of propaganda?

11. How does propaganda differ from education?
12. What are the instruments or outlets for the use of propaganda?
13. What are the requirements for effective propaganda?
14. Name the various media used by propagandists.
15. Why did the mass media weaken the role of diplomacy and strengthen the role of propaganda? Give examples.
16. What are the impacts of *glasnost, perestroika,* and *new thinking* on Soviet propaganda?
17. Why was Mikhail Gorbachev's visit to Bonn, West Germany, in June 1989 a successful propaganda coup?
18. What are the elements of Gorbachev's new thinking in Soviet foreign policy?
19. What is the relationship between sports and propaganda?
20. Why was Secretary-General Waldheim's proposal on the UN agenda to place measures against terrorism rejected in 1972?
21. What kind of UN resolution on terrorism was adopted in 1985?
22. How does the UN definition of *aggression* relate to terrorism?
23. What are the main ingredients of terrorism?
24. How does terrorism differ from *guerrilla warfare*?
25. When does terrorism become *international* terrorism?
26. What are some examples of internal and international terrorist organizations?
27. What are the differences among organizational, insurgency, and state-sponsored terrorism?
28. What are some of the examples of state-sponsored international terrorism?
29. Why is the Fatah considered an enemy by some renegade PLO groups?
30. How did the European Community react to Syrian and Libyan connections to international terrorism?
31. Do other countries support international terrorism? Name them.
32. Why do certain states resort to international terrorism as an instrument of foreign policy?
33. How does the Soviet Union figure in this game?
34. How do you explain the fact that terrorist incidents have been on an increase, casualties on a decrease, and still terrorist operations have had a high success rate?
35. What was the impact of international terrorism in Latin America, the Middle East, Western Europe, and South Asia?
36. Why do European nations prefer diplomacy over military action against international terrorism?
37. Why are Americans and U.S. installations the main targets of international terrorism?
38. How does Enrique Zileri characterize the causes of terrorism conducted by the Shining Path in Peru?
39. What is official U.S. policy toward terrorism?
40. How does L. Paul Bremer III evaluate U.S. success or failure toward terrorism?
41. Why does the United States officially refuse to negotiate with terrorists?
42. Why did the United States unofficially sell arms to Iran in order to free hostages in Lebanon?
43. What was the European reaction to the U.S. bombing raid on Libya?
44. Why does the United States promote the principle of law and order, and then refuse to follow it on the international level?
45. Why is international law considered ineffective against international terrorism?
46. Name some of the American organizations and agencies that deal with international terrorism.

47. What measures does the United States take against terrorism?
48. Why is it so difficult to eradicate international terrorism?
49. What are the prospects for the future as far as international terrorism versus democracy are concerned?

Key Terms

aggression
Cold War
covert operations
disinformation
glasnost
guerrilla warfare

intifada
perestroika
propaganda
psychological warfare
terrorism

Notes

1. For a thoughtful discussion of the concept of influence in foreign policy behavior, see K. J. Holsti, *International Politics: A Framework for Analysis,* 4th ed., (Englewood Cliffs, N.J.: Prentice-Hall, 1983), pp. 144–159.
2. See J. F. C. Fuller, *Tanks in the Great War, 1914–1918* (London: Murray, 1920), p. 320. See also Paul M. Linebarger, *Psychological Warfare,* 2nd ed. (Washington, D.C.: Combat Forces Press, 1954).
3. Bruce Russett and Harvey Starr, *World Politics: The Menu for Choice,* 2nd ed. (New York: W. H. Freeman, 1985), p. 139.
4. For a personal account of the events leading to the ouster of Dr. Mossadegh, see General Hassan Arfa, *Under Five Shahs* (New York: Morrow, 1965), pp. 396–418.
5. See Sandra Burton, "Aquino's Philippines: The Center Holds," *Foreign Affairs* 65, no. 3 (1987): 524–537.
6. See John Barron, *KGB: The Secret Work of Secret Agents* (New York: Reader's Digest Press, 1974); and Ladislav Bittman, *The KGB and Soviet Disinformation* (McLean, Va.: Pergamon-Brassey's International Defense Publishers, 1985). It is interesting to note, however, that there were allegations in the U.S. press that the Reagan administration had used similar techniques against Libya in 1987.
7. See Craig M. Karp, "The War in Afghanistan," *Foreign Affairs* 64, no. 5 (Summer 1986): 1026–1047.
8. See Rosanne Klass, "Afghanistan: The Accords," *Foreign Affairs* 66, no. 5 (Summer 1988): 922–945.
9. Bruce L. Smith, "Propaganda," in *International Encyclopedia of the Social Sciences,* vol. 12, ed. David L. Sills (New York: Macmillan, 1968), p. 579.
10. See Leonard W. Doob, *Public Opinion and Propaganda* (New York: Holt, 1948).
11. See Harold D. Laswell, Daniel Lerner, and Ithiel de Sola Pool, *The Comparative Study of Symbols* (Stanford: Stanford University Press, 1952).
12. Statement by First Deputy Head of the Community Party of the Soviet Union's International Department Vadim Zagladin in an interview to Milan Syrucek in Prague, Czechoslovakia. *Tvorba* 21 (May 25, 1988): 18–19.

13. See *Frankfurter Neue Presse,* June 14, 1989.

14. For the success of Gorbachev's new thinking, see, for example, *"Vneshnaya politika—uroki proshlogo"* [Foreign Policy—Past Achievements], *Mezhdunarodnaya zhizn* 1 (1989): 93–95; for a critical analysis of new thinking, see, for example, Peter Javiler and Hiroshi Kimura, eds., *Gorbachev's Reforms: U.S. and Japanese Assessments* (New York: Aldine & Gruyter, 1988).

15. See Abraham D. Sofaer, "Terrorism and the Law," *Foreign Affairs* 64, no. 5 (Summer 1986): 903.

16. See UN General Assembly, Resolution on Measures to Prevent International Terrorism, January 14, 1986, *International Law Manual* 25 (1986): 239 (A. Res. 40161).

17. See UN General Assembly, Special Committee on the Question of Defining Aggression, April 12, 1984, *International Law Manual* 13 (1974): 713 (A. Res. 3314).

18. Frank H. Perez, Deputy Director, Office for Combating Terrorism, U.S. Department of State, cited in U.S. Department of State Bureau of Public Affairs, Current Policy No. 402, June 10, 1982.

19. See, for example, Timothy B. Carrigan and George A. Lopez, *Terrorism: A Problem of Political Violence* (Columbus, Ohio: Consortium for International Studies Education, 1978), pp. 1–2; Andrew J. Pierre, "The Politics of International Terrorism," *Orbis* 19 (Winter 1976): 1251–1270; Frederic B. Pearson and J. Martin Rochester, *International Relations* (Reading, Mass.: Addison-Wesley, 1985), p. 409; and James Lee Ray, *Global Politics,* 3rd ed. (Boston: Houghton Mifflin, 1987), p. 384.

20. Christopher Dobson and Ronald Payne, *The Terrorists: Their Weapons, Leaders and Tactics* (New York: Facts on File, 1979), p. 71.

21. Ray Cline and Yonah Alexander, *Terrorism: The Soviet Connection* (New York: Crane Russak, 1984), p. 49; cited in Ray, *Global Politics,* p. 386.

22. See Benjamin Netanyahu, "Terrorism: How the West Can Win," *Time,* April 14, 1986, p. 48.

23. Quoted in Robert Oakley, "International Terrorism," *Foreign Affairs* 65, no. 3 (1987): 611. For a list of terrorist organizations, see George Rosie, *The Dictionary of International Terrorism* (Edinburgh: Mainstream, 1986).

24. Oakley, "International Terrorism," pp. 620–621. See also Office of the Secretary of State, Ambassador at Large for Counterterrorism, *Syrian Support for International Terrorism: 1983–86* (Washington, D.C.: Department of State *Special Report No. 157,* December 1986).

25. For a more thorough identification of the various terrorist groups and organizations, see the Vice-President's Task Force on Combating Terrorism, *Terrorist Group Profiles* (Washington, D.C.: Government Printing Office, November 1988).

26. Netanyahu, "Terrorism," p. 49.

27. Central Intelligence Agency, *International Terrorism in 1979.* (Washington, D.C.: Central Intelligence Agency, 1980), p. 3; cited in Pearson and Rochester, *International Relations,* p. 411.

28. Oakley, "International Terrorism," p. 613.

29. See David L. Milbank, *International and Transnational Terrorism: Diagnosis and Prognosis* (Washington, D.C.: Central Intelligence Agency, April 1976); and Chalmers Johnson, *Perspectives on Terrorism, Summary Report of the Conference on International Terrorism* (Washington, D.C.: Department of State, 1976). Both are cited in Carrigan and Lopez, *Terrorism,* pp. 5–6; and Pearson and Rochester, *International Relations,* p. 411.

30. See Office of the Secretary of State, Ambassador at Large for Counterterrorism, *Patterns of Global Terrorism: 1988,* Department of State Publication 9705 (Washington, D.C.: Department of State, March 1989).

31. Ibid., p. 8.

32. Oakley, "International Terrorism," pp. 623–624.

33. Brian M. Jenkins, "Will Terrorists Go Nuclear?" *Orbis* 29 (Fall 1985): 511; cited in Ray, *Global Politics,* p. 387.

34. Walter Laquer, *Terrorism* (London: Weidenfeld and Nicolson, 1977), p. 221; cited in Pearson and Rochester, *International Relations,* p. 411.

35. Central Intelligence Agency, *Pattern of International Terrorism: 1980* (Springfield, Va.: National Technical Information Service, 1981); cited in Todd Sandler, John T. Tschirhart and John Cauley, "A Theoretical Analysis of Transnational Terrorism," *American Political Science Review* 77, no. 1 (1983): p. 37.

36. Sandler, Tschirhart, and Cauley, "A Theoretical Analysis of Transnational Terrorism," p. 52.

37. See L. Paul Bremer III, "Terrorism: Its Evolving Nature," *Current Policy No. 1151* (Washington, D.C.: Department of State Bureau of Public Affairs, March 1989).

38. L. Paul Bremer III, Ambassador at Large for Counterterrorism, Department of State, cited in Current Policy No. 913 (Washington, D.C.: Department of State Bureau of Public Affairs, January 1987).

39. Benjamin Netanyahu, *Terrorism: How the West Can Win* (New York: Farrar, Straus & Giroux, 1986); see also Sofaer, *Terrorism and the Law,* p. 922; and Frank Brenchley, *Diplomatic Immunities and State-Sponsored Terrorism* (London: Institute for the Study of Conflict, 1984).

40. See M. Kidder Rushworth, "Countering the Threat of Terrorism," *Christian Science Monitor,* May 21, 1986. For an assessment of U.S. policy toward terrorism, see the supplemental reading "Terrorism: Its Evolving Nature."

41. Brian M. Jenkins, "Trends in International Terrorism," *World Affairs Journal* 3, no. 2 (Spring 1984): 48.

42. Lawrence C. Hamilton and James D. Hamilton, "Dynamics of Terrorism," *International Studies Quarterly* 27, no. 1 (1983): 52.

Eight

War and Intervention

The human race congratulates itself in this modern age for being civilized, but the sad truth is that the Four Horsemen of the Apocalypse—war, famine, pestilence, and death— have stalked us from the beginning and plague us still. Enlightenment and reason have yet to root out these ills. Famine, pestilence, and death all lie at least partially beyond our control, although we can take some steps to prevent them. But war is another matter; it results primarily from acts of the human will. As such, it should be preventable or at least controllable. History teaches us, however, that war persists. There is hardly an age of history that has not been marked by the scourge of war. In our own century, after the Ages of Reason and Enlightenment, two global wars of great devastation and dozens of smaller conflicts have been fought. More people have died in these wars than in all the recorded wars of history.

At the close of World War II, members of the United Nations promised in Article 2 (5) of the charter that they would "refrain in their international relations from the threat or use of force against the territorial integrity or political independence of any state." A legal basis for prohibiting war was laid. But it rested on the erroneous notion that the UN Security Council would be an effective institution for the maintenance of peace and the prevention and punishment of aggression. As we will see in chapter 9, the Security Council's peace-making role was never fully realized. Force and war remain an integral part of modern international relations today, despite efforts by the UN Charter to reign them in and prevent their use.

Several major wars have been fought in the past decade. The bloodiest by far was the Iran–Iraq war that started in 1980. Hundreds of thousands of lives were lost in that war. In Afghanistan, withdrawal of Soviet troops left the central Afghan government to wage war with Afghan resistance groups. In Kampuchea, fighting goes on between the Cambodian government and Khmer resistance groups. Wars have been fought between Argentina and the United Kingdom (over the Falkland Islands), China and Vietnam, Ethiopia and Somalia, Mali and Burkina Faso (formerly Upper Volta), and Tanzania and Uganda. Civil wars have been even more numerous. There may be a legal presumption against the use of force in the UN Charter, but the practice of many states suggests that war is still an accepted tool of foreign policy.

In this chapter we will examine the various kinds of war that exist in the contemporary international system and review the principal theories about why nations go to war.

Types of Warfare

Before we consider the causes of war, we must draw some distinctions about different kinds of war. In this section we will discuss international versus civil wars, intervention, total versus limited wars, conventional versus nuclear wars, and guerrilla wars.

International Versus Civil Wars

Students of international relations distinguish between international wars and civil wars.[1] **International** or **interstate wars,** such as World War I and II, are fought between two or more states. **Civil wars** are fought between one or more factions vying for control over territory within a single country. However, civil wars can lead to wider international conflict. For example, the ongoing civil war in Chad has drawn in France and Libya. Similarly, international war can lead to civil wars within countries. The success of the Bolshevik Revolution in Russia, for instance, can be attributed in part to the problems associated with Russian participation in World War I.

Intervention

Civil wars are also a common cause of foreign intervention.[2] **Intervention** may be defined in its broadest sense as the interference of one country in the affairs of another. More particularly, we are concerned here with military interference in the territory of another state. It is necessary to distinguish here between *uninvited* and *invited* interventions. Military interventions are considered legal if invited by the lawful government in a country (such as when the latter needs help putting down a rebellion or revolution). Under some circumstances, a country might justify intervention, for example, to protect its nationals from harm or to comply with existing treaty rights, but generally, uninvited interventions are considered a violation of international law.[3]

Military interventions almost always involve a strong state interfering in the internal affairs of a weak state. The United States and the Soviet Union have conducted most of the interventions in the post–World War II period. For example, the United States has intervened successfully in the Dominican Republic (1965), Grenada (1983), and Panama (1989); the Soviet Union has interfered in Hungary (1956) and in Czechoslovakia (1968). In each of these cases—with the exception of Panama—intervention was couched as a collective effort by regional organizations (such as the Organization of East Caribbean States and the Warsaw Pact) to lend the actions some legal legitimacy.[4] Interventions by strong countries into weaker ones are not always successful, as the United States learned in Vietnam and the Soviet Union learned in Afghanistan. Further, military interventions have not been limited to the superpowers. Several nations—such as the United Kingdom, France, Libya, Vietnam, Israel, and Syria—have actively intervened in the civil wars of other countries.

Total Versus Limited War

In this century, students of war have begun to distinguish between total and limited war. **Total wars** engulf many countries, the arena of conflict is global, and the goal is the unconditional surrender of the enemy. World War II was a total war. **Limited wars,** on the other hand, usually involve only a few countries, are confined to a much smaller geographical area, and have limited objectives. The Vietnam war was considered a limited war. The prevention of limited war has taken on more significance in light of the existence of nuclear weapons. The belief is that limited wars must be prevented from escalating into total ones in order to avoid a superpower confrontation and a possible and deadly nuclear exchange.

Conventional Versus Nuclear War

The emergence of nuclear weapons has given rise to a distinction between conventional and nuclear war. In **conventional wars** the participants' armies, navies, and air forces battle each other with nonnuclear weapons (which, nonetheless, may be highly sophisticated and quite destructive). **Nuclear war** is largely a theoretical concept, because one has never been fought. Many scholars contend that there could be no winner in a nuclear war, but others believe that limited nuclear wars could be fought successfully.

Guerrilla War

Yet another distinction can be drawn between conventional and guerrilla war. Guerrilla war is fought by irregular forces that use hit-and-run tactics and avoid direct military confrontation. Guerrilla forces typically attempt to blur the distinction between themselves and the local civilian population, thus complicating the enemy's efforts to search for and destroy them without causing substantial harm to innocent civilians. Guerrilla wars are most common in the recently independent countries of the Third World.

Problems with Defining and Quantifying Wars

Defining war is not an easy task, in part because the line between war and peace is a fuzzy one. Does war exist only when it has been legally declared? The Vietnam war was never formally declared, and yet hundreds of thousands of lives were lost in it. Clearly it was a war in a practical sense. On the other hand, some wars have formally been declared but have resulted in very few casualties and little change. For example, the Ecuadoran–Colombian War of 1863 lasted about a month and resulted in only one thousand battle deaths. Should events such as this be considered wars merely because they were declared? Similarly, international war can legally be fought only by states. Does this mean that wars fought by colonial authorities against indigenous peoples or between indigenous peoples in a colonial area are not wars?

Answers to these questions vary with different students of war. Quincy Wright in his monumental work *A Study of War* dealt with the definitional problem of war by adopting four different categories of warfare: (1) balance of power wars (between and among member states of the international community), (2) civil wars (wars within a state), (3) defensive wars (wars fought in defense of modern civilization and against alien cultures), and (4) imperial wars (wars fought to expand "modern civilization at the expense of an alien culture").[5] Wright also used several criteria for determining when an incident would be classified as a war. These criteria included the legal status of the participants (as states, colonies, indigenous tribes, etc.), the political consequences (significance) of the war, the legal status of the war, and the number of troops involved. Using these criteria, Wright identified 278 wars between 1480 and 1940.[6]

In another widely recognized study, Lewis Frye Richardson rejects all subjective judgments about the legal status of war—such as whether the participants were members of the state system or what the political consequences of the war were—and focuses instead only on statistical measures of war, primarily the number of casualties generated.[7] A war, or as Richardson describes it, a "deadly quarrel," became worthy of study if it resulted in more than 317 battle deaths. The problem with Richardson's approach is twofold. First, the use of 317 deaths as the threshold for defining a quarrel as a war, though statistically derived, is arbitrary. Second, the reliance only on casualties to identify war fails to distinguish between different kinds of conflicts. Clearly a war involves loss of life, but not every conflict that involves loss of life is a war (for instance, a local massacre resulting from communal violence).

Perhaps the most ambitious ongoing study of war is the Correlates of War (COW) project, which got underway in 1963 at the University of Michigan. The purpose of the COW project is to attempt to describe quantitatively the nature and character of war, so that judgments can be made about the causes of war. Drawing on the earlier work of Wright and Richardson, this study distinguishes among three basic kinds of war: (1) interstate wars fought between existing states, (2) **imperial or colonial wars** fought between an existing state and some nonrecognized entity such as a tribal group, and (3) civil wars, which involve military conflict between the central government and at least one competing party.[8]

International wars (interstate, imperial, or colonial wars) are considered wars only if 1,000 battle deaths were sustained by the forces of the existing states. This definition combines one of Wright's criteria (status of the participants) with the only significant criterion used by Richardson (battle deaths). Using this standard, 118 international wars were identified during the period from 1816 to 1980.[9] (During the same time span, 106 civil wars were identified.) Having established this criterion, the COW project goes on to study the magnitude of wars (using the number of nation-months spent at war), the severity of the wars (using the number of battle-connected deaths), and the intensity of the wars (using fatalities as a percentage of the population and armed forces of the participating states). [10]

The COW project staff seem to have found a useful working definition of international war, which takes into account both battle-related deaths and involvement of at least one recognized state. However, by applying these standards, over 200 conflicts were rejected as having been wars. The experts clearly differ on the basic question of how many wars there have been, because they differ on what standards should be used to define war.

Theories on the Causes of War

Throughout the ages, philosophers and politicians alike have speculated about the causes of war. In this chapter we will focus on ten theories of the causes of war and attempt to sort out the persuasive ones. As Kenneth Waltz argued in his classic work *Man, the State and War,* the causes of war can broadly be conceptualized as falling into three categories: (1) those that emphasize the role of human nature, (2) those that emphasize the nature and organization of the state, and (3) those that emphasize the nature and organization (or lack thereof) of the international system.[11] This threefold distinction is a useful departure point in discussing the various theories of conflict.

War and Human Nature

Many people believe war is rooted in the very nature of human beings. Indeed, wars appear to have been around for a long time. The world itself has changed; new forms of political organizations have evolved; and the structure of the international system has varied over time. The only constants, it would seem, have been wars and the people who fight them. Using history as their guide, many scholars have concluded that the primary cause of conflict lies in the nature of the human animal. Thomas Hobbes argued that human beings are by nature aggressive.[12] Others argue that human beings are sinful and weak (for example, prone to greed or revenge).[13] In this section we will consider two prevalent theories about human nature and its connection to war: instinctive aggression theories and war/peace cycles.

Instinctive aggression theories Are human beings, like other animals, naturally aggressive? Individual violence and its social manifestations, such as riots or wars, are seen as evidence of this natural aggressiveness. But is violence something that is innate (hereditary) or is it learned (a product of socialization)? Biological studies of the animal world suggest that aggression serves useful purposes within and between species. Aggressive behavior is important in establishing territorial rights and mating privileges within species. Aggression between species is critical for the survival of certain species. Carnivores, for instance, will attack and kill animals of different species for their food but will avoid killing each other. The survival of the species depends on this kind of behavior. Ironically, *Homo sapiens* is one of the few species that so readily kill their own kind. Biologist Konrad Lorenz has argued that most species that are physically capable of killing easily also develop certain inhibiting mechanisms that prevent them from killing members of their own species when they show submissive behavior. Wolves, for instance, may fight over territory or a mate, but when the weaker bares its neck to the stronger, the fight is over. Instinct tells the stronger animal not to go for the jugular but to allow the weaker animal to scurry away. Unlike wolves that have sharp teeth—a potentially dangerous natural weapon—to use against their fellow wolves, human beings are not born with a dangerous natural physical capacity. Lorenz speculates that this may be why *Homo sapiens* have not developed the same inhibiting mechanisms that dangerous predators possess. Instead, people have relied on their oversized brains to develop all kinds of ingenious tools—weapons—with which to kill each other.[14]

Other students of human aggression believe that there is no innate human predisposition to war or violence. They believe that violence and war are a product of human socialization. Anthropologists, for instance, have studied many isolated communities where violence and crime are largely nonexistent.[15] For example, there is no war among Eskimos. Indeed, Eskimos have numerous words for snow (something that is obviously prevalent in their environment), but there is no word for war in their vocabulary. Could it be, however, that the environment is merely an intervening factor? Could it be that there is a latent aggressive drive that the environment suppresses or enlivens? Placed in another environment, might otherwise peaceful communities become warlike? In other words, it could be that both biological and environmental factors contribute to the aggressiveness of the human species. To the extent that this is true, it offers some hope. For if war is even partly a learned behavior, then there is the possibility that it can be unlearned too.

Indeed, a rather considerable body of literature and argument holds that war is the product of cultural misunderstandings. Ignorance is seen as one of the prime causes of war. This argument suggests that "to know them is to love them." The logic, for instance, behind the creation of the UN Educational, Scientific and Cultural Organization (UNESCO) was that through educational and cultural exchanges, people would gain a knowledge, respect, and perhaps even an affection for other people and cultures. The preamble to the UNESCO constitution states that "ignorance of each other's ways and lives has been a common cause, throughout the history of mankind, of that suspicion and mistrust between peoples... which...have all too often broken into wars." The chances of war in a world of international understanding should be much less likely. Several arguments are posed against this thesis, however. Knowing and loving do not always go hand in hand. Indeed, as Aesop observed, "familiarity often breeds contempt." A high percentage of homicides (especially crimes of passion) involve family members or friends. Finally, even in a world of understanding, there are interests, quarrels, and jealousies. Greater knowledge of others, under these circumstances, may just as well lead to war as to peace. Had the leaders of Europe truly understood Hitler's intentions, instead of appeasing him by allowing the annexation of the Sudetenland in 1938, they might have opposed him with force much earlier.

War/peace cycles   One of the problems with the notion that human nature causes war is that peace is also part of our experience as a species. If human nature causes war, then it must cause peace too. And if it causes both war and peace, then is it of any predictive value? In a way, by explaining everything it explains nothing. Something else must be triggering the war instinct or the peace instinct. Some students of conflict are convinced that war and peace follow predictable cycles.[16] If there are cycles of war and peace—a point that is not at all certain and that is still hotly debated—what could be causing them? One assertion is that in the immediate aftermath of war, people are exhausted and disillusioned by the killing and destruction. They crave a period of peace, stability, and prosperity. The visions of the glory of war have been rudely replaced by the reality of its horrors. Should an occasion for yet another war occur at this time, a war-weary country is unlikely to rush headlong into battle, rather it looks for ways to resolve the problem peacefully. But after a considerable time of peace, it is theorized, as new generations emerge who have not experienced the horror of war, the martial spirit once again emerges. Should an occasion for war occur after a prolonged but growingly restless period of peace, the likelihood of resorting to war increases. The cannons thunder again, teaching yet another generation of leaders and soldiers the hard realities of war, and the cycle repeats itself.

Several questions pose difficulties for the analyst of war/peace cycles in history. Do these cycles exist in the individual experience of nations? Or are they found only in the overall incidence of war in the international system? If there are cycles, what is the length of the periods of peace and war? According to one study, there is no overwhelming support of the thesis that war/peace cycles can be found in nations' individual experiences.[17] On the other hand, authors of several studies suggest that cyclical patterns in the incidence of war do occur in the experience of the entire international system, but they disagree about the length of the cycles.[18]

War and the Nature and Organization of the State

Many students of international relations do not believe that war can be attributed to human nature. Instead they find the cause of war in the political and economic organization of the state; that is, countries with certain kinds of economic or political structures are more aggressive and warlike. Marxists, for instance, have argued that capitalist states are inherently aggressive and that in the search for raw materials and markets they inevitably become involved in imperial wars. Other scholars hold that authoritarian governments (including

Marxist ones) are likely to be more aggressive than democratic governments.[19] Still others point out that the idea of nationalism itself is the most important cause of war and that it transcends any particular economic or political system. In any case these theories share a common view that the nature of the state or nation is the key to understanding why war occurs. In this section we will consider four theories (and several variations), including nationalism, the rally-around-the-flag syndrome, economic causes of war, and the theory of relative deprivation.

Nationalism and its variants   Ultimately, wars are fought not between individuals but between governments that presumably represent the interests of their nations. At the most elemental level we can observe that wars certainly preexisted the rise of modern nationalism. However, the growth of nationalism in the nineteenth and twentieth centuries has been accompanied by conflicts of increasing intensity and magnitude. Moreover, many of this century's civil and international wars have involved countries or groups of people asserting their rights of self-determination against an existing government. Clearly all war is not the direct result of nationalist fervor, but nationalism does appear to be a factor in a large number of contemporary conflicts.

In trying to understand the mechanics of how nationalism causes war, it is useful to draw a distinction between expansionistic nationalism and expressionistic nationalism. **Expansionistic nationalism** is exhibited by countries that seek to expand their territorial control and dominate other countries economically or politically. **Expressionistic nationalism,** on the other hand, is exhibited by groups of people seeking self-determination and independence from the political control of existing nations.

Let us deal first with various kinds of expansionistic nationalism. A particularly virulent form was Nazism before and during World War II. According to the Nazi view, Germans of the Aryan race were superior to all others, thus Germany had a right to expand its territory at the expense of other nations. As a great people, Germans needed **Lebensraum,** literally, living space.[20] If gaining this space meant that Poles or Czechs would have to lose their land, then so be it. The struggle among nations was an evolutionary process in which only the strongest would survive. This exaggerated view of German nationalism was heightened by German resentment of the treatment they had received from the victorious allies at the end of World War I. The outbreak of World War II could be seen as a direct consequence of the expansionistic nationalism not only of Germany in Europe but also of Japan in the Pacific.

Another variant of expansionistic nationalism is **irredentism,** in which a country claims historical rights to a portion of another country's territory and ethnic similarity to the population of that territory. Bitterness can result between countries when the states making the irredentist claims believe that the territory was unjustly stolen from them or lost to them by past and uncontrollable circumstances. Obviously, such claims can be a source of conflict, particularly if the leaders of the country whose territory has been lost wish to further their own political fortunes by inciting popular resentment against the neighboring country. Recently, an irredentist war took place between Somalia and Ethiopia in 1977–1978. In this case Somalia argued that the Ogaden region of Ethiopia, which is populated predominately by Somali nomadic clans, had been unjustly stolen by Ethiopia in collusion with other colonial powers. Sensing that Ethiopia was already weakened by internal turmoil and disruption, the president of Somalia (who had been born in the Ogaden region) invaded Ethiopia and seized this long-lost territory. The attempt ultimately failed; Somali troops were driven from the Ogaden by Ethiopian troops with assistance from Cuba and the Soviet Union. Although the Somali invasion of Ethiopia was an example of expansionistic nationalism, certain aspects of expressionistic nationalism were also involved in that the Western Somali Liberation Front was engaged in a guerrilla war against Ethiopia in the hopes of gaining self-determination for the Ogadeni Somalis.

Expressionistic nationalism most often takes the form of **separatism,** which is the desire of a people to establish a government of their own and thereby to separate themselves (to secede) from the existing government. Often the claim for separatism is based on ethnic, linguistic, or religious differences between the population in the affected region and in the country as a whole. Separatist claims have been made by the Basques in Spain; the Tamils in Sri Lanka; Eritreans in Ethiopia; Kurds in Iraq, Iran, and Turkey; and southern Sudanese against the Arab north in Sudan. Separatist claims are a major cause of civil war, because most existing governments perceive these claims as a threat to their sovereignty and territorial integrity. Separatist movements can cause international conflict if the government and the separatist group call on foreign nations to come to their assistance. Numerous groups around the world still seek self-determination. However, most of the world now falls under the jurisdiction of existing states that are reluctant to give up territory without a fight. Thus, wherever separatist claims are advanced, they constitute a potential cause of civil conflict and even international war.

The rally-around-the-flag syndrome and scapegoat wars   Some people believe that leaders start foreign wars to unify their home front, assuming that people will put aside their domestic differences and quarrels and rally around the flag in the face of a common external threat. The objective of these conflicts is to rejuvenate common nationalist feelings (rally around the flag) or to blame internal problems on external factors (scapegoats). Throughout history leaders have started wars to help overcome domestic conflicts and turmoil. Bismarck started several tactical wars in the latter part of the nineteenth century to promote the unification of the German states. More recently, a beleaguered military government in Argentina precipitated the Falkland Islands war with the United Kingdom in hopes of drawing its population's attention away from a deteriorating domestic economy. Similarly, Ayatollah Khomeini rallied many disparate factions in Iran around a common external enemy, first the United States and then Iraq. Iraq started the conflict, but Khomeini took full advantage of it as a means of mobilizing his population. Indeed, the war with Iraq served several other purposes, including a desire to reclaim the disputed Shatt-al Arab area that had previously been invaded by Iraq and to promote the downfall of the Saddam Hussain regime in Baghdad. Clearly, the rally-around-the-flag strategy can backfire. Indeed, if the war can be won decisively, or the tactical objectives gained in a short time, it may have the intended effect of boosting the prestige of a previously embattled leader. However, if the war drags on, causing many casualties and draining the country's economy, this strategy could cause even greater domestic turmoil. For example, American public and congressional support, strong in the early years of the Vietnam war, waned substantially as the conflict wore on. Eventually the United States experienced significant protests and domestic turmoil that were a direct consequence of the prolongation of the war.

Popular as the rally-around-the-flag and scapegoat strategies are among policy makers, empirical studies have challenged their validity as explanations for war. These studies assume that if external conflicts are started in response to internal conflicts, then there should be a clear correlation between the frequencies of internal and external conflict in the international system. In fact, very little support for the notion that internal conflict causes external conflict can be found in the empirical literature.[21] However, the politicians who cite the existence of the rally-around-the-flag theory do not maintain that it explains every conflict. Indeed, they assert only that it can be used in certain strategic cases as an element of statecraft.

Economic causes of international war   Assertions that war is the result of nationalism suggest a strong political content in motivations to go to war. However, many scholars speculate that nations' economic motivations and the organization of their societies are more central causes of both international and civil wars. Lenin held, for instance, that capitalist countries inevitably conflict with each other as they attempt to expand their economic influence over other countries. This occurred in part, he argued, because capitalist countries keep their working classes impoverished. Impoverished workers, in turn, are unable to purchase the surplus goods they produce, which forces the capitalist elite to find foreign markets as outlets to absorb surplus production. Moreover, if capitalists are not fighting over markets, they are fighting over access to the vital natural resources and cheap labor that they intend to obtain from the underdeveloped countries of the world.[22] In Lenin's view, international wars are essentially imperial wars caused by the conflicting economic interests of capitalist elite in different countries. Therefore, modern war will disappear when capitalism is eliminated. Unfortunately, the working class is duped in the meantime into doing the actual fighting and dying in the vain and illusory pursuit of something called the *national interest,* which in the Marxist view, is the interest of a few rich people trying to get richer.

The Marxists are not alone in blaming wars on small groups of people who stand to benefit, regardless of whether their country wins. Theories that blame any small or particular group of people for war are known as **devil theories.** Some people believe, for instance, that World War I was caused by the arms merchants who manipulated governments into fighting to create a market for their weapons. It may well be that certain influential businesses benefit from war, but many more businesses are actually harmed by war. War, after all, is a very destructive process. Trade, commerce, and financial relations are interrupted. Property is destroyed. Resources are diverted from production of hardware and machinery, which can be used to generate further economic wealth, to production of weapons, which have no long-term positive economic impact. In many cases heavy government military spending and shortages of domestic products result in inflation. None of this is particularly good for business in general. In fact, it is downright bad for most business, including many of the largest and most powerful.

Conventional wisdom seems at odds with this interpretation, however. Indeed, it is quite clear that the American economy did not recover from the Great Depression until World War II began. Only then did unemployment decline significantly (if artificially). While this is no doubt true, one should not infer that war is always and in every respect good for the economy. Indeed, in Europe, where World War II was actually fought, the economic consequences were devastating. European economies took nearly a decade to recover from the destruction. Moreover, while the American economy certainly benefited from World War II, neither the U.S. government nor American businesspeople can reasonably be held responsible for its outbreak.

Although war may in fact have very negative effects on economies, if a nation's leaders or influential economic elites *expect* to gain from war, they may be inclined to seek one, even though the actual outcome may prove disastrous to the nation as a whole. Devil theories base their assumptions on the *expectation* of gain, regardless of whether particular elite groups actually benefit from war.

While some scholars argue that nations resort to war to stimulate sagging economies, others maintain that the most likely time for war is during upsurges in economic growth and industrial productivity. This view holds that economic deterioration is only exacerbated by recourse to war. However, periods of growing prosperity will improve a country's ability to wage war. Some scholars have argued that in an upswing in the business cycle (the boom and bust periods of economic activity), governments are more likely to go to war, either because they are in a better position to do so, or because they fear the coming of the inevitable economic downturn.[23] However, a recent study based on an examination of business cycles in the United States, Great Britain, France, and Germany has found little evidence to support the thesis that the business cycle is in any systematic or regular way associated with the outbreak of war.[24] Others have argued that the changes in the business cycle are relevant but not isolated from other factors such as power relationships, alliances, and willingness to bargain for advantages rather than fight.[25] Economic growth and industrial might are clearly fundamental aspects of a country's power and its war-fighting capability. Although many scholars are fascinated by the role of economic trends on war, the effect of war on economic trends should not be ignored.[26] The effects of economic factors on the outbreak of war obviously are complicated and probably interrelated. It is not surprising, then, that the evidence on economics as a cause of war is mixed, and that definitive conclusions still elude students of international relations.

One of the theories cited as a cause of bellicose behavior is the military-industrial complex.[27] This quasieconomic theory suggests that military leaders, industrial tycoons, and politicians with a political stake in promoting military spending for their districts combine to form a very powerful predisposition to develop weapons systems. This leads to significant military spending, international mistrust, and instability, and eventually to the possibility of war. For many reasons that have been discussed, the military-industrial complex as an explanation for war suffers from a number of flaws. Clearly there are close relations, for instance, between the Pentagon and companies (contractors) that produce weapons. In many cases, retired generals act as consultants for high-technology companies seeking to win defense contracts. That military and industrial enterprises, whether in the United States or other countries (including the Soviet Union), develop very close working relationships is not in question. It is clear that military-industrial complexes exist. The question is how effective are they? Do they really cause wars? Indeed, higher military spending does not in itself cause war. One might even conceive of such spending as a substitute for war. Decisions to go to war rarely are determined solely by the private economic interests of industrialists in conspiracy with military leaders. They more commonly result from a mixture of motives of which the economic one may or may not be significant.

Relative deprivation If economics is a contributing cause of certain international wars, could it be a key factor in civil wars too? The theory of relative deprivation suggests that it is but only when factored through the perceptions of individuals. As people's expectations for economic advancement rise, they may be frustrated by their governments' inability to satisfy them. As the gap between economic expectations and fulfillment of them by the political system grows, so does the degree of frustration, which will likely manifest itself in violence, rebellion, and revolution. This theory does not hold merely that internal conflicts are most likely to occur in conditions of absolute poverty. Indeed, people may lack the physical energy to rise up against their government in such a situation. Rather this theory stresses that internal conflicts are most likely to occur during a period of economic advancement that either reverses or proceeds too slowly to match the peoples' rising aspirations for a better life. What may result in such circumstances is often called a "revolution of rising expectations."[28]

The fact that the vast majority of civil wars, rebellions, and revolutions occur today in the developing world lends a great deal of credence to the relative deprivation thesis. However, the question remains, do civil wars in developing areas result primarily from the governments' poor economic performance or are other factors such as the regimes' political weakness or ethnic dissension more critical? Indeed, lack of political and economic development may be crucially linked as mutual causes of Third World conflict. Moreover, political violence and civil wars may be aided and abetted by external interference. Developed countries are not bashful when it comes to intervening in the domestic affairs of weaker counterparts in the developing world. Indeed, external subversion of weak governments may be a key factor in the larger incidence of internal political violence in the developing states.

War and the Nature of the International System

Many reasonable explanations for the cause of war can be found in the nature of human beings or in the nature and organization of the state. However, we also need to consider the larger environment in which the state operates, in other words, the impact of the international system. As we have frequently noted in this book, the international arena is marked by weak and decentralized executive, legislative, and judicial institutions. The state is the primary and highest legal unit of the system. Is order possible in a world of more than 160 sovereign units that are answerable to no higher authority? Many students of international relations believe that wars occur because of the strong anarchical tendencies inherent in a system of sovereign states. If sovereignty could be superceded by strong international institutions, many scholars believe that war could be made a thing of the past. Until that time, wars are likely to result from the inadequacies of the international system. Because no effective central mechanism exists to control or prevent conflict, states still find it necessary to resort to self-help to protect their interests. The theories considered in this section stress the importance of the nature and organization of the international system as a fundamental cause of war. Let us begin with one of the most frequently cited causes of conflict.

Imbalances of power   One of the primary arguments of balance-of-power advocates is that aggressive countries can only be deterred from warring on their neighbors by opposing them with equal or superior strength. As we have seen in previous chapters, this can be done in two principal ways: national armament (the implications of which will be discussed shortly under the subject of arms races) and alliances. The prudent country will arm itself and also make powerful friends to prevent an aggressive neighboring state from dominating or attacking it. This theory posits that war is most likely when significant disparities exist between a weak nonaggressive state and a strong aggressive one. Such imbalances of power should be corrected if countries wish to deter war. Of course, an imbalance of power in favor of a nonaggressive state would not be as likely to result in war.

But is a rough balance of power a guarantee that war will not occur? Several factors suggest that it is not. Uncertainty in calculating the balance of power is heightened by the fact that power emanates not only from observable military strength, but also from economic and industrial capacity, technological sophistication, organizational efficiency, and strength of will. Because of this uncertainty, there is always the possibility that leaders of a country considering a war with its neighbor will underestimate their adversary's strength. Or the leaders may be well aware of the actual balance of power but still feel compelled for other personal, nationalistic, or domestic reasons to go to war. Others may hope to gain an advantage through surprise attack.

One noted student of international relations has argued that wars are in fact most likely to occur at a time of an approximate balance of power. Organski argues that when a country is experiencing a dramatic increase in military and economic power, the opportunities for war are likely to increase for two reasons. First, the rising state is likely to resent continued treatment as a second-rate power and be inclined to demonstrate its new-found strength by picking a fight. Second, existing major powers, fearing that they soon might be outpaced in strength, may choose to attack the upstart before it can truly gain the upper hand.[29] In other words, war may be a function not of imbalances of power as such, but rather of the uncertainty resulting from rapid changes in the distribution of power among nations. This concern did not begin with Organski. Indeed, writing two thousand years earlier in reference to the Peloponnesian Wars, Thucydides notes that it was "the growth of the Athenian power, which terrified the Lacedaemonians and forced them into war."[30] It seems that students of international relations have been preoccupied with concern for balance-of-power politics for centuries.

Even in our modern age, policy makers are preoccupied with balancing power. In the Middle East, the United States has judiciously provided weapons and military aid to Israel and a number of Arab states (chiefly Egypt and Saudi Arabia). Prior to the Camp David Peace Accords between Egypt and Israel, military assistance was used as a means of adjusting the military balance between the two countries. Leaders constantly talk about the need to maintain regional balances of power. In Central America, U.S. government assistance to the *contras* was justified as a way of countering Nicaraguan aggression against neighboring countries. Similarly, concern was voiced about how an Iranian victory over Iraq might affect the balance of power in the Persian Gulf region.

While one can point to many cases of bigger powers picking on smaller ones, the record of warfare suggests that roughly equal powers spend a lot of time fighting too. Attractive as the imbalance-of-power-leads-to-war argument may seem at first glance, closer scrutiny suggests neither that imbalances necessarily equate to war nor that balances of power are surefire means of avoiding war.

However, could different global power distributions (global alliance relationships) lead to higher frequencies of war? Recall for a moment our discussion in chapter 2 about bipolar and multipolar distributions of power in the international system. Could it be that one or the other of these systems is more stable or less conducive to the onset of war? Some experts have argued that a bipolar system, consisting of two rather large and rigid alliances, is more stable than a multipolar one with constantly shifting alliances.[31] This argument holds that war is less likely in a bipolar international system and more likely in a multipolar one. Others argue quite the opposite. The very rigidity of the bipolar structure and the tension it produced between blocs is believed to have promoted war. Multipolar systems allow for greater mobility in formation of alliances, the maintenance of balance-of-power equilibrium, and thus avoidance of war.[32] Which of these opposing views is correct? In an effort to sort out the impact of multipolar and bipolar international systems on war, one study suggests that neither kind of system is free of war. Rather, wars in bipolar systems tend to be less frequent, but to last considerably longer. Wars in multipolar systems are shorter but more frequent, involve more countries, and lead to more casualties.[33] A more recent study has concluded that neither power equilibrium nor power disparities between individual countries or coalitions of countries predicts a higher or lower likelihood of war.[34] Yet another study focusing on war among great powers finds that, throughout history, alliance formation among the great powers has contributed more to peace than to war.[35]

Can the incidence of the war be affected by other characteristics of the international system apart from global power distributions? For instance, could the lack of international coordination mechanisms contribute to the incidence of war? If this were so, an argument could be made that as the number of international organizations increases—especially those responsible for peacekeeping and dispute settlement—the incidence of war should decline. Empirical studies do not support this thesis. In fact, it appears as if the number of intergovernmental organizations (IGOs) and the degree of state participation in them has little discernible effect on the incidence of war or peace. On the contrary, it seems that war causes growth in the number of IGOs and state participation in IGOs. Apparently leaders create or join IGOs in spurts after very warlike periods, either in the hope of preventing future wars or as a demonstration of their commitment to peace.[36]

Arms races   Because states must rely largely on their own resources to protect their interests in a hostile world, the vast majority have developed military systems. As we have noted, many countries have acquired arms as a means of balancing power and protecting their national security from external threats. While it may be comforting for a country to possess a military arsenal, the fact that other countries also have arsenals is more disturbing because everyone else's weapons pose a potential threat. Thus, the inevitable conclusion is that a nation must bolster its military forces to meet these potential threats. As countries vie to increase their margins of security, arms races result. Some people fear that the likelihood of war increases when arms races spiral out of control. Clearly, a rather significant arms race occurred in Europe in the decade prior to World War I. Indeed, Lewis Frye Richardson suggested that if the European nations had done just a little more trading with one another, and less jostling for a lead in arms production, World War I might have been avoided.[37] Similarly, the armament of Somalia by the Soviet Union in the 1970s put it in a position to attack Ethiopia in 1977. Many other wars have been attributed in part to arms races that exacerbated international tensions.

Do arms races really cause a higher incidence of war? The evidence is mixed.[38] One study suggested that sometimes arms races may be a substitute for war.[39] For instance, one of the most expensive arms races ever is between the United States and the Soviet Union. Both countries have spent vast sums of money not only on conventional weapons systems, but also on nuclear missiles. After more than forty years, however, this superpower arms race still has not erupted into a direct confrontation or war. On the other hand, many limited *proxy wars* (wars between client states of the two superpowers) have taken place. Many regional conflicts have been complicated by the introduction of superpower military assistance.

Many experts point out that arms by themselves do not cause wars. Rather, arms are a symptom of underlying political differences among states. Arms, in this sense, are a consequence of existing tensions and conflicts between states. Arms races may serve to further aggravate these tensions, but they rarely account for them in the first place. The real problem with arms races lies in the fact that when the wars are fought, they run the risk of being far more destructive. Hence, many politicians recognize the need to observe some degree of restraint in the arms race, hoping to bolster stability and prevent escalations in tension that might set off an unwanted war.

War as a means of settling disputes   Because of the institutional weakness in the international system, states have often found it necessary to resort to various bilateral mechanisms to resolve disputes. Sometimes this has been accomplished peacefully through diplomatic channels. On other occasions, however, underlying political disputes have been so fundamental that peaceful resolution has not been possible. In such circumstances, war has frequently been the final method of dispute settlement. Indeed, one of the great students of war, Carl Von Clausewitz, argued that war was the "extension of diplomacy by other means."[40] War, in this view, is a tool of foreign policy that can and should be employed judiciously to advance the state's power and interests. Idealists may view war as a horrible aberration, but to the mind of the realpolitician it is but one instrument in the toolbox of statecraft. War may be necessary at some times and unavoidable at others. Of course, achievement of the state's interests through peaceful means is preferable. But the limited and rational use of war is viewed by the realpolitik school as a legitimate and sometimes necessary exercise.

In today's world, war is still used (although not always skillfully) as a means of resolving intransigent conflicts that defy solution through diplomatic means. Argentina, for example, after several years of unsuccessful talks with the United Kingdom, eventually used force in a vain attempt to retake the Falkland Islands. But the use of war to resolve conflicts is even more dangerous today than in the past.

The Role of Misperception as a Cause of War

One of the key causes of war cited in the literature of international relations is misperception.[41] We deal with it last because it operates at all of the levels we have just reviewed. Misperceptions are a key aspect of human nature. Individuals ultimately make decisions about whether to make war on others. Misperceptions are found (1) in the behavior of governments as they attempt to formulate and implement policies favorable to the national interest; (2) in the relationships between different cultures, races, and religions; and (3) in decision makers' judgments about the balance of power in the international system. Misperceptions arise out of the great potential for anarchy that exists in an international system dominated by around 160 different and often competing states.

In a penetrating and readable study John Stoessinger examines several cases of modern wars.[42] He concludes that misperception was a decisive precipitating factor in virtually every case he studied. Misperceptions were found in the way leaders perceived themselves, as well as in the way they perceived their adversaries' intentions, power, and capabilities.[43] Stoessinger observed that, on the eve of a war, most leaders believe that they will win a quick and decisive victory. Of course, this actually happens only rarely. Leaders often look down on their adversaries, believing them to be either inferior or less virtuous. Often the other countries are perceived incorrectly as a serious threat. When a leader is convinced that another country intends to attack, there is a strong temptation to strike preemptively. Stoessinger points out that when the leaders of two countries both believe that they are about to be attacked, war becomes a "virtual certainty."[44] Finally, Stoessinger underscores that misperception of an adversary's power is the primary cause of war. Typically, he holds, adversaries underestimate each other's strength and miscalculate the balance of power.

Robert Jervis has also pointed out many perceptual flaws in decision-making processes that may lead to miscalculations and to war.[45] First, many policy makers have rigid views of the world, with well-defined notions of who the "good guys" and "bad guys" are. This may make it easier to use force on the perceived "bad guys." Leaders who see the world in less black-and-white terms may be more reluctant to use force. Second, leaders may interpret information they receive in light of their preconceptions of the world. Information that does not fit these preconceptions is often ignored or rejected. Third, information coming from sources that are considered reliable may be trusted implicitly even if shown later to be completely inaccurate, whereas information from sources that have previously been less reliable may be ignored even though completely accurate. Fourth, leaders often perceive themselves as the immediate target of the actions of other nations, when in fact certain policies of other states may not be intended to affect that country at all. When the Soviet Union deploys intercontinental ballistic missiles in Siberia, it is highly likely that they are aimed at China, but American officials worry that they could be used against the United States and insist that they be included in negotiations on strategic weapons control and reductions. Finally, when leaders contemplate using force against an adversary they often misperceive how third parties will react. In the Ethiopian–Somali war of 1977–1978, for instance, the Somali government was quite certain that the United States, its allies, and the Arab world would approve of and perhaps even assist in its invasion of Ethiopian territory. The reasoning was based on the notion that the Western powers would not stand by and watch Ethiopia's Marxist, Soviet-backed government prevail. What the leadership in Somalia failed to understand was that it would be perceived as the aggressor by most states, even if they were sympathetic to Somalia's territorial claims to the Ogaden region. Although Somalia did receive some assistance, it was far less than expected.

One of the aggravating factors in misperceptions between countries is that when they most need to communicate with each other, they tend to cut off diplomatic ties. Psychologists point out how important it is for people to keep communication lines open to one another, especially in times of acute crisis and hostility. Yet one of the most frequent retaliations against a country that has committed an unfriendly or hostile act is to break diplomatic relations. Thus, while miscommunication may be a cause of conflict, lack of communication is even worse.

Stoessinger appears to be quite right in asserting that misperceptions are a key **precipitating cause** of conflict; that is, they trigger a conflict that is already ripe. Rarely are misperceptions the actual fundamental or underlying cause of conflict. Economic and political differences, religious hostilities, disputes over borders, and nationalistic demands are more fundamental causes of conflict. But misperceptions often push a latent conflict over the brink into outright war. If misperceptions are so critical in the actual outbreak of conflicts, what can be done to avoid them?

Avoiding misperceptions that might lead to war requires continuous effort. It presupposes that leaders are aware of some of the basic traps into which they can fall. It further presupposes that leaders desire to avoid misperception. Sometimes, however, leaders use propaganda to distort reality and encourage popular misunderstanding of an enemy. This action is not misperception, rather it is the willful manipulation of popular sentiment to specific ends. For those leaders who want to avoid misperception, there are several things that can be done. First, they can surround themselves with experts from many different backgrounds, and with different political viewpoints, so that full consideration can be given to complicated foreign policy crises that might lead to wars. By doing this, they can protect against simplistic conclusions based on erroneous information or unfounded assumptions about the intentions of other countries. Second, they can attempt to put themselves into the shoes of the other countries' leaders, which will give them a feel for their adversary's worries, problems, and fears. This strategy can also help predict how the leaders of another country might react to steps taken by the other side. Third, they can stay in constant communication with their adversary's leaders and attempt to clarify their own intentions, fears, and concerns. Fourth, they can pay close attention to history and attempt to draw accurate lessons about past mistakes and successes. This assumes that inappropriate past analogies are not mistakenly applied to different contemporary problems. Knowing history, then, is necessary but not sufficient for avoiding misperceptions. Leaders must master the art of correctly applying the lessons of the past to the present before they can be confident that they are avoiding misperception.[46] These four steps would go a long way toward preventing unnecessary war. But even this is no guarantee against the wiles of misperception, which come in many deceptive forms.

One final observation should be made here. Accurate perceptions may cause conflicts as much as inaccurate ones. We are not implying that all wars fought throughout history have been the result of accidents or misperceptions, or that somehow people have fatalistically and mistakenly trudged into the mire of war. War is not the work of fanatics and jingoists alone. It also occurs between countries who take up arms against each another with clear objectives and their eyes wide open.

War and International Relations: The Basic Issues

We have just reviewed a number of basic causes of war that have been asserted by prominent observers of international relations. None of these theories can claim to explain all causes of war, although some appear to explain a good deal more of it than others. This review suggests that single-cause theories are too ambitious. Most wars result from a combination of factors that evolve over time. Some of these factors create a general context that predisposes countries to war; others are more immediate factors that actually precipitate the war. In fact, the record suggests that one cause of war may be previous wars.[47] In other words, wars might be part of a longer feud between nations, with vengeance or resentment being significant motives. For instance, World War II cannot be understood without appreciating the outcome of World War I. Lingering German resentment of their treatment after World War I was a significant cause of the resurgence of German nationalism and the popularity of Nazism. Economic factors and the reluctance of other major powers to check German rearmament and the growth of German militarism also contributed to the outbreak of World War II.

Sorting out the various causes of wars has been one of the major preoccupations of students of international relations. Of necessity, this has required a somewhat backward-looking approach, exploring the pages of history for clues about why nations go to war. But will the future be anything like the past? Even if we could make definitive judgments about why wars occurred, could we be certain that these would apply to the future? Unfortunately, the science of international relations has yet to reach the stage of sophistication that would permit reliable prediction of the future. Indeed, debates over explanations of the causes of past wars continue. Thus as we look to the next decade and beyond for potential trends in the phenomenon of war among nations, we must recognize the tentativeness of the exercise.

As it has been for the past forty years, direct superpower confrontation must be avoided for the general health of the planet. Indeed, even a war between the major powers would seem to be a most dangerous exercise. Thus, it would seem that war can be fought safely only by the less significant powers. This trend is likely to continue in the decade to come as economic and political instabilities continue in the Third World nations.

This prediction of continuing small-power war and a decrease in major-power conflict is at least partially supported in Jack S. Levy's findings in the supplemental reading. He argues that the frequency of Great Power war has been on the decline throughout the last five centuries. He also finds that the magnitude, severity, and intensity of Great Power wars have increased dramatically. Under these circumstances, it is fortunate that Great Power wars have declined in number. Indeed, Levy suggests that the very large human and economic costs of Great Power wars may account for their decreased frequency.

Summary

War has always fascinated human beings. Some are awed by its glory, others disgusted by its effects, and still others frightened by its horrors. We have advanced significantly in our ability to wage war and to destroy our enemies. But the study of war itself is guided by different motives. Some scholars study war to be able to fight it better (Von Clausewitz, for example). Others seek to understand war so that it might be prevented (Singer and Small, for instance). Unfortunately, our knowledge about why war occurs is still largely speculative. Numerous empirical studies have helped clarify some aspects of the origins and incidence of war; however, their results are often mixed. Some studies have sparked lively and continuing debates, while others have raised more questions than they have answered.

Several arguments about why war occurs have been advanced in this chapter. Indeed, nearly every theory cited has a significant number of adherents. Breaking down the causes of war into three basic types—those stressing human nature, the nature and organization of the state, or the nature and organization of the international system—might leave the impression that the causes are to be found only in one of these areas. Many inquiries into the causes of war tend heavily to favor one of these principal sources of war. However, it would seem to be more fruitful to explore the linkages *among* the individual, national, and international levels of analysis. If we assume that there is no single cause of war, then it seems logical also to assume that war, the context in which it occurs, its timing, and its character are determined by a number of factors operating simultaneously at the individual, national and international levels.

A definitive understanding about the multiple causes of war is far in the future. Probably still much further off is the day when all the swords are beaten into plowshares and war fades into the shrouded past to be recorded only as a curious anachronism in the pages of history, never again to scourge our race.

Jack S. Levy

Historical Trends in Great Power War, 1495–1975

It is widely believed that the probability of a war between the superpowers is diminishing but that its potential destructiveness is increasing. Our argument is that this phenomenon, if it exists, is not simply a product of the nuclear age but also a manifestation of long-term historical trends in war that have been underway for many centuries. While the future is a matter of conjecture, the question of past historical trends is eminently suitable for rigorous and systematic empirical research. The aim of this study is to test the hypothesis that war between the Great Powers has been decreasing in frequency but increasing in seriousness over the past several centuries.

These "Great Power wars" are of enormous importance for international politics. They have generally been history's most destructive conflicts and have had the greatest impact on the stability of the international system. For the most part, the interaction of the Great Powers determines the structure and evolution of the system and serves as the basis for most of our theories of international politics. . . . This question of historical trends in Great Power war is more than one of simple historical curiosity, however, for the occurrence of another Great Power war might very well bring an end to contemporary civilization. The Great Power wars of the past provide a rich source of historical data and in many respects provide the best empirical referents for a hypothetical superpower war of the future. While theory provides the best grounds for predictions about the future, in the absence of theory an empirically confirmed explanation of historical

SOURCE: Excerpts reprinted from the *International Studies Quarterly,* Volume 26, No. 2, June 1982, with permission of the International Studies Association, Byrnes International Center, University of South Carolina, Columbia, SC 29208 USA. © 1982 International Studies Association.

trends may be quite useful, particularly if the factors contributing toward the trend show no signs of abating. . . .

The Modern Great Power System

A Great Power can be defined generally as a state which plays a major role in international politics with respect to security-related issues. Operational indicators of Great Power status include the following: possession of a high level of power capabilities, which provides for reasonable self-sufficiency in security matters and permits the conduct of offensive as well as defensive military operations; participation in international congresses and conferences; de facto identification as a Great Power by an international conference or organization; admission to a formal or informal organizaton of Powers; participation in Great Power guarantees, territorial compensation, or partitions; and, generally, treatment as a relative equal by other Great Powers (for example, protocol, alliances, negotiations, and so forth).

. . . [These] criteria . . . are applied to the historical literature and the resulting Great Power system is presented in table 1.

Great Power War: Conceptualization, Identification, and Measurement

A Great Power war is an armed conflict between the organized military forces of two or more Great Powers, operationally defined as involving at least one thousand battle deaths, or an annual average of one thousand, among the

Table 1
The modern Great Power system

France	1495–1975
England/Great Britain	1495–1975
Austrian Hapsburgs/	1495–1519;
Austria-Hungary	1556–1918
Spain	1495–1519; 1556–1808
Ottoman Empire	1495–1699
United Hapsburgs	1519–1556
Netherlands	1609–1713
Sweden	1617–1721
Russia/Soviet Union	1721–1975
Prussia/Germany/	
West Germany	1740–1975
Italy	1861–1943
United States	1898–1975
Japan	1905–1945
China	1949–1975

Powers.... Civil, imperial, and colonial wars do not satisfy the definition and are excluded.... The resulting compilation of Great Power wars is given in table 2.

In order to test the hypothesis that Great Power wars have become less frequent but more serious, we analyze war in terms of several key dimensions in addition to *frequency*. The *duration* of war refers to its total elapsed time (measured in years). The *extent* of war refers to the number of participating Great Powers. The *magnitude* of war, reflecting a joint spatial and temporal dimension and combining the extent and duration indicators, is the total nation-years of war for all participating Powers. The human destructiveness or *severity* of war is measured by the number of battle-connected deaths. Whereas the severity of war

refers to loss of life in absolute terms, the *intensity* of war reflects the human destructiveness in relative terms and is the ratio of battle deaths to European population. The *concentration* of war in space and time is another important dimension and is the ratio of battle deaths to nation-years of war. The sixty-four Great Powers wars since 1495 are measured along all these dimensions....

Frequency of Great Power War

Our first question is whether Great Power wars are becoming more or less frequent over time. There is little doubt about the answer, as seen from figure 1, which plots the frequency

Table 2
Great Power wars

War	Dates[a]	War	Dates[a]
War of the League of Venice	1495–1497	Thirty Years War—	
Neapolitan War	1502–1504	Swedish-French Period	1635–1648
War of the Holy League	1511–1514	Franco-Spanish War	1648–1659
Austro-Turkish War	1512–1519	Anglo-Dutch Naval War	1652–1654
Second Milanese War	1515–1515	Great Northern War	1654–1660
First War of Charles V	1521–1526	English-Spanish War	1656–1659
Ottoman War	1521–1531	Ottoman War	1657–1664 (1661)
Second War of Charles V	1526–1529	Anglo-Dutch Naval War	1665–1667
Ottoman War	1532–1535	Revolutionary War	1667–1668
Third War of Charles V	1536–1538	Dutch War of Louis XIV	1672–1678
Ottoman War	1537–1547	Ottoman War	1682–1699
Fourth War of Charles V	1542–1544	Franco-Spanish War	1683–1684
Siege of Boulogne	1544–1546	War of the League of Augsburg	1688–1697
Arundel's Rebellion	1549–1550	Second Northern War	1700–1721 (1715)
Ottoman War	1551–1556	War of the Spanish Succession	1701–1713
Fifth War of Charles V	1552–1556	War of the Quadruple Alliance	1718–1720
Austro-Turkish War	1565–1562	British-Spanish War	1726–1729
Franco-Spanish War	1556–1559	War of the Polish Succession	1733–1738
Scottish War	1559–1560 (1560)	War of the Austrian Succession	1739–1748
Spanish-Turkish War	1559–1564	Seven Years War	1755–1763
First Huguenot War	1562–1564	War of the Bavarian Succession	1778–1779
Austro-Turkish War	1565–1568	War of the American Revolution	1778–1784
Spanish-Turkish War	1569–1580	French Revolutionary Wars	1792–1802
Austro-Turkish War	1576–1583	Napoleonic Wars	1803–1815
War of the Armada	1585–1604	Crimean War	1854–1856
War of the Three Henries	1589–1598	War of Italian Unification	1859–1859
Austro-Turkish War	1593–1606	Austro-Prussian War	1866–1866
Spanish-Turkish War	1610–1614	Franco-Prussian War	1870–1871
Spanish-Turkish War	1618–1619	Russo-Japanese War	1905–1905
Thirty Years War—		World War I	1914–1918
Bohemian Period	1618–1625 (1621)	Russian Civil War	1918–1921
Thirty Years War—Danish Period	1625–1630	World War II	1939–1945
Thirty Years War—Swedish Period	1630–1635	Korean War	1950–1953

[a] For wars which do not begin as Great Power wars, the date of intervention of the second Power is given in parentheses.

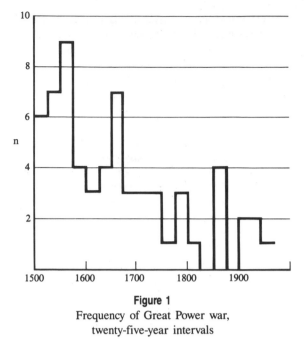

Figure 1
Frequency of Great Power war,
twenty-five-year intervals

Table 3
Average frequency of great power war per decade
for each century

Century	Average Frequency per Decade
16th	2.6
17th	1.7
18th	1.0
19th	0.50
20th	0.66

of Great Power war per quarter-century against time, and from table 3, which computes the average frequency of war per decade for each century. There has been a continuous decline in the number of Great Power wars in each century from the sixteenth to the nineteenth, with a very slight increase in the twentieth century. Over 75 percent of the Great Power wars occur in the first half of the 480-year system (prior to 1735), while less the 25 percent occur in the last 240 years.... The average frequency of Great Power war in the twentieth century is only a fourth of its average frequency in the sixteenth century....

The Characteristics of Great Power War

Having established that Great Power war has been declining in frequency, let us now ask our second question: Given that a Great Power war occurs, is it getting more or less serious in terms of the dimensions of duration, extent, magnitude, severity, intensity, and concentration?... Over the last five centuries Great Power wars have been increasingly serious in every respect but duration. While the *duration* of Great Power wars has remained basically constant since the late fifteenth century, the *extent* of Great Power wars has increased sharply.... Prior to the Thirty

Years War, no conflict involved more than four Powers and most wars involved two Powers; from the early seventeenth century to the early nineteenth century, the number of warring Powers varied from one to six, the median being four; no war in the nineteenth century involved more than three Powers, but the two World Wars in the twentieth century involved seven and eight Powers, respectively....

The *magnitude* of Great Power war has also been increasing.... Great Power wars have also become increasingly destructive in terms of all of the fatality-based indicators....

The *severity* of Great Power war has been increasing at an average rate of 62 percent each year. At this rate, the average number of battle deaths in a Great Power war has doubled every 110 years or so. The *intensity* of war has increased nearly as rapidly (.46 percent per year), doubling every 150 years. The most pronounced trend in Great Power war...is its increasing *concentration* over time. The number of battle deaths has increased at a rate of .67 percent per year, doubling every 100 years.... The data...clearly reveal that these upward trends are not simply the product of the enormous destructiveness of two world wars, but would hold true without them.

Interpretation of the Historical Trends

The preceding data analysis leaves little doubt regarding historical changes in wars between the Great Powers over the last five hundred years. Great Power wars have been rapidly diminishing in frequency but increasing in extent, severity, intensity, concentration, and (to a certain degree) magnitude. That is, Great Power wars have involved an increasing number of belligerent Powers, and nation-years of war, and have become increasingly violent in terms of absolute and per capita battle deaths and their relative number per nation-year of war. Of the important dimensions of Great Power war defined here, only its frequency has diminished and only its duration has been relatively constant over time. The hypothesis that Great Power wars have become less frequent but more serious or destructive is confirmed beyond any reasonable doubt.

The description of historical trends is easier than their explanation, however. Before it could be fully accepted, such an explanation would itself have to be tested against the historical evidence. This would require the operationalization and measurement of the explanatory variables (and plausible control variables as well) in as systematic a manner as we have dealt with the dependent variable. This is an enormous task lying far beyond the scope of this study. Having rigorously and systematically described longitudinal trends in Great Power wars, we can here only hypothesize about their theoretical explanations, by identifying the important variables and suggesting plausible theoretical linkages.

Of all the trends, perhaps most puzzling is the relatively unchanging duration of Great Power war. We might have expected that improvements in communications and logistics would have increased the speed of military operations on the battlefield and that innovations in military technology and the increasing destructiveness of military conflict would have increased the costs of war; both would presumably force an earlier termination of the hostilities. Obviously, there are other variables which counteract this tendency. While the costs of war have become much greater, the gradual industrialization of basically agricultural societies has increased their economic capacity to sustain a war and accept the costs. We might also hypothesize that, in spite of the enormous changes in military technology, the defense has managed to keep up with the offense, so that it takes equally long to obtain a decisive advantage on the battlefield. Finally, the increasing organizational momentum and incrementalism generated by a larger and more firmly entrenched bureaucracy, and the increasing political insecurity of elite (deriving from the decline of dynastic legitimacy) in conjunction with increasing nationalist pressures, both make it ever more difficult to withdraw from a costly but inconclusive war.

Equally interesting is the fact that an ever-increasing number (and proportion) of Great Powers have been participating in these wars. We might hypothesize that this derives in part from the increasing interdependence of the modern Great Power security system. As the Great Powers evolved from dynastic to nation-states, their "national interests," as well as their capabilities to project power in defense of their interests, tended to expand and their commercial relationships also became closer. The Great Powers came increasingly to perceive their own strategic and economic interests as dependent on power relationships in the system as a whole, and were increasingly likely to intervene in external wars to maintain a "balance of power" or their own influence and prestige. Hence the extent (and also the magnitude) of Great Power war has increased over time.

Let us now consider the increasing destructiveness of war in terms of severity, intensity, and concentration. The most obvious explanation, of course, is *technological*: the major changes not only in the destructive power of weapons, but also in their range, accuracy, volume of fire, mobility, and penetrability, and the speed and efficiency of military transport and communications systems. In addition, there has been an increasing economic capacity to produce a larger quantity of weapons and support systems. Much of the increased capacity for violence over the past centuries can be traced to the changes in production and transport generated by the Industrial Revolution; the mechanization of war at the beginning of the twentieth century; the development of air-power a few decades later; and (in terms of potential destruction for the future) the development of nuclear weapons and global delivery systems by the second half of this century.

Technological innovation alone, however, cannot fully explain the increasing destructiveness of Great Power wars in the last five centuries. There are several interrelated political, socioeconomic, and cultural factors contributing to the gradual emergence of total war. Let us briefly consider these in approximate chronological sequence. First was the increasing *rationalizaton* of military power under the state, beginning in the late fifteenth century and intensifying after the legal codification of the existing sovereign state system at Westphalia. The wars for the personal honor, vengeance, and enrichment of kings and nobles in the Middle Ages (which may have contributed to their frequent but limited nature) were increasingly replaced by the "rational" use of force as an efficient instrument of policy for the achievement of political objectives, first by dynastic/territorial political systems and ultimately by nation-states. The seriousness of the wars grew proportionally with the expansion of these political objectives, from personal gain, to the territorial aggrandizement of the state, to the national ambitions of an entire people.

Reinforcing this was the increasing *centralization* of political power within the state. This began with the gradual subordination of feudal interests to centralized state authority in the early sixteenth century, and intensified in the late seventeenth century with the development of an administrative and financial system capable of supporting a military establishment and providing the logistical basis for an expanded military effort.

Contributing further to the power of states and their ability to make war was the *commercialization* of war beginning in the early seventeenth century. There was an increasingly symbiotic relationship between the state and the commercial classes. Commerce generated the wealth necessary to sustain war and war in turn became a means of expanding commerce. In the mercantilist conception, commerce was a continuation of war (with an admixture of other means) and war was a continuation of commerce. The merchants' enthusiasm for war diminished somewhat as this mercantilist system was replaced by free trade in the late eighteenth century, but the link was hardly broken and subsequent economic progress contributed further to the state's capacity for war.

This period also marked the emerging *popularization* of war: the rise of nationalism and popular ideology, the institution of conscripted manpower, and the creation of the "nation in arms." Each of these phenomena contributed to the enhancement of the military power of the state.

The state's ability to utilize these expanding resources was furthered by the *professionalization* of military power in the late nineteenth century. This refers to the development of a peacetime military establishment directed by a new professional military elite that was independent of the aristocracy, headed by a general staff system, run according to new principles of scientific management, and supported by a system of military academies. These developments not only increased the efficiency of the conduct of war; they also enhanced the legitimacy of the military profession and contributed to the trends toward militarism, the acceptance of the values of the military subculture as the dominant values of society. At the same time, the earlier moral and cultural restraints on war associated with the Christian and Humanist traditions were gradually eroded by the materialism and individualism of industrial society.

These trends culminated in World War II with the *scientific revolution* in war: the harnessing, for the first time, of the entire scientific, engineering, and technological capacities of the nation directly for the conduct of the war. This mobilization of the intellectual as well as material and social resources of the nation for the purposes of enhancing military power continues now in peacetime. These political, social, and cultural developments, in conjunction with technological innovation, have been largely responsible for the increasing destructiveness of war.

Let us consider some plausible explanations for the declining frequency of Great Power war. It can generally be argued that the potential benefits of Great Power war have not kept up with their rising human and economic costs. Warfare has involved enormous increases in casualties and human suffering, the physical destruction of industrial infrastructure, and opportunity costs for society deriving from increasing costs of weapons systems, manpower, and logistics. The greater tendency toward external intervention in Great Power war (described above) further raises the costs or reduces the potential benefits from war, whether by adding the military burden of an additional enemy or by necessitating the sharing of the gains with an ally. The declining legitimacy of Great Power war has increased its diplomatic and domestic political costs. Finally, the changing bases of national power and the declining value of territorial conquest have reduced the potential benefits of Great Power war, as has the increasing congruence between state and ethnic boundaries (at least for the Great Powers). These increasing costs of Great Power war relative to its perceived benefits have reduced its utility as a rational instrument of state policy and largely account for its declining frequency. . . .

Study Questions

1. Discuss the difference between (a) international and civil war; (b) total and limited war; (c) conventional and nuclear war.
2. Define *intervention*. How can interventions cause wars? Cite some examples.
3. How does guerrilla war differ from conventional war?
4. When does a war become a war? Discuss several different approaches that have been used to count wars.
5. How does the COW project define war?
6. Kenneth Waltz defines three basic conceptions or images of war. What are they?
7. Do you believe that war is a learned or an inborn behavior trait? Discuss the theories of instinctive aggression and the results of anthropological research in this connection.
8. What is a war/peace cycle? Do you think there is such a thing?

9. Discuss the distinction between expansionistic and expressionistic nationalism. What are some examples of each?

10. What is the difference between a separatist and an irredentist conflict? Provide examples.

11. Do you think nationalism is a basic cause of international or civil wars, or both? Explain.

12. Do you think a major cause of international war is the leaders' desires to overcome internal dissension by creating external conflicts and enemies? Discuss.

13. What is a *devil theory* of war?

14. According to the Marxist interpretation, what are the mechanics of modern-day war? Do you agree with this assessment? Why or why not?

15. Do you think war is generally good or bad for capitalist economies?

16. Define the term *military-industrial complex*. In your opinion, does this phenomenon cause war?

17. Discuss the concept of *relative deprivation*. Does it explain the existence of international or civil war?

18. Imbalances of power cause war. Do you agree or disagree with this statement? Discuss it.

19. How does the global distribution of power (bipolarity and multipolarity) affect the incidence and severity of war in the international system?

20. Discuss the connection between arms races and war.

21. War is the continuation of politics by other means. What is meant by this statement? Is war an effective means of settling disputes?

22. What are some common misperceptions that can lead decision makers into war?

23. What steps can be taken to avoid these misperceptions?

24. Discuss the difference between fundamental and precipitating causes of war. In which category does misperception best fit?

25. Which of the theories discussed in this chapter do you find to be the most persuasive?

26. In your opinion what shape will wars of the future take?

27. Why do you think the number of Great Power wars has declined over the last several centuries?

28. Jack S. Levy examines Great Power wars along several dimensions, including frequency, duration, extent, magnitude, severity, intensity, and concentration. What do these dimensions mean? How has Great Power war changed along these dimensions?

29. Apart from technological development, what factors explain the increased destructiveness of Great Power war (as measured by indicators of severity, intensity, and concentration)?

Key Terms

civil war
conventional war
devil theories
expansionistic nationalism
expressionistic nationalism
imperial or colonial war
international or interstate war
intervention

irredentism
Lebensraum
limited war
nuclear war
precipitating causes
separatism
total war

Notes

1. J. David Singer and Melvin Small, *Resort to Arms: International and Civil Wars, 1816–1980* (Newbury Park, Calif: Sage, 1982), especially at pp. 31–60 and 203–220 for distinctions between international and civil wars.

2. Ibid., p. 234. Singer and Small argue that 20 percent of civil wars become internationalized by intervention of major powers.

3. Gerhard Von Glahn, *Law Among Nations* (New York: MacMillan, 1986), pp. 155–157.

4. For a discussion of the legal implications of the U.S. intervention into Grenada, see Maurice Waters, "The Invasion of Grenada, 1983 and the Collapse of Legal Norms," *Journal of Peace Research* 23, no. 3 (1986): 229–246.

5. Quincy Wright, *A Study of War* (Chicago: University of Chicago Press, 1942, rev. ed. 1965), p. 641.

6. Ibid., pp. 636–646.

7. Lewis Frye Richardson, *Statistics of Deadly Quarrels* (Pittsburgh: Boxwood Press, 1960).

8. Singer and Small, *Resort to Arms,* pp. 54–58.

9. Ibid., p. 118.

10. Ibid., pp. 62–77.

11. Kenneth Waltz, *Man, the State and War: A Theoretical Analysis* (New York: Columbia University Press, 1959).

12. Thomas Hobbes, *Leviathan,* ed. C. B. McPherson (Baltimore: Penguin Books, 1974), pp. 183–188.

13. Rheinhold Neibuhr, *Christianity and Power Politics* (New York: Scribner's, 1940); idem, *Beyond Tragedy* (New York: Scribner's, 1938); Hans Morgenthau, *Scientific Man vs. Power Politics* (Chicago: University of Chicago Press, 1946).

14. Konrad Lorenz, *On Aggression* (New York: Harcourt Brace Jovanovich, 1966), pp. 126–132, 232–235.

15. See, for instance, Margaret Meade, "Warfare Is Only an Invention—Not a Biological Necessity," *Asia* (August 1940), especially at pp. 402–405.

16. Some of the earliest inquiries into this subject found little evidence for a war/peace cycle. See Pitirim Sorokin, *Fluctuations of Social Relationships, War and Revolution,* vol. 3 (New York: Bedminster, 1962), p. 357; Richardson, *Statistics of Deadly Quarrels,* pp. 137–141.

17. Singer and Small, *Resort to Arms,* pp. 143–157, especially at pp. 156–157.

18. Frank Denton and Warren Phillips, "Some Patterns in the History of Violence," *Journal of Conflict Resolution* 1, no. 2 (June 1968): 182–195. In this study a 30-year cycle is identified. A longer cycle of 177 years is identified by Edward Dewey, *The 177–Year Cycle in War, 600 B.C.–A.D. 1957* (Pittsburgh: Foundation for the Study of Cycles, 1964). See also Singer and Small, *Resort to Arms,* p. 156.

19. A number of studies have explored the proposition that democratic societies are inherently more peaceful than authoritarian ones. Perhaps the strongest proponent of this view is R. J. Rummel. See R. J. Rummel, "Libertarianism and International Violence," *Journal of Conflict Resolution* 27, no. 1 (March 1983): 27–71; idem., "Libertarian Propositions on Violence Within and Between Nations: A Test Against Published Research Results," *Journal of Conflict Resolution* 29, no. 3 (September 1985): 419–455. Other studies dispute this claim. See Steve Chan, "Mirror Mirror on the

Wall . . . Are the Freer Countries More Pacific?" *Journal of Conflict Resolution,* 28, no. 4 (December 1984): 617–648. This study found support for Rummel's thesis only in the most recent time period. Erich Weede, "Democracy and War Involvement," *Journal of Conflict Resolutions,* 28, no. 4 (December 1989): 649–664, is less equivocal in his rejection of the libertarian thesis.

20. See James Dougherty and Robert Pfaltzgraff, Jr., *Contending Theories of International Relations* (New York: Harper & Row, 1981), pp. 67–68 for a discussion of Haushofer and the *Lebensraum* concept.

21. Several studies dispute the validity of this theory. These include Rudolph Rummel, "The Relationship Between National Attributes and Foreign Conflict Behavior," in *Quantitative International Politics,* J. David Singer, ed. (New York: Free Press of Glencoe, 1968); Raymond Tanter, "Dimensions of Conflict Behavior Within and Between Nations, 1958–1960," *Journal of Conflict Resolution* 10, no. 1 (March 1966): 46. When controlling for types of government and different kinds of conflict behavior, another study provided some qualified support for the theory. See Jonathan Wilkenfeld, "Domestic and Foreign Conflict Behavior of Nations," *Journal of Peace Research* 1 (1968): 55–59. Another study found a modest correlation between internal and external conflict in pre-industrial societies. See Marc H. Ross, "Internal and External Conflict and Violence," *Journal of Conflict Resolution,* 29, no. 4 (December 1985): 547–579.

22. See J. A. Hobson, *Imperialism: A Study* (Ann Arbor: University of Michigan Press, 1965); V. I. Lenin, *Imperialism: The Highest Stage of Capitalism* (New York: International Publishers, 1939).

23. See, for instance, A. I. Macfie, "The Outbreak of War and the Trade Cycle," *Economic History* 3 (February 1938): 89–97; and G. Blainey, *The Causes of War* (New York: Free Press, 1973).

24. William Thompson, "Phases of the Business Cycle and the Outbreak of War," *International Studies Quarterly,* 26, no. 2 (June 1982): 311.

25. Several studies point to a role of economic factors (among others) as an inducement to war. See Raimo Varynen, "Economic Cycles, Power Transitions, Political Management and Wars Between Major Powers," *International Studies Quarterly,* 27, no. 4 (December 1983): 389–418; Charles F. Doran, "War and Power Dynamics: Economic Underpinnings," *International Studies Quarterly,* 27, no. 4 (December 1983): 419–442; and Robert C. North and Nazli Choucri, "Economic and Political Factors in International Conflict and Integration," *International Studies Quarterly,* 27, no. 4 (December 1983): 443–462.

26. Varynen, "Economic Cycles," p. 407.

27. C. Wright Mills, *The Power Elite* (New York: Oxford University Press, 1956).

28. For discussions of the mechanics of the revolution of rising expectations, see Ted Gurr, *Why Men Rebel* (Princeton: Princeton University Press, 1970), pp. 92–122; and James C. Davies, "Toward a Theory of Revolution," *American Sociological Review* 27, no. 1 (February 1962), pp. 5–19.

29. A. F. K. Organski, *World Politics* (New York: Knopf, 1958), pp. 325–337

30. Thucydides, *History of the Peloponnesian Wars* (New York: Random House, 1951), p. 24.

31. See Kenneth Waltz, "The Stability of a Bipolar World," *Daedalus* 93 (Summer 1964): 881–909.

32. Karl Deutsch and J. David Singer, "Multipolar Power Systems and International Stability," *World Politics* 16 (1964): 390–406.

33. Michael Haas, "International Subsystems: Stability and Polarity," *American Political Science Review* 64 (1970): 98–123.

34. Bruce Bueno de Mesquita, "Risk, Power Distributions, and the Likelihood of War," *International Studies Quarterly,* 25, no. 4 (December 1981): 541–568.

35. See Jack Levy, "Alliance Formation and War Behavior," *Journal of Conflict Resolution* 25, no. 4 (December 1981): 581–613.

36. J. David Singer and Michael Wallace, "Intergovernmental Organization and the Preservation of Peace, 1816–1964: Some Bivariate Relationships," *International Organization* 24, no. 3 (Summer 1970): 520–547.

37. Lewis Frye Richardson, *Arms and Insecurity* (Pittsburgh: Boxwood, 1960).

38. See Michael Wallace, "Armaments and Escalation," *International Studies Quarterly* 26, no. 1 (March 1982): 37–51. He suggests that a correlation does exist between arms races and the onset of war.

39. Samuel Huntington, "Arms Races: Prerequisites and Results," in *The Use of Force,* eds. Robert J. Art and Kenneth Waltz, (Boston: Little Brown, 1971), pp. 365–401. One study found that in the context of nuclear war, arms races and can lead either to war or to the avoidance of war. See Michael Intriligator and Dagobert Brito, "Can Arms Races Lead to the Outbreak of War?" *Journal of Conflict Resolution* 28, no. 1 (March 1984): 63–84.

40. Carl Von Clausewitz, *On War,* ed. and trans. Michael Howard and Peter Paret (Princeton: Princeton University Press, 1976), p. 87.

41. Robert Jervis, *Perception and Misperception in International Politics* (Princeton: Princeton University Press, 1976).

42. John Stoessinger, *Why Nations Go to War* (New York: St. Martin's Press, 1985).

43. Ibid., pp. 202–219.

44. Ibid., p. 209.

45. See Jervis, *Perception and Misperception in International Politics,* for a thorough analysis of the types of problems policy makers should avoid.

46. Richard E. Neustadt and Ernest May, *Thinking in Time: The Uses of History for Decision Makers* (New York: Free Press, 1986).

47. One study concluded that a major cause of war is prior or ongoing war, at least within specific regions. This study provides some support for the thesis that war is "contagious." See Henk Houweling and Jan Siccama, "The Epidemiology of War, 1816–1980," *Journal of Conflict Resolution* 29, no. 4 (December 1985): 641–663, especially at p. 661.

Nine

■

International Organization

Every time you mail a letter to a foreign country, fly an airplane overseas, make a phone call to Europe, read a book translated into English from a foreign language, listen to a weather report about other countries, or fill your car's tank with gasoline, you come into contact with international organization in some way. Each of these activities is affected by regulations and policies established by international organizations. Let's take a closer look at how this works.

When you mail a letter to a foreign country, you can thank the Universal Postal Union, which was created in 1874, for its prompt delivery. This international organization establishes uniform postal rates between countries so that mail can circulate quickly and easily. When you take a trip overseas by plane, your safety is protected in part by international regulations governing flight patterns and air navigation. These regulations were developed by the International Civil Aviation Organization, which was created in 1944 to harmonize international air flight. When you make a phone call overseas, it passes through telecommunications satellites. Telephone communications between countries are regulated by the International Telecommunications Union, which was created in 1865 to promote more efficient international telegraph service. When you read a book written by a foreign author, the material is probably protected by international copyright laws that were given effect by the World Intellectual Property Organization, which came into being in 1967. Ever since 1873, collection and dissemination of global weather information have been promoted by the World Meteorological Organization. Finally, when you pump gas into your car, the price you pay depends substantially on the policies of the Organization of Petroleum Exporting Countries (OPEC). These are only a few examples of the countless ways in which your life is affected by the decisions, rules, and regulations of international organizations.

In this chapter we will explore the historical development and theoretical bases of international organizations and examine several of them, in particular the United Nations.

Background and Basic Concepts

Historical Development of International Organizations

How and why did international organizations come into being? For many years after the Peace of Westphalia interstate relations were largely personal relations between monarchs.

Diplomatic contact was sporadic. Relatively speaking, countries were much less dependent economically on international trade than they are today. International travel and communications took much longer. Then in the early 1800s European governments began to recognize the need for more regular diplomatic contact for two reasons: (1) the disruptiveness of the Napoleonic wars, and (2) the increasing commercial activity resulting from the Industrial Revolution. In 1814, at the Treaty of Chaumont and again a year later at the Congress of Vienna, a number of European states—chiefly England, Austria, Russia, and Prussia—agreed on the need to establish regular and periodic consultations to ensure French compliance with peace agreements in the wake of the Napoleonic wars. By maintenance of a balance of power in Europe, these states hoped to achieve a less violent political order. Although this **Concert of Europe,** as it is sometimes called, broke down after four meetings, the nations continued to consult with one other throughout the nineteenth century on a fairly regular basis to resolve disputes, discuss common security concerns, and create a variety of organizations to deal with more specific technical problems. Although the Concert of Europe was not, strictly speaking, an international organization, it (together with the consultative processes that later emerged) can be viewed as the early steps from which international organizations such as the League of Nations and the United Nations evolved.[1]

Indeed, the Congress of Vienna created the first true international organization in 1815. The Rhine River Commission was established to regulate commercial shipping and prevent disputes between states that used the river for commercial purposes. Although dispute settlement was an important reason for this commission, the economic motivation was also significant. Europe's Industrial Revolution of the late eighteenth and early nineteenth centuries led to a much higher level of commercial activity. The desire to increase and facilitate these commercial ties was an important motivation behind the creation of several other intergovernmental organizations, including the Danube River Commission established by the Congress of Paris in 1856 and the Postal and Telecommunications Unions, which we referred to earlier. During the century that preceded World War I, the number of intergovernmental organizations grew to a total of forty-nine.[2] Today there are over three hundred, and they deal with every conceivable aspect of relations between states.

Why have international organizations proliferated? The answer is chiefly because states see them as a means of controlling conflict and promoting economic and commercial relations. More recently, international organizations promoting social welfare and humanitarian goals have also become more numerous. In short, many countries view these organizations as a tool of foreign policy, as a useful complement to bilateral diplomacy, and as a means of achieving national objectives in regional and global politics.

Defining International Organizations

We have discussed how and why international organizations came into existence. But what exactly are they? How should they be defined? Traditionally, international organizations were described as organizations *between* or *among* any two or more states.[3] However, the term has recently been used to describe both intergovernmental and international nongovernmental groups.[4] For this reason, when referring to organizations whose members are states, we will use the term **intergovernmental organizations** (IGOs). Created by states to facilitate or regulate their mutual interrelations, IGOs can be bilateral, regional, or universal in character. Most IGOs derive their authority from treaties made between or among states, although many are now created under the auspices of existing organizations.[5] Typically, intergovernmental organizations have a budget, regular meetings, a headquarters, and a secretariat that is answerable to a governing body composed of the member-states.[6] In short, IGOs are the creatures of sovereign states, and, except under rather rare circumstances, can do only what states empower them to do. Unlike states, they do not possess sovereignty. However, there are some qualified exceptions to this general rule. When an IGO is given the power and authority to make decisions that the states once made, it is said to have a *supranational* character. For instance, the **European Communities** (EC)—sometimes referred to as the Common Market—is empowered to regulate the coal and steel industries, agricultural policy, and other aspects of its member-states' economies, but only because the latter have given it that authority.[7] The EC is often referred to as a *supranational* organization because it has the authority to make regulations that are binding on its member-states and on individuals and businesses within the member-states. In general, however, states do not intend international organizations to subvert national sovereignty, but rather to provide mechanisms to facilitate, promote, and harmonize state relations in ways that are beneficial to the states concerned. Having no sovereignty of their own, IGOs normally operate between rather than above states. Intergovernmental organizations should not be confused with international **nongovernmental organizations** (NGOs) or **private voluntary organizations** (PVOs).[8] These groups, though more numerous than IGOs, are private and nonprofit.[9] Many NGOs and PVOs have consultative status with the United Nations and perform lobbying functions similar to those of domestic interest groups.[10]

Another term, **transnational organization,** is used to describe religious groups and business enterprises that have interests or conduct operations in more than one country. The Catholic and Mormon churches and multinational corporations such as General Motors, IBM, and Royal Dutch Shell are examples of transnational organizations. As we saw in chapter 4, it is no longer possible to ignore the role of nongovernmental organizations in international relations.[11] In this chapter, however, we will focus primarily on IGOs and the important role they play in the contemporary international system.

Conceptual Bases of Intergovernmental Organizations

As we have seen, international organizations emerged to perform three basic functions. The first and most elemental function was to provide more continuous diplomatic contact between states. The other two functions, controlling conflict and facilitating day-to-day economic interactions, depend on this institutional continuity. It will be useful to explore the theories that underlie these latter functions.

Collective security   The basic premise of *collective security* organizations is that all members agree not to use force to settle disputes among themselves, and that if any member-state should break this agreement, all other members will oppose the aggressor with force.[12] Any member-state that might be tempted to use force would be deterred by the prospect of inviting the opposition of every other member-state. Acting out of self-interest, such states would then seek a peaceful resolution of the dispute. The League of Nations was, and the United Nations is, based at least in part on collective security principles. Regional organizations such as the Organization of African Unity and the Organization of American States also contain collective security elements.

The problem with the collective security theory is two-fold. First, it depends on being able to define *aggression,* which is not always easy. Consider the following situation: Country *A* mobilizes forces and deploys them along its border with country *B*. Country *A* verbally threatens country *B*, which assumes that country *A* is about to attack. Believing that it could not successfully absorb an attack, country *B* decides to strike first and thus gain the advantage of surprise. Which country is the aggressor? Country *B* may have attacked first, but country *A* forced the issue. A preemptive strike by a state facing country *B*'s predicament could be viewed as an act of self-defense rather than one of aggression, even though it strikes first. When one state attacks another with premeditation and without provocation, the aggression is more apparent. However, the international community is often faced with more ambiguous situations.

Second, because the membership in collective security organizations (especially those that aspire to a global membership) is so ideologically and politically diverse, any time a dispute actually leads to war, some states will defend the aggressor, others the victim, and others will choose to remain neutral—none of these actions is permitted under the collective security arrangement. Thus, as figure 9.1 illustrates, the theory of collective security, which calls for unified retaliation against aggression, often devolves, in practice, into a free-for-all in which states make individual choices about how to define and respond to aggression. Collective security has had difficult time superceding the more entrenched practice of the balance of power.

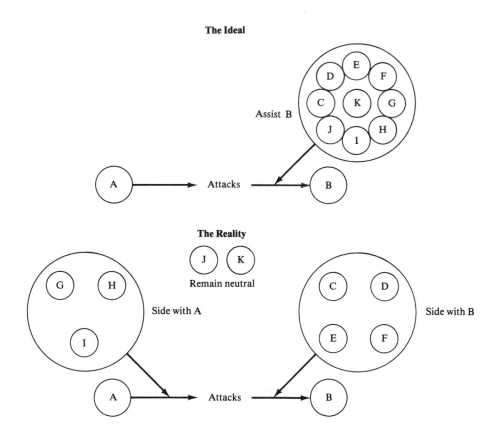

Figure 9.1
Collective security: theory and reality
SOURCE: Adapted from Hans Morgenthau, *Politics Among Nations,* 4th ed. (New York: Knopf, 1967), pp. 401–402. Reprinted with permission.

Regional security organizations differ from collective security ones in the sense that they are not created to protect their members from aggression among themselves, but rather from aggression instigated by nonmember-states, by those outside the organization. These organizations are more in keeping with traditional notions of the balance of power. The North Atlantic Treaty Organization and the Warsaw Treaty Organization are regional security organizations, since each was created to protect its members from the threat of aggression by the opposing alliance.

The purpose of both collective and regional security organizations is to deter aggression, but they go about it in different ways. Collective security organizations attempt to draw states into mutual and cooperative efforts to deter aggression, whereas regional security organizations are alliances among like-minded states against other competing states or alliances.

Functionalism   Many IGOs that were created to facilitate economic, social, cultural, and humanitarian interaction are based on the theory of **functionalism.** This theory holds that when states cooperate to solve economic and social problems, they build up trust that may eventually extend or "spill over" into their political relations. This **spill-over effect,** it is theorized, will eventually allow countries to resolve their political differences more easily. David Mitrany, one of the leading proponents of this theory, once argued that a "spreading web" of international cooperation in technical and non-political areas would inevitably lead to the disappearance of the state system and thus to a world of greater peace and stability.[13]

Several assumptions underlie this theory of functionalism. First, war is seen as a by-product of hunger, disease, ignorance, poverty, lawlessness, and miscommunication. Second, nationalism and the state perpetuate these problems. Third, out of their own self-interest, states will attempt to solve problems by creating IGOs to deal with them. Fourth, by separating the technical solutions to these problems from politics, functional organizations will gradually resolve them. Fifth, as it becomes apparent to people that their lives are increasingly and positively affected by a "spreading web" of international agencies, they will transfer their loyalties from the nation-states to these more pragmatic international institutions. Hence, the nation-state system will slowly but inevitably give way to one governed by international organizations that actually get the work done.

All but one of these assumptions would appear to be debatable. There is little doubt that states have turned to functional agencies to perform much of the necessary, day-to-day coordination of economic, technical, social, and humanitarian affairs. Literally hundreds of such IGOs exist at the bilateral, regional, and global levels. Even the most severe critics of the UN system will admit these facts.[14]

However, it is not at all clear that poverty, ignorance, disease, and so on, are the actual causes of war. Nor is it self-evident that the nation-state is the cause of these problems or the main factor that perpetuates them. Similarly, separating technical from political issues often has proved to be a very difficult process. The United Nations Educational, Scientific and Cultural Organization (UNESCO) would seem, for instance, to deal with nonpolitical subjects. To the contrary, education imparts not only information, but also societal and political values. Scientific knowledge can be used to advance a nation's economic and military sophistication, and culture is often very closely tied to a society's national aspirations. Of all the UN functional agencies, UNESCO has proved to be one of the most controversial. Its efforts to establish a New Information Order through creation of a new system of licensing journalists and controlling the flow of news excited great political controversy. Third World nations insisted such a system was necessary to encourage more balanced coverage in the

Western media of both the good and the bad news in the developing world. Western journalists were seen by developing countries (LDCs) as crisis mongers in search of sensational stories about famines, coups, and massacres, while ignoring accounts of the difficult economic problems faced by the LDCs or the many success stories in dealing with these problems. By contrast, many Western governments saw the New Information Order as a threat to freedom of the press and an effort by Third World governments to control, stifle, and censor international news in much the same way that the majority of them control their domestic news. In short, it appears that technical issues such as the flow of information and news coverage have definite political implications, as do many other technical areas, including regulation of nuclear energy, development assistance lending, and assistance to refugees. Separating technical from political issues is an ongoing and difficult task. Finally, there is very little evidence to support the contention that people will eventually transfer loyalty from their nation to supranational agencies. Quite to the contrary, nationalism seems as strong today as it was forty years ago when the theory of functionalism was gaining wider attention. Some studies even show that more tourism, travel, and contact between people can reinforce nationalist sentiments rather than encourage a more cosmopolitan attitude.[15] Thus, based on a contemporary reading of international relations, the inevitability of functionalist evolution would seem to be in question.

Nevertheless, numerous functional agencies perform important work and help promote economic, social, and humanitarian ties between nations. Indeed, far from challenging the state system, functionalism seems to be compatible with it. Most of these organizations perform their work quietly, efficiently, and beyond the glare of the spotlight; the more obscure ones are often more effective. The numerous specialized agencies of the United Nations (discussed in "Genesis of the United Nations," beginning on page 258, and enumerated in figure 9.2) and other UN bodies deal with a dizzying array of functional activities. Among the regional organizations, the European Common Market is the most prominent organization based explicitly on functionalist theory.

Types of Intergovernmental Organizations

Intergovernmental organizations come in all shapes and varieties and perform a number of general and particular functions, depending on why they were created. Some IGOs serve limited functions; others are unlimited in purpose. Some IGOs have limited memberships and others are universal, or at least nonexclusive in membership.[16]

Limited-purpose, limited-membership IGOs By far most IGOs have been created for limited or very specific purposes. Most limited-purpose organizations are also limited in membership to two or a few states. Examples include international boundary commissions (such as the U.S.–Canadian Boundary Commission) and the numerous bilateral mixed-claims commissions that resolve legal disputes between countries (such as the U.S.–Mexican Mixed Claims Commission). Other examples of limited-purpose IGOs include regional security organizations such as NATO, the Warsaw Treaty Organization, and the Rio Pact. Still other IGOs deal with regulation of various international commodities. The Organization of Petroleum Exporting Countries is the most well known **commodity cartel.** Other international commodity organizations exist for cotton, natural rubber, and copper, to name but a few. Still other commodity organizations exist for the benefit of both producer and consumer states, including the International Coffee Organization, the International Lead and Zinc Study Group, the International Jute Organization, and the International Sugar Organization.

Different IGOs exist to promote research on cancer, rice production, and agricultural research, whereas others are devoted to the conservation of whales, fur seals, tuna, and endangered species of both plants and animals. The list goes on and on and should be illustrative of the diverse array of concerns that individual IGOs have been created to address.

Limited-purpose, broad-membership IGOs   Other limited-purpose organizations have very broad or universal memberships. The UN specialized agencies, for instance, while having limited mandates and specific operational purposes, are open to all states that want to become members. For example, as of 1988, the Food and Agricultural Organization (FAO) had 158 members and the World Health Organization (WHO) had 167. The purpose of the FAO is to raise nutritional standards and improve the production and distribution of food especially in the rural areas of the developing world. The WHO is charged with coordinating public health work, assisting governments to strengthen health care services, and eradicating and controlling the spread of infectious diseases in addition to other health-related functions and purposes. The FAO and WHO are two examples of more than two dozen UN specialized agencies and special programs that perform specific operational and coordinating functions.

Broad-purpose, limited-membership IGOs   A smaller number of IGOs have unlimited or very broad purposes but are limited in terms of membership. These include regional IGOs such as the Organization of African Unity, the Organization of American States, the Arab League, the Nordic Council, and the Association of Southeast Asian Nations. In each case membership is limited by geography or by cultural heritage, as in the case of the Arab League and the Nordic Council. Although limited in membership, these organizations deal with a broad range of international problems, including peace and security issues, economic concerns, cultural relations, and social and humanitarian concerns. The organizations' formal purposes are stipulated in the treaties that created them, but informal goals may also exist. For example, one of the few truly unifying factors among members of the OAU, apart from their successful decolonization campaign, has been opposition to South Africa's **apartheid policy** of racial separation. Similarly, opposition to the state of Israel has been a prime unifying factor for the Arab League.

One of the most extensively studied limited-membership, broad-purpose organizations is the Common Market.[17] Its primary purpose has been to achieve greater economic integration among its European member-states. However, in keeping with functionalist theory, the Common Market's founders hoped that greater political integration would also occur. *Integration* may be defined as the process by which separate nation-states establish common, unified mechanisms and institutions that have the authority to perform political or economic functions once exclusively performed under the jurisdiction of the preexisting nation-states. In a sense, integration means, quite literally, from many to one.

One of the explicit purposes behind the creation in 1951 of the first European institution, the European Coal and Steel Community (ECSC), was to integrate production, processing, and marketing in the strategically important French and German coal and steel industry so thoroughly that no future war between them would be practical. French Foreign Minister Robert Schuman, the architect of the ECSC, believed that if these two crucial industries for wartime production could be placed under international authority and managed as a European enterprise, none of the participating governments would be in a position to quit the ECSC and rebuild its own independent capability—without inviting incredible harm and disruption to its own economy. Hence, the prospects for war would be substantially reduced. The successful efforts of the ECSC were followed in 1957 by the creation of a European Atomic Energy Community (EURATOM) and the European Economic Community (EEC), which established common markets in most other economic areas. The purpose of a **common market** was to promote free trading among its members by eradicating all tariffs and other barriers among the member-states and establishing a common external tariff that would apply to all agricultural and manufactured goods imported into the common market from the outside. These three bodies—the ECSC, EURATOM, and the EEC—were later integrated into a single organization known today simply as the European Communities (EC). Initially, the EC included only six members: France, Germany, Italy, and the so-called Benelux countries (Belgium, Netherlands, and Luxembourg). Today the EC boasts a membership of twelve, including the United Kingdom, Ireland, Denmark, Spain, Portugal, and Greece.[18]

The EC has been a tremendous success in terms of achieving economic integration and stimulating economic growth, but it has yet to achieve significant levels of political integration. The governments have not been willing to develop a common security policy, although there is considerable military and foreign policy consultation and cooperation. Even though efforts to establish a European Defense Community in the 1950s failed, cooperation has always been evident in security affairs. Recently Europeans have worried about the U.S. tendency to pursue unilateral security initiatives, such as the strategic defense initiative commonly known as Star Wars, and intermediate nuclear force cuts with the Soviet Union without consulting them. This concern spurred discussions between France and Germany on the creation of joint military units and joint talks between France and the United Kingdom about their nuclear forces. Still, Europe is far from establishing a common security policy. There has also been reluctance to establish a common European currency, although there has been significant monetary cooperation and by 1992 there is hope that a European central bank will exist and that all barriers to capital flows will be eradicated. There has been no effort to erase the separately constituted governments and political systems of EC member-states, but there has been contact and consultation between political parties of the various countries in the European Parliament. The European Parliament is, itself, somewhat of a misnomer. It does not actually legislate. Once merely consultative, it now has the authority to propose amendments to and force reconsideration of proposals made by the EC's executive body, the Commission. The Parliament also approves the EC budget, and may dismiss the Commission with a vote of no confidence. The other institutions of the EC conduct the organization's real business. The Council of Ministers, whose members are appointed by governments as their national representatives enacts most legislation. The Commission, in turn, proposes legislation to the Council and is responsible for executing its decisions. In addition, the Commission must explain its administrative actions and policies to the European Parliament.

For many years decisions in the Council, which is the decisive EC body in terms of approving new policies, were based on consensus. Since no major proposal could be adopted without unanimity, progress toward economic integration in a wide range of areas could be blocked by a single state. However, the entry into force of the Single European Act in 1987 increased the scope of decisions in which a qualified majority rather than unanimity applied. Thus, under current council arrangements, a total of seventy-six votes are distributed among the twelve members. Four big states—France, the United Kingdom, the Federal Republic of Germany, and Italy—get ten votes each, while smaller members get proportionally fewer votes. Under a qualified majority system, proposals can no longer be blocked by one state. Now a minimum of three governments—two big ones and a small one—is needed to block proposals. The unanimity rule still exists for certain especially sensitive matters, but the qualified majority provisions have been sufficiently broadened to reinvigorate the process of economic integration, which by 1992 will see the last real barriers to economic integration fall.

The EC has proved to be one of the more innovative and successful attempts at international economic integration. It has promoted common trade, industrial production and agricultural, transportation, fisheries, monetary, and environmental policy. Indeed, member-states have ceded sovereignty over trade and agricultural policy to EC institutions. These successes have not yet resulted in actual political integration, but much progress has been made to ensure close political cooperation. Political integration is still a long way off, but momentum toward it remains. Indeed, the EC has clearly demonstrated its utility in facilitating economic interaction among its members, and its expanding membership in recent years suggests that it is viewed positively by the governments of its current and prospective member-states.

Broad-purpose, broad-membership IGOs While limited-membership, broad-purpose organizations such as the EC are not overly numerous, there are still fewer examples of unlimited membership, broad-purpose organizations. Indeed, there have only been two organizations in the history of international relations that have been broad in function and, at least potentially, universal in membership: the League of Nations and its successor, the United Nations. For this reason we will focus much of our attention in this chapter on the United Nations. While it is but one of literally hundreds of international organizations, it is the most all-encompassing and most visible in existence today.

The United Nations System

Negotiations creating the United Nations began during World War II, largely at the instigation of the United States, which hoped to replace the failed League of Nations with a new, more effective, and comprehensive organization that would both control international conflict and gradually eliminate the underlying causes of conflict. To understand how the United Nations differed from the League, it is important to examine some of the key difficulties the latter encountered.

Problems with the League of Nations

One of the more obvious problems the League of Nations faced was lack of participation by key powers. The United States failed to participate in the League from its inception despite the fact that President Wilson had been its main architect. Wilson's arguments failed to sway Republican opponents in the Senate, who so overburdened the Versailles Peace Treaty (which included a covenant that created the League of Nations) with reservations that U.S. ratification would have been meaningless. Nonparticipation for significant periods by other Great Powers such as the Soviet Union and Japan also had a negative effect on the League. However, nonparticipation was not the only problem.

Another drawback was that the League Council, which was responsible for maintenance of peace and security, proved unable to achieve consensus on how to respond to and prevent aggression. Because the League Council operated on a principle of unanimity (unanimous support) when considering substantive proposals, each member could veto and thus prevent any proposed council action it opposed. As a result, the League was often hamstrung in responding to the aggressive actions of its members that were in clear violation of the League Covenant. In 1931, for example, Japan invaded Manchuria. This was a clear violation of the League Covenant, but France and Great Britain opposed efforts to impose sanctions because they were reluctant to contest Japan. Later, when a League Commission of Inquiry found Japan to be the aggressor, Japan simply withdrew from the League, which stood by, powerless either to prevent or punish this aggression. Even when consensus was achieved, the League had only marginal enforcement ability. In 1935 when Italy invaded Ethiopia, the League declared the invasion illegal and imposed economic sanctions. Although these sanctions had adverse effects on the Italian economy, application of harsher sanctions was scrupulously avoided. The League's members were willing to make a moral and symbolic statement, but less eager to impose sanctions that would truly have been effective.[19] The outbreak of World War II sounded the death knell of this first noble if flawed experiment at global collective security, but evidence of the League's ineffectiveness was mounting even before then. The high ideals of that organization were ahead of time, but the architects of the United Nations hoped to learn from the League's weaknesses and improve on its performance.[20]

Genesis of the United Nations

American policy makers hoped that the United Nations would succeed where the League had failed, and this time the United States would be present not only to assist but to promote the effort. During World War II, the United States urged its allies, chiefly Great Britain and the Soviet Union, to join it in creating a new global organization, which it called the United Nations. At several wartime conferences the allies agreed on the structure and role of the Security Council and on provisions for restructuring the post-war economy. The United Nations, like its predecessor the League of Nations, was initially conceived as a collective security organization designed to control conflict and enforce global peace. It continued the concept initiated under the League of addressing the underlying causes of conflict, such as poverty, disease, ignorance, lack of self-determination, and poor legal development. The General Assembly and a variety of subsidiary bodies, together with a refurbished World Court, addressed these latter concerns while the Security Council performed the collective security functions. The Security Council originally included five permanent members—the United States, Soviet Union, United Kingdom, France, and China—and six additional seats occupied by other member-states on two-year rotating terms. Later the nonpermanent seats were expanded to a total of ten, so that the Security Council now has fifteen members. In keeping with the principles of collective security, each UN member-state pledged not to use force in their mutual disputes, and agreed that any state that broke this pledge would immediately be opposed as an aggressor by all other UN members. Most states, it was hoped, would be deterred by a united front of opposition to aggression, which would be implemented by the Security Council through the concerted efforts of its powerful members. On the other hand, a safety valve (or loophole, depending on how one views it) was built into the theory: Each permanent member of the Security Council was given a veto. Thus, if a major power were involved in a dispute, it could veto UN involvement. This seemed prudent, since a confrontation between the United Nations and a major power was not viewed as a good thing. On the other hand, where major powers agreed to enforce the peace, the Security Council would be in a position to do so effectively. The framers of the United Nations hoped by limiting the veto to the five permanent members that the consensus that had so often eluded the League Council could be achieved. It was hoped that conflicts involving nonmajor powers could be contained and resolved without escalating and involving the major powers. The feeling was that peace was "indivisible," that a conflict in any part of the world might become a global conflagration unless contained and controlled.

While the major powers agreed about these essential ingredients of the United Nations, many smaller states voiced disgruntlement at their second-class status in the Great Power proposals for the organization. At the San Francisco Conference near the end of the war, these small states successfully lobbied for the inclusion of the Economic and Social Council as a separate UN organ and for the creation of a Trusteeship Council, which would oversee the progressive decolonization of the world. The Latin American states insisted on a key role for organizations such as the Organization of American States (OAS) in the resolution of regional disputes. Under article 51 of the charter, regional collective security organizations have a role in resolving disputes among their members. For instance, should a threat to peace emerge in Latin America, the OAS may deal with it after notifying the Security Council. If the regional organization fails to resolve the dispute, the Security Council may then take the matter up directly. By providing for this layered system, it was hoped that conflicts could be resolved more flexibly and effectively. While the small powers extracted concessions in several of the areas mentioned above, their assault on the Great Power veto in the Security Council was unsuccessful. The Great Powers made it clear that there would be no United Nations without a Great Power veto in the council.

The upshot of the San Francisco Conference was an organization that consisted (and still consists) of six major organs: (1) a **General Assembly** composed of all member-states, which can consider any issue submitted to it by the members (this body is further divided into six main committees and several standing and procedural committees and other subsidiary bodies; (2) a **Security Council,** which is responsible for the maintenance of international peace and security; (3) a **Trusteeship Council,** which has successfully participated in the progressive movement toward independence of non-self-governing territories; (4) an **Economic and Social Council** (ECOSOC), which reports to the General Assembly and coordinates the vast array of functional agencies and subsidiary organs that are active in the social, economic, and humanitarian areas; (5) the **International Court of Justice** (ICJ), which serves as a constitutional court of sorts for the UN system, delivers advisory opinions at the request of other official UN bodies, and serves as a court of law for states to resolve legal disputes (see Chapter 10 for details); and (6) a **Secretariat,** which administers and manages the work of the entire UN system. These organs and many other UN bodies are illustrated in figure 9.2.

To what extent has the United Nations lived up to its founders' expectation as a collective security organization and as a means of eradicating the underlying socioeconomic causes of conflict?

Collective Security Innovations

If students of the UN agree on anything, it is that the collective security provisions of the UN Charter were never able to develop fully. Almost from the beginning, the United States and the Soviet Union were engaged in a Cold War that prevented superpower agreement on Security Council enforcement of the peace. The Military Staff Committee and other operational aspects of Security Council peace-making machinery never got off the ground, thus depriving the council of the tools it could use to enforce its decisions. With the exception

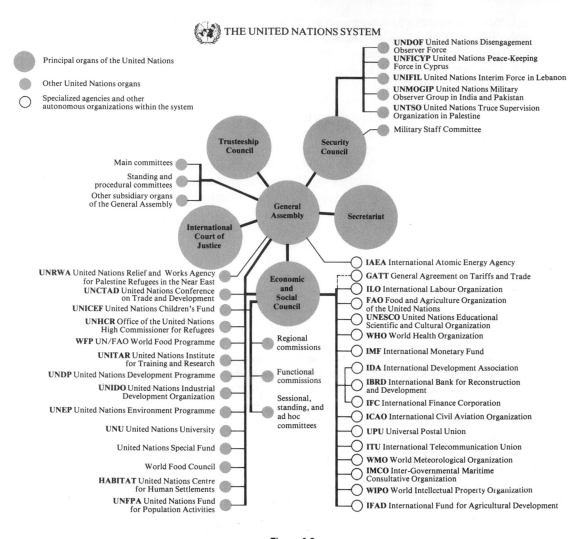

THE UNITED NATIONS SYSTEM

Principal organs of the United Nations

Other United Nations organs

Specialized agencies and other autonomous organizations within the system

UNDOF United Nations Disengagement Observer Force
UNFICYP United Nations Peace-Keeping Force in Cyprus
UNIFIL United Nations Interim Force in Lebanon
UNMOGIP United Nations Military Observer Group in India and Pakistan
UNTSO United Nations Truce Supervision Organization in Palestine
Military Staff Committee

Trusteeship Council

Security Council

Main committees
Standing and procedural committees
Other subsidiary organs of the General Assembly

General Assembly

Secretariat

International Court of Justice

UNRWA United Nations Relief and Works Agency for Palestine Refugees in the Near East
UNCTAD United Nations Conference on Trade and Development
UNICEF United Nations Children's Fund
UNHCR Office of the United Nations High Commissioner for Refugees
WFP UN/FAO World Food Programme
UNITAR United Nations Institute for Training and Research
UNDP United Nations Development Programme
UNIDO United Nations Industrial Development Organization
UNEP United Nations Environment Programme
UNU United Nations University
United Nations Special Fund
World Food Council
HABITAT United Nations Centre for Human Settlements
UNFPA United Nations Fund for Population Activities

Economic and Social Council

Regional commissions

Functional commissions

Sessional, standing, and ad hoc committees

IAEA International Atomic Energy Agency
GATT General Agreement on Tariffs and Trade
ILO International Labour Organization
FAO Food and Agriculture Organization of the United Nations
UNESCO United Nations Educational Scientific and Cultural Organization
WHO World Health Organization
IMF International Monetary Fund
IDA International Development Association
IBRD International Bank for Reconstruction and Development
IFC International Finance Corporation
ICAO International Civil Aviation Organization
UPU Universal Postal Union
ITU International Telecommunication Union
WMO World Meteorological Organization
IMCO Inter-Governmental Maritime Consultative Organization
WIPO World Intellectual Property Organization
IFAD International Fund for Agricultural Development

Figure 9.2
The United Nations system
SOURCE: United Nations Office of Public Information, July 1980.

of the Korean war, the Soviet Union vetoed council reaction to disputes involving East–West interests. In the Korean case, the Soviet Union boycotted Security Council proceedings to protest the council's failure to seat Mao Tse-tung's Communist Chinese regime instead of the Nationalist government in Taiwan. The North Korean invasion took place during this Soviet boycott. Soviet absence enabled the United States and the other Western members of the council to vote for a UN Peace Force to resist North Korea's aggression against South Korea. In addition, the United States successfully lobbied for the passage of the **Uniting for Peace Resolution,** which provided that in future cases when the Security Council was stalemated by a veto, the General Assembly could recommend collective security actions to make peace, and authorize deployment of peacekeeping forces. At the time the United States enjoyed a largely friendly, pro-Western majority in the General Assembly, which gave America a temporary advantage over the Soviet Union. Realizing its error in boycotting council meetings, the Soviet Union hurried back before further damage could be done.

The role of the General Assembly was further enlarged in 1956 when Secretary-General Dag Hammarskjöld proposed the use of a UN peacekeeping force in the Suez war. France and the United Kingdom had joined Israel in attacking Egypt after its nationalization of the Suez Canal. Since both France and the United Kingdom held a veto in the Security Council, it could not act. Consistent with the provisions of the Uniting for Peace Resolution, and with strong backing by the United States, Hammarskjöld seized the opportunity for the non-veto-bound General Assembly to exercise a useful role. A UN Emergency Force (UNEF) was established in 1956, and with the agreement of Egypt, it was stationed in Egypt along its border within Israel to separate the opposing forces. It remained there until 1967 when Egypt's President Nasser called for its withdrawal just prior to the third Arab–Israeli War in that year. Although other UN commissions and observer forces had existed prior to the UNEF experiment, it was the most ambitious. Moreover, the UNEF was the first clear-cut example of overcoming paralysis in the Security Council through General Assembly involvement and administrative action by the secretary-general. As table 9.1 illustrates, the **peacekeeping** practice has been employed in many other situations since UNEF forces were first dispatched to the Middle East. In many subsequent cases, such as the Congo, Cyprus, and UNEF II, the Security Council has been able to take the lead on the insertion of peacekeeping forces.

The practice of peacekeeping that has evolved over the years was not anticipated in the UN Charter.[21] It is sometimes referred to as Chapter "Six-and-a-Half," since it falls between authorities granted to the Security Council in Chapter Six ("Pacific Settlement of Disputes") and Chapter Seven ("Actions with Respect to Threats to the Peace, Breaches of the Peace, and Acts of Aggression"). The idea behind peacekeeping is not to establish an armed force to make the peace. Rather the idea is to achieve a ceasefire agreement between the conflicting parties, and then to place between them a "thin blue line" of neutral UN forces, whose primary object is to separate the parties physically and buy time for the disputants to engage in further negotiations aimed at resolving the underlying causes of the conflict. In most cases, this has meant securing the agreement of the disputing parties, as well as some agreement in the Security Council, about the composition and mandate of the peacekeeping forces and arrangements for financing them. Given this rather daunting list of prerequisites, it is a minor miracle that the list of peacekeeping operations is as long as it is.

Although the collective security provisions of the UN Charter have not been achieved, the United Nations has demonstrated a capacity to respond informally to peacekeeping requirements. Still, several problems continue to plague UN peacekeeping. The Soviet Union, in most instances, has refused to contribute to the financing of peacekeeping operations despite its acquiescence to their use in certain situations. As a result, contributions to these rather expensive operations have usually been made on a voluntary basis by participating states, the combatants, and other nations that have supported the establishment of particular forces. Recent exceptions include UNEF II and related Middle East peacekeeping forces that have been assessed as a regular part of the UN budget. The establishment of a permanent "Ready Force" has yet to be achieved, so that ad hoc arrangements need to be made with governments who are willing to provide their armed forces to the United Nations on a case-by-case basis. Some states have been ready to participate on a fairly regular basis (chiefly Canada, and the Nordic countries of Denmark, Iceland, Norway, and Sweden), but the lack of a readily available force hampers the expeditious deployment of peacekeeping forces.

While numerous problems attend the use of UN peacekeeping forces, their recent deployment in various conflict situations, after nearly a decade in which no new initiatives were undertaken, suggests that they remain a viable option in helping resolve disputes. In 1988 and 1989 UN forces were introduced in Iran and Iraq, Namibia, Angola, Afghanistan, and Central America, and proposals are pending for involvement in the Western Sahara and Cambodia (See Table 9.1).

Eradication of the Underlying Causes of Conflict

Success in the pursuit of its second chief goal—the eradication of the underlying social, economic, and humanitarian causes of conflict—has met with equally mixed success. The UN's first decade was dominated by big power disputes and the chilling effect of the Cold War. Gradually, however, new nations joined as decolonization gained steam.[22] Inevitably, the agenda of the developing world replaced the East–West dispute as the focal point of UN attention. New issues (such as economic development, human rights, the elimination

Table 9.1
UN peacekeeping operations

Operation	Date	Purpose
UN Special Committee on the Balkans (UNSCOB)	1947	Investigate Greek border situation
UN Truce Supervision Organization (UNTSO)	1949	Monitor cease-fire in Arab–Israeli dispute
UN Commission for Indonesia	1949	Monitor cease-fire until Indonesian independence
UN Military Observer Group in India and Pakistan (UNMOGIP)	1949	Patrol cease-fire line in Kashmir
UN Emergency Force (UNEF)	1956–1957	Station observer force along Egypt–Israeli border
UN Observer Group in Lebanon (UNOGIL)	1958	Investigate charges of border infiltration
UN Congo Operation (ONUC)	1960–1964	Stabilize domestic turmoil in the Congo
UN Security Force (UNSF in conjunction with UNTEA)	1962–1963	Stabilize West Iranian situation
UN Yemen Observation Mission (UNYOM)	1962–1964	Supervise disengagement of forces in civil war
UN Force in Cyprus (UNFICYP)	1964–present	Supervise and monitor disengagement of forces during civil war
UN India–Pakistan Observation Mission (UNIPOM)	1965	Patrol border between India and Pakistan
UNTSO–Suez Canal	1967	Monitor cease-fire line
UNEF II	1973–1979	Observe borders in Sinai
UN Disengagement Observer Force (UNDOF)	1975–present	Patrol Israeli–Syrian border in Golan Heights
UN Interim Force in Lebanon (UNIFIC)	1978–present	Monitor Lebanese civil war
UN Good Offices Mission in Afghanistan and Pakistan (UNGOMAP)	1988–present	Implement Geneva Accords in Afghanistan
UN Angolan Verification Mission (UNAVEM)	1989–present	Verify Cuban troop pullout from Angola
UN Transition Assistance Group (UNTAG)	1989–present	Supervise elections and transition to Namibian independence
UN Observer Group in Central America (UNOGICA)	1989–present	Verify cessation of and aid to irregular forces

Note: Forces have also been proposed to supervise elections in the Western Sahara and to keep peace in Cambodia after Vietnamese troop withdrawals.

of racism, and decolonization) occupied the concern of UN bodies. The General Assembly, the Trusteeship Council, the Economic and Social Council (ECOSOC), and a host of subsidiary UN agencies were involved in overseeing the UN response to these issues.

General Assembly   The General Assembly oversees much of the UN's work in the nonsecurity area. Virtually all UN organs report to it. Its seven main committees deal with the whole gamut of UN subjects. The Special Political Committee and the First Committee deal with political issues, the Second Committee with economic affairs, the Third Committee with social and humanitarian affairs, the Fourth Committee with trusteeship issues, the Fifth Committee with administrative and budgetary concerns, and the Sixth Committee with legal questions.

The General Assembly, unlike the Security Council, does not have the authority to make legally binding resolutions on UN member-states. It can make declarations, pass resolutions, and vote for draft conventions (treaties), but they have no legal force except under those circumstances when states clearly indicate that they do or when states acquiesce in such General Assembly actions. States that vote against resolutions and declarations are not required to abide by them, nor can a vote in favor of such resolutions or declarations be construed as acceptance of legal obligation unless states take further actions indicating their acceptance of an obligation. Each member-state's government must ratify UN conventions that are debated and voted on by the General Assembly before they can come into force. No member-state is under legal obligation to ratify UN treaties or conventions. Thus, except for certain internal administrative and budgetary purposes, the legal effect of UN resolutions is marginal and indecisive, although they can pave the way for legal obligations and legally binding multilateral treaties. For example, the General Assembly Universal Declaration of Human Rights, though initially intended as a statement of moral aspiration, marked the beginning of an evolution of human rights treaties and agreements. The declaration has also been incorporated into the constitutions of numerous nation-states.[23] General Assembly resolutions may only have a marginal legal effect in terms of securing the states' compliance in their political interrelations; but within the UN framework, these resolutions are the means by which decisions are made and communicated among UN bodies. The General Assembly has used the resolutions, declarations, and draft conventions to expand the dialogue among nations on a variety of security and nonsecurity issues.

The General Assembly may also be called into special session by the secretary-general to consider issues of urgent and special concern. In recent years, special sessions have been called to deal with disarmament, the creation of a New International Economic Order, and the problem of economic recovery and rehabilitation in Africa. These sessions highlight specific international issues and heighten international attention to them.

Working closely with the General Assembly to address the underlying causes of conflict have been two other UN organs: the Trusteeship Council and ECOSOC.

The Trusteeship Council and decolonization   Efforts by the Trusteeship Council to oversee the movement of colonial territories toward self-determination constitute one of the success stories in the UN's mission to eliminate the causes of conflict. Indeed, this council has been so successful that it has virtually worked itself out of business. The idea behind trusteeship was that a developed country would agree to assist a colonial territory to achieve its independence by promoting economic improvements and development of political institutions. Placement of territories in trust, with the exception of Namibia, was done on a voluntary basis. Because of the rather rigorous responsibilities incurred by the trustee country only eleven territories were placed under trusteeship arrangements. Most were holdovers from the **mandate system** of the League of Nations. Under that system, various independent states were charged with assisting the former colonial territories of the losing (World War I) Axis powers toward eventual self-determination.

The vast majority of LDCs gained their independence outside the specific mandate of the Trusteeship Council. Under the provisions of the UN Charter, states holding control over **non-self-governing territories** (colonies or territorial dependencies) were urged to pledge that they would assist in the development of these areas. Gradually, this became a vehicle by which non-self-governing territories could lobby for independence. Of over 100 countries that joined the United Nations after 1945, the vast majority were from the non-self-governing territories of the Third World. The growth in UN membership from 51 at the signing of the charter to 159 today is chronicled in table 9.2. Many of the recently admitted countries are small, insignificant actors in international relations. These ministates are viewed by their larger colleagues as marginally qualified at best to assume the privileges and duties of UN membership. Indeed, some of the mini-states, such as the Maldive Islands, are so poor that they cannot afford to send a delegation to the UN headquarters in New York.[24]

Table 9.2
Growth of UN membership, 1945–1986

Year	Number	Original Member States
1945	51	Argentina, Australia, Belgium, Bolivia, Brazil, Byelorussian SSR, Canada, Chile, China, Colombia, Costa Rica, Cuba, Czechoslovakia, Denmark, Dominican Republic, Ecuador, Egypt, El Salvador, Ethiopia, France, Greece, Guatemala, Haiti, Honduras, India, Iran, Iraq, Lebanon, Liberia, Luxembourg, Mexico, Netherlands, New Zealand, Nicaragua, Norway, Panama, Paraguay, Peru, Philippines, Poland, Saudi Arabia, South Africa, Syria, Turkey, Ukranian SSR, Soviet Union, United Kingdom, United States, Uruguay, Venezuela, Yugoslavia

Year	Number	New Member States
1946	55	Afghanistan, Iceland, Sweden, Thailand
1947	57	Pakistan, Yemen
1948	58	Myanmar (Burma)
1949	59	Israel
1950	60	Indonesia
1955	75	Albania, Austria, Bulgaria, Democratic Kampuchea, Finland, Hungary, Ireland, Italy, Jordan, Lao People's Democratic Republic, Libyan Arab Jamahiriya, Nepal, Portgual, Romania, Spain, Sri Lanka
1956	80	Japan, Morocco, Sudan, Tunisia
1957	82	Ghana, Malaysia
1958	83	Guinea
1960	100	Benin, Burkina Faso, Central African Republic, Chad, Congo, Cote d'Ivoire, Cyprus, Gabon, Madagascar, Mali, Niger, Nigeria, Senegal, Somalia, Togo, United Republic of Cameroon, Zaire
1961	104	Mauritania, Mongolia, Sierra Leone, United Republic of Tanzania
1962	110	Algeria, Burundi, Jamaica, Rwanda, Trinidad and Tobago, Uganda
1963	112	Kenya, Kuwait
1964	115	Malawi, Malta, Zambia
1965	118	Gambia, Maldives, Singapore

(continues)

Table 9.2 (continued)

Year	Number	New Member States
1966	122	Barbados, Botswana, Guyana, Lesotho
1967	123	Democratic Yemen
1968	126	Equatorial Guinea, Mauritius, Swaziland
1970	127	Fiji
1971	132	Bahrain, Bhutan, Oman, Qatar, United Arab Emirates
1973	135	Bahamas, Federal Republic of Germany, German Democratic Republic
1974	138	Bangladesh, Grenada, Guinea-Bissau
1975	144	Cape Verde, Comoros, Mozambique, Papua New Guinea, São Tomé and Príncipe, Suriname
1976	147	Angola, Samoa, Seychelles
1977	149	Djibouti, Vietnam
1978	151	Dominica, Solomon Islands
1979	152	Saint Lucia
1980	154	Saint Vincent and the Grenadines, Zimbabwe
1981	157	Antigua and Barbuda, Belize, Vanuatu
1983	158	Saint Christopher and Nevis
1984	159	Brunei Darussalam

SOURCE: *UN Chronicle* 27, No. 1 (March 1990).

Economic and Social Council   The wide array of ECOSOC activities in the social, economic, and humanitarian fields has been based on General Assembly resolutions, declarations, and conventions. Several UN bodies have been created by resolution to cope with the social, economic, and humanitarian needs of the developing world.[25] Examples include the UN Conference on Trade and Development (UNCTAD), the UN High Commissioner for Refugees (UNHCR), and the UN Relief and Works Agency for Palestine Refugees (UNRWA). Under the UN Charter, ECOSOC is charged with coordination of these agencies and the many other functional and specialized UN agencies. In addition to this coordination function, ECOSOC has a mandate to deliberate and pass resolutions on social and economic affairs, and to conduct research and issue reports. Although the work is far less glamorous than that involving peace and security issues, as much as three-fourths of the UN budget is spent in support of the ECOSOC program.

Despite all the resources devoted to these programs, efforts to enhance the economic development of Third World governments have been marginally successful at best. Without UN efforts, however, the plight of many LDCs might be even worse. The UN humanitarian agencies can be given high marks for providing emergency assistance to refugees and victims of natural disasters. Efforts to resolve the underlying economic and political circumstances that lead to these disasters have been less successful.

The Political Dimension of Intergovernmental Organizations

Intergovernmental Organizations as Foreign Policy Tools

Nations can have several motives for joining IGOs. One motive is to use the IGO as an instrument of foreign policy to achieve certain goals and objectives that otherwise might be more difficult to attain. A second motive is to benefit from the common service provided by the organization, such as a more orderly system of postal service, telecommunications, aviation, peacekeeping, or trade. These motives are somewhat conflicting, because one stresses the individual benefits the country may gain by using its political influence to manipulate the IGO in a direction compatible with its interests, and the other stresses the common benefits accruing to the entire membership of the organization through cooperation.

In short, international politics does not stop just because states create an organization that has high-minded ideals such as promoting a peaceful order or even more practical objectives such as monitoring nations' use of radio frequencies. Thus, whether it is the UN, the EC, or any other IGO, states will attempt to dominate the agendum and manipulate it to their own advantage. The United States, for instance, dominated the UN's agendum for years. In the 1960s the Third World began to have a good deal more to say in UN activities and redirected the UN's focus away from East–West disputes to the economic needs of the developing world. More recently, however, the United States has flexed its financial muscle by withholding contributions to exact certain administrative and budgetary reforms in the UN system. Simultaneously, the once-strident demands of the LDCs have become more sober. For example, at a recent General Assembly emergency session on the African development crisis, African diplomats accepted responsibility for their own economic predicament instead of blaming the Western industrial nations; they outlined a program for reform in their domestic policies; and they asked for Western help in providing assistance to their beleaguered economies. Thus, although Third World nations have used the General Assembly—where they enjoy a voting majority—at times as an ideological mouthpiece to express anti-Western ideals, they have shown more pragmatism recently.

Efforts to influence the outcome of IGO decisions and activities are seen in other organizations as well. The European Communities has been dominated by the interests of its three most powerful members. France has had a significantly larger influence on agricultural policy as the largest producer of agricultural commodities. West Germany is the industrial powerhouse, and the United Kingdom secured special privileges for its Commonwealth trading partners prior to its entrance as an EC member. Similarly, Saudi Arabia dominates OPEC policies, because it holds the largest oil reserves and enjoys the least expensive production costs of all OPEC members. Saudi Arabia has not hesitated to flex its muscle and even override the majority's wishes on pricing and production policies. In short, countries will use whatever political capital and economic power they have to influence the activities of IGOs, either individually or as members of a bloc of nations with common interests. This is why the reunification of Germany poses a challenge to the EC. Germany already exerts considerable influence. A reunited Germany many be even more formidable, and other EC members understandably wonder whether their interests will be adversely affected.

Bloc Politics

One of the more interesting political phenomena in the United Nations is bloc politics.[26] Over time, several groups of nations have coalesced to achieve certain common objectives. The Group of Seventy-Seven grew out of the nonalignment movement of the 1950s and 1960s. Although initially composed of seventy-seven members, it now boasts a membership of over a hundred. This group has sought to draw more attention to LDC interests. But the Group of Seventy-Seven is not a homogeneous group. It is futher subdivided into African, Arab, Latin American, and Asian groups. Countries in these groups, which had been former colonies of Great Britain, also participate in the Commonwealth Group. Others are members of the Islamic Conference Group. Nor is bloc politics the exclusive domain of the developing countries. The Soviet Union leads the East bloc nations in what, until recently, was one of the most tightly controlled and unified blocs in the United Nations. Rarely did an East bloc country fail to vote with the rest of the bloc on issues addressed at the UN. Competing with the East bloc countries is the Western Group, consisting of most First World countries. The Western group is further subdivided into the Nordic Group, the EC Group, and the Peacekeeping Group, which hopes to encourage the development of a more effective peacekeeping system. In a sense, the United Nations reflects the existing divisions and groupings of states in the international system. These blocs meet, discuss voting strategies, lobby for passage of resolutions that reflect that group's interests, and propose candidates for election to UN organs such as the Security Council and ECOSOC. The vast majority of UN member-states participate in one or more of these groups; only South Africa, Israel, and Albania—which for this and other reasons have often been referred to as "pariah" states—do not participate.[27]

Public Diplomacy

One purpose of IGOs is to provide an open forum for discussion of international issues. This idea began with Wilson's dream of a League of Nations in which decisions would be reached openly and continues with the United Nations. While public international diplomacy provides an opportunity for every member-state to hear and understand the foreign policy objectives of every other state, critics of the UN have found this to be one of the most objectionable features of the organization. In this view, small and powerless countries can use the General Assembly as a platform to propagandize and criticize those nations that pay for the majority of the UN's financial needs. Certainly, to the extent that this is true, it is not necessarily constructive or desirable. In fact, a case could be made that this can worsen rather than relieve international tensions. But it is clear that the United Nations was intended as a forum in which its member-states could thrash out their differences, even when they might result in bruised feelings. Indeed, an overemphasis on UN speech-making ignores the fact that much of the real negotiation and compromise takes place in the corridors and cocktail parties. Private diplomacy continues apace even as the cameras focus on what is said at the General Assembly podium.

Assessing the Value of Intergovernmental Organizations

As we have noted, the chief contributions of IGOs have been to provide states with (1) alternative mechanisms, in addition to traditional diplomacy, to resolve disputes, (2) additional mechanisms to facilitate everyday transnational interactions in the vast array of functional areas that have emerged with economic progress, and (3) a way to share the costs of maintaining order in an increasingly complex international environment.

Because the rate of international conflicts has failed to decline appreciably, one might conclude that IGOs, such as the UN, have made little difference in international relations. But as we saw earlier, the United Nations has been used successfully on numerous occasions to defuse regional disputes. In the area of functional relations, the mind-boggling number and scope of IGOs is more impressive. Put very simply, the explosion in the number of IGOs is a reflection of the complicated nature of today's international system. States form organizations to gain some control over this complexity, achieve greater order, and facilitate more effective international interaction.

The United Nations, in particular, still occupies a special and prominent place in contemporary international relations, although the hopes of its founders have not been fully realized. Hopes or fears that it might formulate the basis of a genuine world government have also not materialized. The UN has very limited capacity to enforce its resolutions, which carry little legal force; however, it is an important forum in which the vast majority of sovereign nations participates. Indeed, for many smaller countries that cannot afford to maintain embassies throughout the world, the UN provides the only focal point for contact with representatives of virtually all other nations.

The United Nations also monitors a far-flung, sizable number of subsidiary organizations that help to facilitate day-to-day relations among nations. It fosters negotiation of treaties that progressively develop international law, promotes social welfare and human rights, and assists refugees and disaster victims. In addition, the UN can potentially be used for settling disputes. In short, it has become an important part of modern international relations. At least, this is one version of the UN's role.

If the UN system has grown in size and importance, it does not necessarily mean that it has become more effective or useful. Indeed, a good many people think that the United Nations is a massive failure, a bloated, inefficient bureaucracy dominated by opinionated Third World ideologues, and an actual hindrance to the maintenance of peace. Consider, for instance, the views of a prominent critic of the United Nations:

> ...the United Nations is an organization out of control. For one thing, it has become exceedingly anti-U.S., anti–West, and anti–free enterprise. Much worse, it has been betraying the spirit and substance of its own charter. It has not been helping those poor, needy, and threatened communities of the world which it was created to serve. It has failed as a peacekeeper and as a protector of human rights. Inefficiency, cronyism, high pay, lavish expense accounts, and even corruption and illiteracy have become the all too common characteristics of the Secretariat and other UN bureaucracies...[28]

Which version is more accurate? Is it an indispensable tool of diplomacy or a worthless nuisance? Or is this too stark a contrast? Could it be that the United Nations is a complex, imperfect organization that sometimes works and sometimes does not? We turn our attention to these questions in the next section.

Basic Issues in Contemporary Intergovernmental Organization Literature

The United Nations and the Management of Conflict

Management of international conflict is regarded as the UN's most important purpose. Although the United Nations has manifestly failed to resolve some disputes (i.e., the Middle East conflict), it has contributed significantly to the resolution of others through a variety of mechanisms other than direct enforcement. For instance, the active role of the secretary-general's office in mediating the Afghanistan war was critical to the achievement of a Soviet withdrawal of forces. Nevertheless, the United Nations does not function effectively in dealing with planned and determined aggression. Nor is it especially effective in highly antagonistic and intense conflicts. In other cases, however, it can buy time for dispute settlement by sending peacekeeping forces to separate conflicting parties, when those parties are agreeable to such a step.[29]

What is the UN's record in the related problem of international crises? One study examined a thirty-year period between 1945 and 1975, finding that the UN participated in nearly 60 percent of the crises but succeeded only 28 percent of the time.[30] Another study by Ernst Haas holds that during the 1970s the UN conflict management system grew less effective—it literally began to decay. Haas does not believe that this was evidence of UN failure, but rather a symptom—indeed, possibly, a temporary result—of state preferences to live with low levels of conflict that did not centrally threaten the integrity of the international system.[31] In the first supplemental reading, John G. Ruggie points out that the United Nations has enjoyed spotty success in dispute settlement but considerable success in the more passive area of peacekeeping.

Most recent studies seem to suggest that the United Nations has performed its conflict management role successfully in about one-fourth to one-third of the cases in which it gets involved. Opinions on how it will operate in the future vary considerably. However, most experts agree that the United Nations has performed useful if limited peacekeeping roles in the past and that it could continue to do so in the future.

Reforms for the Functional Agencies?

A second set of issues, which has been of special concern to the United States, is whether the UN can be made leaner, more efficient, and at least in the case of some technical and specialized agencies, less politicized. This issue is the pet target of many staunch UN critics. Particularly galling to these critics is the fact that eighty countries whose combined contributions to the UN account for barely 1 percent of its budget constitute a majority and thus decide how to spend the money of some twenty-three industrial countries that pay for nearly three-quarters of the UN budget.[32]

To remedy this situation, there have been periodic calls for weighted voting procedures that would emphasize the size of a state's population, gross domestic product, contributions to the UN, energy consumption, or some combination of these factors instead of the one-nation, one-vote rule based on the "fictional" notion of the sovereign equality of nations. Several studies have shown, however, that weighted voting procedures either would not work as well or would not be as easily achieved as their advocates would hope.[33]

Short of forcing weighted votes in the United Nations, the major donor countries have found it useful to consult regularly among themselves to discuss specific programs and proposals for UN reform and to monitor UN reform efforts. The Geneva Group, which John Bolton addresses in the second supplemental reading, is one forum in which donors accomplish this. Various donors have called for UN budgeting based on consensus rather than majority vote. Consensus voting gives the donor countries a greater voice in budget proposals. Under majority voting, major donors are simply outvoted. Under consensus voting, pressure is placed on all member-states to arrive at compromise budgets that will be acceptable to all, including the donors. Consensus voting also reduces pressures to devise complicated and politically unpopular weighted voting schemes.

Many sympathetic UN supporters believe that the United Nations suffers from duplication of effort, poor management policies, budgetary waste, and a lack of effective coordination. Other supporters are bothered by the politicization of UN specialized agencies, leading one prominent scholar to complain about the degradation of the UN's constitutional environment.[34] The UNESCO is commonly cited as a case of unwarranted politicization of technical mandates complicated by a morass of administrative and financial problems. John Ruggie, writing in the first supplemental reading, believes that the process of reforming the UN bureaucracy will be a difficult, though not impossible, task. The difficulty arises from the fact that the United Nations is what it is largely because of the decisions and, in some cases, indecision of its member-states. If reform is ever to succeed, the member-nations must approach it conscientiously and practically.

The reforms most often called for are the professionalization of the UN administration and staffing, the strengthening of internal auditing capacities possibly through allowing greater scope and authority for the UN Joint Inspection Unit (the UN equivalent to an auditor), the promotion of interagency coordination, and a movement away from voluntary contributions to a fixed assessment approach, which allows agencies to plan more effectively.[35]

The last of these reforms is likely to be the most controversial. Under a **fixed assessment** system, countries pay a percentage of the IGOs costs based on some set of criteria, such as the ability to pay, size of the GNP, or the like. If they do not pay, they are said to be in arrears, and, in the case of the United Nations, can lose their right to vote if they are more than two years in arrears. Under a **voluntary contribution** system, no penalty is enforced against noncontributing members; they simply pay as much as they see fit. Obviously, any effort to move toward assessed contributions in those IGOs that do not already have such a system is likely to be resisted by those member-states that prefer the flexibility of the voluntary contribution approach. However, if other significant reforms are to take place, governments must come up with some way to give the UN agencies greater budgetary certainty.[36]

In the second supplemental reading Bolton discusses the Bush administration perspective, which is not unlike that of many other major donor countries. Bolton, who welcomes recent UN reforms, believes that further reforms should be undertaken in each of the specialized agencies, as well as within the context of the organization's overall structures and capacities. He believes that the concept of a "unitary United Nations" should be used to identify and implement continuing budgetary and administrative reforms. In the first reading, Ruggie echoes this sentiment, noting that there is too little accountability between and among agencies, and that the UN system as a whole lacks many characteristics that make classical bureaucracies work efficiently in an unbiased manner. Ruggie also notes that the governments themselves are responsible for much of the duplication of effort and proliferation of overlapping agency responsibilities. The UN agencies are not created and do not evolve in isolation from government decisions.

Bolton subscribes, as do many officials of donor governments, to zero budget growth in the UN system as a whole, although he recognizes that individual agencies may need substantial infusions of resources to meet their mandates. The perspective raised in his article will continue to put UN officials on the spot to demonstrate fiscal responsibility and administrative efficiency. One would hope that an enthusiasm for budget cutting will not so deeply slash UN budgets as to deprive them of the ability to meet the growing demands of global interdependence. As Bolton seems to imply, there is danger that the budget knife can cut too deep.

Regionalism

A final theme that appears in the contemporary literature revolves around the issue of global versus regional approaches to solving international problems. The UN Charter allows for regional handling of peace and security issues. As we have seen, the OAU, OAS, and other IGOs have functioned in this capacity. The theory is that regional responses to regional issues are often more effective than global ones. Regional approaches to international relations are not limited to the security area alone, they have also been applied extensively to the economic sphere, the most celebrated example being the Common Market in Europe. Regional approaches can be very useful, but they can also create larger competitive blocs of states, with each block consisting of states that cooperate on security or economic policies. But intrabloc harmony may lead to interbloc strains and conflict. In other words, regional approaches to international relations can have positive and negative side effects. This is an old concern among students of international organization.[37] But it has been resurrected in recent literature as concern grows that the wealthier Western countries have turned their backs on global solutions in favor of regional approaches to international peace and economic issues. The heads of state of the wealthiest countries now meet regularly to discuss international economic, trade, and monetary issues.

Concern has been raised in recent years about the apparent reluctance of Western nations to consider economic problems from a more global perspective, taking into special account the needs of the poorer LDCs. Regionalism that excludes a larger dialogue with other nations does not serve the interests of the international community.[38] However, there is no reason that regional solutions to security and economic problems must be counterproductive to global solutions. Indeed, regional and global solutions to these issues, at least theoretically, can complement rather than contradict each other. For instance, at the 1988 Toronto Summit meeting of key Western leaders, one high-priority item for discussion was debt relief for the ailing economies of sub-Saharan African countries. The final communiqué of the Toronto Summit gave creditor nations wide discretion in reducing interest rates, rescheduling debts over a longer period, even partially canceling some debts. In subsequent years, Western governments acted on this front, much to the relief of African country economies. As this illustrates, regional meetings in one part of the world can lead to beneficial solutions in another.

Final Observations

The United Nations and other IGOs are mirrors of the imperfect, politically divided world of the states that created them. In this sense they are part of the problem and part of the solution. Intergovernmental organizations will become a more effective part of the solution when states are prepared to give them the opportunity.

Over the next decade, the issues identified in this chapter will become increasingly important. Indeed, the UN system will find itself caught between increasing reluctance from donor countries to provide funding for its programs and an increase in program needs, especially in the Third World. Budgetary retrenchment inevitably will move beyond the domestic programs of individual countries to affect foreign aid outlays. Foreign aid of all descriptions, bilateral and multilateral, will probably continue to suffer. Some governments may even choose to reduce their multilateral contributions further, transferring some of these savings into bilateral assistance over which states have more direct control. All of this could potentially hit the UN system very hard. It will need to find ways to perform its functions—certainly with no more and possibly with less revenue—at a time when more rather than fewer resources are needed. On the brighter side, reduced tensions between the East and the West may allow the UN Security Council to function more effectively and to revitalize its peace-making and peacekeeping roles. Introduction of UN forces into Namibia, for instance, saw the United States aligning with the Soviet Union to ensure a smaller, less expensive operation. Reduced Cold War tensions might also reduce the levels and intensity of regional conflicts worldwide. These would be welcome developments, and UN bodies should aggressively capitalize on them.

When the United Nations entered the 1980s, it had the look and feel of an organization in disarray. Nor did the 1980s lack severe challenges to the budgetary health and organizational purposes of the UN system. However, it would be wrong to conclude that the United Nations has failed to meet these challenges. At the very end of the 1980s, patient diplomatic negotiations, many directly sponsored by the UN, began to pay handsome dividends, as one regional conflict after another proved amenable to at least interim cease-fire measures and insertion of peacekeeping forces. Many conflicts still resist full resolution, but measurable progress toward peace is manifest. On the financial front, the United Nations, under pressure from large donors, has successfully trimmed its personnel by 12 percent, moved toward consensus methods of budgeting, and reduced costs of administration. As the Bolton reading suggests, donor governments are not content to have the reforms stop there; since 1985 efforts by the secretary-general working with the Group of Eighteen have achieved significant reforms. The Group of Eighteen consists of reform-minded UN member states, principally major donors.

The United Nations leaves the 1980s in much better condition than it entered them. The 1990s will prove to be a time for continuing and sober reevaluation of the UN system and of IGOs as a whole. But opportunities for revitalizing its role in international affairs also exist, and it is highly likely that based on its more vigorous role in recent years, the UN may yet contribute substantially to a more peaceful and prosperous world in the 1990s.

John G. Ruggie

The United States and the United Nations: Toward a New Realism

Quantitatively, international governmental organizations (IGOs) are still an expanding force in international relations.... Qualitatively, however, the world of IGOs is not in good shape. Indeed, there is widespread talk these days about a crisis of multilateralism.... North–South economic negotiations in the United Nations have been stalemated for a decade and the decade-long Law of the Seas negotiations failed to produce a universally acceptable treaty. The administrative performance of the United Nations and its agencies is said by many critics to be inferior, the salary and benefit levels inflated. Many of its technical agencies are accused of having become thoroughly politicized. There is a pervasive sense that the system as a whole is somehow out of control....

I focus on two areas of concern. The first is the role of the United Nations in the maintenance of international peace and security.... The other area of concern is the administrative performance of the UN system, including the specialized agencies. Here, the criticisms are that the United Nations comprises so bloated and inefficient a bureaucracy, and that the agencies have so politicized their technical tasks and deliberations, that the United Nations as a whole accomplishes too little of what it was designed to accomplish (and at great expense)....

The Maintenance of Peace and Security

For governments assembled in San Francisco, the primary purpose of the United Nations was to "maintain international

SOURCE: From *International Organization* 39, no. 2 (Spring 1985). Reprinted by permission in abridged form. © 1985 by the Massachusetts Institute of Technology and the World Peace Foundation.

peace and security." Some two hundred international conflicts later, the goal still appears elusive.... The management of actual conflicts among states, involves two distinct tasks: the peaceful resolution of disputes and UN enforcement action. Here the United Nations serves as a forum for concerted action and as an actor in its own right....

[However,] the ability of the United Nations to settle or even isolate disputes reached, with the important exception of the 1973 Arab–Israeli conflict, a nadir by the mid-1970s.... This decline in efficacy roughly coincided with several developments: the arrival in the United Nations of many more developing countries, guarding their newly acquired sovereignty and making consensus more difficult to achieve; the constraint that U.S. military involvement in Vietnam placed on U.S. initiatives in the Security Council for dealing with conflicts elsewhere; and American success in marginalizing the role of the Soviet Union in such critical areas of conflict as the Middle East, thus ensuring Soviet opposition in the Security Council to international approval of U.S. negotiated settlements. The revival of Cold War rhetoric in the 1980s worsened an already bad situation. Virtually by default, then, the focus of UN activity in the peaceful resolution of disputes...shifted to the secretary-general....

As for enforcement action under Chapter VII of the UN Charter, it was a dead letter in 1945.... In recognition of this fact, Dag Hammarskjöld and his staff back in the 1950s invented the more modest notion of peacekeeping forces. These forces have been deployed in a dozen or so instances—in the past, generally to control conflicts attending decolonization that threatened to become globalized along East–West lines. On the whole, peacekeeping has been a success story for the United Nations, as even some of the fiercest critics of the organization are obliged to concede....

When the United Nations works on matters of peace and security, it works to insulate and contain, to provide an environment within which governments can undertake measures to deal with underlying issues.... Taking an issue to the United Nations is, therefore, only the beginning of collective conflict management, not the end. If governments with the means to do so do not follow through, no issue can be resolved. The United Nations has not worked well in the peace and security area...[until recently] because governments...failed to exercise their influence and provide support in behalf of collective efforts....

A reversal of this...state of affairs can be [sustained] only by the permanent members of the Security Council, in particular by the two superpowers.... Tacit agreement or behind-the-scenes efforts by the United States and the Soviet Union to support UN attempts to resolve conflicts from which neither can hope to gain any advantage would not only [continue] to rejuvenate the peace and security mechanisms of the organization, but perhaps also contribute to a [further] easing of. . .tension between the two superpowers. . .Specific institutional reforms in the functioning of the Security Council are also required, but they are meaningless in the absence of substantive agreement and will be achieved more readily in the wake of substantive agreement.

Administrative Performance

If the public at large has been disappointed by the United Nations,. . .government officials in the United States are particularly exercised by its administrative performance. . . and the politicization of the specialized agencies. . . .

Traditionally, activities of the specialized agencies have received little public notice. Of late, however, they have become the object of considerable media and official scrutiny. In the United States this shift has been prodded by several criticisms. The first is that the agencies have become thoroughly politicized and have therefore compromised their technical missions. This argument is not without merit, yet the issue is more complex than it appears at first glance. Great care must be taken to distinguish between two very different kinds of politicization. One, concerning the principles governing an issue area, is inevitable and legitimate; the other, concerning the introduction of extraneous political issues into an issue area, is neither. Take, as an illustration, the case of the International Telecommunications Union [ITU]. The basic rules concerning allocation of the frequency spectrum and registration of frequency bands were determined by the industrialized countries to suit their particular needs, on a first-come, first-served basis. As the frequency spectrum has become more crowded, both because of the rapid growth of telecommunications services and the trebling of membership in the ITU, the developing countries (not surprisingly) have challenged the prevailing principles of allocation. They have sought to replace them with principles that more effectively protect their own long-term interests. To challenge a principle of allocation in any social system is, of course, an act of "politicization," particularly when the challenge is accompanied by rhetorical flourishes, as it is in the case in the ITU, calling for a "new international information order." There is nothing whatever perverse or illegitimate about this activity, however; Americans would do precisely the same were the United States in the disadvantaged position. Appropriate compromises will, we may presume, be worked out in such contexts. . . .

The threshold of admissibility is crossed, however, when governments or groups of governments seek to exploit a technical forum purely for the pursuit of political objectives that have no direct bearing on that realm. Even at the height of the Cold War, East and West managed to circumscribe their ever-present desire to engage in this practice; but the developing countries seem to have been less successful in restraining themselves. In some ultimate sense, everything may well be related to everything else in international politics; acting on this premise in UN agencies, however, produces organizational paralysis, not reform.

The recent UNESCO crisis has brought to public attention another problem afflicting the specialized agencies: Once executive heads are appointed, there are relatively few effective internal checks and balances on their behavior. The UNESCO case may [have been] extreme, combining, as it apparently [did], autocratic leadership, gross cronyism, the explicit abandonment of impartiality, and questionable financial practices. Still, the more general problem is potentially present in all UN agencies: Effective and accountable leadership depends too much on individual professionalism and integrity and not enough on institutionalized restraints. Existing restraints, such as they are, are inadequate for two reasons. First, executive heads are not responsible on a day-to-day basis to any legislative body or executive board; both meet too infrequently to perform such a supervisory role. Second, there exists a symbiotic relationship between the executive heads of international agencies and officials in national ministries who serve as delegates to the governing bodies of those agencies. The two can be of enormous assistance to each other in allocating resources and advancing their respective careers. As a result, the governors are not always eager to govern, and the sole mechanism of accountability that does exist can be too easily compromised.

A third and final point of contention concerns the perennial problem of overlap and duplication in the programmatic activities of UN agencies. The record shows that interagency coordination is marginally more effective today than it was in the past. The record also shows, however, that the problem ultimately cannot be solved at the interagency level. After all, it was not international bureaucrats but national governments that established (as one example) no fewer than four international agencies dealing with food and agriculture alone. Nor is it only officials of international agencies who ignore requests by various central UN organs to coordinate their activities in similar domains. The governing boards of the separate agencies, consisting of national officials, jealously guard the piece of institutional turf for which they are responsible, even against the wishes of their own foreign offices for more efficiency and less duplication.

. . .The United Nations may have become too much of a bureaucracy in the current, pejorative sense of the term, but it is not enough of a bureaucracy in the classic, analytical sense: a system of rationalized authority and administrative relations, capable of rising above particularism and personalism, following generalized rules of procedure, and held strictly accountable on the basis of objective performance criteria. To some extent the United Nations is prevented from becoming more "bureaucratized" in this latter, positive sense by the very nature of the international polity and the particular alignments that prevail within it. Nonetheless, resolution of some of these problems is possible, particularly in budgetary and management techniques, as well as personnel and career development policy. If the proper lessons are learned from the UNESCO affair, it may become possible to invent and institute more effective governing structures in UN agencies as well.

U.S. Policy

American power and resources first breathed life into the many postwar multilateralist schemes, including the United Nations. Subsequently, the United States and the United Nations worked in tandem, over the opposition of the major colonial powers, to catalyze and facilitate decolonization. For the first quarter century or so, U.S. foreign policy included a routine if not central part for the United Nations. It is ironic, therefore, that the United States now plays the multilateral game less effectively than many other states. American leaders tend to focus blame exclusively on the United Nations, but a dispassionate assessment also calls for an examination of the posture and performance of the United States.

One is struck first of all by the inability of the United States to define and maintain any kind of strategic orientation toward the United Nations. The Soviet Union look[ed] to the organization as a vehicle to delegitimize the postwar international order constructed by the capitalist nations, while retaining its own political prerogatives to act unconstrained by multilateral obligations. The Third World [sought] to liquidate the remnants of colonialism and upgrade its position in the international division of labor. The small European states support the United Nations as a potential agency of peaceful change in the face of international forces over which they have no control. Their larger European neighbors see the United Nations as a forum that to some extent endows them with a status and influence they no longer enjoy in the world at large. But what of the United States? Put simply, the visions being debated in UN forums today are the visions of others, not our own. Few can recall the last time the United States initiated a major new action in the United Nations. Our posture toward the organization recently has oscillated wildly between accommodationism, rejectionism, and pragmatism, but at no time has it been guided by a clear strategic concept of the potential contribution of the United Nations to the kind of world order we desire. . . .

Conclusion

. . . Any crisis of multilateralism is a crisis of humankind, for the human agenda is coming to be dominated by more, not fewer, issues of global proportions. International institutions can resolve none of these issues on their own, but neither can national states resolve them without international institutions. For better or worse, then, we are condemned to improve existing international institutions or to invent new ones to take their place. . . .

John R. Bolton

■

The Concept of the "Unitary UN"

It is a special pleasure for me to participate in this my first meeting of the Geneva Group consultative level. This forum, especially through the 1980s, has provided an important and useful opportunity for exchanging views and coming to conclusions on budgetary, financial, and administrative issues affecting the organizations of the UN system. . . .

Together, the members of the Geneva Group represent over 70 percent of the contributions to the assessed budgets of the UN system. Were we to add our voluntary contributions to the extra-budgetary activities of the UN agencies, and to the operational programs such as UNDP [the UN Development Program], . . .the percentage would be at least as high. It is incumbent on members of the Geneva Group to fulfill our responsibilities to our taxpayers and to other members of the organizations by continuing to provide the leadership required for adapting the UN system to its growing responsibilities. With your indulgence, I will take a few moments. . .to discuss with you our concept of the "unitary United Nations."

In the course of formulating the Bush administration's diplomacy toward the UN system, it struck me that we should have a policy that treated the United Nations comprehensively. Instead of a series of unrelated policies toward each UN component, I felt that we needed to address the UN system in much the same way as the U.S. State Department's regional bureaus interact with the governments in their respective regions. Just as an action taken toward one specific country affects overall regional relationships, by analogy, so, too, do the actions of individual UN agencies affect the operation of the entire system. . . .

The unitary United Nations concept provides us with a basis to deal coherently with the UN system on both budgetary and policy grounds. We have all noted the proliferation of committees, councils, conferences, and meetings, all of which cover essentially the same issues. Numerous governing bodies (however denominated) all spend precious time and fiscal resources discussing precisely the same issues, often in several different cities. Moreover, almost all components of the UN system have expanded their programs beyond their originally intended missions and are now duplicating each other's work. Moreover, there is always the risk of creating even more new organizations, with substantial budgetary claims, when existing agencies could handle emerging problems.

Following the unitary United Nations concept would provide us with a principle rule of decision to prune the thicket of UN governing bodies. It would also permit us to redefine the proper limits of each UN component's responsibilities and help avoid both empire building and turf fighting. By adhering to the original intent underlying the creation of each UN component, we should achieve not only budgetary savings but also create a greater sense of political responsibility among member governments and secretariats.

Under a unitary United Nations concept, even if some elements of the UN system were to take on new responsibilities, we are not suggesting that the Geneva Group abandon its policy of zero real growth. Indeed, the possibility of added responsibilities increases the need for maintaining tight budgetary discipline. In fact, I view the unitary United Nations concept as a logical next step beyond the policy of zero real growth, which is now only applied component by component. But in implementing a policy of zero real growth, we must recognize that there will be instances where some agencies must grow to respond to new and emerging developments. Otherwise they will stagnate, and initiatives will be taken by other organizations which do not have the expertise or qualifications to do so in the most effective way possible. Any such growth, however, must be offset by reductions in other organizations so as to maintain zero real growth throughout the UN system. Difficult choices must be made not only by the secretariats but by us, the member governments; ultimately, the burden of identifying and enforcing priorities rests with us. As we have seen, it is not easy to achieve cutbacks in agency functions, but if we want to strengthen the UN system, it is incumbent upon us to take a hard look at the various components in order to rationalize and harmonize their operations.

SOURCE: Published by the U.S. Department of State, Bureau of Public Affairs, Current Policy No. 1191. This is an abridged version of the speech given by Mr. Bolton, Assistant Secretary for International Organization Affairs, before the Geneva Group consultative-level meeting, Geneva, Switzerland, June 29, 1989.

My reference to the concept of the unitary United Nations should not be misinterpreted. I am not now suggesting a change in the mandate of the Geneva Group. I well understand that the Geneva Group does not address the whole of the UN system, and that its mandate explicitly is limited to concern for administrative, budgetary, and financial issues related to the basic infrastructure of the UN system, i.e., the regular assessed budgets of the specialized agencies.... However, we must recognize that this infrastructure influences, and is influenced by, a much larger whole in order to be effective in addressing our concerns about the basic infrastructure.

Let me also make clear that my use of the concept of the unitary United Nations does not mean that I am advocating central control in the UN system. I fully recognize that many of our substantive interests in the UN agencies are fostered and protected by the pluralism of the UN system. I am familiar with the longstanding efforts of some to do away with this pluralism in order to allow the whole of the UN system to be tightly orchestrated by a politicized majority in the UN General Assembly. It is because of the pluralism of the UN system, and our interest in maintaining this pluralism, that I urge the concept of the unitary United Nations. The lack of effective central control in the UN system increases the need for us, the member governments, to guide our participation in the different UN agencies with an eye on the overall system.

One example of the concept of the unitary United Nations at work is in deciding upon the appropriate role of the UNDP for the 1990s. We believe that the UNDP should play a more vigorous coordinating role. Over the years, UNDP has been weakened considerably, since agencies are taking it upon themselves to do what is properly in UNDP's realm. Indeed, if the Geneva Group is to be effective in assuring the best of resources by the United Nations' technical agencies, it will be essential that we assure a clearer division of labor between the UNDP and the technical agencies. Further, there needs to be improved communication among the major donors on the relationships between bilateral and multilateral assistance programs. The current state of play, all too often, means that resources are wasted or that we work at cross purposes in the management of a unitary UN system.

This is important because we recognize the great and growing need for the work of the UN system. In addition to the recent major increase in UN peacekeeping activities, still more can be expected. More directly related to our work at this meeting are the significant transnational problems increasingly being addressed. Certainly, the UN system has the potential to help deal with issues such as drug control, terrorism, refugees, AIDS, ...human rights, and the host of environmental problems....

In conclusion, I want to stress that the United States looks forward to important opportunities in the UN system for dealing with critical world problems. The renewed confidence in the UN system must be further strengthened and maintained; we must guard against allowing the expected return of financial stability to result in renewal of wasteful practices. This will require continued vigor by the Geneva Group in insisting on value for money. However, building on what we have achieved in recent years, we must go a step further in identifying and enforcing priorities for the UN system as a whole in order to be sure that our financial resources are being well used. I urge that—within our governments—we all place more emphasis on what I have called the unitary United Nations.

Study Questions

1. Define the term *international organization*. What are the chief characteristics of IGOs? How do international organizations differ from supranational ones?
2. What are nongovernmental organizations and transnational organizations? How do they differ from IGOs?
3. Why have international organizations proliferated in the last century?
4. What was the Concert of Europe? Why did it come about? Discuss its significance.
5. What is meant by the term *collective security*? How would an organization based on this idea differ from a *regional security* organization like NATO?
6. What is functionalism? Is this a tenable theory? Why or why not? What are some examples of IGOs based on functionalist propositions?
7. Discuss the importance of the European Communities.

8. What were the primary purposes of the United Nations? How is it similar to and different from the League of Nations?
9. Has the United Nations been an effective collective security organization? Why or why not?
10. Discuss the development of the UN peacekeeping function.
11. Are resolutions of the General Assembly binding on member-states? Why or why not?
12. Discuss the various social, economic, and humanitarian activities of the United Nations.
13. Why do states seek membership in international organizations? What advantages do they derive from membership?
14. Discuss the significance of bloc politics in the United Nations.
15. Based on the literature reviewed, would you conclude that the United Nations has been a failure or a success in its role as a crisis manager? Why?
16. What are some of the major reforms critics of the United Nations would like to see implemented? Which of them do you think is most important? most needed?
17. What is the importance of regionalism as a concept in international relations?
18. Based on your reading of John G. Ruggie's selection, do you think the United Nations is largely irrelevant or does it serve any useful purpose in international relations?
19. What does Ruggie mean when he talks about the need for a new realism in U.S. policy toward the United Nations?
20. What does John R. Bolton mean by the term *unitary United Nations*? What are the implications of zero-growth budgeting for UN agencies?
21. Ruggie discusses two kinds of politicization in UN specialized agencies. What are they? Can either one be considered legitimate? Discuss.

Key Terms

apartheid policy
commodity cartel
common market
Concert of Europe
Economic and Social Council
European Communities (EC)
fixed assessment
functionalism
General Assembly
intergovernmental organization (IGO)
International Court of Justice (ICJ)
mandate system

nongovernmental organization (NGO)
non-self-governing territories
peacekeeping
private voluntary organization (PVO)
regional security organizations
Secretariat
Security Council
spill-over effect
transnational organization
Trusteeship Council
Uniting for Peace Resolution
voluntary contributions

Notes

1. For a more extensive discussion of the Congress of Vienna and subsequent historical developments, see Harold Jacobsen, *Networks of Interdependence: International Organizations and the Global Political System* (New York: Knopf, 1984), pp. 1–33.

2. Ibid., p. 9.

3. For a traditional treatment of international organizations, see Inis Claude, *Swords into Plowshares* (New York: Random House, 1964).

4. The more recent use of the term *international organization* is explained in detail in the appendix to volume I of the *International Organization Yearbook,* 21st ed. (Munich: K. G. Saur Verlag, 1984), p. 1631.

5. Edward H. Buehrig, "The Resolution-Based International Agency," *Political Studies* 29, no. 2 (June 1981): 217–231.

6. See David J. Finlay and Thomas Hovet, Jr., *7304: International Relations on the Planet Earth* (New York: Harper & Row, 1975), p. 290.

7. For an excellent treatment on the history of the European Communities, see Leon Lindberg and Stuart Scheingold, *Europe's Would-Be Polity* (Englewood Cliffs, N.J.: Prentice-Hall, 1970).

8. See Robert F. Gorman, ed., *Private Voluntary Organizations as Agents of Development* (Boulder: Westview, 1985).

9. For data on the numbers of international organizations, see the forward to the *International Organization Yearbook.*

10. For a discussion of NGOs in the UN system, see Chiang Pei-heng, *Non-Governmental Organizations at the United Nations: Identity, Role, Function* (New York: Praeger, 1983).

11. For a discussion of nonstate actors in international relations, see Richard Mansbach, Yale Ferguson, and Donald Lampert, *The Web of World Politics: Non-State Actors in the Global System* (Englewood Cliffs, N.J.: Prentice-Hall, 1976).

12. For classical treatments of the concept of collective security, see Frederick H. Hartmann, *The Relations of Nations,* 5th ed. (New York: Macmillan, 1978), pp. 375–396; and Hans Morgenthau, *Politics Among Nations,* 4th ed. (New York: Knopf, 1967), pp. 285–298.

13. David Mitrany, *A Working Peace System* (Chicago: Quadrangle Books, 1966).

14. See Burton Pines, ed., *A World Without a U.N.* (Washington, D.C: Heritage Foundation, 1984), p. xvi.

15. See, for example, Ithiel de Sola Pool, "Effects of Cross-National Contact on National and International Images," in *International Behavior,* ed. Herbert C. Kelman (New York: Holt, Rinehart & Winston, 1965).

16. This typology among international organizations is carefully detailed in Finlay and Hovet, *7304,* p. 287–290.

17. See Lindberg and Scheingold, *Europe's Would-Be Polity;* and Werner Feld, *The European Community in World Affairs: Economic Power and Influence* (Port Washington, N.Y.: Alfred Pub. Co., 1976).

18. Austria and Turkey are also considering membership in the EC.

19. For a discussion of League sanctions in these cases, see M. S. Daoudi and M. S. Dajani, *Economic Sanctions* (London: Routledge & Kegan Paul, 1983), pp. 56–72.

20. For a discussion of the problems encountered by the League as well as a sympathetic treatment about some of the important advances made by this organization, see A. LeRoy Bennet, *International Organizations* (Englewood Cliffs, N.J.: Prentice-Hall, 1986).

21. Several useful works on UN peacekeeping can be cited: Larry Fabian, *Soldiers Without Enemies: Preparing the United Nations for Peacekeeping* (Washington, D.C.: Brookings, 1971); David Wainhouse, *International Peace Observation* (Baltimore: Johns Hopkins University Press, 1966); and Indar J. Rikhye, Michael Harbottle, and Bjorn Egge, *The Thin Blue Line: International Peacekeeping and Its Future* (New Haven: Yale University Press, 1974).

22. See David Kay, "The United Nations and Decolonization," in *The United Nations: Past, Present and Future,* ed. James Barros (New York: Free Press, 1972).

23. For a classic legal discussion on the role of the General Assembly in the development of law, see Rosalyn Higgins, *The Development of International Law Through the Political Organs of the United Nations* (London: Oxford University Press, 1963).

24. On the ministate issue, see Michael M. Gunter, "What Happened to the United Nations Ministate Problems," *American Journal of International Law* 71 (January 1977): 110–124.

25. Buehrig, "The Resolution-Based International Agency."

26. The classic treatment of this phenomenon in the UN is found in Thomas Hovet, Jr., *Bloc Politics in the United Nations* (Cambridge: Harvard University Press, 1960).

27. Actually, the United States does not formally participate in any of these bloc groupings. However, for purposes of UN voting, the United States is included in the Western Group.

28. Pines, *A World Without a U.N.,* p. x.

29. For an explication of these views, see Raimo Varynen, "Focus On: Is There a Role for the United Nations in Conflict Resolution?" *Journal of Peace Research* 22, no. 3 (1985): 191–196.

30. Jonathan Wilkenfeld and Michael Brecher, "International Crises 1945–1975: The UN Dimension," *International Studies Quarterly* 28, no. 1 (1984): 45–69. See also Jock Finlayson and Mark W. Archer, "The United Nations and Collective Security: Retrospect and Prospect," in *The US, the UN, and the Management of Global Change,* ed. Toby T. Gati (New York: New York University Press, 1983), p. 173.

31. Ernst Haas, "Regime Decay: Conflict Management and International Organizations, 1945–1981," *International Organization* 37, no. 2 (Spring 1983): 189–235.

32. See the Heritage Foundation, *The United Nations: Its Problems and What to Do About Them* (Washington, D.C.: Heritage Foundation, 1986).

33. William Dixon, "The Evolution of Weighted Voting Schemes for the UN General Assembly," *International Studies Quarterly* 27, no. 3 (1983): 295–315.

34. Leo Gross, "On the Degradation of the Constitutional Environment of the UN," *American Journal of International Law* 77, no. 3 (July 1983): 569–584.

35. For an insightful treatment of the impact of national politics on the selection and staffing of the UN Secretariat, see Seymour M. Finger and Nina Hanan, "The United Nations Secretariat Revisited," *Orbis* 25, no. 1 (Spring 1981): 197–208. While not sparing the UN Secretariat from criticism, Finger and Hanan attribute many of its administrative problems to political pressures by governments, which almost preclude rational administrative procedures from being adopted.

36. For a treatment of the UN's financing problem, see Robert F. Meagher, "United States Financing of the United Nations," in Gati, *The U.S., the UN, and the Management of Global Change,* ed. Toby T. Gati (New York: New York University Press, 1983), pp. 101–128.

37. See, for instance, Joseph Nye, *Peace in Parts: Integration and Conflict in Regional Organization* (Boston: Little, Brown, 1971).

38. Robert O. Keohane and Joseph F. Nye, Jr., "Two Cheers for Multilateralism," *Foreign Policy* no. 60 (Fall 1985): 148–167.

Ten

■

International Law

Ask an average American about international law, and he or she will probably expound on its irrelevance. You might hear comments such as "Treaties aren't worth the paper they're written on," or "If there is any such thing as international law, nobody pays any attention to it." Indeed, in our disorderly world where terrorism and violence are pervasive, international law does seem largely irrelevant. For instance, where are the international mechanisms for making, enforcing, and interpreting international law? Is there really law if such central mechanisms do not exist? On the other hand, what would international relations be like without international law? Before we explore these questions, we need to compare the international legal order to the domestic legal orders of states.

Background and Basic Concepts

Comparing International Law to Domestic Legal Systems

Police, judges, juries, courtrooms, legislatures, and statutory codes are the elements we normally associate with law. In domestic legal orders, well-defined, constitutionally legitimized institutions usually exist to legislate, execute, and interpret law. Lawbreakers can be apprehended, tried, and punished, and the law itself can usually be found in specific codes. In domestic legal systems courts have specific and compulsory jurisdictions, the police are sanctioned to enforce the law, and citizens usually recognize the necessity to obey the law. When they break the law, they know they run the risk of being caught and held accountable.

By comparison, international law lacks central executive, legislative, and judicial functions and, for the most part, is not centrally *codified,* that is, brought together in a written code. The very idea of state sovereignty works against the formation of centralized legal institutions. Under the Westphalian system, states are answerable to no higher authority. International law, then, exists between states, not above them.[1] It is a law of coordination rather than subordination. Under these circumstances, can international law truly be considered law? Some scholars would say no because it lacks fully developed institutions and enforcement capacities. But this view relies on a very restrictive definition of law. If we adopt a slightly broader focus, we can say that international law is law but that it certainly is not as fully developed as a nation's domestic legal system, and it has more imperfections.[2]

Compliance to International Law: Executive Functions

States have always recognized and abided by certain legal obligations that exist in their mutual relations. Why is this if they are free not to? Usually states conform to international law because it is in their interest to maintain order. If they did not accord privileges and immunities to one another's diplomats, if they did not protect the rights of resident aliens, if they did not respect the territorial claims and jurisdictions of other nations, they would not be able to enjoy the fruits of international trade, travel, and commerce. States create a great number of international laws to accommodate their reciprocal interests, and most adhere to these laws out of a principle of reciprocity; that is, a state agrees to grant other states certain legal privileges knowing that these states will give the same privileges in return. Thus, although we often read about major breaches of the law, such as the Iranian seizure of American diplomats as hostages or the American mining of Nicaraguan harbors, most of the time states routinely and strictly observe international law, whether out of mutual self-interest, reciprocity, or expedience.[3]

Much of international law works well because it describes what nations actually do. It is useful, then, to make a distinction between the vast body of utilitarian law that nations routinely observe, such as the laws of diplomacy and the regulatory regimes established by UN functional agencies, and the more political areas of law dealing with the regulation of force and the settlement of disputes, which were highlighted by the 1989 U.S. invasion of Panama. In these latter areas the imperfections of international law become apparent. But even in this more contentious arena, some basic principles exist. What happens when states actually violate international law?

As figure 10.1 shows, international law provides a number of alternatives to states that seek to resolve a dispute or to punish an offender. Basically they can go in two directions to resolve disputes legally: one direction leads toward peace and the other toward war. Indeed, many classical works in international law were written with two bodies of law in mind: the Law of Peace and the Law of War. Hugo Grotius, who is known as the father of modern international law, first made this distinction in 1625 in his classic text *Three Books on the Law of War and Peace.* The distinction survives even now.

If nations choose to resolve their dispute in a peaceful manner, they can begin by negotiating directly with each other. If this does not work, they might invite the UN

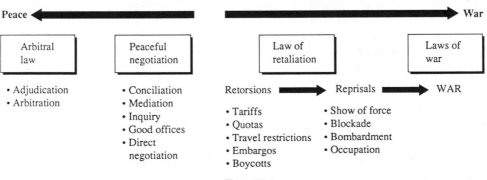

Figure 10.1
Laws of retaliation and dispute settlement
SOURCE: Adapted from Urban G. Whitaker, Jr. *Politics and Power: A Text in International Law* (New York: Harper & Row, 1964), p. 536.

secretary-general to assist the negotiations—to provide his **good offices**—or to make a formal **inquiry** into the facts. More active third-party efforts to resolve the dispute might involve **mediation** or **conciliation.** In these approaches the third party actively participates in the negotiations, suggesting possible solutions. Under some circumstances, the parties to a dispute might agree to invoke **arbitration** or **adjudication,** in which case they might agree in advance to be bound by the decision of an ad hoc arbitral panel or permanent court. All these steps lead to a peaceful resolution of a dispute. But what happens if the nation that committed the initial offense is unwilling to negotiate? What recourse is there then?

When states break international law, they can be held accountable. Although there is no international police force, the framers of the UN Charter had hoped that the Security Council would be able to perform this function. Indeed, in theory the Security Council could still exercise an enforcement function if its five permanent members—the United States, the Soviet Union, China, the United Kingdom, and France—and four other members could agree to do so. As we saw in Chapter 9, however, the Security Council has been hamstrung by lack of agreement among the permanent members. But this does not prevent a state or group of states from punishing breaches of international law, that is, from resorting to the traditional provisions of self-help when no other practical recourse is available. The sovereign states perform the executive function. They can punish other states that break international law by retaliating against them. The international law of **retaliation,** or *lex talionis,* allows a state that has been injured by the illegal act of another state to take action against the original offender provided it first attempts to achieve redress through peaceful means, and if this fails, if its response is proportional, to the original offense.[4] This is a primitive and imperfect form of enforcement because states have an infinite capacity to disagree about what is illegal, who is really at fault, and what constitutes a proportional response. The threat of widespread retaliation by other states, however, probably does have a certain deterrent effect.

International law draws a distinction between two kinds of retaliation: retorsions and reprisals. A **retorsion** is any legal but unfriendly act taken in response to an equally unfriendly but legal act committed by another state. For instance, suppose country *A* imposed stringent import quotas or tariffs on the imports it received from country *B.* Country *B,* viewing this as an unfriendly act, would be legally entitled by right of retorsion to impose similar restrictions on country *A*'s exports to it. The acts are unfriendly but legal. A **reprisal,** on the other hand, is an unfriendly (hostile) *and* illegal act that can be justified if undertaken in response and in proportion to a prior unfriendly and illegal act committed by another state. A reprisal is not legal under normal circumstances, but it can become legal if it is undertaken in response to an illegal act. Normally, under the provisions of the UN Charter, reprisals should be undertaken collectively under the aegis of the Security Council. However, the Charter's collective security provisions, as we saw in chapter 9, have largely been inoperative, and states have often resorted to unilateral reprisals.

As figure 10.1 illustrates, reprisals can potentially escalate into all-out war. This is one reason that the principle of **proportionality** is so important. By requiring that reprisals be proportionate to initial offenses, the law attempts to put a brake on the deterioration of retaliation into war. For instance, if one country illegally seizes and imprisons another country's diplomats, the latter would be entitled to expel some of the former country's diplomats, to break diplomatic relations, or to call on international sanctions against the offending state. But bombing the other country's capital city or invading a portion of its territory would not be legal because they are not proportional to the original offense. This does not mean that states always respond proportionately, but there is a legal expectation that they do so.

Nothing prevents a state from pursuing retaliatory and peaceful strategies simultaneously, however. Indeed, the simultaneous use of carrots and sticks or promises of peace and threats of war is a time-honored aspect of international relations. It is not unusual to see countries negotiating with each other, while at the same time maneuvering against each other through the application of retorsions and reprisals.

Finally, in those cases where retaliation eventually leads to war, an extensive body of international law, appropriately called the Law of War, comes into effect. We will return to this subject later in the chapter.

Two recent examples illustrate the problems of enforcement and retaliation in international law. In 1979 Iranian students seized the U.S. embassy in Tehran and took American diplomats hostage. The Iranian government subsequently approved this action, despite the fact that it was in direct violation of bilateral and multilateral treaties and customary international law. The act was condemned by countries all over the world, but the Iranians persisted. President Carter, despite strong public pressure, chose not to respond with immediate military force. Instead he froze Iranian assets in the United States, boycotted the purchase of Iranian oil, severed diplomatic relations, and called for other countries to take similar retaliation against Iran. These steps were all retorsionary in character. Some states responded, and at least in regard to the oil boycott, Iran began to feel the economic pinch. In the meantime, Carter quietly pursued possible third-party diplomatic options and even explored direct negotiations with specific members of the Iranian government. He also took the matter through a variety of UN channels, including the Security Council and the International Court of Justice; both bodies ruled in the favor of the United States. Only after several months was a military rescue of the hostages attempted. American restraint in this case was due to the fear that stronger retaliatory measures might lead to the death of the hostages. However, the United States acquitted itself well in terms of observing the rules of international law on retaliation. Carter responded to a widely recognized and serious violation of international law through a variety of economic and diplomatic means. He tried to resolve the matter peacefully, and his retaliatory measures were clearly proportionate to the original offense.

In a more recent case, the situation was more ambiguous. The United States bombed Tripoli, Libya, in April 1986 in retaliation for the bombing of a Berlin nightclub in which two Americans were killed and more than sixty injured. President Reagan claimed that this bombing, together with many other previous acts, including earlier bombings at the airports in Rome and Vienna, had been committed by terrorists who were sponsored directly by Libya. Within ten days of the Berlin incident, the United States attacked Tripoli, bombing the residence of Muammar Gaddafi, several military installations, and apparently by accident, a nonmilitary section of the city where numerous civilians were killed. Later, doubt was cast on the Libyan role in the Berlin bombing. Some evidence suggested that Syria may have been more directly involved. Had the United States retaliated legally? The original act—the terrorist bombing in Berlin—was clearly illegal, but there was doubt about the extent of Libya's culpability in that specific instance, though its involvement in other previous terrorist activities had been well documented. Only a short time elapsed between the Berlin bombing and the U.S. retaliation. There was little effort to pursue the matter through peaceful and diplomatic channels, although how can one state negotiate with another state that is known for sponsoring terrorism? More people were killed in the American bombing of Libya than had been killed in the terrorist attack in Berlin, casting doubt on the proportionality of the act. However, on the night of the raid, then Secretary of State George Shultz emphasized that the retaliation was proportionate to the original offense. Indeed, if the victims of the prior acts in which Libya had participated were included, the U.S. position seemed more justifiable. Moreover, proportionality is not based solely on a body count. More tenuous is the larger issue of whether the United States had the right to bomb a foreign city because of a presumed connection between that nation and terrorist acts committed on the soil of a third country. Clearly, the United States saw a legal need to justify its retaliation, which it did without apology. But as the smoke cleared and the dust settled, some doubt lingered about the legal legitimacy of the U.S. retaliation in this instance. In the months following this incident, however, several European states expelled Libyan (and Syrian) diplomats because of involvement in terrorist activities.

These examples suggest that retaliation is a limited tool at best for punishing offending states. Especially when dealing with terrorism, it can invite an escalation of violence. On the other hand, states may refrain from illegal acts if they fear retaliation by other states. Imperfect as it is, retaliation remains one of the few punitive tools available to states for seeking redress of a wrong. Rarely can a state break international law without paying some kind of price. Thus, in addition to the strong motivations of mutual self-interest that lead to compliance, states also adhere to international law because of the potential costs of not doing so.

If the executive function of law in the international arena is performed by the same states that are in a position to break it, what of the judicial function?

Judicial Functions in International Law

Enforcement of the law usually implies a capacity to settle disputes and to determine breaches of the law through some judicial process. Judicial bodies usually have a clear and often compulsory jurisdiction, and their judgments are usually enforced by the government's executive authority. **Compulsory jurisdiction** implies that a court can determine what kinds of cases are subject to its jurisdiction according to the relevant statutes and legislation in the particular legal system. It also means that when a court hears a case it may summon people before it under legal penalty. At least that is how things usually work in domestic legal systems. The international system, however, does not have a strong and centralized judiciary. The International Court of Justice (ICJ) exists both as the legal organ of the United Nations, which enables it on request of other UN bodies to render advisory opinions on the constitutional interpretation of the UN Charter and on the operating relations of various UN organs, and as a court of law to which states may resort for legal decisions regarding the interpretation of treaties and law and the determination of culpability and measures of redress for breaches of the law. The court could serve as a centralized judicial body in this latter capacity, however, because the ICJ has no compulsory jurisdiction over cases, it is a pale shadow of the state courts. As a result most highly contentious political disputes do not find their way to the ICJ.[5]

The ICJ has no compulsory jurisdiction because most states do not want to be forced to defend their actions in disputes with other states before the court. Indeed, the ICJ Statute, which it inherited from the Permanent Court of International Justice associated with the League of Nations, contains a provision known as the **Optional Clause,** which permits states to choose compulsory jurisdiction if they so desire. In other words, although all members of the United Nations are automatically party to the court's statute, they are not subject to the court's limited compulsory jurisdiction unless they specifically agree to it by a separate acceptance of the Optional Clause. In effect, the framers of the statute realized that states would be reluctant to become members of a court having compulsory jurisdiction. So they gave them the option of becoming members without being subject to compulsory jurisdiction, while providing them the additional opportunity to accept this jurisdiction freely.

In fact, over two-thirds of the UN's members have not accepted the court's limited compulsory jurisdiction under the Optional Clause. Of those nations that did accept it, only a handful have done so without reservation. Some of the reservations are so extensive that they have weakened the Optional Clause and, in some cases, have made acceptance of it meaningless. For instance, the United States, apart from other reservations, accepted the court's limited jurisdiction under the Optional Clause but with the understanding that it would not apply to disputes on matters under U.S. domestic jurisdiction, *as determined by the United States.* In other words, the United States would determine on a case-by-case basis whether the "compulsory jurisdiction" of the court applied!

Even states that have accepted the court's optional compulsory jurisdiction can terminate their acceptance with six months' prior notification to the UN secretary-general. In fact, the U.S. government did just that when it decided in October 1985 to announce its intention to withdraw its acceptance of the Optional Clause, a decision that became effective in April 1986. The withdrawal took place in the wake of Nicaragua's ICJ suit against the United States concerning its support of the *contras* and mining of Nicaraguan harbors. Although U.S. termination of its acceptance of the Optional Clause took place after the ICJ determined, over U.S. objections, that it had jurisdiction over this case, the U.S. government refused to participate in subsequent litigation on the merits of the case and refused to accept the court's controversial and largely unfavorable decision.[6]

Clearly, in most cases states are under no obligation to use the ICJ to settle their disputes. Indeed, as we saw earlier, adjudication under the ICJ, or for that matter under any other international legal body, is usually optional. Although the ICJ's docket is not very cluttered, a number of cases have been brought before it. Usually cases are brought to the court because the suing state, referred to as the **applicant,** believes that it will gain some political advantage. Typically, the state being sued, referred to as the **respondent,** will deny that the court has jurisdiction, as Iran did when the United States brought the hostage seizure case to the court, and as the United States did when Nicaragua brought the case of American mining of Nicaraguan harbors to the court. In other cases, respondents may choose to settle the issue with the applicant before a judgment is reached, thus avoiding a potentially embarrassing situation.

Once the court renders judgment, the next obstacle is to enforce the decision: that is, to gain **compliance.** Because the international system lacks centralized executive functions, compliance must be achieved under the same voluntary conditions that brought the case to the court in the first place. In other words, states that are party to a dispute will often agree in advance to the court's jurisdiction to hear a case and to abide by the court's final judgment. Indeed, most ICJ awards have been duly implemented by the losing state. Failure to comply with an ICJ judgment calling for compensation or some other steps to rectify a situation gives the offended state a right to seek further redress in other international bodies or to take other retaliatory measures.

The ICJ is not the only judicial body that rules on international law. Every year states refer hundreds of legal disputes to bilateral mixed-claims commissions, arbitral panels, and their own national courts. Indeed, most international law is enforced by state courts. The U.S. Supreme Court hears international law cases, and its decisions are enforced by the executive branch of the U.S. government. In other words, just as the executive function is carried out by the various sovereign states, so too is the judicial function in the vast majority of cases.

The Legislative Function in International Law

One might be tempted to argue that there is no such thing as a legislative function in international relations. For instance, where is a global legislature? The UN General Assembly, as we have seen, can pass resolutions, but barring the most exceptional circumstances, they are not legally binding. If there is no central or permanent legislature, in what sense is there a legislative function in the international system? The answer lies in the fact that nations create much of the international law. Especially in recent years, many important international conferences have been called, sometimes by the UN General Assembly, at which nations have negotiated multilateral treaties that have subsequently been ratified by large numbers of countries. Examples include the Vienna Convention on the Law of Treaties and the Law of the Sea Treaty. These treaties often help clarify existing customary laws and create new laws for certain technical areas of international relations that states agree require more systematic standards of law and regulatory activity. Thus, while there is no specific international legislature that can make binding international law, such conferences can be called on an ad hoc basis to deal with pressing problems. A discussion of the legislative function leads next to a search for the location of international law. In other words, what are its sources?

The Sources of International Law

International law also varies from domestic law in terms of where it can be found. In most domestic legal systems, laws or statutes can be found in a specific statutory code. International law, on the other hand, is less easily located. There is, in effect, no single international legal statutory code, rather law is found in a variety of scattered sources. Generally, five sources of international law are cited by international law experts: customs, treaties, general principles of law, judicial decisions, and writings of respected authorities and jurists. The major sources of international law are customs and treaties (and to a lesser extent general principles) because the states themselves create them. Writings of authorities and jurists and judicial decisions are considered secondary sources because they issue from observers's interpretations of state behavior, rather than from the will of the state. They may help to explain or understand the law, but they do not make it; this privilege is reserved to the states. Let us examine in greater depth each of these sources of international law.

Custom Out of the actual practice of nations has grown a body of international law that is customary in nature. Until this century, the most dominant form of international law was **custom.** In the international arena, customs describe what states actually do out of a sense of legal obligation. Violations of customary law invite potential retaliation. But how is a custom identified, as distinct from nations' **nonobligatory practices?** Indeed, these practices may evolve into customs. When do we know that a customary rule of law has come into existence?

Several factors can be used to determine the existence of customary law. A number of these factors concern factual issues such as whether the practice enjoys widespread, uniform, and continuous observation over a significant time span. Should the practice meet these criteria, it might be a candidate for a customary rule, but the key factor is whether the states engaged in the practice actually consider it to be legally binding. If the common expectation of the states in question is that the law should be observed, then the practice is said to have "ripened" into a customary law. At times, even this can be a very difficult determination to make. Sometimes countries do not clearly indicate their recognition of a legal obligation: Instead they simply abide by the rule as though it were legal. In these cases, judicial decisions or writings of key publicists may help clearly define where custom exists. The classic illustration is the famous *Scotia* case rendered by the U.S. Supreme Court.[7] An American and a British ship had collided on the high seas resulting in the loss of the American ship; the owners sued in U.S. courts, claiming the fault of the collision rested with the crew of the British ship. The Supreme Court ruled that, to the contrary, the British ship's crew had observed the widely practiced display of colored lights and steering regulations and that the American ship had been derelict in observing these rules. Although these rules were nowhere enacted in treaty, they were widely and generally practiced by all maritime nations, and so, the Court argued, had ripened into a custom. In applying this custom, the Court ruled against its own nationals in favor of the British. Further evidence of customs can be found in diplomatic correspondence, government statements, and opinions of governmental legal experts. As can be seen, customs are not easily defined and interpreted, but they do exist and are often described or referred to in secondary sources of international law.

Customs can be strictly bilateral, binding only two governments, or they can be more general, even to the point of being universally binding. The extent depends on how widespread in practice and adherence the custom is. Universal customary practice includes, for example, the laws of diplomatic privilege and immunity and freedom of navigation on the high seas. Regional customs include the practice among Latin American nations of extension of diplomatic asylum and the two hundred–mile territorial sea limit. Nations that comply with another nation's claim to a specific right, such as a two hundred–mile territorial sea claim, recognize it as a legal right, whereas those governments that protest such a claim are under no obligation to observe it. The U.S. government, for example, has encouraged U.S. tuna fishermen to disregard Latin American territorial sea claims because it considers most of these areas as part of the high seas. It not only reimburses fishermen for any boats and equipment seized by the Latin American countries, but also deducts the sum from the foreign aid outlays to those countries that refuse to reimburse U.S. fishermen for their losses.[8] Similarly, the United States justified its naval maneuvers in the Gulf of Sidra, which Libya claims as part of its territorial waters, by recourse to the principle of freedom of navigation on the high seas.

In a sense, then, states can choose which customs they will observe as law. Indeed, when a state asserts a new right, others may so quickly follow suit that a new customary principle can emerge. Such was the case after World War II when the United States claimed exclusive rights to exploit the continental shelf along its coasts for various resources. Within a matter of years, most other coastal countries had made similar claims to their continental shelves, giving rise to a new customary principle of international law. However, if other states had resisted the U.S. claim and had not made similar ones of their own, the U.S. action would still constitute at best a unilateral assertion of a right.

While states normally have control over which customs they are obliged to observe, there are exceptions. For instance, when new states come into existence, they are required to observe all universally accepted principles of customary international law as a condition of their admittance to the community of nations.

Treaties In this century, treaties have surpassed customs as the predominant means of creating international law. Customs recently have proved to be an awkward and inappropriate way to respond to the fast-paced changes in international relations. By contrast, treaties can be negotiated and come into legal effect more quickly, and there is less ambiguity about when its provisions become law.

Treaties constitute states' explicit acceptance of specific rights and duties among themselves. Sometimes treaties serve to codify existing rules of international law by formalizing existing customs (the Vienna Convention on Diplomatic Relations is an example of codification). At other times treaties are legislative in character. Legislative treaties create new law, new rights, or obligations that the parties of the treaty are expected to observe. On occasion, a treaty may both codify and legislate, as did the Law of the Sea Treaty. Like customs, treaties bind only those states that have agreed to them, in this case by formal acts of **ratification** (an official announcement by a state executive to other states that the state will abide by the provisions of the treaty). Under international law ratification is not a legislative act. For example, the president, not the U.S. Senate, ratifies treaties. Technically, the Senate only advises and consents to the ratification of treaties. Since there is no central source that officially monitors nations' treaty obligations, each nation must keep track of its own bilateral and multilateral agreements to ensure its compliance, as well as the compliance of other states. The United Nations encourages states to register treaties with it, but they are not obliged to do so. However, treaties that are not registered with the United Nations cannot be cited as evidence or sources of law by states that may later appear before a UN body such as the ICJ.

General principles of law General principles of law constitute the final primary source. Actually the difference between these principles and customary principles is a rather fine one. For practical purposes there is little difference at all, but legal scholars have categorized them separately. Examples of general principles include the doctrine of sovereign equality, the expectation that aliens will exhaust all available domestic remedies for injury incurred in a foreign country before appealing to their state of nationality to press a claim on their behalf, and the related expectation among states that one another's nationals will receive fair treatment.

Judicial decisions Among the secondary sources of international law are judicial decisions. They are categorized as a secondary source because they only interpret and apply the law, they do not make it in the first place. Nevertheless, as we have seen, judicial decisions can help clarify the prior existence of customary rules and identify rules that are outdated or have little meaning in the behavior of nations.

Unlike many domestic legal systems, a judicial decision in the international system does not create a binding legal **precedent;** that is, previous cases do not have a controlling effect over later decisions. The reasoning is based on the fact that only states make international law. In domestic legal systems, courts interpret and apply the law and make definitive statements about what the law is. Subsequent legal decisions then rest on these earlier interpretations. International courts also pay attention to earlier decisions, but are less bound by them than by changes in the law effected by states since the earlier opinion was issued. In addition, nations' domestic courts are often responsible for the application of international law. Thus, it would not be realistic to assume that the U.S. Supreme Court would be bound by previous decisions made by a high court in France or the Soviet Union, or vice versa.

Decisions made by international courts, on the other hand, might be viewed as less biased interpretations of the law and therefore are more apt to be respected by governments. In any case, in addition to other available and more reliable sources of law such as treaties and customs, courts will review relevant prior judicial decisions when hearing a case to find evidence about the existence of legal obligations.

Writings of jurists and publicists Over the years, many highly respected authorities have written treatises about international law. Indeed, writers such as Hugo Grotius had a significant impact on the early development of international law. These experts do not create the law, but they often help clarify it, point out its weaknesses, and make suggestions for improvement. In fact, states will often rely on the opinions of judges and legal scholars to bolster their legal positions.[9]

Principles of Continuity and Change in International Law

To be effective, every legal order must deal with the requirements of change and continuity. If there is no continuity or stability to laws, people will find them difficult to obey. On the other hand, if laws cannot be changed to reflect basic changes in a society, they will become outmoded and irrelevant. Once this happens, people are likely to ignore the law and lose respect for it. In domestic legal systems, the legislatures and courts act like a thermostat, interpreting and applying existing law in new contexts, preserving those laws that are required to efficiently regulate society and changing those that have become too burdensome or outdated.

International law also has principles of continuity and change, but they are less efficient—there is no central thermostat. With respect to treaties, states are governed by the principle of *pacta sunt servanda;* literally, treaties must be served. This principle of continuity requires states to abide by those obligations it has agreed to honor in treaties.

But treaties can become outdated. Are states required to abide by them when circumstances have changed so much that the original purpose of the treaty is no longer relevant? In international law a principle known as *rebus sic stantibus,* or the doctrine of fundamentally changed circumstances, gives nations the right to seek, through negotiation or some judicial remedy, a means of being relieved of the burdensome provisions of the treaty. (They cannot, however, unilaterally renounce their obligations.) Rarely has there been a need to resort formally to this principle. Instead, states have a variety of ways to revise treaties that have become outmoded or especially burdensome for one party. Panama, for instance, convinced the United States to renegotiate the Panama Canal Treaty, arguing that the original 1903 agreement was flawed and no longer acceptable. President Nixon agreed to new negotiations, and President Carter later signed a new treaty. Most treaties negotiated today contain provisions for amendments, periodic review, and denunciation after notification by states that may later wish to be relieved of the duties stipulated. These methods allow treaties to respond to the changing needs of international relations. This is more difficult and uncertain with customary laws, which, by their very nature, usually take much longer to develop and are less easily modified. This accounts in part for states' increasing reliance on the use of treaties, which can respond more quickly to rapid changes in contemporary international relations.

Is International Law Really Law?

We have drawn a number of comparisons between domestic legal systems and international law. Clearly international law is different from domestic legal systems. Its institutional mechanisms for law making, execution, and interpretation are less reliable. It is less codified and more sensitive to political interests. Instead of a central sovereign authority, there are around 160 sovereign states. It is an imperfect legal system, but it does exist. States continue to demonstrate a need to make international law and, on those rather rare occasions when they break it, to legally justify their transgressions. Indeed the transgressions, as we have previously noted, are rather infrequent compared to the vast areas of law that are routinely observed.

The actual nature of international law has been the subject of debate throughout the centuries. In the early development of the international legal order, debate raged between the positivists and the natural law school.[10] The **positivists** held that law could only be based on the existing treaty or customary norms accepted by states. The **natural law school** held that law issued from existing principles in nature that were divine in origin. The task of defining law, according to this school, was to correctly determine what the natural law was. Then the correct behavior for the states could be determined. Other scholars argued that law could be derived through both state practice and natural law. By the beginning of this century, the positivist interpretation was almost universally accepted. Law was not what "ought to be" but rather what is. The problem for the natural school was that almost every state could argue that its policies were morally right. The more practical and realistic positivist views allowed states to accept a fairly significant amount of treaty and customary law as binding.

An overemphasis on the positivist interpretation, however, can cause problems. If the positivist insists on accepting only the law that is, there would be little room for evolution and change: Continuity would be achieved at the expense of necessary change. In other words, paying too little attention to what "ought to be" might deprive the legal order of any vision or sense of direction. For this reason, many legal scholars have modified the absolute positivist position that dominated legal thinking at the turn of the century to account for the reality of and the need for evolution in international law.

The **Universal Declaration of Human Rights** of 1948 is an example of a nonlegally binding document that affirmed the law that "ought to be." Most of the rather significant number of human rights treaties can trace their origins to principles enunciated in this declaration. Indeed, subsequent state action helped give many of its provisions greater legal authority. A slavish adherence to the positivist doctrine might have prevented this evolution from occurring. Obviously, there is room in international law for law that embraces what ought to be and law that actually describes what is.

It should also be obvious that those aspects of international law that describe what states actually do will be more closely observed than those areas of the law that seek unrealistic adjustment or change in state behavior. For example, in 1928 the Kellogg-Briand Pact outlawed the use of war, except in cases of self-defense or in collective actions aimed at restraining aggression. Slightly more than a decade later, the world plunged into the most devastating war in history. The ideal of a world without war was shattered by the reality of war as an instrument of state policy.

Two final points about the nature of international law are in order before we move to a discussion of various contemporary challenges to international law. The international legal order has always been closely tied to the interests of the most powerful states. As powerful states insist on certain legal rights or privileges, previous principles of international law may change. The views of the powerful, in other words, are more likely to be enforced and enshrined as legal principles. The Law of the Sea is an example. In the fifteenth and sixteenth centuries the dominant maritime powers, Spain and Portugal, sought to reserve the seas under their own exclusive jurisdiction. They argued a position of *mare clausum* (closed seas). But aspiring maritime powers, such as Great Britain and Holland, wanted a piece of the action. They argued for a principle of *mare liberum* (freedom of the seas). Not surprisingly, Grotius, who was Dutch, argued strongly in favor of the latter. Indeed, over time new maritime powers entered the scene, and the freedom-of-the-seas doctrine eventually prevailed.

The second point is a related one. International law is especially sensitive to politics. Countries seek the widest possible freedom of action in pursuing their foreign policies. Hence, when wishing to avoid compliance with international law, states frequently resort to the argument that the law is unsuitable or unrealistic, or they find some other legal argument to justify their action. Opposing states, however, will make known their expectation that existing laws should be observed. When the shoe is on the other foot, states typically will make the opposite arguments. Consistency in international law, or for that matter in international relations generally, is not a common phenomenon. Law is usually a secondary consideration and is subordinated to the primacy of politics in the relations of nations.

Compare, for instance, the U.S. invasion of Panama in December 1989 and the Soviet invasion of Afghanistan in December 1979. Both interventions were violations of the UN Charter (and, in the Panamanian case, of the OAS treaty as well). The United States and most other nations condemned the Soviet Union's invasion of Afghanistan. A decade later, almost to the day, the Soviet Union and most other nations condemned the American intervention in Panama. The Soviet Union justified its invasion by arguing that it had been invited in by the Afghan government. The problem with this claim was that the government that extended the invitation had been placed into power by the Soviet Union after the previous leader was killed in a Soviet-engineered coup. The United States similarly installed a government in Panama that subsequently praised the American intervention. Although there are similarities, the two cases differ in important ways. The Afghans resisted Soviet military occupation, whereas the Panamanian people welcomed the American military presence. Once a legitimately elected government was installed in Panama and order restored, the American military forces began to withdraw. Moreover, the United States could further justify its intervention because Manuel Noriega had declared war on it. Politically speaking, if not legally, the American action, though widely criticized in official diplomatic circles, was privately applauded even by some Latin American diplomats.

Legally speaking, states are to avoid military intervention in their mutual relations. Any enforcement actions that must be taken to restore order and prevent events in a country from threatening international peace should be done under the auspices of the United Nations or some other appropriate regional organization. In some cases states may justify intervention to restore order along a common border with another state, provided their intention is not to occupy territory permanently. In other cases states justify intervention to protect their citizens from danger or to prevent a humanitarian disaster. Of course, if a country's legitimate government asks for military assistance, intervention is considered legal. But intervention often takes place without an invitation in situations where the humanitarian or security justifications are ambiguous and the motivations for the action are of highly dubious legality. So it was in both the Afghan and Panamanian cases.

Ultimately, the validity of an action is judged in part by its outcome. On this score, the U.S. invasion of Panama will probably prove to be a political success, despite its dubious legality, whereas the Afghan intervention will go down as a gross violation of international law (a point recently conceded even by Soviet officials) and a political failure.

Basic Issues in the Literature on International Law

Contemporary Challenges to International Law

Modern international law, as we saw in chapter 1, is fundamentally rooted in principles that are three and a half centuries old. The Westphalian principle of sovereignty and its corollary that a state is bound only by those rules to which it agrees are both the cornerstones of international law and the primary obstacles preventing the establishment of a more effective global legal order. For many years, international law regulated only fairly limited areas of European state relations, such as diplomacy, certain aspects of warfare, and the acquisition and maintenance of colonial territories. Most of this law grew up as customs that states practiced in their mutual relations. However, as international relations expanded, as international trade and commerce grew, and as former colonial areas sued for their independence, the demands on international law grew as well. Essentially European in origin, international law now has global application in a multicultural world. Indeed, it is in some ways rather remarkable that most states have accepted many of the legal principles originating in Europe. However, non-Western and Marxist states challenge other aspects of international law. To them, some principles of international law are biased, backward-looking, and unfair. For instance, many revolutionary or Marxist governments have been reluctant to observe international rules requiring compensation for foreign-owned property that has been nationalized. Developed Western states have resisted incorporating the legal traditions and concepts of poor and Marxist countries into the larger corpus of international law because it would dilute their influence and threaten their dominance of the international legal order.[11]

Another challenge to international law has come from the tremendous technological advances of the past century, especially in the post–World War II era. Deep seabed mining, nuclear energy, nuclear weapons, space flight, air travel, and electronic communications are only a few of the technologies that have complicated exclusive state jurisdiction over territory. Economic interdependence challenges the principle of sovereignty. States have coped by developing treaties and international organizations to regulate these new areas of interstate activity. But just as the ink dries on an agreement, new technologies and shifts in economic and political realities often challenge its provisions. Agreements reached in the late 1950s on jurisdiction over the exploitation of the continental shelf were quickly overtaken by the development of deep seabed mining capabilities and the discovery of significant deposits of valuable manganese nodules on the deep seabed floor. A new Law of the Sea Negotiation was called to develop a new regime for deep seabed exploitation and to regularize a wide array of additional ocean management issues, including access through straits, territorial sea claims, fisheries management, pollution, and marine scientific research. Similarly, agreements not to use outer space for military purposes or to place nuclear weaponry in outer space were penned at a time when the technology was nonexistent. Today, these once-fantastic dreams seem technologically feasible, thereby challenging earlier legal agreements.

Another area in which international law has been challenged by technological and political considerations is the Law of War. One of the key, and most widely recognized, principles of the traditional Law of War was the distinction between military combatants and civilian populations. Many of the specific principles of the Law of War existed to preserve this distinction: Soldiers were to wear uniforms so that they could be clearly identified from the civilian population. Battles were to be fought, as far as was practicable, away from urban population centers. When cities were to be attacked, time was to be allowed to evacuate civilians. War was to be fought by well-defined armies, and innocent civilian lives were to be protected. Two variants of modern war—global war and guerrilla war—have challenged these traditional principles.

In this century's two global wars new military technology and warfare practices were developed. In World War I, the use of the submarine and the airplane revolutionized naval and land battle tactics, but their use also made distinguishing between military and civilian targets more difficult. Indeed, in World War II wholesale fire bombings of industrial centers took a widespread toll on civilian lives in Europe, and in Japan the use of nuclear weapons wiped out whole cities. Did military necessity require or justify these actions? One argument made at the time was that in an industrial age a country's war capacity is no longer limited to the battlefield. The factories that produced military aircraft, missiles, and tanks were also a part of the war effort. Achieving victory under these circumstances meant destroying the economic base of the opponent's war machine. (The bombings of Hiroshima and Nagasaki in Japan, were justified on different grounds; namely, to bring an early end to the war and thus save countless millions that might have died in an invasion of Japan.) In practice, destruction of the industrial base of the war effort also meant compromising the distinction between civilians and armed forces, although some effort is still required to limit damage as much as possible to military targets. Certainly there is no more potent a symbol of the problems encountered here than the nuclear weapon, which destroys everything in sight without distinction.

Fortunately, the international system has not experienced a third global war. But there is no dearth of civil wars around the world, and they, too, have an insidious effect on the traditional principles of the Law of War. If the key objective in traditional warfare is to distinguish between civilians and soldiers, in civil wars involving guerrilla tactics, the objective is just the opposite. Indeed, the more guerrillas look like civilians, the better. They thereby gain two advantages: (1) they can attack the enemy more easily by hiding their movements and escaping retaliation, and (2) when the enemy does retaliate innocent civilians are likely to be victimized, further galvanizing popular support for the guerrilla forces. Under the traditional Law of War that was observed under custom and later included in the Hague Conventions of 1899 and 1907, irregular forces must wear a uniform or some other fixed, identifiable emblem that is visible at a distance, carry arms in the open, be a part of a military chain of command, and obey the Law of War. Individuals not adhering to these regulations would be considered illegal participants in the war and would be subject to trial and execution as war criminals. This has not prevented the widespread use of guerrilla and terrorist tactics in the last several decades. More disturbing still is the apparent willingness of major powers, including both superpowers when it has served their interests, to support various groups fighting "wars of national liberation" that are known to have flouted the traditional principles of the Law of War.

In short, the legal and political environment in which modern-day warfare has been fought has deteriorated significantly. Several Geneva conventions have been promulgated since World War I to reestablish some semblance of order in international and "internal" or civil wars.[12] In addition, as the Nuremberg trials after World War II affirmed, military officials can be held accountable for war crimes. At these trials numerous Nazi officials were found to have violated war crimes and were punished for their deeds. The regular armed forces of many nations operate under manuals detailing the Law of War, and where military forces are not adequately trained, the International Committee for the Red Cross, which is charged with promoting adherence to the various Geneva conventions and protocols, makes training available. Despite these measures, the trends of modern warfare are disquieting from both a practical and a legal standpoint.

Coping with the Challenges

One of the basic issues facing international law today is whether it can effectively cope with the challenges of the contemporary world we have just described. The supplemental reading selections in this chapter address the basic issues of the effectiveness and relevance of international law, and, more specifically, what role the International Court of Justice should play in modern international relations.

Friedrich Kratochwil takes the issue of the relevance and effectiveness of international law head-on. He rejects the notions that international law does not exist as true law, and that if it does exist, that it is ineffective and regularly abused by the powerful. He points out that law serves not only to constrain and punish but to facilitate. As he notes, literally thousands of international transactions are facilitated by international norms of law. Abuse of force and violence are still present, as they are in any legal system, but the consequences in international relations are far greater, thus giving rise to the perception of the weakness and irrelevance of international law. In fact, Kratochwil argues that the problem lies not in the prescriptive weakness of the law but in the nature of the political order that militates against effective prevention of violence. Without international law, matters would likely be worse. International law is primitive in the sense that compulsory legal settlement of disputes does not automatically apply to the citizens of the international order (i.e., states). But this weakness results from the political order in which international legal processes operate, not from the legal order itself.

Richard Falk's essay is more specifically tied to the ICJ as an institution, but it is placed squarely in the larger context of international relations and law. Falk asserts that the ICJ has clearly failed to meet expectations as an effective tool for the settlement of disputes. The appropriate response to the decline of the ICJ is for jurists to actively carve out a new role for themselves in a fast-changing international arena, rather than wait passively, hoping that the court will one day assume a more significant role in effectively applying international law.

An obstacle to such judicial activism is the fact that, despite broader representation of different cultures on the ICJ today, most jurists have been socialized into essentially conservative patterns of thinking. They view the role of adjudication in international relations along traditional lines—as a tool that can be used by states as they see fit to resolve their disputes. Falk believes that judges should develop a value-oriented jurisprudence with the primary aim of educating others about the legal needs of a multicultural, ever-changing international arena. Serving in this capacity, judges should help government elite and "planetary citizens" see what the future should look like. They should teach us about how to achieve equity in international relations, be sensitive to ecological concerns, and avoid conventional and nuclear war.

Legal positivism, which stresses the importance of law that is as opposed to law that should be, and the very principles of sovereignty are powerful obstacles to an active judicial role. Falk is aware of the formidable nature of these legal doctrines, but he feels that unless they are attacked directly and changed, the future of our planet is at peril. He describes his strategy as visionary and potentially futile, given the continued potency of nationalism and state sovereignty. In effect, he believes that the ICJ has very little to lose in adopting an activist strategy, since it already has such marginal influence on international relations.

Recent literature suggests a continued interest in the role and effectiveness of the court. Some scholars believe, for instance, that although the ICJ has not been able to coerce unwilling sovereign states, it has been a useful tool in the settlement of some disputes. One study of governments' prelitigation behavior found that they often use the ICJ as a tool in the broader process of dispute settlement.[13] These findings corroborated those of previous studies.[14] Apparently, states choose to use the court for a variety of reasons, which may or may not be intended primarily to achieve a positive legal judgment. In some cases, for instance, a country may resort to the court because of substantial popular or domestic political pressure to take action against another state. By going to the ICJ, a government may only seek to relieve this domestic political pressure, knowing that the case itself is unlikely to bear fruit. In other cases, states may seek litigation to force another state to negotiate a settlement more earnestly or to break a stalemate in a negotiation. States on friendly terms with one another might use the ICJ as a way to isolate a mutual problem in such a legal forum and thus keep it from adversely affecting their overall political relations. In addition, states might agree to go before the court to clarify a legal principle that may be of wider legal and political value.[15]

These studies suggest that although the court may not enjoy widespread use, it has been resorted to on a number of occasions by states seeking limited objectives. Seen in this light, the lack of a large number of definitive judgments is not necessarily alarming. The court can, in short, perform a useful if more limited role than was initially intended. Falk is uncomfortable with this view. He would like to see the court break out of its role as a bargaining tool into a more active, aggressive posture. Other scholars disagree about whether there is a need to do so or whether a more active approach is desirable or practical. Clearly, the debate about whether the ICJ should play a passive or active role in international relations will continue.

Some Additional Issues

Also evident in the contemporary literature is a concern for how international law will respond to a number of continuing challenges, including (1) the regulation of new technologies for exploitation of the ocean and the militarization of outer space, (2) response to demands for new international regimes by developing countries, (3) coping with international conflict and terrorism, and (4) promotion of human rights and the dignity of the individual.

The Law of the Sea Perhaps the most closely observed and studied event in the recent history of international law was the Third International Conference on the Law of the Sea, to which we have already made several references in this chapter.[16] This conference spanned a decade from its initiation in 1973 until a treaty was concluded for ratification in 1982. The conference dealt with a wide range of activities because different countries entered the negotiations with different concerns. For the United States and the Soviet Union, the key issue was to maintain a legal order that would permit largely free access for their military vessels through international straits. Related to this was their desire to limit exclusive claims by some coastal states to jurisdiction over larger areas of the high seas, which in turn might limit ocean navigation and compromise the security and military interests of the superpowers.[17] Most coastal states wanted to establish their exclusive right to exploit their continental shelves and their more limited right to preferential use of fishery resources through the creation of economic zones off their coasts.

The interests of the coastal states and the superpowers were largely met. Agreement was reached that countries could claim a territorial sea of twelve miles (the standard prior to then had been three miles). This agreement might have effectively closed access to some two hundred international straits, but governments agreed that seagoing countries would retain a right of innocent passage through those straits that had been traversed as part of the high seas under the three-mile rule but that now fell under national jurisdiction with the extension of the territorial sea to twelve miles. Coastal states were given the right to exploit the resources of the continental shelf up to two hundred miles from shore.[18] They also were given the right to control marine research, fishing, and pollution within a two hundred–mile economic zone.

Landlocked states had different concerns. They worried about having a right of access to the sea and complained that, unlike coastal states, they were not in a position to gain from the economic benefits of coastal status. It was in their interests to limit coastal claims and to emphasize that any resources found on the deep seabed beyond the limits of national jurisdiction be considered the "common heritage of all mankind," from which all countries should benefit. This was the position of many of the developing countries (LDCs) too. They argued, in effect, that the profits gained from the exploitation of deep seabed mining, should go into a common pool of resources governed by an **International Seabed Authority (ISA).** Not all LDCs were as excited about this. Many of them produced the very metals found in the mineral nodules to be recovered. They worried that overproduction of these metals could reduce market prices for the metal exports on which their livelihood depended. Thus, the treaty included provisions that took into account their interests.

But who was to do the mining? Only a few developed countries had the technology. The developing countries insisted on the creation of the **Enterprise,** an international business that would compete with private mining enterprises. States having the requisite technology would transfer the knowledge to the Enterprise, which would be governed by the ISA. Many countries that had the mining technology were not excited about the provisions relating to seabed mining in the treaty. They wanted to maintain control of this advantage, but eventually they agreed to a **parallel system** in which they would mine one site for their own benefit and another site of equal value for the international community. Despite the apparent agreement, many powerful nations, such as the United States and Germany, have refused to ratify the Law of the Sea Treaty because of these and other provisions. So far, other principles agreed on during the negotiations have found their way into the customary practice of nations, seemingly assuring their preservation even if the treaty should fail to gain widespread adherence. For instance, states have widely adopted the economic zone principle, which gives them preferential rights to fish to a limit of two hundred miles from their coasts. Other states are permitted to fish in these zones, but they are subject to quotas established by the coastal state. These practices seem to be fairly well-established. But the mining issue could still become a very sore point among nations, should those countries that already have the technology unilaterally assert their claims while ignoring the political interests and needs of the developing states.[19] This could lead to an unraveling of the consensus on other issues, perhaps threatening innocent passage through straits or any number of other subjects contained in the treaty as well.

As of 1989, the treaty had only forty-two of the sixty ratifications needed to bring it into force. It could be some time, then, before the treaty takes effect. In the meantime, pressures continue to build to allow countries access to the deep seabed resources. In 1982 the United States, the United Kingdom, France, and West Germany signed a reciprocal Dispute Resolving Agreement regarding potential seabed mineral claims. Many scholars and governments see this agreement as a competitive legal regime and a potential threat to the Law of the Sea Treaty. A preparatory committee established by the treaty to lay the groundwork for its eventual entry into force has been negotiated with potential pioneer investors to protect the treaty's integrity. Indeed, by 1987, France had been lured into the pioneer investment scheme, as had other major powers such as the Soviet Union, Japan, and India. Whether these negotiations will ultimately result in a workable compromise with all the dispute resolving states is yet to be seen. Until then, the fate of the important seabed mining provisions and many other provisions of the treaty will remain in limbo.

Demands for equity in the distribution of international economic wealth   Another area of difficulty for international law is the tremendous disparity of wealth between nations. Falk suggests that the international system must soon take into account the demands of the leadership of the developing world for redistributive justice, for a greater share of the world's resources and wealth. But not all students of international law agree. Some suggest that the international system is not organized in a way that such redistribution can be legally insisted on. This perspective suggests that demands for reform of international law based solely on the desire of some poorer states to have a greater share of global resources ignores the larger issue of how wealth is distributed within countries. International law cannot dictate the latter, nor can it dictate how wealth is distributed between countries. This does not prevent states and groups of states from seeking an international legal order that is more advantageous to themselves, rather it suggests that no state is obligated to accept the arguments of other states that any particular global redistribution of resources is a sacred duty.[20]

The role of the individual in international law   Finally, the role of the individual in international law remains a major consideration on the global agendum in the years ahead. Much progress has been made in the human rights area since World War II. Numerous human rights treaties have come into being, including the Covenants on Civil and Political Rights and Economic and Social Rights that have been widely ratified. However, relatively few states have ratified the Optional Protocol to the Covenant on Civil and Political Rights, which includes provisions for more effective enforcement against potential violators of the covenant's provisions. In short, despite the existence of new human rights laws, the individual is still largely subject to the sovereignty of the country of nationality. Erosion of this principle has occurred in very few cases; in Europe, however, individual cases can be appealed directly to the European Commission of Human Rights. In most other cases international human rights agreements call for states to incorporate and implement treaty provisions through their domestic law.

On the other hand, the individual can be held personally responsible for war crimes, piracy, and other violations of international law. But it is one thing to have duties such as these and quite another to be the subject of direct international rights which could be used to protect individuals from their own governments. International law still recognizes the predominance of the state in dealing with its own citizens, and only in those circumstances where states explicitly have created mechanisms for individuals to seek redress in international courts have individuals been accorded truly direct rights. This dilemma will remain as long as states continue to guard their sovereign rights of control over their citizens. In the meantime, human rights to a large extent will depend on the enlightened policies of governments. Where enlightened policies do not prevail, pressure from human rights groups and other governments can be undertaken to embarrass offending regimes or to encourage them to behave more humanely.[21]

Recent literature shows a continuing interest in the future progress of human rights. Basically, students of human rights make two distinct arguments, which closely resemble the views of the positivist and natural law schools discussed earlier in this chapter.[22] First, some argue, from a more positivistic perspective, that the individual is unlikely to enjoy any significant expansion of rights under international law, despite the appearance of human rights treaties. For such an expansion to occur, a dramatic transformation would have to take place in the nation-state system itself. In this view, the weak enforcement provisions of new human rights legislation are not evidence of the beginning of an inevitable erosion of state sovereignty, but rather they are a sign of the jealousy of states in guarding their sovereignty. Moreover, widespread violation of human rights still exists, suggesting that states may preach human rights but take frequent exception to them in practice.[23]

The second view of human rights accords more closely to the natural law school emphasis on what ought to be, as opposed to what actually is. Proponents of this perspective argue that the battle for human rights may be an uphill one, but it is a battle that should be fought by individuals and their governments to secure a more civilized world. In this view, human rights ought to be a major issue among nations, and those nations that practice progressive human rights policies ought to put pressure on those who do not.[24] For adherents of this view, one of the primary aspects of international relations in the next decade or so will be whether stronger and more effective human rights agreements can be enacted among nations, and once enacted, whether they can be enforced to the benefit of humankind.

Future Prospects

The future health of international law depends on governmental willingness to regulate the use of force and protect human rights. The most significant challenges to international law concern the use of force and intervention. There is plenty of customary and treaty law already governing the use of force. Customary law regarding retaliation, reciprocity, and intervention provide legal guidance to states in times of actual or potential conflict. As far as treaty law is concerned, the UN Charter proscribes war as an instrument of member-state policy, except in instances of self-defense and collective action. All this notwithstanding, governments often have resorted to legally dubious intervention and force, in part because of the UN's inability to maintain security in a world marked by bitter ideological divisions. However, with the passing of the Cold War, we may well see a regeneration of state compliance to and respect for legal norms that protect state sovereignty and prohibit intervention.

The protection of human rights, however, paradoxically depends to some extent on a higher level of international scrutiny of and, potentially, interference with a state's domestic policies. Indeed, one reason given by the Reagan administration for its interventions in Nicaragua and Grenada, and by the Bush administration for its invasion of Panama, was the promotion of democracy and respect for human rights. Clearly, international law cannot be based on the principle that any state may intervene in the affairs of another in accord with its own definition of human rights, whether or not a powerful state can get away with such actions. Such a principle attacks the very foundations of the legal order. Yet progress toward ensuring human rights and democracy are viewed, in the UN Charter and in the eyes of many governments, as important goals for the international community. Does this mean that the goals of human rights and sovereignty are completely irreconcilable? A careful conclusion would suggest that in spite of the inherent tension between these two norms, they are not totally contradictory. To the extent that governments incorporate and enforce human rights laws for the benefit of their own citizens, progress can be made while state sovereignty is respected. In such a world, intervention would be less necessary, and less justifiable, but such a world has not yet been fully achieved.

Can international law respond to the challenges we have enumerated? No one really knows. Part of the drama of the next decade will depend on how well states can abide by existing international norms and can create new ones to cope with a fast-changing global arena. International law clearly does exist, but how it will look in another decade and what kind of shape it will be in is a matter of conjecture, although recent increases in global cooperation hold promise for an expanded role for international law.

Friedrich Kratochwil

...On the Relevance of Norms and the Study of Law for International Relations

Many students of international relations voice...objections concerning the status of legal prescriptions in the international arena. In a realm governed by great insecurity, marginally rather than widely shared values, and great competitiveness,...three...objections appear relevant:... (1) international law does not exist, i.e., any norm which might exist in the international arena is not legal; (2) if legal norms exist, they are ineffective; and (3) even if legal norms exist and are relevant to decisions, they are constantly abused in the interest of the powerful. For these reasons the idea of an impartial regulatory system is fanciful indeed.

...The first and most radical objection, but also perhaps the easiest to refute, is based on a particular definition of law. A conceptual clarification can quickly show the inadequacies of a preconceived idea of law derived exclusively from a particular subset of legal prescriptions. For example, using criminal law as the model means to mistake a part of law for law in its entirety. This shows two things. First, the question of the existence or nonexistence of international law cannot be answered by nominal definitions as, e.g., in Austin's theory: law is the command of the sovereign; since there is no sovereign in international relations therefore there is no law. As a corollary, it is only against the background of a broader definition of law that the question of the status of international law can be discussed intelligently.

The second aspect...deals with the influence of norms upon decision making and, in particular, the constraining force of prescriptions. To focus exclusively on the constraining aspect of prescriptions—as opposed to a fuller

SOURCE: From the *Journal of International Affairs* 37, no. 2 (Winter 1984), pp. 343–356. Reprinted by permission in abridged form.

account which includes the justificatory, enabling, and communicative aspects of norms—leads to serious distortions concerning the efficacy of law in social life. Law, therefore, is not simply a "constraint," it also functions to orchestrate and thereby facilitate societal interaction.

The final objection focuses on the jurisprudential issue of the link between a set of legal prescriptions and the requirements of a formal or substantive conception of justice. This in turn not only includes the specification of such criteria as fairness, impartiality, or equity, but entails a critical appraisal of the actual strategies by which a more principled and just order can emerge from the interactions between states....

From this preliminary analysis it becomes obvious that the conception of law as a coercive order needs revision. The efficacy of law cannot be assessed simply in terms of the compliance or noncompliance with prohibitions. Such a procedure would be inaccurate, because it mistakes laws for commands, and because complying with prescriptions is an intensely dynamic process as opposed to passively following rules....

It appears not only that one cannot equate rules with commands, but that a variety of different rule types exist, each of which exhibits characteristic differences in the incentives for compliance. Although prohibitions are adequately represented as constraints, rules that empower or enable are not. Thus while enforcement according to the "cops and robber" model of criminal law may increase compliance with a certain type of prescription, and thus the effectiveness of a certain part of the legal order, it is clearly irrelevant to the compliance patterns of enabling rules. A serious effort in ascertaining the effectiveness of legal prescriptions in general would entail: first, the differentiation of several types of rules; second, an analysis of the social situation to which these rules correspond; and third, an empirical account of actual compliance patterns. It should be obvious that such an enterprise is at odds with the facile arguments about the ineffectiveness of the legal order mentioned above in the second...objection. Actors, in the domestic as well as the international order, are not simply constrained by rules. Rules enable them to act, to pursue goals, to communicate, to share meanings, to criticize claims and justify actions....

These theoretical considerations conform with an unprejudiced assessment of the empirical evidence. While it is true that the international legal order is not very successful in preventing international violence, the relevance of norms in international life is manifest in the thousands of transactions that take place every day. It is precisely because policy-making machinery has become bureaucratized that it increasingly needs standard operating procedures by which to function. These conditions can be best structured by the application and invocation of norms.

The fact that legal prescriptions are not particularly effective in preventing violence in international, as well as in the domestic, context is not new. In both arenas the legal order is continuously violated. What distinguishes the failure of international law from that of the domestic legal order is less the frequency of violations than the catastrophic consequences these failures have for international relations. While the daily death toll from violent crimes in American cities alone might amount to thirty victims, it does not have the same saliency as a guerrilla attack or military expedition which claims ten or twenty lives and which is quickly adduced as proof for the failure of international law.

In addition, the scope of war distinguishes it from private acts of unauthorized violence. The destruction wrought, and the possibility of escalation, clearly sets international violations apart from even the worst failures of the domestic legal order, with the exception of internal strife and civil war. The issue, therefore, is not the weakness of the international prohibitions against violence but rather more effective prevention of violence. . . .

A legal order can be conceived of as a particular system of communicative action. It informs the participants about the nature of the game by determining the type of actors who can make claims; it sets the range of permissible goals the actors can pursue, specifies the steps necessary to ensure the validity of their acts, and assigns priority and weight to different claims. The legal order represents one of the primary means of organizing social life because it makes more specific the shared general notions in practical matters which allow for interdependent decision making. Finally, the legal order deals with the problems that arise due to scarcity and the nonidentical preferences of a multiplicity of actors. These last remarks deserve further exploration and will be helpful in clarifying the concept of a "primitive" order. . . .

The international legal system is most obviously primitive in that it does not automatically subject its members to the compulsory settlement of disputes by legal means. This weakness is not specific to international law, because the settlement of disputes through court proceedings is always difficult once organized groups are involved and once issues cannot be separated from the wider social context. The lack of institutionalization of the world political process limits the more effective utilization of the legal process. Although international law provides for a rudimentary informal organization of social life among independent actors, there are no effective formal organizations that can translate interest and issues into policy. The world political

process remains, in spite of all communications, sporadic, and is often characterized by bargaining and coercive moves rather than by persuasion and by appeals to common standards, shared values, and accepted solutions. Thus not only can the legal process not be separated from the political process, but the impartiality of legal reasoning is crucially impaired by the lack of authoritative decisions concerning the applicability and scope of legal norms.

International adjudicative institutions are more often than not quite limited in their ability to determine what the law is. This is either due to general jurisdictional limitations incorporated into the statute that brings such a "court" into existence, or to the further limitations under which the parties to a dispute agree to ask for a judicial decision. Thus, quite apart from the. . .institutional problem of how authoritative decisions of international tribunals can be enforced, the problem of determining the applicable legal principle is often impaired by the narrow limits to the jurisdictional domain of such tribunals. This has two corollaries: first, if the relevant legal rule or principle cannot be authoritatively established, many issues remain unclear. An unknown rule can neither be followed nor violated. In this way one of the major advantages of a legal settlement is diminished; i.e., that future quarrels can be avoided by taking the authoritatively established rule into account. The second corollary is that substitutes have to be found so that such impasses do not become totally disabling characteristics of the legal order. In this context advisory opinions, decisions by national institutions, and scholarly expositions have to be mentioned.

In an arena that does not accept the principle of *stare decisis,* opinions defining the scope of legal principles are of decisive importance. Their weight, however, will largely depend upon their persuasive power rather than their institutional authority. Only in this sense does the importance of advisory opinions by the International Court of Justice become understandable. This also explains why legal scholars' writings are considered a "subsidiary source" of international law.

National institutions often fail in establishing "the law" because of their partisan nature. The observer is then confronted with practices varying from state to state. The most obvious example of the partisan nature of decision making is evident in the regulations of administrative agencies, whose rulings are bound by national policy. But even the independent courts have considerable difficulty acting in a detached fashion. They might have to defer to the executive agencies because of constitutional considerations or are bound by national legislative interpretations or precedents. Thus while the decision of a national court settles a particular dispute which has international legal ramifications, and while its decision might be authoritative as a precedent within a given domestic legal system, it will often fail to be considered an authoritative decision on the international law level.

The lack of international credibility of domestic decisions has important implications for an assessment of international law as an instrument that impartially protects the interests of all claimants. It is clear that those parties which have the most developed domestic organizational structures as well as the most far-reaching interests can adjudicate the largest number of disputes. Although no modern nation is currently in the same privileged position as England was with respect to maritime trade, differentials of development and power still matter. . . . An even-handed assessment must admit. . .that national courts occasionally deviate from established national policies and try to come to terms with the changing structure of international society, thereby providing important new crystallization points for the development of international law.

Finally, the lack of effective channels for an authoritative determination of what the law is and how it can be modified, changed, or rescinded sheds new light on the problem of compliance and legal change. Noncompliance is usually conceived of in terms of transgressions in which an actor works for advantages in hopes of not being discovered. Even in the domestic arena, however, there are cases of noncompliance in defense of a valued position and with the explicit purpose of changing an objectionable rule. Although the latter strategy might open the door for all types of extralegal considerations and thus weaken the strength and autonomy of the legal order, significant distinctions exist between these two cases. Cynical acts of rascality, therefore, are treated differently than actions of civil disobedience. Nothing in the nature of the international legal order allows the neglect of such crucial differences. Precisely because the means of peaceful change in the international arena are few, and by and large ineffective, the violation of a legal norm is often not a pure act of lawlessness but rather part and parcel of a larger bargaining game for change. It would be a legalism of the worst kind to reduce the problem of compliance to the technical problem of ensuring norm conformity at the least cost through the elaboration of repressive techniques, while leaving the issue of justifying actions in terms of broader principles, demands for justice, and pleas for peaceful change to history and philosophy.

International relations specialists would do well to remember the limitations of the positivist approaches and to reflect critically upon them. An international jurisprudence in which the critical and reflective attitude is preserved is essential for the education of future decision makers. Only in this way can the human project in the domestic and international arena be examined as a continuous creative effort. It is not determined by the "objective forces" of history or fate, but is a project for which everyone bears responsibility.

Richard Falk

The Role of the International Court of Justice

Attitudes toward the role of law in international relations, and in particular toward judicial activity in the international arena, have greatly changed over the past fifty years. From a somewhat naive hope for fundamental change in the nature of international affairs due to the establishment of international institutions and tribunals, pessimism, even cynicism, about the prospects for a just order emerged. . . .

Faced with the failure of the World Court, even jurists seem disenchanted with international legal institutions. Many now suggest that the true function of the court should be assessed less in terms of its effectiveness in settling international disputes than in terms of its contribution to the development of international law. A prudent evaluation of the future of the court seems to suggest a "wait-and-see" attitude, dedicated to preserving this institution in the hope that sometime in the future, its existence will facilitate the effective application of international law.

This attitude might seem to be wise counsel in view of both the reluctance of states to use the court for important disputes and due to the deep-seated ideological and cultural differences that currently exist among states. Nonetheless, a passive juridical approach will not preserve options for the future, but instead might seriously threaten the viability of the entire legal enterprise in international politics. A more farsighted understanding of the problems facing the court and the need for a series of reforms and altered attitudes are necessary. . . .

Underlying these difficulties there exists a legal culture which, in spite of all rhetorical differences, is shared by most jurists and is based on a largely mistaken conception

SOURCE: From *Journal of International Affairs* 37, no. 2 (Winter 1984), pp. 253–268. Reprinted by permission in abridged form.

of the place of adjudication in politics. Because of the persistence of this shared culture and consensus, creative innovations which might help resolve world order problems are unlikely to occur. . . .

The world order system of the late nineteenth and early twentieth centuries was a simpler affair, yielding simpler solutions. A relatively small number of actors dominated the world, actors who shared generally a religious, cultural, and political tradition which they believed superior to others, and who were confident that a science-based industrial economy would continue indefinitely to make the material conditions of life easier. This application of reason to human affairs was believed to have displaced the authority of religion and led reformers to suppose they could "devise solutions" to solve problems. Juristic rationalism was merely one symptom of a larger societal disorder, that of presupposing the capacity of reason to fashion sensible institutional solutions for all human problems.

The Russian revolution was the culmination of a continuing process undermining confidence in rational reform of relations among sovereign states. Marxism–Leninism, as a philosophy and then as an ideology, challenged the legitimacy of the entire jural temperament and its underlying theoretical presuppositions. Change was based on armed struggle made inevitable by a capitalist society deeply riven by class conflicts. Law and the state were the political instruments of the ruling classes that were engaged in exploitation of dependent classes and peoples. Such a structure could not be reformed precisely because the reformers were civil servants in the state bureaucracy and thus were exploiters themselves. From such a revolutionary perspective, the state could not be gradually reformed, it had to be smashed. In short, Marxist and Soviet views on the role of international law emphasize revolutionary social forces as the catalysts of change. The only proper socialist relationship to the institutions of the existing legal order, including the United Nations and the court, is to neutralize their capacity to serve as instruments for international class domination by the capitalist majority. Operating from a minority position, the Soviet group of states has participated in the world legal system to facilitate its own ends and to neutralize the system's ability to intervene in the historical process. In this sense, the Soviet government has never repeated its error of 1950 when its absence from the Security Council enabled that organ to assert a formal mandate for the defense of South Korea. The ideological and geopolitical split in the West since the Russian revolution has nullified the consensus on the means and ends of global reform, especially on the place of law and international institutions in this process.

With the collapse of the colonial system, the process of dissension spread further. Non-Western outlooks have become important in international affairs. The heritage of international law has been regarded with skepticism because it formerly provided a legitimating rationale for colonialism, and was associated with the functioning of what the non-Western world experienced as a grossly inequitable international economic order. At best, this legal heritage was regarded as an unfamiliar product of an alien civilization. The new states of Asia and Africa and the more emancipated states of Latin America, despite the array of their differences, have established a Third World identity that has been marked by considerable solidarity on many international issues. Underlying this solidarity is often a kind of Marxist–Leninist interpretation of international history, which prevails even in countries where the governing elite is rabidly anti-Marxist and pro-Western. The essence of this Third World outlook in relation to law, in some ways typified by the predominantly conservative alliance of the OPEC oil producers, is that struggle and political power are the main engines of meaningful change in the current world system and that law and judicial remedies represent snares and delusions. The Third World brings a new agenda of economic priorities into the international arena which fractures further the illusion that reason translated into international institutions is the path to peace and justice.

In such an international environment, it is not surprising that there has been a decline in the legal dispositions of the United Nations relative to its predecessor, the League of Nations. There has been a decline in the status and function of international adjudication if a comparison is drawn between the Permanent Court of International Justice and the International Court of Justice. A successful legal order depends on an underlying agreement among its members as to the acceptability of the existing political framework. There may be grievances, even wars, in an adequate legal order, but the framework of values and political guidelines that conditions the behavior of actors is not often questioned. When such a consensus no longer exists, the legal process loses its capacity to generate respect from the community as a whole. Its role becomes marginalized, and tears of regret and frustration are shed by its former champions, who had expected and led others to expect a steady strengthening of the legal dimension of international life.

The evolution of international society in recent decades has created an even more problematical context for the discharge of judicial functions as conventionally conceived by international law specialists in the Euro-American tradition.... Views on "law" and "judicial function" are inevitably culture-bound, geopolitically shaped, and historically conditioned. There exists no single prescriptive model for what the World Court should be. Its own statute is vague and ambiguous. To rely on the Permanent Court of International Justice as a suitable model for the court (a tendency reinforced by judicious references to its operations as "the golden era of international adjudication") overlooks the International Court's drastically different context of operation. Perhaps much of the superficiality of assessments of why international adjudication is not working can be traced back to the original uncritical extension of the Permanent Court's framework to the altered world of 1945.

Immediately after World War II, because of the experience of the East–West anti-Axis alliance, it was natural that continuities with the past would be stressed. But reference to the nature of judicial function in the period of the Permanent Court, as if it automatically pertained to the International Court of Justice period, has discouraged a reevaluation of basic issues of craft and orientation. For instance, it has been mechanically argued that the present court should necessarily discharge its advisory role in the spirit of a "responsible magistrature," because this was the approach adopted by the earlier court. The Permanent Court no longer provides, if indeed it ever did, a positive model for international adjudication at the global level.

No matter how similar the formal structure and procedures might appear, changes in the international political environment, specifically changes in the patterns of conflict and the globalization of participation, have inevitably made the court a very different kind of institution. The essence of that difference is the collapse of the earlier consensus among the active participants in international society about its normative character, as well as a far greater diversification in the cast of characters....

[However,] Third World and Soviet bloc presence in the court with few notable exceptions has been inconsequential in reshaping the image of the court or in endowing the critical notions of law and judicial function with a new and more appropriate content.... The members of the court have been socialized into accepting a certain conception of the range of permissible jurisprudence and of its appropriate derivation. They have also been trained, by and large, to adopt a style of legal reasoning that falls within rather narrow logical confines. These features of legal education have been "received" as if they were beyond questioning, whereas the apparent objectivity of their status is partly a matter of history, partly a question of geopolitics. Cultural hegemony as a mode of domination partially explains the jurisprudential "consensus." There are certain factors taken for granted even though they are actually a legacy of one form or another of domination. Educational patterns in the legal profession have been overwhelmingly based on Euro-American presuppositions and textual materials. Very few independent reexaminations of these supposedly value-free presuppositions about the nature of the judicial function and their relation to the needs of the ex-colonial peoples or various underclasses of the world have been made. Little social criticism of the court along these lines as a judicial institution exists. As a consequence, legal thinking does not adequately take into account changing global contexts, arenas of international law often seem sterile, and the great issues of the day are obscured rather than illuminated even when the World Court directly confronts them. . . .

The court will not be able to overcome its current difficulties until its members come to embody a spirit of cultural *autonomy* and *pluralism* which in turn reflects the principal attitudes in the world system on leading normative issues, including a range of views about the lawmaking processes at work in international life. The conservative idea of banishing the big case, of reserving the court for technical, routine issues which stress. . .procedural matters, is not *politically* viable. . . . New questions arise concerning judicial style and jurisprudence suitable for a world system constituted by the diversity of states, cultures, and ideologies now active in the global arena. To what degree can Euro-American judges be induced to be responsive to the needs and aspirations of this new international setting?

To achieve a spirit of autonomy involves both form and substance. It requires the court to reconsider the audience for its proceedings and its overall role in the world system. More concretely, such autonomy would naturally lead to a value-oriented and educative jurisprudence. . . .

The most important aspect of a new jurisprudence for the court would entail a commitment to an educative mission in which the primary audience of the court, in addition to the parties to a dispute, would become a nonprofessional constituency of concerned *planetary* citizens. One crucial priority for this audience involves an awareness of the adverse normative effects of international hierarchy in its various political, economical, and cultural dimensions. The normative profile of such a jurisprudence would be generally progressive, although contrary interpretations would also be represented. The World Court could become a much more genuine judicial arm of the United Nations sensitive to the way the organization has evolved. The court could in the process become, temporarily at least, an anathema to Euro-American or Western-oriented legal professionals who have hitherto generally given it their support. Yet, to be global in its orientation, the new judicial culture would have to reach beyond a Third World agenda

of global reform to embrace the interrelated agenda of concerns associated with a visionary world order for all peoples and stages of development, including the problems of avoiding nuclear war. . . .

My argument is directed particularly toward the policy-making constituency of the world political system, especially in the Third World, where there may be a more receptive audience among leaders and their advisors than in the West. The essence of the appeal is to reevaluate the role and the character of the World Court from a visionary perspective. It is necessary to promote the self-interest of the non-Western countries in a global system in which the structures of power and authority are weighted against change. The potentials for a reorientation of consciousness within the United Nations has barely been explored. One structure where such a creative possibility exists is the World Court. It is an intriguing possibility because virtually everyone agrees that the court is not working well. The standard diagnosis of international lawyers has been to account for the disappointment by blaming it on a regressive refusal by sovereign governments to entrust their disputes to third-party procedures. My diagnosis suggests that national governments have indeed been regressive, but in a different sense. They have failed to reconstitute the court in light of values and goals *freely* considered.

In a formal sense, I am proposing that normative life be breathed into Article 9 of the court's statute:

> At every election, the electors shall bear in mind not only that the persons elected should individually possess the qualifications required, but also that in the body as a whole the representation of the main forms of civilization and of the principal legal systems of the world should be assured.

And as for qualifications, Article 2 says:

> The Court shall be composed of a body of independent judges, elected regardless of their nationality from among persons of high moral character, who possess the qualifications required in their respective countries for appointment to the highest judicial offices, or are jurisconsults of recognized competence in international law.

. . .What is the content and the drift of an educative jurisprudence? Is there any point in extending and reproducing the ferment and partisanship of the General Assembly in the calmer confines of the World Court? I believe that the search for "judicial innovators" generally acceptable to the General Assembly through the nominating and electoral process result in three kinds of change:

- an upsurge in reliance upon the court's advisory functions by coordinated organs of the United Nations;
- a greater willingness by the court to engage in judicial activism to deal with the inequities of the past and present, especially as these are evident in North–South relations; and
- a concern about longer term issues of world order, including questions touching on war and peace, mass poverty, oppression of various types, and ecological decay.

Yet why should citizens of the United States (or any other trilateral or OECD [Organization for Economic Cooperation and Development] country) support such a proposal? Is this not an example of a disguised form of altruism which assumes the shape of "Third Worldism" and is attractive mainly to intellectuals in the First World who feel alienated from the governing process and value patterns of their own society? I am convinced that this proposal to reorient the World Court could become part of a broader strategy of international adjustment to the changing realities of international life.

. . . Accommodating the flow of history, . . . supposes that the stability of the state system in the nuclear age will finally depend upon combining equity and ecological planning to a sufficient degree to discourage large-scale recourse to warfare.

Even if this kind of analysis holds true, the short-term reaction of First World elites and their citizens is likely to be highly antagonistic to any effort to confer a potential for legislative action upon the World Court. . . . The court seems likely to relent quite rapidly when a defendant state rejects its authority. Certainly one would expect an immediate reaction of hostility to this proposed reorientation in professional and official circles dominated by the Euro-American ethos. The reaction may in turn produce a wave of rebuttals against the present degree of acceptance by these states of compulsory jurisdiction. It is even probable that the reliance on the court for contentious proceedings, at least by First World governments and those closely aligned with them, would diminish to the vanishing point. Yet, given the current marginality of the court, any further decline along this dimension would be slight and should not be feared.

Study Questions

1. Define *international law*. In your opinion is it really law?
2. Describe the key principles involved in the *lex talionis*. Is this an effective means of enforcement? Why or why not? What is the difference between a retorsion and a reprisal?
3. How does international law differ from the domestic legal orders of countries?
4. Why does the International Court of Justice lack compulsory jurisdiction? How does the Optional Clause deal with this problem?
5. In what sense does international law have a legislative capacity?
6. What are the primary and secondary sources of international law? Why are some considered primary and others secondary?
7. Under what conditions does a practice become a legally binding customary law?
8. What advantages do treaties have over customary law?
9. What is positivism? Discuss the implications of this theory for international law.
10. When Friedrich Kratochwil describes international law as primitive, what does he mean?
11. What is the difference, according to Kratochwil, between legal and moral rules?
12. What are the three objections about the existence of international law, and how does Kratochwil address them?
13. According to Richard Falk, has the ICJ been a success or failure? Why?
14. Discuss the performance of courts such as the ICJ in dispute settlement and as interpreters of the nature of international law. Which in your view is more important? Why?

15. Falk argues that the ICJ should promote a more value-oriented and educational jurisprudence. What does he mean? Do you think this is a realistic proposal? a necessary one?
16. What are the primary challenges to contemporary international law?
17. What are the chief threats to the protection of civilian populations during a war?
18. How has technological progress created a need for new legal principles and agreements? Name some examples.

Key Terms

adjudication
applicant
arbitration
compliance
compulsory jurisdiction
conciliation
custom
Enterprise
good offices
inquiry
International Seabed Authority (ISA)
mediation
natural law school
nonobligatory practice

Optional Clause
pacta sunt servanda
parallel system
positivists
precedent
proportionality
ratification
rebus sic stantibus
reprisal
respondent
retaliation
retorsion
Universal Declaration of Human Rights

Notes

1. For authoritative definitions of international law, see Lassa Oppenheim, *International Law,* ed. Hersch Lauterpacht, vol. I, 8th ed. (London: Longmans, 1955), p. 4; and Georg Swarzenberger, *A Manual of International Law,* 5th ed. (New York: Praeger for the London Institute of World Affairs, 1967), p. 3.
2. See Gerhardt Von Glahn, *Law Among Nations,* 5th ed. (New York: Macmillan, 1986), p. 4.
3. Ibid., pp. 1–14.
4. For an authoritative description of the law of retaliation, see Oppenheim, *International Law,* vol. 2, pp. 134–144.
5. A critical analysis of the ICJ is offered in John Gamble and Dana Fischer, *The International Court of Justice: An Analysis of a Failure* (Lexington, Mass.: Lexington Books, D. C. Heath, 1976).
6. For justification of the U.S. decision to withdraw its acceptance of the Optional Clause, see *Department of State Bulletin* (Washington, D.C.: Department of State, January 1986), pp. 67–71. For an excellent and wide-ranging analysis of the court's decision in *Nicaragua* v. *United States,* see various articles and comments in *American Journal of International Law* 81, no. 1 (January 1987). The U.S. revocation of its acceptance of the

Optional Clause does not affect cases where the United States and another litigant may mutually agree to refer a dispute to the ICJ, or where the United States may be party to a treaty that calls for ICJ dispute resolution.

7. *U.S. Supreme Court,* 1872, 14 Wallace. 81 U.S. 170 (1872).

8. See Susan O'Malley Wade, "A Proposal to Include Tuna in U.S. Fishery Jurisdiction," *Ocean Development and International Law* 16, no. 3 (1986): 255–304, especially at p. 262.

9. On the sources of international law, see J. L. Brierly, *The Law of Nations,* 5th ed., ed. Sir Humphrey Waldock (Oxford: Clarendon Press, 1955), pp. 57–69. This source is highly recommended to all students as a brief but highly authoritative and readable classic on international law, despite the fact that it is dated on a number of subjects.

10. For a more extensive discussion of the development of those legal schools, see Von Glahn, *Law Among Nations,* pp. 44–55.

11. A general discussion of the problems of multicultural legal perspectives can be found in Josef Kunz, "Pluralism of Legal and Value Systems and International Law," *American Journal of International Law* 49 (1955): 370–376.

12. Of the four Geneva Conventions of 1949, the fourth, Protection of Civilian Persons in Time of War, most directly reiterates the primary distinction between civilian and armed forces. In 1978 two additional protocols to the Geneva Conventions entered into force: Protection of Victims of International Armed Conflicts and Protection of Victims of Non-International Armed Conflicts. While the Geneva Conventions enjoy rather widespread adherence, the protocols are weakened by lack of strong enforcement measures and nonratification by a number of major powers. Nevertheless, these instruments represent an effort to reestablish the time-honored distinction between civilian and armed forces and to promote humanitarian treatment of victims and prisoners of war.

13. Dana Fischer, "Decisions to Use the International Court of Justice: Four Recent Cases," *International Studies Quarterly* 26, no. 2 (June 1982): 251–277.

14. William Coplin, "The World Court in the International Bargaining Process," in *The United Nations and its Functions,* eds. R. W. Gregg and M. Barkim (Princeton: Van Nostrand, 1968); and A. Rovine, "The National Interest and the World Court," in *The Role of the International Court of Justice,* ed. Leo Gross (New York: Oceana Publications, 1976).

15. Fischer, "Decisions to Use the International Court of Justice," pp. 270–274.

16. From 1974 to 1983, the *American Journal of International Law* featured, on almost an annual basis, articles on the developments at the UN Conference on the Law of the Sea (UNCLOS III). Bernard Oxman authored or coauthored most of these articles. These articles represent one of the most authoritative assessments of UNCLOS III and the Law of the Sea issues in general. Interest in the Law of the Sea issues has continued unabated in the pages of this journal, which is one of the most respected international law journals of the world. Another journal regularly featuring technical and legal articles on the Law of the Sea is *Ocean Development and International Law.*

17. The security issues were the initial impetus for the conference. For an insightful group of articles on security concerns in the Law of the Sea, see David Larson, guest ed., *Ocean Development and International Law,* 17, no. 4 (1986), "Security Issues and the Law of the Sea."

18. States whose continental shelves extend beyond two hundred miles are expected to pay a portion of profits obtained from seabed mining to the International Seabed Authority,

which was established by the treaty to govern the exploitation of deep seabed resources beyond the limits of national jurisdiction.

19. Daniel Cheever, "The Politics of the UN Convention on the Law of the Sea," *Journal of International Affairs* 37, no. 2 (Winter 1984): 247–252.
20. See Terry Nardin, "Distributive Justice and the Criticism of International Law," *Political Studies* 39, no. 2 (1981): 232–244.
21. For a useful discussion of human rights and its connection to the Law of War, see Terry Nardin, "The Moral Basis of the Law of War," *Journal of International Affairs* 37, no. 2 (Winter 1984): 295–309.
22. An entire issue of *Daedalus* 112, no. 4 (Fall 1984) was devoted to the subject of human rights.
23. For a lucid statement of this perspective, see John G. Ruggie, "Human Rights and the Future International Community," *Daedalus* 112, no. 4 (Fall 1984): 93–110.
24. This argument is cogently put by Stanley Hoffmann, "Reaching for the Most Difficult Human Right as a Foreign Policy Goal," *Daedalus* 112, no. 4 (Fall 1984): 19–49.

Eleven

███

International Economics

In this chapter we will review some basic historical features of international economic relations, discuss several realities of the contemporary international economy, and identify several key issues in international economic relations that will be of continuing political significance in the decade to come.[1]

Historical Aspects of the International Economy

The instinct to travel to exotic places, to find exotic treasures and luxuries, and to exploit markets in foreign-produced commodities has lured venturous souls to foreign lands throughout human history. For the Europeans in the fifteenth and sixteenth centuries, silks and satins from China, ivory and ebony from Africa, incense from the Middle East, jewels from India, teak and mahogany from Southeast Asia, and furs from the New World were exotic and attractive. Sugar, tobacco, cotton, and other agricultural products from the tropics also lured traders across the seven seas. Trade with remote areas of the world opened up as explorers sought new lands. This process of exploration began long before the Treaty of Westphalia ushered in a new framework for international relations. European powers began to expand their overseas activities in earnest in the 1700s and 1800s, as if in competition to see which one could control and exploit the economic fruits of vast areas of the New World. Portugal, Spain, Britain, Holland, Germany, Italy, and Belgium competed for colonies. The Age of Imperialism had begun.

The concept of imperialism has been defined in a variety of ways.[2] A neutral definition of **imperialism** might be as follows: The political, economic, and psychological domination of one nation or people over another. Imperialism results when countries seek to conquer and control other people—when they seek to establish empires. Wherever there have been empires—in ancient Egypt, Greece, Rome, or China—there has been imperialism. The colonial era was an age of European imperialism.

Several historical factors produced this interest in foreign colonies. Especially after the Industrial Revolution, European economies needed external resources and raw materials, as well as markets in which to sell their surplus manufactured goods. Competition for foreign markets was strong. But once colonies were established, their economies could be fashioned in ways that benefited the parent state. **Mercantilism** was born. Colonies were an ideal way to secure larger supplies of labor and raw materials and to develop new markets for the colonizer's manufactured products. Under the mercantilist system, colonies became storehouses of agricultural goods, minerals, and other commodities. These resources were shipped to the mother country and processed there, thus contributing to industrial growth in Europe. The manufactured goods were either sold at home or exported abroad, often to the colonies where settlers were obliged either to purchase these highly expensive goods or nothing at all. The European powers encouraged little industry in the colonies. When manufacturing did develop, as with textiles in India, foreigners generally controlled the shipping, insurance, and marketing abroad, where most of the profit was to be made.[3] Mercantilism worked to the strong disadvantage of colonized areas, while European countries reaped the economic advantages of their privileged position. Some countries, such as the United States, were fortunate to escape the clutches of this disadvantageous situation before their resources were exhausted or their trade sector completely dominated. Other countries were not as fortunate.

Apart from economic relations between colonial powers and their colonies, the nineteenth and twentieth centuries saw trade expand rapidly between fully sovereign states. Commerce among nations exploded, and new forms of international interaction were needed to deal with it. As the volume of trade increased, direct bartering became too clumsy. Gold financed international transactions, but eventually national currencies, such as the British pound sterling, were accepted in payment for goods and services too. New monetary systems emerged to support the growing trade relationships.

Trading economic goods obviously involves a great deal of cooperation between states, but it can also cause considerable tension.[4] Competition over resources and markets can lead to war, just as trade can encourage peaceful relations. International economic relations cannot easily be separated from nations' political interests. For this reason, it has become fashionable in recent years to talk about the international **political economy.**[5] Clearly, the political differences between modern capitalist and communist countries have been based at least in part on their very different economic systems. Similarly, economics can be used as a political weapon, as it was by Arab oil-exporting states when they embargoed oil sales to countries with pro-Israeli political stances. And, of course, colonialism, which was inspired by both political and economic competition between European countries, led them to dominate vast areas of the rest of the world. In short, politics affects economics, and economics affects politics. There is almost universal agreement that a clear understanding of international relations is not possible without considering the relationship between the political and economic activities of both states and nonstate actors. To achieve such an understanding, it is important to consider several key realities of international economics.

Realities of the International Political Economy

Imports and Exports

The first reality of international economics is that most countries are not self-sufficient in raw materials and manufactured goods. To get these domestically unobtainable resources, they must engage in international trade. In short, they must import goods from the outside world. In order to do this, they must be in a position to purchase these goods. Most countries earn money to buy imports by selling their products (exporting) to other countries. This is one way a country can earn enough foreign exchange (money) to purchase imports.

Trade may take place because a country either does not possess certain resources or products, or because they are in too short a supply to match domestic demand. However, in other cases, countries may actually import and export the same product at the same time. The United States, for instance, exports and imports cars. There is little doubt that the United States could meet all of its domestic demand for cars through domestic production. But if it prevented the importation of cars from other countries (such as West Germany and Japan), they might in turn retaliate by reducing imports of cars or other products from the United States. Countries have numerous incentives to export products. Exports open up external markets for domestic producers, help increase domestic employment, and reduce the cost of products on the domestic market. For instance, by producing cars for export, producers can reduce the cost of all their cars, including those sold at home. But the ability to export is closely tied to a country's willingness to import goods and products from other countries. When a country opens its markets to other countries, however, it takes a chance. If the goods of other countries are more competitively produced and less expensive, domestic producers may be run out of business and unemployment will grow. Under these circumstances, why would a country want to take the chance on importing goods if it can meet its own domestic needs?

The answer to this question lies, at least in part, in an old and widely believed theory: the **theory of comparative advantage.**[6] The author of this theory, David Ricardo, a famous English economist, argued that trade between two countries would be profitable for the inhabitants of both countries if the comparative costs of production of certain goods within each country differed and if each country specialized in the product it produced most efficiently while trading for others. Let us use an example to illustrate this theory: Assume that the United States produces both cars and televisions, as does Korea. Let us further assume that the United States can produce one car for the same expenditure of labor, materials, and energy that it costs to produce fifty television sets. The production of cars is highly efficient and large numbers are produced. The television industry is also rather large, but it is not quite as efficient as the auto industry. Let us assume, however, that in Korea the situation is the opposite; the auto industry is not as well developed as in the United States, but Koreans are extremely adept at producing televisions, so much so that they can produce one hundred televisions for the expense of producing one car. A simple cost ratio emerges: in the United States, the comparative cost of production is one car to fifty televisions, while in Korea it is one car to one hundred televisions. Under these conditions, and assuming that the costs of shipping are not excessive, it would be profitable for the United States to specialize in the production of cars and trade them for Korean televisions, while Korea would benefit by specializing in TVs and trading them for cars. Why? In this example, the United States can manufacture only fifty televisions at the cost of producing a single car. In other words, it sacrifices the production of one car to produce fifty televisions. But if it trades a car to Korea it might get seventy-five or eighty televisions in return. It might even get up to a hundred televisions depending on the actual supply and demand for cars and televisions and the shipping costs. In other words, by shifting all of its attention to cars, producing them both for domestic sales and for export to Korea, the United States could have all the cars it needs plus a lot more television sets than if it sacrificed auto production in favor of making televisions. Korea, on the other hand, would have to sacrifice the production of one hundred televisions to produce one car at home. It would be better for Korea, therefore, to import cars because it would only have to spend seventy-five or eighty televisions sets for each car. Korea could get more cars this way than by diverting its labor from producing televisions to producing cars. In other words, if each country were to specialize in the product in which it enjoyed a comparative advantage, each economy would be better off: Each would enjoy a larger number of cars and televisions. This would be true even if the absolute costs of production for both cars and televisions were cheaper in the United States than in Korea. The key lies in the costs of production of goods *within* each country.

In the real world, however, things are not so simple. There are many goods produced and traded by a large number of countries. Domestic producers of certain goods are not interested in going out of business just because they are not as competitive as some other domestic or foreign industry. The benefits of comparative advantage will not exist if one or both trading partners price their products unrealistically high or if labor interests lobby for their governments to protect certain industries from foreign competition. These are potential obstacles to the unfettered operation of the law of comparative advantage. But the Ricardian notion of comparative costs is appealing, and many countries have recognized the economic advantages of participating in international trade.

Part of the reality of imports and exports is that a country can only sell those goods that it has in sufficient supply to export and that other countries are willing to buy. The ability to make a good return on trade depends, in turn, on the type of export the country has to sell. Since World War II, manufactured goods, for instance, have increased in value at a faster rate than have agricultural commodities. Thus, countries relying on agricultural exports to earn foreign exchange have been at a disadvantage. The prices they pay for manufactured imports have increased faster than the return they get on their agricultural goods. Their **terms of trade,** as the economists refer to it, have not been advantageous. But not all commodities are in an equally bad position. For instance, oil-producing countries generally receive a better return on their oil than do countries that rely on bananas, coffee, or peanuts as their primary export commodities. The more important a country's commodities or goods are to other economies, the greater its ability to sell them will be.

Another dimension of trade competitiveness has to do with the productivity and efficiency of a country's production capacities. Indeed, one of the arguments behind free trade is that it should promote global economic efficiency: Competitive industries and companies will survive and less competitive ones will perish. Assuming the equivalence of labor and other costs, if a country invests heavily in modern production technologies, eventually it will be able to undersell industries in other countries that rely on outmoded production techniques. The dilemma of the U.S. steel industry is that labor costs are high *and* technology is outmoded. The Japanese steel industry, on the other hand, is equipped with state-of-the-art technology. Should the country with the declining industries interfere with free trade under these circumstances? The ethic of free trade suggests that it should not. However, countries do impose trade restrictions when their industries become less competitive. Usually they justify their actions by arguing that the competition has sought unfair advantages, denied free access to its own economy, or dumped products on foreign markets at artificially low prices to put competitors out of business (a charge that U.S. government officials have recently made about Japanese computer microchip firms). This leads us to a discussion of protectionism, a problem that has received much attention in the news lately.

Protectionism

The second reality of international trade is somewhat in conflict with the first. If every country produced only those goods that it could make most competitively while trading for the rest, the trade system would be entirely free. But the real world is not that simple. Within each country, industries make goods that can be produced much more cheaply in other countries. If absolutely free trade and competition existed, these producers would go out of business. Instead they put pressure on their governments to impose tariffs on the more competitive foreign imports, so that the price domestic consumers pay for them is artificially increased. By putting tariffs on imported goods, a government makes them more expensive and the domestic products more attractive to local consumers. Historically, countries that have tried to develop their young (infant) industries, tried to shelter them from the better established and more competitive industries of other countries. Using tariffs and other devices such as import quotas is known as **protectionism,** since such strategies are intended to protect domestic businesses from foreign competition. Another term used to describe countries that aggressively seek to expand their exports and reduce their imports at the expense of other states is **neomercantilism.** Obviously, if one state pursues neomercantilist policies and ends up running substantial trade surpluses, other countries will be running deficits. Because trade deficits lead to substantial unemployment, most governments resent other nations' neomercantilist policies. During most of the post–World War II period, Japan, for instance, has pursued very restrictive import policies while aggressively developing export markets. When American auto workers began to lose their jobs because of the flood of Japanese automobiles into American markets, political pressure began to build to place restrictions on Japanese auto imports. The U.S. government urged Japan to adopt voluntary export quotas to the U.S. market. Japan cooperated out of fear that even more restrictive policies might ensue if it did not. The dilemma for a neomercantilist country such as Japan is that if it pushes its exports too aggressively it can excite protectionist reactions among its trading partners. Thus, countries that tend to run chronic trade surpluses have some incentive to reduce them over time and to take steps that will help their deficit partners bring trade back into equilibrium.

Protectionist measures come in a variety of forms. We have already mentioned tariffs. These and related steps such as import taxes are tacked onto the price of a product to make it more expensive for domestic consumers to buy. The problem with tariffs is that they can stimulate inflation and provide an artificial "quick fix" to domestic industries that might choose to defer investments that would increase productivity and competitiveness. Potentially even more ominous is that tariffs invite retaliation by the affected countries. If the imposition of tariffs gets out of hand, a trade war can ensue that will prevent the free, efficient flow of products among nations. Hoping to avoid such an outcome, Western governments have engaged in periodic negotiations under the **General Agreement on Tariffs and Trade (GATT)** to promote free trade and to gradually reduce tariffs and other trade barriers.

Countries can use other trade barriers to discourage the purchase of imports by consumers; one example is an import quota, which limits the amount of a particular product that can be imported. In some cases nations may bar importation of a product altogether. Import prohibitions are even more onerous to the affected country than tariffs, in the sense that it is denied all access to another country's market, and the impact is more immediate.

More subtle than the effect of tariffs or import quotas are such practices as imposing licenses, restrictions on advertising imported products, and passing health, safety, sanitation, or environmental legislation that could be used to restrict the importation of certain products. These and similar measures are the result of conscious decisions or policies of governments that in turn restrict trade. However, the problem is even more difficult when consumers have an ingrained and cultural preference for homemade products. Such is the case in Japan, where foreign products have a hard time competing on Japanese markets even when they are allowed access. In turn, American corporations have gone on a "buy American" advertising binge in recent years to stimulate the American consumer's patriotic instincts, to reduce the demand for foreign-made products, and thereby to stimulate domestic production.

In addition to the steps countries can take domestically to discourage imports, they often attempt to get other countries to adopt **voluntary export restraints (VERs)** or **orderly marketing arrangements (OMAs),** which place the burden on the exporting country to limit its exports to another country. The difference between these protectionist measures and outright tariffs or import restrictions is that they are negotiated between countries and hence take effect voluntarily. Of course, countries that agree to exercise export restraints often do so out of fear that if they do not more excessive and potentially damaging domestic protectionist measures might be taken by their trading partners.

Balancing Trade and Balancing Payments

The third reality of international trade is that somehow a country must be able to keep its income and expenses in rough balance. Countries maintain a **balance of payments** by keeping the outflow of money from their economy roughly equal to the inflow of money. Trade (imports and exports) is a major component of the balance of payments. If the value of the goods a country imports is roughly equal to the value of the goods it exports to other countries, then its trade is said to be in balance. However, if its trade is out of balance, if its imports exceed the value of its exports, then it must somehow make up the imbalance. One way to do this is by exporting more or importing less. Countries do not have to maintain a strict balance of trade, however. They can make up for a trade imbalance by attracting money from foreign countries or by preventing the outflow of money to other countries. They might choose to attract foreign investment or to borrow to cover the imbalance in trade. Table 11.1 illustrates the factors that contribute to the calculation of a country's balance of payments.

Table 11.1
Factors affecting the national balance of payments

Net Inflow	Net Outflow
Export of goods or services	Import of goods or services
Receipt of foreign aid	Provision of foreign aid
Receipt of foreign investment	Investment abroad
Repatriation of capital	Return of capital to foreign countries
Collection of fees	Payment of fees
Collection of debt	Payment of debt
Collection of interest on debt	Payment of interest on debt
Tourism by foreigners	Tourism by nationals abroad

Obviously, not every component of the balance of payments needs to be in balance all the time. However, the overall payments situation should be in balance. Thus, if a country imports significantly more than it exports, it might try to stay in balance by receiving foreign aid or investment, cutting down on the aid and investment it sends to other countries, collecting previous debts, encouraging foreigners to visit and spend money while discouraging its own citizens from traveling and spending money abroad. Finally, if a country should have chronic balance-of-payments problems, it might decide to devalue its currency relative to the currencies of other states. **Devaluation** would make its products more competitive on foreign markets and discourage domestic purchase of foreign imports, which would become more expensive. Theoretically, this should promote a favorable trade balance and help rectify an imbalance of payments. Consider the following example: Let us assume that the United States devalues the dollar. Before the devaluation the dollar was equal to four German deutschmarks. Afterward, it was equal to two. What effect would this have on the American and German economies? In Germany a consumer could buy an American car for half of what it cost before devaluation. The price of the car in dollars did not change, but the German deutschmark has now doubled in value in relation to the dollar (four deutschmarks once bought one dollar in exchange, now four deutschmarks buys two dollars). In other words, Germans are suddenly able to purchase American imports much more cheaply after devaluation. In the United States the situation is the reverse. German cars are now twice as expensive, so Americans are discouraged from buying them, opting instead for cheaper domestic cars. The overall effect is that American exports become more competitive, and the exports of other countries become less competitive in American markets. Another way to achieve the same effect would be if Germany revalued its currency upward, while the dollar's value remained unchanged. In a sense countries are much like individuals: They need to keep a balanced checkbook. If countries exceed their means, they need to cut back on their lifestyle or take other steps such as those listed in table 11.1.

The Role of Currencies

The fourth reality is that a country can only buy foreign goods with currencies that are acceptable to the selling country. Sudan cannot buy oil from Saudi Arabia with its national currency—the Sudanese pound. This currency is not highly valued by the Saudis, who normally demand U.S. dollars in payment for oil because they know that they can use dollars to buy things they need. The dollar is what economists call a **hard currency;** that is, most countries gladly accept payment in dollars for their exports because they know that the dollar is backed by the strength of the American economy. Everybody will accept payment in dollars because everyone else will. But the same is not true of the Sudanese pound. It is a **soft currency** because no one has confidence in the strength of the Sudanese economy. Quite simply, nobody wants Sudanese pounds, because nobody else does.

Currencies play a number of important roles in the international economy.[7] First, currencies represent a unit of value. The government often dictates the domestic value of the currency. The value on international markets varies with the currencies of other countries depending on the relative strengths of each economy. Today the values of currencies fluctuate almost daily, as anyone who has traveled abroad can testify. Tourists wanting to convert U.S. dollars into the currency of the countries they visit find that exchange rates change frequently. An **exchange rate** is the value of one currency relative to another. Table 11.2 illustrates the fluctuations in the exchange rates of several key international currencies since 1967. Notice that the dollar in 1985 was more highly valued against other currencies than

Table 11.2

Exchange rates of major currencies relative to the U.S. dollar[a]

Year	Belgian Franc	Canadian Dollar	French Franc	German Mark	Italian Lira	Japanese Yen	British Pound	Swiss Franc
1967	2.01	92.69	20.32	25.08	0.176	0.276	275.04	23.10
1969	1.99	92.85	19.30	25.50	0.159	0.279	239.01	23.19
1971	2.06	99.02	18.15	28.77	0.162	0.288	244.42	24.32
1973	2.58	99.98	22.54	37.76	0.172	0.369	245.10	31.70
1975	2.73	98.30	23.35	40.73	0.153	0.337	222.16	38.74
1977	2.79	94.11	20.34	43.08	0.113	0.373	174.49	41.71
1979	3.41	85.39	23.50	54.56	0.120	0.458	212.24	60.12
1981	2.70	83.41	18.49	44.36	0.088	0.454	202.43	51.02
1983	1.96	81.13	13.18	39.23	0.066	0.421	151.59	47.66
1985	1.70	73.23	11.22	34.25	0.052	0.422	129.56	41.06
1987	2.80	76.30	17.40	58.80	0.080	0.745	175.59	71.40

[a] These exchange rates are expressed in U.S. cents. Rates are given in two-year increments from 1967 to 1987.

SOURCE: Adapted from the *Economic Report of the President* (Washington, D.C.: Government Printing Office, February 1986 and 1988).

during the mid-1970s. This meant that American tourists could get better buys in 1985 than they did in the mid-1970s. This was true in Europe but not in Japan, since the yen increased in value during that period. For American businesses seeking to export goods, however, the strong dollar in 1985 meant reduced exports since foreign consumers could no longer as easily afford American-made products. The situation changed quite precipitously by 1987, when the dollar's value plummeted against all major currencies. Although the dollar's lower value made travel overseas far less attractive, many foreign tourists flocked to the United States where their currencies enjoyed considerably higher buying power. Similarly, American exports grew more competitive, while foreign imports became less competitive.

Another important function of currencies concerns their role in pricing goods and services. Currencies are used to establish prices. In effect when a person buys a gallon of milk, he or she trades a dollar or two for it. The currency both establishes a price and serves as a medium of exchange for goods and services.

Currencies also represent a store of wealth, a potential means to pay for things in the future, or a kind of savings account. When currencies are held in savings, they are referred to as **reserves.** Let us explore this more closely. When a country trades with other countries, it receives currencies in payment for its exports, and it pays for imports with currency. If a country exports a good deal more than it imports (if it is running a trade surplus), it will build a large accumulation of currencies from its trading partners. In other words, its reserves will be increasing, and this represents future buying power. On the other hand, if a country imports more than it exports (if it has a trade deficit), it will be using up its reserves (savings). Obviously, a country will eventually get into trouble if it runs a chronic trade deficit. It will soon chalk up debts to other countries that it cannot pay because its reserves will have been depleted. Couldn't such a country simply print more of its currency to pay for its debts? Theoretically it could, but at some point other countries would refuse to accept its currency because of their concern about that country's failing economy and the fact that the currency would have little future value (the predicament faced by Sudan in our earlier example). Countries caught in such a situation need to take steps to reduce their trade deficits. If their traditional trade partners and allies are running trade surpluses, they will have reserves that could be used to purchase goods from the deficit country. Under these circumstances they might be willing to reduce their tariffs on that country's goods, revalue their currencies upward relative to the deficit country, or otherwise make that country's goods more attractive to their consumers. This assumes, however, that the trading partners are cooperating. If they are not, the deficit country may feel the need to take protectionist measures such as increasing tariffs or imposing import quotas on the trade surplus countries. If the deficit country believes that its problem has less to do with failing competitiveness than with unfair trading practices, cooperation might vanish in favor of trade wars. Clearly, the adjustment of trade deficits between countries is a continuous process.

Increasing Economic Interdependence

So far we have dealt with international trade and monetary relations as though they take place between discrete entities called nation-states. A fifth, and growing reality of the international political economy, is that states are not in complete command of their trade and monetary relations, in part because of the growth of multinational corporations and the internationalization of the production process for so many goods. Cars are no longer completely built at one site or even in one country. The chassis may be built in Detroit, the engine in Japan, the axles in Europe, and the electronic components in Taiwan. Under these circumstances, the corporation is doing the importing and exporting. Even in those cases in which governments impose trade restrictions, companies may choose to take steps to minimize their negative effects. Japanese (Honda) and German (Volkswagen) automakers, for instance, have opened plants in the United States. In this way they can produce and sell cars without worrying about the effects of tariffs.

International capital (money) markets demonstrate similar interdependence. The dramatic increase in the U.S. stock market during 1986–1987, was due in part to the influx of foreign investment capital seeking to take advantage of the U.S. stock market surge. Huge, privately owned corporate banks now lend massive sums of money to governments. Indeed, government central banks are no longer in command of their money supply. Many large corporations hold large sums of currencies privately. They can act as banks by lending it out to other businesses or even to governments. The term **Eurodollar** market, for instance, refers to the rather large sums of dollars held by private corporations or banks in Europe, over which governments have very little control.

Foreign Aid

A sixth reality of the international political economy concerns the widespread use of foreign aid. As we have already seen, foreign aid rarely is provided without certain strings attached. Thus, when a country needs money to balance its payments or to develop its economy, it can expect that the aid will have certain conditions. Foreign aid can be bilateral or multilateral in character. Wealthy countries often employ bilateral aid as a way to assist friendly countries and deepen their political and economic ties with them. (See table 11.3 for data on the top aid-giving countries.) By withdrawing aid, displeasure can be shown toward countries whose behavior is considered offensive. Similarly, aid can be used to reward countries that show support for an aid-giver's foreign policy. Bilateral aid is especially sensitive to politics. Multilateral aid, on the other hand, tends to have fewer political strings attached because it is provided through international institutions rather than directly by

Table 11.3
Leading OECD[a] and OPEC foreign aid–giving nations

Rank	Country	Total Aid (in millions of dollars)	Rank	Country	Aid as Percentage of GNP	Rank	Country	Per Capita (in U.S. dollars)
1	United States	9,395	1	Saudi Arabia	4.29	1	Kuwait	397
2	Japan	5,761	2	Kuwait	2.90	2	Saudi Arabia	297
3	France	4,876	3	Norway	1.43	3	Norway	219
4	Federal Republic of Germany	3,651	4	Denmark	1.30	4	Denmark	165
5	Saudi Arabia	3,571	5	Netherlands	1.20	5	Sweden	137
6	Italy	2,424	6	Sweden	1.06	6	Netherlands	116
7	Netherlands	1,747	7	France	0.82	7	France	89
8	United Kingdom	1,667	8	Finland	0.58	8	Finland	71
9	Canada	1,606	9	Belgium	0.57	9	Switzerland	65
10	Sweden	1,167	10	Federal Republic of Germany	0.50	10	Canada	62
11	Norway	921	11	Italy	0.50	11	Federal Republic of Germany	60
12	Denmark	842	12	Canada	0.44	12	Belgium	52
13	Australia	817	13	Australia	0.43	13	United Arab Emirates	51
14	Kuwait	715	14	Switzerland	0.37	14	Australia	51
15	Belgium	516	15	Japan	0.37	15	Japan	48
16	Switzerland	424	16	United Arab Emirates	0.35	16	Italy	43
17	Finland	350	17	United Kingdom	0.33	17	United States	39
18	Austria	202	18	Ireland	0.32	18	United Kingdom	29
19	New Zealand	73	19	New Zealand	0.30	19	Austria	27
20	United Arab Emirates	72	20	Austria	0.27	20	New Zealand	22
21	Ireland	58	21	United States	0.22	21	Ireland	16

[a]Organization for Economic Cooperation and Development.

SOURCE: Adapted from the World Bank, *World Development Report 1988* (Washington, D.C.: World Bank, 1988).

governments. However, multilateral aid is not completely unaffected by political considerations. An International Monetary Fund loan may require countries to undertake very difficult economic reforms—such as reducing imports and removing food subsidies—that may have significant domestic economic and political implications. Bilateral foreign aid includes military, economic, technical, and humanitarian assistance. Multilateral aid typically takes the economic, technical, and humanitarian forms.

Few countries provide bilateral development assistance for purely humanitarian reasons. Aid is often given in the form of loans that must be repaid with interest. Even when outright grants are made, most aid givers expect to realize economic or commercial gain or some degree of political influence as a result of providing assistance to other countries. Often the recipient is required to use the aid to purchase products or services from the nation giving the aid. **Tied aid** of this sort helps the aid-giving country stimulate its exports. In other words, much of what it gives eventually returns to its economy. Soviet bloc countries, in contrast to developed Western countries, rarely give loans; they are not in the charity business either. Rather they grant credits that are tied to the development of particular projects or to the purchase of East bloc equipment. In many cases, the socialist countries will claim first rights to products made by factories built with their inputs. Aid is given in this way rather than as cash loans because, like the Third World countries generally, the socialist nations lack adequate reserves of hard currencies.[8]

Given the political aspects of foreign aid, why would a country accept it? Foreign aid may be one of the few ways a country can acquire resources to develop its infrastructure, acquire technology, educate its population, develop export industries, or in the case of military assistance, provide for its security. Critics of foreign aid claim that it only further impoverishes a country, increases its future debt, makes it more beholden to the political interests of others, and thus reduces its independence. However, very few countries do not play the aid game, either as a donor or a recipient. As figure 11.1 shows, foreign aid outlays increased dramatically during the 1970s, peaking around 1980. These increases reflected the growing needs for aid in the developing world, needs that continued to grow even during the early 1980s when foreign aid outlays plateaued, before rising again in the mid-1980s.

Much of the assistance represented in figure 11.1 was given to middle-income states in the developing world—primarily to those in strategic or tension-ridden areas—rather than to the poorest countries. In this connection, it is also important to recognize the difference between actual economic assistance as opposed to what can be called "security" or military-related aid. The United States, for instance, includes as part of its economic development aid a category known as Economic Support Funds (ESF). These funds, which comprise a portion of the development aid budget, are little more than an additional source of security assistance for developing countries. Despite some of these qualifications, foreign aid is still an integral part of the international political economy. It continues to be a tool of foreign policy as countries struggle to win friends, outflank foes, and attract capital for development.

Wealth and Poverty

A seventh reality of international economics is that some countries are rich and others are poor. There are different explanations about why this is so and how poor countries could become less poor. Marxists argue that poor countries will stay poor as long as they participate in an international capitalist economy that is stacked against them.[9] In this view the deck is rigged in favor of the rich capitalist countries, which are in turn governed by wealthy capitalist elite. According to dependency theorists, poor countries will stay in the

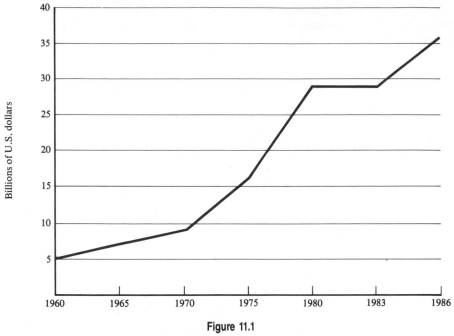

Figure 11.1

Trends in official development assistance

(Organization for Economic Cooperation and Development Countries)

SOURCE: World Bank, *World Development Report 1988* (Washington, D.C.: World Bank, 1988).

clutches of this system unless they pursue socialist revolutions, overthrow the local elite who have been co-opted and corrupted by international capitalism, and withdraw from the capitalist economic system in order to develop their economies on their own terms.

Liberal economists take an entirely different view; they believe countries are poor for a variety of internal domestic reasons, such as lack of labor productivity, overpopulation, lack of incentives for entrepreneurship, overcentralization of the economy, corruption, and lack of capital and economic infrastructure.[10] To overcome these problems, the liberal school argues that poor countries need to participate more openly in the international economy, rather than isolate themselves from it. They need foreign aid, foreign investment, and foreign trade.

Others, such as economist Raul Prebisch and reformists who have called for a New International Economic Order, have argued a middle position.[11] They agree that poor countries can only improve their lot by participating in the international economy. However, that economy should be restructured in ways that will be fairer to the special economic circumstances of the poor countries. One major problem, in this view, is that poor and agricultural countries have a difficult time getting fair terms of trade for their commodities as compared to the prices they must pay for manufactured goods imported from industrialized countries. Developing countries (LDCs) faced a disadvantageous terms-of-trade situation in the 1960s. During the 1970s, this situation changed dramatically, so that by the early 1980s they enjoyed a rough parity with the developed market economies. But the tremendous rise in the price of oil accounted for most of the dramatic price increase for LDC commodities in the 1970s. Unfortunately, only a few LDCs export oil, while the vast majority import it. This left many even worse off than they were in the 1960s. For a significant majority, the terms of trade situation continues to be very poor. So reformists continue to press for **commodity indexation agreements** that will keep prices for these goods on a par with those of manufacturers. Reformists also have argued that aid should be provided on less restrictive terms and that poor countries should be given a chance to develop less competitive manufacturing sectors. We will return to the problem of international poverty in chapter 12. Whichever view is held—Marxist, liberal, or reformist—however, there is a common recognition that the international economy generally will reflect the interests of the most powerful countries in the system at any particular time. This insight leads us to a final reality of international economics.

Persistent Change

A final reality is that international economic relations are marked by persistent change. Trade relations among nations require constant accommodation, as trade surplus and trade deficit countries struggle for economic advantage. Economically powerful countries in one century become second-rate powers in another.[12] Depressions and recessions constantly reshape the distribution of economic wealth between nations. As new technologies and energy sources are discovered, the fortunes of nations change. War can shatter the economic capacities of some nations, while catapulting others into a position of prominence. The realities of international economics persist, but because of the shifting economic and political fortunes of nations, the specific rules and institutions that govern international economics vary. To understand how these changes occur, we turn to a discussion about how our contemporary international economic system has developed.

The Contemporary International Economic System

Post-World War II Dilemmas

World War II brought big changes in the international economy. Prior to the war, the global economy had experienced the worst depression in modern memory. International trade was hampered by nations' strong protectionist policies. The war helped the U.S. economy lurch out of its lethargy, but for many countries it was even more devastating economically than the Depression had been. The powerful European countries were devastated. Factories were in rubble. Agricultural productivity had declined. Millions of people were homeless; thousands were perched on the brink of starvation. Japan, a major military and economic power before the war (like Germany), was a broken and vanquished nation. Although emerging as a strong military power, the Soviet Union also faced significant economic hardship. Only one country was in a position to resurrect the global economy from this widespread devastation: the United States.

The key need in the international economy at this time was for capital, that is, money for reconstruction. Where would this money come from? Gold could not be mined in sufficient quantities or fast enough to refinance the billions of dollars of reconstruction that was necessary. A strong currency was needed that could be distributed in large quantities throughout the world and that could be backed by gold. In other words, the world needed what economists call **liquidity:** It needed a resource that could be readily used to finance international reconstruction and economic growth. All eyes turned toward the United States.

Its economy, unlike so many others, was humming along quite nicely. Moreover, by the end of the war the United States held about 70 percent of the world's gold reserves. Other countries were confident that the dollar, backed by gold, could serve as the international currency they needed to get back on their feet. The United States, for its part, was eager to play the role of the world's banker, a role that would secure its expanded economic and political influence around the world.[13]

The Bretton Woods System

The Bretton Woods Conference established an international economic system, known as the **Bretton Woods System,** based on several key principles. First, governments would exercise considerable autonomy in their domestic economic policy, including sensitive areas such as taxation, maintenance of employment, and economic growth. Second, the U.S. dollar would serve as the principal international currency, and it would be backed by gold; that is, countries holding American dollars could convert them into gold, which was in turn valued at thirty-five dollars an ounce. (During the early years of this system, most countries chose to hold onto their dollars rather than convert them.) Third, all other national currencies would be valued at fixed rates in relationship to the dollar. Fourth, countries having balance-of-payments problems (i.e., they were spending more money than they were earning) could borrow from the International Monetary Fund (IMF) to cover short-term deficits. Fifth, countries needing longer term loans for reconstruction and development could seek them from the World Bank and other international lending institutions.[14]

The World Bank has grown into something more than a mere source of official long-term assistance. Many LDCs now rely on the bank for financial policy advice. The bank itself, which began operation in 1945 as the International Bank for Reconstruction and Development (IBRD), now lends primarily to countries at more advanced levels of development. Another arm of the bank, the International Development Association (IDA), was created in 1960 to provide concessional credit to the least developed countries that might not otherwise qualify for loans. The IBRD and the IDA, combined, lend to over seventy countries. They have become, in many cases, crucial focal points for governmental lobbying. The World Bank can often make or break a country's development plans and is quite influential in the establishment of LDC financial policies. Donor governments, of course, also play a significant role in World Bank policy making, because they ultimately provide the bank with the resources or guarantees that allow it to leverage private capital markets. The United States contributes about a fourth of the IDA's resources and is the largest single contributor to the IBRD as well. The latter, however, relies not only on donor country contributions but is also able to borrow on private capital markets, with guarantees of repayment given by its member governments. This allows it to leverage additional resources at lower rates of interest and to pass them on to the LDCs.

In 1956 a third arm of the bank, the International Finance Corporation, was established to provide credit directly to private enterprises in developing countries. This approach attempts to stimulate economic development directly by promoting development of private enterprises. More recently, in 1988, a fourth bank institution, the Multilateral Investment Guarantee Agency, was established to encourage further private investment in LDCs by insuring investors against the common political risks of investment in the Third World, such as expropriation, civil war, and government efforts to prevent foreign companies from converting and repatriating earnings in local currency into foreign currencies.

The bank, then, has grown in scope, size, and importance since the days of Bretton Woods. Together with the IMF, the World Bank remains the multilateral focal point in the economic planning of Third World governments. Donor and host country roundtable meetings hosted by the bank set the development planning agenda of many LDCs today. The bank finances a wide range of development programs including economic infrastructures, such as roads and power systems, as well as programs for health, education, housing, and agricultural development.

Critics of the bank point out that it sometimes finances environmentally disastrous projects such as Brazil's Amazon road project, which is leading to vast deforestation. Others believe that much of the money lent to governments gets lost in international and national bureaucracies, with little of it trickling down to the poorest people in poor countries. Still others criticize the World Bank—and its sister agency, the IMF—for placing governments in the uncomfortable position of implementing severe economic austerity programs, which hurt the poor most, to qualify for further bank loans. These criticisms have some merit. But it is equally true that the bank and the IMF have assisted many governments on the road to sounder financial and economic policies. They have grown more sensitive to the potential environmental consequences of its projects. The bank has also been more attuned in recent decades to the need to sponsor grass-roots development efforts, to promote basic human needs assistance, and to stimulate direct assistance to private entrepreneurs, thus bypassing national government bureaucracies. In other words, the bank is responsive to changing needs, and if the number of participating governments in its programs, either as donors or borrowers, is any indication, it remains a vital part of the global development system.

To be a member of the bank, a nation must belong to the IMF, an institution that serves not only to adjust nations' short-term balance-of-payments needs, but also to promote stable currency exchange relations that will enhance global prosperity and promote orderly monetary relations. In its early years during the period of fixed exchange rates, the IMF worked principally with the developed countries, lending them short-term funds to cover balance-of-payments deficits. Later, as fluctuating exchange rates became the norm, developed states required less short-term assistance, since the currency market automatically adjusted currency values to reflect the deficit or surplus positions of various countries. At the same time the rapid growth in the numbers of developing countries led the IMF to focus its short-term lending on them, because many LDCs had become chronic debtors. The short-term loans are based on the willingness of debtor governments to undertake structural adjustments in their economies to promote growth, exports, and a more stable balance-of-payments posture. The IMF has 152 member states; 133 are LDCs. In recent years the IMF together with the World Bank and major donors have engaged in comprehensive efforts to help the poorest countries make difficult but necessary economic reforms to promote genuine development and alleviate crushing poverty.

Substantial increases in IMF reserves (which can be used for future lending) are anticipated over the next decade as the needs of the developing world continue and as the integration of Eastern Europe and the Soviet Union into the world economy takes place. These troubled economies will rely heavily on multilateral loans, both short-term ones from the IMF and long-term ones from the World Bank, as they make painful adjustments to market economies.

In addition to its concern about the need to restructure the post–World War II international financial structure, the United States was convinced of the need for free trade among nations. Many experts believed that the protectionist policies pursued during the interwar years had aggravated the economic situation and contributed to the prolongation of the

Depression. After World War II, the General Agreement on Tariffs and Trade was created to monitor international trade and, through ongoing negotiations, to encourage countries to reduce tariffs and other trade barriers so that international trade could move more freely and efficiently. Reductions in tariff barriers were expected to be undertaken reciprocally. **Reciprocity** meant that if country *A* reduced tariffs on its imports from country *B*, country *B* would also be expected to reduce tariffs on goods it imported from country *A*. To assist in the progressive lowering of tariffs, countries were encouraged to grant most-favored nation (MFN) status to trading partners. What this meant was that the country granting MFN status would give the trading partner's products the lowest (most-favorable) tariff rates already enjoyed by other trading partners. Finally, the trading system was expected to work more smoothly because the dollar would become the universal medium of exchange, or at least the benchmark against which all other currencies would be measured. Thus, international transactions would be more predictable.[15]

This trade and monetary system worked as intended for a number of years. The system was not accepted by most members of the Soviet bloc, who were reluctant to subject their socialist economic systems to potential capitalist penetration. However, despite the growth of two competing economic systems, even the socialist bloc could not entirely avoid the effects of the much more dynamic capitalist economy.[16] Nor was the developing world satisfied with the global economic institutions created by the dominant capitalist countries. The LDCs were especially concerned about the GATT emphasis on reciprocal trade agreements. Since their primary commodities, as we have already noted, were not competitively priced with industrial products for many years, reciprocal trade agreements worked to their disadvantage. They wanted a **preferential trade system,** which would lower tariffs on their primary export commodities to developed economies, while permitting them to keep high tariffs on manufactured imports so that they would have a chance to develop their less competitive infant industries. The **UN Conference on Trade and Development (UNCTAD)** was created in 1964 to address LDC economic needs that were often ignored by the GATT.[17] The eventual adoption of a General System of Preferences for the commodities and semimanufacturers of developing states is one of the chief successes of UNCTAD.

As for virtually the rest of the world, the Bretton Woods system had an even more significant impact. The economies of Europe and Japan revived rapidly as American dollars flooded the international economy. Global trade increased dramatically. American corporations invested in foreign lands. American tourists spent large sums of money overseas. The U.S. government gave millions of dollars in foreign aid, first to European countries during the Marshall Plan and later to the poor and newly emerging countries of the Third World. American military expenditures overseas also increased, especially as Cold War tensions and the East–West dispute intensified during the 1950s. For any other country such a massive outflow of currency would have been unacceptable, since it was also expected to maintain a balance of payments. But the United States was running trade surpluses that helped offset these expenditures. Moreover, as long as the U.S. economy was strong, other countries needed and wanted the U.S. dollar.

Erosion of the Bretton Woods System

Global confidence in the U.S. economy and in the dollar gradually eroded, however. By the 1960s the European and Japanese economies were not only back on their feet, but they were beginning to compete with the United States. The United States was spending prodigious sums to fight the Vietnam war and pay for expanded domestic social programs, without corresponding increases in taxes. Domestic budget deficits mounted. The U.S. trade surpluses also began to turn into deficits as Americans began to import more than they exported. Then U.S. gold reserves dwindled, as some countries, most notably, France, insisted on converting the dollars they held into gold. Other countries grew more concerned that the United States might unilaterally devalue the dollar or perhaps even refuse to redeem dollars for gold. Indeed, as figure 11.2 illustrates, the percentage reserve holdings of the United States decreased rapidly over the post–World War II period. While it enjoyed 50 percent of international reserves in 1952, this figure declined to 28 percent by 1962 and to only 8 percent in the 1970s and 1980s. This decline occurred largely because of the dollar's role as the instrument of liquidity and global international economic growth. During this time confidence in the U.S. economy deteriorated rapidly, as the U.S. balance-of-payments

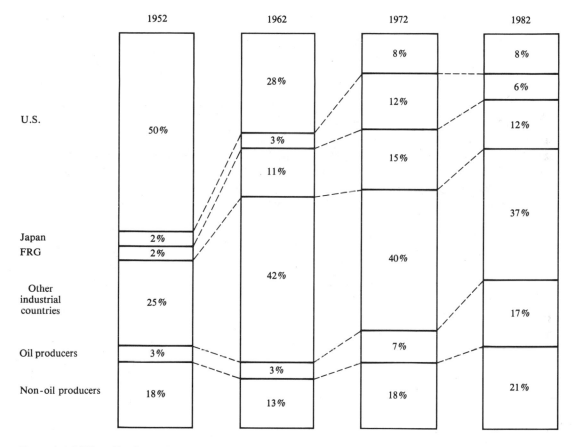

*Reserves include SDRs, gold, and reserves in the IMF and foreign exchange holdings.
Data excludes Eastern Bloc countries (USSR, East Europe, and Cuba after 1960).

Figure 11.2
International reserves (1952–1982)*
SOURCE: Adapted from data in the *Economic Report of the President* (Washington, D.C.:
Government Printing Office, February 1986).
*Reserves include Special Drawing Rights, gold, reserves in the IMF, and foreign exchange holdings.
Data excludes Eastern bloc countries (Soviet Union, Eastern Europe, and Cuba after 1960).

deficits grew larger and more chronic, and as the U.S. trade balance, reserve holdings, and domestic economy deteriorated.

By the early 1970s, the situation had become critical. With gold reserves dwindling rapidly, President Nixon announced that the dollar would no longer be convertible into gold. In addition, the dollar was devalued on two occasions (in other words, its value was decreased relative to gold and to other currencies). Finally, the dollar was cut loose altogether from a fixed price in gold and allowed to "float" on its own. This meant that the dollar's values would change frequently relative to other currencies. Obviously, this made international trade more complicated and less predictable.[18] Correspondingly, the protectionist impulse has grown stronger, as countries seek to shelter their own industries from foreign competition. Advocates of free trade now find themselves swimming upstream to fend off protectionist policies that they believe could stifle international trade.[19]

Not all of the Bretton Woods system came to an end in the 1970s, however. Fixed exchange rates and convertibility of the dollar into gold were gone, but the World Bank, IMF, GATT, and other institutions remained.[20] The dollar no longer reigned supreme, but it was still one of the most important currencies of exchange. Currencies of other countries with strong and stable economies joined the dollar in this capacity. Also created during this difficult period for the international economy was the **Special Drawing Right (SDR).** One of the problems with the dollar, or any other international currency, is that confidence in it as a reserve asset depends on the economic performance of the reserve currency country. As we saw, confidence in the dollar declined because of the chronic balance-of-payments deficits run by the United States in the 1960s. But such deficits were themselves a product of the dollar's role in providing international liquidity. The SDR was an attempt to get around this problem by creating an international reserve asset that would be managed by the IMF and apportioned to countries based on an established system of quotas. The SDRs joined gold, dollars, and other internationally accepted reserve currencies as a way to help resolve accounts among countries. They were intended to take the pressure off gold and currencies during periods of rapid economic expansion by providing another asset that could be used to resolve balance-of-payments accounts. Like currencies, SDRs have value in settling national accounts because countries have agreed to create and accept them as a monetary tool.

American economic supremacy has clearly declined relative to the immediate post–World War II period. The United States enjoyed considerable political influence by virtue of its preeminent economic position during the 1950s and 1960s.[21] Scholars still debate whether economic domination or a genuine fear of communism motivated American decision makers during this time. No doubt both concerns played a role. Certainly, U.S. policy makers justified expanded military presence throughout the globe as an effort to thwart what they viewed as Soviet subversion and communist threats to the Free World. However, it was inevitable that a high-profile, expensive American presence throughout the globe would become burdensome for even the strongest economy. Competition from European countries and Japan in foreign trade, and the rise of Arab oil power in the 1970s only hastened the process. By the 1970s American policy makers were looking for ways to reduce overseas military obligations and expenditures. American influence over world affairs was bound to decrease in the process. The Reagan administration sought to reverse this trend in the early 1980s. However, apart from perhaps a renewed sense of national pride, the restoration of American power to the level that was enjoyed during the heyday of the post–World War II period, has not been achieved, nor is it likely to be. To a very large extent, the reason is economic in character: Global hegemony is costly, and no country can afford to maintain it indefinitely. Great Britain was unable to maintain its leadership of the international economy in the 1800s. Nor has the United States been able to maintain the dominant position it enjoyed after World War II.[22] The difference today is that no nation appears to be willing or able to replace the United States as the dominant country. The U.S. role in the international economy is still a formidable one, despite its diluted influence. Nevertheless, with U.S. economic leadership in decline, one of the few options to avoid international economic anarchy appears to be continued multilateral cooperation.[23]

In summary, in the forty years since World War II, the international economy has undergone a good deal of change. The realities of international economics are still present, but the specific rules of the trade and monetary games have been modified to reflect changes in the international political and economic situation. This always has been, is now, and will continue to be a basic fact of life in international relations. The task we face is to identify key problems that will require attention in the near future and devise rules and institutions that will promote a healthy international economy.

Basic Issues

A review of recent literature suggests that four key international economic issues currently concern scholars and policy makers alike. First, can and how might the global debt crisis be resolved? Second, are international commodity cartels such as OPEC continuing influences or spent forces in the international economy? Third, is the world moving away from free trade to protectionism, and what will be the consequences? Finally, are economic sanctions a useful foreign policy tool in an age of interdependence? Let us deal with each of these issues in the order in which they have just been presented.

The Global Debt Situation

Our first issue—the global debt crisis—has attracted an impressive degree of attention in the scholarly literature, perhaps more than any single contemporary economic issue.[24] At the heart of this crisis is the simple fact that in the 1970s key donor countries and private banks lent very large sums of money to countries whose economies seemed to hold great promise for growth. Later, as a result of changes in the international economic situation, the economies of these countries went sour. (See table 11.4, for a list of the countries with the highest levels of foreign external debt.) This put many of these nations, such as Mexico, Argentina, and Brazil, in the position of not being able to pay back their debts. The fear most experts express is that a default on a loan by a major debtor nation could send shock waves through the international monetary system, leading at a minimum to the collapse of the affected financial institutions and perhaps to a more severe domino effect in which one major bank after another collapses. Fear so far has produced a remarkable degree of cooperation between the lenders and debtor countries; they have negotiated a series of debt rescheduling agreements.[25] A symbiotic relationship exists between lenders and debtors: It is in neither's interest to have debtors default because this would put the banks out of business and the debtor would be in no position subsequently to borrow money to cover continuing development needs. There is disagreement about why the debt crisis came into being and who was responsible. Some blame creditors, others debtors, and still others structural changes in the international economy.[26] Whatever the cause, most analysts agree that this crisis has been a dangerous threat to global economic stability. Lenders and debtors

Table 11.4
Global external debt

Debt Crisis Countries[a]			Countries with Debt in Excess of $10 Billion		
Country	Total Debt (in millions of U.S. dollars)		Country	Total Debt (in millions of U.S. dollars)	
	1984	1986		1984	1986
Argentina	45,839	48,908	Algeria	13,811	17,929
Bolivia	3,913	4,619	Colombia	12,285	14,619
Brazil	104,384	110,675	Egypt	23,206	28,556
Chile	19,959	20,741	Greece	14,369	20,862
Mexico	97,307	101,722	India	30,678	41,088
Peru	13,164	15,303	Indonesia	32,480	42,090
Philippines	24,383	28,172	Israel	23,449	23,775
Portugal	15,012	16,658	Nigeria	19,742	21,876
Turkey	22,267	31,808	Pakistan	11,656	13,620
Uruguay	3,288	3,770	South Korea	43,057	45,109
Venezuela	34,247	33,891	Thailand	15,278	17,959
			Yugoslavia	19,844	21,364

Lowest Income Countries with Debt in Excess of $2 Billion (1986)			
Country	Total Debt (in millions of U.S. dollars)	Country	Total Debt (in millions of U.S. dollars)
Ethiopia	2,139	Kenya	4,504
Bangladesh	7,868	Zambia	5,300
Burma	3,766	Sudan	8,272
Madagascar	2,899	Pakistan	13,620
Tanzania	3,955	Ghana	2,385
India	41,088	Sri Lanka	4,119
China	22,724	Senegal	2,990

[a] The debt crisis countries have been identified by the World Bank. Debt crisis is a function not only of the size of the debt, but also of other economic factors (e.g., lack of foreign exchange) that impede repayment.

SOURCE: Adapted from the World Bank, *World Development Report 1986* (Washington, D.C.: World Bank, 1986), pp. 208–209; and idem, *World Development Report 1988* (Washington, D.C., World Bank, 1988), pp. 252–253.

seem to have coped with it successfully for now, but coping and solving a crisis are two different things, and many analysts are still concerned as the debt of many Third World countries continues to mount.

One side effect of the debt situation in several LDCs has been a reduction in imports. Ironically, the current U.S. trade deficit can be attributed in part to the decreased purchase of U.S. goods by debt-ridden countries such as Mexico and Brazil. These countries have been forced to cut back on imports to save foreign exchange to pay off their debts. The debt situation, in other words, is closely tied to problems in the international commerce of nations.

Meanwhile, as a result of chronic trade and balance-of-payments deficits, as well as gigantic budgetary deficits, the United States has become the world's largest debtor nation in the past decade. Given the size of the American economy relative to that of the world, this potential debt problem may one day exceed those of the Third World in importance.

Commodity Cartels

Cartels are organizations of countries (or companies) that seek to control the price of a commodity by manipulating its supply. Several factors are crucial to a cartel's success: (1) the degree to which the commodity is an essential to other countries and for which there are no readily available substitutes, (2) the members control a substantial portion of the global supply, and (3) the membership is sufficiently small and homogeneous to permit concerted action.

Of the cartels created in the 1970s, OPEC was clearly the most influential and successful. Unlike producers of copper, tin, or bauxite (which also had cartels), the OPEC countries initially best satisfied the factors just mentioned. However, high prices for oil (achieved in large part as a result of OPEC efforts) stimulated exploration and conservation by other countries. Gradually, as new supplies of oil were found, the global supply increased and prices eventually dropped. The existence of a large number of different oil producers in the world bodes poorly for the continued influence of OPEC.[27] Indeed, as the economies of many oil producers were adversely affected by dropping prices, they responded by increasing their volume of export, thus further contributing to the price declines. For several consecutive years the OPEC nations failed to agree among themselves to specific production quotas for each member. Only recently, after a purposeful effort by the Saudi Arabians to glut the market and drive prices below the breakeven point for many non-OPEC oil producers, has OPEC been able to agree on a new quota scheme. However, it is yet to be seen if North Sea producers such as the United Kingdom will buckle to OPEC pressure and come into line with its pricing and quota policies. It seems doubtful that they will ever collaborate closely with OPEC. However, the Soviet Union, which is the world's fourth largest oil producer, has recently shown a willingness to coordinate its exports with OPEC to firm up global oil prices.

If other cartels have floundered in relative obscurity, OPEC seems to have fallen on hard times. But its capacity to affect oil markets, and that of its individual members such as the Saudis, should not be discounted just yet. Its once rather impressive clout, though considerably diminished today, may one day be regained.

Trade Wars

A third key issue in contemporary literature focuses on the direction of trade relations between states. The world trade balance, and trade balances between particular countries, is a very sensitive political issue because it can affect the availability of jobs in countries. In recent years, the U.S. trade deficit has skyrocketed, whereas other countries such as the Federal Republic of Germany and Japan have enjoyed substantial trade surpluses. Table 11.5 illustrates these basic trends. The U.S. trade deficit has shot upward in the 1980s, from a $40 billion deficit in 1981 to $143 billion in 1985. In 1986, although not shown in the table, the deficit grew to nearly $175 billion.[28]

It should come as no surprise that labor groups and politicians in the United States have become increasingly alarmed at these statistics. They charge that Japan and European countries have unfairly prevented access to American agricultural and manufactured goods. The threat of trade wars between the United States and Japan over manufactured goods (particularly electronics) and between the United States and European Community (EC) countries over agricultural trade loomed large in early 1987, as protectionist interests in the United States pressed for relief from what they characterized as unfair foreign competition. Trade tensions came to a head in March 1987 when the Reagan administration slapped

Table 11.5

The world trade balance[a]

Country	1965	1970	1975	1981	1982	1983	1984	1985
Developed Countries	-7.4	-11.4	-33.6	-102.0	-84.5	-76.6	-110.6	-129.3
United States	4.3	0.5	2.2	-39.6	-42.6	-69.4	-123.3	-143.8
Canada	-0.3	2.5	-2.1	2.4	12.8	11.4	11.8	10.8
Japan	0.2	0.4	-2.1	8.6	6.9	20.6	33.5	39.6
European Community	-5.4	-5.3	-7.0	-32.9	-25.4	-16.3	-14.7	-12.7
France	-0.2	-1.0	-0.9	-14.5	-19.0	-10.5	-6.1	-6.6
Federal Republic of Germany	0.3	4.3	15.3	12.2	21.0	16.5	18.7	23.8
Italy	-0.2	-1.8	-3.7	-15.7	-12.7	-7.7	-10.9	-15.8
United Kingdom	-2.3	-2.5	-9.9	-0.5	-2.7	-8.5	-11.1	-8.5
Other Developed Countries	-6.2	-9.5	-24.6	-40.5	-36.2	-22.9	-17.9	-23.2
Developing Countries	-1.4	-0.5	22.8	46.4	-5.9	3.3	33.9	18.2
OPEC	3.9	7.0	59.6	117.4	43.5	30.3	37.6	24.6
Other	-5.3	-7.5	-36.8	-71.0	-49.4	-27.0	-3.7	-6.4
Communist Countries	0.7	0.8	-10.5	5.1	20.8	22.3	20.0	-2.5
Soviet Union	0.2	1.1	-3.7	6.2	9.4	11.3	11.1	3.0
East Europe	0.2	-0.3	-6.0	-3.7	4.3	5.0	6.2	5.5
China	0.2	0.0	-0.3	2.1	5.0	3.8	0.7	-10.7

[a] Figures are in billions of U.S. dollars.

SOURCE: Adapted from the *Economic Report of the President* (Washington, D.C.: Government Printing Office, February 1986).

trade sanctions on Japan, accusing it of having dumped microchips illegally on the American market, thus unfairly undercutting American microchip producers.

In Congress and in the corporate boardrooms of America, a new buzz word dominated discussions about the role of the United States in international trade: **competitiveness.** This concept includes elements of protectionism such as tariffs and import quotas for American industries that have been hit especially hard by foreign competition. However, it also implies the need to update the American industrial plant, to introduce the latest technologies in outmoded industries, and even to consider new tax policies that would put American exporters on a more equal footing with foreign competitors.[29] Other scholars believed that an overvalued dollar was the chief reason for the tremendous U.S. trade deficits. They predicted that once the value of the dollar fell to a level that was more appropriate with other currencies, U.S. exports would become more attractive. Indeed, early in 1987 the U.S. government encouraged the dollar to fall on world markets, hoping that eventually U.S. exports would become more competitive on foreign markets. But the rise in the U.S. trade deficit was not arrested and reversed until the spring of 1988.

Opinion on protectionism varies. Some fear a return to protectionist policies as a means of retaliating against violators of trade agreements. Almost everyone agrees that the days of steady progress in reducing trade barriers are gone. Many of the original principles on which the GATT was based (nondiscriminatory or reciprocal trade, steady reduction in trade barriers, and mediation of trade disputes) have been eroded by the practice of states.[30] Some experts fear the return of protectionist impulses in international trade. For example, Robert Reich writes that the "recent collapse of free-trade ideology into retaliatory protectionism attests to the bankruptcy of that ideal in the present international economy."[31] Nor are these judgments limited to American experts. Some Europeans have suggested that free trade may have ceased to be an organizing principle in the international economy, and they worry about how free trade in Europe might be preserved in the face of increasingly strong protectionist impulses.[32]

Although a large number of international trade specialists fear the consequences of protectionism, another school of thought suggests that reciprocity, bilateralism, retaliation, and regulatory restrictions on trade can serve as effective means of ensuring compliance to otherwise self-enforcing trade agreements.[33] In this view, because the GATT operates on a kind of honor system of self-enforcement, strong temptations exist for countries to cheat. One way to stop cheating is for other countries to retaliate against the offenders. Thus, what is currently viewed as an onslaught of protectionism may only be a correction process. Another way to stop cheating is to ask the GATT to form a review panel to deal with trade disputes.

In this chapter's first supplemental reading, Susan Strange goes even further by rejecting most of the liberal assumptions about free trade. In her view most of the problems of the international economy are due to dislocations in monetary policy, shifts in capital flows, recession, and other structural changes in the international economy, such as the movement of manufacturing industries to the Third World, not to protectionism.[34] Indeed, through careful maneuvering, newly industrialized countries such as Korea, Taiwan, and Singapore have minimized the adverse effects of protectionist policies of developed countries and have gained economic advantage in the process.[35]

Only time will tell which of these views on protectionism is correct. Strange's argument is attractive, but it is quite clear that many other students of the international political economy are jittery over the possible implications of a global devolution into protectionism and are counseling policy makers to show as much restraint as possible in the face of strong domestic protectionist constituencies.

In the second reading, John Conybeare suggests that the size of competing countries affects international economic conflict. Trade wars between large countries should be short-lived because each will recognize the mutual harm incurred by prolonged protectionism. On the other hand, trade wars between a big and a small power are unlikely to occur in the first place because the weaker party normally will not be in a position to start or sustain a trade war. Prolonged and damaging trade wars, Conybeare argues, are unusual. As for the current trade climate, he believes that it could be improved by ridding the GATT of the most-favored nation (MFN) principle, which discourages countries from entering GATT negotiations and instead encourages bilateral trade deals. The problem with MFN is that by giving a trade concession to one country, all others in the GATT gain without making a reciprocal concession. Instead Conybeare proposes a system of points that could be used by a country to protect certain of its most vulnerable industries but not all of them.

Protectionism is strongest in those countries that lose employment to foreign competitors. Free trade is often viewed in these countries as the primary enemy. However, another problem—**overcapacity**—seems to be accounting increasingly for the decline of a whole range of industries in many countries. Overcapacity results when too many factories produce so much of a product that global supply exceeds demand. Under these conditions, all producers will begin to feel a pinch, prices will drop, and plants will close. Steelworkers in Pennsylvania may blame the more technologically sophisticated steel industries in Germany and Japan for the problem. But today, steel companies in those countries are also hurting badly. They are facing a market in which Korea, Taiwan, Brazil, and Mexico are producing large quantities of cheap steel using the very latest production technologies and cheaper labor. But other steel-producing countries are not yet ready to get out of the business. The upshot is that the world has more steel than it needs, and more steel plants than can be operated economically.[36]

According to experts, the problem is not limited to steel, it is also true of automobiles, televisions, computers, and petrochemicals.[37] As more countries begin to industrialize, the degree of overcapacity is bound to grow. Free trade might solve this problem by forcing the least-efficient plants out of business. However, once countries have invested heavily in an industry, and thousands of jobs hang in the balance, domestic political pressures to protect the industries are bound to grow. Only painful adjustments can solve overcapacity: a decrease in the number of factories and the level of production. The struggle in international relations concerns which countries' industries will survive and which will not. This struggle is joined by the domestic political question of whose jobs will be lost.

From the perspective of overcapacity, it may not be enough for some American industries to become more competitive. If there is too much capacity for production and too much production around the world, even competitively priced goods may go unsold. In the long run, overcapacity could be solved in one of two ways: (1) by the least-competitive enterprises going out of business (thus reducing production capacity and supply), or (2) by a substantial widening of the market (an increase in demand), which might be achieved, for example, if developing countries accumulated more wealth and purchasing power in the process of industrializing.

As we leave this discussion of trade wars and competitiveness, it is important to underscore three points. First in the area of international trade it is almost impossible to separate domestic and international politics. Trade sits squarely at the intersection of global and domestic economies. It affects domestic employment, inflation, and the balance-of-payments posture. Domestic political interests alternatively press for liberal or restrictive trade policies.

Second, despite the strong domestic tendencies toward protectionist trade policies, GATT and other international economic institutions continue to provide multilateral channels for resolution of trade disputes. For instance, in 1986, the Uruguay Round of GATT Negotiations, involving ninety-two countries were initiated in Punta del Este, Uruguay. Among the global trade issues being discussed are (1) export subsidies and import barriers in agricultural trade (a ticklish dispute involving the United States and the EC), (2) new guidelines for trade in services for which no international rules exist, and (3) trade-related investment and protection for intellectual property. In addition to the GATT forum, bilateral negotiations enable states to resolve trade disputes. For instance, persistent negotiation between U.S. and Japanese government officials bore fruit in April 1990, when Japan agreed to remove barriers to U.S. lumber exports. Earlier, Japan had agreed to open its markets to U.S. satellites and supercomputers. Japan thus avoided being placed on a retaliation list, as required under congressional legislation, and escalation of the U.S.–Japanese trade dispute was averted.

Third, the current concern about trade wars illustrates that economic competition can lead to a deterioration of political relations among countries.[38] Economics in this case drives politics. However, there are also times when politics dictates economic policy. We turn next to a discussion of trade embargoes and economic sanctions as foreign policy instruments that are often employed to achieve certain political goals.

Economic Sanctions

The final issue that we will consider concerns the effectiveness of economic sanctions and trade embargoes. An **economic sanction** is the coercive use of economic means to deny resources to an opposing government, to punish a country for something it has done, to deter a nation from taking an objectionable action, or to force a nation to reverse an objectionable policy.[39] Sanctions may also be employed for domestic reasons, such as winning political favor with particular groups by showing toughness toward unpopular governments. Economic sanctions may include a wide range of activities, including trade embargoes (refusing to sell products to the target country), disinvestment (encouraging corporations to pull out of the target country), boycotting the purchase of other countries' products, cutting off foreign aid, halting the travel of citizens to the target country, preventing the extension of loans, and freezing assets of the target country held under the jurisdiction of the country imposing the sanctions. These are a few examples of economic sanctions. How effective are they in achieving their goals?

The conventional wisdom is that economic sanctions are not an effective tool of foreign policy.[40] However, several recent studies point out that although economic sanctions may not achieve all of their initially stated objectives, target countries may be adversely affected in unanticipated ways.[41]

Most students of this subject agree that economic sanctions, whether effective or not, continue to be a popular policy option. Why? One reason may be that other forms of international coercion such as military intervention, covert action, or severing diplomatic relations may be even more ineffectual and, in some cases, more dangerous than economic sanctions. But if economic sanctions may be less dangerous, are they more effective? According to Huffbauer and Schott, who examined over a hundred cases of sanctions, their success depends on the kinds of goals states want to achieve, the context in which sanctions are carried out, and the type of sanctions employed. They found that sanctions were successful in more than a third of the cases studied; success was more prevalent when the goals sought were more modest and far less prevalent when the goals were more ambitious. Sanctions work best when they are employed against economically weak countries, when they are applied quickly and decisively, and when the costs to domestic firms are minimized.[42] Others have argued that trade embargoes are most likely to succeed when the initiating country can forego the benefits of trade, when the products are of importance to the target country, when the target country has little capability to substitute for the product or find alternative suppliers, and when the target country is not readily able to retaliate.[43]

Clearly, economic sanctions will continue to be one tool in the states' arsenal as they seek to influence the behavior of their fellow states and express disagreement with or even outrage at the policies of other governments. In the last few years the U.S. government has employed sanctions on numerous occasions: to punish Libya as an agent of international terrorism, to destabilize Nicaragua as a newly emerging Marxist state (presumably because of its subversive actions against neighboring countries), to slap South Africa on the wrist for failure to reform its racial policies, to punish the Soviet Union for its intervention into Afghanistan, to deter European countries from participating in the gas pipeline project between the Soviet Union and Western Europe, and to weaken the undemocratic and corrupt former regime of General Noriega in Panama. The popularity of sanctions, then, has not diminished significantly, nor is it likely to decline during the decade to come despite the general tendency of scholars to dismiss sanctions as ineffectual.

Summary

In this chapter we have focused on several key economic issues, but our analysis has not been exhaustive. For now we have left several ongoing questions largely untouched: What are the effects of continuing disparities of development? How can poor states develop their economies? Should there be a New International Economic Order that will be more favorable to the economic needs of the poor countries? We will return to some of these questions in chapter 12.

Some final reflections are in order as we leave our discussion of the international political economy. The world we live in today is in a period of economic transition. Preferences for global solutions to trade and monetary problems have given way to more regional or bilateral solutions. And yet the global and interdependent nature of the economy cannot be completely ignored, despite the at-least partial failure of multilateral efforts to manage it. The big question is whether we will see a return to economic nationalism and bilateral management or whether new multilateral trade and monetary regimes can be devised to cope with the increasingly complex and difficult problems that will continue to vex the international political economy in the years to come.

Susan Strange

Protectionism and World Politics

...The main tenet of liberal economics regarding international trade is that the less governments intervene to obstruct the flow of trade, the better. The more generally liberal policies are adopted toward foreign competition, the better the national welfare and global welfare will be served. Free trade, it is held, allows the most effective allocation of resources to the production of goods and services and thus maximizes the production of wealth for the community. Protection, conversely, encourages inefficiency and impoverishes both individual consumers and the society as a whole.

Much conventional liberal opinion goes on to argue that protectionism adopted by one country provokes retaliatory protectionism in others, setting off a vicious spiral. To avoid this vicious spiral, it is held essential to maintain the momentum of multilateral diplomacy aimed at the reduction of trade barriers. The more protectionist policies multiply, the more imperative for world order it becomes that the states that have signed the General Agreement on Tariffs and Trade (GATT) should...stop the rot. Moreover, it is sometimes argued, the economic effects are apt to spill over into politics, poisoning international relations and contributing if not actually leading to conflict between allies and to war between states that might otherwise have been content to coexist.

Like most other simple doctrines, liberal economics is held with enormous passion but with rather less than unassailable logic or strict regard for historical facts. The chief fallacies, false premises, and historical misrepresentations that sustain the liberal doctrine can be fairly briefly stated....

The basic premise that state policy should, or even can, be based on the single criterion of maximizing efficiency in the production of goods and services for the market is demonstrably false. Efficiency never has been, *and never can be,* the sole consideration in the choice of state policies. Given an international political system in which the world is divided territorially among states over whom there is no reliable higher authority to prevent conflict among them, security from external attack and the maintenance of internal order are and always have been the first concern of government in each state. Efficiency can be given priority only if the provision of security, internally and externally, is taken for granted—as indeed it is by many if not most liberal economists....

Efficiency, in short, is only one of four basic values that any politically organized society seeks to achieve for its members. Wealth, order, justice, and freedom...are the basic elements of politics[s]....

Government, consequently, is a matter of finding an appropriate trade-off between these four basic values... when it comes to making state policy. On occasion it may be necessary to sacrifice some freedom and accept binding rules (as under the GATT), if it is thought the rules are just and that greater wealth through faster economic growth will thus be attained. At other times it may be necessary to assert independence over efficiency in order to preserve... national unity....

[A] second myth is...that the individual pursuit of private gain is consistent with the general welfare of the society, since the hidden hand of the market ensures that the producer will make what the consumer wants and at the lowest price, or else he will go out of business.... [Similarly,] the pursuit of national interests by individual states is [held to be] consistent with the general welfare of international society—or, in short, that the world economy will be well served if each individual government or state observes the law of comparative costs and sells on the world market what it produces best.

The fallacy here is that the political or economic security of the state may *not* in fact be best served by observing the law of comparative costs.... In theory, states can freely adapt either to the changing prices of factors of production or to the changing demands and conditions of the world market. In reality, the political as well as material costs of having to...change from one production sector to another are by no means inconsiderable, especially for poor countries or ones that do not share the high degree of

SOURCE: From *International Organization* 39, no. 2 (Spring 1985), pp. 233–259. Reprinted by permission in abridged form. Copyright © 1985 by the Massachusetts Institute of Technology and the World Peace Foundation.

conformism, respect for authority, and adaptability of, for instance, Japanese society. These costs, moreover, are probably higher now than they used to be as the pace of technical change accelerates and the cost of capital investment in the latest technology appreciates. Prompt adjustment may be in the collective interest, but it will not always be in the interest of the individual state. The law of comparative costs is an essentially static concept, ever more open to question as the world economy becomes more dynamic. . . .

[Another] . . . myth of liberal economics . . . concern[s] the interpretation of twentieth-century economic history. . . . Regarding the world depression of the interwar years, the conventional wisdom of liberal economics is that though it may have started with financial crisis, a main cause of shrinking markets was the raising of trade barriers. The major problem was protectionism; the system was trapped in a vicious spiral of beggar-thy-neighbor policies, in which each country retaliated against the others for barriers raised against its own products. The result was that all suffered and no one benefited.

But this is not what the economic historians say—or rather, what they said when, a few years later, they finally got around to sifting the evidence and looking at the figures. Unfortunately, that was just the time when all over the world people's attention was already turning to the impending outbreak of another world war, or when that war had actually started, threatening the very survival of states and political systems. The result was that the economic historians' verdict on the Depression was little heeded and soon forgotten. What they said was that tariffs, though substantially raised, had made surprisingly little difference either to the volume of world trade or to its direction. . . . Nor had retaliation been the significant motive. There was not much tit for tat. It was just that as markets shrank, politicians were everywhere under pressure to handicap foreign producers against domestic ones, to keep jobs open at home if it could be done. Yet the handicaps actually did little to alter the pattern of trade flows. . . . The effects of tariffs . . . were minimal.

Why, then, did the myth gain such popularity that it persists to this day? The answer is simple. Americans correctly perceived themselves as the strong traders of the postwar world, both because they were technologically more advanced and because American corporations were better organized to produce for and to sell to a mass market of consumers. They also regarded British and other Europeans' sheltered colonial markets as obstructing their conquest of the world market after the war, and the destruction of preferential barriers against American exports was the first target of U.S. commercial policy. The myth that protectionism had been the main cause of the prewar Depression . . . was echoed by U.S. policy makers. The Europeans, including the British, accepted the argument, recognizing that whether or not trade barriers had done much harm, they certainly had done little good, and that a fresh start at the end of the war would probably be in everyone's interest.

Another historical myth holds that the postwar recovery of Europe and the unprecedented growth of all industrialized countries' economies in the 1960s was primarily the result of multilateral tariff reduction conducted under the aegis of the GATT. . . . That these tariff-bargaining rounds were an important innovation in economic diplomacy and that they helped make business more confident about expanding markets for most capital and consumer goods is not in doubt. But were tariff reductions the *main* cause of postwar prosperity? . . .

In this case it seems to me far more probable that prosperity permitted liberalization. Trade revived after the war, and continued to grow, because the United States injected large doses of purchasing power into the system at a rate that pretty well matched the physical ability of enterprises to increase production. . . . Eventually, of course, and especially after the mid-1960s, the injection of dollar purchasing power became increasingly inflationary as the U.S. government also took on the financing of social welfare. But that it was instrumental for a generation in spreading purchasing power more widely throughout the whole economy is hardly in doubt.

When it comes to more recent history and the present state of the world economy, one must be careful not to overstate what the liberals say. There are, of course, substantial differences of emphasis both in their analyses of past events and in their prescriptions for future policy. But three general observations crop up again and again. . . . One is that the main problem afflicting the world economy is deterioration in the trade system. . . . Another is that if the drift toward protectionism is not arrested, things will get a lot worse. . . .

The final historical myth is the unwarranted but very widespread assumption that the only hope lies in multilateral agreement, negotiated through international organization. This assumption rests, of course, on that biased interpretation of postwar history which ascribes so much importance to multilaterally negotiated reductions in trade barriers and so little to other factors. It greatly underrates the importance of some key bilateral relationships within the American alliance, specifically those of the United States with Britain, with Canada, with Germany, and with Japan. Each of the four had its own reasons for complying with the American policy objectives. It also underrates the steady creation of credit first by the U.S. government, then through the investment of dollars abroad by U.S. corporations, and finally, after the first oil price rise of 1973, by international banks lending through the Eurodollar and other Eurocurrency markets. . . .

Even the most cursory examination of recent trends in world trade shows that while world trade. . .declined only a trivial 1 percent, growth rates, output, and employment suffered a much more severe setback. In the early 1980s the world passed through quite a severe recession. . . . Yet recession did not have nearly so violent an effect on the volume of international trade as the Depression of the 1930s. The reasons for this paradox are not at all well understood, but one plausible explanation implicates the growth of. . . production for a world market by large corporations that operate with a global strategy and not only sell abroad but actually produce in more than one country. . . .

Whatever the reason, trade in manufactures has grown very much faster than trade in primary products. Moreover, there is far more trade between industrialized countries than trade between them and the developing countries. The conventional notion holds that trade is determined by differences in resource endowment. But, . . .technology and the accelerating rate of technical change has a lot more to do with the drive to produce for the world market. For, as technology becomes more complex, and expensive, each new plant or process a company installs is dearer and is destined to more rapid obsolescence than the one it replaces. In most industries it becomes impossible to recoup the investment fast enough by selling on only a local or national market. One result is that trade in semimanufactures—half-finished goods—has also grown faster than the average rate of growth. Thus a totally Swedish Volvo car or a totally American Boeing aircraft, even a totally South Korean ship, no longer exists. Components are put together from all over, and the figures on trade collected by international organizations tell only half-truths inasmuch as they allow us to continue to think in these obsolete terms of trade as an international exchange of national products.

A second point is that developing countries' penetration of industrialized countries' markets has been faster in manufactured goods in the 1970s than ever before. . . . Protectionism does not work as a check on the industrial development of developing countries. Very precise arrangements, bilaterally negotiated between industrialized countries such as Japan and the United States, for well-defined products, do apparently check market penetration. Quota restrictions and tariffs, and even voluntary export agreements reached with developing countries. . .do not. . . .

The new international division of labor appears to be unstoppable. The move of manufacturing industry to the

Third World is structural, not cyclical. Though more visible in the export-oriented economies of South Korea and Taiwan, it is also happening in India and Brazil where an expanding mass market—for clothes, radios, even computers —is increasingly satisfied by domestic production rather than by imports from the old industrialized countries. . . .

Protectionism is far less important to LDCs than the rate of growth in the world economy as a whole. Although it may well be. . .that these exports would have been greater still had it not been for the barriers they encountered, the rate of growth remains astonishing. It is far beyond anything anticipated by economic forecasts made in the 1960s. The record of the four leading East Asian Newly Industrialized Countries [or NICs,] (South Korea, Taiwan, Hong Kong, and Singapore) is of course streets ahead of the ASEAN [Association of Southeast Asian Nations] group and still further ahead of the Latin American countries. Nevertheless, the point is still valid that if protectionism has not effectively held back the leaders (those whose products pose the greatest threat to the domestic industries of the developed countries), then protectionism cannot be the main problem. . . .

All the evidence, in fact, points to volatility in the availability of credit as the dominant factor. Here, the Latin American experience differs vastly from the East Asian, and mainly because it was the Latin Americans who borrowed most heavily in the Eurocurrency markets, led to do so by the big U.S. banks. . . . When credit ran out and the mounting burden of interest rates made it necessary to reschedule Latin American debts under IMF surveillance, an immediate consequence. . .was a drastic cut in imports. The GATT noted that in 1982 the total deficit in LDCs fell from $74 billion in 1981 to just over $60 billion in 1982—an "improvement" of $14 billion and one achieved largely by *not buying abroad*. Argentina, Mexico, and Chile all cut their imports by half, according to GATT. . . . But as the loans dried up, so did U.S. exports. . . . By the first half of 1983, U.S. exports were less than two-thirds of what they had been a year earlier. . . . Trade declined primarily because of a lack of purchasing power.

Significantly, this lack has affected LDC trade with the industrialized countries more than it has their trade with each other. More than one-third of their exports of manufactures now go to other LDCs, and in some cases even more than that. Over half of South Korea's growing exports of cars and trucks go to other LDCs, even though ten years ago the industry did not exist. The explanation for this expanding trade in manufactures within the Third World may lie in the growing number of regional and bilateral trade arrangements between the countries concerned. . . .

By about the mid-1980s, however, in Mexico and in several other previously protectionist countries, a change was beginning. It was due less to the exhortations of liberal economists or the urging of international organizations than to the urgent need to earn foreign exchange. Governments of all political kinds began to perceive the handicap that protection imposed on national competitiveness in world markets and to extol the advantages of opening the home market to more competition. . . .

. . .One very strong reason why protectionism is not such a great threat. . .is that developing countries are getting much better at finding ways to wriggle around the barriers raised against them. In the well-known case of Hong Kong, quotas on low-cost textiles and clothes forced exporters to go up-market, where barriers were fewer, thus actually increasing the total value of exports. . . . There are always third-party go-betweens ready and willing to pass on consignments above the producers' quota as their own exports.

Most important of all in explaining why protectionism is not working to keep out LDC manufactures is the connivance of the transnational corporations. Between them and the governments of developing countries there is a strong symbiotic relationship that accelerates the shift of manufacturing industry from North to South. It is this symbiosis that leads [corporations] to negotiate between complex bargains with other corporations and with state enterprises and governments around the world. Some estimates of the proportion of world trade which is actually trade between different sections of transnational corporations suggest that intrafirm transfers account for as much as half of some countries' total imports.

Many developing countries, in consequence, recognize that bargaining—which the government conducts with the private sector—is a good deal more important than ordinary diplomacy with other states. Ecuador's negotiations with Gulf Oil in recent years, for example, have probably been more important to the country than its diplomatic relations with its neighbors. In this new form of diplomacy the state's control of territory gives it control over access to its markets as well as to its natural resources, its work force, and its financial resources and borrowing capacity. The corporation, on its side, can be taxed for revenue and often has new technology based on its Research and Development capacity; it has managerial experience and the capacity to market products in other countries, all of which it can exchange for the access that the state alone can give or withhold. A mutuality of interest exists which both

parties acknowledge when they bargain with each other but which both often deny in public. . . .

Such spotty and uncoordinated evidence as we have, chiefly from the financial press, strongly suggests that this bilateral network of contracts is not only sustaining—despite the financial disorder—the continued expansion of world trade but is actually doing a great deal more than debates in the United Nations to achieve the much-discussed New International Economic Order. This quiet commercial diplomacy produces more tangible results in the shape of new investments, new jobs, and new production in the South than all the resolutions, codes of conduct, guidelines, and declarations on which so much official time has been spent. . . .

What has happened between the 1930s and the 1980s is that international corporations have taken over in large part from governments in arranging trade deals across frontiers. This bilateralism is regarded with disdain in international organization circles and by liberal economists, but their attitudes are more than a little biased, by self-interest in the first case and by ideology in the second. It seems at the least arguable that the model of a web of bilateral contracts is capable of producing a more durable and generally satisfactory trade-off among the basic values of political economy than any other. It would appear capable—always given the necessary monetary management—of sustaining growth and efficiency in the production of wealth. By aiding the changing international division of labor to benefit the NICs, it is also bringing about some more just and equitable distribution of benefits of economic integration. And it is certainly giving greater freedom to states to be openly inconsistent (instead of covertly, as before) in their trade policies. For political security reasons they may choose to be protectionist in one sector. . .while open and competitive in others. . . . The choice is theirs, and there is no reason why governments should not change their mind in either direction.

In any case, the next few years will show whether world trade can continue to survive despite the deadlock in the GATT and despite a certain amount of increased protectionism. My contention is that a combination of political and economic interests, reinforced by structural change in the international division of labor brought about by the mobility of capital and technology, is preventing a world depression from seriously arresting or reversing the steady growth in world trade. . . .

John A. C. Conybeare

Managing International Trade Conflicts: Explanations and Prescriptions

. . . During the past twenty years, trade issues have become part of the realm of "high politics," the subject of major interstate threats, negotiations, and occasionally even trade wars. In the current age of "interdependence," trade issues are thought to have a major impact on national welfare, and are therefore too important to be left to lower levels of bureaucracies. Trade policy, some have argued, will determine whether or not we may avoid a global recession of the magnitude of the 1930s, and may have major implications for world political alignments.

Such claims are undoubtedly exaggerated. A major trade war would cost the United States little more than 2 percent of its national income. Unless a country is small and highly trade dependent, the effect of trade policy is small, compared to other types of policy. It is also highly unlikely that U.S. trade policy alone could effect any major change in international political relationships. Yet trade policy is still a worthy object of study, since a relatively small part of national income may be a large absolute value, and trade policy does have a propensity to spill over into political affairs, irritating otherwise friendly relations. Domestically, trade policy may be of great legislative importance, if it affects concentrated groups of strategically placed actors, even though the absolute and relative value of the trade may be small.

. . . Most trade bargaining issues may be explicated in terms of size: Relatively equal-size countries generally reach cooperative solutions, and larger countries usually impose asymmetric solutions on smaller countries. . . . There are other factors that may distort the simple size

criterion for assessing trade conflicts; I deal with these under the rubric of the length of time of the conflict, numbers of bargainers, linkage to nontrade issues, and transaction costs.

A Framework of Analysis

. . . [One] trade relationship is that which may prevail between two large countries. Each country has a strong incentive to impose optimal tariffs as a way of taxing the other and shifting the maximum possible amount of income to itself by changing the prices at which goods are traded. Each can gain by imposing unreciprocated taxes on the other's trade, but both lose (relative to free trade), when mutual trade barriers are imposed. This situation is analogous to that faced by two supermarkets engaging in a price war: Both would be jointly better off if they colluded and kept prices high, but each would be better off individually if it undercut the other's prices. When both engage in price cutting, both experience mutual losses. The problem is often referred to as the Prisoner's Dilemma game, the dilemma being that each has an incentive to implement a predatory policy (trade taxes or cutting prices), regardless of what it thinks the other will do. If the other does not take similar measures, the initial predator will be much better off; if the other also imposes restrictions, the predator will still be better off than if it had allowed itself to be exploited.

The dynamic prognosis for such conflicts is not quite so dismal. If the interaction is one that persists for a reasonable amount of time, the two parties may actually end up in a highly cooperative pattern of behavior. If each adopts the tactic of "tit-for-tat," punishing the other for predatory practices, they may reach an equilibrium in which they cooperate because mutual cooperation is preferable to mutual conflict. The equilibrium is fragile, however, since the incentive to cheat is ever present. Furthermore, in situations where there are a large number of major negotiating powers, the threat of retaliation may be insufficient to induce cooperation, for reasons that I will discuss below.

A [second] variation on the structure of trade negotiations is that which may prevail when a larger power faces a small power. The small power will only hurt itself by imposing trade restrictions against the larger power, either unilaterally or in retaliation. The large power may gain by imposing predatory trade taxes on the small power, even if the small power retaliates. When the structural asymmetries in the bargaining situation are of this magnitude. . . the outcome is likely to be one where the small country suffers the large country's tariffs, and makes large concessions in order to try to alleviate the degree of predation. . . .

SOURCE: From the *Journal of International Affairs* 42, no. 1 (1988), pp. 75–91. Reprinted by permission in abridged form.

Large Power Trade Conflicts

There have been numerous trade conflicts between large countries able to inflict mutual harm on each other.... The simple theory applicable to such disputes would predict the evolution of a pattern of cooperation through the exercise of strategies of contingent retaliation such as tit-for-tat. Yet such cooperation has often not occurred, or has taken many years to do so....

...Most large power trade disputes arise during periods of...depression. Economic hardship will...raise the incentive to indulge in predatory income transfers, even in the face of retaliation.... Recent U.S.–EC trade conflicts over steel have occurred at a time when the steel sector of the industrial countries has been suffering a slow and painful decline. Several European tariff wars occurred during the agricultural recession of the last thirty years of the nineteenth century, when larger European countries shut out their smaller suppliers.

...Trade conflicts between major powers may not evolve into cooperation when there are problems in accurately directing sanctions. The Anglo-Hanse wars provide one example of this: The Hanseatic League suffered from attacks on its shipping by English privateers and, being unable to retaliate against the privateers, compensated its merchants by seizing the goods of English merchants, who would in turn obtain a "letter of reprisal" from the English authorities to do the same, leading to ever-escalating rounds of retaliation.

In the modern period there is a similar problem: The most-favored nations (MFN) rule, which requires tariff concessions negotiated between two parties to be extended to third countries. When countries A and B agree on a tariff reduction on commodity i, country C, which also exports commodity i, will derive free benefits. If this problem of "free riding" becomes too great, the trade negotiating system will break down, as did occur during the Smoot–Hawley tariff wars of the 1930s.

Asymmetric Trade Conflicts

Cases of small countries involved in trade disputes with large countries exhibit less variation, mainly because small countries realize their vulnerability and either take care not to provoke larger powers or give in quickly when disputes do arise. A few deviant cases do exist...

[However,] in recent times, small countries have been more cautious in their dealings with larger powers.... Most small countries [are] careful not to retaliate directly against large countries, preferring to seek the protection of a regional hegemon or to attempt to band together with other smaller powers.... The small countries hurt by, for example, U.S. textile and steel quotas, have not retaliated....

A Synthesis

A theory of international economic conflict based on relative size would predict that such conflicts should rarely escalate into sustained trade wars (i.e., periods of repeated, prolonged, and high-intensity mutual retaliation). This should be true because of the ease of conveying threats that are both credible and effective—either because strategies of contingent retaliation will quickly remove the gains from predatory policies between large countries, or else because asymmetry will be quickly manifested in a manner that will usually...induce the weaker party to back down and accept the best deal it can get. This generalization is historically well supported: Trade conflicts rarely do escalate to the point of trade war. Yet it is also true that the size-based prediction of cooperative conflict resolution is not always consistent with outcomes. Credible threats do not always work, and in order to explain why trade conflict may escalate into war, one may need to introduce other variables that affect outcomes.

...[There are] several reasons why trade conflicts may escalate in spite of the existence of asymmetries or tit-for-tat punishment, both of which ought to shorten such disputes. These are time, numbers of actors, linkage to nontrade issues, and transaction costs.

The introduction of a time dimension may help dampen trade conflicts, as it provides the opportunity for the making and implementing of credible threats of retaliation. However, there are at least two ways in which time may also promote more lasting conflicts. First, a dynamic conflict may inspire one or both sides to prolong the battle in order to exhaust the other party and force them to withdraw.... Many trade wars have undoubtedly been prolonged by such incentives.... Second, time may discourage settlement of trade conflicts if one of the parties believes that the situation will become more unfavorable over time....

A second problem occurs when trade conflicts involve large numbers of actors.... The problem exists at both the domestic and the international level. At the international level, the major issue is adherence to MFN rules, which encourage nonparticipation in the tariff reduction process, and free-riding behavior of the kind pursued by the United States in the 1920s. The primary solution is to constrain the operation of the MFN rule. The sanctioning issue also operates at the level of domestic interest groups....

It is in the interests of the U.S. steel industry to lobby for protection, even if it knows the EC will retaliate, since the EC can only retaliate against other U.S. industries. Here the solution is simply to have stronger central control of trade policy in order to internalize these effects.

Third, the linkage of trade issues to other political matters may inhibit the solution of the former. Linkage is usually introduced as a means of making it costly for the other party to refuse cooperation. . . .

Finally, transaction costs can be a brake on any negotiations. . . . High transaction costs may arise simply through the presence of large numbers of negotiating parties. In the extreme case, transaction costs may be high enough to prevent any negotiations at all. . . .

Institutional Management

The problems discussed above are not insurmountable, but clearly require some careful institutional innovation. The type of trade negotiating system required (assuming that our goal is the global good) is one that will make transaction costs low, encourage countries to believe that they will be punished for uncooperative behavior, proscribe hegemonic predation, and discourage tactics of linkage to wider political issues. The GATT certainly scores high on several of these criteria: it provides a forum for negotiation that lowers transaction costs, it tries to isolate trade from other more contentious issues, and it provides universal rules for retaliation. However, it has one major fault. GATT's MFN rule introduces the public good sanctioning problem, and the incentive for countries to hold back from negotiations.

So far, this has been constrained by two practices. One is the principal supplier method of negotiation. Most GATT negotiations have been based on this technique, with the result that the bulk of trade concessions are exchanged between a small group of large countries. The other is the tendency to remove trade negotiations from GATT altogether. The major trade barriers today consist of bilaterally negotiated quotas. Neither of these solutions are conducive to global welfare gains.

The policy question is, then, how to retain GATT's central role of reducing transaction costs, legitimating sanctions and spreading the benefits of negotiation globally, while avoiding the tendency for an MFN-based system to break down due to free-riding problems. Allowing negotiations to continue to drift away from GATT will result in the loss of GATT's obvious benefits. Negotiation purely on a principal supplier basis will restrict negotiations to a small group of

countries. Some have proposed to give GATT stronger powers, but this is more likely to simply drive its members further away.

The first objective would be to recapture the diversification of trade barriers away from tariffs into nontariff barriers, such as quotas. Since such measures are too well entrenched to be proscribed, the best we could do would be to devise a common method of measuring them, so that each country's level of protection across industries could be [made] comparable. . . .

Once this has been done, the problem would be to devise a GATT-based bargaining system that would encourage globally beneficial negotiations. One possible solution would be to devise a global "points" system. Once all trade barriers were converted to a common index, their negative effect on global welfare could be calculated and countries could be assigned a base level of points, representing the total amount of global welfare reducing protection allowed to them. These points could then be traded across countries. This would allow countries that have a high demand for protection in certain industries (perhaps for domestic political reasons) to buy protection points from other countries, either with financial payment or by trading points.

The scheme might combine the ease of bilateral negotiation (avoiding the MFN problem of free-riding), with avoidance of the negative consequences of the principal supplier solution to the MFN problem (the tendency for negotiations to be restricted to small groups of large countries). Under the old principal supplier method, a large country has no incentive to negotiate a tariff reduction that would benefit a number of small countries, since once it had negotiated the reduction (for a small return concession), all of the small countries would get the concession for free. However, if the "points" are valued according to world welfare losses, a country could get "credit" for tariff reductions that would not occur in a principal supplier framework. If the United States, for example, wished to add protection to a politically important industry, it would need to "buy" some protection points, which it might do by reducing protection on a good (or goods) exported by a larger number of small countries. . . .

Such a system might save the United States considerable embarrassment. At present time the United States attempts to take the high ground in GATT negotiations, arguing for general free trade, while at the same time massively violating the principles it is recommending to the international community. The United States claims not to have quotas; it has "voluntary export restraints." The EC is constantly criticized for its agricultural protection, yet the United States restricts agricultural imports with quotas on, for example, sugar and beef. The developing countries are castigated for restricting the export of U.S. services (e.g., banking, data processing), at the same time as the United States imposes "voluntary" quotas on their exports of steel and textiles. A "points" system may help move it away from such unproductive and pseudo-moralistic posturing, recognizing that domestic politics will always require some deviations from free trade, but allowing these deviations to be measured and traded in an efficient and equitable manner.

Conclusion

The factors that produce and prolong trade disputes are many and complex.... It is unlikely that any negotiation forum can simultaneously ameliorate all of these problems. Yet it may be that with a bit of imaginative institutional innovation, GATT could do a better job of bringing back within its purview much of what it has lost, as trade negotiations have steadily moved off into bilateral talks outside of its formal rule structure.

Study Questions

1. Define *imperialism*. How would a Marxist and a realist differ in their definitions of this term?
2. What were the primary motives behind the European drive for colonies?
3. Define *mercantilism*. What was its impact on the colonies?
4. Discuss the meaning of the term *international political economy*.
5. Why do countries trade?
6. What is meant by comparative advantage?
7. In what ways can a country reduce a balance-of-payments deficit?
8. Discuss the political implications and differences between bilateral and multilateral aid.
9. What is the difference between a hard and a soft currency? What political implications does this have?
10. Discuss the role of currencies in international trade.
11. What is a special drawing right?
12. What does a policy of protectionism mean? How would a country implement one? Why? What might be the implications? Discuss the difference between tariff and nontariff barriers to trade.
13. What is the difference between the notions of reciprocal trade and preferential trade? Which concept is upheld by GATT and which by UNCTAD?
14. What is meant by most-favored nation status?
15. Discuss the views of Marxists, conventional theorists, and reformists on why countries are poor. Which view do you think is most valid?
16. Describe the role played by the United States in establishing global economic institutions after World War II.
17. What does liquidity mean? What was its importance after World War II?
18. What were the five key features of the Bretton Woods system?
19. What is GATT? What are its purposes?
20. Why did the Bretton Woods system fall apart in the early 1970s?
21. How did the decline of American economic preeminence affect its foreign policy?
22. What is the global "debt crisis"? Why is it a crisis? Who is involved? What are its potential implications?
23. What are some factors that increase the success of commodity cartels?
24. Do you think protectionism is dangerous? Why doesn't Susan Strange think it is?

25. According to Strange, why have newly industrialized countries been insulated from Western protectionist policies in recent years?
26. What are the primary criticisms Strange levels at the free-trade theorists?
27. How, according to John Conybeare, does size affect the likelihood of an outbreak or prolongation of trade wars?
28. What conditions tend to prolong trade wars?
29. How does the MFN principle, according to Conybeare, complicate trade relations?
30. Discuss the phenomenon of overcapacity. What are its consequences for international trade?
31. Under what circumstances are economic sanctions most likely to succeed?

Key Terms

balance of payments
Bretton Woods system
commodity indexation agreements
competitiveness
devaluation
economic sanctions
Eurodollar
exchange rate
General Agreement on Tariffs and Trade (GATT)
hard currency
imperialism
liquidity
mercantilism
neomercantilism

orderly marketing arrangements (OMAs)
overcapacity
political economy
preferential trade system
protectionism
reciprocity
reserves
soft currency
Special Drawing Right (SDR)
terms of trade
theory of comparative advantage
tied aid
UN Conference on Trade and Development (UNCTAD)
voluntary export restraints (VERs)

Notes

1. For a useful discussion of the role of economics and politics in international relations, see Robert C. North and Nazli Choucri, "Economic and Political Factors in International Conflict and Integration," *International Studies Quarterly* 27, no. 4 (1983): 443–461. Another interesting study is Ruth Arad and Seev Hirsch, "Peacemaking and Vested Interests: International Economic Transactions," *International Studies Quarterly* 25, no. 3 (September 1981): 439–468. This study focuses on the Egypt–Israeli case, showing how economic trade can be used to the advantage of previous belligerents to promote peace and mutual economic gain.
2. For very different views on imperialism, see V. I. Lenin, *Imperialism: The Highest Stage of Capitalism* (New York: International Publishers, 1939); and Hans Morgenthau, *Politics Among Nations* (New York: Knopf, 1966), pp. 41–68.

3. W. Arthur Lewis, *The Evolution of the International Economic Order* (Princeton: Princeton University Press, 1977), pp. 22–23.

4. See, for instance, Herbert Wulf, "East–West Trade as a Source of Tension," *Journal of Peace Research* 19, no. 4 (1982): 301–322.

5. This does not imply that the term is of only recent origin. In fact, it was used widely in the late 1800s. See Henry Teune, "Human Development in a Global Political Economy" (Presidential address to the International Studies Association), *International Studies Quarterly* 25, no. 4 (December 1981): 523–539, esp. at pp. 523–524.

6. See Jan Pen, *A Primer on International Trade* (New York: Vintage Books, 1967), pp. 12–20.

7. For a discussion of the role of international currencies, see David Blake and Robert Waters, *The Politics of Global Economic Relations* (Englewood Cliffs, N.J.: Prentice-Hall, 1983), pp. 58–59.

8. Ruben Barrios, "The Political Economy of East–South Relations," *Journal of Peace Research* 20, no. 3 (1983): 239–252.

9. See Harry Magdoff, *The Age of Imperialism* (New York: Monthly Review Press, 1969); and Paul Baran and Paul Sweezy, *Monopoly Capital* (New York: Monthly Review Press, 1966).

10. See, for instance, Walt W. Rostow, *The Stages of Economic Growth* (London: Cambridge University Press, 1960).

11. See Raul Prebisch, "Towards a New Trade Policy for Development" in the documents of the *UN Conference on Trade and Development* Vol. 2 (New York: United Nations, 1964), pp. 5–64. Prebisch served as secretary-general for the conference.

12. For a provocative analysis of the economic fortunes of nations, see Mancur Olson, *The Rise and Decline of Nations* (New Haven: Yale University Press, 1982). Commentary on this work can be found in the *International Studies Quarterly* 27, no. 1 (March 1983): 3–37.

13. See Raymond Vernon, "International Trade Policy in the 1980s," *International Studies Quarterly* 26, no. 4 (December 1982): 484–490.

14. See Richard N. Cooper, "A Monetary System for the Future," *Foreign Affairs* 63, no. 1 (Fall 1984): 166–184, especially at pp. 167–171.

15. On the development of the approaches to trade see Vernon, "International Trade Policy in the 1980s," pp. 484–490.

16. Over time most communist bloc countries have become affiliated with the IMF and GATT. The Soviet Union until recently has spurned contacts with these agencies. However, as a result of the significant drop in oil prices in recent years, and with borrowing needs on the increase, the Soviet Union is now seeking observer status in GATT and is rethinking its position toward the IMF and the World Bank. See John Yemma, "Soviets Rethink Economic Ties," *The Christian Science Monitor,* August 28, 1986, p. 21.

17. Jock Finlayson and Mark Zacher, "International Trade Institutions and the North/South Dialogue," *International Journal* 36, no. 4 (1981): 732–766.

18. On the economic dislocations of the early 1970s, see Michael Hudson, *Global Fracture: The New International Economic Order* (New York: Harper & Row, 1977), especially at pp. 59–77. On the problems of international trade and protectionism, see Robert B. Reich, "Beyond Free Trade," *Foreign Affairs* 61, no. 4 (Spring 1983): 773–804.

19. Two recent publications underscore the urgency perceived by some analysts regarding the international trade predicament. See C. Michael Aho and Jonathan D. Aronson,

Trade Talks: America Better Listen! (New York: Council on Foreign Relations, 1986); and Miriam Camps and William Diebold, Jr., *The New Multilateralism: Can the World Trading System Be Saved?* (New York: Council on Foreign Relations, 1983 and 1986). However, contrast these works with the views of Susan Strange (in the first supplemental reading of this chapter), who is not nearly so concerned about the possible negative effects of protectionism.

20. Cooper, "A Monetary System for the Future," p. 171.

21. Stephen Ambrose, *Rise to Globalism: American Foreign Policy Since 1938* (New York: Penguin, 1985).

22. For a discussion of the benefits and frustrations of national dominance in the international economy, see Charles Kindleberger, "Dominance and Leadership in the International Economy," *International Studies Quarterly* 25, no. 2 (June 1981): 242–254.

23. David Lake, "Beneath the Commerce of Nations: A Theory of International Economic Structures," *International Studies Quarterly* 28, no. 2 (June 1984): 143–170, esp. at p. 167.

24. In addition to numerous articles in several journals, *International Organization* and the *Journal of International Affairs* devoted special issues to this subject in 1985 and 1984, respectively.

25. Miles Kahler, "Politics and International Debt: Explaining the Crisis," *International Organization* 39, no. 3 (Summer 1985): 357–382.

26. Richard Weinert, "Coping with LDC Debt," *Journal of International Affairs* 38, no. 1 (Summer 1984): 1–10.

27. Mohammed E. Ahrari, "OPEC and the Hyperpluralism of the Oil Market in the 1980s," *International Affairs* 61, no. 2 (Spring 1985): 263–277.

28. David R. Francis, "Dollar Plunge Unsettles Allies," *Christian Science Monitor,* January 16, 1987, p. 6.

29. Ron Scherer, "Competitiveness" (interviews with key U.S. business leaders), *Christian Science Monitor,* February 2, 1987, pp. 18–20.

30. Vernon, "International Trade Policy for the 1980s," p. 483 and passim.

31. Reich, "Beyond Free Trade," p. 774. For additional discussion, see Lawrence A. Fox and Stephen Cooney, "Protectionism Returns," *Foreign Policy,* no. 53 (Winter 1983/84), p. 74.

32. Albert Bressand, "Mastering the World Economy," *Foreign Affairs* 61, no. 4 (Spring 1983): 752. See also Wolfgang Hager, "Protectionism and Autonomy, How to Preserve Free Trade in Europe," *International Affairs* 58, no. 3 (Spring 1982): 413.

33. Beth V. Yarbrough and Robert M. Yarbrough, "Reciprocity, Bilateralism, and Economic 'Hostages': Self-Enforcing Agreements in International Trade," *International Studies Quarterly* 30, no. 1 (March 1986): 7–21.

34. The view that structural changes have occurred in the manufacturing sector in particular, with corresponding shifts of corporate activities to a number of formerly nonindustrial countries is underscored in James Caparoso, "Industrialization in the Periphery: The Evolving Global Division of Labor," *International Studies Quarterly* 25, no. 3 (September 1981): 347–384.

35. David Yoffie, "The Newly Industrializing Countries and the Political Economy of Protectionism," *International Studies Quarterly* 25, no. 4 (December 1981): 569–599, esp. at pp. 596–597.

36. For an insightful treatment of the overcapacity issue see, "Business Bloat," "MacNeil Lehrer News Hour," November 6, 1986, Transcript #2899, pp. 6–7.

37. Ibid.
38. Lake, "Beneath the Commerce of Nations," p. 167.
39. Wulf, "East–West Trade as a Source of Tension," p. 311.
40. See, for instance, Margaret Doxey, "Oil and Food as International Sanctions," *International Journal* (Spring 1981), p. 344; and John Mayall, "The Sanctions Problem in International Economic Relations: Reflections in the Light of Recent Experience," *International Affairs* 60, no. 4 (Autumn 1984): 631.
41. Mohammed Daoudi and Munther Dajani, *Economic Sanctions: Ideals and Experience* (London: Routledge & Kegan Paul, 1983), pp. 161–169. See also Mayall, "The Sanctions Problem in International Economic Relations," p. 638; and James M. Lindsay, "Trade Sanctions as Policy Instruments: A Re-Examination," *International Studies Quarterly* 30 (June 1986): 153–173.
42. See the excellent and systematic study by Gary Huffbauer and Jeffrey Schott, assisted by Kimberly Elliott, *Economic Sanctions Reconsidered: History and Current Policy* (Washington, D.C.: Institute for International Economics, 1985). For a brief synopsis of the findings of this larger work, see Gary Huffbauer and Jeffrey Schott, "Economic Sanctions and U.S. Foreign Policy," *PS* 726 (Fall 1985): 727–735. (*PS* is published quarterly by the American Political Science Association, Washington, D.C.)
43. Wulf, "East–West Trade as a Source of Tension," pp. 311–312.

Part IV

Tension and Harmony in the International System: The Issues

Twelve
Issues of Potential Conflict: Regional Conflict, Disparity of Development, and the Global Arms Race

Thirteen
Issues of Potential Cooperation: Humanitarian Policy, the Global Environment, and Regional Integration

Twelve

Issues of Potential Conflict: Regional Conflict, Disparity of Development, and the Global Arms Race

International relations is marked by persistent patterns of both conflict and cooperation. We have explored many aspects of each in the preceding pages. In this chapter, we will focus on unresolved global issues that produce tensions between states and that could lead to conflict. We will begin this chapter with a discussion of regional conflict. We will then address two issues of potential conflict with more global significance: (1) the implications of continued disparities in development between rich and poor states, and (2) the impact of the arms race on international relations. We will argue that arms races and national security policy are closely linked, at least in the budgetary sense, with success in achieving economic development. A guns-or-butter dilemma of a sort is faced by all nations, rich and poor, though the results of overspending on security are almost always more devastating for the poor countries that can least afford to unwisely invest their often meager resources.

These and other issues of *potential* conflict need not actually lead to conflict among nations. Indeed, every issue over which conflict might occur also provides an opportunity for governments to accommodate their differences through cooperation. In a very real sense, then, the tension-producing issues we will address in this chapter are issues of both potential conflict and potential cooperation.

Patterns of Conflict

East–West and North–South Tensions

As we saw in chapter 2, students of international relations have begun to look at the world as being composed of several different worlds. The First World consists of the industrialized, economically advanced capitalist countries, whereas the Second World includes the industrialized socialist countries of the Eastern bloc. One of the primary conflicts of recent international relations centered on the struggle between the East and the West, between the communist and capitalist worlds. This contest was not merely an ideological one; it also involved competition between two very different political and economic systems. It has been marked by military confrontation, bitter propaganda exchanges, massive increases in weapons development, and the ever-present threat of nuclear annihilation. Thus it should not be surprising that most students of international relations in the post–World War II period have been preoccupied with the East–West dispute. However, this dispute may decline in importance in the future as a result of Gorbachev's new "political thinking" in the Soviet Union and political and economic reforms in Eastern Europe. As cooperation between the superpowers gains momentum, what seemed to be ingrained hostility may continue to wane. At the same time, however, the Soviet Union faces increasing internal upheaval as non-Russian regions clamor for more autonomy, and political instabilities in Eastern Europe continue to be worrisome.

Moreover, a new dimension of North–South conflict has been added to the East–West dispute. Developing countries of the Third and Fourth worlds are increasingly preoccupied with their own, sometimes desperate, economic needs. The East–West dispute may complicate matters for them, but it is not their primary concern. They are concerned about the incredible wealth of the North (whether socialist or capitalist) and the considerable poverty of the South, and how to rectify the discrepancy.

Intraworld Tensions

Many students of international tensions tend to focus on either the East–West dispute or on the North–South problem. But considerable tension and possibilities for conflict also exist within these categories of states. Conflicts over international trade have caused tensions within the Western bloc. Similarly, differences over nuclear policy and how to deter the Soviet Union have caused breaches in the Western alliance structure. France, for instance, withdrew from the NATO military structure and pursued its own nuclear capability rather than rely on the U.S. nuclear umbrella. More recently, the United States and New Zealand squabbled about the rights of U.S. nuclear-equipped ships to dock at New Zealand ports under the ANZUS (Australia, New Zealand, United States) treaty agreement.[1] Nor is the Eastern bloc immune from internal conflicts. The Soviet Union intervened twice in Eastern Europe to prevent liberalization movements in Hungary (1956) and Czechoslovakia (1968). These movements threatened to undermine Soviet domination by allowing greater private economic activity, a lessening of communist party control over the economy and greater tolerance of individual rights (such as free speech) and political dissent—goals that, ironically, were achieved in the amazing wave of change that swept across Eastern Europe in 1989. A third intervention in Poland in the early 1980s was only narrowly averted after a successful clampdown by the Polish government on the Solidarity movement. Ironically, Solidarity now governs Poland. In addition to these problems, Yugoslavia spurned close association with the Soviet Union for decades, while Romania pursued, from the Soviet perspective, an annoyingly independent foreign policy. In addition, major rifts existed between the Soviet Union and China, between China and Vietnam, and between Vietnam and Kampuchea. Each of these countries is socialist in character, although only the Soviet Union can be described as a substantially industrialized and developed country. If there has been West–West tension, there has been plenty of East–East tension too. Nor, as we observed a moment ago, have Gorbachev's new policies of openness placated these tensions. In Eastern Europe, in the Soviet Baltic states and central Asia, and in China, tensions growing out of reform efforts bedevil the socialist world. This will continue as formerly communist states attempt to make difficult political transitions to democracy and more liberal economic policy.

Nor are only the First and Second worlds prone to internal tensions. Tensions among Third World countries have also been evident, despite their common interests of securing a global economic system that more favorably addresses their needs for development. For example, while the OPEC countries got rich in the 1970s when prices for crude oil skyrocketed, the hardest hit countries were already the poorest ones of the Fourth World. Like the richer energy consumers of the North, they had to pay the higher prices for oil, gas, and almost everything else that rose in price in response to energy price increases. The difference was that they could least afford it. The boon of oil price increases for some Third World countries was a terrible bane for others. Fortunately, the more recent declines in oil prices helped ease the economic position of the poorest LDCs, and efforts by OPEC members to give some foreign aid to the most seriously affected countries helped heal some of the wounds caused by the oil shocks of 1974 and 1979.[2]

Regional Conflict and Civil War

Apart from economic tensions that have strained relations among Third World countries, many bilateral and regional disputes have often resulted in bloody and disastrous conflicts. Frequently, these regional disputes—sometimes collectively referred to as **hotspots**—have been marked by great power intervention and the intrusion of the East–West dispute. Conflicts between Pakistan and India, Ethiopia and Somalia, Israel and the Arab states have involved substantial foreign influence and, in some cases, outright intervention.

Political problems within particular states have also given rise to regional instabilities and external interventions. The Vietnam war, the crisis in Central America centering on Nicaragua, the Angolan and Rhodesian civil wars, internal turmoil in South Africa, and domestic instability in Afghanistan have invited interventions or influence attempts by either one or both of the superpowers. Regional conflicts, then, often become internationalized. Arms shipments to these unstable areas increase and the toll in human life mounts as opposing foreign powers seek to strengthen friendly forces and weaken those favored by their opponent. Moreover, the human toll in the regional disputes can be measured by the large numbers of refugees they produce—some 15 million worldwide according to one respected estimate.[3]

It might appear to the reader that the world is quite free of conflict, at least insofar as war is concerned. For instance, the United States has not been involved in a war since its withdrawal from Vietnam in 1975. It has engaged in a few minor interventions (Lebanon and Grenada) and has supplied weapons to several resistance movements (i.e., the *contras* in Central America and resistance fighters in Afghanistan, Kampuchea, and Angola). Apart from this, outright war has been avoided. But this does not mean that the world is without conflict. Indeed, dozens of regional and civil disputes continue to occupy the attention of governments around the world, as table 12.1 shows.

Recognizing that regional conflicts affect many areas of the world, let us take a closer look at one of the most persistent and volatile cases: the Middle East. It is not uncommon for students to see the Middle East primarily as a place where Arabs and Jews fight one another. But the Arab–Israeli dispute is only one feature of this vast geographical area, which is composed of at least twenty-one countries and perhaps as many as twenty-five depending on the definition of the Middle East used. Middle Eastern countries include Israel, Iran, Iraq, Turkey, Syria, Lebanon, Jordan, Kuwait, Saudi Arabia, North and South Yemen, Oman, and the Persian Gulf states of Qatar, Bahrain, and the United Arab Emirates; these nations are located on the Asian continent and the Arabian Peninsula. The Middle East also includes Egypt, Libya, Tunisia, Algeria, and Morocco; these countries are located in North Africa. The island of Cyprus in the Mediterranean Sea is also considered a Middle Eastern country. Although some scholars view Pakistan and Afghanistan as central Asian

Table 12.1
Ongoing regional and civil conflicts

Border Disputes	Regional Hotspots or Tension Areas	Civil Wars/Ongoing Insurrections
Iran/Iraq	The Middle East (Arab–Israeli dispute)	Afghanistan
China/Vietnam	The Horn of Africa	Angola
Belize/Guatemala	Indochina	Azerbaijan
Burkina Faso/Mali	Central America	Burma
Argentina/United Kingdom (Falklands)	Southern Africa	Chad
Ethiopia/Somalia	Persian Gulf	Colombia
Pakistan/India		El Salvador
North Korea/South Korea		Ethiopia
Libya/Chad		Guatemala
Greece/Turkey		India
Thailand/Laos		Indonesia
Mauritania/Senegal		Kampuchea
		Kurdish Liberia Insurgency (Iran, Turkey, and Iraq)
		Mozambique
		Nicaragua
		Peru
		Philippines
		South Africa
		Sri Lanka
		Sudan
		Surinam
		Uganda
		Western Sahara

countries, both are heavily influenced by Islam and have other ties to the Middle East. Sudan and Somalia, both African countries, are also Islamic and members of the Arab League.[4]

The Arab–Israeli dispute is not the only divisive force in this region. Even among the Arab states there are significant differences. First of all, several Middle Eastern countries do not consider themselves to be Arab. Apart from the obvious example of Israel, which is a Jewish state, Turkey is populated by Turks, Iran by Persians, and Morocco by Moors and Berbers. Although Islam provides a link among most countries in the area, the long-lasting disputes between the Islamic Sunni and Shi'ite sects, which can be traced back to disputes over the line of succession from the prophet Muhammad less than fifty years after his death in 632 A.D., still foster tension among Islamic countries. Iran is almost entirely Shi'ite. The majority of Iraq's population is Shi'ite, while smaller pockets of Shi'ites are found elsewhere in Pakistan, Syria, Oman, Yemen, and Lebanon. Sunnis, however, are the dominant sect, constituting the vast majority of Muslims in most Middle Eastern countries.

Still more forces divide the Middle East. Some countries are fantastically wealthy, including Saudi Arabia, Kuwait and the gulf states. Others such as Egypt and Jordan are relatively poor. Political ideology and bilateral disputes also produce tension among Middle Eastern countries. Syria and Libya profess pro-Soviet leanings. Iran proclaims an ideology of revolutionary Islamicism. Iraq professes to be socialist in orientation. On the other hand, Saudi Arabia, Kuwait, and the conservative states of the Persian Gulf look more to the West. So does Egypt, although at one time it professed a socialist ideology. Algeria is a socialist country, whereas its neighbor Morocco is a conservative, pro-Western monarchy—as is Jordan. The political diversity of Middle Eastern countries is complicated by numerous territorial disputes. The Iran–Iraq war was based in part on a long-standing dispute over control of the Shatt-al-Arab waterway. Algeria and Morocco have clashed over disputed territory in the Sahara desert. Syria harbors claims to territory in Lebanon, while Libya and Egypt have experienced very tense relations from time to time. Conflicting claims to the West Bank of the Jordan River have caused serious disputes and rifts between Jordan and the Palestine Liberation Organization (PLO), although King Hussein of Jordan recently abandoned claims to the area in favor of the PLO. North and South Yemen have also squared off militarily against each other.

The seeds of division are found in the PLO as well. Claiming to represent the displaced people of Palestine, the PLO itself is a faction-ridden coalition of constantly bickering groups, which seem at times to mirror disputes among the Arab states.[5] Table 12.2 identifies the main factions of the PLO. The key faction, Al-Fatah, is led by Yasir Arafat. His leadership has been challenged at one time or another by almost every other faction or by coalitions of the factions listed in table 12.2. Generally the pro-Syrian factions of the PLO (the Popular Front for the Liberation of Palestine—General Command, the Palestine Popular Struggle Front, and Saiqa) have been very anti-Arafat. In 1983, together with renegade Al-Fatah members, they formed a Palestine National Alliance in opposition to Arafat. In the same year, the Democratic Alliance—composed of the Popular Front for the Liberation of Palestine, the Popular Democratic Front for the Liberation of Palestine, the Palestine Liberation Front, and the Palestinian Communist Party—also opposed Arafat but later came to terms with him to prevent a complete split in the PLO. Apart from these eight main factions,

Table 12.2
Factions of the Palestinian Liberation Organization

Faction	Affiliation
Al-Fatah	Yasir Arafat
Popular Democratic Front for the Liberation of Palestine (PDFLP)	Marxist
Palestinian Liberation Front (PLF)	Split from PDFLP—GC in 1977
PLF Abbas Abbas Faction	Pro-Arafat (Tunisia)
PLF Talaat Yaqoub Faction	Anti-Arafat (Syria)
Popular Front for the Liberation of Palestine (PFLP)	Pro-Syrian, Marxist
Arab Liberation Front (ALF)	Pro-Iraqi
Saiqa (Vanguard of the Popular Liberation War)	Syrian-backed
Popular Front for the Liberation of Palestine—General Command (PFLP—GC)	Syrian-backed
Palestine Popular Struggle Front (PPSF)	Syrian-backed
Fatah Revolutionary Council (Black June movement—Abu Nidal)	Split from Al-Fatah in 1973 (pro-Syrian)
Al-Intifada (The Uprising—Abu Musa)	Pro-Syrian
The Black September Movement	Radical splinter group
The 15 May Group (Abu Ibrahim)	Radical splinter group
Palestinian Communist Party (PCP)	Marxist

SOURCE: *The Middle East and North Africa, 1987*, 33rd ed. (London: Europa Publications, 1986), p. 92.

which have from time to time recognized the authority of an umbrella organization called the Palestinian National Congress (PNC), a number of smaller groups have also made the news, including the Abu Musa faction known as "the Uprising" and the Abu Nidal faction known as "the Black June movement." These groups, together with the Black September movement and the May 15 group under the leadership of Abu Ibrahim, have promoted a great deal of the terrorism that has rocked the world in recent years. Clearly, the PLO is only a loose umbrella group for a badly divided organization. The divisions in the PLO have often been aggravated by Arab countries. Syria, for instance, has made no secret recently of its distaste for Arafat and has openly supported factions opposed to Arafat's continued dominance. The PLO seems to be a hopelessly divided organization in an equally divided Arab world.

Ironically, it sometimes seems that among the few unifying factors for the Islamic countries of the Middle East are the common reverence for the prophet Muhammad and the existence of the state of Israel. Israel and the Arab states have fought four wars since 1948. The last one was fought in 1973–1974, but an uneasy tension still pervades the area, and Lebanon serves as a constant reminder of the larger tensions in the Arab–Israeli dispute. Although it is beyond the scope of this book to examine the Arab–Israeli dispute in great detail, it is useful to review some of the essential background. In the aftermath of World War II, Jewish immigration to Israel increased dramatically, and pressure built for the United Kingdom (which had occupied Palestine as a mandate territory under the League of Nations since the end of World War II) to withdraw. In 1948 the United Nations created an Arab and Jewish state in Palestine. War broke out almost immediately between the fledgling Jewish state of Israel and her Arab neighbors. During this war, Israel actually gained more territory than had been granted initially. The Arab states refused to recognize Israel, and two more wars, the Suez War of 1956 and the Six-Day War of 1967, were fought. The latter was an especially humiliating defeat for the Arabs in which the Israelis gained control of the Sinai Peninsula in Egypt, the Golan Heights in Syria, and the West Bank of the Jordan River, which had previously belonged to Jordan. In 1973 Syria and Egypt attacked Israel in the Yom Kippur War. Arab forces acquitted themselves much better in this war, and it set the stage for eventual peace negotiations between Egypt and Israel.

The uneasy peace that has reigned in the Middle East for the last decade and a half can be attributed in part to the fact that Israel and Egypt decided to bury the hatchet and in part to aggressive U.S. mediation that eventuated in the Camp David Accords. Egypt recognized Israel in 1979, and Israel withdrew its forces from the Sinai. Radical Arab states deeply resented Egypt's action, but without Egypt's significant military might behind the anti-Israeli cause, successful war against Israel was not possible. But even though outright war has been avoided in the past decade and a half, significant tensions still linger. Fomented with support from Iran, Libya, and Syria, terrorist activities in the Middle East continue. Lebanon is a continuing focal point of conflict. War raged between Iraq and Iran for nearly a decade. Governments in the Middle East are armed to the teeth with Soviet, American, and European weapons. And there is the ominous possibility of the superpowers being drawn into the conflicts in this strategic, oil-rich region. It is little wonder, therefore, that even rumors of war in the Middle East are enough to send shock waves through financial markets and jitters through the halls of governments throughout the world.

The peace breakthrough between Israel and Egypt suggests that cooperation is possible in this conflict-ridden region, but only when the warring parties tire of conflict and when sufficient diplomatic encouragement is brought to bear by third parties. Ultimate resolution of the dispute between Israel, the other Arab states, and the PLO will depend on some mutual concessions. The basic principles for a settlement were contained in UN Security Council Resolution 242, which was formulated in 1967 after the Six-Day War. That resolution called for Israel to return to its prewar boundaries and for Arab states to recognize Israel's territorial security. It is clear that these conditions must be met, but Israel and most of her Arab neighbors have yet to accept fully the terms. In 1988 the PLO's Yasir Arafat created new opportunities for negotiation by renouncing terrorism and accepting Resolution 242, including the provision of Israel's right to exist. Clearly, recognition of Israel's existence by other Arab states is essential. But some compromise on the rights of the Palestinian people to a state of their own will also be essential. Unless this issue is resolved, there will be continual tension and terrorism in the Middle East. Indeed, Arafat himself has taken a dangerous gamble in his bid to lure Israel into negotiations.

An uneasy peace—with the exception of the Lebanese civil war—has prevailed now for fifteen years between Israel and her Arab neighbors. Israel's domestic peace, however, has been disturbed by an increasingly restive Palestinian Arab population. The increasing number of Arabs in Israel and their refusal to be treated as second-class citizens has led to violent demonstrations and confrontation, especially in the West Bank and the Gaza Strip. The Arabs call this uprising, which grew to fever pitch in 1988, **intifada.** Although the PLO has tried to fan the flames of discontent, it cannot be held responsible for the emergence of intifada, which was a genuine outgrowth of the disgruntlement of the indigenous Arabs. Israel's deteriorating domestic situation sparked renewed interest in pressing for a Middle East peace that somehow accounts for the aspirations of Palestinians for a state of their own.

Peace might be achieved here through a variety of means including a comprehensive peace conference, bilateral agreements approximating the Israeli–Egyptian model, UN intervention, or the natural evolution of some other informal modus vivendi. Some countries, such as the Soviet Union, have pressed for a comprehensive settlement. The Israeli government is of two minds: some members prefer bilateral initiatives, others would be willing to consider a comprehensive agreement. In 1988 former Secretary of State George Shultz tried unsuccessfully to promote a combination of bilateral negotiations and a comprehensive international peace conference. Ultimately, the instrumentalities of attaining peace are not so important as long as the parties to the dispute are serious about settling their differences. The road to peace in the Middle East will be strewn with obstacles and hazards, but the logic of continued terrorism and conflict is still more hazardous, as the governments and peoples of the region must one day realize.

Coping with regional conflicts in Central America, Indochina, Afghanistan, numerous regions of Africa, and the Middle East continues to be one of the major tasks of modern international relations. Regional conflicts are not likely to disappear soon nor are the tensions that give rise to them. The task we face is to contain and resolve regional tensions so that they do not escalate into wider, more dangerous conflicts. This is the chief lesson to be learned from the Middle East conflict, and one that applies to regional disputes throughout the globe.

Disparities of Development

Scope of the Problem

Theoretically, at least, the existence of massive poverty in a majority of the world and of incredible wealth in a minority of nations is potentially destabilizing. It is clear that there

Table 12.3

Indicators of disparity of development

	Developed Countries		Developing Countries	
	Average	Highest	Average	Lowest
Percentage of population with safe drinking water	94	100	51	1
Life expectancy (in years)	73	77	59	37
Protein supply per capita (in grams)	100	158	58	32
Literacy rate (percentage literate)	99	100	60	8

SOURCE: Adapted from data in Ruth Leger Sivard, *World Military and Social Expenditures* (Washington, D.C.: World Priorities, 1985), pp. 38–43.

are significant disparities of development among states. According to World Bank statistics, the least developed countries have per capita GNPs of $400 or less, with the average being about $260. Ethiopia, the world's poorest country, has a per capita GNP of only $110.[6] In highly developed industrial nations, on the other hand, per capita GNPs average $11,060. By this measure Switzerland is the richest industrial-market economy, enjoying a per capita GNP of $16,290. Ironically, the world's richest countries are in the Third World: the United Arab Emirates and Kuwait. Both countries are major oil exporters and have very small populations.

As table 12.3 shows, disparities are also found in many other measures of development. People in poor countries have far fewer educational opportunities, much poorer health care and nutrition, and far shorter life expectancies. In poor countries, infant mortality rates are significantly higher. The average number of infant deaths per one thousand live births in developed and developing countries is sixteen and ninety, respectively. In some developing nations, the infant mortality rate exceeds two hundred.[7] These are rather sobering statistics. Similarly, as figure 12.1 illustrates, per capita consumption of energy is much lower in Africa, South America, and Asia than in North America, Europe, or the Soviet Union.

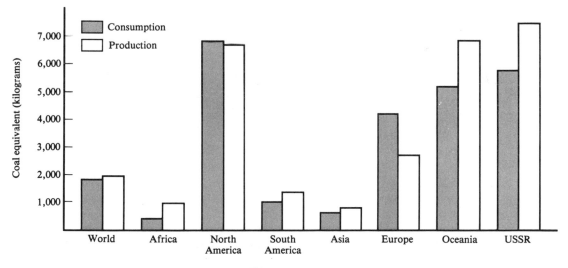

Figure 12.1

Per capita consumption and production of commercial energy by region (1982)
SOURCE: *UN Statistical Yearbook* (New York: United Nations, 1982), p. xlviii.

Certainly, domestic political systems that display such wide disparities of wealth (or development) are subject to potential societal upheaval, instability, and even revolution. Indeed, in many of the poorest countries, wealth is concentrated in the hands of a very few, while the masses live in crushing poverty. It is not surprising that many of these countries have experienced significant domestic instability.

Could the international system suffer similar problems if global disparities in development are not addressed? Might Third World nations become increasingly belligerent with their richer counterparts? Or might the impact of massive poverty in the Southern Hemisphere have other, more subtle tension-producing effects? For instance, Third World poverty might become so overwhelming that massive spontaneous migration to the richer countries would result. The trends in migration seem fairly clear: Immigration into North America and Europe is already quite significant.[8] It is quite possible that disputes over migration could lead to tensions between poor and rich states in the coming decades.

The Role of Population

This leads to yet another question: What are the implications of uncontrolled population growth? The world's population is expected to reach about 6 billion by the end of this century. Moreover, 90 percent of those born between now and then will be citizens of the Third World. As figure 12.2 shows, population rates in the Third World—Latin America, Asia, and Africa—are significantly higher than in Europe or North America. The specter of famine, which is already uncomfortably familiar, will no doubt take a greater toll in the future if economic development does not keep pace with population growth in the Third World. The population bomb will initially affect the poorest countries, but can the consequences of rapid population growth be contained there? The likelihood is that they cannot, and that migration pressures, within the Third World and between the Third World and the developed world, will become a source of increasing tension in the coming decades.[9] This scenario might be softened, however, if massive infusions of resources are pumped

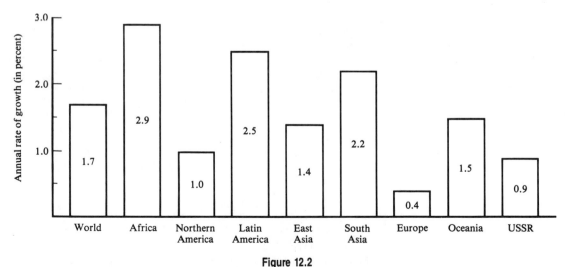

Figure 12.2
Growth of world population by regions (1975–1980)
SOURCE: *UN Statistical Yearbook* (New York: United Nations, 1982), p. xxxii.

into the least developed and developing countries to strengthen their economic capacities to house, feed, and employ millions of new citizens. Otherwise, these people will join in the already significant stream of immigrants from poor states in the Southern Hemisphere to the wealthy states of the Northern Hemisphere where greater opportunities lie.

Studies show that population growth rates decline as countries develop economically and as education—especially among women—becomes more widespread.[10] One theory suggests that poor countries experience high growth rates after the introduction of medical technologies, which decrease infant mortality and overall death rates. However, birth rates continue at a relatively high level as people adjust to the fact that having large families is no longer the asset it once was perceived to be. For example, when over half of the children die before age five, people have a strong incentive to have many children, hoping that a percentage of them will survive to provide for their parent's needs when they become too old to do so for themselves. In other words, children in many traditional societies are a kind of social security policy. Birth rates are affected by this kind of socialization, by education, and by other customs and mores in rearing families. As economic development occurs people begin to delay marriage, have smaller families, and practice various forms of family planning and birth control.[11] Fertility is also checked when women become more educated. This gradually leads to a relative equalization of birth and death rates and a corresponding decline in overall population growth rates, as shown in the theoretical model in figure 12.3.

If this is true, it may behoove wealthy states to invest in future global stability by assisting the poor countries to achieve higher levels of education and development. An alternative for the wealthy countries is to attempt to wall themselves off from the poverty of the South and from the impact of population increases there. But it is difficult to figure out how this could be done effectively, especially by the Western democratic states, which

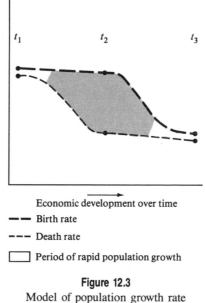

Figure 12.3
Model of population growth rate
reductions over time with increased
economic development

take pride in their traditions of promoting individual rights, justice, and humanitarian assistance. Still another alternative would be to provide larger sums for population control and economic assistance to the developing world.

Several issues have arisen from this discussion. In view of the growing population pressures, how will poor countries cope with increasingly greater food and energy needs and how will they overcome other disparities of development? To what extent will disparities of development lead to conflict in international relations? Under what conditions might migrations contribute to conflict among nations?

Overcoming Disparities

Whether the poverty of the developing world is blamed on the international system or on the failure of domestic policy, the poor countries will continue to be under tremendous economic pressures in the years ahead. To cope with these pressures, governments and international institutions must adopt new policies and approaches. Domestic policies aimed at increasing local food production must be coupled with an efficient international food reserve system. In the area of energy, poor, nonoil-producing countries would be hard-pressed to conserve energy or to move away from high-cost capital and energy-intensive development plans. The choice would be to find domestic energy alternatives. But for some countries, neither is a likelihood. Indeed, not all developing countries face the same food and energy problems. Some are in much better shape; others are in much worse.

The gaps between developing countries on these issues, in turn, make it more difficult for them to bargain successfully as a group with the developed countries. Instead, most countries try to cope through bilateral or regional strategies, such as securing foreign aid, access to credit, and South–South trade. These efforts may not be optimal, but they are better than nothing, and they represent realistic options in light of the continuing inability of developing countries to make any headway with their richer counterparts to the North on establishing a New International Economic Order more favorable to Southern interests. A comprehensive approach to ease the pressures on their economies would be desirable, but this may be unattainable for now. In the meantime, each country must "muddle through" on its own. This is likely to lead to increasing differentiation among developing nations, as they compete for scarce resources. Newly industrialized countries (NICs), such as Taiwan, South Korea, and Singapore, will dominate trade among the developing nations and between the developing nations and the developed world. Non-NICs are likely to languish in relative poverty as their relatively better-off, newly industrialized counterparts enjoy some upward mobility. In short, although North–South tension may still be present, considerable South–South tension may be in the offing in the years to come.[12]

Alternative Paths to Development

The literature on the problems caused by disparity of development, their causes, and strategies for redressing them is extensive. As noted in chapter 11, there are basically three schools of thought about how poor countries might become less poor. Marxists argue that withdrawal from the capitalist international economy is the only prescription for overcoming disparities of development.[13] Conventional theorists say that only through increased aid, trade, and investment can poor countries expect to attract the monetary resources needed to develop their economies.[14] The reformists argue that certain reforms are needed in the international economy to reduce structural barriers to development and give poor countries a fair chance to compete.[15] They have called for a New International Economic Order (NIEO), which would help redistribute international wealth more fairly. Conventional theorists have been split on how far to accede to poor countries demands for more concessional aid, debt rescheduling or cancellation, commodity indexation, and preferential trade rights. Some have rejected all attempts to institutionalize such principles. Others have been favorably disposed to certain of these ideas and opposed to others.[16] Marxists, on the other hand, have viewed any "planetary bargain" along these lines as a mirage.

These schools of thought do not contest the fact of economic disparity. They vary only on how to cope with it. Most observers agree that global efforts to negotiate an NIEO have ground to a near-halt. Poor countries, having tried global negotiating strategies, appear to be resorting to bilateral and regional approaches to resolve these rather significant disparities. It is clear that while the NIEO initiative may be moribund, the problems it proposed to address are not. What will happen if they are not somehow addressed? Will desperately poor countries be content to muddle through? Will they face rising internal stability and revolution as the Marxists suggest? Or will they turn their frustrations on their neighbors or the wealthy countries of the North to obtain by blackmail what they cannot achieve by negotiation or by self-help?[17] That many observers of international relations ask these speculative questions suggests that not everyone is comfortable with the growing absolute and relative poverty in the global arena.

A more practical and immediate question concerns how poor countries can become less poor. Whatever one's ideological beliefs, it seems clear that poor countries need to address an awesome range of tasks in order to develop their economies. They need to control population growth, educate their populations, increase economic productivity, stimulate agricultural production, reinforce the rural economic infrastructure, maintain political stability, reduce military expenditures, and avoid costly military adventures. To accomplish this, they need enlightened leadership to mobilize domestic resources or to attract capital from the outside. The fact is it costs a great deal to develop an economy. Whether these resources are attracted through outside aid, trade, investment, or purely domestic efforts is largely a matter of a government's individual preferences. In general, *autarkic policies*—that is, policies that emphasize isolation from other countries—have not been very successful or popular. Albania, one of the few countries still practicing such a policy, is hardly a major success story. Most other countries that have flirted with this approach, including China and Kampuchea, experienced grave economic difficulties.

If autarky, on one hand, and universal initiatives such as the NIEO, on the other, hold out little promise, then how can countries mobilize needed resources? The range of bilateral and regional options is limited. Poor countries can try regional trade strategies to strengthen their mutual economic situation. Organizations such as the Economic Community of West African States, the Association of South-East Asian Nations, or the Andean Pact are prime examples. Poor countries can also attempt to form cartels to gain economic leverage in international markets (see chapter 11). They can seek bilateral or multilateral aid or private foreign investment, realizing that in doing so they will be under certain political or economic constraints imposed by the lending or investing agents. In today's international economy, countries are largely on their own in grappling with poverty. Whether their struggle continues to be a quiet one, or whether it leads to growing frustration and international tension remains to be seen.

The Global Arms Race

If disparity of development is the primary concern of the North–South dispute, there can be little doubt that the global arms race is the chief preoccupation of the East–West dispute, so let us address a few basic concepts and issues that undergird the current nuclear arms debate.

The Security Dilemma

All but a very small number of states have determined that their security depends on the development of military systems and arms to protect themselves from the aggressive actions of other countries. The idea is to amass sufficient military strength to prevent other nations from erroneously assuming that they can attack without paying a very high cost. A major objective of developing military strength and arms is to deter other countries from attacking. Unfortunately, there is good reason to feel insecure about the military strength of other nations, since countless examples of using force for offensive purposes can be cited.

This leads to a ticklish problem in international relations: One country's security becomes another's insecurity. Whether a nation's intentions are strictly defensive, other countries are likely to view its strength as a potential threat. They, in turn, are likely to increase the size of their military, produce larger numbers of arms, or develop more sophisticated weapons systems to protect themselves from this perceived threat. Still other countries will see this as a threat and respond with arms buildups of their own. The paradox of arms races is that in the pursuit of security states become intimately involved in a spiral of increasing insecurity. It is little wonder then that the contemporary international system is marked both by considerable insecurity and by a large number of bilateral, regional, and global arms races.

Arms Control and Disarmament

The idea of peace through strength, of keeping peace through preparing for war, is an old one. Whether greater military capabilities lead to peace or war is debatable.[18] The problem with arms races is that they can lead to greater insecurity and greater destructiveness when wars are fought. For these reasons, peace advocates have argued for the necessity of controlling and curtailing the arms race. Arms races can be controlled or curtailed in basically four ways: (1) arms limitation or control, (2) arms freezes, (3) arms reductions, or (4) disarmament. **Arms control** allows countries to deploy weapons under predetermined quotas or limits. An **arms freeze** implies that countries may not develop a particular new weapon or weapons but may keep their old arsenal intact, without increasing the number of weapons. **Arms reductions** imply that states must reduce the number of weapons, whereas **disarmament** aims at the elimination of arms or particular kinds of arms altogether.[19]

A simplistic view of arms control and disarmament is that war can be prevented by controlling or getting rid of weapons. A more sophisticated view is that war is not caused by arms as such, but by countries that sometimes have very different and conflicting interests. Arms control and disarmament do not eliminate the underlying political differences, but they can foster stability and promote diplomatic contact between potential adversaries, which can help them manage their relationship short of outright war. Thus wherever there are arms races, arms control or disarmament may be a useful means of managing interstate relations and preventing unwanted wars.

Indeed, although numerous arms races continue to characterize international relations, many countries have recognized the importance of trying to brake them when they overheat or at least prevent their expansion into other areas. Prior to World War I, for instance, the Hague Conventions of 1899 and 1907 prohibited the use of various weapons. The Geneva Protocol of 1925 proscribed the use of chemical and bacteriological weapons, which many countries had already found impractical during wartime. Since World War II, spurred by the development of nuclear weapons, numerous additional arms control agreements have come into being. Table 12.4 lists the significant arms control agreements that have been initiated in the post–World War II period.[20]

There have been basically five tracks on which arms talks have moved over the past decade and a half: (1) strategic arms talks between the two superpowers, (2) intermediate-range nuclear force talks between the superpowers that involved consultation with their allies in Europe at various stages, (3) the Conference on Disarmament in Europe, also known as the Stockholm talks, (4) the multilateral discussions under the auspices of the UN Conference on Disarmament, and (5) the Mutual and Balanced Force Reduction talks between the NATO and Warsaw Pact alliances, which are now proceeding under the title of Conventional Stability Talks. A brief look at each of these negotiation tracks is useful.

Strategic arms talks   The Strategic Arms Limitation Talks (SALT I and SALT II), which were bilateral negotiations between the United States and Soviet Union, focused on the long-range strategic weapons issue. SALT I limited the deployment of antiballistic missile (ABM) systems to two sites (later reduced to one site) in each country with no more than

Table 12.4

Arms control agreements since World War II

Agreement	Year
Antarctic Treaty	1959
Partial Nuclear Test Ban Treaty	1963
The "Hot-Line" Agreement	1963
The Outer Space Treaty	1967
Treaty on Prohibition of Nuclear Weapons in Latin America	1967
Nuclear Non-Proliferation Treaty	1968
U.S./USSR Communications Link Agreement	1971
U.S./USSR Nuclear War Risk Reduction Agreement	1971
Treaty on the Prohibition of the Emplacement of Nuclear Weapons on the Seabed	1971
Convention on Bacteriological and Toxic Weapons	1972
The Antiballistic Missile (ABM) Treaty	1972
The Strategic Arms Limitation Talks I (SALT I)	1972
Threshold Test Ban Treaty[a]	1974
France/USSR Agreement on Prevention of Accidental Nuclear War	1976
Convention on Prohibition of Environmental Modification Techniques	1977
U.K./USSR Agreement on the Prevention of Accidental Nuclear War	1977
The Strategic Arms Limitations Talks II (SALT II)[a]	1979
South Pacific Nuclear Free Zone	1985
The Intermediate Range Nuclear Force Treaty	1988

[a]The United States has signed but never ratified the Threshold Test Ban Treaty and SALT II. Nevertheless, many of the provisions of these two agreements have been observed by both the United States and the Soviet Union.

SOURCE: Stockholm International Peace Research Institute (SIPRI), *SIPRI Yearbook 1987* (United Kingdom: Oxford, 1987), pp. 457–461.

100 interceptor missiles. SALT I also placed ceilings on the number of strategic missiles based on land and in submarines at sea. SALT II limited the number of total launch vehicles (heavy bombers, intercontinental ballistic missiles, and submarine-launched ballistic missiles) to 2,400 for each country. These talks clearly focused on the long-range strategic weapons forces of the two superpowers. Although the United States never ratified the SALT II treaty, most of its provisions have been honored by both the Soviet Union and the United States. To replace the SALT talks, President Reagan called for the inauguration of the Strategic Arms Reductions Talks (START) in 1982. These talks were intended to move beyond arms control to actual disarmament (progressive arms reductions). They broke down a year later, only to be resurrected in 1985 as part of a much broader negotiating agenda including intermediate-range nuclear forces and space weapons.

Intermediate-range nuclear force talks   Another category of weapon is the **intermediate-range nuclear forces (INF),** most of which were located in Europe. The INF reduction talks were initiated in 1981 but broke down in 1983 and, like the START talks, resurrected in 1985 as part of a package of related but separate negotiations. Eventually they led to the ratification of an INF agreement between the United States and the Soviet Union in 1988. This agreement was particularly significant because it represented the first major breakthrough in arms discussions in nearly a decade, it provided for total elimination of a class of weapon, and it called for **on-site inspection** to ensure that both sides actually dismantled INF forces under each other's direct observation.

The Stockholm talks   The third track on which disarmament talks have been conducted is at the European level. Strictly speaking, the Conference on Disarmament (CDE), or the Stockholm talks, is not a disarmament talk, despite the reference to disarmament in its title. Rather the CDE's purpose is to develop confidence-building measures between the opposing members of the NATO and Warsaw Pact alliances. Confidence-building measures include notifying other countries of impending military maneuvers, limiting force sizes participating in such maneuvers, and allowing outside observers to attend them. These talks, which grew out of the Conference on Security and Cooperation in Europe held in Helsinki, Finland, in 1975, are seen as a way to promote a safer political and security climate in Europe, which might have a positive effect on bilateral superpower negotiations.

UN Conference on Disarmament   The fourth track is the only global multilateral negotiating body, the forty-member UN Conference on Disarmament. Formerly the UN Committee on Disarmament, this body changed its name to the Conference on Disarmament in 1984 and now meets twice annually to discuss a broad range of arms control and disarmament issues. Among its members are the five nuclear arms countries—the United States, the Soviet Union, the United Kingdom, France, and China. The United Nations has sponsored special sessions of the General Assembly devoted to disarmament and has been broadly supportive of disarmament efforts at the European regional level. Past UN multilateral efforts have led to a number of multilateral nuclear arms agreements. But these efforts have only had a marginal impact on the crucial bilateral arms control negotiations between the superpowers.

Mutual and balanced arms reduction talks   Since 1973 NATO allies and the Warsaw Pact have pursued a fifth track of armaments discussions known as the Mutual and Balanced Force Reductions (MBFR) talks. These talks were aimed at reducing the dangerously high levels of nuclear and conventional forces in Europe. The assumption was that reduction in these forces would produce a more stable military situation in Europe. Roughly equal reductions would be necessary in weapons and troop deployments on both sides in order to achieve a stable military balance. These talks have taken on new significance with the entry into force of an INF agreement calling for the total removal of all intermediate-range nuclear weapons from Europe. NATO experts have long believed that such weapons were a must in the Western arsenal to deter a conventional attack by what they viewed as numerically superior Warsaw Pact conventional forces. Now that INF forces are dismantled, many NATO defense experts feel that Europe is exposed to a greater danger of conventional attack, and so they are keen to see reductions in the Warsaw Pact conventional forces. With these concerns in mind, rejuvenation of MBFR discussions continues under the title of Conventional Stability Talks, sometimes referred to as the Conventional Force in Europe (CFE) negotiations. Indeed, the idea of conducting conventional force reductions gained renewed momentum in December 1988 at the United Nations when Mikhail Gorbachev dramatically announced Soviet intentions to unilaterally withdraw large numbers of Soviet troops and tanks from Eastern Europe. In May 1989 the first installment of fifty thousand Soviet troops and five thousand tanks were withdrawn. President Bush countered later in the same month, announcing at NATO meetings his intention to cut U.S. NATO forces by 10 percent. He also proposed further deep cuts in aircraft and tanks by both NATO and Warsaw Pact forces to reach a rough balance in conventional forces. In 1990 Bush and Gorbachev agreed to carry out even greater reductions in force. The current race to cut arms seems remarkable set against the backdrop of the unprecedented arms race the world has experienced for the last four decades—a period that we now must explore.

The U.S.–Soviet Arms Race

Despite the many efforts at arms control, the global arms race and the superpower nuclear arms race continued largely unabated until recently. In this section we focus on the U.S.–Soviet arms race, because it is the one fraught with the gravest consequences and it has implications for many other arms races around the globe.

As the United States and the Soviet Union squared off in a Cold War after World War II, each pursued technological advances in nuclear weaponry—the United States in most cases to stay ahead of the Soviet Union, and the Soviet Union to catch up to U.S. technological advances. In 1945 the United States was the only nuclear power. But by 1949 the Soviets had developed an atomic weapon. A short time later, in 1952, the United States developed a thermonuclear weapon (a fusion or hydrogen bomb), which was even more devastating than earlier atomic weapons. The Soviet Union (which had detonated a partial-fusion weapon some months before the United States) developed a full-fusion bomb within a year of the successful American tests. But having bombs was one thing and delivering them to potential targets on other continents was another. Each superpower energetically set about devising delivery systems that would make their nuclear threat credible. The United States deployed strategic intercontinental bombers in 1948; the Soviet Union did not do so until 1955. However, Soviet technology produced the first ICBMs in 1957. The United States countered with ICBMs of its own a year later. The escalation in both technological sophistication and quantity of the weapons grew dramatically throughout the 1960s. The United States deployed submarine-launched ballistic missiles (SLBMs) in 1960. It took the Soviet Union eight years to match this achievement. In short, during the early phases of nuclear competition the United States enjoyed a substantial edge in terms of numbers of weapons and delivery capability. None of these advantages, however, lasted very long. The bottom line was that by the late 1950s and early 1960s each superpower had developed a capacity to destroy the other's population centers with long-range nuclear weapons.

As the nuclear arms race entered the 1970s, the Soviet Union began to challenge American nuclear superiority, both in terms of technology and quantity of weapons. The United States introduced the first multiple independently targeted reentry vehicle (MIRV) warheads in 1970. With these weapons, as many as ten nuclear warheads could be housed on a single missile, and each warhead could be targeted on a separate target. The Soviet Union countered with similar weapons in 1975. In 1982 the United States introduced long-range cruise missile technology. These weapons fly so closely to the ground that they cannot be easily detected with conventional radar. The Soviet Union developed similar technology in 1984. Clearly the pattern of action and reaction in the superpower nuclear relationship follows the classical pattern of an arms race. Each side casts about for new, exotic technologies to counter existing weapons systems and gain an edge. Any move by one superpower was matched by the other, usually within a matter of a few years. After forty years of nuclear competition, American and Soviet nuclear arsenals are brimming with enough nuclear missiles and warheads to destroy the world many times over. Still neither side enjoys overall superiority in the arms race. As of 1985 the United States enjoyed a slight lead over the Soviet Union in numbers of strategic and tactical nuclear weapons: about 27,000 warheads to the Soviets' 21,000.[21] The Soviet Union, on the other hand, enjoyed a lead in the destructive capacity (megatonnage or explosive power) of its warheads. Indeed, an age of rough nuclear parity has prevailed for over a decade.

With the numbers of weapons and the changes in technological sophistication, it should come as no surprise that nuclear strategic doctrines would change as well. Certainly, if a nation is going to have so many weapons of such awesome destructive capacity, there should be some idea about their purpose. In the early years of American nuclear superiority, the doctrine of **massive retaliation** guided U.S. strategic thinking. This doctrine held that should the Soviet Union attempt to invade Western Europe, or even other areas of the world considered strategically important, the United States would retaliate with the full force of its nuclear power. John Foster Dulles, secretary of state under President Eisenhower, used this threat of massive retaliation in a number of Cold War standoffs with the communist world. This was known as a policy of **nuclear brinkmanship,** a sort of game of nuclear chicken or a test of will and nerves. This threat, it was hoped, would deter any expansionist impulse the Soviet Union might have. However, this doctrine became clumsy and dangerous as the Soviet Union began to catch up with the United States in the nuclear field. Indeed, even by the late 1950s, policy makers began to talk about the need for **flexible response** to the Soviet threat. The threat of nuclear devastation of Moscow would not prevent the problems of guerrilla war and communist intervention in the Third World. Nonnuclear forces—that is, conventional military systems—needed to be buttressed to provide other means of resisting the perceived expansion of Soviet influence.[22]

By the 1960s, with each superpower fast gaining the capacity to destroy the other, unilateral policies of massive retaliation were too dangerous. In the United States flexible response became firmly entrenched as the chief method of deterring Soviet aggression abroad. But how could a direct nuclear attack be deterred? Flexible response was not enough. It was soon joined by the doctrine of **mutual assured destruction,** known—quite appropriately—by its acronym, MAD. According to this doctrine, each superpower had developed a thermonuclear capacity to destroy the other several times over, even if attacked first. Neither superpower could use these awesome weapons to attack the other because it would mean sure suicide when the other side retaliated, since both sides could annihilate each other and since neither would be foolish enough to invite its own incineration by attacking the other first. Under these circumstances, **mutual deterrence** could be achieved. But this policy of deterrence rested on the grim premise that peace could be maintained only if the cities of the two superpowers remained vulnerable to attack by the nuclear weapons of the other side. If, on the other hand, one superpower should gain the ability to wipe out all the missiles of the other side through a **first-strike attack** (or counterforce strategy), it would no longer be vulnerable to a **second-strike attack** (countercity or countervalue attack) by the other side. (See figure 12.4 for an illustration of the logic of mutual assured deterrence). Assuming that the superpower could effectively prevent an attack on its cities, it might be tempted to use these weapons first or at least to threaten their use to get its way during a crisis or dispute. Fortunately, both the United States and the Soviet Union have managed to retain their second-strike capability—that is, a capacity to retaliate even after absorbing a first strike—and no nuclear exchange has occurred.

But maintaining a stable system of mutual deterrence has not been easy or tension-free. A complicating factor in determining the relative nuclear balance is the fact that the United States and the Soviet Union have somewhat different kinds of weapons based in different kinds of modes. The United States, for instance, has historically pursued a policy of a **triad;** that is, the U.S. bases its nuclear capability in three roughly equal legs: bombers, ICBMs, and SLBMs. The theory is that if one leg of the triad—let's say ground-based ICBMs—is wiped out in a first strike, the other legs could retaliate. By preserving the triad, the United States retains a second-strike capability and thus strengthens deterrence. On the other hand, the Soviet Union has lagged behind the United States in its submarine and bomber capability and has relied more heavily on building its ICBM force. About 70 percent of the USSR's nuclear force is based in an ICBM mode.

This single fact presents special difficulty. Because ICBMs represent the most accurate basing mode, they are the most reliable first-strike weapon. Missiles of great accuracy and warheads of significant power are needed to destroy the missile sites of another country. Soviet rockets have always been more powerful than their American counterparts and thus carry larger warheads. Until recently the United States could compensate for the powerful Soviet rockets because its missiles were far more accurate. But the Soviet Union has closed

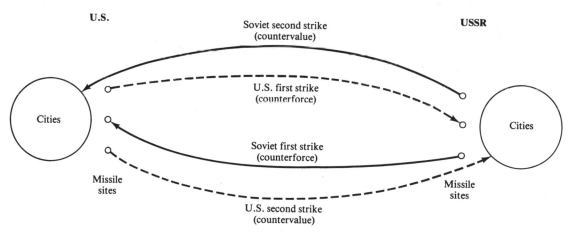

Figure 12.4
The logic of mutual assured destruction (MAD)

the accuracy gap. This development has led many American strategic thinkers to worry that the Soviet Union's large ICBM force could effectively wipe out the smaller U.S. ICBM force and, with it, the command and control systems needed to mount a retaliatory strike. If the Soviet leadership perceived such an advantage, they might be willing to strike first, betting on the fact that the United States would be reluctant to use its bombers of SLBMs to attack Soviet cities and military bases in retaliation, since this would in turn invite immediate Soviet retaliation and the annihilation of U.S. cities as well. Faced with either capitulation or annihilation, the only other choice for American leaders would be to launch the American ICBM force on the warning of a Soviet first strike. But this, too, would invite a wholesale nuclear exchange. It should be obvious that the nuclear arms game is not just based on numbers of weapons, but on perceptions. For example, when U.S. strategic thinkers assume that Soviet leaders would be willing to risk total nuclear annihilation on the chance that U.S. leaders would lose their nerve under attack, they are making assumptions about how Soviet leaders might think and act.

Another perception in the United States is that the large Soviet ICBM force is a destabilizing threat. Moscow argues, however, that its nuclear forces are vulnerable because ICBMs are not mobile and are easy targets for an American first strike. They worry about the greater mobility of American nuclear forces (the submarines and bombers) and point out that they need to counter the advantages the American forces enjoy with a larger ICBM force. Moreover, they point out that virtually all missiles outside the Soviet Union are aimed at the Soviet Union. Moscow has to worry about not only the U.S. nuclear force, but also the United Kingdom's, France's, and even China's.

Another complicating factor in the nuclear arms game concerns the specific situation in Europe; that is, the role of INF and short-range nuclear forces (SNF).[23] For a time the defense of Western Europe from possible Soviet invasion was based largely on the potential use of these weapons. Some strategists argued that the INF and tactical nuclear missiles, which are used in a conventional mode but carry nuclear warheads, were needed to deter a Soviet invasion or, should one ever be attempted, to halt it. In the early 1980s NATO deployed a large number of Pershing II and cruise missiles in Western Europe to answer this potential threat and to offset the growing number of Soviet SS-20 class medium-range missiles that had been deployed in the European theater. Just how were these missiles to count in any further arms control agreements? Soviet SS-20s could be used to attack Europe but not the United States. On the other hand, NATO nuclear weapons based in Europe are capable of hitting Soviet targets. Should the missiles in the European theater be counted as part of the larger Soviet–American nuclear competition? Or should they be seen as a separate regional problem? The Soviets tried to link them, while the Europeans and Americans resisted doing so. Moreover, even if arms reductions treaties were negotiated, how could compliance be verified as long as each side denied the other access to its sensitive security sites?

In the early 1980s high levels of distrust, tension, and competition between the superpowers continued to pose problems for mutual agreement on limiting the arms race. However, dramatic progress on many of the issues that hindered past negotiations took place during the Geneva Nuclear Arms talks, which, as we noted earlier, began in 1985 and were intended to deal with reductions in long-range ballistic missiles, the INF situation, and the issue of space weapons. Three separate tracks of negotiations developed along these lines, with success being achieved first in the INF talks. After much maneuvering, both sides agreed to the so-called "zero option"—that is, a complete removal of all intermediate nuclear weapons in Europe. Even more dramatic was their agreement to allow on-site inspection to ensure mutual compliance. This spectacular breakthrough meant that, under the watchful eye of each other, the Soviet Union would dismantle about five warheads for every U.S. warhead. But despite this seeming advantage, the NATO alliance was left wondering how it could deter a Soviet conventional attack. In the bargain the Soviet Union gave up a clear superiority in INF weapons, while the United States and Europe decided to live with a lower level of deterrence against conventional attack to eradicate this species of weapon. The INF agreement paved the way for progress on the far more serious issue of reductions in ICBMs and in the strategic nuclear arsenal. For nearly three years after the INF success, negotiations to produce a Strategic Arms Reductions Talks (START) treaty continued. This treaty, which is slated for conclusion by the end of 1990, will not achieve the overall reductions in nuclear warheads initially promised by Reagan and Gorbachev during their summit meetings. It will call for substantial reductions in the number of warheads deployed on ICBMs: 35 percent for the United States and 50 percent for the Soviet Union. However, the cuts in ICBM warheads will be offset by allowable increases in warheads carried by strategic bombers or sea-launched cruise missiles. By deliberately undercounting the number of weapons carried in these modes, each side has breathing room in which to build and deploy more and newer warheads. Those who believed the advance billing that the START treaty would produce deep cuts in nuclear arsenals may find it to be a major disappointment. Nevertheless, the treaty does break new ground in arms negotiations. First, unlike the prior SALT agreements, START limits the actual number of nuclear warheads (even though it permits a modest buildup in certain basing modes). The SALT agreements limited the number only of missile launchers, not warheads. Second, the treaty does reduce deployment of warheads on ICBMs —the largest, most accurate, destabilizing and dangerous weapons in both sides' nuclear arsenals. Third, the treaty anticipates more than a dozen different kinds of mutual verification and inspection procedures to ensure compliance with the agreement. These advances build on progress made in INF toward OSI and mutual verification. Finally, however disappointing the treaty may be overall, it does underscore superpower willingness to work incrementally toward prospective reductions in nuclear forces. Once the START agreement is concluded, further negotiations are likely to focus on broader reductions in the nuclear arsenals. But difficult issues will be faced, including how to count mobile land-based missiles, how to treat cruise missiles of all varieties, and how to cope with strategic defense issues.

Despite the success of INF and START talks and recent breakthroughs in conventional force reductions, numerous arms control issues remain problematical. Short-range nuclear forces (SNF) potentially complicate arms talks. They were considered essential by most NATO countries, but West Germany, where these weapons are principally deployed and where they would be used in the event of a Soviet attack, would like to see them dismantled eventually. Other NATO partners argued that they should be modernized to compensate for the loss of NATO Pershing II missiles under the INF accord and for possible reductions in NATO troop levels. The USSR countered by threatening to renege on the INF treaty should NATO proceed with SNF modernization. Despite the remaining obstacles, agreement on a START treaty, a CFE treaty, and even bans on the production and storage of chemical and bacteriological weapons are likely in the months and years ahead. In September 1989 preliminary agreements on several of these subjects were concluded by the U.S. and Soviet governments at ministerial-level meetings held in Jackson Hole, Wyoming. Later, at the Bush–Gorbachev summit in June 1990, further progress was made, several agreements signed, and agreement in principle reached on the START treaty.

Can the superpowers hope to completely dismantle their nuclear arsenals, even if these problems are overcome? This seems unlikely because the closer both sides get to complete disarmament, the more significance their remaining forces take on as a hedge against cheating or a sudden breakout of rearmament by the opponent. **Nuclear proliferation** presents another dilemma for superpower nuclear disarmament, because the spread of nuclear weapons technology to many other countries means that the superpowers have become more vulnerable to the nuclear forces of other nations. Total nuclear disarmament, in other words, would have to be global in scope and would prove most difficult to verify with confidence. Total disarmament, then, seems unlikely, although substantial reductions remain a real likelihood in the current climate of international relations. Progress along these lines, however, continues to be pestered by the lingering question of the role of strategic defense, which grew in importance with the announcement by the Reagan administration in 1983 that the United States would undertake a **Strategic Defense Initiative (SDI)** as an alternative approach to the MAD doctrine.

The Evolution of the Strategic Defense Initiative

Some people are convinced that the Soviet Union is bent on achieving a first-strike capability and that Soviet military doctrine calls for the development of a capacity to win limited nuclear wars. If so, they argue, it would be prudent for the United States to develop a defensive system that would be capable of shielding its population centers from attack or at least of maintaining deterrence by ensuring the survivability of its own missiles. Other experts worry about the accidental use of these destructive weapons. Some of them, too, have argued that it was wrong to base deterrence on a policy of leaving the population vulnerable to annihilation by a crazed dictator or even an unintentional mistake that could lead to a wholesale nuclear exchange. For all these reasons, some people argue that it would be better to develop a defensive capability, a way to destroy any or all incoming missiles before they could destroy the country. A new logic of defensive deterrence based on these principles has emerged.

Similar arguments were made in the 1960s by supporters of the development of an antiballistic missile (ABM) system. But in 1972 the superpowers agreed to limit deployment of ABM systems. Each superpower was initially allowed to develop two ABM sites, but later this was limited to one. Clearly, this was not enough to protect all of their cities from nuclear destruction. Comprehensive ABM systems were rejected at the time because they did not seem feasible and because of concern that they could potentially destabilize mutual deterrence. However, the attractiveness of a defensive nuclear system that would shield the cities from devastation excited the continued attention of some U.S. scientists and politicians. In 1983 President Reagan proclaimed his intention to pursue the SDI, believing that a determined research effort would make it a technically feasible approach within a decade or so. It would be better, he argued, to base nuclear strategy on a more humanitarian and defensive posture than the traditional MAD doctrine.

Alternative Views on the Strategic Defense Initiative

Initial reaction to the SDI proposal was mostly negative. Doubts about the technical feasibility of this system, the huge production cost, its vulnerability to rather effective and inexpensive countermeasures, and the potentially destabilizing effect it might have on the traditional concept of deterrence concerned many skeptical experts and public officials. But President Reagan persisted and eventually gained both allied support and congressional approval for a research program. Predictably, the Soviet Union was opposed to SDI. The staggering costs of such a system no doubt gave the Soviet leadership pause to consider the financial impact of such a new, if defensive, arms race. Suddenly SDI was a major stumbling block to progress on arms control talks, as the Soviet Union pressed for its inclusion on the negotiating agenda, and the United States refused to treat it as a bargaining chip. In the Reagan–Gorbachev summit in Reykjavík, Iceland, matters came to a head as Gorbachev linked deep cuts in nuclear arms to limitations on SDI research, an approach that Reagan rejected.

Opponents and proponents of SDI take issue with each other on a number of counts: (1) whether SDI can be effective, (2) whether a less than 100 percent effective system is valuable or cost effective, (3) whether deployment would lead to a crisis among NATO allies, (4) whether SDI research and deployment violates existing treaties, (5) whether arms control negotiations will be adversely affected, and (6) whether deterrence and crisis stability will be enhanced or weakened.[24]

Opponents and supporters of SDI disagree on all six counts, mainly because they can only speculate about a very uncertain future. No one can say with certainty whether SDI will stabilize or destabilize deterrence, poison or improve relations among allies, help or hurt arms control. No one can say for sure whether a defensive shield is technically feasible or even precisely how expensive it would be to deploy one. Most of the technology an SDI shield would rely on does not even exist. And so the speculation continues, as does research on SDI. As this research continues, questions about the basic issues probably will be clarified. Recent technical assessments by the U.S. Congress and the U.S. Joint Chiefs of Staff have resulted in a scaled-down version of SDI. A full-defense shield is not seen as being feasible anytime soon. But even opponents of SDI, such as Democratic Senator Sam Nunn, have proposed a more limited ballistic missile defense directed against accidental launchings or attacks by third parties, such as a crazed dictator.

In the final analysis, the SDI program can only be justified if it adds significantly to nuclear deterrence and stability. Can the cost of and effort to build a full-scale SDI system be justified in those terms? Let us consider for a moment the ancient but pertinent story of King Pyrrhus. Pyrrhus, king of Epirus in ancient Greece, planned to extend his power beyond Greece into Italy. His wise counselor, Cyneas, admonished him to beware of ambition in the following dialogue:

Cyneas: Well, Sir, to what end do you make all this mighty preparation?
Pyrrhus: To make myself master of Italy.
Cyneas: And what after you have done this?
Pyrrhus: Sicily next holds out her arms to receive us.
Cyneas: And will the possession of Sicily put an end to the war?
Pyrrhus: No. These are but the forerunner of greater things, for then I will go subdue Africa, after which no enemy could resist me.
Cyneas: None, Sir. But when all this is in your power, what will you do?
Pyrrhus: We will then live at our ease, drink all day, and keep pleasant conversation.
Cyneas: For God's sake, sir, what hinders us now, if the goal is to be merry and entertain ourselves, since we have at hand already those things which you propose to achieve at the expense of much blood, great labor, and infinite hazard?[25]

Pyrrhus did not heed Cyneas's advice, though it troubled him much. Instead he embarked on his grand design, and, at great loss of life, fought unsuccessfully for six years in Italy and Sicily.

For all intents and purposes, the superpowers have achieved a condition of mutual nuclear deterrence. The ultimate end of SDI is to achieve just that, except based on a defensive rather than an offensive posture. But, like Cyneas, we might ask why so much expense and effort should be exerted to achieve a state-of-affairs that is ultimately little different from what we already enjoy. Why not attempt instead to save resources and energy by pursuing disarmament and diverting our energies and resources to the daunting problems of poverty, disease, and environmental degradation? If the threat of SDI can be used as a bargaining chip to encourage progress towards disarmament, so much the better. If continued research produces less expensive ways to increase security against accidental launches of nuclear missiles, again so much the better. Let us only hope that today's leaders act wisely and that they do not, like Pyrrhus, rush headlong in pursuit of expensive and dangerous dreams, which ultimately promise to leave us no better off, and perhaps much worse off.

Arms Races and Disparity of Development: The Link

As we conclude this chapter, it is important to note that the issues of economic development and the global arms race are not unrelated. It may seem that they are wholly different— one a butter issue, the other a guns issue. But in a fundamental sense, the two issues *are* a unified guns-versus-butter issue.[26] Every minute of every day about $2 million is spent on arms worldwide.[27] Such massive expenditures can be justified if the emphasis is on defensive systems meant to deter aggression by other countries. However, consider for a moment some other costs. How would a similar expenditure on tractors, plows, or tools affect economic growth? Resources spent on such goods have a far more positive impact on economic growth, since they can be used to produce other valuable goods. By contrast, missiles and tanks cannot be used to harvest crops or make cars. In other words, exaggerated military spending, even for defensive purposes, can have certain economic drawbacks.

On the more ominous side, when arms actually are used they destroy economic infrastructure, not to mention human lives. It would be better if countries could accommodate their differences, reduce expenditures on arms, and apply more resources to economic development. In fact, they seem most reluctant to do this, in part because many nations face what they perceive to be genuine threats to their security from other nations.

And so the global arms race continues. The U.S.–Soviet conventional and nuclear arms races divert resources that might otherwise be used to strengthen their economies or given as economic aid to desperately needy countries. It is ironic that much of the aid given by the superpowers and other major powers to the poorer countries of the world takes the form of military aid rather than economic assistance. Second- and third-generation weapons systems are exported to poor countries, which often use them against their own populations or in regional arms races with their neighbors. As table 12.5 shows, the spending priorities of many Third World governments, in turn, reflect a heavy emphasis on security. The figures in the table are based on the percentage of the government's budget devoted to defense. Ethiopia, for example, spends as much as a third of its domestic budget on defense, while substantial portions of its population barely survive and often starve.[28] Nor is Ethiopia alone. Many other poor countries suffer economically in part because of overemphasis on spending for imported arms.

Theoretically, some degree of military organization should have positive consequences for the development of poor countries. Military systems provide order, help a country overcome regional and ethnic divisions, provide education to recruits, give people opportunities for personal advancement, and develop a corps of professional officers and enlisted persons.

Table 12.5
Third World government expenditures devoted to defense

Country [a]	Percentage of Total Government Expenditures Devoted to Defense
Low-Income Countries	
Ethiopia	39.0 [b]
Burkina Faso	17.1
Burma	19.0
Uganda	19.8
India	20.2
Pakistan	33.5
Middle-Income Countries	
Yemen Arab Republic	35.5
Zimbabwe	17.3
Morocco	16.5
Thailand	20.6
Turkey	15.2
Jordan	24.8
Syria	37.7
Malaysia	15.1
South Korea	31.3
Yugoslavia	50.4
Israel	30.3
Singapore	22.9
High-Income Oil Exporters	
Oman	49.4
United Arab Emirates	36.4

[a] Only those countries with expenditures exceeding 15 percent of the government's budget are included.
[b] Figures for Ethiopia are taken from *Africa South of the Sahara 1986* (London: Europa Publishers, 1985), p. 419.

SOURCE: Data compiled from the World Bank, *World Development Report 1986* (Washington, D.C.: World Bank, 1986). Data are for 1982.

Presumably this should help the process of nation building in recently independent countries. Armies also contribute to national stability by providing logistical systems, which can be useful even in times of nonmilitary emergency.[29] While there may be some general positive effects from the development of military systems, some scholars have argued that excessive military spending is harmful to economic development. One recent study of 116 countries has shown that the relationship of military spending, military participation in developing societies, and military control of the governments and their effect on the general welfare of a society is complex.[30] Using the Physical Quality of Life Index (PQLI) as a general measure of societal welfare, this study found that military participation in developing countries can have a positive effect on societal well-being. (The PQLI measures a nation's general well-being based on its economic production and the availability of education and medical and social services.) High levels of military spending were also found to correlate with societal welfare. But when the researchers broke down military spending between spending on human resources (i.e., for salaries and training recruits) and other kinds of spending (e.g., purchasing major weapons systems), they found a different result. When expenditures for manpower were discounted, military expenditures were found to have a negative effect on general societal welfare. This finding seemed to confirm the theory about the nation-building effect of armies. Money spent increasing an army's human resources and training recruits seems to have a positive impact. But excessive spending on weapons, especially if they are imported from abroad and not produced at home, apparently deprives a country of resources that could be used for economic development and the betterment of social welfare.[31] The same study found that military governments are no better or worse than civilian ones in providing for the general welfare. The key, apparently, is whether governments employ military manpower in ways that promote development and order or whether they spend excessively on expensive capital-intensive, imported weapons. The quality of life suffers in countries that ignore the former and engage in the latter.[32]

Governments obviously have choices about how to spend their resources. They often choose to treat military security as a higher priority than the attainment of a better economic life for their people. One thing is certain, weapons (as distinct from armies) are not designed to feed people, prevent famine, cope with spontaneous migration, and provide productive employment. Recent evidence suggests that the level of arms imported by developing countries finally began to taper off in the mid-1980s, but overall levels of expenditures still remained quite high and continued to impose a substantial economic burden on a large number of developing countries.[33]

The chief theme of this chapter has been that governments' national security policies are linked to their broader policies of economic development, especially in budgetary terms. In this chapter's supplemental reading, Mohammed Ayoob explains that in some cases there may be an important psychological linkage between development and security, especially in the case of Third World countries, which often take seemingly contradictory stances in their national security and development policies. Ayoob sees the national security emphasis of these governments as a function of nation and state building. Not infrequently, the national security—defined in military terms—is given priority over economic development. Indeed, developing countries are often inherently unstable and poor. When push comes to shove, these governments frequently give preference to guns rather than butter as a means of preserving their territorial integrity. Often they rely on more powerful governments for both military and economic assistance. They resent both this dependency and their incapacity to influence the setting of a global agendum—a process dominated by the Great Powers. This makes LDCs appear a bit schizophrenic, but Ayoob suggests that their behavior is better explained by the problems associated with their maturation as nations and states.

Summary

The issues of conflict in international relations are numerous. They range from bilateral disputes over territory (e.g., the Iran–Iraq war), illegal migration, and unfair trade practices, to global concerns about the arms race and disparity of development. Every conflict affords an opportunity for cooperation to resolve the dispute. When cooperation fails, countries sometimes resort to conflict to resolve their differences.

The two major tension-producing issues we have discussed include disparities in development between rich and poor countries and the global arms race. Whether tensions arising out of these problems will produce conflict or cooperation in the decades to come is a difficult matter to answer. If the past is any guide, they will probably lead to a mixture of both, as governments and other actors struggle to cope with the complex problems of our time.

Mohammed Ayoob

■

The Third World in the System of States: Acute Schizophrenia or Growing Pains?

Introduction

This paper is an attempt to think through the problem of the Third World's place in the international system and to analyze how the new entrants into the system, the Third World states, have interacted with the system, how much have they influenced the mores governing the system, and how much have they been influenced by the established norms that they encountered upon becoming full members of the system of states. [This inquiry] strives to correct a lapse apparent in most analyses of the roles of Third World states in the international system. In general, these analyses have failed to penetrate beyond the most superficial level to provide credible answers to the questions: What makes Third World states a different category of international actors? What are the factors that explain their patterns of behavior in the international arena? [We attempt] a preliminary answer to these questions by pointing to the double role that Third World states play in the international system; the different pressures that are brought to bear on their decision-making centers as a result of the two roles they play; their efforts to reconcile these dual pressures; and, finally, Third World leaders' overriding concern with security (broadly defined). This preoccupation with security, the paper argues, underlies Third World leaders' actions in both their spheres of activity—as leaders of individual states and, after the Second World War, as members of the "intruder element" in the established Eurocentric system of states. . . .

SOURCE: From the *International Studies Quarterly* 33 (1989): 67–79. © 1989 International Studies Association. Reprinted by permission in abridged form.

The Dual Role of Third World States

This problem is particularly acute in the arena of Third World foreign policies or international relations, or in other words, in locating and understanding the role of the Third World in the international system as it is currently organized. Such an analysis is difficult for two reasons. The first has to do with historical antecedents and the fundamental state-centric nature of the international system, and the second with the Janus-faced interaction of the states constituting the Third World within that system. The seemingly schizophrenic attitude toward the international system on the part of the collectivity called the Third World is the result of the fact that Third World states interact with the international system simultaneously at two levels. At one level they interact with the international system . . . as individual states with certain interests to protect and relatively discernible objectives to achieve. At another level they interact with and impinge on the system collectively as the major "intruder" element whose main objective seems to be to change important rules, particularly those relating to the distribution of global resources, by which the game of international politics has been played since the Peace of Westphalia (1648) and certainly since the Congress of Vienna (1815).

This combination of two roles has made it difficult for analysts of Third World states' external behavior patterns to find a satisfying answer to the question of how Third World states relate to other states and to the international system as a whole. The second facet of the Third World states' role in the international system, their collective characteristic as an intruder element in that system, is probably as important as the first, especially in terms of the long-term future of the system. In fact, it could be argued that in some ways it is even more important because of the gradual, almost imperceptible, changes that have been and continue to be brought about in the mores governing the international system as a result of the "Third World majority" in the United Nations, in its affiliated institutions, and in various other international fora.

While at various junctures in the earlier history of the modern system of states newcomers or intruders have joined the system (e.g., Russia, Turkey, and Japan), these intruders have always been numerically inferior to the established members at the time when they were accepted as members of that system. It has therefore been relatively easy for the system to accommodate the intruders without undergoing much trauma and dislocation. . . .

The rapid process of decolonization following World War II, however, led to an unprecedented expansion of the system of states in an unprecedentedly short time, thereby globalizing what had been basically a European system of states. This system had also come to incorporate the American and Australasian extensions of Europe plus a few selected states from Asia that had for one reason or another escaped formal colonization by the major European powers and were at the same time considered "civilized" by the major chanceries of Europe. Therefore, the post–World War II expansion of the states-system posed more than a problem of quantitative adjustment. It posed a much greater qualitative problem for the system. For the first time since the establishment of the system of sovereign states the intruders far outnumbered its established membership, which had shared a certain similarity of civilization, religion, political philosophy, and even racial prejudice.

Furthermore, this transformation coincided with the setting up of the first truly universal international organization, the United Nations. Although the nominal equality of its universal membership was qualified by the creation of a category of permanent members of the Security Council with the right to veto, enough of the UN's egalitarian thrust survived in the halls of the General Assembly (and in the later proliferation of specialized agencies affiliated with the UN) to have an apparently significant impact on the norms of state behavior. In the postwar world, with their bias towards universality of membership and increasing concern with "international opinion," international organizations in general and the UN in particular have...disproportionately increase[d] the collective visibility and audibility of the Third World newcomers in the international system, particularly on issues related to international morality and the reallocation of global resources. This phenomenon is all the more striking because this high profile on the part of Third World states bears little relationship to the political, military, economic, and technological capabilities—the traditional indices of "power"—that they possess.

Concomitant with this increasing visibility, however, is increasing evidence of a contradiction in Third World international behavior—a contradiction that might be characterized as "schizophrenia." On the one hand, as intruders and have-nots in the international system, Third World states generally tend to favor (some more selectively than others) structural changes in global economic and political systems to encourage a redistribution of the world's resources and capabilities. On the other hand, their enthusiasm for such changes, which could often have de-stabilizing consequences, is tempered—indeed, it is frequently neutralized —by their role as *states* with a vested interest in the preservation of predictable norms of state behavior. One could argue in fact that their very weakness as states, their lack

of "unconditional legitimacy" for their state-structures as well as for most of the regimes that preside over these state-structures, gives them a greater stake in international order than the established states within the system. After all, any significant weakening of international order could have far graver consequences for the weak newcomers to the system than for the established states which are comparatively strong as *states* individually, as well as collectively strong as *powers*. The tension between the two roles that Third World states play in the international system results, then, from the apparently contradictory demands made upon them by considerations of justice (at the collective plane where they function as the have-nots in the international system) and of order (at the level of individual states preoccupied with the maintenance of political and economic stability).

Security, Autonomy, and Status: Reconciling Key Demands

The problem is further exacerbated by concrete considerations of state and regime security that force Third World decision makers to concentrate primarily on immediate regional environments populated by other Third World states. Threats to Third World states and regimes emanate largely from within their regions, if not from within these states themselves. This is a result both of geographic proximity and of weak state-structures and narrowly-based regimes lacking unconditional legitimacy, which invite intrastate security problems that often get transformed into interstate conflicts among neighboring political entities. Not surprisingly, these security concerns are perceived by Third World governments as more pressing than abstract considerations of the relative merits of justice versus order in the international system.

However, this relatively acute sense of insecurity on the part of most Third World governments generally predisposes them favorably toward the maintenance and promotion of international order—a goal congruent with a strong status quo orientation. It also promotes the building of security links between many Third World governments on the one hand, and major centers of global power on the other, thus further reinforcing the former's commitment to the global status quo. The proliferation of mutual security agreements, peace and friendship treaties, and less formal security arrangements between Third World states and one superpower or the other bears adequate testimony to this phenomenon. Such security links provide Third World ruling elites the assurance that a major power will come to their aid if they are threatened by domestic or external opponents. In turn, these security links provide the superpowers the opportunity to extend their influence within the Third World, especially within its strategically important regions, and to acquire bases and facilities as part of their continuing global competition with each other. This means that many, if not all, Third World states act as collaborators with the international establishment in preserving an international order which, at the same time, they consider iniquitous. Even those states that do not have security alignments with the superpowers and are, therefore, politically nonaligned, are linked to the centers of international power because of their dependence on the advanced industrial countries for trade, aid, investment, and technology. . . .

While recognizing the primacy of these security concerns in the policy calculus of Third World ruling elite, and, therefore, their stake (with some exceptions, like postrevolution Iran or Maoist China) in the maintenance of the existing international order, one should not totally dismiss their aspirations for independence from the economic and political managers of the international system. These aspirations are often buried under the more weighty immediate concerns of "reason of state." Nevertheless, they are products of a historical process of unequal interaction—in military, economic, political, cultural, and technological terms— between the populations and, more importantly, the elite of these countries and their former colonial masters.

Although economic historians may be correct in hypothesizing that trade with the Asian and African colonies did not contribute substantially to the economic development and industrial advancement of the metropolitan powers in the colonial era, this does not detract from the fact that the colonial process is viewed in the Third World, particularly by its elite, as having brought disproportionate economic and financial benefits, not to speak of political and military advantage, to the colonizing powers. . . .

. . . Benefits are commonly perceived in the Third World as having accrued to the metropolitan powers because of the colonized peoples' lack of political, cultural, and economic autonomy vis-à-vis their imperial overlords. Accordingly, most Third World elites aspire to change that situation, which they see as continuing to this day, by changing the status of their countries from that of mere "objects" of international relations to one in which they can be recognized as "subjects" as well. Their quest for autonomy, manifested in various ways, is based on the fundamental assumption that the unequal terms of interaction between the developed and the developing countries need to undergo drastic revision. . . .

Paradoxically, this feeling of deprivation is augmented by two contradictory tendencies in the international system as it is currently organized on the basis of strategic bipolarity and nuclear deterrence. First, the current stratification within the international system between the "developed" and the "developing" worlds allows for the exportation of the developed world's conflicts, in which the two superpowers play the role of the chief protagonists, to the Third World. Second, despite such exportation, the same stratification in the global hierarchy by and large effectively insulates the "core" of the international system, the two superpowers and their respective alliance systems in the industrial heartland of the globe, from the conflicts and instabilities prevalent in the Third World—thereby, drastically curtailing the impact of the Third World's security concerns on the international system's security agenda. As a result, Third World states get the worst of both worlds. They are unable, on the one hand, to prevent the penetration of their polities and regions by superpower rivalries and conflicts. They are equally incapable of affecting, except marginally and in selected cases, the global political and military equation between the two superpowers and their respective alliances.

This dual impotence reinforces the feeling among many Third World intellectual and political elites that there are in fact, if not in law, two types of actors in the international system: the primary actors, the superpowers and their European allies plus Japan, and the secondary actors, comprising the Third World of Asia, Africa, and Latin America in almost its entirety, with the striking exception of China (which has been able to break the power barrier between the two sets of actors by achieving nuclear-weapons capability). However, in light of China's own domestic economic and political contradictions, even Beijing's membership in the category of primary international actors appears rather tenuous. It would seem to be based largely on the sufferance of the two superpowers and on their calculations of China's importance in their respective global strategies, primarily aimed against each other.

Nonetheless, the additional respect and privileges accorded to China by the international establishment following the demonstration of its nuclear-weapons capability drove home the lesson to Third World ruling elite, especially those of the larger and regionally powerful states, that there is a positive correlation between the acquisition of nuclear weapons and a country's international status. This conclusion was strengthened by the fact that China's enhanced standing in the international system, which depended principally on superpower perceptions of Beijing's role in global affairs, was not affected adversely even by the turmoil China underwent during the decade of the Cultural Revolution, which followed close on the heels of its first nuclear explosion in 1964.

This perception on the part of leaders of Third World states had much to do with their ambivalence toward, and in some cases outright opposition to, the Nuclear Non-Proliferation Treaty (NPT), which was opened for signature in 1968 and came into force in March 1970. In the light of the Chinese experience, no Third World leadership aspiring to graduate to the status of a primary actor in the international system could feel comfortable about giving up its nuclear option. The successful exercise of that option seemed to have become the standard by which the status of international actors was judged.

The controversy surrounding the NPT helped to highlight both the resentment of leading Third World states toward what was considered a modern version of an unequal treaty, and the concrete state-security interests of some major Third World actors like India, Pakistan, Argentina, and Brazil that effectively precluded their accession to the treaty. The controversy demonstrated that specific security interests could on occasion coincide with broader considerations of justice within the international system in the foreign policies of at least some Third World states.

The concept of "nonalignment" in general and the membership of the Non-Aligned Movement (NAM) in particular also serve to reconcile particular state interests of Third World countries with the general political and economic interests of the weak, intruder elements of the international system in a strategically bipolar and economically stratified world. For the major Third World founders of NAM—India, Indonesia, and Egypt, who were also the preeminent powers in their respective regions—nonalignment was a means of minimizing, if not totally excluding, political and military intervention by the Great Powers and their involvement in regional affairs. But even smaller and weaker powers, who needed Great Power patrons partly to resist the hegemonic tendencies of the "regional influentials," subscribed to the philosophy of nonalignment and competed with each other in gaining membership in NAM.... Despite the reservations that many members of NAM continue to have about the movement, they value membership in the movement and swear allegiance to the principle if not the practice of nonalignment....

As a result of [a] broad interpretation of nonalignment, many members of NAM have been able to retain the privileges of membership while maintaining security links with one or the other superpower. Although this has no doubt given rise to tensions within the movement (most clearly witnessed at the Havana Summit of 1979 when Cuba unsuccessfully tried to sell the thesis that the Soviet Union was NAM's "natural ally"), the vast majority of the movement's membership obviously feels that the benefits from continued membership outweigh the negative effects of tensions and bickerings within NAM.

These benefits lie not merely in collective economic bargaining with the developed countries. To be sure, economic issues have become an increasingly important part of the NAM agenda since the mid-1970s. But since the Third World's economic grievances and demands also can be aired in other forums—for example, meetings of the Group of 77, UNCTAD, and Special Sessions of the UN General Assembly—they do not provide the fundamental rationale for the existence, indeed the popularity, of NAM. The main reasons for NAM's existence and expansion are political and are closely related to the Third World's quest for independence from the dominant global powers.

Interestingly, membership in NAM provides even the most aligned of the nonaligned countries a modest amount of freedom of maneuver in their relationship with the major powers. In many cases, it helps the bilaterally aligned Third World states resist pressures from their superpower patrons for closer alignment of their policies with those of either Moscow or Washington and increase their own leverage with the superpowers. For example, even at the height of the conflict in the Persian Gulf, Saudi Arabia and Kuwait were able to resist pressure from the United States for base facilities or at least for more visible alignment with Washington by citing, among other things, their commitment to a nonaligned foreign policy....

In short, the contradictions perceived in the foreign policies of certain NAM members between their commitment to nonalignment and their actual alignment with one of the superpowers reflects the dual pulls of state and regime security on the one hand and, on the other hand, the inherent desire of most Third World elites to retain as much flexibility and maneuverability as possible in the international arena so as not to irredeemably compromise their newly acquired status as full members of the system for sovereign states. Membership in NAM helps even those countries most vulnerable to superpower pressure reduce the intensity of such pressure if not neutralize it totally.

The discussion so far makes it clear that the states of the Third World are subject to these diverse pulls and pressures not only in the context of their membership in NAM but also as a part of the entire process of their interaction with the international system. These pressures emanate partly from their attempt, as new entrants into the system of states, individually to act *as states* within that system. In the process they have to emulate the behavior of the established members of the international system and internalize their value system. This process is made difficult but not impossible by the fact that many new Third World entrants, unlike their established and industrialized counterparts, have not yet acquired unconditional legitimacy in the eyes of their own citizens either for their state-structures or the regimes that preside over these state-structures. This is partly because the citizenry has not yet learned to identify with these new structures and partly the result of the narrow social and political bases of most Third World regimes.

A different set of pressures operate on Third World regimes in their role as part of the collectivity which can only be defined as the intruder element in the system of states. Given the historical baggage of colonization and discrimination inflicted on them, they collectively operate from a position of inferiority vis-à-vis the established states, whether measured in terms of economic, military, or technological capabilities. . . . To correct at least some of these imbalances and to protect themselves from the deleterious effects of the inequality of power and influence, these states are forced to act within the system as some sort of opposition (however loose and ill-organized) to the international political, technological, and economic establishments. Since Third World states now happen to hold a numerical majority in the system of states, the noise they can create globally is considerable. However, their actual power to influence events, while it may not be negligible, is certainly dramatically inferior to their level of visibility and audibility inside and outside international forums.

Security: Primary Concern and Overarching Concept

These two types of pressures can and do often pull Third World governments in different directions. This, in turn, permits their policies to be portrayed by an image of role-confusion, especially when their rhetoric points in one direction and their actions point in quite another. But this confusion should not be considered unique to Third World states or a permanent component of their international diplomacy. With the passage of time they are likely to become more adept at reconciling their individual interests with their collective goals as members of the Third World.

However, if a fundamental conflict of interest arises between the two sets of objectives, the decision makers in Third World states are unlikely to hesitate in favoring their state and regime interests over the more diffuse and general interests of the collectivity known as the Third World. This is the logic that the state-centric nature of the international system demands of them. Those who fail to respond to that

logic will find their capacity to act as full members of the system irreparably damaged. But, in the absence of such fundamental conflicts of interest over many issues likely to dominate the global agenda during the next decade and beyond (e.g., those relating to global resource reallocation, residual decolonization, transfer of technology, etc.), most Third World states reasonably can be expected to continue to espouse both sets of objectives. They would do so because, in the final analysis, both enhance their capacity to act as rightful members of the system of states. Therefore, the present phase of adjustment to the international system, which includes the reconciliation of their membership in the system as states with their collective grievances against the international establishment, is for most Third World states analogous to the growing pains of adolescence rather than to the schizophrenia of the demented.

Moreover, even the second set of pressures on Third World decision makers, which emanates from the collective position of these states as the intruder element into the system of states, has a major security dimension built into it. This proposition may not be evident on cursory examination. It is based on the recognition that issues of *status* and of *security* cannot be treated in mutual isolation, particularly when discussing perceptions of Third World ruling elites. Elite perceptions and, even more, the perceptions of their domestic constituencies of the way their states relate to the international system, especially to the major centers of global power, are largely colored by the experience of colonialism that these societies have undergone. Even the second or third generation of leaders of postcolonial societies, some of them avowedly technocratic, share much of this historical baggage. Given the prevailing inequality of power within the international system that is heavily weighted in favor of Europe and its cultural and racial offshoots, issues of status in the perception of Third World elites easily turn into issues of security as a result of their memories of European domination. The perceived security if not the survival of these states largely hinges on the terms on which they interact with the dominant powers of the global "North." Thus, even the most technical aspects of the Third World negotiating agenda on North–South issues, whether they relate to the "New International Information Order" or the "New International Economic Order," are in essence issues of both security and status as far as these elites and their domestic constituencies are concerned.

This does not mean, however, that a situation of unmitigated confrontation exists or is likely to exist in the future between the Third World and the more established members of the system of states. . . .

[Such a] view grossly distorts reality by viewing the Third World's participation in the international system as nothing short of disaster and by hypothesizing a permanent and pervasive contradiction between the new entrants into the system and its established (Euro-American) membership. While a certain degree of tension between new entrants and established members is to be expected in any institution, elevating this tension to the level of an irreconcilable contradiction takes this logic to its absurd limits, . . . [especially] when the new entrants to the international system are trying desperately to mold themselves in the fashion of the established members by accepting and internalizing the fundamental state-centric values on which the system is based, those of sovereignty, nonintervention, hierarchy, and the balance of power.

Furthermore, as has been argued earlier, the security and developmental concerns of individual Third World states make most if not all of them dependent to varying degrees on the superpowers and their allies for arms, political support, capital, and technology. These ties are in most cases strong enough to neutralize, for all practical purposes save occasional rhetoric, the confrontational tendencies of Third World ruling elites. Moreover, many analysts, especially in the West, do not realize that the distinction between the Third World states' foreign policy concerns as individual members of the international system and their collective concerns about improving their position within that system is more apparent than real. The two sets of concerns, as has been argued earlier, are in essence the two sides of the same security coin for these new members of the system of states. They may find different manifestations at different times and in connection with different issues, but they result from the same preoccupation, if not obsession, with the overriding concerns of state and regime security on the part of Third World ruling elites.

Therefore, any paradigm with sufficient power to explain the behavior of Third World states in the international system will have to be built around an expanded concept of security, encompassing internal as well as external security, regime as well as state security, and economic as well as military security. Given the pervasiveness of insecurity in the Third World, in itself a function of the recent collective experience of full membership in the modern system of states, considerations of security in one way or another will continue to determine the Third World states' interaction with the international system. A clear understanding of this point could prove to be the beginning of wisdom for analysts interested in finding common threads in the Third World states' behavior in the international arena.

Study Questions

1. Provide examples of East–West tension, North–South tension, and South–South tension.
2. What indicators or measures can be used to illustrate disparity of development among nations? How can one distinguish, for instance, between a developed and a lesser developed country?
3. What are some of the potential negative effects of large and continuing disparities of development between states?
4. When people talk about the population bomb, what are they referring to?
5. Is there any connection between population growth rates and the economic development of countries?
6. In your view, which school of thought—Marxist, conventional, or reformist—best addresses how countries can overcome poverty? Why?
7. Discuss the utility of each of the following strategies as a means by which developing countries could attract resources and overcome poverty: autarky, the New International Economic Order, blackmail, cartels, regional trade organizations, liberal aid, trade, and foreign investment.
8. What is the "paradox" of arms races?
9. Discuss the differences between arms control and disarmament.
10. In your judgment, do arms races cause conflict?
11. What is meant by the following terms: *flexible response, massive retaliation,* and *nuclear brinkmanship*?

12. Define the term *MAD*.
13. Discuss the logic of mutual deterrence.
14. Why was the limitation of antiballistic missile forces considered essential to effective mutual deterrence in the early 1970s?
15. How does the Strategic Defense Initiative change the logic of mutual deterrence and the previous attitude about limiting ABM defenses?
16. Describe the link between the global arms race and disparity of development. Do high military expenditures in and of themselves lead to deterioration of basic human needs and economic development? Explain.
17. What does Mohammed Ayoob mean by the "dual role" of Third World states?
18. Why do most Third World governments place a greater emphasis on security than development?
19. Why do Third World states resent the implications of the Non-Proliferation Treaty?

Key Terms

arms control

arms freeze

arms reduction

disarmament

first-strike attack

flexible response

hotspots

intermediate-range nuclear force (INF)

intifada

massive retaliation

mutual assured destruction

mutual deterrence

nuclear brinkmanship

nuclear proliferation

on-site inspection

second-strike attack

Strategic Defense Initiative (SDI)

triad

Notes

1. On recent U.S. problems with ANZUS, see Andrew Mack, "Crisis in the Other Alliances: ANZUS in the 1980s," *World Policy Journal* 3, no. 3 (Summer 1986): 447–472.
2. See Bijan Mossavar-Rahmani, "OPEC and NOPEC: Oil in South–South Relations," *Journal of International Affairs* 34, no. 1 (Spring–Summer 1980): 41–58.
3. U.S. Committee for Refugees, *World Refugee Survey: 1989 In Review* (New York: American Council for Nationalities Service, 1989).
4. See *The Middle East and North Africa* annual editions (London: Europa Publications, Ltd.) for extensive treatments of each of the countries in this region. On the foreign policy of the area, see George Lenczowski, *The Middle East in World Affairs,* 4th ed. (Ithaca: Cornell University Press, 1980).
5. For annually updated treatments of the Palestinian Liberation Organization, see *Middle East Contemporary Survey,* annual ed. (Tel Aviv: Tel Aviv University).
6. World Bank, *World Development Report* (Washington, D.C.: World Bank, 1986), pp. 175–179.
7. For data on infant mortality rates, see Ruth Leger Sivard, *World Military and Social Expenditures* (Washington, D.C.: World Priorities, 1985), pp. 38–43.

8. Michael Teitelbaum, "Right vs. Right: Immigration and Refugee Policy in the United States," *Foreign Affairs* 59, no. 1 (Fall 1980): 21–59.

9. See Robert MacNamara, "Time Bomb or Myth: The Population Problem," *Foreign Affairs* 62, no. 5 (Summer 1984): 1107–1131.

10. For a discussion about the connection between development and population, see Lester Brown, ed., *The State of the World, 1985* (New York: Norton, 1985), pp. 200–203. See also Parker Marden, Dennis Hodgson, and Terry McCoy, *Population in the Global Arena* (New York: Holt, Rinehart & Winston, 1982): pp. 9–16.

11. Brown, *The State of the World, 1985,* pp. 205–208.

12. Robert Rothstein, "Dealing with Disequilibrium: Rising Pressures and Diminishing Resources in Third World Nation-States," *International Journal* 39 (Summer 1984): 551–576.

13. These views are expressed in an extensive body of literature that is often referred to as the dependency school of thought. See Andre Gunder Frank, *Capitalism and Underdevelopment in Latin America,* rev. ed. (New York: Monthly Review Press, 1969); Emmanuel Arghiri, *Unequal Exchange: A Study of the Imperialism of Trade* (New York: Monthly Review Press, 1972); and Celso Furtado, *Economic Development in Latin America* (London: Cambridge University Press, 1970), to name a few classic examples. For a more recent collection of differing views, see Mitchell Seligson, *The Gap Between Rich and Poor: Contending Perspectives on the Political Economy of Development* (Boulder: Westview, 1984).

14. Representative of this viewpoint are Richard Gardner and Max Millikan, eds., *The Global Partnership: International Agencies and Economic Development* (New York: Praeger, 1968); and Lester Pearson, *Partners in Development: Report of the Commission on International Development* (New York: Praeger, 1969). A more recent treatment on the evolution in Western perspectives on development is Prate Cranford, "From Pearson to Brandt: Evolving Perceptions Concerning International Development," *International Journal* 35, no. 4 (1980): 623–646.

15. A number of works sympathetic to the reformist perspective appeared during the late 1970s and early 1980s. See, for instance, Roger Hansen, *Beyond the North–South Stalemate* (New York: McGraw-Hill, 1979). See also James O'Leary, "Toward a Northern Response to the South," *Orbis* 26, no. 2 (1982): 431–451.

16. See, for instance, Robert Tucker, *The Inequality of Nations* (New York: Basic Books, 1977). Tucker would support extension of tariff preferences to developing nations but oppose indexation, which, he believes, would institutionalize inflation. See pp. 182–183.

17. Robert Heilbroner, *An Inquiry into the Human Prospect,* (New York: Norton, 1974), p. 43.

18. See, for instance, Samuel Huntington, "Arms Races: Prerequisites and Results," in *The Use of Force,* eds. Robert Art and Kenneth Waltz (Boston: Little, Brown, 1971), pp. 365–401. Huntington argues that arms races may lead to wars or serve as a substitute for war, depending on whether power relationships between the countries engaged in the arms race are roughly different or equal.

19. A classic on arms control and disarmament is Hedley Bull, *The Control of the Arms Race* (New York: Praeger, 1965).

20. For an extensive collection of arms agreements, with commentary, see Jozef Glodblat, *Arms Control Agreements: A Handbook* (New York: Praeger for the Stockholm International Peace Research Institute, 1983).

21. See Sivard, *World Military and Social Expenditures,* p. 50.

22. Henry Kissinger, *Nuclear Weapons and Foreign Policy* (New York: Harper & Brothers, 1957).

23. For a discussion of short-range (tactical) weapons and their relationship to intermediate nuclear weapons, see Thomas Hirschorn, "Tactical Nuclear Weapons in Europe," *Washington Quarterly,* Winter 1987, pp. 101–121.

24. For a compilation of recent articles on SDI, see Franklin Long, Donald Hafner, and Jeffrey Boutwell, *Weapons in Space* (New York: Norton, 1986). Several articles appeared in the *Journal of International Affairs* 39, no. 1 (Summer 1985).

25. This dialogue is adapted from Plutarch, *The Lives of the Noble Grecians and Romans* (New York: Modern Library, n.d.), pp. 476–477.

26. UN Department of Economics and Social Affairs, *Disarmament and Development* (New York: United Nations, 1972).

27. About $940 billion were estimated to have been spent on arms in 1985, according to the U.S. Arms Control and Disarmament Agency (ACDA), *World Military Expenditures and Arms Transfers, 1985* (Washington, D.C.: ACDA, 1985), p. 3. This breaks down to about $1.8 million per minute in arms expenditures around the globe.

28. For specifics on Ethiopia, see *Africa South of the Sahara 1986,* 15th ed. (London: Europa Publications, 1985), p. 419. Using another measure, Ethiopia invests 11 percent of its entire GNP on military expenditures. Nicaragua spends over 10 percent on similar expenditures.

29. On the role of the military as a positive inducement to political development, see Samuel Huntington, *Political Order in Changing Societies* (New Haven: Yale University Press, 1968); and Morris Janowitz, *The Military in the Political Development of New States* (Chicago: University of Chicago Press, 1964).

30. See William Dixon and Bruce Moon, "The Military Burden and Basic Human Needs," *Journal of Conflict Resolution* 30, no. 4 (December 1986): 660–684.

31. Ibid., p. 666.

32. Additional research on the impact of military expenditures reaches mixed conclusions. One study found that, in general, military expenditures have a negative impact on economic growth and development. See Saadet Deger and Ron Smith, "Military Expenditures and Growth in Less Developed Countries," *Journal of Conflict Resolution* 27, no. 2 (June 1983): 335–353. Another study found that military spending contributes to economic growth in states with unconstrained access to credit. On the other hand, military spending has no discernible negative or positive impact in countries with very poor credit. See Robert E. Looney and P. C. Frederiksen, "Defense Expenditures, External Public Debt and Growth in Developing Countries," *Journal of Peace Research* 23, no. 4 (1986): 329–337.

33. U.S. Arms Control and Disarmament Agency, *World Military Expenditures and Arms Transfers,* pp. 7–8.

Thirteen

![black square icon]

Issues of Potential Cooperation: Humanitarian Policy, the Global Environment, and Regional Integration

As we noted in chapter 12, there is a fine line between cooperation and conflict in international relations. We focused on two key issues of potential conflict: disparity of development between rich and poor countries and the global arms race. Although each of these problems could eventually lead to significant conflict in international relations, they could also be accommodated through negotiations. Potential conflicts such as these often result in a degree of cooperation. In this chapter we will focus on several issues that call for considerable international cooperation. Indeed, in each case a fair degree of cooperation has already been demonstrated, although the potential for deterioration into conflict remains. The issues of potential cooperation that we will examine in this chapter include (1) humanitarian cooperation on behalf of refugees, (2) various global environmental problems (ozone depletion, acid rain, depletion of the forests), and (3) economic integration among various countries. Before considering these issues, however, we need to explore the role of cooperation in international relations.

Cooperation in International Relations

Tools of Cooperation

Although students of international relations have focused much of their attention on conflicts among nations, history demonstrates that cooperation among nations is equally common, if not more so. We have already examined several manifestations of international cooperation in previous chapters. International law, international organizations, economic intercourse, and diplomacy are four primary methods by which states seek to coordinate their affairs constructively. States have used these tools of cooperation to promote order and facilitate their political and economic interrelations. Nations have resorted to conflict as well, but unceasing conflict is disruptive and counterproductive to long-term interests. Hence, governments usually find it in their interests to control conflict and promote a fair degree of cooperation. Order and stability are preconditions for growth and prosperity in both domestic and international politics. However, the job of maintaining order in the international arena is more difficult because there are no widely recognized and effective central mechanisms for legislation, execution, and adjudication of rules of behavior. Instead a premium is placed on the ability of some 160 or more sovereign and independent entities to coordinate their affairs.

Motives for Cooperation

Enlightened self-interest   States have numerous motives for cooperation. Two of the most prevalent motives are enlightened self-interest and expedience. If a country's political and economic interests can be met by cooperating with other nations, it has little incentive to threaten conflict to achieve the same ends. Persuasion and compromise often are more effective ways for a government to promote its interests. Threats may be useful on occasion, but a steady diet of threats and conflict is likely to encourage resistance from other governments that do not wish to be pushed around. Hitler managed to gain considerable concessions (including the annexation of the Sudetenland from Czechoslovakia) from European states before World War II by blandishing threats. But his invasion of Poland was the last straw that unleashed perhaps the most devastating war in history. The European powers that had first accommodated Hitler became his chief opposition. In the process Nazism in Germany was demolished. Militarism had been counterproductive for Germany and very destructive for Europe.

Maintaining peace   Indeed, wars in the last few centuries seem to spur governments to engage in closer cooperation. As we saw in chapter 9, the Napoleonic wars led to greater cooperation among European countries—a phenomenon referred to as the Concert of Europe. After World War I, the League of Nations and a host of additional international organizations sprang into being. World War II was followed by an explosion in the number of international organizations. Wars seem to jolt governments with the realization that overt conflict is destructive. Once brought back to reality, they recognize the value of cooperation, compromise, and peaceful relations. Hence, in an ironic way, one motive for cooperation is to heal the wounds caused by war. Another motive is to find ways to avoid future wars. Gauging from the fact that nations continue to resort to conflict, the latter goal has been less successful than the former. Still, with the increasing destructiveness of modern war, a stronger incentive exists today to avoid unnecessary conflict and to promote cooperative relations among nations.

Encouraging economic prosperity   Another strong inducement to cooperation has emerged with the incredible growth of international commerce. Nations' economic well-being has grown increasingly dependent on international trade, aid, and investment. This is not a recent development; its roots can be traced to the European Industrial Revolution. However, in this century, and particularly since World War II, the degree of global interdependence has clearly intensified. Conflict under these circumstances has greater consequences for nations. War runs the risk of severing trade, aid, and investment links with the rest of the world, leading potentially to significant economic dislocation.[1] Interdependence, then, would seem to provide a strong incentive for cooperation, but as we have seen, it can also be a cause of tension and conflict. Economic interdependence does not mean that countries cease trying to gain advantages over one another. The recent trade wars between the United States and Japan illustrate how greater economic interdependence can heighten tension, particularly if countries believe that their companies' products are being treated unfairly. But the fact of interdependence clearly shapes the responses of nations to their trade partners.

For example, Japan and the United States are unlikely to go to war over trade differences. Economic ties may suffer, tariffs may be imposed, trade may be adjusted, but a complete break in relations is most unlikely.

Dealing with Externalities

Countries' political and economic activities are not pursued without cost. The negative side effects of wars and domestic turmoil include the destruction of property and the generation of refugees. The negative side effects of economic activity include pollution and resource depletion. Economists often refer to these negative side effects as **externalities.** Negative externalities cannot be solved without some agreement, cooperation, and compromise within and among nations. But is coordination among nations to deal with the negative consequences of their domestic and foreign policies and activities possible? In the three major topics discussed in this chapter—humanitarian assistance (e.g., to refugees), environmental dilemmas, and economic integration—we will see that coordination of nations' behavior is possible but often difficult to achieve.

Cooperation in Pursuit of Humanitarian Goals

Refugees as an Externality

Two of the chief by-products of international and domestic conflict and turmoil are refugees and displaced persons. International and civil wars destroy homes, interrupt economic activity, and produce great insecurity for people. When large numbers of the inhabitants flee from these conditions, they present a problem for the areas into which they migrate. When they cross international boundaries as refugees, seeking protection and assistance from countries neighboring their own, they often impose a burden on the host country, particularly if it is a poor one. Under such circumstances, they become a problem for the international community as a whole. In this sense, refugees are an externality of conflict. Their predicament is often the result of domestic turmoil, persecution, and conflict. But protecting and assisting them becomes a problem for the host countries and the international community.

Even when people fail to cross an international boundary as refugees, they can present a significant problem for the international community. For example, in the Ethiopian famine of 1984–1985 a large number of Ethiopians fled into neighboring Sudan. International aid agencies assisted them as if they were refugees. However, an even larger number of Ethiopians from rebel-held areas fled from their drought- and war-ravaged homes into government-held areas of Ethiopia. Technically, these people were not refugees because they did not cross an internationally recognized boundary, but they needed food and medicine as badly as their refugee counterparts who fled into Sudan. Millions were at the brink of starvation, and hundreds of thousands eventually perished. Presented with a humanitarian disaster of the highest order, the international community responded with an outpouring of assistance. Global rock concerts were held. "We are the World" became the rallying cry as governments, the United Nations, and private agencies rushed in to save lives in Ethiopia and in other war-ravaged and drought-stricken areas of Africa.

Refugees and internally displaced persons are potent symbols of conflict. But they are equally potent symbols of cooperation. Indeed, the spirit of humanitarian concern that marks the international community's effort to assist them is one of the great stories of international cooperation.

Mechanisms for Coping with Refugees and Displaced Persons

There are about 15 million refugees, and several million displaced persons in various parts of the world today. The vast majority of these, about 90 percent, are located in the developing world. These poor countries, for the most part, are not in a position to absorb the costs of assisting large numbers of destitute people. Fortunately, there is a significant and complex network of governments and organizations that is devoted to providing assistance to the victims of war, political turmoil, and disasters.

The UN High Commissioner for Refugees (UNHCR) takes the lead in protection and assistance for refugees. The UNHCR was created in 1951 to resolve the problem of millions of post–World War II refugees in Europe. Located in Geneva, Switzerland, the UNHCR can trace its origins back to the League of Nations, which established the first international office dealing with refugees, primarily Europeans. As the European refugee situation was slowly resolved, the UNHCR found its attention turning to the developing world, where dozens of new, politically unstable states gained independence. Today, the UNHCR maintains over eighty offices around the world—the vast majority in the Third World—in an effort to monitor the global refugee situation.[2]

The UNHCR is an intergovernmental organization. Accordingly, although it is charged with the responsibility of looking out for the welfare of refugees, it must also be responsive to the governments that constitute it and that contribute to its budget. Governments are not always motivated by humanitarian instincts and so the UNHCR cannot avoid political realities. However, governments do provide the majority of funds for refugee aid. Not all governments are active donors of humanitarian assistance. The Soviet Union and most East European countries, for instance, are not members of the UNHCR and contribute nothing to its assistance programs. At the same time, nearly half of the world's refugees have fled from Soviet-backed governments. The UNHCR's major donors are the United States, the West European democracies, Canada, Japan, and Australia.

In addition to governmental financial support, there is also broad agreement on the fundamental rights of refugees, the role of the UNHCR, and the duties of governments toward refugees. Refugees, for instance, may not be sent back (repatriated) to their countries of origin against their will. The UN Convention of the Status of Refugees prohibits this practice. Not all countries are party to this treaty, but there is a general expectation, nonetheless, that countries should not involuntarily repatriate refugees. Violators of this principle run the risk of diplomatic protests from other governments that take the principle seriously, including most major donor countries. Most countries find it expedient under these circumstances to observe this refugee right.

In addition to the governments and the UNHCR, many other important actors provide humanitarian assistance to refugees, including other UN agencies (such as the World Food Program and UNICEF), the World Bank, and the World Health Organization. Perhaps even more important are the nongovernmental organizations (NGOs) such as CARE, World Vision, Africare, and Save the Children. Since the UNHCR is not actually equipped to implement assistance programs, it relies on the NGOs to do the job. Literally hundreds of these groups around the globe do the legwork for the UNHCR. They staff the medical facilities, mete out emergency food aid, transport food and medicine from the ports to the refugee-affected areas of countries, and implement small-scale self-help projects to improve living conditions in refugee settlements. Because they work so closely with refugees, the NGOs also tend to become strong advocates for the needs of refugees and an important source of information about whether the host government (and sometimes even the UNHCR) is abiding by its international responsibilities toward refugees. Although the particular interests and styles of governments, IGOs, and NGOs may vary somewhat, they do share a common sense of responsibility to meet the humanitarian needs of refugees and to search for solutions to the refugee problem.

Finding solutions for refugees calls for significant political cooperation. The international community recognizes three durable solutions to the predicament: voluntary repatriation, local settlement, and third country resettlement. **Voluntary repatriation** is considered the best solution for the refugees. Under this approach, refugees choose to return to their original country. This occurs most frequently when a solution has been found to the conflict that caused them to flee in the first place. After the Rhodesian civil war, for instance, most refugees from Zimbabwe went back home. When voluntary repatriation is not feasible, the next best solution for refugees is to seek **local settlement** in their country of first asylum. Many Angolans sought local settlement in Zambia, as did many Eritreans in Sudan. But if host governments are reluctant to accept large numbers of refugees for permanent settlement, as was the case in Southeast Asia for many of the boat people who left Vietnam in the 1970s, **third country resettlement** may be the only available humanitarian solution. Over 1.5 million Indochinese refugees have been resettled from their temporary countries of asylum in Southeast Asia, because of the reluctance of countries such as Thailand, Malaysia, and Indonesia to accept them permanently.[3] Malaysia feared that large numbers of refugees would upset its already difficult ethnic balances, whereas the other nations worried that militant refugees along their borders might cause a deterioration in relations with the neighboring states the refugees came from. In this case, Western governments interceded with the Asian countries, prevailing on them to stop sending unseaworthy boats full of refugees back out to sea, where they often sank or became easy prey for pirates. Part of the deal was that the Western governments would provide assistance and eventual resettlement for the refugees, provided these governments would accept them on a temporary basis. Despite a difficult political situation, humanitarian instincts eventually prevailed.

The ultimate solution to refugee problems is to resolve the underlying causes of conflict that give rise to their predicament in the first place. This places the situation squarely in the spotlight of international politics. Indeed, wherever there are significant international conflicts, there are refugees. The *contras* in Central America were refugees. They received U.S. assistance while the former Sandinista government they sought to overthrow received Soviet aid. Many of the 5 million Afghan refugees who fled into Iran and Pakistan continued to support the Afghan resistance against the Soviet Union. The United States also supported the Afghan resistance. Palestinian refugees promote a significant degree of the terrorism that has rocked the world in recent years. In this sense, refugees can be as much a part of the problem in resolving disputes as a part of the solution. Nevertheless, until such political disputes are resolved, there will continue to be large numbers of refugees around the world and a need to cope with the long-term effects of their presence in poor countries.

Turning for a moment from refugees to displaced persons, we find a somewhat different set of international institutions to cope with their needs. Because internally displaced persons have not crossed an international boundary, they are not refugees and the UNHCR has no mandate to assist them. Other UN agencies respond to their needs. The UN Disaster Relief Organization may become involved if people have been displaced by a natural disaster (such as drought). Other agencies, such as the World Food Program, typically provide food assistance. The UN Development Program (UNDP) may coordinate in-country assistance efforts by several other UN development and emergency agencies. When civil war is the key cause of internal population movements, the International Committee of the Red Cross will often be on the scene, making sure that food and medical aid makes it into strife-torn areas of countries.[4] As with refugee assistance, governments provide the bulk of the resources provided to displaced persons, and NGOs often serve as implementing agencies, just as they do with regard to refugee assistance.

One of the major problems in humanitarian assistance, whether it takes the form of refugee aid or emergency aid to displaced persons and victims of natural disasters, has to do with the distinction governments make between emergency aid and development assistance. Faced with a humanitarian emergency, many countries are willing to provide aid, even to a country with a hostile government. The United States, for instance, provided more than 50 percent of the emergency food aid received by Ethiopia during the 1984–1985 famine, even though Ethiopia is a close ally of the Soviet Union and hostile to U.S. interests. Despite its close ties to Ethiopia, the Soviet Union donated very small amounts of rice and some helicopters and planes to transport food. However, donor governments are often reluctant to provide aid to hostile governments that might be used for the long-term development of that country's economy. Thus, while the United States gave grain to Ethiopia, it refused to donate trucks to transport the grain, since the trucks might later be used to ferry troops or to haul economic goods. Similarly, irrigation projects and other agricultural programs are developmental in character, even though they may have the effect of preventing future emergencies. Since Ethiopia pursues socialist agricultural policies, including collectivized and state farms (forcing farmers into group cooperatives where land is farmed collectively and individual ownership of land reduced to small plots for gardens), the U.S. government was not inclined to provide any kind of agricultural aid. Saving lives during a famine is one thing, promoting socialism is another. The upshot is that, lacking long-term development assistance, Ethiopia will continue to be vulnerable to drought and famine.

The distinction between long-term development assistance and short-term emergency aid also causes problems for refugee assistance. When refugees descend in large numbers into a poor country, they can place a substantial burden on an already weak economic infrastructure, such as roads, schools, hospitals, and clinics. Humanitarian or emergency aid to the refugees may address their needs but ignore the needs of the local population, which may be in an equally bad position. Refugees compete for common property resources, such as water, fuel, wood, and land, thus putting a strain on available supply. They compete for jobs that local people might otherwise perform, thus reducing wages for some host country nationals. Many refugees settle spontaneously in their host countries, placing additional demands on health care, education, and social service facilities. These burdens cannot be addressed unless either refugee or development assistance takes into account the developmental impact of the presence of refugees. Recently, UN refugee (UNHCR) and development (UNDP) agencies have made efforts to coordinate their assistance activities so that these needs are addressed.[5]

Cooperation among states is not always easy. But the record of state behavior suggests that a good number of countries have a genuine concern about meeting humanitarian needs. These humanitarian motives are sometimes strong enough to overcome the naked political interests. One could argue, for instance, that the United States had no interest in providing aid of any sort to the Ethiopian government, and perhaps a strong interest in giving aid only to the rebel groups fighting that government. But such a policy would run counter to the basic moral precepts that most Americans share, and so the humanitarian need was addressed, however reluctantly. Similarly, when refugees flee from a strife-torn land, there is a network of international organizations, private agencies, and interested governments that will respond to the need. Politics often supercede humanitarian instincts. The existence of refugees represents a victory of politics over humanitarianism. But politics can also be put to the service of meeting humanitarian needs. The work of humanitarian agencies around the globe suggests that humanitarian goals can be, and often are, achieved.

Cooperation in Pursuit of a Healthy Environment

When looking at the earth from outer space, astronauts testify that the most striking feature is the lack of visible borders. From 26,000 miles in space, the political boundaries that separate the earth into territorial units of competing nationalities are invisible. From the vantage point of space, earth resembles a ship hurtling through the vastness of the universe. Its inhabitants, from this perspective, are fellow travelers on a magnificent life-bearing vessel.

Indeed, for centuries, the riches of this planet have supported the needs of its inhabitants. People have exploited the earth's resources—cutting down forests for farmland, building material, and fuel; mining for precious metals; hunting animal species; fishing in the rivers, lakes, and oceans. When the global population was much smaller, it was possible to do these things without straining the carrying capacity of the environment. Today, with the global population predicted to exceed 6 billion by the turn of the century, exploitation of the environment has more ominous implications. Environmentalists question how much longer industrial pollutants can be pumped into the atmosphere and the oceans. They grow increasingly concerned about whether the rapid deforestation of the globe will lead to disastrous climatic changes. They worry about the rapid depletion of the earth's resources.

Historical Behavior of States Toward the Environment

Historically, environmental issues have not been the major concern of governments. Indeed, when governments ran up against environmental limits they tended to engage in several common behaviors. Finlay and Hovet identified these as escapism behavior, denial behavior, greed behavior, and eternal optimism behavior.[6] Migration to a new land was a simple answer for a country facing overpopulation of its land; it was a means of escaping the environmental limits of a confined territory. Indeed, if uninhabited land could not be found, then occupied territory was wrested from its current inhabitants and exploited for the benefit of the new population. Colonialism is a primary example of *greed behavior.* Nations have now claimed almost the entire land surface of the globe. There are no places to escape to, and taking land by force is a dangerous business. But nations still deny the environmental limits of their immediate and the global environment. Pollution of the atmosphere, rivers, lakes, and oceans was widespread and unchallenged until recent decades. It continues still in many countries, especially in the developing world, where the costs of pollution control are a difficult burden. Overexploitation of fishing resources was treated as a territorial issue among nations, not as a biological question of preserving the capacity of fisheries to reproduce themselves. Only in this century, and primarily in the last two decades or so, have people begun to realize that there are biological and environmental limits that cannot be denied.

Still, even today, there is a large degree of optimism about the ability of our technology to avoid the limits of our environment, to forestall depletion of energy resources, to increase agricultural production, and to control pollution. Perhaps our technological virtuosity will allow us to avoid making serious changes in the way we manage the earth's resources. But we should not allow this optimism to blind us to the existence of environmental limits and the need to take reasonable steps to protect the environment. Indeed, one of the encouraging signs in recent years has been the growing willingness of countries to study and learn more about how economic and even security activities affect the environment. For instance, open-air testing of nuclear weapons has been prohibited by the Nuclear Test Ban Treaty. The use of chemical and bacteriological weapons is similarly proscribed. Countries have enacted marine pollution standards to protect their coastlines. Numerous nations are taking steps to clean up air and water pollution within their territories. Some cooperation among nations is apparent. However, to what extent is it possible to achieve global environmental protection agreements? To answer this question, it will be helpful to consider some of the problems encountered when people share certain common resources.

The Tragedy of the Commons

Do people exhibit any consistent behavior when they must manage a shared resource? Garrett Hardin has argued that they do and that the consequences can be disastrous if steps are not taken to protect common resources.[7] First of all, what is a common resource? Put simply, it is any resource that all people have equal access to and that they can use as much of as they want. Air is a common resource. We can all breathe it, and we can breathe as much of it as we want. For fishermen, the fish in an ocean or a public lake are a common resource. For ranchers, the range is a common resource. To illustrate the kind of problems people have in managing these kinds of resources, Hardin asks us to consider the example of an English village. Most traditional English villages had a commons area, or a green, that the villagers could use to graze their animals. The commons was of limited size, but each villager had access to it and could graze as many animals on it as he or she wanted. Problems began to arise as each villager calculated his or her individual economic gain as against the interests of maintaining the viability of the green as a common resource. Individual villagers knew that they could make more money by doubling the number of animals they grazed in the commons. They knew as well that if all the villagers did the same thing, the commons would be overgrazed, destroyed as a source of free food for the animals. But the loss of the commons would be a shared loss, while any gain realized by selling more fattened animals would profit specific individuals. On the other hand, each villager calculated that if he or she did not increase the herd size, others would, and he or she would be the loser. If he or she increased the herd size and others didn't, he or she stood to gain. The villagers were led by this logic to increase the size of their herds. Each villager, acting as a rational, self-interested actor, made the same decision, resulting in the ruin of the commons. Hardin refers to this process as the **tragedy of the commons.**

This is a logic that is not limited to traditional English villages. Indeed, it is a common problem in modern political systems and in the international arena.[8] Consider the problem of pollution of the air by automobiles. Assuming that government regulations do not require pollution-control equipment in cars, how many people would voluntarily pay for expensive catalytic converters that counter pollution but also reduce gas mileage? A car owner realizes that if everyone refuses to put this equipment in their cars, the air she breathes will remain polluted, and perhaps adversely affect her health and everyone else's as well. But she could end up paying for a converter and still breathe bad air if no one else puts converters in their cars. Under this circumstance, she is out several hundred dollars with no appreciable difference in air quality. Thus, there is little incentive to absorb the personal cost of cleaning up a common resource.

Similarly, countries that dump waste into the oceans recognize that if every country did the same thing, the seas could become sumps. But the cost of reducing land-based pollution that ends up in the sea or of discarding garbage on the land instead of in the ocean may be too high. Calculating that other countries will continue to dump garbage into the ocean, any country may come to the conclusion that the possible gains from not polluting the ocean are offset by the cost of finding alternatives to the pollution.

Wherever a common resource exists, the potential for its ruination by otherwise rational actors also exists. Is it possible to prevent this? The assumption we have been making is that individuals (or governments) live in a world where decisions are made by individuals or by individual governments. When we introduce the possibility of regulation through cooperative efforts of individuals or governments, a different picture emerges. To prevent the ruination of the village commons, a village council may establish regulations on how many animals a villager is allowed to graze. A city, state, or national government may require car manufacturers to include catalytic converters as standard features in all cars sold and may fine car owners who disconnect them. Governments may charge an international organization with the capacity to establish standards of pollution control to protect the oceans. In other words, the key to preventing the ruination of the environment is cooperation and mutual regulation. Regulatory bodies with the power to make decisions about how to regulate resources are necessary. These organizations can determine how to provide incentives (such as tax breaks) for conservation or protection of the environment and disincentives (penalties, such as fines) for acts that degrade the environment. Within countries, these functions are performed by local and national governments. In the international system such cooperation is considerably more difficult since governments ultimately make decisions without any higher authority to countermand them. This places an even greater premium on nations' abilities to coordinate their policies in defense of the global environment. In the balance of this section we will explore several areas in which some cooperation is manifest and others in which it is not but perhaps should be.

The Politics of Ozone

For many years scientists have been concerned about the adverse effects of chlorofluoro-carbons (CFCs) on the atmosphere's ozone layer. These CFCs are used as refrigerants in cooling systems and even as propellants in spray cans. When CFCs make their way into the upper atmosphere, they destroy ozone, a particular form of oxygen that absorbs the harmful ultraviolet rays of sunlight. Depletion of the ozone layer would allow these rays to reach earth. Some scientists have predicted that this would lead to a massive increase in the incidence of skin cancers and crop losses. In a very real sense, ozone is a global resource. Its depletion will adversely affect all nations. On the other hand, CFCs are an important economic resource that many nations, especially the least developed ones, will be reluctant to give up. A tragedy of the commons is in the making unless countries can agree to cooperate.

Efforts to reduce the harmful effect of CFCs on ozone first began in the United States and Canada. In 1978 both countries banned the use of CFCs as propellants in aerosol-spray cans. But CFCs continued to be used in the U.S. and Canada and most other countries for a wider range of applications. For some time the U.S. government has urged other governments to deal with the growing evidence of the harmful effects of CFCs on the ozone layer. Scientific investigations at the South Pole have indicated that a massive hole has already appeared in the ozone layer, although the exact cause is not known. Nevertheless, this finding added to fears that a depletion of the ozone layer was already well underway. In the midst of these growing concerns, several countries began to lay the groundwork for a Protection of the Ozone Treaty limiting CFCs. In 1987 a meeting to strengthen this treaty was held under the sponsorship of the UN Environmental Program at Geneva, Switzerland. Thirty-one countries attended the meeting, and twenty-four eventually signed the resulting treaty known as the Montreal Protocol, which reflected a growing consensus that depletion of the ozone layer was a real problem, but that industries would need some time to find alternatives to CFCs. Representatives of the participating governments agreed to freeze production of CFCs at 1986 levels beginning in 1990, followed by further reductions in production and consumption of CFCs by 1992. The U.S. government had hoped to achieve a more sweeping reduction of CFC production but faced strong opposition from domestic industries and reluctance by many other countries to move any faster. American wishes were fulfilled, however, within a short time. In May 1989 the sense of urgency about ozone depletion convinced one-hundred governments meeting at Helsinki, Finland, to strengthen the Montreal Protocol by calling for a total phase-out of CFCs by the year 2000. More recently, Western governments agreed to set up an ozone fund to help LDCs shift from CFCs to more expensive ozone-friendly refrigerants. Environmentalists view these agreements as significant steps in the right direction.[9] They illustrate that cooperation among nations to preserve our common environment is difficult but well within the capability of states.

The Politics of Acid Rain

The problem of acid rain is slightly different from that of ozone. What is acid rain? Pollution from heavy industry, especially from the smelting of metallic ores, combined with pollutants from the combustion of fossil fuels, leads to high levels of sulfur dioxide and nitrogen oxides. Entering the atmosphere, these compounds are chemically transformed into acids that fall to the earth in various forms of precipitation, such as rain and snow.[10] As acid levels in the soil and water increase, forests begin to die and fish perish. Realizing that concentrated pollution is a health hazard, many smelting operations have built very tall smokestacks, thus distributing pollutants over a much wider area. These compounds drift into the upper winds, and are often deposited in other countries. What might have been a domestic pollution problem becomes an international one. Indeed, when industries in the American Midwest and Northeast or in the Ruhr Valley of Germany spew pollution into the atmosphere, the effects are felt most acutely in Canada and the Scandinavian countries, respectively, where thousands of lakes no longer support fish and where the forests are slowly dying. Needless to say, these countries resent the damage to their environment and economy that results from acid rain, and they have not stood still. Canada, for instance, has demanded that the United States place restrictions on industries contributing to sulfur dioxide emissions. Acid rain was a key agendum item at the summit between Prime Minister Mulroney of Canada and President Reagan in 1987.

Unlike the ozone problem, fingers can be pointed much more directly to particular sources of acid rain. Bilateral relations between the polluting country and the victim can be strained. But the need for cooperative solutions to the situation has led them into dialogue and discussion on the issue. Indeed, forest damage is so well documented in many European countries that even the nations primarily responsible for sulfur emissions are beginning to recognize the potential environmental and economic consequences. The biggest polluters in Western Europe have been the United Kingdom and West Germany, and they have fought stricter pollution control regulations. But the West Germans have grown increasingly alarmed at the extent of their own forest damage and have shown some support for Scandinavian proposals to limit sulfur emissions in the future.[11] To complicate matters, most countries both export and import pollution. Some countries export a lot of pollution and import only a little. The United Kingdom is one example. On the other hand, other nations do very little polluting but receive a lot of emissions from other countries. Finland, Norway, and Sweden fit into this category. Pollution recognizes no borders. As a result, acid rain and other manifestations of pollution are now on negotiating tables around the world as countries try to hammer out acceptable compromises to prevent environmental catastrophes and protect economic interests.

Deforestation

Deforestation has a number of direct causes. Population increases, for instance, create pressure for more food production, industrialization, and urbanization. Trees are cut down to make way for expanding cities and farmlands. Pollution, soil degradation, cattle grazing, and demands for fuel and building materials cause further deforestation. According to some experts, these pressures may lead to "irreversible degradation" of forest land.[12] Deforestation has occurred throughout the world, but it is happening most rapidly today in the developing countries, where population pressures are greatest. Each country has a right to exploit its resources as it sees fit. However, the forests play a significant role in the global climate. Too much deforestation will lead to expanding deserts, less cultivable land, changing rainfall patterns, and increased global temperatures. Forests' photosynthetic processes produce a substantial amount of the oxygen in the atmosphere. As forests are depleted, levels of carbon dioxide will increase. Incidentally, the burning of fossil fuels, such as oil and coal, is thought to contribute significantly to the same effect. Higher levels of carbon dioxide in the atmosphere, it has been argued, will lead to a gradual global warming trend since carbon dioxide intercepts and reflects back to earth some of the heat normally radiated into space. This so-called greenhouse effect could lead to an expansion of the oceans, by retaining heat and melting the polar ice caps, thus threatening coastal areas around the world.[13] Indeed, some scientists have measured significant global warming trends already and predict that very substantial heating will occur within the next fifteen years. Apart from the environmental consequences of deforestation, the exhaustion of wood resources would lead to considerable economic dislocations and significant hardship, not to mention the loss of one of the world's natural wonders and sources of recreation.

It would seem, then, that countries would have an incentive to protect forest resources. Indeed many countries have undertaken programs of reforestation and conservation to regenerate and protect forest lands. But the most rapid deforestation today is taking place in the developing world, in West Africa, Brazil, and Indonesia. Poor countries rarely can afford reforestation, and conservation is difficult given the pressures to clear land for cultivation, to provide for fuel needs, and so on. Ironically, poor countries may be sacrificing their future well-being to avoid immediate economic hardship. Forest policies are made at the national level, despite the fact that there are broader environmental consequences. In 1977 the United Nations sponsored a conference on desertification, which concluded that reforestation must become a matter of high priority for the international community as a whole. But many governments are cutting trees at a much faster pace than they are planting them. This trend, many believe, must be reversed or significant environmental degradation will result.

Economic Dimensions of Ecological Policy

We have argued that the pursuit of economic interest by individuals and countries creates negative side effects or externalities, not the least of which are considerable environmental dilemmas. We have also argued that the negative side effects of economic activity have an economic cost of their own. When these costs become too great, pressure eventually grows to regulate the economic activities responsible. At the international level, this is possible only through cooperative measures. In recent years, environmental issues have risen on the list of important policy concerns among nations. There is a wider awareness that industrial activities in one country may have harmful environmental impacts in another. Only recently have governments paid much attention to the degradation of their own environments. So the fact that the environment is the subject of debate and negotiation among nations is an encouraging sign.

The increasing salience of the ecological issues, however, is largely attributable to the fact that industrially developed countries have actually encountered the economic consequences of uncontrolled pollution and potential depletion of resources. Typically, the industrial nations are now pressing for greater global attention to the consequences of industrial growth. On the other hand, the poor countries are suspicious. They are in the early stages of industrial development and resent the argument of the wealthier states—most of which polluted their way to industrial status—that developing countries should pay the additional costs of limiting industrial pollution. From the poor country's viewpoint, they are being asked to undertake economic sacrifices that the industrialized countries did not make, and this represents a veiled attempt to forestall their development and keep them poor. They will be most reluctant to take the brunt of the costs associated with cleaning up their industries. Ultimately, preserving the global ecology will require bargaining and compromise by all countries. Governments have demonstrated a capacity to negotiate on these topics, but the degree of progress has been very small. Thus the environment still holds promise as a prime area in which states could promote cooperative relations. Agreements will not be achieved easily, since nations' specific economic interests vary with each environment issue. But in a very real sense, it is in every state's interest to preserve the integrity of global ecology as a whole. To pursue any other course but cooperation is to invite disaster for all.

Malthusian Dilemmas

In the late 1700s and early 1800s Thomas Malthus, an English economist, predicted that the world's population growth would outpace food supply, leading to mass starvation, disease, and death.[14] To prevent this, he argued, population growth must be controlled. His prediction about the inability of the food supply to keep pace with population growth thankfully has proved inaccurate to date. Modern-day Malthusians, however, are growing increasingly concerned about whether the limits of the earth's carrying capacity are being strained. To what extent can the earth support continued rapid population and industrial growth?

In the early 1970s a nongovernmental group of experts, called the **Club of Rome,** conducted computer modeling of numerous factors related to industrial and population growth. This study, known as the *Limits to Growth,* concluded that continued rapid population and industrial growth would eventually lead to resource depletion, high levels of pollution, and degradation of farmland.[15] In turn, these events would lead to environmental stress and collapse, decreases in food production, a collapse of industrial production, and widespread starvation and death. Even under optimistic assumptions, this study held that unless population and industrial growth were checked by the early 1980s these outcomes would be inevitable.[16] In later studies the sense of urgency was toned down and greater emphasis placed on the need to create international institutions to accommodate ecological and economic interests—institutions that were seen as crucial to a healthy future for the planet.[17]

These and similar studies have resulted in a growing awareness of the perils of unchecked and uncoordinated industrial development. In addition, in a growing number of international and regional conferences governments have addressed these daunting problems of population, food, the environment, human settlements, and desertification. Most of the conferences listed in table 13.1 were attended by more than one hundred nations. They were truly global in scope, and they are evidence that governments recognize that they live in a global commons. The interests and the views expressed by governments at these conferences have varied. Indeed, in most cases a global consensus on the causes and solutions to these problems does not exist. Countries are still in the early stages of grappling with the implications of life in a global commons and of realizing that some degree of cooperation will be essential to long-term survival.

Economic Integration and International Cooperation

Perhaps the most intense form of international cooperation occurs when countries seek to integrate their economies. Indeed, successful economic integration among countries usually occurs where there has already been significant economic cooperation over a period of time.

Table 13.1
Important international conferences

Conference	Site	Year
UN Conference on the Human Environment	Stockholm, Sweden	1972
UN Conference on the Law of the Sea	Caracas, Venezuela; New York; and Geneva, Switzerland	1973–1982
World Population Conference	Bucharest, Hungary	1974
World Food Conference	Rome, Italy	1974
Conference on International Economic Cooperation	Paris, France	1975
UN Conference on Human Settlements	Vancouver, British Columbia, Canada	1976
UN Water Conference	Mar del Plata, Argentina	1977
UN Conference on Desertification	Nairobi, Kenya	1977
Conference on Technical Cooperation Among Developing Nations	Buenos Aires, Argentina	1978
Conference on Agrarian Reform and Rural Development	Rome, Italy	1979
UN Conference on Science and Technology for Development	Vienna, Austria	1979
UN Conference on New and Renewable Sources of Energy	Nairobi, Kenya	1981

Economic cooperation might take the form of trade agreements, monetary cooperation, or mutual investment activities. Once economies become closely tied to one another through either informal or formal economic relations, they become potential candidates for economic integration and possibly even political integration. Whether economic integration occurs depends on a number of factors. For instance, Japan and the United States share significant trade ties, important monetary relations, and mutual investment activities. But the two countries are unlikely to become a single economic unit. The cultural differences, the significant geographic distances, and the considerable differences in domestic economic practices that separate them do not augur well for the creation of a single U.S.–Japanese economic system. On the other hand, the members of the European Community (Common Market) have gone a long way toward integration of their economies. They have eradicated tariffs among themselves, established common external tariffs, developed a common agricultural policy, harmonized their monetary relations, and opened borders to the free flow of labor and capital among EC members. The European countries involved in this enterprise shared a common historical tradition, strong trade ties, geographical proximity, similar democratic political institutions, and a desire to gain from the common benefits of freer trade and economic activity. Moreover, after reeling from the effects of two devastating world wars, European nations were eager to take steps in the economic sphere that might lead to political cooperation and avoidance of future wars.

Sectors of Integration

In chapter 9 we defined integration as a process by which separate countries establish common, unified mechanisms and institutions that have the authority to perform political or economic functions that were once exclusively performed by national governments. Normally, economic cooperation exists before countries even begin to develop common trade policies, common markets, and so on. Similarly, economic integration normally precedes political integration. Political integration, as distinct from economic integration, implies that governments have ceased to exist as separate, independent, and sovereign entities and have ceded sovereignty to a new and common central authority that makes policy for them.

Governments perform a number of political and economic functions that could be subject to potential integration. Foreign affairs, including military security policy, diplomatic relations, and foreign commercial activity, constitute one major area for potential integration. Domestic political activities, such as the maintenance of domestic order, political participation, and civil rights, are key functions of a sovereign state. Full political integration of previously sovereign governments would imply that these areas would come under the jurisdiction of the new central government. Economic and quasieconomic activities that could eventually be subject to integration among nations, without implying full political integration, include social welfare policy, promotion of education, budgetary policy, fiscal policy, agricultural protection, economic development and planning, natural resource policy, transportation policy, media regulation, monetary policy, balance-of-payments policy, antitrust policy, and labor–management relations.[18] Of course, substantial cooperation in these economic areas may eventually require states to engage in significant political coordination as well.

Political integration may take either a confederal, federal, or unitary form. In the *confederal union,* the weakest form, countries coordinate their external affairs (foreign policies) and certain aspects of their economies. But a confederal government's decisions do not apply directly to individuals, and the constituent governments can nullify central government enactments. In a *federal union* the constituent governments and individuals are bound by enactments of the central government. Interstate trade and commerce, fiscal and monetary policy, and foreign policy are regulated or made by the central government. The constituent governments may have certain reserved powers and authorities and separate legislative capacities. In a *unitary* union, the constituent governments cease to exist as separate legislative units and become mere extensions of the central government apparatus. Throughout history there are numerous examples of countries that entered into confederal relations with others, but few examples of federal unions formed from previous independent entities. The United States and Switzerland are the two most prominent examples of federal unions formed by free decision. There are no existing unitary unions of formerly independent countries today, although many countries have a unitary form of domestic administration.

We have identified a range of activities and functions that could be subject to integrated policies by governments. The degree to which integration occurs may vary considerably. At one end of the spectrum is the mere recognition by governments that they share a mutual problem, such as ocean pollution, which they study jointly with a view toward coordinating their separate national policies. At the other end of the spectrum are those rare cases where the states create common institutions to administer and enforce rules that have been adopted collectively. An example would be the European Coal and Steel Community; its member-states have granted it the authority to establish binding regulations. The degree to which governments wish to cede direct control over a particular activity to a collective international authority depends to a very large extent on whether they perceive any particular advantage to collective rather than independent national action.

Why Integration Occurs

Economic integration among nation-states has occurred in various parts of the world. The most impressive example is the European Community, but numerous additional examples also exist. What conditions gave rise to the creation of these integration efforts? Students of economic integration have argued that several factors promote regional integration. Some of these factors may be classified as background factors and others as expectations about future benefits. Several background factors have been identified by students of international integration.[19] For instance, some degree of shared values appears to be necessary at a minimum. One-party socialist or communist states do not engage in economic integration with capitalist democracies. A measure of ideological commonality appears to be essential. A similar cultural and historical background or at least a tolerance of cultural diversity is also useful. Coupled with this is the need for reasonably good relations between the prospective members of a common market and a fairly well-established track record of economic cooperation. Normally, these factors are more likely to exist if the prospective countries are reasonably equal in size and close to one another geographically. The greater the economic inequalities and the distance among nations, the less the likelihood that they will successfully integrate their economies. Finally, in most cases of regional integration, a fair degree of external impetus exists. Prospective participants in a regional integration scheme may want to offset the influence of a major external economic competitor. For example, both the EC and the Latin American Free Trade Association were motivated, at least in part, to strengthen each region's capacity to compete with and counteract the economic influence of the United States.

Several future expectations are also key to the initiation of integration. Participating states must perceive that they will experience significant benefits. Creation of a common market, for instance, may require them to change their trade relations with traditional outside partners, but it may also promise to increase their domestic production and trade opportunities in certain sectors with respect to trade partners inside the common market. If every country in a prospective common market perceives a degree of benefit resulting from participation, then integration is more likely. Similarly, integration is more likely when the countries perceive that the costs of participation to their domestic economies and foreign relations are minimal. Finally, if integration is valued, particularly by the governmental elite, as a means of promoting peaceful and productive relations, then it is more likely to take place. Certainly in Europe, this was a key impetus to the formation of the EC. Strong elite support was crucial to the formation of other regional integration schemes including the Andean Common Market and the Economic Community of West African States.

Factors in Successful Integration

Spillover   As we noted in chapter 9, one of the assumptions behind the functionalist theory was that cooperation in one area would lead to the need for cooperation in related areas. The concept of *spillover* refers to this process. For instance, as the trade barriers were reduced in the European Common Market, businesses found that their ability to participate in trade was affected by the variable tax policies of the member-states. This led EC members to establish a common value-added tax policy to ensure fairness in the trade sector.[20] Similarly, as capital in the EC began to flow away from the poorer, agricultural countries and regions of Europe to the wealthier, industrial regions, member-states found it necessary to establish a regional policy of economic redistribution of income. Of course, problems can also arise that harm previous integration efforts. Not all spillover effects have only positive effects on future integration. However, when countries are basically satisfied with the operation of common institutions—when they believe that they have benefited from previous integration efforts—they are more likely to support the extension of integration and policy coordination into other related sectors.

Rising economic interaction   A second effect of economic integration is an increase in the amount of economic interaction among members of a common market. To cope with these rising interactions, governments may recognize the need to strengthen or enlarge the common institutions they established in the first place. Whereas spillover may call for the expansion of integration efforts into additional sectors, rising transactions among member-states may only call for a bolstering of the capacity of existing institutions to handle the increasing volume of interactions within a particular sector. This might mean strengthening the budgets of regional institutions, increasing staff, or fine-tuning legal authorities and mandates.

Interaction of the elite   As governments implement regional integration agreements, they have increasing opportunities for contact with one another. Bureaucracies are created to administer common markets and are staffed by people from various countries. As these people interact with one another, they may begin to develop a common set of values. More cosmopolitan and less nationalistic values may result from increased contact of this sort. Since many people in common market institutions later return to government service in their own countries, cosmopolitan values may permeate the bureaucracies of the member-states, thus reinforcing support for integration. As one authority on integration noted, government bureaucrats are one of the strongest potential sources of opposition to integration. To the extent that they participate in the decision-making processes of common market institutions, they can be co-opted as supporters of integration.[21] However, multinational staffing of regional integration organizations is far from a perfect situation. Sometimes hostilities and tensions based on nationality can emerge.

Emergence of regional interest groups   As regional integration institutions are created and begin to function, nongovernmental groups that stand to gain or lose from certain regional policies are likely to emerge. These organizations are cross-national in character. Farmer's groups and unions, for instance, may lobby regional institutions directly for favorable policy decisions. Such groups usually continue to lobby national governments as well. Appeals by such groups to regional organization institutions lends greater legitimacy to the organizations.

Mass public support   The emergence of elite support and regional interest groups are clearly important to the success of regional integration efforts. However, in the long run, there must be mass popular support for such endeavors if they are to thrive and grow. To the extent that public opinion in the participating countries identifies regional integration with prosperity and growth, positive attitudes for further integration are likely to persist. The longer institutions for integration exist, the more the mass public perceives them as permanent. Individuals, businesses, and groups begin to factor regional institutions into their decisions about trade and investment. Once regional institutions have become ingrained in the fabric of economic life, their survival is probably ensured. Whether they are able to expand and grow, thus further integrating the members' economic systems, depends on continuing perceptions of their success in meeting common goals.

Legal development   Regional integration bodies create regulations, policies, decisions, rules, guidelines, and laws that member-states agree to abide by. Legal development is an important factor in promoting integration. Without some common legal standards, friction between participating countries, their businesses, and their citizens is likely to grow. Thus, in Europe a body of law has arisen that increasingly defines the relationship between EC institutions, member-states, private organizations, and individuals. The EC Court of Justice is perhaps the most prominent example of a regional legal institution that grapples with the application of EC law to these entities. A key stumbling block to integration is whether the regional organization's law takes precedence over the domestic law of member-states. Governments are most reluctant to recognize the existence of any legal authority higher than their own. Nevertheless, in some important respects the Court of Justice is an example of an existing supranational legal character.

External factors   The continuing success of integration efforts depends at least in part on a favorable international climate, as did the initial formation effort. One effect of a common market is the erection of a common external tariff on goods imported to the market from all outside countries. Combined with the removal of tariffs among market members, this external tariff is intended to stimulate common market trade. But it may have a negative effect on the economies of traditional trade partners outside the common market. If they respond negatively by raising tariffs of their own or taking other punitive action over a long period, the health of the common market could be affected. Similarly, significant changes in the international political economy can challenge integration efforts. The growth of OPEC and the drastic increase in the price of oil in the 1970s put severe strains on European economies and sparked the emergence of various national energy policies. The EC's role diminished as countries scrambled to preserve their own national energy security.

Assessing success Determining the success of various integration attempts is not necessarily easy, even using the rather clear criteria set forth in this section. At one level, the mere survival of a regional integration effort is a measure of some success. But survival is one thing, and healthy growth is another. If integration takes the form of a common market, then success should be judged to a large extent on the degree of economic activity and growth stimulated by the arrangement. An ability to adapt to changes and challenges would also seem to be important. The ability to grow and adapt depends in turn on the numerous factors just considered, including elite and mass support, legal development, and a favorable external climate. Moreover, success may not necessarily be permanent; a regional integration organization may grow phenomenally for a time, only to stagnate during another. Indeed, disintegration is always a possibility.

Contemporary Regional Integration Efforts

Cooperative integration efforts have taken place in virtually every region of the world, including Asia, Europe (both East and West), Africa, and Central and South America. Conflict may be a pervasive phenomenon today, but apparently so are efforts toward intense cooperation and integration. Of all the regional integration efforts attempted, the European Community has been the most successful and most widely studied. As we saw in chapter 9, the EC was a by-product of the desire in Europe to prevent a repeat of the First and Second World Wars. Despite the great hostility that had existed between several EC members-states, they shared at least a common history, cultural background, and relatively close economic relations. After World War II, European elites were ready to bury the hatchet and pursue strategies of peace and prosperity, and the general populace was supportive of these efforts as well. In addition, the countries were all industrialized, and no single country was in a position to overpower the others economically. The background factors for successful integration were present. But the EC's success has been based on its performance as well. The creation of a common market led to an explosion in trade and almost unprecedented economic prosperity for the initial six members. Its membership later expanded to nine, then ten, and now stands at twelve. Today the EC has the largest share of international trade in the world.[22] The success of the common market made it easier for member-states to extend integration into many other sectors. Common policies for agriculture, coal and steel, and value-added taxation were developed. Free movement of capital (investment money) and labor quickly followed. Spillover effects were evident everywhere.

The EC has not evolved without difficulty. However, its institutions have grown stronger and gained legitimacy both among the elite and the mass populations of the member-states. Monetary relations have been coordinated, although countries still retain separate currencies and ultimate control over their monetary and fiscal policies. Economic integration among member-states has been significant, but the hoped-for next step of political integration has not been achieved, nor is it likely to be anytime soon. The members have agreed to consult and collaborate with one another in an informal and nonbinding process they call **European Political Cooperation (EPC).** In 1987 EPC was formalized by treaty. Desire for eventual political union is stronger in some countries than in others, but as EC member-ship expands, so does the political and economic diversity of its member-states. This has reawakened a debate about whether EC members desiring to move faster toward more complete economic union and even political union should proceed, allowing the others to follow along at their own pace.[23] Some subscribe to this view, while others insist on the need for consensus. The EC's increasing diversity will be a continuing challenge even as it presses to achieve its goal of unfettered movements of capital, people, goods, and services by 1992.

The movement toward greater integration can be complicated not only by internal diversity, but also by external events. For example, the dramatic events in Eastern Europe soon created complications for the 1992 program. With the two Germanys taking active steps toward reunification, EC governments began to worry about the political and economic consequences for the Community as a whole, and their own particular interests as member states. Germany was always a major economic force and political player in EC politics, but a reunified Germany would dwarf any other member state in terms of its economic productivity. Moreover, how well could socialist East Germany make the transition to a capitalist market economy? Certainly, from a political standpoint, liberalization in Eastern Europe and the reunification of Germany were welcome changes after years of Cold War. But for the EC, these developments continue to pose significant challenges that are bound to complicate its drive for greater integration and to delay for some time certain elements of the 1992 program.

Apart from the EC, several other regional integration efforts have been undertaken, including the Council for Mutual Economic Assistance in Eastern Europe, the Andean Common Market (Andean Pact), the Latin American Free Trade Association (LAFTA), and the Central American Common Market (CACM) in Latin America, and the East African Common Market (EACM) and the Economic Community of West African States (ECOWAS) in Africa. None of these organizations has achieved the level of success enjoyed by the EC. The EACM is defunct, and only the CACM, the Andean Pact, and ECOWAS have enjoyed even moderate long-term success. The EC has been more successful for several reasons, some of which we have already mentioned. The member-states have relatively modern, sophisticated, industrial economies and well-developed agricultural sectors. Their economies vary in size and strength but not to a wide extent. Because of their stronger economies, EC members have been better able to withstand the ups and downs of the international economy than their Third World counterparts. By contrast members of most other regional integration schemes have widely variable economic capabilities, with many countries having weak economies. Disparities in economic level mean that some countries will enjoy greater economic benefits from free trade agreements. Unless agree-able means of redistributing the gains from trade can be reached, support for integration will be eroded, as was the case with LAFTA. Political stability is another factor in suc-cessful economic integration. The EC members have enjoyed relative political stability, while members of several of the other integration schemes cited have been subject to substantial political upheaval. Although regional integration efforts in other parts of the world have not been able to duplicate the rather breathtaking successes of the EC, a few—such as the Andean Pact, the CACM, and ECOWAS—continue to offer some prospect for positive contributions to the economies of their member-states and some hope for regional cooperation.

Prospects for International Cooperation

We have examined how countries have chosen to cooperate, at least to some extent, in pursuit of humanitarian goals, environmental improvements, and economic integration. Each of these areas lies, for the most part, in the so-called nonsecurity aspect of international relations. Humanitarian, environmental, and commercial policies are not found at the top of many nations' foreign policy agenda. Perhaps some states can engage in significant degrees of cooperation in these areas because they attach less significant concern to them.

Does this suggest that cooperation is not possible in military–security affairs or other significant political issues? Although it may be easier for states to cooperate on issues relating to economic and humanitarian affairs, it should not be assumed that cooperation is not possible on issues on the high political agenda. As Charles Lipson has noted, "economic issues are characterized far more often by elaborate networks of rules, norms, and institutions, grounded in reasonably stable, convergent expectations."[24] But while admitting that well-organized and formal rules for security issues are far less common, Lipson also notes that:

> . . . it is seriously misleading to assume that security issues do not present the opportunity for significant joint gains or at least the prevention of joint losses. Even adversaries like the United States and the Soviet Union wish to avoid nuclear war. And both could profit from restraints on arms racing: limits on the number of launchers and warheads, reduction of conventional forces in Europe and so forth.[25]

Lipson believes that cooperation is more prevalent in economic issue areas such as trade and monetary policy, because the negative consequences for cooperation when other countries fail to keep their obligations are not as great as in the area of military security. Similarly, if one country cheats on a bilateral trade agreement, reciprocal retaliatory measures can be applied by the injured country without severe risk to the integrity of either nation. But if a country cheats on an arms control or disarmament measure, the risk to the party that honored the agreement is greater, as are the risks of retaliation for both nations. Lipson recognizes that cooperation is still possible in military–security relations among nations even if it is more difficult to achieve and more dangerous.

To illustrate the problem of cooperation in international relations, let us assume that two countries—the United States and the Soviet Union—have an opportunity to cooperate with each other by honoring an arms control agreement. As figure 13.1 shows, by cooperating, each country realizes a positive benefit of 25 points, which we will assume is the benefit of nuclear stability and the savings realized by avoiding a massive arms race. But let us assume that both countries understand that if one of them abides by the agreement and the other does not, the defector will realize a gain of 50 points, which we will assume is the added strategic advantage gained by cheating. Under these circumstances, the cooperating country has been suckered and actually loses 50 points, because the cheater has now developed a lead in nuclear technology. Let us also assume that if both countries cheat, or fail to cooperate, they both experience a loss of 25 points, which is the cost of a continued arms race, and a higher level of nuclear instability, which is now compounded by deeper mutual distrust, since both sides cheated on their legal obligations. Assuming

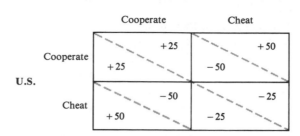

USSR

	Cooperate	Cheat
Cooperate	+25 / +25	+50 / −50
Cheat	−50 / +50	−25 / −25

U.S.

these kinds of rewards and penalties, we have a gamelike situation that can be expressed in the matrix in figure 13.1.

Under these conditions, there is a strong incentive for each country to cheat on the arms agreement. For each country the "I cheat/they cooperate" situation leads to the optimum payoff (+50, −50). Mutual cooperation leads to the second-greater payoff (+25, +25). Mutual cheating leads to the next-to-worse payoff (−25, −25). However, the "I cooperate/they cheat" situation leads to the worse possible payoff (−50, +50). The big problem with this kind of situation is the constant fear that the other side will cheat, leaving the cooperator at a great disadvantage. But there is also a strong temptation to cheat to gain an advantage. Given the reward/penalty payoff structure in this example, the fear of cheating and the cost of being suckered may drive countries to cheat. But suppose that the advantage of mutual cooperation was 40 points and the penalty for mutual cheating was a loss of 40 points. Under these circumstances, each country would have a stronger incentive to cooperate, since both the costs of mutual cheating and gains of mutual cooperation are substantially increased.[26] In other words, changes in the payoff structure affect the outcome.

This is one reason that cooperation is more prevalent in nations' economic relations than in their security relations. The benefits of cooperation may be no greater, but a state's failure to cooperate does not lead to an overwhelming and dangerous advantage over states that do cooperate. Moreover, economic retaliation against a cheater is not as dangerous a threat as military retaliation against cheaters on security agreements.

Because it is a hypothetical model, this kind of game theory approach should be seen only as an interesting way to point out some of the strategies countries engage in. International relations is played out over time as countries bargain with one another, punish one another for failure to cooperate, and develop reputations as being trustworthy or untrustworthy. Also the world is composed of more than just two countries. Arms control may be a significant issue in U.S.–Soviet relations, but their bargaining in this area takes place in a complicated context in which many other countries, including adversaries and allies, have a stake. In addition, countries have numerous interrelated contacts with one another. The games they play in the real world are often linked in very complicated ways. In times past, for instance, the United States has linked progress on arms control with the Soviet Union to a decrease in Soviet military adventurism throughout the world. So our example is an oversimplified one.

Students of game theory believe that cooperation is possible among nations when they have mutual interests that can be furthered by cooperation, when they are concerned about the negative effects of noncooperation on future relations and interests, and when the number of relevant actors is reasonably small, allowing for manageable systems of regulation to emerge.[27]

Although cooperation on security issues may be difficult, other experts have pointed out that cooperation even on economic issues, which are more imperative now than ever before, is also growing more difficult. Ernst Haas, for instance, has argued that the growth of a large number of new states that do not fully accept current international regimes for trade, monetary relations, ocean development, and so on, has increased demands for change.[28] On the other hand, he argues that the most powerful states (hegemons) have declined in terms of power and influence, and so defense of existing cooperative regimes grows weaker. In the face-off between many new states clamoring for change and a few declining hegemons, the result may well be indeterminant negotiations, failure to agree on new regimes, or the replacement of old regimes and ways of doing things with less stable new regimes and ways of doing things. The Law of the Sea negotiations, which involved some 140 nations and virtually the whole spectrum of ocean resource issues but which ultimately failed to attract universal support, are cited as an example of this phenomenon.

While cooperation has become a more complicated affair, Haas also points out that force and conflict have also grown increasingly outmoded:

> . . .there seems to be greater reluctance to use force in the solution of economic disputes. Governments no longer dispatch their navies to collect foreign debts or to open up ports to trade; they no longer conquer neighboring countries in order to gain access to oil, copper, or gold. They do not even use the threat of military force to foist an unwanted trade agreement on a weaker country.[29]

We conclude this chapter with two supplemental readings. Robert Axelrod and Robert Keohane explore several of the means by which cooperation is achieved in international relations. Indeed, as they suggest, the key to a safe and sane future in international relations does not rest so much on whether states should pursue cooperation in their mutual relations, but how they can go about doing it effectively. Joseph Grieco suggests that cooperation even among allies can be difficult to achieve. Nations worry about their current friends' economic gains because one day they may be foes. He suggests that the realist approach reflects contemporary international relations more accurately than Axelrod and Keohane's neoliberal approach. Whichever perspective is most accurate, there can be little doubt that cooperation will continue to serve the interest of states in wide areas of their interrelations.

Robert Axelrod and Robert Keohane

■

Achieving Cooperation Under Anarchy: Strategies and Institutions

Achieving cooperation is difficult in world politics. There is no common government to enforce rules, and by the standards of domestic society, international institutions are weak. Cheating and deception are endemic. Yet, . . .cooperation is sometimes attained. World politics is not a homogeneous state of war: Cooperation varies among issues and over time.

. . .Cooperation is not equivalent to harmony. Harmony requires complete identity of interests, but cooperation can only take place in situations that contain a mixture of conflicting and complementary interests. In such situations, cooperation occurs when actors adjust their behavior to the actual or anticipated preferences of others. Cooperation, thus defined, is not necessarily good from a moral point of view.

Anarchy also needs to be defined clearly. As used here, the term refers to a lack of common government in world politics, not to a denial that an international society—albeit a fragmented one—exists. Clearly, many international relationships continue over time, and engender stable expectations about behavior. To say that world politics is anarchic does not imply that it entirely lacks organization. Relationships among actors may be carefully structured in some issue-areas, even though they remain loose in others. Likewise, some issues may be closely linked through the operation of institutions while the boundaries of other issues, as well as the norms and principles to be followed, are subject to dispute. Anarchy, defined as lack of common government, remains a constant; but the degree to which interactions are structured, and the means by which they are structured, vary. . . .

SOURCE: From *World Politics* 38, no. 1 (October 1985), pp. 226–254. Reprinted by permission in abridged form.

Decision makers themselves perceive (more or less consciously) that some aspects of the situations they face tend to make cooperation difficult. So they work to alter these background conditions. Among the problems they encounter [are] the following:

1. how to provide incentives for cooperation so that cooperation would be rewarded over the long run, and defection punished;
2. how to monitor behavior so that cooperators and defectors could be identified;
3. how to focus rewards on cooperators and retaliation on defectors;
4. how to link issues with one another in productive rather than self-defeating ways. . . .

A fundamental strategic concept in attaining these objectives is that of reciprocity. Cooperation in world politics seems to be attained best not by providing benefits unilaterally to others, but by conditional cooperation. Yet reciprocity encounters many problems in practice. . . . Reciprocity requires the ability to recognize and retaliate against a defection. And retaliation can spread acrimoniously.

Actors in world politics seek to deal with problems of reciprocity in part through the exercise of power. Powerful actors structure relationships so that countries committed to a given order can deal effectively with those that have lower levels of commitment. This is done by establishing hierarchies. . . .

Another way to facilitate cooperation is to establish international regimes. . . . International regimes have been extensive in the post-1945 international political economy, as illustrated by the international trade regime (centered on the GATT [General Agreement on Tariffs and Trade]) and the international monetary regimes (including the IMF as well as other organizations and networks). Since the use of power can facilitate the construction of regimes, this approach should be seen as complementary to, rather than in contradiction with, an emphasis on hierarchical authority. Regimes do not enforce rules in a hierarchical sense, but they do change patterns of transaction costs and provide information to participants, so that uncertainty is reduced. . . .

International regimes do not substitute for reciprocity; rather, they reinforce and institutionalize it. Regimes incorporating the norm of reciprocity delegitimize defection and thereby make it more costly. Insofar as they specify precisely what reciprocity means in the relevant issue-area, they make it easier to establish a reputation for practicing reciprocity consistently. Such reputations may become important assets, precisely because others will be more willing to make agreements with governments that can be expected to respond to cooperation with cooperation. Of course, compliance is difficult to assure; and international regimes almost never have the power to enforce rules. Nevertheless, since governments with good reputations can more easily make agreements than governments with bad ones, international regimes can help to facilitate cooperation by making it both easier and more desirable to acquire a good reputation.

International regimes may also help to develop new norms. . . . Major banks today are trying mightily to strengthen norms of repayment (for debtors) and of relending (for banks), but it is not at all clear that this will be successful. Better examples of creating norms may be provided by the evolution of thinking on chemical and biological warfare, and by the development, under GATT, of norms of nondiscrimination—which are now. . .under pressure. Evidently, it is difficult to develop new norms, and they often decay in reaction to conspicuous violations.

Establishing hierarchies, setting up international regimes, and attempting to gain acceptance for new norms are all attempts to change the context within which actors operate by changing the very structure of their interaction. It is important to notice that these efforts have usually not been examples of forward-looking rationality. Rather, they have been experimental, trial-and-error efforts to improve the current situation based upon recent experience. Like other forms of trial-and-error experimentation, they have not always worked. . . .

Eventually, any institution is likely to become obsolete. The question is under what conditions international institutions—broadly defined as "recognized patterns of practice around which expectations converge"—facilitate significant amounts of cooperation for a period of time. Clearly, such institutions can change the incentives for countries affected by them, and can in turn affect the strategic choices governments make in their own self-interest. . . .

The experimental groping by policy makers does not necessarily lead to stronger and ever more complex ways of achieving cooperation. The process proceeds by fits and starts. The success of each step is uncertain, and there is always danger that prior achievements will come unstuck. New experiments are often tried only under obvious pressure of events (as in debt rescheduling). And they are often dependent upon the active leadership of a few individuals or states who feel a serious need for change and who have the greatest resources. . . .

But. . .states are often dissatisfied with the structure of their own environment. . . . Governments have often tried to transform the structures within which they operate so as to make it possible for the countries involved to work together productively. Some of these experiments have been successful, others have been stillborn, and still others have collapsed before fully realizing the dreams of their founders. We understand the functions performed by international regimes, and how they affect strategies pursued by governments, better than we did a number of years ago. . . . Even within a world of independent states that are jealously guarding their sovereignty and protecting their power, room exists for new and better arrangements to achieve mutually satisfactory outcomes, in terms both of economic welfare and military security.

This does not mean that all endeavors to promote international cooperation will yield good results. Cooperation can be designed to help a few at the expense of the rest; and it can accentuate as well as alleviate injustice in an imperfect world. Yet the consequences of failure to cooperate —from warfare to the intensification of depressions—make us believe that more cooperation is often better than less. If governments are prepared to grope their way toward a better-coordinated future, scholars should be prepared to study the process. And, in a world where states have often been dissatisfied with international anarchy, scholars should be prepared to advance the learning process—so that despite the reality of anarchy, beneficial forms of international cooperation can be promoted.

Joseph M. Grieco

Anarchy and the Limits of Cooperation: A Realist Critique of the Newest Liberal Institutionalism

Realism has dominated international relations theory at least since World War II. For realists, international anarchy fosters competition and conflict among states and inhibits their willingness to cooperate even when they share common interests. Realist theory also argues that international institutions are unable to mitigate anarchy's constraining effects on interstate cooperation. Realism, then, presents a pessimistic analysis of the prospects for international cooperation and of the capabilities of international institutions.

The major challenger to realism has been what I shall call liberal institutionalism. Prior to the current decade, it appeared in three successive presentations—functionalist integration theory in the 1940s and early 1950s, neofunctionalist regional integration theory in the 1950s and 1960s, and interdependence theory in the 1970s. All three versions rejected realism's propositions about states and its gloomy understanding of world politics. Most significantly, they argued that international institutions can help states cooperate. Thus, compared to realism, these earlier versions of liberal institutionalism offered a more hopeful prognosis for international cooperation and a more optimistic assessment of the capacity of institutions to help states achieve it.

International tensions and conflicts during the 1970s undermined liberal institutionalism and reconfirmed realism in large measure. Yet, that difficult decade did not witness a collapse of the international system, and, in the light of continuing modest levels of interstate cooperation, a new liberal institutionalist challenge to realism came forward

SOURCE: From *International Organization* 42, no. 3 (Summer 1988), pp. 485–507. Reprinted by permission in abridged form. © 1988 by the World Peace Foundation and the Massachusetts Institute of Technology.

during the early 1980s. What is distinctive about this newest liberal institutionalism is its claim that it accepts a number of core realist propositions, including, apparently, the realist argument that anarchy impedes the achievement of international cooperation. However, the core liberal arguments—that realism overemphasizes conflict and underestimates the capacities of international institutions to promote cooperation—remain firmly intact. The new liberal institutionalists basically argue that even if the realists are correct in believing that anarchy constrains the willingness of states to cooperate, states nevertheless can work together and can do so especially with the assistance of international institutions.

This point is crucial for students of international relations. If neoliberal institutionalists are correct, then they have dealt realism a major blow while providing the intellectual justification for treating their own approach, and the tradition from which it emerges, as the most effective for understanding world politics.

. . . In fact, neoliberal institutionalism misconstrues the realist analysis of international anarchy and therefore it misunderstands the realist analysis of the impact of anarchy on the preferences and actions of states. Indeed, the new liberal institutionalism fails to address a major constraint on the willingness of states to cooperate which is generated by international anarchy and which is identified by realism. As a result, the new theory's optimism about international cooperation is likely to be proven wrong.

Neoliberalism's claims about cooperation are based on its belief that states are atomistic actors. It argues that states seek to maximize their individual *absolute* gains and are indifferent to the gains achieved by others. Cheating, the new theory suggests, is the greatest impediment to cooperation among rationally egoistic states, but international institutions, the new theory also suggests, can help states overcome this barrier to joint action. Realists understand that states seek absolute gains and worry about compliance. However, realists find that states are *positional*, not atomistic, in character, and therefore realists argue that, in addition to concerns about cheating, states in cooperative arrangements also worry that their partners might gain more from cooperation than they do. For realists, a state will focus both on its absolute and relative gains from cooperation, and a state that is satisfied with a partner's compliance in a joint arrangement might nevertheless exit from it because the partner is achieving relatively greater gains. Realism, then, finds that there are at least two major barriers to international cooperation: state concerns about cheating and state concerns about relative achievements of gains. Neoliberal institutionalism pays attention exclusively to the former, and is unable to identify, analyze, or account for the latter.

Realism's identification of the relative gains problem for cooperation is based on its insight that states in anarchy fear for their survival as independent actors. According to realists, states worry that today's friend may be tomorrow's enemy in war, and fear that achievements of joint gains that advantage a friend in the present might produce a more dangerous *potential* foe in the future. As a result, states must give serious attention to the gains of partners. Neoliberals fail to consider the threat of war arising from international anarchy, and this allows them to ignore the matter of relative gains and to assume that states only desire absolute gains. Yet, in doing so, they fail to identify a major source of state inhibitions about international cooperation.

In sum, I suggest that realism, its emphasis on conflict and competition notwithstanding, offers a more complete understanding of the problem of international cooperation than does its latest liberal challenger. If that is true, then realism is still the most powerful theory of international politics.

Study Questions

1. What are the chief motives states have for cooperating with one another?
2. What is an *externality*? Provide examples.
3. Discuss how refugees can be considered an externality.
4. Discuss the ways in which nations cooperate to deal with refugees and displaced persons.
5. Identify the three key durable solutions to refugee problems.
6. How does the distinction between emergency and development aid complicate meeting the humanitarian needs of refugees and displaced persons?
7. Discuss the four principal behaviors states have engaged in historically with respect to the environment.
8. What is the *tragedy of the commons*? Why is it significant for international relations? Discuss this concept with reference to the problems of ozone depletion, acid rain, and deforestation.
9. Why do poor countries resent discussions about the protection of the international environment?
10. What was the conclusion of the *Limits to Growth* study, and how is it related to the earlier work of Thomas Malthus?
11. How have states responded to the challenge of protecting the international environment?
12. What are the chief background factors that promote economic integration?
13. Define the concept of *spillover*.
14. Discuss the factors that are likely to encourage successful economic integration. Which of these factors, in your opinion, is most important?
15. Why is the European Communities such a successful example of regional integration?
16. What problems have prevented Third World regional integration efforts from achieving significant success? Of the Third World regional integration efforts, which have been the most successful? Why?
17. Why is cooperation in economic relations more prevalent than in military–security affairs?
18. In what sense has cooperation in economic affairs become more difficult today?
19. How do Robert Axelrod and Robert Keohane define *cooperation*? *anarchy*?
20. According to Axelrod and Keohane, what are four problems decision makers run into in trying to promote cooperation?

21. How does reciprocity encourage cooperation?
22. How do regimes encourage cooperation?
23. According to Joseph Grieco, what does the realist school believe about cooperation in international relations? the neoliberal approach? Which in your view is the more accurate approach?

Key Terms

Club of Rome
European Political Cooperation (EPC)
externalities
local settlement

third country resettlement
tragedy of the commons
voluntary repatriation

Notes

1. Ironically, dependency theorists argue that war diverts the attention of imperial powers from their normal domination of weaker trade partners, leaving many smaller countries to develop on their own terms. Andre Gunder Frank, for instance, argued that Latin American countries experienced economic growth during World Wars I and II, because of the lessened grip of the United States on their economies. See his *Capitalism and Underdevelopment in Latin America* (New York: Monthly Review Press, 1969), pp. 297–298.
2. See Louise Holborn, *Refugees: A Problem of Our Time,* 2 vols. (Metuchen, N.J.: Scarecrow Press, 1975). For a more recent assessment of the contemporary refugee situation, see William R. Smyser, "Refugees: A Never-Ending Story," *Foreign Affairs* (Fall 1985) 154–168.
3. See Barry Wain, *The Refused: The Agony of the Indochina Refugees* (New York: Simon & Schuster, 1981).
4. For an analysis of the history of the ICRC, see David Forsythe, *Humanitarian Politics: The International Committee for the Red Cross* (Baltimore: Johns Hopkins University Press, 1977).
5. See Robert Chambers, "Hidden Losers," *International Migration Review* 20, no. 2 (Summer 1986): 245–263; and Robert Gorman, *Coping with the African Refugee Problem: A Time for Solutions* (Dordrecht, Netherlands: Martinus Nijhoff with UNITAR, 1987).
6. David J. Finlay and Thomas Hovet, Jr. *7304: International Relations on the Planet Earth* (New York: Harper & Row, 1975), pp. 100–126.
7. Garrett Hardin, "The Tragedy of the Commons," *Science* 162 (13 December 1968): 1244–1245.
8. For discussions of international issues affected by the commons dilemma, see Per Magnus Wijkom, "Managing the Global Commons," *International Organization* 36, no. 3 (Summer 1982): 511–536; and Marvin Soroos, "Commons in the Sky: The Radio Spectrum and Geosynchronous Orbit as Issues in Global Policy," *International Organization* 36, no. 3 (Summer 1982): 665–685.

9. Robert C. Cowan, "Balancing Ecological and Economic Realities for Life on Earth," *Christian Science Monitor,* May 12, 1987, p. 23; and Marshall Ingwerson, "Summit Pushes Environment at World Level," *Christian Science Monitor,* July 19, 1989, p. 8.

10. Sandra Postel, "Protecting Forests," in *State of the World, 1984,* ed. Lester R. Brown (New York: Norton, 1984), pp. 74–94. For a specific treatment of acid rain, see pp. 79–82.

11. See Sandra Postel, "Protecting Forests from Air Pollution and Acid Rain," *State of the World, 1985,* ed. Lester R. Brown (New York: Norton, 1985), pp. 118–121.

12. B. Bowonder and S. S. R. Prasad, "Global Forests: Another View," *Futures: The Journal of Forecasting and Planning* 19, no. 1 (February 1987): 52.

13. Lester Brown, ed., *State of the World, 1985* (New York: Norton, 1985), p. 15.

14. Malthus's work *An Essay on the Principle of Population* was published anonymously in 1798.

15. Donella Meadows, Dennis Meadows, Jorgen Randers, and William Behrens III, *The Limits to Growth* (New York: Universe Books, 1972).

16. Ibid.

17. One influential report to the Club of Rome Studies was Jan Tinbergen, Antony Dolman, and Jan van Ettinger, *Reshaping the International Order,* (New York: Dutton, 1976).

18. Leon Lindberg, "Political Integration as a Multidimensional Phenomenon Requiring Multivariate Measurement," in *Regional Integration: Theory and Research,* eds. Leon Lindberg and Stuart Scheingold (Cambridge: Harvard University Press, 1971), p. 60.

19. Several of the criteria cited in this chapter are compiled nicely in Joseph Nye, "Comparing Common Markets," in *Regional Integration: Theory and Research,* eds. Leon Lindberg and Stuart Scheingold (Cambridge: Harvard University Press, 1971), p. 199–217.

20. Ibid., p. 200.

21. Ibid., p. 204.

22. "Europe—the Future," *Journal of Common Market Studies* 23, no. 1 (September 1984): 73.

23. For a discussion of the idea of different rates of integration within the EC membership, see William Nicol, "Paths to European Unity," *Journal of Common Market Studies* 23, no. 3 (March 1985): 199–206.

24. Charles Lipson, "International Cooperation in Economic and Security Affairs," *World Politics* 37, no. 1 (October 1984): 12.

25. Ibid., p. 13.

26. Ibid., pp. 7–8.

27. Robert Axelrod and Robert Keohane, "Achieving Cooperation Under Anarchy: Strategies and Institutions," *World Politics* 38, no. 1 (October 1985): 228–238.

28. Ernst B. Haas, "Why Collaborate? Issue-Linkage and International Regimes," *World Politics* 32, no. 3 (1979): 357–406.

29. Ibid., pp. 357–358.

Part V

■

The Future of the World Order

Fourteen
The Changing International System: Issues for the Future

Fourteen

The Changing International System:
Issues for the Future

In the preceding chapters our primary focus has been on contemporary global politics. We noted that the international political system is dynamic and that it is the result of certain processes that depict both constancy and change. In chapter 2 we discussed the "sources of change" leading to the development of the contemporary international system. We tried to explain, through a host of concepts, the meaning of recurrent practices (or continuity) in international politics and deviations from them (or change). Among the many, varied changes in today's global system, we find several new types of subnational and transnational actors, with quite different internal characteristics, seeking unconventional political objectives; an increased number of nation-states making their unprecedented influence felt through economic power, rather than political or military power; a noticeable impact of technological innovation on the choices of foreign policy goals; and a disruption of long-standing patterns of relationships among states due to the culmination of piecemeal developments that render old practices useless or impractical. It is reasonable to assume that these changes take place in the world arena because they are driven by more powerful forces than continuity and thus move at an accelerated pace toward convergence. This might suggest that a transformation of the international system is well under way—if, indeed, it has not already occurred. One manifestation of a metamorphosis in the global system is the emergence of numerous new issues and problems articulated by nation-states in their foreign policies. Our aim in this chapter is to identify those issues and analyze their implications for the future of global politics.

In 1989 the Seventy-Sixth American Assembly described the 1990s as the watershed years in global affairs. This decade represents a significant turning point in post–World War II, political, economic, and security relations: Western Europe will attain greater economic and political unity. Japan will share its great economic achievements by assuming larger world responsibilities. The Soviet Union and the nations of Eastern Europe might move further from doctrinaire communism and closer to economic and political reforms. The People's Republic of China will find combining economic reforms with totalitarian practices to be an impossible struggle. And many developing countries will continue to set examples in achieving political and economic reforms. In other words, the assembly saw the 1990s as relatively peaceful and prosperous, propelled by a fast-moving, multidimensional technological revolution that has heightened the increasing interdependence of nations.

On the other side of the ledger, the assembly saw growing dangers in trade and other economic imbalances that have been permitted to accumulate and in the lack of global economic growth, further liberalization of trade, and effective measures to cope with illegal drug use and environmental deterioration. The road to a peaceful and stable transformation of the international system, the assembly felt, requires the creation of "a new architecture for international economic cooperation," which would address the myriad issues facing the world's industrialized countries.[1]

Global Interdependence, the Nation-State, and Economic Issues

As we pointed out earlier, the world has grown increasingly complex and interdependent since the Peace of Westphalia in 1648, which gave birth to the nation-state system. Ever since the end of World War II, contact, communication, and exchange among the actors in the state system have steadily increased, and the number of nation-states and other nongovernmental actors has multiplied by leaps and bounds. During the past four decades, we have witnessed the unfolding of two counteracting forces, which has left a distinct mark on the capabilities of the present international system. On the one hand, we have seen the emergence of certain centrifugal forces that are responsible for the increased range of possible mutually beneficial exchanges between states and the creation of many cooperative ventures across national boundaries. On the other hand, we have encountered certain centripetal forces as possible sources of disagreement leading to tension and conflict. Thus, as the world has grown smaller—primarily because of the scientific and technological breakthroughs in our lifetime—it has also become more complex, unstable, and less manageable. In spite of these opposing trends, political power remains embedded primarily in the central decision-making institutions of the national actors that make up the international system. This fact underscores the traditional state-centric focus of the theory of political realism in international relations.

According to certain critics, however, nation-states are no longer capable of playing certain historic roles or of meeting desperate human needs. Such notions as the independence of nations, sovereignty of governments, and reliability of alliances can no longer be taken for granted because the nation-state system is losing its effectiveness. In some countries, such as the former **Soviet bloc** where the **Brezhnev doctrine** of limited sovereignty was in use until Mikhail Gorbachev came to power in 1985, nations had to sacrifice their sovereignty for ideology. The lack of an effective defense against possible nuclear attacks makes it more difficult for governments to perform their principal function, which is to protect the lives, liberty, and property of their people. Nor is the nation-state system an effective instrument for promoting world order; there were about forty ongoing conflicts in the world at the beginning of 1988, and despite a renewed vigor of UN peacekeeping activities, disputes among state actors were seldom brought to the world court or resolved by international arbitration. The nation-state system is making little progress in closing the gap between the "have" and "have-not" nations. For these and countless other reasons, the position of the state as the preeminent actor in international affairs is challenged by a growing number of nongovernmental actors. Corporations, terrorists, insurgent groups, and nonprofit agencies operate independently of governments, sometimes directly challenging their authority and even the existence of particular states. The emergence of a large number of poor, weak states in the last three decades has magnified the importance of nongovernmental actors. Nevertheless, corporations are often financially more powerful than many newly independent countries. Moreover, these new nations are further weakened by direct challenges to their sovereignty from various internal rebel organizations.

Today, almost no state is economically self-reliant. Economic interdependence challenges a nation's ability to control its domestic economy, promote economic independence, and use military power effectively. Events in one country can have devastating effects on the economies of faraway lands. Contemporary international economics is a truly global affair. For example, environmental pollution recognizes no boundaries and increasingly presents nations, as well as the entire international system, with some serious dilemmas. The harmful impact of acid rain, ozone depletion, and deforestation on the global environment and on the political relations of states is receiving more widespread attention.

Another example of economic interdependence seriously impacting on the effectiveness of the nation-state system is the debt problem. At the beginning of 1988, developing countries owed about $1.2 trillion to the developed world's governments and banks—up from $752 billion at the end of 1982. More than two dozen nations have faced problems in servicing their debt since the debt crisis erupted in 1982. Latin American countries owed about 34 percent of the $1.2 trillion total; African countries owed 22 percent. In 1988 the leading debtor nations included Mexico with about $108 billion, Brazil with $110 billion, Argentina with $52 billion, Egypt with $44 billion, Venezuela and the Philippines with $34 billion each, and Nigeria with $23 billion. The debt crisis underscores the interdependent character of the global financial system. When debtors cannot meet their financial obligations, creditors are the first to suffer. American commercial banks have about $123 billion in outstanding debt to developing countries, the top nine U.S. banks owe two to three times their equity. European and Japanese banks, however, account for about 70 percent of the total commercial bank loans to the Third World. The problem is that the economies of many Third World countries are not growing fast enough to enable them to meet the interest payments on their debt, which amount to over $90 billion annually, much less reduce their principal. As already mentioned in chapter 11, unsound economic policies in some developing countries have constrained growth, and rising interest rates and falling commodity prices have further compounded the problem. Two opposing schools of thought about how to deal with the world debt problem surfaced in 1985. Then Secretary of the Treasury James Baker proposed calling for balanced government budgets, a larger role for market forces and private enterprise, and greater reliance on capital investment and less on borrowing. President Fidel Castro of Cuba and others advocated debt forgiveness and government bailouts. The main argument against this latter plan was that it was "leading developing countries down a dead-end road, a road which will not bring long-term growth and integration into the world economy."[2] Although the "sustained growth" program, in existence since October 1985, achieved some progress, in March 1989 Secretary of the Treasury Nicholas Brady submitted a new proposal to strengthen the debt strategy. His proposal, endorsed by the 1989 Paris summit of the **Group of Seven (G-7)** nations, emphasized stronger growth, economic policy reforms, external financial support by creditors, and individualized treatment of each country's needs and problems. Brady's approach also allowed for debt service reduction, some debt forgiveness, new investment, and flight capital repatriation.

Developing countries with low foreign borrowing and high capital investment (e.g., South Korea, Singapore, Malaysia, Hong Kong, and Taiwan) have low foreign debts, a high rate of domestic savings, and a high domestic output. On the other hand, developing countries such as Brazil, Mexico, and Argentina are victims of capital disinvestment. From 1983 to 1985, for example, almost $14 billion more flowed out of Mexico than flowed in. Although a creative refinancing program has since stimulated a mild inflow of foreign investment capital, the debt problem in Mexico, as elsewhere in Latin America and Africa, still lingers.

Foreign capital investment in a country's domestic economy usually bodes well for economic success; however, in some cases, as in the United States, it can be a double-edged sword. The $1.5 trillion invested in the United States by foreigners in 1988 led several presidential candidates to appeal to the voters during the primary elections with the campaign slogan "prevent the selling of America." The reference was to an unprecedented number of real estate transactions showing foreign purchases of hotels, banks, high-tech companies, and other businesses. However, the largest amount of foreign investment went into U.S. bonds and other securities, which also led to speculation that should these foreign investors decide to withdraw all their investments, or even a major portion of them, the withdrawal could throw the United States into a recession. Incidentally, to appease the voters, the same candidates promised new business and job opportunities in depressed areas of the country under the threat of trade protectionism. However, attempts to prevent further decline in U.S. manufacturing capability, and therefore a possible rise in unemployment through high tariffs and other measures of trade protectionism, could trigger a negative response from U.S. trading partners resulting in increasing U.S. economic isolation, depression, and global financial chaos. Under conditions of global interdependence, decisions made in the United States have important implications and consequences for other nations. Conversely, decisions made in other countries have serious consequences for the United States. For example, efforts to increase U.S. exports by lowering the value of the dollar encouraged the Japanese to invest more heavily in the United States because the overvalued yen could buy twice as much in 1988 as in 1985. However, U.S. exports to Japan continued at only a slightly increased level, while the gap in the balance-of-payment trade between the two countries continued to increase in favor of Japan. On the other hand, the decrease in the value of the dollar adversely affected the balance-of-payment positions of many less developed countries because international trade, transacted in dollars, bought them fewer dollars and therefore more debt.

As the world has grown more interdependent economically, the distinctions between foreign policy and domestic policy and between national security policy and foreign economic policy have become more blurred and the link between politics and economics more reciprocal. As a result, the issues of interdependent world economy have been subjected to a number of competing analytical perspectives in an effort to unravel the significance and influence of the distribution of material wealth on the exercise of power in the global arena. The three prevailing paradigms or approaches to understanding international political economy are sovereignty-at-bay (or liberal), dependencia (or Marxist), and mercantilist (or the nationalist).[3] The **sovereignty-at-bay model** argues that increased economic interdependence and technological advances have undermined the nation-state's control over economic affairs and made the multinational corporations, the Eurodollar market, and other international institutions better suited to the economic needs of humankind. The **dependencia model** challenges the partners-in-development motif of the sovereignty-at-bay model, arguing that the world order is hierarchical and exploitative. This model contends that the flow of wealth and benefits moves from the underdeveloped periphery to the centers of industrial financial power and decision, producing affluent development for some and dependent underdevelopment for the majority of humanity. In other words, what the liberal school calls transnationalism, the Marxist proponents consider imperialism. The **mercantilist**

model, by contrast, states that the future is determined primarily by the way in which nation-states pursue their national interests. The emergent world order is characterized by intense international economic competition for market, investment outlets, and sources of raw materials. Global interdependence will be followed by a fragmentation of the world economy into regional blocs and, to avoid a global conflict, the exercise of mutual self-restraint.

As noted in chapter 11, the international economy is characterized by complex relationships that cut across national boundaries and affect the entire global arena. Not all countries are equally involved in the international economy and not all receive the same benefits from the flow of international trade and other economic activities. Neo-realists like Robert Keohane and Joseph Nye, for example, remind us that international organizations, banks, and multinational corporations provide cooperative links that have developed across national boundaries and are deeply enmeshed in economic interdependence. As a matter of fact, some sovereign governments deliberately set barriers that inhibit economic transactions among states. To remove these impediments and integrate the international economy through global institutions, a set of principles, norms, rules, and decision-making procedures, called a trade regime, was established in the final days of World War II.[4] This international trade regime, under the auspices of the General Agreements on Tariffs and Trade (GATT), has served the world well for about three decades. The period from about 1945 to 1975, for example, saw the world gross national product grow three times faster than ever before. Now, however, GATT is under serious attack, and the road to future reconstruction of the world economy is paved with hardship and uncertainty. As the institutional mechanism through which industrialized countries promote development of an open, multilateral trading system, GATT is unable to cope with the protectionist tide now engulfing the world. Differences in GATT members' policies and trade behavior and in their willingness to accept international obligations have resulted in discrimination and destabilization of the world economy.

The United States, which after World War II offered assistance to former adversaries, now depends on investments from those countries. The U.S. trade deficit is roughly equal to the trade surpluses of Japan and West Germany. Their surpluses translate into more than 4 million full-time manufacturing jobs. Still, the United States must attract foreign funds with higher interest rates, even if higher interest rates upset domestic markets. This is a problem that neither the executive nor legislative branch of the U.S. government can solve alone. Only a bipartisan policy can address the sensitive issues of why Americans borrow more than they save, spend more than they earn, and consume more than they produce. As demonstrated in the case of Japan, the combination of high output and the capacity to transform goods and services from consumption to other ends constitutes economic power. The capability to solve domestic macroeconomic problems depends on the recognition and application of policy and the economy's responsiveness to the policy. Both conditions, however, are predicated on the will of the nation, which includes ingredients such as discipline, cohesion, and purpose. Without this national will, no economic miracle will work.

In November 1975 then French President Giscard d'Estaing initiated the first economic summit conference to attempt to remedy some of the problems associated with economic malaise in the Western Alliance. Six heads of government met at Rambouillet, France, for three days to deal with three major problems: unemployment, inflation, and energy. Since then, similar meetings are held every year to discuss pressing economic issues that require cooperation among the more advanced industrial nations that constitute the Group of Seven—Canada, the Federal Republic of Germany, Great Britain, France, Italy, Japan, and the United States. (Canada was brought into the Group of Seven as a participant in 1977 and into the Commission of the European Communities in 1978.) A coordinated policy among the major Western industrial nations—particularly the United States, Japan, and West Germany—is imperative to save the world from possible economic and financial disaster. After all, these three countries generate about half of the world GNP. Cooperation, however, requires certain sacrifices and perhaps the relinquishment of some national economic sovereignty. As to the future, in the words of one astute observer, Martin Wolf, "the best that can be hoped is a more or less comprehensive network of continually renegotiating international cartel arrangements; the worst could be a complete breakdown in international cooperation and a return to the chaos of the 1930s."[5]

Whether economic cooperation among the major industrial partners of the West will increase or decrease in the 1990s is a matter of conjecture. The impending formation, in 1992, of a unified, dynamic European Community (EC), in which virtually all trade, financial, and investment barriers will be eliminated, has some business people and politicians in the United States, Japan, Korea, Taiwan, Singapore, and the developing world concerned, while others are anxiously awaiting to compete in the favorable new environment. The concerned parties argue that the 1992 effort will lead to increases in protectionism and discrimination against outsiders and perhaps to the creation of a "Fortress Europe."[6]

If the events in Eastern Europe since the summer of 1989 are a reliable indicator, then Western Europe will become not a fortress but a magnet for non–EC member European states. The wave of East German immigrants to West Germany at summer's end and, earlier in the year, the dismantling of the barbed-wire fence between Hungary and Austria by Hungarian border guards, were human manifestations of the magnetism. In August 1989 Poland became the first East European government to have a noncommunist government in more than forty years. Then Hungary, East Germany, Czechoslovakia, Romania, and Bulgaria followed this example. Both the United States and the Soviet Union were swept along with the tide of change, neither nation anticipating the swift and far-reaching consequences of these events. The independence shown by the East European countries is making the term *Eastern bloc* obsolete and is threatening the very foundation of Soviet dominance in the geographic region. The Bush administration originally proposed that Washington manage the Eastern aid operations; however, at the July 1989 summit of the G-7 nations in Paris, the American president had to take a backseat because the task to coordinate the summit nations' aid to East European countries was given to the EC leadership, headed by Commission President Jacques Delors. While the change in transatlantic relations in the West could be labeled an evolutionary transference of power, the diminishing Soviet control in Eastern Europe is being challenged by more radical demands for change. A good example is East Germany.

On February 13, 1990, the Soviet Union agreed with the United States and its major allies and with East Germany on a two-stage formula to reunite Germany. In the first stage, East and West Germany would meet on legal, economic, and political issues. In the second stage, the foreign ministers of the two Germanys would meet with the foreign ministers of the United States, France, Britain, and the Soviet Union to discuss external aspects of achieving German unity, including the issue of security of the neighboring states. On March 18, 1990, in East Germany's first-ever free parliamentary elections, the voters (with a 93% turnout) rejected the "independence" of the German Democratic Republic (GDR). They chose instead to cooperate with the Federal Republic of Germany (FRG) in establishing a united Germany. The election results made it clear that the East Germans desired a constitutional system of government that would protect civil liberties, a democratic rule of law, social justice, and a market economy. Above all, they wanted to be reunited with their brothers and sisters in West Germany.

Although the United States has always supported a peaceful reunification of the two Germanys, the Soviet Union has expressed second thoughts. One month after the March 18th elections, the Soviet Union told East German Prime Minister Lothar de Maiziere that it opposes his plan for quick reunification with West Germany because it would allow East Germany to be quickly integrated into the NATO military alliance. As Mikhail Gorbachev sees it, the unification of the two Germanys concerns not only East and West Germany but the entire European process. Ever since the Eastern bloc began to crumble and the Warsaw Pact to disintegrate, Gorbachev has on numerous occasions suggested replacing NATO and the Warsaw Treaty Organization with new structures on a Pan-European basis. He believes this would eliminate military confrontation between the alliances; it would also create a new economic environment, by permitting all kinds of cooperation based on equity and mutual respect for the union of states with common institutions. Although the European Community leaders agreed in late April 1990, to unite politically by January 1993, the unification plan does not include the Soviet Union or the former members of the European bloc. It does call for the incorporation of East Germany when it is reunited with West Germany. And that is the problem the Soviet Union wants to use to its advantage. Because the Soviet Union is one of the Four Powers that must agree on how their joint responsibility for Germany and Berlin is to end, or on terms for a possible transitional period, the USSR can pressure not only West Germany but also the United States, Britain, and France into terms agreeable to Moscow. The Soviet Union has already tested the option of a reunified neutral Germany, but without success. The realization of a European confederation or Pan-European integration is in the distant future and, therefore, the idea is not very practical. With 380,000 Soviet troops stationed in East Germany in 1990, the Soviet Union is willing to listen not only to guarantees that a "united Germany in a united Europe" will be no threat to the USSR, but also to promise that West Germany would be willing to subsidize the Soviet troops until they leave Germany and to help the Soviet Union with much-needed loans and technology to rebuild and modernize its economy.

In East Germany and in other East European countries, the immediate task in the 1990s will be economic and political recovery from the damages inflicted under communism. While the latter will move at a relatively fast pace, the former will be a slow and tedious process. Economic development will be uneven because of the differences in the culture and history of each country. In some countries, the transformation is more advanced, but economic and social obstacles remain. Fundamental reform is needed to keep pace with rising expectations and cope with growing social unrest.

The more far-reaching question for the 1990s is what dramatic changes will occur within the Soviet Union itself? As pointed out in the previous chapters, Mikhail Gorbachev's policy of *glasnost,* or openness, has taken the lid off decades of ethnic and regional frustrations. Nothing it seems is sacred any longer. Even the logic and principles of Vladimir I. Lenin, the founder of the Soviet state, are being questioned. The call for self-determination in the Baltic states of Lithuania, Estonia, and Latvia and the ethnic unrest and struggle for independence in the Caucasus region and elsewhere are serious obstacles impinging not only on Gorbachev's policies of *glasnost* and *perestroika* but on the integrity and sovereignty of the Soviet state under one-party domination. Or as Foreign Minister Eduard Shevardnadze warned, secession of republics would not only cause military, political, and economic problems for the regions but could result in a major destabilization of the existing international structure. While at this juncture it is unclear what the outcome of all these demands and aspirations unleashed under *glasnost* will be, it is logical to surmise that what has happened in terms of changes in the Soviet Union is irreversible. The new approach to

Soviet foreign policy will have to be based on common sense, not dogma. It is not surprising, therefore, that Gorbachev's "new thinking" in foreign policy envisions a "common European home," which he describes as a vast economic space from the Atlantic to the Urals where the Eastern and Western ports would be strongly interlocked. Although such a grand design is imaginable, it is not very practical at this time. Not everyone in the West is convinced that the time is right for expanding the European house eastward. Jacques Delors and other prominent EC leaders believe that the twelve nations of the European Community should take care of their own house before building a broader European house to include the East European countries and the Soviet Union in whatever shape or form. Therefore, the immediate objective for the EC leaders is to complete the Western section of the much touted "European home" by December 31, 1992.

Assuming that Europe can achieve this goal, there are many other issues of contention, in addition to protectionism and a single economic powerhouse that will be far better equipped to compete with the United States and Japan than the old European Community. After all, this is not the first time that European nations have set aside their differences in the name of international competitiveness. Will they go as far as to encourage some protectionist external barriers? It will be interesting to see if community directives call for reciprocity and establish preferences to discriminate against outsiders who negotiate regulatory standards for the community, and on what basis outsiders can receive mutual recognition of standards, and how bilateral quotas on cars and textiles are converted into EC-wide quotas. Since the European Community is making incremental changes in policies that discriminate against outsiders, it is possible that future U.S. trade frictions will not be so much with Japan as with the European Community.

What if "Project '92" should fail? Then, Europe and the United States as well would have to pay a high price for failure. According to this scenario, Europeans could perceive Americans as the cause of failure and take their frustrations out on the United States. In practice, it could bring about increased protectionism, an unwillingness to participate in NATO-related programs, and perhaps a shift to neutrality and demilitarization of Europe.

Regardless of whether the program fails or succeeds, certain developments will probably complicate the unification process before the end of 1992. For example, Mikhail Gorbachev's *perestroika* and the "new thinking" in foreign policy have already made a noticeable dent in the perceptions and attitudes of West Germans; in the spring of 1989 Gorbachev visited Bonn and invoked the old metaphor "common house of Europe," first used in Bonn in 1981 by Leonid Brezhnev. The meaning of the concept in 1981 and in 1989 is to exclude the Americans from the unification process.[7] The very same Soviet policy could have a negative influence on the revival of defense cooperation in the Western European Union and on U.S. reassessment of defense strategy and pressure for increased burden sharing and the future vitality of NATO.

Transnational Security Issues

A similar uncertainty is noticeable in the area of world security and the preservation of the human race. The global environment is punctuated by the threat of violence and the fear of possible annihilation. This trend is persistent in spite of the attempt made in 1928 to outlaw war as an instrument of foreign policy. In that year, almost every nation signed and ratified the General Treaty for the Renunciation of War—a document known as the

Kellogg–Briand Pact, or the Pact of Paris. The signatories condemned recourse to war for the solution of international disputes and pledged to use only peaceful means to resolve their disagreements. Sixty years later, however, individuals and nations have yet to remove the motivation for violence, and the international political system still lacks effective central institutions that are capable of conflict management and resolution. Consequently, nation-states—large or small, rich or poor—are preoccupied with defense preparations to promote national security. The drive for security and self-preservation continues to make people rely on military power as a deterrent against potential enemies. Since military power is primarily a political tool, its strength, strategy, and tactics vary from country to country, depending on the political system and the role of the military in it. Although the United States and the Soviet Union follow opposing concepts of military doctrine (defensive versus offensive), both nations consider the role of military might to be decisive in world politics. Scholars such as Robert J. Art, for example, defend this position by arguing that "as long as the physical use of force remains a viable option, military power will vitally affect the manner in which all states in peacetime deal with one another."[8]

However, advocates of military power do not suggest that force must actually be employed to be politically useful; they consider the value of force more as a bargaining device to pressure opponents to make compromises under a credible military posture or as a balancing device to create a political climate conducive to peace. They reject the arguments that nuclear weapons make war between the superpowers unthinkable, or that humanity's common problems have made war and military power passé, or that the world's nations have become so economically intertwined that military power is no longer a credible alternative. They believe that, although a superior military position can give one state a bargaining edge over another in the conduct of their bilateral economic relations, superiority in arms by itself does not guarantee superiority in economic leverage. Whether we look at the world as an armed camp or as a commercial beehive, the ultimate question for nations seeking global preeminence is whether to rely on force or on trade as the most useful means of achieving power or influence in the international political system. Richard Rosecrance, for example, asserts that "the trading state" has demonstrated greater advantages in this regard than the state committed to the acquisition of power and influence through territorial control and military buildup. While the latter state is doomed to weaken its global leadership role, the former state is gaining in prominence and prosperity.[9] According to Rosecrance, the military-political world is armed to overkill, but at the same time it is overextended, overburdened, and oversubscribed. On the other hand, the trading world is becoming richer, more stable, and more competitive. Seaports and airports are alive with international commercial transactions, foreign travel, cultural contact, and economic activity. Such activity is greater today than at any other time in human history. We live in an age of markets that force the hands of governments as well as other actors in the international arena. The markets, not the governments, are the "shakers and movers" in today's world. Japan is a good illustration of the soundness of economic stability: Only about 1 percent of the Japanese GNP is spent on defense, while foreign trade that amounts to 20 percent of the GNP fuels a prosperous economy. The United States spends half of its research and development budget on arms; Japan spends practically all of it on civilian production. Rosecrance's criticism notwithstanding, is it feasible for all nations in the international political system to relinquish military power and substitute trade as a means of security? Is the economic success of trading nations attractive enough to change the behavior of nations that adhere to the arms race, aggression, military intervention, and war? Is it possible for nation-states to be successful trading partners while maintaining a strong military capability?

The most urgent questions for both opponents and proponents of military force as a means of national security seem to be how to prevent a possible nuclear war and how to reduce the enormous cost of armaments. "The nuclear arms race," according to Carl Sagan, "has now booby-trapped the planet with some sixty thousand nuclear weapons—far more than enough to obliterate both [superpowers], to jeopardize the global civilization and perhaps even to end the million-year-long human experiment."[10] Nations spend over $1 trillion annually—about $2 million every minute—on arms. Nuclear arsenals are so large that the world could be destroyed many times over. The awareness of the devastating effects of nuclear weapons and war underscores the urgency of finding solutions to a multitude of issues that nuclear weapons pose.

Since the atomic age began in 1945, the members of the nuclear club, and the entire world, have experienced **chronic tension.** It is different from the older **acute tension,** which is more dynamic, more predictable and, therefore, more controllable—even though, in most instances during modern history, acute tension led to war. Chronic tension is deeper, encompassing total antagonism; it is less dynamic in its manifestation and can persist without explosive consequences. For decades after World War II, scholars and politicians believed that chronic tension could neither be maintained nor reduced by design. Since it could not be controlled by direct methods, some argued, chronic tension also contributed to equilibrium, particularly between the superpowers, which is based on the concept of reciprocal deterrence. In other words, a strategy of threatened punishment or denial convinces others that the costs of their anticipated action would outweigh the gains. Or to state it differently, we would be able to do to our opponents' cities and countryside whatever they might threaten to do to ours; that is to say, erase it from the surface of the earth. For all practical purposes, the superpowers cannot escape the circumstances to which they have both contributed—mutual assured destruction (MAD).[11] As a result, deterrence was transformed into an apocalyptic threat to commit suicide by both the attacker and the defender.

With the rise in power of Western Europe, Japan, and the People's Republic of China, American fear of Soviet aggression gradually diminished, and the old concept of deterring only a total strategic attack was modified to incorporate a discriminate deterrence based on selective and strictly military use of nuclear weaponry. Consequently, both superpowers now rely on highly accurate but less destructive long-range strategic weaponry, including procurement of the now-feasible nonnuclear strategic weapons.[12] Perhaps for these and similar reasons, President Reagan and General Secretary Gorbachev signed the Intermediate-Range Nuclear Forces (INF) Treaty on December 8, 1987; and in November 1985 in Geneva, Switzerland, and in October 1986 at Reykjavík, Iceland, they agreed to reduce strategic offensive nuclear arms by 50 percent.[13]

The ability of the Soviet and American negotiators to reach an agreement on nuclear weapons signifies a degree of flexibility and willingness to compromise on both sides. In the meantime, however, the English and the French retained their independent nuclear capabilities; before the breakdown of the Eastern bloc, this was of great concern to the Germans, who felt that unless short-range missiles (with a range of under three hundred miles) were also eliminated, Germany could become the victim of a possible war in Europe. For the Germans, the issue was how to prevent their soil from becoming the major battleground with conventional and nuclear weapons in a future war. Without a "double-zero" (zero intermediate and zero short-range missiles), Germany could have been "singularized" and "victimized" in a showdown between the two military alliances—NATO and the Warsaw Treaty Organization. Before the INF treaty was signed, the Federal Republic of Germany had agreed to modernize its short-range nuclear weapons. However, since 1988, because of serious domestic opposition to such upgrading of nuclear weapons, the West German government, under Chancellor Helmut Kohl, had been unable to reach a successful solution to the problem. Therefore, in May 1989 at the NATO summit, U.S. President George Bush and British Prime Minister Margaret Thatcher agreed to postpone modernization of the U.S.–built Lance launchers, deployed mostly in West Germany, until 1992. However, because of the political changes in Eastern Europe in early 1990, the plan to modernize the Lance launchers was abandoned. Weapons modernization could have unleashed political forces seeking a denuclearization of Europe and American disengagement from NATO and brought about the defeat of the Kohl government and the victory of the Social Democrats who were opposed to weapons modernization from the very beginning.

In addition, there are influential people in France who believe that the United States and the Soviet Union reached the INF agreement without regard for the security of the West European states. Since the French generally agree that nuclear deterrence has kept Europe free from war for the past forty-five years, they consider the INF treaty to be a sellout of European security interests. Therefore, their immediate concern is to prevent the Americans and the Soviets from forcing France and Great Britain to reduce their independent nuclear forces. The signing of the INF treaty and the ongoing negotiation regarding further reductions in nuclear arms do not mean that the arms race is over.[14] The Soviet Union and the United States will each retain thousands of other strategic and theater nuclear weapons, while they continue to develop new weapons that threaten to destabilize the balance of power between them. Although the INF treaty has eliminated a whole class of nuclear weapons on both sides, humanity is still threatened by nuclear annihilation, and it is still unclear whether Gorbachev's "new thinking" in foreign policy is a change of means rather than a change of ends.[15] Some world political leaders, George Bush among them, believe that Soviet "new thinking" has not yet totally overtaken the old. As long as the Soviet Union keeps producing more tanks, planes, submarines, and missiles than it did before Gorbachev's declaration of a unilateral reduction in Warsaw Pact conventional forces in December 1988, the critics are cautious not to rely on promises or wishful thinking in matters that can have dire consequences. Consequently, international security and defense against nuclear attack are still priority concerns for most nation-states, especially the United States. The past seven American presidents, for example, had no choice but to admit to their constituents that the government could not defend them against a first-strike nuclear attack. Therefore, it should not have been surprising when former President Reagan announced the launching of the Strategic Defense Initiative (SDI), also known as "Star Wars," on March 23, 1983. That initiative, as we saw in chapter 8, was predicated on the assumption that deterrence would be based more on the ability to defend rather than on the ability to retaliate with predictably tragic devastation. The president claimed that such a defense would render nuclear weapons impotent and obsolete.[16]

Although many scholars and politicians believe that the Star Wars ballistic missile defense is unlikely to be realized, others argue that a shift in strategy and weapons systems toward defense of heavy population centers is feasible and desirable.[17] American critics of the SDI system are not alone; they were joined from the beginning by Soviet leaders who characterized the program as an effort to reestablish military superiority over the Soviet Union, an effort to acquire a first-strike capability, or subterfuge for developing a war-winning capability.[18] Of even greater concern to Moscow is the possible shift in the arms race from strategic nuclear weapons to SDI competition. Should Reagan's prediction of SDI aims render nuclear weapons "impotent and obsolete," Soviet military power, which earned the Soviet Union the title of superpower in the 1960s, would be in jeopardy. Alternatively, should the Soviet Union accept the challenge and engage in SDI competition, Gorbachev's priority of economic reforms could suffer serious consequences. Perhaps the worst possible scenario for the Soviet decision makers would be to press on with the projected economic reforms and at the same time sacrifice certain advantages in their strategic nuclear posture for arms reduction agreements that might benefit the United States and its allies. In retaliation, however, the Soviets could employ their propaganda skills to promote themselves as the champions of world peace and disarmament, while tainting the United States as a warmonger bent on world domination. Whether the Soviet Union eventually accedes to any agreement that seeks to replace the present nuclear stalemate with a new relationship dominated by defenses on both sides is contingent on Soviet military theory, which until 1989 considered offense to be the linchpin of Soviet strategy and active defense only a backdrop for a counterforce strategy.

While the United States and the Soviet Union are key players in determining the future course of the nuclear arms race, many other players in the global arena will also decide whether we live in a peaceful or violent world. As we have pointed out in previous chapters, humanity's capacity for violence has increased precipitously—subject, of course, to the actor's financial or technological means. Although, in the past, only a few nation-states have been able to acquire the most sophisticated weapons to inflict greater violence with fewer personnel, these weapons are now available to anyone, including *terrorists*. In 1987, for example, a Roper poll asked Americans to name topics that they wanted the government to act on. Terrorism was named more often than nuclear arms reduction or Middle East peace. Terrorism has become the leading foreign policy issue for many Americans as well as for the citizens of other nations.

In chapter 7 we noted that terrorism is measured not only by the number of terrorist actions, but also by whether these actions can destabilize a society and show that the targeted government is incapable of coping with terrorism. There are numerous terrorist groups driven by a variety of motivations. Some are nationalist–separatists; others are revolutionary internationalists; still others are fanatics or religious fundamentalists. For instance, the "Khomeini movement" (which by the way is political as well as religious) represents a twelfth-century type of Islamic movement that involves spreading the Shi'a fundamentalist revolution to other Islamic states and driving Western influence from the Middle East. Although in general terrorists have been successful in achieving their immediate goals relative to the costs incurred, their larger aspirations (e.g., the changing of the world political and economic order, the elimination of Western influence from the Middle East, or the creation of an independent homeland) still remain only wishful thinking. Whether it is in the Middle East, Southeast Asia, or Spain, the assumption is that the creation of a homeland would not necessarily stop dissatisfied radicals from terrorist acts.[19] On the other hand, many Third World observers argue that terrorism is often the only available weapon of the oppressed who are deprived of a homeland. For example, they reason that to censure PLO violence against Israel and to condone South African oppression of Namibia are contradictions perpetrated by the United States and other industrialized states. Based on the logic that one person's "terrorist" is another person's "freedom fighter," the world's governments are not universally opposed to terrorism. This fact is also evident from the relatively low number of signatories (less than one-third of the UN membership) on the International Convention Against the Taking of Hostages, drafted in 1979. The convention provides that states shall prosecute or extradite all hostage takers, while recognizing the rights of **national liberation movements**.[20] Yet, on December 9, 1985, the UN General Assembly unanimously passed a resolution containing a blanket condemnation of all terrorism. A similar condemnation was issued on January 16, 1989, by thirty-five nations meeting in Vienna, Austria, to sign a new East–West agreement on human rights.[21]

Perhaps because terrorism is a subjective phenomenon, strategies for how to deal with it vary from country to country. Although the effects of terrorism are the same (to frighten and intimidate large numbers of innocent people and to capture public attention), the demands vary. Consequently, nation-states committed to combat terrorism cannot agree on (1) how to free hostages (e.g., by negotiating with the terrorists, by attempting a rescue, or by taking hostages for the purpose of exchange as Israel did in July 1989 [this action led to the execution of kidnapped UN Military Observer Lt. Col. Richard Higgins]); (2) how to reduce terrorism (e.g., by using military action or by relying on peaceful means); and (3) how to deal with states that support terrorism (e.g., by launching retaliatory strikes as the United States did against Libya in 1987 or by imposing economic restrictions as the United States did on Iran after the occupation of the U.S. Embassy in Tehran in 1979). There are no clear-cut answers or pat formulas to these questions. Political leaders, experts, intelligence analysts, and scholars who study terrorism disagree over the proper responses for combating terrorism. Regardless of whether the response is a unilateral national policy or a coordinated global effort, whether it is a highly visible display of force or behind-the-scenes intelligence work, whether it is directed at government sponsors of terrorism or at terrorist groups themselves, terrorism continues to be a major threat. Moreover, many counterterrorist strategies and tactics fail to alleviate the root causes of the problem and thus provide no solution to international terrorism.[22]

Transnational Ecological Issues

As we noted in chapter 13, global ecology issues are moving toward the top of the international agendum. A recent report by the World Commission on Environment and Development appealed to the conscience of the world community of nations with a plea for effective cooperation to manage ecological interdependence. This appeal is based on the somber findings that nature had been disastrously pillaged for profit; that life itself is threatened by toxic emissions, waste, dust, smoke, soot, pesticides, and chemical additives; and that the suicidal pollution of the oceans, the mass destruction of the forests, and the squandering of precious natural resources is rapidly approaching a crisis situation. The "eleventh-hour appeal" is actually a warning to all nation-states that the world is faced with imminent ecological collapse if they fail to cooperate in finding global solutions to transnational ecological issues.

The Global 2000 Report to the President issued similar warnings as early as 1980. The report's projections of impending disaster prompted an overwhelming response (there are hundreds of agreements on international and regional levels[23] dealing with ecological problems); however, not all of the environmental accords have produced results. In several instances environmental conservation lacks legal clout; and in other cases the loopholes in the agreements are large enough for the signatories to evade the issue and continue business as usual. Or as another "global pessimist" put it, the absence of either higher law or higher authority in the international system and the persistence of the principle of sovereignty encourage struggle and the pursuit of self-interest, not collaboration.[24] Many countries find it difficult to reconcile ecological and economic interests, and as a result, they are depleting forests and turning vast mining areas into wastelands, and rivers and seas near cities into cesspools. This is particularly true in more than one hundred developing countries, despite the existence of environmental conservation in these countries. Therefore, it is reasonable to assume that if these nations do not soon implement conservation programs and stop following the industrial nation's example in pursuing economic growth at all costs, the outcome will be disastrous not only for them but for our entire planet.

One plausible explanation for worldwide ecological negligence is the response by the "global optimists" to the pessimistic conclusions drawn in *The Global 2000 Report*. As a matter of fact, some of the report's projections have already proved wide of the target. So far, the diminution of global food production and energy supply has failed to materialize. On the contrary, by the mid-1980s global food production scored gains far more impressive than some had expected; between 1950 and 1985, there was an increase of 125 percent. In spite of the long war between Iran and Iraq, and several cutbacks in OPEC oil production, the global supply and price of oil stabilized during the 1980s. Some global optimists, like Julian L. Simon, argue that the reason for the overly pessimistic projections in *The Global 2000 Report* is false assumptions leading to unrealistic conclusions. "If we lift our gaze from the frightening daily headlines and look instead at wide-ranging scientific data as well as evidence of our senses, we shall see that economic life in the United States and the rest of the world has been getting better rather than worse during recent centuries and decades...I do not say that a better future will happen automatically or without effort. It will happen because men and women will use muscle and mind to struggle with problems that they will probably overcome, as they have in the past."[25]

Another plausible explanation for ignoring the seriousness of global ecological problems, especially in the Third World countries, is the disproportion in UN agencies between budgetary contributions and influence in determining how the money is spent. The United States, for example, has only 1 vote out of 159 in the General Assembly but contributes 25 percent of the UN's regular budget. As already mentioned in chapter 10, eight countries (the United States, the Soviet Union, Japan, Germany, France, Great Britain, Italy, and Canada) supply over 70 percent of the funds but have only 5 percent of the votes, while more than one hundred members, for the most part developing countries, pay less than 2 percent of the budget but determine who gets what. Therefore, the United States or other industrialized countries may propose larger allocations of funds for family planning or ecological programs in the Third World, but these developing nations will dispose of the funds as they see fit.

The global pessimists and optimists agree that the demands emanating from an ever-expanding population and the ability of the earth's delicate life-support systems to support its burgeoning billions require attention. However, they disagree on the proposed solutions. World population, now 5.2 billion, grew an unprecedented 90 million in 1987—that is, 247,000 a day or 170 people a minute. It is not clear whether the world population will finally level off at 8, 10, 12, or more billion. Certainly, however, population growth will profoundly affect the habitability of our planet. Population growth in many Third World countries is causing explosive increases in the population of already overcrowded cities (see the first supplemental reading, "Cities Without Limits") and poses grave threats to economic development, environmental balance, and political stability. A 1988 report by the UN Fund for Population Activities stated that thinning of the earth's protective ozone shield,[26] toxic chemical waste, pollution of water supplies, loss of soils and forests, and extinction of species are directly tied to rapid world population growth.

Population is static or declining in Western industrialized countries, but it is soaring in many parts of the Third World. Basing their arguments on the fallacious theory that population growth has a positive effect on economic development by increasing the potential for innovation (i.e., the more hands, the more brains), many developing societies have fallen victim to unabated population pressures. In China, for example, population pressures on land forced the development of rigid systems of landholding and government, which may have caused the late arrival of an industrial revolution. As the examples of Japan and Brazil demonstrate, there is a direct relationship between lower levels of fertility and per capita income. In 1960 Brazil's per capita GNP was $900 and Japan's was $1,400. Both countries have had similar economic growth rates; however, according to World Bank data, in 1984 while the GNP per capita in Brazil was only $1,720, Japan's was $10,630 (see figure 14.1). Brazil's higher fertility rate reduced its economic expansion to a relatively low level. Yet some scholars from the developing countries caution that "to imply that rapid population growth is the cause or even one of the main causes of the problem of poverty is clearly an oversimplification of the problem."[27] The basic cause of poverty in developing countries is usually the economic backwardness or stagnation of the rural areas where the vast majority of the population live.

Within the framework of the North–South dialogue, the spokespeople for the South argue that its mass of humanity would not be such a problem if more wealth were available to distribute among its people. Representatives of the North, however, urge the South simply to control its numbers. Thus, the problem remains: How to produce improved economic conditions in the Third World when such progress is hampered by the very population growth it could curb? The North is fully aware of the results of the demographic transition that European countries have experienced during the post-industrialization period and of the projections that, after the turn of the century, more than half the human race will live in urban areas. Latin America is already 70 percent urban[28] and Africa's urban population, which is now smaller than North America's, will be three times greater by the year 2025. Therefore, spokespeople from the North argue that any effective strategy to deal with rapid population growth, poverty, and ecological problems will succeed only if it is supported by successful efforts to educate and train people in family planning and technological advancement.

The last World Population Conference held in Mexico City in 1984 made it abundantly clear that developed and developing countries have a common interest in avoiding the consequences of current population trends, which were symbolized as a time bomb with important political, social, and economic implications that transcend national borders. Without controlling the burgeoning population growth, we cannot effectively manage our global resources. There can be no resource conservation in the Third World, unless the developed countries provide financial support for such conservation and unless intergovernmental organizations provide more internationalized management of these resources. The developed countries are not in full agreement on several of these issues. They disagree about the rights to "mine" the global commons and to derive profits from natural resources and about the priorities of conservation, pollution control, industrial expansion, and energy self-sufficiency. Scholars and politicians alike seem to agree that we must be wiser in the management of our global commons than we have been. Our success or failure depends on cooperation among the actors that have a vested interest in the management of our ecosphere. These actors include not only nation-states, but various subnational interest groups, multinational corporations and nongovernmental organizations, and IGOs. New technological developments have spurred the creation of international legal regimes to coordinate state behavior in areas such as air travel, telecommunications, space flight, ocean exploitation, nuclear energy, and meteorology. Impressive strides have been taken to deal with disasters and disease throughout the world. What is lacking in this impressive array of coordinative mechanisms

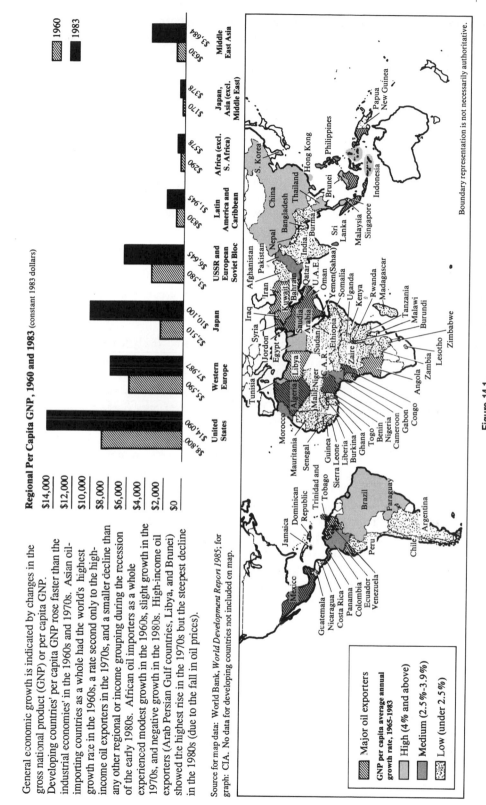

General economic growth is indicated by changes in the gross national product (GNP) or per capita GNP. Developing countries' per capita GNP rose faster than the industrial economies' in the 1960s and 1970s. Asian oil-importing countries as a whole had the world's highest growth rate in the 1960s, a rate second only to the high-income oil exporters in the 1970s, and a smaller decline than any other regional or income grouping during the recession of the early 1980s. African oil importers as a whole experienced modest growth in the 1960s, slight growth in the 1970s, and negative growth in the 1980s. High-income oil exporters (Arab Persian Gulf countries, Libya, and Brunei) showed the highest rise in the 1970s but the steepest decline in the 1980s (due to the fall in oil prices).

Source for map data: World Bank, *World Development Report 1985*; for graph: CIA. No data for developing countries not included on map.

Regional Per Capita GNP, 1960 and 1983 (constant 1983 dollars)

Figure 14.1

GNP growth rate in developing countries

SOURCE: Harry F. Young, *Atlas of United States Foreign Relations* (Washington, D.C.: Department of State Publication 9350, December 1985), p. 76.

is a strong, centralized mechanism for ensuring that general (global) interests prevail over special (national) interests.[29]

Future Prospects

We may begin our crystal-ball gazing by asking the question: Is the international system one unit with a single division of labor and multiple cultural systems,[30] or is it a horizontal organization of authority relations that explain how systemic properties act as a constraining and disposing force on the interacting units that constitute it?[31] In either case, competition between the governments of sovereign nation-states remains the dominant feature of the international system, although private and public nonstate actors are part of an ever-expanding web of human relationships that cut across state lines and impact global politics. This is a complex system not only in terms of the multitudes of actors interacting in the global arena, but also in terms of the range of issues that concerns them. Global issues converge in at least three areas—economic well-being, peace and military security, and ecopolitics and cultural identity—thus providing an impetus to press international cooperation for the sake of preserving humanity.

Although the number of states in the international system is not likely to expand much further, several small island territories may yet become full-fledged legal members of the interstate system. Most nations will no longer be preoccupied with attaining independence but rather with nation-building, both in terms of achieving political stability and economic viability (see the second supplemental reading, "The World and the United States in 2013"). One of the chief obstacles to nation-building in the Third World, particularly in Africa, will be the many competing nationalistic claims to self-determination. However, if nation-building continues in the developing world, a declining incidence of civil wars and insurrections would be expected as governments gain a stronger hold on the loyalty of their populations and the security of their territories.

The number of states may have neared its upper limit, but the population of the human race has not. By the turn of the century, in a little more than a decade, the global population will be a little over 6 billion. By 2040 to 2050, the earth's population will probably have doubled once again to a total of 12 to 15 billion. The vast majority of these people will inhabit Latin America, Africa, and Asia. As population in the Third and Fourth worlds skyrockets, we might well see changes in the ideological struggles and divisions that have marked international politics in the last forty-five years. For instance, although the East–West dispute between communism and capitalism has been the dominant preoccupation in our time, the key dividing line in future global politics may be rich versus poor nations. Ironically, the United States and the Soviet Union might eventually come to the conclusion that they have more common interests than competitive ones, provided the restructuring and openness that is now taking place in the Soviet Union frees it from its ideological constraints and replaces communist totalitarianism with democratic pluralism. Even if the Soviet Union and other socialist countries resist endeavors to oust the outmoded one-party dictatorships, global interdependence might increase to the point where efforts to solve major societal problems will be vested more and more in global IGOs like the United Nations or in regional IGOs like the Association of South-East Asian Nations. A multipolar world, with the two superpowers playing a dominant role, is slowly emerging. In this world one might expect growing cooperation among the Great Powers as they attempt to exercise a global responsibility in the absence of a world government.

However, as the momentum for interdependence increases and technological and other developments threaten to undermine the nation-state's sovereignty, some national governments may seek to reduce interdependence and return to a state-centric system.[32] In other words, as in physics, the movement toward global interdependence, representing the centripetal forces, will be challenged by state-centric supporters, representing the centrifugal forces. According to social anthropologists, there are as many as fifteen hundred distinct nationality or ethnic groups in the world. Potentially, each group is seeking full cultural identity and, in many cases, political independence. If this is not recognized to the satisfaction of the indigenous people, they may take matters into their own hands. If so, the process of realignment of power seeking a stable world order might not be as swift and smooth as the global problems would demand.

As a result of global interdependence, we might witness a further emergence of Third World regional associations that demonstrate a means for pragmatic cooperation to solve concrete day-to-day problems. However, many Third World nations still adhere to patriarchal institutions. Indeed, in some parts of the Third World, such as Africa, women perform nearly 80 percent of the agricultural work but are not treated as equal economic partners. The agenda for development of the Third World regional organizations are long and complex. Nevertheless, these organizations are in a better position to deal with their problems than either the United Nations or the individual Third World governments.

In economic terms, despite the slow increase in the world's industrial production, it is estimated that the young Third World will leap from 18 percent of world revenues in 1970 to 34 percent by the turn of the century—a figure equivalent to the United States's revenues in 1970, which is projected to drop to around 20 percent by the year 2000. In reality, this jump will mean an equalization process between the trading partners in which the so-called threshold countries will provide the "old" industrial nations with increasing competition. To meet this and other challenges, industrialized nations will continue to make significant investments in the scientific and technological innovations that are necessary to achieve an improved standard of living around the world. In Europe, for example, the emphasis is no longer on the eighteenth century dream of a "United States of Europe" to be achieved by reshaping different national identities into a "European" one, but on the formation of a homogeneous market, including finances, brain power, laws, and industrial policy. The aims of European integration as set forth in the 1992 goals are to harmonize the centripetal forces with the centrifugal ones to achieve economic well-being and cultural freedom in a secure environment.

As exemplified by the experiences of the Soviet Union and Japan, the limits of military power are far greater than those of economic power. In 1960 the Soviet Union's share in per capita world GNP was four times higher than Japan's and second only to the United States's. By 1986, however, the Soviet Union's share was not only lower than Japan's but also below that of the United States and the European Community. Economic stagnation in the Soviet Union resulted in a decline of about 12 percent in the Soviet share of per capita world GNP between 1960 and 1986. Not surprisingly, therefore, the Soviet Union is now compelled to make swift adjustments from military to economic expenditures. Since the United States has experienced similar, but not as severe, economic pressures resulting from the arms race (i.e., a slowing down of growth rate and standard of living), the following question arises: How long will the two superpowers be able to exert their unchallenged influences in the global arena? The answer, of course, depends not so much on the individual actors that might desire to replace either one or both superpowers, but rather on the conditions and circumstances that would necessitate the creation of powerful coalitions that could erode superpower influence on global affairs. Ultimately, it is not what a country can accomplish on its own, but what it can accomplish in concert with other nations that will determine which regions of the world thrive and grow and which countries see a substantial increase in power. For instance, the growth of Asian economic power may focus global concern on the Pacific Rim countries instead of on Europe and the Middle East. Before the bloody suppression of the peaceful student movement for democracy in Beijing's Tiananmen Square in June 1989, the prospects for stronger trade and commercial ties between Japan, the People's Republic of China, Hong Kong, and Taiwan looked promising. A continuation of Chinese economic and political liberalization and the return of Hong Kong to Chinese sovereign control by the end of the century would have brought about an economic alliance that could have presented a formidable challenge to the rest of the world. However, Beijing's decision to revert to Maoist tactics reminiscent of the "cultural revolution" represents a serious setback on the road to progress and democratization not only for China but for the entire region.

Will the 1990s and thereafter be more peaceful and secure than the 1980s? The interdependent world we live in has rendered new opportunities for cooperation, but it has also introduced new sources of disagreement. As contact, communication, and exchange among international actors have increased, so have mutual dependence and the number of potential rivalries, antagonisms, and disagreements. A world that has grown smaller does not necessarily become a more peaceful world. Power and influence still dominate global affairs, and spending on armaments has not changed precipitously since the superpowers agreed to eliminate INF strategic weapons. Even if the United States and the Soviet Union agree on significant strategic nuclear arms reduction, which is not only possible but probable in the not-too-distant future, controlling nuclear proliferation will remain a major arms control issue. To many countries, especially the United States, the problem of controlling global violence through international terrorism is probably one of the most urgent issues concerning security. The concept of global responsibility for preventing certain wanton acts of terrorist violence (e.g., hijacking and assassinations) and for apprehending terrorists has slowly been gaining acceptance; however, because of the international character of much contemporary terrorism, unilateral efforts to combat the problem are not as likely to succeed as concerted efforts taken by several governments acting together. So far, only a few draft conventions exist, and they have many loopholes and few enforcement provisions. It is unlikely that international terrorism will soon subside or that the international community will develop a consensus on how to combat terrorism.

Finally, the quest for security in an insecure world will depend on the management of global resources and **ecopolitics**—the relationship between world political and ecological issues.[33] Whether greater international cooperation in managing global resources is forthcoming will depend on the urgency of the matter caused by unforeseen natural disasters affecting not only one region but the entire world. The accumulation of carbon dioxide caused by burning coal and other fossil fuels is thought to produce a "greenhouse effect," that is, heat is trapped and the earth's temperature is raised. Some climatologists have estimated that the accumulated carbon dioxide has already raised global temperatures by $0.25°$ C which is enough to trigger abnormal droughts and economic disasters in certain agricultural areas. Since the sudden climatic changes threatening our ecosystem are caused by human pollutants, tropical deforestation, overgrazing, and overfarming, the logic of ecopolitics would dictate that earth's human inhabitants finally learn to manage global resources for the preservation of humanity.

Rafael M. Salas

Cities Without Limits

The world has embarked on a course which will transform it into a predominantly urban planet. By the time population stabilizes at the end of the next century, truly rural populations will have become a very small minority.

More than 40 per cent of the world population currently live in urban areas. This figure will increase to more than 50 per cent shortly after the turn of the century. Developed regions have been more than 50 per cent urban since the mid-20th century. Developing countries are expected to pass the 50 per cent mark in the first quarter of the next century.

Within the less developed regions there are important differences. The developing countries of Africa and Asia are less than 30 per cent urban. Latin America, on the other hand, is nearly 70 per cent urban, reflecting the region's stage of development and the special features of its urban structure and history.

By the Year 2000: 5 "Super-Cities" of 15 Million

Most of the world's urban population today lives in developing countries. In 1970 the total urban population of the more developed regions was almost 30 million more than in the less developed. Five years later the position was

Rafael M. Salas, of the Philippines, is an Under-Secretary-General of the United Nations and executive director of the United Nations Fund for Population Activities, which he has headed since it became operational in 1969. A graduate of the universities of the Philippines and of Harvard (USA), he has served as a Minister and occupied other high-level posts in the Philippine Government.
SOURCE: Rafael M. Salas, "Cities Without Limits," *UNESCO Courier* 40, no. 1 (January 1987): 10–17.

reversed and by 1985 the difference had widened to more than 300 million. By the year 2000 the urban population of developing countries will be almost double that of the developed countries. By the year 2025 it will be almost four times as large.

At present the urban population of Africa is smaller than that of North America, but by the beginning of the next century it is expected to be substantially greater, and three times greater by the year 2025.

The proportion of the world population living in the largest cities will almost double between 1970 and 2025, because of the growth of such cities in developing countries. By the year 2025 almost 30 per cent of the urban population in the developing regions will be living in cities of over 4 million, more than double the figure for the more developed regions. Although only a small proportion of the African population today lives in very large cities, by the end of the first quarter of the next century this proportion could be higher than that of any other continent. In developed countries, moreover, there is a trend towards deconcentration.

By the year 2000 there will be five "super-cities" of 15 million or more inhabitants, three of them in the developing regions. Two of them, in Latin America, will have populations of around 25 million. In 1970, nine of the twenty largest cities in the world were in the less developed regions; in 1985 there were ten and by the year 2000 there will be sixteen.

This change signals the end of the close relationship between large cities and economic development. Until recently such cities were because of their size centres of international political and economic networks, a situation which may now begin to change.

The urban population in developing countries is currently increasing three times more quickly than that of developed countries, at a rate of about 3.5 per cent a year, a doubling time of only twenty years.

There are important differences between the developing regions. Latin America has the lowest rates of population growth, followed by Asia. Africa, especially East Africa, has the highest. The current growth rate for Africa is 5 per cent a year, implying a doubling of the urban population every 14 years. The current figure for East Africa is above 6.5 per cent, a doubling time of little more than ten years.

Migrants to the Cities

Such extremely rapid urban growth is without precedent. It confronts the cities, especially in the developing countries,

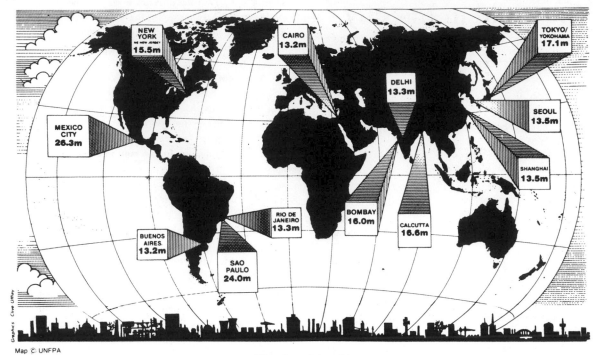

The rise of the cities

with problems new to human experience, and presents the old problems—urban infrastructure, food, housing, employment, health, education—in new and accentuated forms.

Furthermore, despite migration to the cities, rural population in developing countries will continue to increase, at a rate of around one per cent annually.

Five important points emerge from an analysis of United Nations population figures:

- The world's rural population is now more than 2.5 thousand million;
- Rural population density is already very high in many parts of the less developed regions. Standards of living, while improving, remain low. It is doubtful whether added demographic pressure will benefit agricultural development—on the contrary it may jeopardize the development of many rural areas;
- Increasing rural population in developing countries will make it difficult to reduce the flow of migrants to the cities;
- The natural growth rate (the difference between the number of births and the number of deaths) of the rural

population is higher than the one per cent rate—often more than double. The difference is due to the number of migrants to the cities;
- For most of Africa, unlike the rest of the developing world, rural populations will continue to increase until well into the next century.

Although urban fertility in developing countries tends to be lower than rural fertility, it is still at least twice as high as that in developed countries.

When natural increase in urban areas is high and migrants contribute substantially to it, the migrants' future fertility becomes an important factor. The high fertility typical of rural areas may be carried over into the urban environment; more optimistically, migrants plunging into new endeavours in a different context may adapt rather quickly to urban values, including lower fertility.

Those who consider urbanization to be a blessing hold that migration to the cities is part of a dynamic development process. Those who think that it is a burden believe that rural surplus population becomes an urban surplus, producing "over-urbanization," in which an inefficient and

The child in the city

For Third World parents the city may seem the best place to bring up a child—education and health services are usually better than in the country side. But there are disadvantages too: the city child will spend much more of the day away from the family and at greater risk of exploitation.

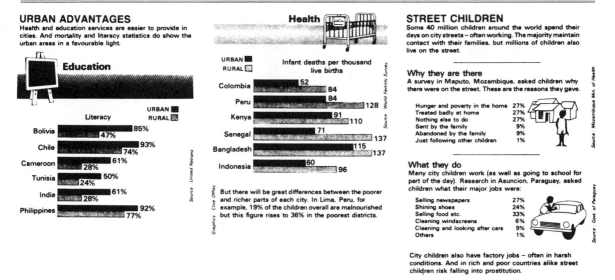

URBAN ADVANTAGES
Health and education services are easier to provide in cities. And mortality and literacy statistics do show the urban areas in a favourable light.

Education

URBAN ■
RURAL ▨

Literacy

Bolivia	47%	85%
Chile	74%	93%
Cameroon	28%	61%
Tunisia	24%	50%
India	28%	61%
Philippines	77%	92%

Source: United Nations

Health

URBAN ■
RURAL ▨

Infant deaths per thousand live births

Colombia	52	84
Peru	84	128
Kenya	91	110
Senegal	71	137
Bangladesh	115	137
Indonesia	60	96

Source: World Fertility Survey

But there will be great differences between the poorer and richer parts of each city. In Lima, Peru, for example, 19% of the children overall are malnourished but this figure rises to 36% in the poorest districts.

Graphics: Clive Offley

STREET CHILDREN
Some 40 million children around the world spend their days on city streets – often working. The majority maintain contact with their families, but millions of children also live on the street.

Why they are there
A survey in Maputo, Mozambique, asked children why there were on the street. These are the reasons they gave.

Hunger and poverty in the home	27%
Treated badly at home	27%
Nothing else to do	27%
Sent by the family	9%
Abandoned by the family	9%
Just following other children	1%

Source: Mozambique Min. of Health

What they do
Many city children work (as well as going to school for part of the day). Research in Asuncion, Paraguay, asked children what their major jobs were:

Selling newspapers	27%
Shining shoes	24%
Selling food etc.	33%
Cleaning windscreens	6%
Cleaning and looking after cars	9%
Others	1%

Source: Govt. of Paraguay

City children also have factory jobs – often in harsh conditions. And in rich and poor countries alike street children risk falling into prostitution.

The child in the city

unproductive "informal sector" consisting of street vendors, shoeshine boys, sidewalk repair shops and other so-called marginal occupations becomes more and more important.

Urban life has its positive aspects, but they emphasize employment rather than what workers get for their labour. A city worker may earn more than a rural counterpart, but is it enough to cover the basic needs of food, health, housing and education?

Two important aspects of urban life are income distribution and the number of city-dwellers living below an acceptable and culturally adjusted "poverty line." Reliable data are lacking, but it is probably true that the distribution of incomes is more inequitable in urban than in rural areas, in that there are proportionally more very rich and very poor people in the cities.

This may be as much an indication of economic development in the urban areas as of the privileges enjoyed by urban élites. Rapid demographic growth among the urban masses also contributes to the inequality of income distribution and swells the numbers of the poor.

A Massive Housing Deficit

The most visible manifestations of the problems of rapid urban population growth are the makeshift settlements on the outskirts of every city in the developing world. They are usually in the worst parts of town as regards health and accessibility, lacking basic services and security of tenure. They are by their nature overcrowded—average occupancy rates of four to five persons per room are common.

The names given to these settlements graphically express their characteristics. In Latin America the word *callampas* (mushrooms) refers to their almost magical overnight growth. The term *bidonvilles* (tin can cities), is often used in Francophone Africa to describe their makeshift nature. There are many other labels, usually given by outsiders: those who live in these settlements might describe them differently, perhaps even considering them as starting points on the path to a higher standard of living.

There is a massive housing deficit in many large cities. The World Bank estimated in 1975 that the poorest quarter of the population in most African and Asian cities

How cities grow

The urban population of developing countries will be almost double that of developed countries by the year 2000—according to the 1986 'State of World Population' report from the UN Fund for Population Activities.

BUILDING FROM BELOW

The major architects of today's Third World cities are poor families building their own homes. The diagram below shows the percentage of squatters and slum dwellers in four major cities.

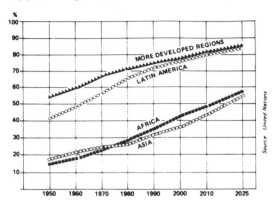

60% KINSHASA

46% MEXICO CITY

67% CALCUTTA

55% MANILA

Graphics : Clive Offley

Source : Assignment Children 57/58

CONTINENTAL CONURBATIONS

Latin America has some of the largest cities of the developing world – but Africa is now urbanizing at a rapid rate. The chart shows the percentage of the population living in urban areas.

MORE DEVELOPED REGIONS

LATIN AMERICA

AFRICA

ASIA

Source : United Nations

How cities grow

cannot afford even minimal housing. Wood and cardboard packing crates, sheets of plastic or corrugated iron, flattened tin cans, leaves, bamboo and beaten earth are the main sources of materials.

Space is also a problem. Landlords may add illegal floors to existing buildings, only to watch their dreams of wealth collapse along with the buildings and the lives of the unfortunate inhabitants. In some cities several workers will use the same "hot bed" in shifts over the twenty-four hours. In Cairo squatters have occupied a large cemetery; the tombs of the wealthy have become homes for the poor.

Colonies of squatters occupy the last areas to be settled, and may be perched on steep hillsides subject to frequent landslides, or installed by rivers or on swampy ground which is flooded regularly. In Mexico City about 1.5 million people live on the drained bed of a salt lake, bedevilled by dust storms in the dry season and floods in rainy months. In Lagos, Nigeria, the proportion of wet land to dry land settled has worsened, while the absolute area of dry land occupied has doubled.

Where squatter settlements have been established near workplaces, the inhabitants may run the risk of pollution and are exposed to dangers such as the leak of poisonous gas in Bhopal, India, or the explosions at oil refineries in Mexico City.

Squatter settlements typically lack water, sewage and waste disposal facilities, electricity and paved streets. In Mexico City, 80 per cent of the population have access to tapwater, but in some squatter settlements the figure is less than 50 per cent. Water consumption in the wealthy quarters of Mexico City is at least five times as high as in the poorer areas. In Lagos, water is strictly rationed and in some parts of the city residents must walk long distances to obtain water from a few pumps which are turned on only in the early morning.

According to a study carried out in Lima, Peru, lower income groups spent three times more per month on water from vendors but consumed less than a sixth as much as those with running water at home.

It is estimated that three million inhabitants of Mexico City do not have access to the sewage system. In São Paulo, Brazil, the absence of sewage systems have turned the two main rivers into moving cesspools.

Because they occupy land owned by the government, private individuals or communal organizations, squatters are frequently subject to harassment, which increases their feeling of insecurity and the precariousness of their existence. Illegal or barely legal occupation does nothing to encourage squatters to improve or even maintain the shaky structures in which they live.

A number of schemes have been devised to give more security to squatters, but there are risks. One is that improving living conditions in the city will encourage people to move there. Another is that improvements to property will increase its value and encourage squatters to sell, while moving it out of the reach of other low-income families.

Two Urgent Problems: Child Health and Education

The health of the poor may be worse in urban than in rural areas. Infant mortality in the Port-au-Prince slums is three times higher than it is in the rural areas of Haiti. In some of the *favelas* of São Paulo, infant mortality is over 100 per thousand live births. The overall infant mortality rate for the slums of Delhi is 221 per thousand, twice that for some castes. In Manila infant mortality is three times higher in the slums than it is in the rest of the city. (Tuberculosis rates are nine times higher; the incidence of diarrhea is twice as common; twice as many people are anemic and three times as many are undernourished.) In Panama City, of 1,819 infants with diarrheal diseases, 45.5 per cent came from the slums and 22.5 per cent from squatter settlements. Children living in the best housing were not affected.

In most cities in developed countries, young people under 19 constitute less than 30 per cent of the population. In developing countries, the proportion is typically over 40 per cent and may reach 50 per cent in cities such as Manila, Jakarta and Bogotá. If the education system breaks down under this sort of pressure, it will add immeasurably to problems of employment delinquency and allied problems caused by the existence of "street children."

Education is probably the most pressing of urban problems. A lower rate of population growth would immeasurably help the situation, but such a decrease partly depends on the spread of education. Family planning programmes will certainly be useful, but they must be accompanied by renewed efforts to bring education to the urban masses.

How Will the Cities Be Fed?

How will agriculture respond to the tremendous pressure of urbanization and the growth of urban population? A recent study by the United Nations Food and Agriculture Organization (FAO) and the United Nations Fund for Population Activities (UNFPA) draws attention to some of the likely effects.

First, urban populations demand cheap food. By weight of numbers they force governments to keep retail prices down. Governments may make up the difference by subsidizing farmers but experience has shown that, once established, such subsidies are difficult to withdraw.

Second, as urban populations grow and indigenous agriculture fails to keep up with demand (for lack of incentive to increase supply), more food is imported. This drains off hard currency intended for capital imports with a view to long-term development.

Third, urban population increase means that rural populations and the agricultural labour force will grow more slowly. But to meet urban needs agricultural productivity should be increasing by 17 per cent for each agricultural worker in developing countries between 1980 and the year 2000. This figure seems high, but recent experience in Asia and Latin America shows that it is possible.

For Africa, however, the increase per worker will have to be almost 25 per cent, an eventuality that seems very doubtful in view of recent events. Research in Africa has shown that lower production gains were made in countries with high rural-urban migration. This contrasts with experience in other regions, where rural-urban migration has been at least partly the consequence of higher agricultural labour productivity.

Fourth, tastes in food change under the influence of urban life-styles, as traditional staples are partly replaced by foods such as bread, meat and vegetables.

Fifth, the growth of urban population intensifies competition for land, water and energy. Cities gobble up agricultural land, often the best land because its fertility was the original attraction which stimulated urban growth. Between 1980 and the year 2000, according to one study, cities will devour four million hectares of land with the potential to feed 84 million people.

Sixth, while malnutrition may be more widespread among rural populations, the urban poor suffer more acutely. People in the lowest income groups normally have to spend more than half of their incomes on food.

Balanced Approaches to an Urban Planet

The transformation from a rural to an urban planet offers both great blessings and heavy burdens. The transition from agrarian to urban has always been considered a positive step, part of the process of modernization. However, the rapid growth of urban populations in societies rapidly changing in other ways is fraught with enormous tension and tremendously complex problems.

In its search for solutions to problems of urban population dynamics, UNFPA puts continuous emphasis on three fundamental objectives: economic efficiency, social equity and population balance. It recognizes that the solution for many urban problems will only come through economic efficiency and vast growth of the productive forces. Economic growth is essential to any solution of urban problems. At the same time social equity should be pursued, with emphasis on equal opportunity for all.

Neither economic efficiency nor social equity can be attained without demographic balance—balance within and between urban and rural areas, balanced population distribution and balanced population growth.

Daniel Bell

The World and the United States in 2013

Introduction: A Cautionary Tale

Can we predict the future? If we mean by that the exact configuration of world society, or even of the United States in 2013, not likely. The imponderables are primarily the political–ideological currents that are too complex and not easily charted.

Consider: Few analysts before World War II predicted the collapse of the old colonial systems—the British, French, Dutch empires—and the rapid emergence of the Third World and the vast number of new nations that are today relevant actors on the world scene. Few writers a decade ago predicted the rise of Khomeini and the transformation of Middle Eastern politics, or the use of terrorism as an instrument of national policy.

The future: What will happen in Cuba after the demise of Castro? Will it be like Ghana after the passing of Nkrumah? Does anyone remember Nkrumah today? Yugoslavia lapsed into a lethargic Balkan state after the death of Tito. Will this be true of other autocratic states? Spain negotiated the difficult transfer to democracy after more than forty years of rule by Franco. Will this be true of Brazil or Argentina or Chile? Most important, perhaps: Can Gorbachev modernize and even liberalize the Soviet Union? We do not know.

. . .We tend to project the present configurations onto the future. But, by the mid-1990s and the year 2000, will there be a closer unity of the two Germanys and a realignment with the Soviet Union? This happened in Rapallo, in 1922, when the Soviet Union and Germany made a pact, and the Russians retrained the German army in violation of the Treaty of Versailles. And there was a Hitler–Stalin pact in 1939. Some such possibility is at least conceivable for two reasons: the Russians would benefit enormously from German technology; Germany, losing out in world markets, would have a huge customer in Russia, taking Russian raw materials in exchange. On the political level, this would certainly break up NATO (which is, in any case, becoming sclerotic) and give the Russians a security zone. Possible? Perhaps. Impossible? Not so.

One can do forecasting when one has an algorithm (a decision rule) that tells us into which "slots" phenomena may go. There are no algorithms in politics. . . . The world society is like a set of giant Calder mobiles, shifting in uneasy balances in accordance with the winds of change, but the exact configurations are difficult to capture— especially for twenty-five years from now.

What, then, can one do?

. . .Within a limited frame—yet, I believe, one challenging enough—one may be able to identify *basic structural frameworks* that are emerging, that form the matrix of people's lives. . . .

1. The Shift to the Pacific Basin

The major question is whether, by the year 2013, the Pacific Basin will be the center of economic power. If so, the East Asian countries, led by Japan and China, the Southeast Asian nations, and the United States and USSR, will be the major economic players in the world*. . . .

If there is an economic shift, which is probable, will there also be a political shift? And, if so, is it possible for a country to be a major political power without also, in time, becoming a major military power? Unlikely. What, then, of the reemergence of Japan, of the emergence of China, as important military powers?

The major "line of economic force" is from Japan to Australia. Japan has few natural resources and produces little food of its own. Australia has large deposits of coal and uranium; it is a major granary. We could have here, in a new form, the resumption of the old Japanese "East Asian Co-Prosperity Scheme." . . .

*Though it is often forgotten, the Pacific Rim also touches eleven Latin American countries, six island nations (including Fiji, Papua–New Guinea, the Solomon Islands), six Asian countries (including Indonesia, Malaysia, Thailand), three newly industrialized countries (South Korea, Taiwan, Hong Kong), and the five advanced industrial societies of the West, outside of the Soviet Union and China.

SOURCE: Daniel Bell, "The World and the United States in 2013," *Daedalus* 116, no. 3 (Summer 1987): 1–32. Copyright © by Daniel Bell.

2. The New International Division of Labor

The old division of labor, which shaped the world economy for the two hundred years from 1780 to 1980, created a set of *core* manufacturing societies (the United Kingdom and Germany, then the United States, then the USSR and Japan), together with a *periphery* of countries, principally in the Third World, that provided raw materials and primary products for the core countries. This is now breaking up and no simple, single pattern has emerged. Yet basic industrial manufacturing of standardized mass-production products is being "pulled out" of the Western world and located in East Asia and, to a lesser extent, in Brazil and the Mexican–Caribbean region.

The United States and Japan have become postindustrial societies; the predominant sectors are the service and high-tech sectors. By 1990, almost 75 percent of the U.S. labor force will be in services. The word *services* conjures up images of fast-food, low-wage employments. This is misleading. (In fact, the expansion of those sectors is in almost equal proportion to the decline of doing things at home, especially as more women go to work)....

In the new manufacturing, the proportion of raw materials steadily diminishes as a percentage of use and costs. In the advanced countries, the basic change is a move away from heavy, materials-intensive products and processes: one hundred pounds of optical fibers in a cable can transmit as many messages as one ton of copper wire.

Raw materials diminish in importance, not only because of miniaturization (e.g., chips) and the reduction of energy requirements, but also because of the revolution in materials science. One asks less for specific materials—tin, zinc, copper—and more for the properties needed (e.g., tensility, conductivity) and the material combinations that can provide those properties.

If the first change is in the multiple centers of manufacturing, the second is in the centers of finance: The United States becomes a headquarters economy for large parts of the world. London, halfway between New York and Tokyo (in time), becomes a financial services node.

The chief point is the *internationalization of capital.* This was foreshadowed before the end of the century by the vast hoard of "stateless" Eurodollars (dollars held by banks and countries outside the United States) that was not subject to U.S. financial regulation.

The existence of this vast hoard meant that banking and corporate groups could direct their capital in search of higher returns, even when such action went against the domestic interests of individual countries. *This means that few countries, if any, are able to control their own currency. There is a loss of one of the main levers of power and influence....*

Some new international monetary systems will have to emerge to form the backbone of the new international economy. Gold is a simple solution: Prices are dominated in gold; gold is fungible. Yet, it is also subject to manipulation; it cannot function easily as an independent standard outside political controls. The Soviet Union and South Africa are large gold producers and are able to skew the standard. Also, gold is too rigid, largely unavailable to most of the smaller, less-developed countries.

Two other possibilities: a "basket" of major currencies, or a "basket of commodities" in which countries deposit commodities and draw credits for them. A far-out solution, yet rational: an international Federal Reserve-type system, as a supercontrol for the national central banks, performing a "Paul Volcker role" against the Treasury authorities, as proposed by Richard Cooper.

All this may seem esoteric; yet, without some new international structural arrangement, the world economy will remain erratic and unstable. A new monetary system does not rule out instabilities, but makes these more manageable within national contexts....

3. Time Bombs: Polity and Demography

...We have today an international economy, heavily interdependent and almost integrated, tied together in "real time." With some major changes in transportation, it could be tied together physically as well. Consider the possibility of supersonic ballistic aircraft. The Concorde today is limited in its speed; but the development of ballistic aircraft would mean that the distance from New York to Tokyo, or from London to Tokyo, would be about five hours. The distance from Tokyo to Sydney would be about three hours; from New York to Sydney, about five hours. The world is being banded together by communication, possibly by transportation.

Yet while the international economy is increasingly integrated, many polities are fragmenting. The process is accordion-like, expanding and contracting at particular moments. In Belgium the fragmentation is linguistic and national; in Canada it is linguistic; in Northern Ireland it is religious; in Spain it is based on local nationalism; in Nigeria it is tribal. In any of these nations the divisions follow the historic "fault lines" of these countries. But because it seems to be happening in so many different places, one ought to suspect a common underlying structural problem. It is, I believe, this: *The nation-state is becoming too small for the big problems of life, and too big for the small problems of life.*

It is too small for the big problems of life because there are no effective international mechanisms to deal with the problems of capital flows, commodity imbalances, the loss of jobs, and the several demographic tidal waves that will be developing in the next twenty years.

It is too big for the small problems of life because the flow of power to a national political center means that the national center becomes increasingly unresponsive to the variety and diversity of local needs, and local centers lose the ability to effectively control resources and make their own decisions.

In short, there is a mismatch of scale.

A historical retrospect: What was the New Deal of Franklin D. Roosevelt? For some it was "creeping socialism," for others it was "saving capitalism." Perhaps so, but not the central point. In effect, and without much forethought and planning, *it was a response to a change in scale.* From 1900 to 1930, there was a growth in national markets and in national corporations. But the effective economic and countervailing power remained in the hands of the states. What the New Deal did was to create effective national mechanisms to deal with national economic problems: a Securities and Exchange Commission to regulate financial markets; a National Labor Relations Board for collective bargaining; a national social security system; federal help for unemployment assistance.

There is no such matching of scales today. And, given the multiplication of national sovereignties as a result of the breakup of the old colonial system, it is not likely to happen soon. The United Nations is ineffective; the United Nations Educational, Scientific, and Cultural Organization and the International Labor Organization are even more so. In short, there are few, if any, effective international economic or coordinating agencies to match international economic power. And the national political state becomes increasingly ineffective in coping with this problem. *So we see international economic integration and national political fragmentation. . . .*

. . .World population today is about 5 billion persons. Given present projections, it could double in forty years, to about 10 billion. By the year 2000 it would be 6 billion. Can we feed all these people? Will there be sufficient jobs? These are the ways the questions are usually put. I suggest that both the estimates and the questions are misplaced. They are projections, and for a large variety of reasons, they will not hold. (They are not holding, for in the logistic-curve plotting, the rate of growth is already tapering off.) The question of food is equally misplaced.

Are there, then, no problems? Not at all. There are several distinct problems, one of which, in fact, will constitute a threatening time bomb in the next twenty years. . . . It is this: *the widening gap between the age cohorts in different parts of the world.* To break down the jargon: In all of Africa, the proportion of young people under fifteen years of age is between 40 and 50 percent of the population. In almost all of Latin America—in particular, in Central America and the Caribbean—the proportion of young persons is about 40 percent of the population. In most of Asia, the proportion is between 30 and 40 percent. In the United States and Canada, the proportion is about 22 percent. With the exception of Ireland, in Europe it is about 20 percent or below.

These population imbalances mean that, in the next twenty years, we will see demographic tidal waves sweeping the world. In the heavily weighted countries, this will mean more than a doubling of the rates of entry into the labor forces.

Consider Mexico. Mexico today has a population of 80 million, 42 percent of whom are under fifteen years of age. What will happen to these young people? Unemployment is effectively at roughly 20 percent (including underemployment). The capital stock cannot be expanded easily. Inflation has been rampant. Logically, there are only three things Americans can do to help the Mexicans:

1. give them money (capital)—which they cannot now absorb because of a heavy past debt;
2. buy their goods—which may take jobs away from Americans;
3. take their people—which we have already done to some extent, though many are illegal aliens.

In the quarter-century after World War II, Europe had the same problem. . . . The European part of the Soviet Union follows the pattern of a declining population growth. The Central Asian sections are spurting ahead at an almost 3 percent annual increase. Those areas are largely Muslim. By the turn of the century, the Russian population will probably be a minority in the Soviet Union. Given the age distributions, perhaps 35 percent of the Soviet Army will then be Muslim.

The Soviets are in a bind: whether to take populations from Asia into their European land mass, very difficult because of the lack of housing and services, together with the prospect of the multiplication of ethnic tensions; or to allocate large resources to expand economic activities in the Asian areas, to provide jobs for a young population. This requires a diversion of present resources; also the possible loss of some political control of those regions. (This may provide one reason for a Soviet move toward rapprochement with Germany.) . . .

4. Resources

By "resources" I mean food, water, energy, metals and minerals, forests and wetlands, the ozone problem. Contrary to received and popular opinion, these are not crucial shock areas, or even major constraints. I shall have to be abrupt, and even preemptory: The simple point is that all the estimates, from the Club of Rome's to Global 2000's, are based on projections; they overestimate the demand side and are often wildly wrong on the supply side. . . .

. . .Ten years ago there were only about five major exporters of cereals and grains: the United States, Canada, Australia, Argentina, and, marginally, one or two other countries. Today, almost every country in the world is just about self-sufficient in food, and seeking export markets. India is a prime example. The only major importer of grains today is the Soviet Union, and that too may change.

. . .Global 2000 concluded that the world demand for food would increase steadily for twenty years, that food production would fall in the developed countries, that real food prices would double. This was in 1980. But global food production has increased everywhere, particularly in the United States, where farmers went deeply into debt to expand their acreage. Today we have a worldwide glut.

How about famines? Until the twentieth century, a famine was recorded almost every year somewhere in the world. Today famines are rare. The one in Ethiopia and surrounding regions was caused by a combination of drought *and the destruction of the small-trading storage system* by the political authorities.

This is the key point in almost all instances: The problems of food production are *political*. In Ethiopia, Mengistu destroyed the old system in order to resettle populations; a famine that might have been averted, spread. Burma, traditionally a rice-exporting country, has had to import rice since the military dictatorship of Ne Win; yet the topography of the country remains the same. The wheat-growing areas of the Soviet Union are geographically akin to those of the North Dakota–Saskatchewan region; we produce gluts, they import. The reason (weather aside) is that collectivization does not work, and the Russians are trying slowly to get out of that bind.

While famine is not a "problem," malnutrition surely is; but this derives from poverty, and the failures of economic growth; those are political and cultural.

. . .Whether we will "run out" of oil by the year 2013 is problematic. Present projections indicate an oil crisis in the early to middle 1990s. We do not know what new sources may be available directly (e.g., China) or through better extraction (shale, geothermal). That is not the issue. Better management and conservation have been the most effective means of utilizing energy. By the year 2013, there will be new technologies on the horizon: light-emitting diodes, which will replace light bulbs and traffic lights; superconductivity which will enlarge power grids, possibly through windmills and solar panels.

. . .[Water is] a growing problem, especially in the United States, but largely a problem because of waste and mismanagement and pollution. Again, not a resource problem primarily, but an economic and political one: the need for better management of scarce resources.

5. A Summation

Can one draw an integral, coherent picture of the world in 2013? Given simply the political imponderables sketched here, the answer is probably no.

Can one identify major policy issues? If one wishes to concentrate on the principal problems, the most explicit ones would be the demographic, age–cohort imbalances. The most diffuse yet crucial one would be the political fragmentation. Of the structural changes, the rise of the Pacific Rim is clearly the major change in the offing, and it is of extraordinary historic and economic importance. . . .

Study Questions

1. What are the symptoms of change in the current international system?
2. Why did the Seventy-Sixth American Assembly refer to the 1990s as the watershed years in global affairs?
3. According to the assembly report, what are the growing dangers in the 1990s?

4. What have been the two opposing trends in the nation-state system since the end of World War II?

5. What is the evidence for the criticism that nation-states are no longer capable of playing certain historic roles?

6. What entities or institutions are challenging the state's position in international relations?

7. Why aren't states in today's world economically self-reliant?

8. Why is the world debt problem an example of economic interdependence?

9. What are some of the proposals for solving the world debt problem?

10. How has economic interdependence impacted the separation of domestic and foreign policy?

11. What are the three prevailing paradigms to understanding international political economy?

12. What are the aims and purposes of the "trade regime" under the General Agreement on Tariffs and Trade?

13. What is the link between GATT and the discrimination and destabilization of the world economy?

14. What are the prerequisites for economic power?

15. Why are economic summit conferences important?

16. After outlawing war in 1928, why are nation-states still preoccupied with preparations for defense and national security?

17. What are the views put forth by advocates of the use of military power?

18. Why is the trading state gaining in preeminence and prosperity and the military–political state overextended and overburdened?

19. Why are markets, not governments, the "shakers and movers" of the world?

20. What is the difference between *chronic* and *acute tension*?

21. What are the theories of deterrence?

22. Is partial nuclear disarmament achievable? Give examples.

23. Why are international security and defense against nuclear attack still priority concerns of most nations?

24. What is the controversy surrounding the Strategic Defense Initiative?

25. Why has terrorism become the leading foreign policy issue for Americans as well as other people throughout the world?

26. What is *international terrorism,* and what is its aim?

27. What are the issues of terrorism on which nation-states and experts disagree?

28. What are some of the ecological threats to our planet?

29. Why are some of the projections in *The Global 2000 Report* considered unrealistic? Give examples.

30. What are the arguments of the "global pessimists" and the "global optimists?"

31. Why don't all nation-states cooperate in the management of global resources?

32. Why is rapid population growth by itself not the main culprit behind world ecological problems?

33. What are some fallacious theories about population growth and its impact on economic development?

34. What are the main arguments between the Northern and Southern Hemispheres concerning population growth and its impact on economic development and ecology?

35. What are the projected economic, security, and ecopolitical trends in the transcending interdependent global system?

Key Terms

acute tension
Brezhnev doctrine
chronic tension
dependencia model
ecopolitics
Group of Seven (G-7)

Kellogg–Briand Pact
mercantilist model
national liberation movement
sovereignty-at-bay model
Soviet bloc

Notes

1. See William E. Brock and Robert D. Hormats, eds., *The Global Economy, America's Role in the Decade Ahead* (New York: Norton, 1989).
2. See the address by Deputy Secretary of State John C. Whitehead before the Council on Foreign Relations, New York City, October 21, 1987; reprint, *Third World Dilemma: More Debt or More Equity* (Washington, D.C.: Department of State, Bureau of Public Affairs, October 1987), p. 5.
3. See Robert Gilpin, "Three Models of the Future," *International Organization* XXIX, no. 1 (Winter 1975): 37–60. For the neo-realist perspective, see Stephen D. Krasner, *Structural Conflict: The Third World Against Global Liberalism* (Berkeley: University of California Press, 1985), which criticizes the three models for neglecting the real driving force behind the workings of the international economy.
4. See Charles Lipson, "International Cooperation in Economic and Security Affairs," *World Politics* XXVII, no. 1 (October 1984): 1–23.
5. See Martin Wolf, "Fiddling While the GATT Burns," *World Economy* (London) IX, no. 1 (March 1986): 16. An edited version of the article was reprinted in *The Global Agenda: Issues and Perspectives,* 2nd ed., Charles W. Kegley, Jr., and Eugene R. Wittkopf, eds. (New York: Random House, 1988), pp. 299–307.
6. See H. Garrett De Young, "Shape of the Future Europe 1992," *CFO,* October 1988, pp. 38–46; Pierre-Henri Laurent, "The European Community: Twelve Becoming One," *Current History,* November 1985, pp. 357–360, 394; and Edward Heath, "European Unity over the Next Ten Years: From Commonwealth to Union," *International Affairs* 64, no. 2 (Spring 1988): 199–207.
7. See *Frankfurter Allgemeine Zeitung,* July 1989.
8. Robert J. Art, "To What Ends Military Power?" *International Security* IV, no. 4 (Spring 1980): 3.
9. See Richard Rosecrance, *The Rise of the Trading State: Commerce and Conquest in the Modern World* (New York: Basic Books, 1986).
10. Carl Sagan, "The Common Enemy," *Parade Magazine,* February 7, 1988, p. 4.
11. For an explanation of the mutual deterrence doctrine, see Spurgeon M. Keeny, Jr., and Wolfgang K. H. Panofsky, "MAD Versus NUTS: Can Doctrine or Weaponry Remedy the Mutual Hostage Relationship of the Superpowers?" *Foreign Affairs* 60, no. 2 (Winter 1981–1982): 287–304.
12. See the Commission on Integrated Long-Term Strategy, *Discriminate Deterrence* (Washington, D.C.: Government Printing Office, January 1988).

13. See "The INF Treaty: Negotiation and Ratification," Current Policy No. 1039 (Washington, D.C.: Department of State, Bureau of Public Affairs, February 1988); and David Mellor, "The INF Agreement: Is It a Good Deal for the West?" *NATO Review* 35, no. 6 (December 1987): 1–5.

14. See Paul H. Nitze, "START: Reducing and Bounding the Threat," *Arms Control Update* (U.S. Arms Control and Disarmament Agency), July 1988, pp. 1–5; and Richard K. Betts, "NATO's Mid-Life Crisis," *Foreign Affairs* 58, no. 2 (Spring 1989): 37–52.

15. See, for example, V. Zhurkin, S. Karaganov, A. Kortunov, "Vyzovy bezopasnosti-starye i novye" (Challenges to Security—Old and New), *Kommunist* (Moscow), no. 1 (1988): 42–50; and "Gorba Claus," *New Republic,* January 2, 1989, pp. 5–7.

16. Remarks by President Reagan at a briefing on the Strategic Defense Initiative, Washington, D.C., August 6, 1986. Current Policy No. 858 (Washington, D.C.: Department of State, Bureau of Public Affairs, August 1986).

17. See, for example, Jerome Slater and David Goldfisher, "Can SDI Provide a Defense?" *Political Science Quarterly* 101, no. 5 (1986): 839–856; and P. Edward Haley and Jack Merritt, eds., *Strategic Defense Initiative: Folly or Future?* (Boulder: Westview, 1986).

18. See Benjamin S. Lambeth, "Soviet Perspective on the SDI," in *Strategic Defenses and Soviet-American Relations,* Samuel F. Wells, Jr., and Robert S. Litwak, eds. (Cambridge, Mass.: Ballinger, 1988), pp. 37–77.

19. Walter Laquer, "Reflections on Terrorism," *Foreign Affairs* 65, no. 1 (Fall 1986): 86–100.

20. See Harry H. Almond, Jr., "The Legal Regulation of International Terrorism," *Conflict* 3, no. 2 (1981): 144–165.

21. For the full text of the document, see *New York Times,* January 17, 1989, pp. 1, 12.

22. Cf. Conor Cruise O'Brien, "Thinking About Terrorism," *Atlantic Monthly,* June 1986, pp. 62–66; Neil Livingstone and Terrell Arnold, eds., *Fighting Back: Winning the War Against Terrorism* (New York: Livingstone, 1986); Uri Ra'anan, Robert Pfaltzgraff, Richard Schultz, Ernst Halperin, and Igor Lukes, eds., *Hydra of Carnage* (New York: Lexington, 1986); and Amir Taheri, "Islamic Terrorism: A Growing Peril," *Le Point* (Paris), reprint, *World Press Review,* May 1987, pp. 17–19.

23. See Donald L. Rheem, "Environmental Action: A Movement Comes of Age," *Christian Science Monitor,* January 15, 1987, p. 19.

24. See William Ophuls, *Ecology and the Politics of Scarcity* (San Francisco: W. H. Freeman, 1977), p. 208 ff.

25. Julian L. Simon, "Life Is Getting Better, Not Worse," *Futurist* 17 (August 1983): 7–14; idem, *The Ultimate Resource* (Princeton: Princeton University Press, 1981); and Lindsey Grant, *The Cornucopian Fallacies,* (Washington, D.C.: The Environmental Fund, 1982).

26. On April 5, 1988, former President Reagan signed the Montreal Protocol, originally endorsed by twenty-four nations and the European Community, to safeguard the ozone layer.

27. Ambalal Somabhai Patel, "Poverty and Progress: Class, Caste and Power," *UNESCO Courier* 40, no. 1 (January 1987): 26–27.

28. See the first supplemental reading: Rafael M. Salas, "Cities Without Limits," *UNESCO Courier* 40, no. 1 (January 1987): 10–11.

29. For a survey of international cooperation and noncooperation, see Lincoln P. Bloomfield, ed., *The Management of Global Disorder: Prospects for Creative Problem Solving* (Lanham, Md.: University Press of America, 1988). See also Harlan Cleveland, "The Future of International Governance," *Futurist,* May/June 1988, pp. 9–12.

30. Immanuel Wallerstein, *The Capitalist World Economy* (New York: Cambridge University Press, 1979), p. 5.

31. Kenneth N. Waltz, *Theory of International Politics* (Reading, Mass.: Addison-Wesley, 1979), p. 72.

32. See the second supplemental reading: Daniel Bell, "The World and the United States in 2013," *Daedalus* 116, no. 3 (Summer 1987): 13–15.

33. See Jessica Tuchman Mathews, "Redefining Security," Foreign Affairs 68, no. 2 (Spring 1989): 162–177.

Glossary

Acute tension (see also *chronic tension*). Pent-up mass emotions and an awareness of a potential conventional conflict between two or more adversaries due to acts of escalation of hostility between the parties; it is more predictable, more controllable, and more dynamic than chronic tension.

Adjudication. Submission of disputes by states to a court for a judicial decision.

Aggregate data. Unlike survey data, aggregate data numerically summarize (or aggregate) the characteristics of individuals or groups or transactions of events (e.g., per capita income or GNP of a nation-state).

Aggression. An armed struggle, intervention, or any other violent act by an outside group or nation against a sovereign entity of another nation that enjoys the protection of peace under the UN Charter, except in cases where people are struggling for self-determination.

Ambassador. The highest-level diplomatic official appointed by one government as representative to another government.

Apartheid policy. Policy of the South African government that calls for the complete separation of the races.

Applicant. A government (plaintiff) that brings suit against another government in an international court.

Arbitration. An agreement between governments to submit a dispute to a panel of arbitrators selected by the parties for a final and binding decision.

Arms control. Efforts to check or slow the pace of the arms race by placing ceilings or upward limits on numbers of weapons.

Arms freeze. A policy of halting arms increases and holding the number of arms at a no-growth level.

Arms reduction. A process by which arms are reduced in number but not to the point of elimination.

Balance of payments. A measure of total national monetary inflows and outflows.

Balance of power. A distribution of power among states, usually characterized by shifting alliances wherein no one state can exercise hegemony over all.

Bargaining. An interaction that occurs when two or more negotiators attempt to agree on a mutually acceptable outcome in a situation in which their orders or preference for possible outcomes are negatively correlated.

Behavioralists. International relations scholars who use "scientific" methods (e.g., quantitative analysis) to develop and test theories explaining the behavior of international phenomena.

Belief. A conviction that a description of reality is true, proven, or known.

Bilateral aid. Any form of aid or assistance given by a donor to a recipient country.

Bipolarity. A global distribution of power in which two states predominate, and other much weaker states ally themselves to one of the two superpowers.

Boycott. The refusal of one country to purchase goods from another country.

Bretton Woods System. Post–World War II monetary system established in 1944 based on a fixed dollar value in gold, dollar convertibility into gold, fixed exchange rates for other currencies, World Bank financing of long-term development, and International Monetary Fund financing to offset short-term payments deficits.

Brezhnev Doctrine. A Soviet foreign policy, invoked in 1968 against Czechoslovakia, that holds that the laws of international socialism are above the national laws of any member of the socialist community and thus justify intervention by other members of the community to restore socialism in countries where those laws have been violated.

Bureaucratic politics model. A model of decision making that depicts the in-fighting between various agencies of a government and that, in the process of pursuing organizational interests, often produces a foreign policy based more on domestic politics than on national interest or national security.

Capitalism. An economic system advocating private property and profit making, based on the principles of a free market economy.

Chronic tension (see also *acute tension*). A persistent, worldwide feeling of insecurity and helplessness due to the potential threat of a nuclear war among the members of the "nuclear club." Chronic tension encompasses total antagonism and lack of dynamism, yet it can persist without explosive consequences.

Civil war. Armed conflict between competing factions within a country.

Classification. The orderly arrangement of subject matter in categories or classes according to perceived similarities and differences in the various objects of inquiry.

Club of Rome. A group of private experts who met in Rome in the early 1960s and warned the international community about the environmental limits to population and industrial growth.

Cognition. Data (information) derived from the environment, which can be substantiated through physical evidence or perceptual observation; an empirical belief about the nature of humans, politics, international actors, and their interaction.

Cold War. An extended period after World War II of psychological tension, political competition, and occasional military confrontation between the Eastern (communist) and Western (capitalist) blocs.

Commitment. A promise made by a negotiator in the bargaining process with the intent of changing the opponent's expectations about the bargainer's future conduct by changing his or her incentives.

Commodity cartel. Cooperative organization consisting of producer groups that seek to control the market supply and price of their export commodities.

Commodity indexation agreements. Schemes among commodity producing and consuming countries to establish a link between the prices a developing country receives for its exports and the prices it pays for imports from developed countries, thereby stabilizing its terms of trade.

Common market. Government agreements to eliminate trade barriers among themselves, while erecting common barriers to external trade.

Communication paradigm. A body of thought that seeks to explain processes of information sending, receiving, storing, and utilization as they relate to the international system.

Communism. A deterministic Marxist–Leninist ideology and movement advocating the use of single-party rule, central government planning, and state ownership, which will ultimately evolve into a stateless and classless society.

Comparative foreign policy analysis. A body of research that attempts to examine systematically the determinants and behavior patterns that states exhibit in the foreign policy process.

Compellance. In the bargaining process, the attempt by one state to persuade another state to do something the latter generally does not wish to do.

Competitiveness. The capacity of a country's exports to compete in foreign markets with the products of other nations.

Compliance. The degree to which governments abide by the decisions of international courts.

Compulsory jurisdiction. The capacity of a court to hear and rule on a case in which litigants are obliged to participate.

Concert of Europe. A series of meetings held among European powers during the early 1800s to coordinate security policies and avoid the resurgence of French imperialism.

Conciliation. Attempts by third parties to a dispute to soften the positions of the disputants, to prevent hardening of positions, and to encourage dialogue and peaceful settlements. Disputants are free to reject the recommendations of individual conciliators or conciliation commissions.

Conventional war. Armed conflicts fought with nonnuclear weaponry of naval, air, and ground forces.

Cosmopolitan school. A normative school of thought in international relations that seeks to extend the framework of morality and just action beyond the borders of the nation-state into the global arena.

Covert operation (see also *psychological warfare*). An act plotted and committed in secrecy or an activity performed through clandestine means with the aim of achieving specific political or military goals (e.g., conspiracy, subversion, or espionage).

Crisis decision. A foreign policy decision made in situations characterized by high threat and potential gravity, an element of surprise, a short time frame, and the involvement of the highest level of authoritative decision makers.

Cuban missile crisis. The U.S. naval blockade of Cuba in October 1962 to force Soviet withdrawal of offensive missiles after the discovery of the Soviet intent to deploy them on the island against the United States.

Custom. Practices and usages that over time become recognized as obligatory and legally binding.

Decision making. A foreign policy analysis of interactions between states or decision makers involved in a particular decision.

De facto recognition. Government acknowledgement of the factual existence of another state or government short of full legal recognition.

De jure recognition. Formal, legal recognition granted by one government to another government or state.

Dependencia model. A school of thought in international relations that follows a Marxist view that the international economy consists of two sets of states: the wealthy, dominant North and the poor, weak South, the former exploiting the latter in a hierarchical world order.

Deterrence. The attempt by one state to dissuade another state from some act, especially an act of military aggression.

Devaluation. Official reduction in the value of a country's currency relative to others, usually undertaken to increase the competitiveness of a country's exports, to reduce imports, and to stimulate domestic economic production.

Devil theories. Theories about the causes of war that blame a particular group for conspiring to start a war for personal profit or gain.

Diplomacy. The conduct of relations between nation-states through their accredited officials for the purpose of advancing the interests of the appointing state.

Disarmament. A process by which particular weapons are progressively reduced in number to the point of elimination.

Disinformation (see also *psychological warfare*). The practice of feeding erroneous information, which is disseminated by overt or covert action, among adversary groups, organizations, or political systems competing for power; the goal is to confuse the adversary, causing them to make erratic and inaccurate decisions.

Disintegration theory. A branch of *integration theory* that seeks to explain how the deterioration of certain criteria representing communal loyalty and cohesion can lead to the process of internal disintegration of a large community.

East–West dispute. The clash of ideologies and economic and political systems of Western capitalist states and those of the Eastern socialist bloc.

Economic and Social Council (ECOSOC). The fifty-four-member UN organization responsible for addressing the social, economic, and humanitarian causes of conflict among nations.

Economic sanctions. Punitive economic actions taken by one state against another to retaliate for prior objectionable behavior.

Ecopolitics. The politics of managing global resources to resolve various ecological issues affecting an interdependent world.

Embargo. The refusal of one country to sell goods to another country.

Embassy. A permanent mission established by a national government in a foreign country to represent its interests in that country.

Empirical research. Research relying on data and knowledge acquired by observation and experimentation.

Enculturation (see *socialization*).

Enterprise. A public international corporation that will serve as the operational arm of the International Seabed Authority to conduct commercial seabed mining once the Law of the Sea Treaty enters into force.

Eurodollar. Dollars (or other hard currencies) held in private banks or corporate accounts.

European Communities (EC). The combined authorities of the European Coal and Steel Community, EURATOM, and the Common Market, composed of twelve European states for the purpose of integrating their economies.

European Political Cooperation (EPC). A formalized process of political consultation and cooperation among European Common Market heads-of-state.

Exchange rate. The value of one currency relative to another.

Expansionistic nationalism. Nationalism that finds its expression in a desire to conquer neighboring territories and dominate other peoples.

Expressionistic nationalism. Nationalistic sentiments that lead to a desire by a particular people for self-determination.

Extension agreement. An agreement providing for a formal ratification and continuation of existing arrangements.

Externalities. The side effects generated by economic activities (e.g., pollution).

Fact. A peculiar ordering of reality according to a theoretical interest.

First-strike attack. Scenario in which a nuclear power decides to launch its missiles, without warning, against an adversary's nuclear arsenal to destroy it and thereby prevent a second strike or retaliation against its own territory.

First World. Western, industrialized, capitalist states.

Fixed assessment. A procedure whereby an intergovernmental organization (such as the UN) determines mandatory dues, which are levied on its member-states to pay for its budget.

Flexible response. Successor to the doctrine of massive retaliation, this doctrine argues that aggression by communist states throughout the globe should be met by diplomatic, political, or conventional military means, rather than by outright nuclear retaliation.

Foreign policy. A set of authoritative decisions taken in the name of the state that are intended to achieve certain goals in the international arena.

Fourth World. About thirty-four of the world's poorest nation-states, designated by the United Nations in 1971 as the "least developed countries" of the Third World.

Functionalist school. A school of thought arguing that as international contacts and cultural exchanges improve understanding and cooperation among divergent societies, governments will learn to collaborate on political issues, leading gradually to surrender of sovereignty and ultimately a supranational community.

General Agreement on Tariffs and Trade (GATT). A UN specialized agency charged with conducting periodic negotiations aimed at reducing tariff and nontariff barriers to free trade.

General Assembly. The main UN organ having broad scope and authority and in which all members have representation.

Geopolitical school (also known as "geopolitics"). A deterministic approach to foreign policy that attempts to explain and predict political behavior and military capabilities in terms of a nation's physical environment.

Glasnost (see also *new thinking*). An element of Mikhail Gorbachev's policy that seeks to introduce greater political liberalization (openness) into Soviet society and thus stimulate increased citizen participation in economic modernization and production.

Globalist school. According to this school of thought, the state-centric explanation of the struggle for power and security is only one aspect of world politics; the more complete understanding requires a look at nonstate actors and at economic and nonsecurity issues in an interdependent world.

Good offices. The practice of using third parties as a go-between to transmit messages, to encourage communication, and to create a favorable climate for eventual direct negotiations between disputing governments.

Group of Seven (G-7). The heads of seven leading industrial nations in the West—Canada, the Federal Republic of Germany, Great Britain, France, Italy, Japan, and the United States—who meet annually to discuss problems of unemployment, inflation, and energy.

Group of Seventy-Seven (G-77). A group of more than 120 Third World countries, which functions as the largest caucusing group at the United Nations and in other international conferences in favor of development aid, human rights, and the creation of a New International Economic Order.

Groupthink. A social–psychological phenomenon whereby the pressures for group conformity may lead individual members of a decision-making group to suppress any personal doubts about the emerging group consensus.

Guerrilla warfare. Hit-and-run tactics used by small bands of irregular forces against an invading army or by indigenous groups in rebellion against established authorities.

Hard currency. Any currency—usually of highly developed countries—that is readily accepted by governments as payment for provision of goods or services.

Hard data (see also *aggregate data* and *empirical research*). Numerically measurable data obtained through "objective" or empirical observation.

Hegemony. When one government, because of its greater power, exercises preeminent influence over other governments (usually its neighbors).

High politics. The military, security, and political affairs of states.

Historical school. A deterministic approach to foreign policy emphasizing historical evolution by reconstructing the past to predict the future.

Hotspots. Areas of the world marked by flare-ups of heightened tensions and often violent conflict.

Hypothesis. A statement of an expected relationship between variables that may be tested empirically to determine its validity; an assertive statement to be confirmed or denied.

Idealist school (see also *traditionalists*). A school of thought advocating international understanding and cooperation through moral justice and law implemented by international organizations.

Ideology. A structured set of beliefs, attitudes, and understandings about how politics should be organized and about the kinds of policies that should be pursued.

Idiosyncratic factors. The characteristics of individual decision makers that can affect a state's foreign policy.

Image (see also *socialization*). An individual's perception of his or her environment (the world) that tends to color, and sometimes distort, reality; a mental or emotional filter that permits the registering of some "facts" more readily than others.

Imperial (or colonial) wars. Armed conflicts between a state and a nonstate group (e.g., a tribe), including wars of independence.

Imperialism. The political, economic, cultural, and psychological domination of one people or country by another.

Indigenization. A policy employed by governments to ensure greater financial and managerial participation in and control over multinational corporations' investments.

Innovation agreement. An agreement calling for new arrangements that benefit both parties but not always equally.

Inquiry. An official investigation by a third party, usually an international agency, to clarify the circumstances surrounding a dispute, especially when there is a difference over facts.

Integration theory (see also *communication paradigm*). A theory that explains how political and economic units tend to merge together and transfer loyalty to a larger community.

Interdependence. The interrelatedness of national societies that are in varying degrees sensitive and vulnerable to each other's policies.

Intergovernmental organization (IGO). An institution created by states to coordinate their interrelations in an ongoing or permanent fashion.

Intermediate-range nuclear forces (INF). Missiles formerly placed in Europe (but now banned by a 1988 treaty) that could have been used to attack targets in the European theater but fell short of intercontinental range.

International Court of Justice (ICJ). The legal organ and constitutional court of the United Nations; the ICJ delivers advisory opinions at the request of other UN organs and, though lacking compulsory jurisdiction, may hear cases brought voluntarily by governments.

International relations. All forms of interaction between the members of separate societies, whether government sponsored or not.

International Seabed Authority (ISA). An intergovernmental organization established by the Law of the Sea Treaty that will administer and oversee international exploitation of the high seas, the seabed, and subsoil thereof, beyond the limits of national jurisdiction.

International system. Any collection of independent political entities that interact with considerable frequency and according to regularized processes in a general setting in which international relations occur at any time.

International system structure. The effect of the international system on the behavior of the actors in their choices of foreign policy making.

International (or interstate) war. A condition of open, armed hostility between two or more governments or states.

Intervention. Armed interference by one state in the domestic affairs of another with the intention of maintaining or changing the existing order of things.

Intifada. An uprising by Arab Palestinians in the Israeli-occupied territories of the West Bank during 1988–1989.

Irredentism. The aspiration of a people to recover from another country territory that has historically been inhabited by people of their ethnic background.

Kellogg–Briand Pact. a multilateral treaty concluded in 1928 that called for outlawing war as a means of settling disputes between members of the international community.

Lateral pressure. The relationships among technology, resources, and population that forced European decision makers before World War I to make a choice between war and no war.

Lebensraum (see also *geopolitical school*). A term meaning "living space," used by some governments to justify expansionistic or imperial foreign policies (e.g., Nazi Germany).

Legitimacy. The perception or the fact of being lawful, right, or justifiable, especially in reference to the use of power by authorities.

Less developed (or developing) countries (LDCs). A wide assortment of about 130 states—the *nouveau riche,* "newly industrializing countries," and "Third and Fourth World countries"—whose annual per capita GNP is below $2,000.

Limited war. Armed conflicts among small numbers of states in localized areas and with limited objectives.

Liquidity. The capacity to finance international transactions rapidly, usually on a cash basis.

Local settlement. A policy of refugee-hosting countries to permit refugees to settle indefinitely and to seek economic integration.

Low politics. The economic, cultural, social, and humanitarian relations of governments and peoples.

Macro-decision. A foreign policy decision that involves relatively large, general concerns (e.g., foreign assistance programs) and that is designed to establish guidelines for specific situations as they arise.

Mandate system. A post–World War I League of Nations system that placed losing Axis colonies at various stages of preparedness for independence under the administrative authority of other League members.

Massive retaliation. The earliest nuclear strategic doctrine employed by the United States; it called for all-out nuclear response to deter Soviet aggression.

Mediation. The insertion of a third party (state, individual, or international agency) at the request or consent of the contending parties to actively assist in obtaining settlement of a dispute.

Mercantilist model. A school of thought advocating the use of free enterprise and international economic competition for market, investment outlets, and sources of raw materials.

Micro-decision. A foreign policy decision that involves choices that are relatively narrow in scope, that are low in threat, and that can be handled at the lower levels of the government bureaucracy.

Military–industrial complex. A mutually supportive, ongoing relationship between a nation's defense-related industries and its military forces.

Most-favored nation principle. The principle, adopted by GATT, that holds that whenever one member-state lowers tariffs on certain kinds of imports from another member-state, all member-states are entitled to the same favorable treatment with regard to their goods.

Multilateral aid. Any form of aid or assistance transacted among several donor and recipient countries.

Multinational corporations (MNCs). Large business enterprises having operations in three or more countries.

Multipolarity. A global distribution of power among several states, each possessing roughly equal degrees of power.

Mutual assured destruction (MAD). A strategic doctrine of deterrence in which each adversary preserves the capability to absorb a first nuclear attack by the other and still retaliate with devastating nuclear force (i.e., inflicting unacceptable damage on the attacker).

Mutual deterrence. A condition of nuclear balance in which each adversary maintains a credible second-strike capability.

Nation. A group of people, usually living in proximity, who share a common historical tradition, culture, customs, a similar language, often a common religion, and who perceive themselves as distinct from other peoples.

Nation-state (see also *state*). A national political unit in which the population has a common sense of nationhood.

National attribute factors. The demographic, economic, military, and governmental characteristics of a nation-state that can affect the foreign policy of that state.

National interests (see also *realist school* and *state-centrism*). Those conditions or outcomes, defined by the government, that best serve the well-being of an entire people or nation. These interests usually include security, economic well-being, and self-determination.

Nationalism. Devotion to the interests of one's nation, often in exaggerated cases to the detriment of the common interests of all nations.

National liberation movement. An armed struggle for independence waged by indigenous groups against a foreign colonial power exercising authority over the land.

Natural capabilities. Elements of power based on the size, quality, and distribution of a nation's material resources and population.

Natural law school. A school of thought that holds that certain standards of behavior, principles, and rights exist in the natural order of things and that governments must observe them.

Negotiation. A formal interaction through which individuals explicitly try to reach an agreement.

Neocolonialism. The subtle domination of another country through economic penetration rather than through direct subjugation by force.

Neofunctionalist school. A school of thought that identifies certain sectors of intergovernmental cooperation as more likely to lead to further cooperation than others.

Neomercantilism. Apart from the formal colonial system of captive markets, any policy aimed at promoting exports over imports.

Neutralism (see also *nonalignment*). A policy that disavows participation in the East–West dispute.

New diplomacy (see also *diplomacy*). As a reaction to "old" diplomacy, new diplomacy involves negotiations at open conferences, not necessarily by professional diplomats but by representatives of governments with equal status (weight).

New International Economic Order (NIEO). A plan, supported by Third World countries, that would change international economic policies to reflect the interests and needs of poor nations.

"New thinking." Mikhail Gorbachev's foreign policy of scaling down Soviet external ambitions, including the past endorsement of class warfare (revolutions), proletarian internationalism, and limited sovereignty (the Brezhnev doctrine).

Nonalignment (see also *neutralism*). A policy pursued primarily by Third World governments that espouses neutrality in the East–West dispute.

Nongovernmental organization (NGO). Any private, non-profit agency representing nongovernmental interests, often based on religious or professional affiliations and sometimes enjoying consultative status with the United Nations.

Nonobligatory practices. Non–legally binding habits or behavior of governments in their interrelations.

Non-self-governing territories. All territories whose people have not yet attained a full measure of independence; under the terms of Article 73 of the UN Charter, these territories can expect assistance from the administering state toward eventual self-government.

Normalization agreement. The termination of an abnormal situation in relations between two parties by reestablishing diplomatic relations after a breach of relations.

North–South dispute. The clash over distribution of global wealth between rich, industrialized countries of the Northern Hemisphere and poor countries found primarily in the Southern Hemisphere.

Nuclear brinkmanship. The threat of nuclear retaliation to deter a conventional military attack.

Nuclear proliferation. The spread of nuclear weapons to previously non-nuclear countries.

Nuclear war. An attack between states involving the launching of nuclear missiles against each other's missile forces, cities, or command and control facilities.

On-site inspection (OSI). Land-based verification of arms reductions through use of expert teams from the adversary nation.

Optional clause. Found in Article 36 of the ICJ Statute, this provision permits states to declare their acceptance of the compulsory jurisdiction of the International Court of Justice.

Orderly market arrangements (OMAs). Bilateral trade agreements intended to regulate the flow of imports and exports between two nations to minimize economic dislocation to domestic industries.

Organizational process model (see also *bureaucratic politics model*). A model of decision making that assumes that every national government is made up of a conglomerate of loosely allied organizations that function according to standard patterns of behavior and are fairly predictable because of their bureaucratic nature.

Organization for Economic Cooperation and Development (OECD). A regional economic organization consisting of twenty-four members established in 1961 to promote economic growth and freer trade and to expand and improve Western aid to the less developed countries.

Organization of Petroleum Exporting Countries (OPEC). An organization of thirteen less developed countries that together account for a major portion of the world's oil exports.

Overcapacity. Excess productive capacity for a given product relative to global demand.

Pacta sunt servanda. The principle of continuity in international law, which holds that treaties are to be observed by the governments that ratify them.

Paradigm. A scientific world view or model based on one or more past scientific achievements that helps to organize one's thoughts about a set of phenomena and give direction to research.

Parallel system. An approach to deep seabed mining whereby a prospective mining concern identifies two sites of roughly equal value, one to mine for its own profit and the other for the benefit of the international community.

Peacekeeping. A customary device used by the United Nations, in which a UN force is inserted between two warring parties, with their consent, to serve as a buffer to prevent open hostilities and allow time for peaceful resolution of the dispute.

Peace of Westphalia. A series of treaties, adopted in 1648, that ended the Thirty Years War and established the legal framework for modern international relations.

Perestroika (see also *new thinking*). An element of Mikhail Gorbachev's policy aimed at restructuring the Soviet economy toward a modern competitive system in order to strengthen Soviet socialism.

Pluralist school. A major school of thought that argues that international relations is a "cobweb-like" network of numerous crisscrossing relationships among a great variety of actors responsible for major events in a world society.

Political economy. The study of interacting political and economic factors that shape trade, monetary, tax, investment, and aid policies within and among nations.

Positivists. A legal school that holds that the only binding law is that specifically agreed to by states in treaties and customs.

Possibilist school. A school of thought interpreting the properties of the physical environment in the light of human knowledge, equipment, and social organization.

Post-behavioralism (see also *behavioralists*). A stage of development in international relations theory building from about 1970 onward, which resulted in a triangular interparadigm debate among realism, pluralism, and structuralism in the assumption of a state-centric world.

Power. The relative capability of a nation-state to get other states to do things they otherwise would not do, whether by means of persuasion or force.

Precedent. A principle recognizing the binding nature of previous judicial decisions. Though prevalent in domestic legal systems, precedent is not recognized by international law.

Precipitating causes. The immediate incidents of circumstances that prompt countries to go to war.

Preferential trade system. A nonreciprocal trade relationship favored by developing countries in which party *A* receives reductions in tariffs on its exports to party *B*, without in turn being required to reduce its tariffs on imports from party *B*.

Primary actor. In international relations, an actor having sovereignty and the legal capacity to take coercive actions against other actors and make binding rules on them.

Private voluntary organization (PVO). A term used in the United States for nongovernmental organizations.

Propaganda (see also *psychological warfare*). A method of communication aimed at influencing the thinking, emotions, or actions of a group or the public; it is the deliberate manipulation, by means of symbols, of other people's values and behavior.

Proportionality. In international law, the consistency, in scope, nature, and magnitude, of a retaliatory action in relation to the original offense.

Protectionism. Policies designed to shield domestic industries and products from foreign competition by arbitrarily imposing taxes, tariffs, quotas, or other restrictions on imported goods.

Psychological capabilities. Elements of national power based on perceptual factors such as morale, willingness to use power, and quality of leadership.

Psychological warfare (see also *propaganda* and *covert operation*). Deliberate selection and manipulation of data or political, military, economic, and social activities targeted at a potential enemy for purposes of influencing the enemy's thinking and behavior.

Quota. A method of protecting domestic producers from foreign competition by imposing a limit on the maximum volume of allowable imports.

Rapprochement. A reconciliation of interests of rival states after a period of estrangement. In diplomacy a policy of attempting to reestablish normal relations.

Ratification. An executive act by which a government indicates its intention to be bound by the terms of a treaty.

Rational actor model. A model of decision making in which one carefully defines the situations, specifies goals, weighs all conceivable alternatives, and selects that option most likely to achieve the goals.

Realist school. A school of thought that argues that international relations consists of the struggle for power among states in an anarchic environment, each state pursuing its competitive interests.

Rebus sic stantibus. The legal principle asserting that treaties can be unilaterally denounced when the circumstances that gave rise to the legal contract have fundamentally and radically changed.

Reciprocity. A mutual exchange of benefits or privileges. In international economics a mutual reduction in tariffs between trade partners. In international law any mutual extension of legal rights or privileges.

Redistribution agreement. An agreement that benefits one party at the expense of another.

Regimes. In a given area of international relations the sets of implicit or explicit principles, norms, rules, and decision-making procedures around which actors' expectations converge.

Regional security organizations. Alliances among countries within a particular geographical area to protect themselves from external military threats (e.g., NATO).

Reprisal. A hostile act taken by one government in response to a previous illegal and equally hostile act by another. Reprisals may be legal if undertaken after efforts at peaceful settlement, in response to a previous illegal act, and if proportional to the prior offense.

Reserves. Holdings of hard currency, special drawing rights, and precious metals that represent national savings.

Resistance point. A negotiator's irreducible goal in the negotiation process—the minimum objective that he or she is willing to settle for.

Respondent. A government (defendant) being sued by another in an international court.

Retaliation. Any response, whether legal or not, taken by one government against a previous hostile or unfriendly act committed by another government.

Retorsion. A legal but unfriendly act taken in response to a previous legal but equally unfriendly act.

Role. Because of the office or position they represent, authoritative decision makers who make and carry out foreign policies as "role" players are not always free to use their personal ethics, beliefs, or prejudices.

Secondary actor. Entities that can influence international relations by their policies and actions, but that lack sovereignty.

Second-strike attack. The capability of a nuclear power to retaliate against another country's territory even after absorbing a first strike against its nuclear arsenal. In theory a second-strike capability deters a first-strike nuclear attack.

Second World. Eastern, industrialized, socialist states.

Secretariat. The organ of the United Nations, under the direction of the Secretary-General, that administers the UN system.

Security Council. A fifteen-member organ of the United Nations charged with encouraging peaceful settlement of disputes, taking enforcement action to make peace, containing threats to peace, and punishing acts of aggression.

Self-determination. The principle that a people or nation should have the right to their own government.

Separatism. An act or policy of withdrawing from a political union to establish a separate, independent nation.

Shuttle diplomacy (see also *diplomacy*). A term applied to the diplomatic efforts of former U.S. Secretary of State Henry Kissinger to resolve the Arab–Israeli conflict in the Middle East through his extensive travels among Washington, Cairo, and Jerusalem in 1975–1976.

Socialization. The process whereby the nation's attitudes, values, and customs are taught to its citizens; the learning process by which individuals acquire orientation toward government and political life.

Soft currency. Currencies that are not accepted by governments as payment for goods and services.

Soft data. Data primarily consisting of descriptive information and generalizations with subjective value judgments.

Sovereignty. A state's capacity—supreme authority—to regulate its internal affairs and foreign relations.

Sovereignty-at-bay model. A school of thought in international relations that argues that increased economic interdependence and technological advances have undermined the nation-state's control over economic affairs and made the multinational corporations, the Eurodollar market, and other international institutions better suited to humanity's economic needs.

Soviet bloc. A caucusing group of nation-states in the United Nations under the leadership of the Soviet Union; they adhere to Marxist–Leninist ideology and belong to organizations such as the Warsaw Pact and the Council of Mutual Economic Assistance (CMEA).

Special Drawing Right (SDR). A form of international reserve currency provided to states by the International Monetary Fund to resolve short-term balance-of-payments deficits.

Spill-over effect. The process whereby interstate cooperation in one technical or economic area requires further cooperative steps in related areas that build upon earlier cooperative efforts.

State. A legal entity that possesses a territory, a population, an independent sovereign government exercising jurisdiction in and over the territory and people, and recognition by other states.

State-centrism (see also *post-behavioralism*). A position advocated by the realists that focuses on nation-states and their governments as the major actors in global politics.

Strategic Defense Initiative (SDI). A Reagan administration proposal to make nuclear deterrence a defensive posture by shielding the United States from a retaliatory strike.

Structuralist school. A school of thought in international relations that argues that the international system is like a "multiheaded octopus" with powerful tentacles that constantly suck wealth from the weakened peripheries toward the powerful centers.

Subsidiaries. In international business those overseas operations created by a parent company that fall under its ultimate authority and supervision.

Summit diplomacy. Direct, personal contact and negotiation between heads of state.

Superpower. A state that possesses global influence and overwhelming economic or military power.

Synthetic capabilities. Elements of national power based on the capacity to exploit and utilize natural and human resources.

Systemic factors. External factors, such as the physical environment, international interactions, and international system structure, that affect a nation-state's foreign policy.

Tacit negotiation. Informal, indirect communication through words and actions that is designed to signal one's intentions or the importance attached to some issue in the negotiation process.

Tariff. An import tax imposed on foreign products entering a country.

Terms of trade. The relative value of a country's export products compared to those it imports.

Terra nullis. Territory that does not legally belong to any state and that is therefore subject to discovery, exploration, and occupation by existing states.

Terrorism. The illegal use of violence for purposes of political extortion, coercion, and publicity for a political cause.

Theory. A logically related set of propositions stating relationships between variables for the purpose of explanation, prediction, or both.

Theory of comparative advantage. An economic theory propounded by David Ricardo that stipulates that trade will be profitable to all countries if each specializes in a product that its domestic economy produces with the greatest relative efficiency while trading for other products, even if it can produce all products more efficiently than its trade partner.

Third country resettlement. Movement of refugees out of their country of first asylum to a third country that agrees to accept them for settlement.

Third World. The less developed countries, located mainly in the Southern Hemisphere, with generally poorly developed, agricultural or commodity-based nonindustrial economies.

Threat (see also *bargaining*). In international bargaining a statement addressed to the opponents that they will suffer certain consequences if they do not comply with a desired behavior.

Tied aid. Economic assistance given to a recipient with the understanding that it be used only to purchase products or services originating in the donor country.

Total war. Armed conflicts unlimited by the place of battle or number of participants; the purpose is the adversary's unconditional surrender.

Traditionalists. Scholars who base their analysis on insights gained from written secondary sources, memories, and philosophical treatises rather than on the "scientific" methods used in the social sciences.

Tragedy of the commons. When people have equal and unregulated access to shared (common) resources, the tendency to overexploit and ruin them.

Transnational organizations. Centrally directed, hierarchical bodies, such as churches, political parties, or multinational corporations, that maintain organizations and membership in several countries.

Transnational relations. Interactions between private individuals and groups across national boundaries.

Triad. Deployment of nuclear arms in three legs or modes—land-based, sea-based, and air-based—to preserve a second-strike capability.

Trusteeship Council. The UN organ charged with overseeing the progress toward independence of territories entrusted to the supervision and administration of various UN members.

United Nations Conference on Trade and Development (UNCTAD). UN-sponsored negotiations aimed at resolving trade and development issues affecting developing nations.

Uniting for Peace Resolution. A device whereby any dispute stalemated by a Security Council veto may be taken up by the General Assembly for potential enforcement action if approved by a two-thirds majority vote.

Universal Declaration of Human Rights. A nonbinding declaration made in 1948 by the UN General Assembly that set forth human rights ideals and aspirations for governments.

Value. A preference for one state of reality over another; a judgment about the goals that ought to be pursued in political life; the moral quality of political objects and events.

Variable-sum game. In game theory a type of game in which both parties can simultaneously win something, even though one might benefit more than the other.

Voluntary contributions. Nonobligatory donations given by governments to finance the budgets of intergovernmental organizations, when fixed assessments do not apply.

Voluntary export restraints (VERs). Bilateral agreements in which exporting countries limit the amount of a product exported to another country, often to avoid imposition of import quotas by that country.

Voluntary repatriation. The right of refugees to return freely and of their own will to their countries of original nationality.

Zero-sum game. In game theory a type of game in which whatever one party wins the other party automatically loses (i.e., conflict is total).

Index

disputes, 62
dissonance, 56
distance, 122
distribution of power, 60, 64
Dobson, Christopher, 221n
domestic politics, 17, 18, 67, 69, 125, 128, 131, 133, 137, 163, 166, 417
domestic upheaval, 129
dominant nation, 65
Dominican Republic, 224
Doob, Leonard W., 220n
double zero option, 423
Dougherty, James E., 84n, 85n
drug trafficking, 3, 4, 415
Dubček, Alexander, 193
Dulles, John Foster, 366
Dutch colonialism, 30, 31
Dutch East Indies, 125
duties, 11

East, Maurice A., 86n, 151n, 152n, 154n
East African Common Market, 402
East Berlin, 199, 206
East Central Europe, 65
East Germany, 111, 196, 198, 402, 419, 420
  Soviet troops in, 420
East-West dispute (see also Cold War), 33–35, 262, 266, 273, 326, 350–352, 362, 430
East-West regional arrangements, 123
Eastern bloc (see also Soviet bloc), 124, 419, 420, 423
Eastern Europe, 4, 32–34, 65, 123, 191, 351, 387, 414, 419, 421
  EC and, 402
  political changes in, 424
  resurgent nationalism of, 41
  Soviet intervention in, 351
  tensions within, 351
Easton, David, 82n
EC (see European Community)
ecological cooperation, 196, 426, 432
ecological interdependence, 426
ecological negligence, 427
ecological system, 58
ecological triad, 66
ecologists, 14
economic assistance, 139, 196
economic attachés, 162
economic classes, 60, 61
Economic Community of West African States (ECOWAS), 361, 399, 402
economic competition, 418
economic cooperation, 5, 419
economic development, 127, 420, 428, 431
economic growth, 19, 415, 428
economic influence, 171–173
economic integration, 50, 68, 431

economic mode of production, 15, 61, 126, 127
economic needs, 172, 420
economic power, 3, 4, 12, 65, 67, 125, 126, 431, 432
economic reforms, 127, 420, 425, 432
economic rights, 62
economic sanctions, 329, 334
  definition of, 335
  effectiveness of, 335
  Iran hostage crisis and, 284
  League usage of, 258
  purposes of, 335
economic stability, 19
Economic Support Funds, 321
economic system, 60, 126, 127
ecopolitics, 432
ecosphere, 2
ecosystem, 2, 432
Ecuador, 340
Ecuadoran-Colombian War, 225
Eden, Anthony, 130
education problems, 437
egalitarianism, 176
Egypt, 24, 27, 95, 123, 124, 130, 158, 234, 261, 311, 352–355, 378, 416
Eisenhower, Dwight D., 127, 142, 366
El Salvador, 35
Eldridge, Albert E., 83n
elite, 128, 194
embassy, 11, 159–162, 163
empires, 60
empirical approaches, 58
empirical generalizations, 50, 51
empirical testing, 63, 64, 68, 79
energy resources, 199
England (see also United Kingdom), 27, 55, 250, 303, 342
Enterprise (of the Law of the Sea), 297
entity-environment relationship, 66
environmental conservation, 427, 428
environmental issues, 384, 390–396
  economics and, 395
  human behavior toward, 390
  industrial development and, 395–396
  international conferences and, 396
  pollution and, 350
  resource depletion and, 40, 395, 396
environmental possibilism, 66, 124, 129
environmental probabilism, 66
environmental problems, 11, 14, 17, 18, 129, 415
environments, 65–67, 126, 129, 130, 140, 143, 208, 419, 420, 431
envoy, 158
equilibrium, 64, 65, 423
Eritrea, 28, 230, 388
escapism behavior, 390
Eskimos, war and, 228

global debt crisis (*continued*)
   donor–lender relations and, 325
   imports and, 330
   United States and, 330
global economy 11, 12
global environment, 11, 62, 133, 416, 421, 426
global modelers, 14
global oil prices, 11
global optimists, 427
global pessimists, 426
global politics, 16, 414, 430
global problems, 5, 7, 67, 166
global resource depletion, 40
global society (*see also* world society), 2, 3
global system (*see* international system)
global transformation, 16
global village, 2, 15
global war, 3, 18
global warming, 394
globalists, 106
globology, 67
Golan Heights, 355
Goldfisher, David, 445m
good offices, 283
Gorbachev, Michail S., 7, 55, 90, 126, 127, 130,
   165, 195–197, 351, 365, 369, 371, 415, 420, 421,
   423–425
government, role of, 176
governmental organizations, 3, 125, 128, 129, 131,
   133, 137, 138, 140, 142, 146
governmental systems, types of, 128
governments, 59, 130, 136, 137, 193, 208, 415, 416,
   418, 422, 425, 430, 431, 432
grain embargo, 168
Grant, Lindsey, 445n
Great Britain (*see also* United Kingdom), 4, 9, 11,
   29, 33, 54, 57, 64, 65, 77, 111, 124, 169–171,
   198, 232, 338, 418, 419, 423, 424
   colonial expansion of, 30–31, 311
   Commonwealth of, 266
   hegemonial power of, 328
   role in UN of, 258
   Scotia Case, 288
Great Depression, 231, 323, 326, 338, 339
Great Design, 133
Great Power war, 239, 240, 241
   bureaucracy and, 243
   commercialization and, 243, 244
   duration of, 240–242
   elite insecurity and, 243
   frequency of, 240–242, 244
   military professionalization and, 244
   popularization of, 244
   power centralization and, 243
   rationalization of military power and, 243
   scientific revolution in, 244
   technological advancement and, 243

great powers, 14, 164, 431
Greece, 124, 158, 200, 206, 256, 311, 371
greed behavior, 390
Greek city-states, 24, 194
Greeks, 12
greenhouse effect, 17, 394, 432
Greenstein, F.I., 149n
Gregorian, Hrach, 153n,
Grenada, 38, 93, 131, 135, 208
   U.S. intervention in, 38, 224
Grieco, Joseph, 405
Groom, A. J. R., 22n, 84n, 85n, 154n
gross national product (GNP), 4, 11, 125–128, 419,
   422, 428, 431
Grotius, Hugo, 282, 290, 292
Group of Eighteen, 272
Group of Seven (G-7), 416, 419
groups, 56, 60, 63, 64, 68, 138, 140
groupthink, 138, 139, 141, 144, 146, 147
Guatemala, 4, 144
guerrilla warfare, 198, 199, 208
guerrillas, 198
guided missile, 3
Gulf of Sidra, 52, 53, 55, 57, 288
Gulf Oil Corporation, 39, 340
Gulf States, 35, 352, 353

Haas, Ernst B., 189n, 269, 405
Habeeb, William Mark, 188n
Hague Conventions of 1899 and 1907, 294, 363
Haiti, 35, 92
Haley, P. Edward, 445n
Hall, A. J., 85n
Halperin, Ernst, 445n
Hamilton, Alexander, 20
Hamilton, James D., 222n
Hamilton, Lawrence C., 222n
Hammarskjöld, Dag, 261, 273
Hammer, Armand, 106
Hammond, P. Y., 149n
Hanoi, 102
Hanseatic League, 342
Hanson, Elizabeth C., 153n
hard currency, 317, 321
Hardin, Garrett, 391
Havana (Cuba), 131
Havana Non-Aligned Summit (1979), 171
Havanna Summit of 1979, 378
Hawaii, 138
health problems, 437
Healy, Brian, 85n
heartland, 65, 121
Heath, Edward, 444n
Heathrow airport, 199
hegemony, 61, 405
   contemporary IR and, 405
   definition of, 28

moral principles, 59, 62, 63, 139–141

Morgenstern, Oscar, 188n

Morgenthau, Hans J., 14, 30, 41, 63, 64, 67, 84n, 85n

Mormon church, 251

Morocco, 352–354

Moscow, 33, 55, 165, 169, 193, 195, 197, 366, 368, 378, 420

Mossadegh, Mohammad, 192

most-favored-nation (MFN) principle, 173

most-favored-nation (MFN) status, 326, 333, 342, 343

  free riding and, 342

Motorola Corporation, 90, 99

Mubarak, Hosni, 55

Mueller, John E., 84n

Muhammad, the prophet, 353, 355

mujahedeen, 193, 198

Mulroney, Brian, 393

multicentric system, 60

multilateral actions, 129

multilateral aid, 173

multilateral diplomacy, 166, 174

Multilateral Investment Guarantee Agency, 324

multilateral relations, 3, 20, 166

multinational corporations, 19, 32, 35, 37–40, 60, 61, 90, 98–101, 104, 418, 428

  characteristics of, 99

  limits on power of, 99, 101

  subsidiaries of, 99

  Third World origin of, 99

multipolarity, 12, 32, 33, 35, 430

  war and, 234

Musa, Abu, 355

Mutual and Balanced Force Reduction Talks (MBFR), 363–365

mutual deterrence, 367

mutual security, 19

mutually assured destruction (MAD), 172, 366, 367, 370, 423

Nagasaki, 294

Namibia, 262, 263, 271, 425

Napoleon, 29

Napoleonic wars, 250, 385

Naroll, Raoul, 189n

Nasser, Gamal Abdel, 55, 261

nation, definition of (*see also* nation-state), 27

nation-state(s) (*see also* state), 13, 14, 23, 59, 62–65, 67, 68, 112, 120, 123–125, 127, 135, 139, 140, 159, 164, 166, 172, 174, 191, 194, 201, 208, 243, 414–416, 418, 424, 426, 430, 431

  commerce and, 113

  culture and, 113

  definition of, 28

  dimensions of, 112

nation-state(s) (*continued*)

  environment and, 114–115

  public order and, 112–113

  resources and, 113

  security and, 374

  system of the, 112–115

national attribute factors, 124–129, 131, 133, 136, 140

national boundaries, 5, 14, 68

national goals, 63, 64, 70

national interests, 14, 29, 42, 59, 62–64, 69, 71, 128, 137, 167, 418, 430

  conceptual weaknesses of, 29, 30

  definition of, 30, 31

  functionalist thesis and, 254

  interdependence and, 39, 40

  war and, 231

national level, 13

national liberation groups, 91

national liberation movement(s), 207, 425

national morale, 96

National Security Agency (NSA), 159

National Security Council (U.S.), 55, 136–138, 142, 143, 191

national security policy, 59, 136, 417, 422, 423

nationalism, 3, 30, 31, 41, 107

  as a check on legal reform, 295, 296

  definition of, 27

  war and, 229–231, 244

NATO allies (*see also* Western allies), 169

natural capabilities, power and, 97

natural law school, 291, 299

natural resources (*see also* economic resources), 65–68, 124, 125, 126, 172, 432

Nauru, 37, 93

Nazi Germany, 27

Nazism, 229

  war crimes and, 294

negotiation(s), 12, 50, 72, 75, 158, 162–168, 174, 423

  defined, 166

Nelson, A. K., 149n

neocolonialism, 126

neofunctionalism, 408

neoliberal approach, 405, 408, 409

  vs. realism, 408, 409

neo-Marxists, 14

neomercantilism, 315

neorealism, 59

neorealists, 14, 63, 418

Netanyahu, Benjamin, 201, 221n, 222n

Netherlands, The, 31, 122, 256, 311

Neustadt, Richard E., 149n, 150n

neutralism, 35

new diplomacy, 164–166

New Information Order, 253 254, 379

New International Economic Order, 32, 263, 322, 336, 340, 350–361, 379

Operation Prairie Fire, 52, 55
Ophuls, William, 445n
opinions, 56
Oppenheim, A. N., 154n
opportunities, 7, 17, 18
optional clause, 284, 285
Optner, S. L., 86n
Orderly Market Arrangements (OMAs), 316
Organization of African Unity (OAU), 104, 109, 111, 159, 251, 255, 270, 292
Organization of American States (OAS), 251, 255, 270, 292
  relations with UN of, 259
Organization of East Caribbean States, 224
Organization of Economic Cooperation and Development (OECD), 307
Organization of Petroleum Exporting Countries (OPEC), 7, 35, 125, 249, 254, 266, 305, 329, 351, 427
  EC and, 401
  recent problems of, 331
  relative success of, 331
  tensions with LDCs and, 351, 352
organizational process model, 69, 135, 137, 140
organizational terrorism, 199, 200
Organski, A. F. K., 64, 85n, 152n, 234
Ortega, Daniel, 195
Ottoman Empire, 31
outer space, 18, 67, 293
outer-space exploration, 65
Oval Office, 143
overcapacity, 333, 334
overpopulation, 19
overseas missions, 159
ozone depletion, 384, 392, 393
  Montreal Protocol and, 393

Pacific Rim, 19, 125, 432, 439
pacta sunt servanda, 290
Page, Benjamin, 153n
Pahlavi, Mohammad Reza, 192
Pakistan, 9, 33, 111, 193, 202, 352, 353, 377, 388
Palestine Liberation Front, 354
Palestine Liberation Organization (PLO), 28, 104, 107, 198, 199, 207, 354, 355, 425
  factions of, 354, 355
  renunciation of terrorism by, 356
Palestine National Alliance, 354
Palestine Popular Struggle Front, 354
Palestinian cause, 55, 125
Palestinian Communist Party, 354
Palestinian Democratic Alliance, 354
Palestinian National Congress, 355
Palestinian refugees, 388
Palestinian terrorists, 55
Palestinians, 125, 169, 204, 205
  nonmilitant, 199

Pan-Arab legacy, 55
Pan-European integration, 420
Pan-Islamic Conference, 103
Panama, 4, 38, 192, 335
  Panama Canal and, 290
  U.S. intervention in, 38, 224, 282, 292, 299
Panama Canal Treaty, 290
Panjdeh territory, 77
Panofsky, Wolfgang K. H., 444n
paradigms, 15, 58–60, 63, 70, 417
parallel system, deep-seabed mining and, 297
pariah states, 267
Paris, 106
Paris Peace Conference (1919), 130
Patel, Ambalal Somabhai, 445n
patterns of interaction, 61
Pax Britannica, 64
Payne, Ronald, 221n
peace, 7, 13, 18–20, 59, 63–65, 68, 171, 197, 422
peace conferences, 166
Peace of Westphalia, 24, 25, 26, 42, 91, 113, 245, 249, 311, 375, 415
  balance of power in, 28
  colonization and, 30
  international law and, 281
  national interest and, 29
peace through law, 62
peace through strength, 133
peaceful change, 3, 19, 125
peacekeeping, 235, 260–263, 277
  financial apects of, 261
peacekeeping force, 9, 19, 125, 267, 415
Pearl Harbor, 125, 138
Pearson, Frederic S., 152n, 153n, 154n, 188n, 221n, 222n
Peking (*see* Beijing)
Peloponnesian Wars, 234
Pennsylvania, 33
Pentagon, the, 232
People's Republic of China, 3, 9, 73, 122, 127, 130, 173, 414, 423, 428, 432
perceptions, 11, 13, 15, 50, 51, 55–57, 66, 69, 70, 129, 130, 133, 135, 137, 138, 164, 172, 193, 194, 208, 421
perceptual systems, 51, 52, 55, 56
perceptual teamwork, 55
perceptual theorists, 51
perestroika, 123, 124, 126, 127, 195–197, 420
Perez, Frank H., 221n
Permanent Court of International Justice, 285, 305
  as precursor to the ICJ, 305
  League of Nations and, 285
permeability, 67
Pershing II missiles, 195, 368, 369
Persian Gulf, 9, 121, 199, 234, 352, 378
Persian Gulf War, 9
Peru, 208, 216

proportionality, 283–285
  retaliation and, 283–285
prosperity, 63, 68
protection of the Ozone Treaty, 393
protectionism (*see also* trade wars), 7, 314–316, 323, 328, 329, 331–334, 337–340, 419, 421
  dangers of, debated, 332, 333
  definition of, 315
  European perspectives on, 333
  myths of liberal economic theory and, 337, 338
  NICs and, 339
Protel, E., 84n
Protestant Reformation, 24
protracted struggle, 56
Provisional Irish Republican Army, 198
Prussia, 250
psychological capabilities, power and, 97
psychological milieu, 66, 129
psychological warfare, 190–193, 195, 207, 208
public opinion, 54, 57, 128, 162, 193, 195, 196, 206
public policy, 18, 165
Punta del Este, Uruguay, 334
Pyrrhus, 371, 372

quantification, 58
Qatar, 352
Quebec, 111
quotas, 172

Ra'anan, Uri, 445n
Radio Liberty, 195
Radio Moscow, 191
Raichur, Satish, 153n
Ramberg, Bennett, 22n, 188n
Randers, Jorgen, 86n
Rapoport, Anatol, 188n
rapprochement, 130
ratification, 289
  definition of, 289
  as an executive act, 289
rational actor model, 69, 135, 136, 140
Ratzel, Friedrich, 65
Ray, James Lee, 221n, 222n
Reagan, Ronald W., 55, 56, 90, 131, 165, 168, 195, 284, 299, 328, 331, 369–371, 393, 423, 424
Reagan administration, 52, 192
Reagan–Gorbachev summit, 371
realism, 15, 59, 63, 65, 415
realist approach, 15, 405, 408, 409
  pessimism of regarding cooperation, 408, 409
  regimes and, 408
  relative gains and, 408, 409
  vs. neoliberalism, 408, 409
realistic foreign policy, 63
realists, 14, 41, 59, 60–63, 106
reality, 51, 55, 59, 63, 67, 69, 129, 136
rebus sic stantibus, 290

recession of 1983, 7
reciprocity
  cooperation and, 403, 406
  international law and, 282
  power and, 406
  regimes and, 406
  retaliation and, 403, 404
  trade and, 326, 333
recognition
  belligerents and, 96
  de facto, 26
  de jure, 26
  insurgents and, 96
  legal implications of, 26
  sovereignty, 26
  Westphalian implications of, 25
Red Army, 129
Red Cross, 103
redistribution agreements, 167
redistribution of wealth, 62
refugee camps, 125
refugees, 268, 384, 386–390
  common property resources and, 389
  developing countries and, 387
  in Europe, 387
  as externalities of conflict, 386
  international responses to, 387–390
  numbers of, 387
  repatriation of, 387, 388
  solutions for, 388
regional conflicts, 9, 123, 169, 352–356
  civil war and, 352–356
  refugees and, 352
regional integration, 68, 432
regional level, 13, 122, 426
regional organizations, 13, 418, 430, 431
regional relations, 13, 432
regional security organizations, 253
regional systems, 13
Reich, Robert, 332
relative deprivation, 232, 233
religions, 3, 58, 376
  international relations and, 101–103
religious movements, 14, 58, 200
reprisals, 283, 284
  definition of, 283
research and development, 127, 422
research methods, 14, 59
researchers, 57, 58
resistance point, 167, 170, 174
respondent, 286
retaliation, 283
  to breaches of customary law, 287
  proportionality and, 283–285
  U.S. bombing of Tripoli and, 284, 285
  U.S.–Iranian hostage crisis and, 284
rethinkers, 3, 17, 18

short-range nuclear forces (SNF), 368, 369
Shubik, Martin, 188n
Shultz, George, 285
shuttle diplomacy, 26, 164, 174
Siberia, 237
Sicily, 371
Siher, Roger, 170
Sikhs, 103, 107
Sills, David L., 188n, 220n
Simon, Herbert A., 87n, 149n
Simon, Julian L., 83n, 84n, 427, 445n
Sinai Peninsula, 130, 355
Singapore, 35, 333, 339, 360, 416, 419
Singer, David J., 21n, 22n, 86n, 239
Single European Act (1987), 256
Sivard, Ruth Leger, 153n
Siverson, Randolph M., 152n, 188n
Six-Day War of 1967, 355, 356
skyjacking, 208
Slater, Jerome, 445n
Small, Melvin, 239
Smith, Bruce L., 220n
Smith, Steve, 21n
Snyder, Richard C., 69, 86n, 87n
social democracy, 127
social interaction, 60
social movements, 61
social structures, 66
socialism, 126, 168, 193, 197, 430
sociosphere, 2
Sofaer, Abraham D., 221n
soft currency, 317
Solidarnosć, 102, 168, 351
Somalia, 223, 229, 230, 237, 353
    war with Ethiopia, 229, 230, 235, 352
Sorensen, Theodore C., 150n
Soroos, Marvin S., 42
South Africa, 9, 90, 99, 105, 171, 198, 255, 267,
    335, 352, 425
South America, 357
    integration in, 401
South Asia, 205
South Korea, 35, 260, 304, 339, 360, 416
South Mollucans, 107
South Pacific Forum, 109
South Pole, 392
    ozone hole at, 392, 393
South Yemen, 127, 200, 201, 352, 354
Southeast Asia, 311, 388, 425
Southeast Asian Treaty Organization (SEATO), 33
sovereignty, 23, 30, 42, 61, 68, 101, 113, 139, 140,
    159, 170, 174, 407, 415, 416, 419, 420, 426, 431
    challenges to, 32, 101
    definitions of, 24, 25, 112
    development of, 24, 25
    human rights and, 298, 300
    IGOs and, 251

sovereignty (*continued*)
    interdependence and, 38
    international law and, 281, 293
    judicial activism and, 295, 296
    nonstate actors and, 102
    recognition and, 26
    separatism and, 230
sovereignty-at-bay model, 417
Soviet aggression, U.S. fear of, 423
Soviet bloc (*see also* Eastern bloc), 131, 200, 415
Soviet military threat, 7, 12, 123, 127, 168
Soviet Strategic Rocket Forces, 129
Soviet Union, 4, 7, 9, 29, 32–35, 37, 43, 51, 55, 74,
    90, 92, 93, 96, 121–124, 126–128, 137, 168, 169,
    171–173, 191–194, 197, 198, 201, 224, 229, 232,
    235, 237, 256, 259, 266, 271, 273, 289, 351,
    357, 364, 378, 387–389, 403, 404, 414, 420,
    422, 423, 425, 430–432
    Afghanistan and, 224, 292–293, 335
    armed forces of, 127
    arms races and, 365–371
    Baltic states and, 351
    collusion with OPEC of, 331
    cooperation with U.S. by, 169
    dominance by, 419
    economy of, 126, 127, 431
    effects of WWII on, 323
    foreign aid policies of, 171, 321
    foreign policy of, 7, 126, 127, 130, 196, 197, 421
    imperialism of, 65
    internal upheaval in, 351
    Law of the Sea and, 296–298
    League of Nations and, 257
    media of, 193, 196
    Middle East policy of, 355
    military doctrine of, 172, 422, 425
    nationalism within, 41
    nuclear policy of, 364
    policy on LDCs, 7
    propaganda of, 194, 195, 197
    reforms in, 420–421
    reprisals by, 55
    role in UN of, 258, 283
    split with China and, 351
    troop withdrawal by, 193
    views on international law of, 304
    views on SDI of, 370, 371
Spaceship Earth, 2
Spain, 27, 54, 206, 256, 292, 425
    Basque problem in, 111, 230
    colonial expansion of, 30, 311
Spanier, John W., 85n, 87n
Special Drawing Right (SDR), 328
special envoy(s), 164
sphere of influence, 59, 123, 124, 126
Spiegel, Steven L., 153n
spillover effect, 253, 401

United Kingdom (*continued*)
Commonwealth of, 266
Law of the Sea and, 298
nuclear capability of, 368
as oil producer, 331
in Palestine, 355
United States, 3–5, 7, 9, 11, 12, 14, 20, 29, 32–35,
    37, 40, 43, 44, 51, 54, 55, 57, 65, 68, 74, 92,
    93, 96, 99, 103, 104, 107, 110, 121–126, 128,
    130, 131, 133, 136, 164, 169, 171–173, 190, 191,
    193–198, 201, 205, 206, 230–232, 235, 237,
    256, 259–261, 266, 271, 274, 283, 288, 307,
    312, 313, 317, 339, 352, 364, 378, 385–388,
    397, 398, 403, 404, 417–422, 425–427, 430,
    432
  arms races and, 365–372
  auto industry of, 315
  balance of payments deficits of, 328, 330
  bombing of Libya by, 52–54, 57, 206, 284, 285
  Central America and, 234, 286
  colonialism and, 312
  continental shelf claims of, 288
  as a debtor nation, 330
  dollar devaluation of, 323
  dollar diplomacy of, 317, 318, 326
  economic decline of, 326–329
  economy of, 7
  federalism of, 398
  foreign aid policies of, 321, 338
  free trade policies of, 325, 326
  genesis of the UN and, 258, 275
  global position after WWII of, 323, 324
  gold reserves of, 324, 327
  humanitarian aid of, 389
  independence of, 30
  international standing of, 4, 5, 7
  interventions of, 38, 224, 282, 292, 299, 352
  investment of Japan in, 319
  Iran hostage crisis and, 284
  Law of the Sea and, 296–298
  Middle East policy of, 234, 355, 356
  Nicaragua and, 286, 299
  nuclear policy of, 351, 364
  optional clause and, 286
  ozone and, 392, 393
  policies of in Angola, 39
  post-WWII hegemony of, 33
  recognition of China and, 26
  relations with EC of, 331, 334, 342–344
  sanctions and, 335
  steel industry of, 314
  stock market of, 319
  Supreme Court of, 286
  territorial sea claims of Latin America and, 288
  trade deficit of, 331, 332
  trade protectionism and, 315
  trade ties with Japan and, 331, 332, 334

United States (continued)
  treaty ratification process of, 289
  UN reform and, 275–277
  Vietnam and, 130, 139, 224, 230, 273, 352
  World Bank and, 324
United States Information Agency (USIA), 159, 190,
    194
United States of Europe, 431
Uniting for Peace Resolution, 260, 261
Universal Declaration of Human Rights, 62, 263,
    291
Universal Postal Union, 249, 250
University of Michigan, 226
Upper Volta (*see also* Burkina Faso), 223
Uprising, the, 355
urban population growth, 433–435
Uruguay Round, 334
Ury, William, 169, 188n
U.S. aid, 171
U.S. allies, 12, 52, 54, 425
U.S. antiterrorist organizations, 206
U.S. armed services, 129
U.S.-Canadian Boundary Commission, 254
U.S. Catholic Bishops Pastoral Letter on Nuclear
    War, 107
U.S. Congress, 17, 128, 129, 139, 164, 173, 190, 370,
    371
U.S. counterterrorism, policy of, 207, 211, 212
U.S. decision makers, 55
U.S. Department of State, 135, 136, 164, 190
U.S. foreign policy, 133, 142, 192, 195, 206, 207
U.S. government, 9, 11, 199
U.S. influence, 123, 125
U.S. Joint Chiefs of Staff, 371
U.S.-Libyan dispute (1986), 51–56
U.S.-Mexican Mixed Claims Commission, 254
U.S. officials, 55
U.S. Senate, 289
  treaty ratification and, 289
U.S. Sixth Fleet, 55
U.S. Supreme Court, 286, 289
  international law and, 286
  Scotia case of, 287
U.S. trade deficit, 418
use of force, 56, 59, 71–73, 125, 165, 171, 198, 206
USSR (*see* Soviet Union)
utopians (*see* idealists)

value judgments, 57
values, 51, 56, 58, 136, 139, 141, 171, 193, 208
Vance, Cyrus, 164
variable-sum game, 169, 170
Vatican, 102
Venezuela, 159, 416
Venice Economic Summit (1987), 121
Verba, Sidney, 21n, 87n
Versailles, 14